G000145827

BRITISH AIRWAYS

BA 501242

NM PACHECO

Systems Analysis and Design

With CASE Tools

Systems Analysis and Design

With CASE Tools

Len Fertuck

University of Toronto

Book Team

Editor *Edward G. Jaffe*
Developmental Editor *Linda M. Meehan*

 Wm. C. Brown Publishers

President *G. Franklin Lewis*
Vice President, Publisher *George Wm. Bergquist*
Vice President, Operations and Production *Beverly Kolz*
National Sales Manager *Virginia S. Moffat*
Group Sales Manager *Vince DiBlasi*
Assistant Vice President, Editor in Chief *Edward G. Jaffe*
Associate Executive Editor *Earl McPeek*
Marketing Manager *Craig S. Marty*
Advertising Manager *Ann M. Knepper*
Managing Editor, Production *Colleen A. Yonda*
Manager of Visuals and Design *Faye M. Schilling*
Production Editorial Manager *Julie A. Kennedy*
Production Editorial Manager *Ann Fuerste*
Publishing Services Manager *Karen J. Slaght*

WCB Group

President and Chief Executive Officer *Mark C. Falb*
Chairman of the Board *Wm. C. Brown*

Cover design by Christopher E. Reese

Copyright © 1992 by Wm. C. Brown Publishers. All rights reserved

Library of Congress Catalog Card Number: 91–71023

ISBN 0–697–12069–4

Printed in the United States of America by Wm. C. Brown Publishers,
2460 Kerper Boulevard, Dubuque, IA 52001

10 9 8 7 6 5 4 3 2 1

To my wife, Helen;
my children, Kirsten, Stephen, and Tania;
and my mother, Maria.

Contents in Brief

Table of Contents

Chapter 6. Database Definition ... 248

Preface

Changing
Environment

The methods used to design systems depend on what the major constraint is in the design process. In the past, the major constraint in the design of computer systems has been the need to fit the solutions to large problems into relatively small and expensive machines. With this constraint in mind, the methodologies used were designed to focus on economic and technical feasibility. Feasibility constraints were identified early so that compromises could be made in the requirements and the design. The main emphasis was on developing efficient code that would use as few machine cycles as possible.

More recently, there has been a recognition that maintenance costs are as significant a problem as machine costs. The response has been to develop structured methods which produce a structured design that can be implemented and maintained in code that is still machine efficient. The development methods attempt to reach a compromise between machine efficiency and programmer efficiency. The need for machine efficiency has forced developers to use procedural languages. These languages achieve efficiency at the expense of simplicity. The result has been a proliferation of small disconnected systems. They are not integrated because designers cannot cope with the complexity of an integrated design and the complexity of procedural development tools at the same time.

We have finally reached a stage where the major constraint on our ability to build effective systems is most often our inability to understand the full scope of the problem. For many systems the technical constraints of machine and software capability are not important. Very large computers exist at relatively low prices compared to a number of years ago. Very powerful and comprehensive database management software exists to eliminate a large part of the coding complexity. Powerful Computer Aided Software Engineering (CASE) tools and Fourth Generation Languages (4GL) exist to drastically reduce the effort needed to construct input screens, generate reports, and program batch applications.

With these tools, the focus shifts from technological constraints to problem-oriented constraints. For many problems it is now possible to use the available technology to cope with the complexity of our problems rather than reduce the complexity of our problems to fit within the constraints of our technology.

There are still some systems that are so large that they cannot fit into the largest available machines. Airline reservation systems and large banking systems are examples of such applications. Designers will still have to use current methodologies to solve these technology-constrained problems. This book does not address such problems. It focuses on those systems where understanding is the scarce resource. These systems can be found in very many organizations. They occur whenever an organization finds that it has many overlapping applications with redundant data. They can be found when a major effort is required to reorganize existing data whenever management needs to answer even the simplest questions that were not anticipated in the original design.

Teaching
Objectives

There are many Systems Analysis and Design texts on the market. Given the rapid changes in the field, they can be broadly classified by the historic period in which their main paradigm applies. They can prepare students to work in the past, the present, or the future. Each of these periods has a particular approach to analysis and design.

Preparing for the Past

Early books on the subject shared a number of characteristics.

- **Technical constraints** are assumed to be the major problem to be overcome. Design is seen as an exercise in overcoming technical problems. Batch processing techniques dominate the design.
- **Written specifications** are the main product of the analysis effort.
- **Single projects** are the focus of each new effort. There is no attempt at integration because the technical constraints make integration too complex.
- **Project management** is a major concern. The analysis and design are organized around the traditional System Development Life Cycle. Complex specifications must be provided to meet specified milestones in the cycle.
- **Data** are stored in files uniquely designed for each project.
- **Art** is more important than science in the analysis and design process. Texts give a conceptual view without indicating how to implement the concepts.

Preparing for the Present

These texts reflect the current situation in which most analysts realize that there are problems with the old methods, but are struggling to identify ways to overcome the problems.

- **Systems** is a favorite buzzword. However, the project is the main focus of the books and the methods are still based on the System Development Life Cycle. Written requirements, specifications, and project milestones are still the central themes of most books in this class. Methods for evaluating subjective benefits in assessing project priorities are limited.
- **Structured techniques** are used to bring rigor to the analysis process. However, the link between data modeling, structured analysis, and structured design is often very tenuous.
- **Databases** are designed using a relational model. There is rarely any attempt to create an Enterprise Model which will integrate the data from several projects. If an Enterprise Model is considered, it is usually a problem for some ill-defined Data Base Administrator, rather than being an integral part of the analysis and design effort.
- **Modern tools and techniques** are treated as next-generation methods that may someday enter the mainstream. They are often treated in a sidebar, box, or chapter tacked on to the end as an afterthought. Enterprise Models, Joint Application Design, Function Point Analysis, Screen Generators, Application Generators, Real-Time Systems, Object-Oriented Systems, and Expert Systems are often treated in this superficial way.
- **CASE tools** are discussed, but their use is restricted to producing diagrams and documentation for a structured method. CASE tools are rarely treated as a

tool that permits new methods of increasing quality, reducing maintenance, and integrating applications. The major changes in the life cycle required to capitalize on CASE tools are usually ignored.

- **People-oriented skills,** such as interviewing, are emphasized more. However, methods—like prototyping and Joint Application Design—which capitalize on greater involvement with the user are used sparingly, if at all.

Preparing for the Future

The most progressive systems groups are using the most modern support tools in new and innovative ways. An examination of the methods used by them shows that the future of systems analysis will be quite different from the present.

- **CASE tools,** such as Excelerator or Information Engineering Workbench (IEW), are used to define Enterprise Models, Entity-Relationship models, Data Flow Diagrams, Structure Charts, prototype screens, and prototype reports as part of a continuous process. The different parts are linked using a Data Dictionary, encyclopedia, or repository to ensure completeness and consistency. The result is integrated systems, with greatly reduced numbers of errors, that match the client's needs more closely.
- **Relational Data Base Management Systems,** such as DB2, Oracle, or Ingress, are used to define and manage a database that is independent of individual application programs. This produces flexible systems that are easy to modify and extend.
- **Fourth Generation Languages and Application Generators,** like SQL, Telon, and Cross-System Product, facilitate rapid prototyping and development of screens, reports, and batch application programs. This increases user-involvement and user-ownership of the design. This in turn leads to higher quality designs with fewer design errors.
- **Interactive online data entry and query** facilities give users direct access to the current database for validation of entries or answers to queries. These facilitate end-user computing and increase flexibility.
- **Independent system components** are developed separately. The database, screens, reports, and batch applications are developed in relative isolation and delivered continuously over an extended period. Continuous delivery shows the user that progress is being made and builds commitment to the system.
- **Group processes** like Joint Application Design and prototyping are used to identify needs and build connections with the users. An often antagonistic relationship with users is converted into a working partnership.

Intended Use

This book is intended as a Systems Analysis and Design text for college and university courses that emphasize the use of modern CASE tools and group processes. It assumes that the student is being prepared for the environment of the future in which CASE tools, Relational Data Base Management Systems, application generators, group processes, and end-user computing are common. It is intended to appeal to instructors and students who want to be a part of the solution to information systems obstacles, not part of the problem.

This text is the result of examination and use of most of the tools and techniques described in it. It has benefited from the experience of many of the most advanced thinkers in the field. Lessons learned in a number of different specialties are synthesized in the most comprehensive way possible. Techniques that have traditionally been separated into Enterprise Modeling, database design, and application design have been integrated into a seamless whole.

Approach

These tools lead to an analysis and design approach very different from the traditional System Development Life Cycle (SDLC). The traditional SDLC is oriented toward design and implementation of single applications in isolation from the other applications in an organization's portfolio. Each application contains its own data files, input routines, processing, and reports. They often overlap with other applications resulting in redundancy, duplicated effort, incompatible files, and difficult maintenance problems. The methods used in the new environment differ from traditional methods in the following ways:

- **Enterprise Modeling** is used to produce an integrated architecture that identifies the data base, inputs, reports, and processing needed by the whole organization, without duplication.
- **Data-driven design produces an Integrated Data Base.** The database is designed and implemented first to provide a solid foundation for the screens, reports, and programs needed by all the different users who interact with the data. The database is an early deliverable that establishes credibility with the users. It is designed so that other applications can easily access the same data.
- **Data base, screens, reports, and applications are designed independently** to maintain maximum flexibility and ease of maintenance. Once the data base has been designed, design and construction of the other components can proceed independently.
- **Prototyping is used** to design and implement screens and reports as soon as the data base is implemented. This maintains a close link with the users and provides another early deliverable.
- **Testing occurs at every stage** of design and development. Errors are detected and corrected early in the design process. This reduces surprises at the final integration testing stage.
- **Formal specifications and signoffs are reduced.** Phased implementation, continuous contact with the users, and continual testing of requirements reduce the need for legalistic specifications designed to protect the implementers. Dialog and improvement replaces contracts and arguments.

Differences from Traditional Texts

Instructors in traditional systems analysis and design courses may find that their course outlines will need some modification. This text breaks with many traditions in order to prepare students for the design and implementation methods of the future instead of following the methods that have been used in the past. Traditional methods were suited for an environment in which CASE and prototyping tools were unavailable, coding was a major part of the development effort, and integrated systems were impractical with the available tools. The CASE, DBMS, 4GL, and group process environment relaxes many restrictions and permits the design of larger, more integrated systems. The instructor will notice the following changes in content, order, and emphasis:

- **Enterprise Models** are covered in Section I as a preliminary phase that identifies the different systems that an organization needs, partitions them into non-overlapping projects, and sets priorities on the projects. Entity-Relationship models and Business System Planning (BSP) models are used as a basis for this section. The section can be left out of introductory courses that wish to concentrate on the implementation of a single project.

- **Database Design** is treated as the first stage of an implementation project. Extended Entity-Relationship models, normalization, and SQL implementation are covered. Hierarchical, network, and native file structures are ignored, since it is assumed that they will be covered in a separate database course, if needed. Forms analysis, file analysis, and Joint Applications Design are the major techniques used to analyze the database requirements.

- **Screens and reports** are designed by prototyping. They are treated as separate applications rather than being a part of the system. This is because the tools used to design them, the people that use them, and the time at which they are used are typically different from those of a batch application. The chapter on screens and reports can be taught immediately after the database has been designed. However, an introduction to Data Flow Diagrams helps to put these components in perspective.

- **Batch applications** are designed using the traditional approaches of Data Flow Diagrams, Structure Charts, Action Diagrams, and Structured English. Prototyping is usually not suitable because there are rarely any visible components for the user to see.

- **Data Flow Diagrams** emphasize identifying the processes that are used to transform data, since the database has already been designed. Diagnostics identify errors at each stage. The concept of isolation is introduced to identify modules that should stand alone because they might be needed by different people, at different times, or in different places. This provides a way of separating interactive screens and reports from batch processes.

  Data Flow Diagrams are divided into Context Diagrams that deal with external terminators, Event Diagrams that identify a process to handle each external event, and File Diagrams that link processes to files. The concept of event-handling provides a rationale for the initial partitioning of Data Flow Diagrams and leads to more cohesive modules because each focusses on operations related to a single event.

- **Testing** is not treated as a separate chapter. It is integrated through the text by showing how each phase of the analysis process can be tested to make sure that the design is as nearly correct as possible. A Clue/Cause/Cure format is used to identify problems that can be corrected. Prototyping and JAD are used to prevent specification errors by close interaction with users.

- **Deliverables** are functional components instead of documentation. CASE tools automatically document the various stages of the analysis and design process. It is usually not possible to continue until each phase has been completed. Development is treated as a continuous process characterized by constant interaction with the users. Documentation is produced as needed to facilitate interaction with users which, in turn, leads to correct designs. When the analyst and user agree on a solution, the documentation is complete and the next stage can progress. The main deliverable is the finished system, which is delivered in stages as each component is completed. The database, screens, reports, and batch applications are treated as separate deliverables.
- **Specific CASE tools and 4GLs** are not used to illustrate the analysis and design process. Generic notation and methods are used to explain concepts. These can be applied in most CASE tools. There are too many different products available and they change too quickly to be properly dealt with in this text. Some features of specific tools are discussed in a section at the end of each chapter to show how the techniques can be used in specific products.
- **Distributed Systems, Real-Time Systems, and management problems** are each covered in separate optional chapters at the end of the book. They may be left out of courses that do not need this material.

Pedagogical Aids

Objectives, summary, figures, keywords, problems, a project, and a case are included in each chapter. A glossary of terms and graphic symbols is included at the end of the book. A project workbook is available as a student assignment. Adopters can integrate the Excelerator product into the assignments.

- **Objectives and summary** in each chapter help the student review topics. A highlighted table at the beginning of each chapter shows what part of the analysis and design problem is being addressed in each chapter.
- **Over 250 figures** are used to illustrate concepts in the book.
- **Clue/Cause/Cure diagnostics** are provided at the end of many chapters to help the student identify common errors in applying the described methods.
- **Keywords, Review questions, and problems** are included at the end of each chapter. Keywords and review questions are included as a self-study aid. Self-contained problems are provided at the end of most chapters. These are designed to test the student's ability to apply the techniques in each chapter.
- **A glossary** at the end of the book defines all important terms used in the book. All keywords listed at the end of each chapter are included. A separate graphic glossary repeats the graphic notation introduced in the text.
- **A continuing case illustration** based on a student records system is used through most of the chapters to provide continuity and show how the techniques relate to each other.
- **A continuing case assignment** may be assigned individually or in groups after each of Chapters 5 to 10. This assignment allows the student to practice the techniques taught in each chapter in the context of a single continuing project. As an alternative, a generic project assignment is provided at the end

of each of these chapters. The project assignment is general enough to allow students to design a system of their choice.

- **A project book is available.** This book provides background information and chapter assignments to simulate working on a real project in a hospital admissions context. It can be used as an alternative to the continuing case assignment or a student selected project. It can be combined with the use of a commercial CASE tool.

- An online, interactive tutorial is provided to show students how to use Excelerator. Students use the features of this CASE tool as they move through a menu-driven tutorial.

- A videotaped joint-application design (JAD) session, produced by JATec Designer Systems, is available to adopters through the WCB Software and Video Catalog.

- The *Instructor's Manual to accompany Systems Analysis and Design with CASE Tools* offers course outlines, Excelerator instructions, solutions to exercises, and transparency masters of selected figures and other lecture materials. The instructor's manual also contains a test item file, which includes multiple choice, true/false, and matching questions.

- WCB's TestPak 3.0 is a computerized testing service that provides adopters with a call-in/mail-in testing program and the complete test item file on diskette for use with an IBM PC or Macintosh. In addition to random test generation, TestPak allows for new questions to be added, or existing questions to be edited.

Organization

This book is arranged to deal with the design problems in the order that they occur in a CASE-oriented environment. The first chapter provides an introduction to the problems of the existing development methods and the changes that are required when understanding is the constraint instead of technology.

Section I—consisting of Chapters 2, 3, and 4—deals with the definition of an enterprise model. This is done at an aggregate level. Chapter 2 shows how to identify the entities and relationships that will become the building blocks of the database. Chapter 3 shows how to identify the activities that will require computer systems to support them and how to group these activities into subsystems. Chapter 4 shows how to set priorities to identify the order in which subsystems must be developed.

Section II—consisting of Chapters 5 and 6—deals with the detailed design of a database. Chapter 5 shows how to identify the files and detailed attributes or fields that will be needed in a database. Chapter 6 shows how to normalize these files into a stable non-redundant design that eliminates storage and update anomalies. It also shows how the database design can be coded in SQL, a standard language for database implementation.

Section III—consisting of Chapters 7, 8, 9, and 10—deals with the identification of user requirements and the design of screens, and programs to satisfy those requirements. Chapter 7 shows how to use data flow diagrams to identify the functions that application programs must perform. Chapter 8 shows how to design screens for input, inquiry, update, and deletion of data and how to design reports that order and summarize information in files. Chapter 9 shows how to organize the functions into a hierarchical structure of modules that maximize cohesion within a module and minimize coupling between the modules. Chapter 10 shows how to document each module in sufficient detail that programmers can produce the required code.

Section IV—consisting of Chapters 11, 12, and 13—deals with special issues in the design of complex systems. Chapter 11 shows how the database and the application programs need to be modified when they will be used in a network consisting of more than one computer. Chapter 12 extends the methods to include the design of real-time systems that must stay synchronized with external processes such as a chemical reactor in a production plant. Chapter 13 deals with the changes required in the organization to accomplish the transition from the present methods to a method suitable for an integrated CASE environment.

The book takes a practical point of view. It shows how users and existing documents and file structures can be used to identify components of the new design. Diagnostic tests are provided at the end of each chapter to determine whether the results of each stage of an analysis are correct. A section at the end of each chapter identifies which of the described techniques are implemented in a number of existing CASE tools. A single example is used through most of the chapters to illustrate the methods. This makes it easier to understand how the method is applied at different levels.

Course Outlines

This text can be used in a number of ways. It can be a standard book for senior students, a beginner's book on system analysis, a text for a capstone course, or a text in a course for students or programmers who want to learn to use CASE methods. The different courses should cover a different selection of chapters and emphasize topics differently.

- **Standard Systems Analysis Course.** A course for students who already know how to program in a procedural language should cover chapters 1 to 10. If they have already had a database course, Chapters 2, 5, and 6 can be reviewed quickly to show how databases are integrated with systems analysis. Chapters 11 to 13 can be included to give such students more new material. A project can be included in the course to make sure that each phase is understood. Emphasize both the techniques and methods of detecting errors.
- **Introductory Course.** A course for students who have had no previous courses in information systems, database, or systems analysis should cover Chapter 1 and Chapters 5 to 10. The emphasis should be on the techniques of Extended Entity-Relationship Diagrams, normalization, Data Flow Diagrams, Screen Design, Structure Charts, and Structured English in that order. Relatively little emphasis should be placed on the problems of error-checking, since the students will be busy with new concepts including programming. If a CASE tool is available, a case or project can be assigned using the tool. If a

CASE tool is not available, the diagrams can be drawn by hand. A database language like dBase III or IV could be used to implement parts of the project.

This same course could be used as an introduction to systems design and end-user computing for business students. The emphasis is on designing a personal system and using existing databases. Chapter 13 should be included to identify the business problems of converting to an integrated environment.

- **Capstone Course.** A course for students who know a programming language and have taken a database course and a traditional systems analysis course should emphasize the integration of the material and how CASE methods differ from traditional methods. The chapters should be covered to review the relevant material and show how the techniques are integrated. Section I on generating an enterprise model is likely to be new material. The emphasis of the course should be on the use of CASE tools in a major project. An integrated DBMS, like Oracle, could be used to implement a project.

- **CASE Course.** This text could also be used in a course for students or practitioners who have learned in a traditional environment and want to learn the use of CASE tools and code generators. The text provides a method that is different from the traditional SDLC that they are used to. The emphasis in the course should be on the way that this method differs from the traditional SDLC and why it needs to be different in a CASE environment. As much time will be spent on unlearning old ways as on learning new ones. Again, the course can make use of a separate CASE tool text and a project to illustrate how the design process flows through the different phases.

Acknowledgements

This book began seven years ago while I was teaching a Systems Analysis course in the People's Republic of China. Perceptive questions from the students about how and why we do each of the steps in a traditional analysis led me to question many "self-evident truths". The change of environment gave me a chance to rethink the process. The availability of CASE tools soon after made it practical to implement many needed changes in the analysis and design process.

Authoring a book is mostly a lonesome craft. It takes an author, a computer, a telephone, and a lot of reference material. It also takes a lot of quiet time for organizing haphazard thoughts into coherent ideas. The apple blossoms outside my window have turned to apples several times over during this process.

It comes almost as a surprise that I have had so many helpers. The most numerous and most diligent have been students in courses at the undergraduate and graduate level. Their background has ranged from undergraduate students with virtually no computer background to graduate business students with extensive systems experience. Their technological sophistication ranges from those who are intimidated by a microwave oven to computer hackers who are not intimidated by anything. They have contributed in many ways including finding split infinitives, testing problems, and questioning basic assumptions.

Their ego-bashing of the instructor has produced a manuscript that has gone through two major revisions with significant reorganization in several chapters.

This extensive classroom testing has produced a book that approaches a revised version in quality. The students studied electronically published manuscripts in final form, so they were able to critique both form and substance.

Their questions and critiques have resulted in a book that is clearer and more integrated than anything I could do alone. The students are too numerous to list here, but to each of them I express my deep appreciation for their contribution.

The manuscript has been thoroughly reviewed by a number of instructors. I have not always agreed with every criticism, but I have appreciated them nevertheless. Each has caused me to rethink the material that must be presented and the way in which it is presented. Most comments have led to improvements in content or presentation.

I would particularly like to thank Becky Reuber at the University of Toronto who made copious helpful suggestions, including providing the basis for the Cal Oreez case assignment.

I would also like to thank several reviewers who provided critiques and helpful insights. They are Donald L. Amoroso, University of Colorado at Colorado Springs; Thomas A. Browdy, Washington University; Gail Corbitt, San Diego State University; Sergio Davalos, Pima Community College; Dale D. Gust, Central Michigan University; Carolyn A. Hershberger, Olympic College; Charlotte Hiatt, California State University—Fresno; Robert Klepper, Southern Illinois University at Edwardsville; and Jacqueline Wyatt, Middle Tennessee State University.

Thanks also to the team at Wm. C. Brown Publishers who piloted the manuscript through the organizational and technical shoals that sometimes threatened to scupper the whole enterprise. Special thanks go to Matt Loeb who recognized the potential of the manuscript in its early stages, to Ed Jaffe and Earl McPeek who encouraged its publication, to Linda Meehan who carried the project to completion, and to Darlene Schueller who has expedited many requests for help.

Finally, thanks to my trusty 386 microcomputer which made it possible to prepare and revise the manuscript. The manuscript was written using Word 4.0. RightWriter 3.0 was used to check grammar and identify complex passages. As a result, the manuscript has a grade 11 to 12 reading level in spite of its technical subject matter. Most graphics were prepared using GEM Draw. Various other programs were used to generate examples and capture screens for illustrations. The components were combined using Ventura Publisher 2.0. The publisher generated camera-ready copy directly from files produced by Ventura Publisher.

These tools burden the author with tasks that are normally performed by the publisher, but they also provide the author with creative control over the book. They also allow students and reviewers to critique the manuscript in its final form. The result is a faster, clearer, more current manuscript. I am convinced that this is the best way to produce a book with the complex illustrations required in this field.

Len Fertuck,
Toronto, Canada.

Systems Analysis and Design

With CASE Tools

Chapter 1

Introduction to Analysis & Design

Objectives

The systems analyst acts as an interface between the client, who has a need for new computer systems, and the programmer, who has the technical skills to produce such programs. The analyst has the task of understanding the needs and capabilities of both parties and translating the requirements of the client into specifications that the programmer can understand. This communication and translation function is the added value which the analyst brings to the development process.

The development process is divided into phases which are collectively known as the system development life cycle. This process can be made significantly more efficient and less error prone when Computer Aided Software Engineering (CASE) tools and Fourth Generation Languages (4GL) are available.

CASE tools and 4GLs involve new software technology and new analysis and design methods. This chapter provides an introduction to the features of the software, an overview of the appropriate design methodology, and an outline of the subsequent chapters of this book. Specifically, the reader learns:

- The Systems Development Life Cycle stages and products.
- The features of CASE tools.
- How the traditional System Development Life Cycle has to be modified to gain the benefits of CASE tools.
- What components have to be modeled during the analysis and design process.
- When each component is modeled.
- The limitations of CASE tools.

Introduction

The process of systems analysis and design is the process of designing computer software to serve the needs of some community of users. The analyst acts as an intermediary between two quite different groups. On one hand the analyst deals with users who understand the job that they have to perform within their organization, but do not understand how a computer works or how to make it do what they want. These users have indicated that they need a computer system to help them in successfully completing their work. They approach the systems analyst to design such a system for them.

When the analyst has determined what the users need, and designed a suitable system, the design is turned over to programmers. They typically do not understand the users' needs. They do understand how a computer system works and how to write programs to perform the users' functions.

The analyst's job is to bridge this gap between the knowledge that the user has about the functions that must be performed and the technology that can be used to perform those functions. The analyst must know enough about each of these groups to be able to translate their needs to each other. The needs are specified unambiguously in a language that the users understand into specifications stated unambiguously in a language that programmers can understand. When the analyst does not understand what the user needs, the analyst must know how to ask questions that get clear responses. Then the analyst must be able to restate the requirements unambiguously to the user to check that the requirements have been completely understood.

Figure 1-1 symbolizes this dual role in which the analyst must have some of the characteristics of both users and programmers. In addition, the analyst may need the wisdom of Solomon, the patience of a saint, and the thick skin of a rhinoceros to act as a good intermediary.

Some of the Computer Aided Software Engineering (CASE) tools discussed in this book are taking over more of the programming function. Some code generators are able to translate the analyst's specifications directly into computer code. As this trend continues, the analyst still has the same problems understanding users, but is translating user needs directly into the language of more

Figure 1-1

The dual role of the systems analyst.

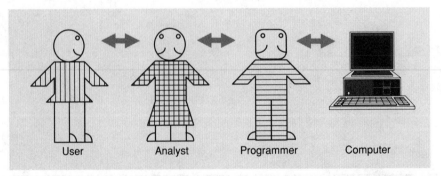

User   Analyst   Programmer   Computer

intelligent computer systems. Many programming functions will gradually be taken over by these CASE tools.

The System Development Life Cycle

The development of software systems is a complex process, usually involving many people with a variety of special skills. The process is usually broken down into stages or phases that deliver several intermediate outputs on the way to the final system. These stages together are called the System Development Life Cycle (SDLC). Different methods may have different names for the stages and they may include some different functions in each stage. All of them contain some variation of requirements definition, analysis, design, specification, coding, testing, and implementation. This section discusses each stage briefly to provide an overview of the process.

Requirements Definition

This stage determines the needs of the proposed users of the system. It produces a broad outline of the system that identifies the functions to be performed, the technology to be used, and the expected cost of the system. There is usually some method of determining which of several competing projects is given highest priority and developed first.

The request for a new system is usually initiated by a group of users, such as the manufacturing division. The scope of the project is usually specific. For instance, they may ask for a new inventory control system.

Most methodologies do not integrate a single project like this into an overall design. The inventory system may overlap with the purchasing system that gets the inventory items and the manufacturing bill of materials system that determines what items are used. However, these are often developed as separate projects. The separate projects often duplicate significant parts of the overall system.

This stage defines broad requirements, but it is not very specific. At the end of this stage there is nobody who yet knows what specific components the system will contain or exactly what they will do. The next stage works out the details of what the users need to perform their jobs.

Analysis

The analysis stage translates broad requirements into detailed requirements. The analyst does this by going back to the users to determine exactly what they do. Most organizations do not have documentation of the functions performed by users in enough detail to be of use to the analyst. Usually the analyst starts by documenting the process using Data Flow Diagrams.

The final system consists of data files and programs that manipulate the data. The analyst has to identify the data that is used and the manipulations of that data that have to be embodied in programs. A Data Flow Diagram views the process from the point of view of the data. As the data progresses through the system, it is transformed by processes.

Figure 1-2 illustrates a very simple high-level Data Flow Diagram for the proposed inventory system. It identifies three processes: Record Deliveries, Record Orders, and Ship Orders. Deliveries, Stock, Orders, and Invoices are the names of aggregate data items that are flowing through the process. The Record Deliveries process transforms data on deliveries into data that records stock on hand. The figure must be expanded in much greater detail to capture all of the data and processes involved in the system.

The analysis stage is actually a learning process in which the analyst tries to gain an understanding of what the user does. The Data Flow Diagram is an intermediate product that allows the analyst and the user to communicate unambiguously. It summarizes the information that the analyst needs during the design stage. It does it in a clear graphic way that the user can understand. The user needs to understand it, because the user may have to point out errors in the analyst's understanding of the system. The final result of this stage is an understanding of the system documented by Data Flow Diagrams.

Design

When finished with recording the processes in the system, the analyst has to change hats and become the designer of a new system that programmers can implement. Just as the Data Flow Diagram serves as a communication language with the user, a Structure Chart serves to communicate with a programmer.

The programmer has to produce blocks of code called subroutines that work together as a logical system. The structural connection between these modules is illustrated in a Structure Chart. The Structure Chart is often a transformation of

Figure 1-2

A simple Data Flow Diagram for an inventory system.

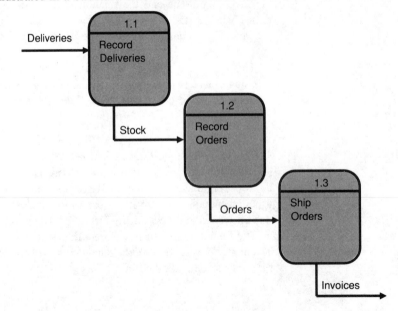

the Data Flow Diagram that maps processes into modules as illustrated in Figure 1-3. However, there are several modifications that frequently have to be performed to make sure that the modules are as independent as possible. Independence between modules reduces the number of problems encountered in maintaining and modifying the modules during their useful life.

Figure 1-3
A simple Structure Chart for an inventory system.

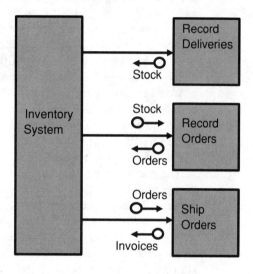

Specification

In addition to specifying the relationship between modules of a system, the designer must specify the contents of each module. These specifications are usually given in a language called Structured English. It is a language half-way between English and a computer language. It is general enough that it can include broad statements like "calculate interest owed." It is specific enough that it eliminates ambiguities that are commonly present in statements written in a natural language like English.

Structured English is often written with commands and indentation that make it look like code in a computer language. For this reason, it is sometimes called pseudocode. Figure 1-4 illustrates a set of instructions that might be found in the Record Deliveries module.

Figure 1-4
Structured English specification of the Record Deliveries module.

```
FOR EACH DELIVERY
      Record INVOICE_ID, SUPPLIER in RECEIPTS
      FOR EACH ITEM
            Record ITEM_ID, QUANTITY, PRICE in RECEIPT_LINE
            Compute new INVENTORY
            Record ITEM_ID, INVENTORY in ITEMS
      END FOR EACH
END FOR EACH
```

Database Analysis

In many methodologies, the specification of file structures and contents is performed either before or after the program specification stage has been completed. In these methodologies a file structure is derived from the information in the data flows of the Data Flow Diagram. Some methodologies treat the definition of a database as a separate process that again involves analysis, design, and specification. This approach is taken here.

If a data file is used by only one system, it is designed in a way that is most suitable for that single system. Unfortunately, data are usually used by many systems, so files must be designed to serve them all. Thus there is a need for methods to analyze and design a system of files, called a database, that is independent of particular application programs or systems. Such methods provide an overview and a detailed view of the database for the system just as the Structure Chart and Structured English provided an overview and a detailed view of the system functions. The overview is provided by Entity-Relationship Diagrams. The detailed view is provided by normalized tables.

The Entity-Relationship approach to data design views all data as being about some particular thing that is generically called an entity or about the relationship between these particular entities. Figure 1-5 illustrates an Entity-Relationship Diagram for four entities that are involved in the inventory system example. At the overview level it is relatively easy to establish that there are at least four entities that the system requires information about: suppliers, parts, bins, and customers. It may not be clear at this stage exactly what items of information are required about each of these entities. It is clear that these entities are the things about which information is recorded.

In addition, the analyst can establish which entities are related to each other and what the relationships are. Suppliers supply parts. Bins store parts. Customers buy parts. Suppliers and customers have no relationship to bins. The relationships can be further characterized by the number of members of each entity that can be related to each other. The arrowheads on the relationship lines can be used to indicate that a part can be in many bins but a bin can contain only one kind of part. A supplier can provide many different parts and a part can be provided by many different suppliers. These entities later become the names of files, called data tables, that need to be created.

Figure 1-5
An Entity-Relationship Diagram for the inventory system.

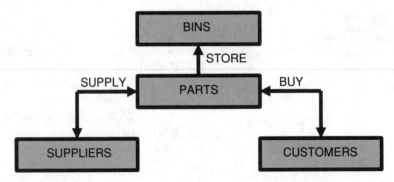

Database Design and Specification

Each entity can be expanded into a table that contains details, called attributes, about the entity. For instance, the customer table contains at least a customer identification, a name, a phone number, and a credit rating. There are techniques, called normalization, to determine whether the tables have been properly structured to eliminate potential problems like duplicated data and inconsistent updates. When the design is completed, the tables can be defined using a database language like SQL. Figure 1-6 illustrates part of the customer table with attributes in the columns and sample entries in the rows.

Once the tables have been defined, it is easy to define the screens that are needed to enter data into the system. Similarly, it is easy to define the reports that can be produced from the data. In traditional methodologies, the screens and reports have usually been treated as part of the functions. They are identified and described during the specification of the Data Flow Diagram, Structure Chart, and Structured English Specification. In modern database systems, screens and reports are often treated as part of the database implementation.

The functions and data both have to be identified and then specified. The difficult question of which are analyzed first is dealt with later.

Coding, Testing, and Implementation

The analyst specifies the functions and data tables that the system must contain. Programmers then code these in a particular computer language and test the resulting system to make sure that it conforms to the specifications. Testing is usually performed first on individual modules to make sure that they do their job and do not contain errors, usually called bugs. Then the whole system is tested to make sure that the modules integrate together. This process is called the bottom-up approach to testing.

Finally programmers implement the system on the selected machine, provide documentation, and train users. The analyst usually does not get involved in coding, testing, and implementation. As modern CASE tools come into common use, this situation is changing. CASE tools simplify the programming process, making it easier for analysts to produce the final product than to specify requirements to a programmer. Sometimes users can produce programs themselves.

Figure 1-6

Selected rows and columns of the Customer data table.

CUSTOMER-ID	NAME	PHONE	RATING	. . .
1047	JONES	444-8172	A	. . .
2115	CHEN	324-5517	A	
3172	BOUVIER	632-9852	B	
3375	SETHI	678-2426	A	
3914	McKAY	491-2376	C	
4120	SENKO	243-4727	A	
. . .				

CASE Tools for the Analyst

Until recent years, the systems analysis and design field was one of the least automated areas in an organization. It was another example of the old adage that "The cobbler's children have no shoes." As a result, many of the development approaches that rely heavily on graphics have not been widely used. Diagrams such as Entity-Relationship Models and Structure Charts are difficult to draw and update manually. As a result they have been avoided, even though using them makes significant improvements in the quality of a design.

This situation is changing rapidly. There are now several software tools that can be used on microcomputers or mainframes. These tools can simplify the design process and eliminate much of the drudgery that goes with the process. They are doing for systems analysis and design what Computer Aided Design and Computer Aided Manufacturing (CAD/CAM) are doing for manufacturing of mechanical and electronic components.

These tools are referred to as CASE (Computer Aided Software Engineering) tools. There is no consensus on what the terms CASE and Fourth Generation Language (4GL) mean. Every vendor who wants to project a progressive image claims that its product is CASE or 4GL. Many times there is little justification for this claim. Currently, the terms refer to a collection of different software tools that provide aid during specific parts of the System Development Life Cycle. The different classes of tools and the phases of the development cycle that they support are illustrated in Figure 1-7. Fisher[2] and McClure[4,5] list and review specific tools for each class.

Figure 1-7

Tools available during the System Development Life Cycle.

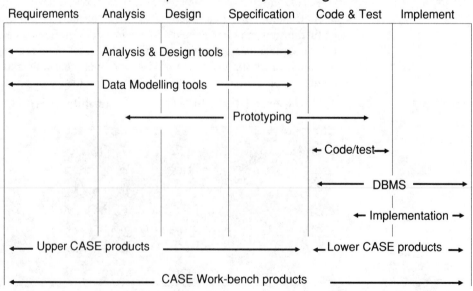

Development Life Cycle Stages

Requirements	Analysis	Design	Specification	Code & Test	Implement

Each class of tools contains several different components. Sometimes several are integrated into a single package. Often a package supports only one or a few of the functions. Together they can be thought of as a set of tools that all analysts should have on their workbenches. Sometimes they are subdivided into front-end products to support the analysis and design stages and back-end products to support the coding, testing, and implementation stages. The front-end and back-end products are sometimes called Upper CASE and Lower CASE tools.

The tools typically found in each class are:

- **Analysis, design, and specification tools.** These include tools to help create Data Flow Diagrams, Structure Charts, and Structured English specifications. They may also contain tools that analyze program complexity. Often they contain a Data Dictionary or repository that provides a complete description of the elements in the design.

- **Data modeling tools.** These include tools to maintain a Data Dictionary, create Entity-Relationship Diagrams, and perform data normalization. The dictionary describes the entities, attributes, and relationships in the database being designed.

- **Prototyping tools.** These tools help to create screens, build menus, specify report layouts, and simulate screen dialogues. This category can also include Fourth Generation Languages that can be used directly by the analyst to define databases, screens, or reports in the presence of the user. Using these tools, it is often simpler to produce parts of the finished product than to produce an unambiguous specification that can be given to a programmer.

- **Coding tools.** These include Data Base Management Systems, Fourth Generation Languages, screen painters, code generators, and program templates. Each one is designed to speed up the production of code in a somewhat different way. In addition, there are tools that restructure code to run more efficiently and tools that translate code into other languages.

  - **Data Base Management Systems.** A DBMS is a utility that allows the designer to define data files; issue commands to insert, update, and delete data; and maintain data by performing validation, backup, and recovery operations. The characteristics of the database are permanently described in a Data Dictionary that is part of the DBMS. The DBMS provides a complete service for storing, retrieving, and manipulating data. It is independent of other application programs, so many programs can share the use of the data without having to design new files for each program.

  - **Fourth Generation Languages.** A 4GL is distinguished from a Third Generation Language (3GL) by the point of view and the amount of detail that the programmer has to provide. With a 3GL, the program must be written from the point of view of the computer with every operation and decision specified in sequence. With a 4GL, the program is written from the point of view of the user with only the required outputs being specified. The 4GL determines the data that must be obtained and the calculations that it must perform. This nonprocedural approach usually leads to a reduction of about 90 percent in the amount of code that has to be written.

The 4GL achieves this saving by maintaining a Data Dictionary that describes the characteristics of the database and by using standard default formats for screens and reports. Some 4GLs combine high level operations with procedural features that can be used for difficult problems. This capability allows the language to grow with the sophistication of the user.

- **Screen generators.** These are tools specially designed to simplify the job of building interactive screens. They can produce quick and easy default screens using the specifications in the Data Dictionary. They can also produce production screens used for regular data entry. A single screen may access multiple files. Screen painters normally provide facilities to maintain the integrity of the database by checking for invalid data. They also provide facilities for creating associated help screens. A single screen may often be used to inquire, insert, update, or delete data in a file.

- **Code generators.** A code generator is similar to a 4GL in that it uses a high level specification language. However, it produces a program in a 3GL such as COBOL. Vendors of code generators claim greater machine efficiency. However, this is often at the cost of higher development and maintenance costs. The code generators do not always use a Data Base Management System and an interactive Data Dictionary that documents the structure of the database.

- **Program templates.** These consist of prewritten skeleton programs that can be customized for specific application problems. For instance, the skeleton of a screen display program would recognize all needed commands and process them. It would have to be customized to access a particular file and display a particular format. Templates are an intermediate between 3GL and 4GL—a 3.5GL.

- **Code restructuring and Reverse Engineering.** These tools take badly written programs and reorganize them automatically to have a more maintainable structure. They cannot integrate separate programs into a set of programs with consistent files and user interfaces. They also cannot convert logic that was produced for an old batch-mode hierarchical file system into logic suitable for a modern interactive database system. The problem is somewhat akin to the problem of taking the result 1+1=2 and restructuring it to derive the original expression:

$$\ln[\lim(1+1/z)^z] + (\sin^2 x + \cos^2 x) = \Sigma[\cosh y(1-\tanh^2 y)^{1/2}]/2^n$$

Despite the near impossibility of the task, the idea appeals to many because they hope that somehow the billions of lines of obsolete code that they have can be magically recycled into modern interactive applications.

- **Code translators.** These tools can translate a program written in one 3GL into another 3GL. Sometimes they translate code written in a 4GL into a 3GL language to increase efficiency. Again, they cannot integrate separate programs into a set of programs with consistent files and user interfaces.

- **Testing Tools.** These tools include on-line debugging facilities, test data generators, test comparators, and simulators. Test comparators check that the results of new versions of programs are the same as the results of old versions. Simulators imitate such conditions as large transaction loads.

- **Implementation tools.** These tools are used to produce documentation, manage libraries of programs, and import or export data from other systems.

Various CASE products contain subsets of the above features. No single product provides all the described features or even a majority of them. Product vendors are now integrating these features to provide a "complete" womb-to-tomb solution to the problem of designing and developing software systems. These integrated systems contain tools that support both the Upper CASE and the Lower CASE functions. Many CASE products have an open architecture that permits customization for the needs of a particular installation. They are very user-friendly with constructive advice and many diagnostics. Some even contain logic to check for specification errors.

CASE tools provide several benefits that increase productivity and improve the quality of software. These benefits are standard methods, graphics, integration, intelligence, and automation.

- **Standard methods.** CASE tools help to enforce standard methods on a project or in a whole organization. Such systems encourage the production of standard tested components that can be reused without being redeveloped. This simplifies the maintenance task and increases productivity during development.
- **Graphics.** Structured analysis makes heavy use of many kinds of diagrams which are difficult to draw manually. CASE tools simplify the production and revision of the graphics that are essential in structured techniques. This results in documentation that is more current and more correct. One organization claimed that this rapid documentation allowed them to actually implement systems before they became obsolete.
- **Integration.** CASE tools store all the design information generated during the system analysis in a repository. This is a database that stores all information needed in the design process. The description of the database, the processes, the user needs, existing systems, and many other facts are stored in the repository. Since all data are stored in a standard form, it is possible to link them and make sure that all parts of the system are integrated. Computer systems no longer have to consist of independent unconnected components.
- **Intelligence.** Since all of the information in the repository is interconnected, it is possible to check it for consistency. Expert systems and other tools can be used to amplify the intelligence of the analyst and perform many of the tedious checks that actual analysts never seem to have time for.
- **Automation.** Some CASE tools are able to transform the design specifications automatically into computer code. This reduces the work required to produce code and eliminates the errors that result from misunderstood specifications.

The most important benefit of CASE tools is that they make it possible to deal with larger problems. When people had only a shovel, they never dreamed that building the Suez canal was possible. When they acquired the steam shovel, the horizon of their ambitions expanded. In the same way, CASE tools make it possible to consider building an integrated information system for an organization, a task that was not possible with traditional methods.

System Development Life Cycle Problems

There are general principles that apply to the functioning of all systems, whether they are biological, mechanical, organizational, or computerized. The most important ones for analysts are:

- **Every system is part of a larger system and can be broken into smaller subsystems.** It is important to define the problem boundaries correctly. Choosing a system that is too large makes it impossible to implement it in a reasonable time, or possibly to understand it at all. Choosing too small a system excludes factors that may be important to the problem. It may lead to duplicated systems to deal with factors that were ignored in the original system. It may also lead to excessive maintenance and modification of an incomplete system.

- **The components of a system must communicate with each other.**   In computer systems, this communication is accomplished through databases and program interfaces. The functioning of the system is extremely dependent on the design of the communication system.

- **The most specialized systems are the least adaptable.** This has been shown to be true for biological systems many times. It is also true for computer systems. A system that exactly mirrors one organization is unlikely to be useful in any other organization, or in the same organization if it changes.

- **Systems grow and change.** Since the system—of which the user is part— also changes, the computer system must be adaptable if it is to continue to match the user's needs. Organizations change continually, so it is essential that computer systems that support them be able to respond to these changes.

The System Development Life Cycle permits large projects to be broken down into smaller implementable stages. It has allowed these projects to be managed in an orderly manner so results can be delivered at a predictable cost within a reasonable time. However, the System Development Life Cycle has also suffered from some problems. It usually does not have a global planning phase so it promotes a narrow project orientation that leads to fragmentation of effort and a host of uncoordinated systems. It focuses on production cost and delivery time at the expense of quality. It leads to misunderstandings between users and developers about what is to be delivered.

Some of these problems are due to performing the steps of the design in the wrong order. Others are due to separating analysis functions that need to be carried out simultaneously. These problems are examined in detail in the following sections.

Project Orientation

The most common SDLC assumes either that the current project is unrelated to any other project or that someone else looks after the inter-relationships between projects. Usually neither of these cases is true. Each project is a component of the overall information system that is needed by the organization. The information used in one subsystem is frequently needed by other subsystems.

Unless these inter-relationships are considered, wasteful duplication occurs in many of the subsystems. One organization found that in a group of 40 application programs, the same data were gathered an average of ten times. Some information is collected and processed several times by several different subsystems. Other needed information may be left out of all systems and not processed at all. Users are unable to access information that is partially available in each of several subsystems, but is not integrated.

By focusing on a single project, the SDLC implicitly ignores the needs of other projects and interested parties. It emphasizes efficiency of single components rather than effectiveness of the whole system. Separate systems trap data in file ghettos. Information must be liberated from these isolated islands of data. Analysts must be proactive problem-solvers instead of reactive order-takers.

The SDLC needs an integration stage that identifies all the projects and all their inter-relationships. This previous stage ensures that the development of each project can be coordinated to produce a synergistic system that is greater than the sum of its parts. This additional phase is the conceptual analysis and design stage. It must come before any of the projects. Like the steel skeleton of a building, it provides a framework within which the other projects can fit like individual floors. It also identifies common features that tie the projects together as elevators tie the floors of a building together. The architectural design helps to anticipate the needs of the users.

In the conceptual analysis and design stage, the analyst deals primarily with the database, the activities, and sometimes the communications network used by the organization. Each is examined at a very aggregate level to partition it into closely related groups that can be implemented as individual projects.

The most common conceptual analysis and design tools are based on the Business Systems Planning (BSP) method. In this method, the analyst identifies the activities that an organization performs and the entities that it gathers data about. An intersection table called an Activity-Entity Diagram is created which identifies, with an X, the data entities that are needed by each activity. This information is then used to cluster the activities into groups of related activities.

Figure 1-8 shows a part of an Activity-Entity Diagram for a university. Three clusters of activities are separated by horizontal lines. When these groups of related activities have been identified, implementation priorities can be set for each group. The middle group is shaded to indicate that it has the highest priority for implementation. This group is then treated as a project with its own development life cycle. As the different projects are implemented, a complete system—without overlapping activities or data—is constructed.

Figure 1-8

An Activity-Entity Table that partitions activities into subsystems.

		Buildings	Rooms	Equipment	Scholarships	Students	Refereees	Programs	Courses	Sections	Meetings	Skills	Tasks	Job-Descriptions	Faculty	Staff	Positions	Subordinates	Grants	Departments
Planning	Demand Analysis				X	X		X	X	X					X					
	Budgeting					X				X							X		X	X
	Applications				X	X	X													
	Financial Aid				X	X	X													
Student	Registration	X	X			X		X	X	X	X				X					
	Student Evaluation					X		X	X	X					X					
	Graduation					X		X	X	X										
	Course Scheduling	X	X	X				X	X	X	X				X					
	Program Admin.									X	X									
Staff	Manpower Planning					X						X	X	X	X	X	X	X	X	X
	Personnel Eval.												X	X	X	X	X	X	X	X
	Promotion													X	X	X	X	X	X	X

Cost, Time, and Quality Tradeoffs

The 3GL environment is characterized by the use of procedural languages such as COBOL and PL/1. Files have usually been defined using the data structures within these languages. File definition and programming in these languages is a complex task requiring a great deal of skill and time. Even single projects, such as an accounting system for a large company, can take dozens of person-years to design and implement. Once implemented, the programs are difficult to maintain. A survey[1] indicates that:

- 93 percent of data processing organizations have a three year backlog.
- Half of all applications take more than a year to develop. A third of them require at least two years.
- Maintenance costs exceed development costs for 90 percent of programs.
- Only 8 percent of data processing budgets are allocated to new application development.
- Personnel costs are 56 percent of data processing budgets. Hardware costs are 31 percent.

This survey clearly shows that we currently have a slow, inflexible, people-intensive system that is complex and unresponsive to organizational needs.

A tradesman once told me that most of his customers want their work done cheaply, quickly, and well. He tells them that they can have any two of the three. Most implementations of the System Development Life Cycle focus on controlling cost, delivery time, and quality—in that order. Cost and delivery time are easy to measure, so there is a lot of emphasis on them in most project management systems. Quality is hard to measure, so it is often ignored. Important elements of quality are flexibility and adaptability which are often ignored completely in the system design.

One project manager explained that if a project ran over budget, there would be a major investigation before further funding could be approved. If it was running late on delivery, there would be a rebuke. If quality was poor, it would become someone else's maintenance problem. Thus, when making trade-offs between cost, schedule, and quality, the factor that suffers most is quality.

The bottom-up approach to testing suffers from a number of problems:

- **There is no feedback from users.** The users rarely see a system between the preparation of the specifications and the delivery of the system. Testing confirms that the system conforms to the specifications. If the specifications were wrong, this would not be known until the system is delivered. By that time it is too late to change it.
- **Serious errors are found last.** The most serious and costly errors are those that result from poor design of the overall architecture of the system. These are not discovered until the final integration stage of testing. An error discovered at this stage likely requires changes to many different modules that depend on the environment that is implicit in the initial architecture.
- **Nothing is done until everything is done.** The final integration test must be completed before the builders can be sure that each of the modules works within the system. None of the modules can be delivered before this test. As a result, it is difficult to show any progress to the client until completion. If a problem is discovered in the final test, it may be a long time before it is fixed. This makes it difficult to adhere to delivery schedules.

The CASE environment deals with these problems by providing tools that reduce the coding and testing effort. Top-down testing is used to test the architecture before the lower modules are built. This reduces the chance that costly errors persist until later stages of coding. CASE provides standard models—like Entity-Relationship Models and Data Flow Diagrams—that help to increase flexibility. It also provides user-oriented methods that reduce specification and design errors. Involving the user in the process reduces the chances that major errors remain in the design. Since it costs much more to correct a design error at the implementation stage than at the design stage of the life cycle, these techniques also reduce costs.

User Mis-understandings

The SDLC used in a 3GL environment tries to identify what the user gets by specifying a list of requirements that must be satisfied. Unfortunately, computer users—and all other mortals—are not very good at visualizing results that fit a set of abstract requirements. The result is illustrated in Figure 1-9. The users may specify that they want a vehicle to transport them around the neighborhood and make the neighbors notice them. They envision a racing bicycle. The analyst interprets the request as a motorcycle and writes specifications that resemble a car. The implementer eventually delivers a truck that satisfies the specification but not the real requirement.

An illustration of communication problems between the user, the designer, and the programmer.

What the requirements stated.

What the designer specified.

What the programmers implemented.

What the user wanted.

The same thing happens with written specifications for computer systems. Languages, like English, are ambiguous and imprecise. The registrar of a university tells the analyst to compute a grade point average. The analyst does not ask further questions because an average is a simple concept. The analyst includes a formula for averages in the specifications to the programmer.

Neither the analyst nor the programmer realize that special rules sometimes apply. When a student has taken a course twice to improve a grade, one grade may have to be deleted. When a student has taken more than the required number of courses for a degree, some may not be counted. Neither is prepared for the registrar who will soon change the rules to allow courses with only a pass/fail grade. The user and the analyst operate in different systems. They have not communicated because each made assumptions about what the other understood.

Designers and users are aware of this problem, but neither can propose solutions. The designers wish that users would specify clearly what they want rather than use vague terms or continually change their minds. Users wish the designers would learn to build systems that are more flexible. These systems must respond to needs that do change frequently in an actual operating environment.

The designers, being in charge of the process, begin to take a legalistic approach to the problem to protect themselves from charges that they do not provide what is needed. They produce voluminous Requirements Specifications. They require the users to sign off and certify that the specifications are the complete requirements of the proposed system.

The users frequently find these documents are loaded with diagrammatic specification charts and jargon that they cannot understand. They are left completely baffled. They usually sign the documents anyway because they feel that a confusing or incomplete system is better than none.

When the system is finally delivered—sometimes years later—the users complain. However, they are told that the system is exactly as described in the specification of requirements and can no longer be changed. The users find that they have, in effect, signed a contract to like whatever is delivered.

The users then send down a blizzard of requests for modifications to be done by maintenance programmers. The requests are collected until the pile is big enough to justify a major system improvement. Meanwhile the maintenance staff works on a backlog of requests for other systems and hopes that the wait teaches users to think more about their requirements before requesting future systems. This becomes the information systems equivalent of a work-to-rules strike.

Users are much better at recognizing what they like—or do not like—when they see it. The part of an information system that users see is the input screens and the output reports. The input screens are the key component from the users' point of view. The output reports are transformations of the input and can be modified relatively easily if the correct input data are available. This indicates that the analyst should concentrate on the data in the input screens as early as possible. That way users can see the interface that they will use and can see the data that will go into the system. If the users do not like the proposed system, there is an opportunity to change it before the rest of the system is developed.

The analyst can give the user an early look at the system by eliminating the emphasis on specifications and moving to a rapid prototyping method. This reduces the total system cost by eliminating a large part of the maintenance cost. Some maintenance still has to be done to adjust the system to conform to new operating policies and new regulations as the user's system changes. The large body of maintenance effort needed to convert the system that was specified, into the system that was wanted, is virtually eliminated.

Figure 1-10 illustrates a typical screen painting program being used to design a new screen. The screen painter is easy to use. It provides pop-up menus from which the designer can select any allowable options, such as the attributes of a data field. A prototype screen may be designed in fifteen minutes in the user's presence. The user then specifies corrections to create a finished screen.

Report generators are ideal for prototyping reports. Meador et al[6] found several reasons, involving reporting and data analysis, for prototyping Decision Support Systems. Functional specifications are hard to develop for unstructured decisions where detailed requirements are unknown. Users do not know what they want and designers do not know what they need.

A small prototype system gives both parties something concrete to which to react. In the process of using a system, users discover insights into their decision process and find uses which were previously unpredicted. Users differ in the way they make decisions. Thus standardization is not possible and the flexible, personal approach of prototyping is needed.

The input screen provides an early deliverable with which the user can interact. People usually find it much easier to change something that exists than to invent something new. They use the input screen that they see as an opportunity to identify missing data and begin to understand the processing environment. They do this within an approximation of the actual future operating environment rather than in some abstract diagrammatic language that they find hard to use.

Figure 1-10

A Screen Painter being used to specify the attributes of a prototype screen.

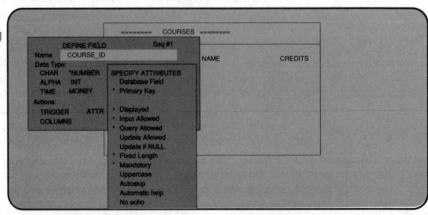

There is some need to repeat this process as users identify new data requirements, but this first prototype serves as a good basis for improvement. The features of a Data Base Management System make it relatively easy to redefine the data structure. Thus analysts have the tools to produce prototypes quickly while the user is present and interested.

Working in the actual operating environment reduces the need for explanation and training. Often large amounts of documentation can be eliminated because the system becomes self-documenting. The Data Base Management System documents the structure of the data it contains. The screens can contain menus to select options and prompts. They can contain helps to indicate what data the system allows. The input data can be automatically validated to make sure that they are consistent with other data in the system. These features reduce the need for paper documentation to guide users through the system.

A prototyping method also reduces the need for requirements documentation. A rough requirements statement coupled with interaction with the users replaces much of the detailed documentation of requirements. This is a saving because requirements documents are used only once in the development process.

Once the data files and input screens are identified and constructed, it is immediately possible to produce reports that summarize the input data. 4GL Query Languages, such as SQL, make it possible for some users to define many needed reports themselves. In fact, any report that does not alter the contents of the database can be safely delegated to the user. Authorized users can be given read-only permission to access the database. They are not able to harm the data in any way. This approach is called end-user computing.

Many users can learn query languages like SQL relatively easily. Not all of them want to, but those who do can modify their own reports as needs change. There is always the possibility that amateur users can produce incorrect reports. However, this is unlikely since the reports are in their own domain of expertise.

Furthermore, the users are very concerned about getting the query right because they are responsible for decisions made while using the reports. In addition, they can tailor the outputs to transfer data to other tools such as spreadsheets, graphics packages, or statistical packages for further analysis. Users may initially make foolish requests, but they learn to improve.

Once the database, screens, and reports have been defined, the only part of the system left to be built is the programs that modify the contents of the data table. Programs, like payroll processing or order generation, are typically batch processes. They take input data on such things as hours worked and transform them into table entries and outputs that reflect payments made. Alternately, they may be transaction processors that interface with other systems such as a credit card validation system. These large critical applications cannot be delegated to users. Professionals must assure that the system has been developed and tested under organizational guidelines on security, accuracy, and compliance with various regulations and audit standards.

The operations of batch programs are largely hidden from users because they are usually triggered at set times or by other processes. They may involve sequential processing of batches of transactions. Prototyping techniques are less applicable to these programs. So the analyst often relies on traditional design techniques to specify requirements and processing steps. Even when a CASE tool is used, these techniques may still be needed. However, they are needed only for a relatively small part of the system. The database, the input screens, and the output reports are all generated by prototyping.

What analysts and developers are doing in the 3GL System Development Life Cycle is entombing the warm living body of user requirements in the cold lifeless concrete of program code. Periodically, during a ritual called maintenance, they reopen the tomb and try to bring their embalmed creation back to life. If this turns out to be impossible, they at least rearrange the bones.

The CASE tools make it very easy to define data structures, generate input screens, validate input, generate reports, and enforce security requirements. That leaves only the routine batch-oriented transaction processing part of the 3GL environment which is relatively unchanged. These tasks still require some of the traditional systems analysis techniques of Data Flow Diagrams, Structure Charts, and Structured English specifications.

In a CASE environment, the user and analyst do not have to be in a legalistic adversary position haggling over the terms of a requirements specification. They are freed to be part of a team that is cooperating in a dynamic process to produce a system that satisfies the users' needs.

Order of SDLC Phases

Current design approaches progress from required outputs to processes that produce them to data required to support them. The design process is driven by the required end product. Unfortunately, in the Information Systems field the outputs must change frequently as external circumstances change or as users learn to use new kinds of information. However, most of the possible outputs are derived from the same set of input data needed to support basic organizational functions. These data were identified long ago and have been collected in forms and files for many years.

The data requirements of an organization are usually the most stable and most pervasive component of the organization. It is usually hard to envision a change in the organization or the environment that creates a need for more than a minor change in the basic data needed to run the organization. For instance, it does not matter whether an organization divides itself into regional, product-oriented, or customer-oriented divisions. The same basic inventory, sales, and accounting data are needed. The processes may change somewhat and the required reports may be quite different, but the data do not change much.

Data are also very pervasive because the same data are often used in many parts of the organization for different purposes. Yet this project-oriented design method encourages design of data files for a very restricted set of needs. It encourages structuring the data so it supports only this restricted set in an efficient manner. The result is a system that is very unresponsive to the dynamics of the organization.

The next most stable part of the organization is the processes needed to support the functions of the organization. In the above example, the same inventory, sales, and accounting processes have to be carried out regardless of the organizational structure.

The least stable components of the organization are the required outputs. These depend on the individuals using the systems, the structure of the organization, and the changing external constraints. As different individuals are rotated into functional positions, they need different information to support their different knowledge levels, needs, and preferences.

As the organization changes from regional to product-oriented, information has to be presented by product instead of by region. The different organizational structure may also place emphasis on different kinds of information such as profitability reports instead of cost reports. As customer needs or government regulations change, new reports have to be generated even though they contain essentially the same data in a new form. As users become more knowledgeable, they discard old information that they no longer find useful. They ask for new information that they have learned to use.

The traditional design paradigm focuses on the least stable part of the system, the outputs. It uses the unstable outputs to constrain the most stable and pervasive parts, the data and processing methods. Analysts identify the needs, build an infrastructure of data and programs to serve those needs and then find that the infrastructure cannot support new needs. This is because the system was not organized in a general enough way to respond to changing needs.

This approach, based on outputs, comes from the historical view that the computer program that implements the process is the central component of the system. The inputs and data files are needed to support the process and the outputs are a by-product of the process. Both programs and data are assumed to die eventually. Figure 1-11 illustrates this viewpoint. The viewpoint is correct for small temporary programs designed to perform an ad hoc analysis of data. It is perpetuated because these are the kinds of problems commonly given to students when they are learning to program. Programmers continue to use this viewpoint because it simplifies the delivery of a single project. No time is spent on identifying the data needs of other projects.

The CASE environment requires that designers take a different view of the information system. The central component is the database, as shown in Figure 1-12. It is assumed to continue to exist forever in some form. Data changes its function as it ages. An order becomes a sale, a delivery, a receivable, a payment, and eventually an archival record as the underlying process continues. The inputs from screens, outputs to reports, and processes that modify the database are components that maintain the database and produce useful outputs from it. Data

Figure 1-11
The process-centered
view of information sys-
tems emphasizes the
programs that imple-
ment processes.

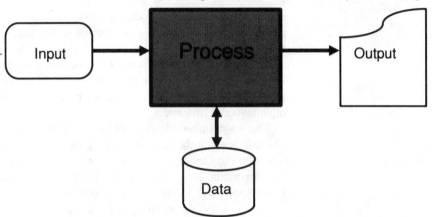

are no longer viewed as things that flow in pipes between programs. They are
now things stored in reservoirs into which programs dip their pipes.

This view of the system contains the same components as the previous view.
The difference is in the emphasis. By viewing the database as the central component, the analyst concentrates on defining the data correctly. Later the analyst
worries about inputs, reports, or programs that transform the data in the database.
The System Architecture is based on the things that make up the enterprise and
on what the enterprise does. The architecture is not based on how the enterprise
is organized to do these things. An objective, neutral architecture is not based on
personalities, politics, and biases.

The data-centered view does make it easier to separate an application into
independent components. Since the database is a permanent central feature of the
system, all the other components can independently use the database whenever
they need to. Any process that is executed at a different time or controlled by a
different person can be developed as a separate application. The database auto-

Figure 1-12
The data-centered view
of information systems
emphasizes the DBMS
that stores the data
needed by the system.

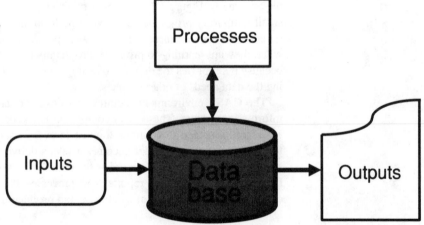

matically connects them into an integrated application (unless there are important timing considerations).

Independence means that inputs can be split into separate on-line and batch systems. The on-line systems validate and update data immediately. The batch systems post batches of transactions periodically from magnetic media. Similarly, output can be split into interactive queries and standard batch reports or other transactions, such as bills. Processes can be split into sequential processes that periodically transform or aggregate data. Aging accounts receivable is an example of a periodic transformation. A monthly sales summary is an aggregation.

Realizing that every system is part of a larger system and that the components of a system must communicate with each other allows the analyst to concentrate on the database. This is the most important part of the organizational communication system.

Inflexibility

The Information Industry is now at the stage that the transportation industry was in during the early part of the twentieth century. At that time the transportation industry was coping with the change from a train-oriented system to a car-oriented system. Airplanes were still at the research stage. Trains were large complex inflexible systems designed to move people and freight between specified points at set times. The users of the system had to adapt their needs to fit within the capabilities and timetable of the railroads. Customization for individual needs was difficult or impossible. Trains had to be operated by specialists and users could never hope to have or operate their own trains because of their complexity and expense.

Most existing computer systems are much like trains. They are large complex inflexible systems designed to move and process specific pieces of data for identified users under conditions and schedules defined by the operators of the system. Customization for individual needs has been difficult or impossible. Computers have had to be operated by specialists. Users could never have or operate their own computer systems because of the complexity and expense.

When automobiles were developed, it became possible for users to afford their own transportation. The technology was simple enough that individuals could operate a vehicle. They were no longer at the mercy of a large organization that set services and schedules to which users had to conform. Now the users could decide where they wanted to go and when.

The one component that still must be provided by a large organization is the road system. Engineers must design and construct safe roads that connect places to which people wanted to travel, and have the capacity to handle the volume of use. Training programs, traffic signals and divided roads are needed to control access to the system. They insure that the system is used only by authorized users in a way that is safe. Roads are treated as a public good, provided centrally for the benefit of all because they are needed by everyone.

Modern computer systems are somewhat like roads and automobiles. Personal workstations allow individuals much more control over how and when they use a computer. CASE and 4GL systems are simple enough that many users are able to operate components of the system themselves.

The one component that still has to be provided by a large organization is the database and the associated communications network. Systems staff have to design and construct a database that contains the data that people need, is safe for individuals to use, and has the capacity to handle the volume of use. Training programs, security controls and validity checks are needed to control access to the system. They insure that the system is used only by authorized users in a way that is safe. The database is treated as a public good, provided centrally by the organization for the benefit of all, because it is needed by everyone.

Automobiles did not eliminate trains. Both coexist as shown in Figure 1-13. The use of trains was redirected to hauling heavy freight between major centers. The rest of the traffic is hauled by individually controlled vehicles. Some interconnections between systems are supported. Cars and busses take people to meet trains. Trucks pick up freight at trains and distribute it locally.

CASE and 4GL systems will not eliminate 3GL systems either. 3GL systems will be restricted to handling heavy applications. Examples are airline reservations or bank transactions. These are handled more economically by a customized application that provides a limited set of services. The rest of the applications will be controlled by individuals who have freedom to design their systems to suit individual needs. Interconnected systems will exist. Users will take data from central systems and manipulate them locally. This will be easy if standard interfaces are provided to allow users to pick up the information that is directed to them. This approach ensures that the new system is as flexible and adaptable as possible.

There is another similarity between cars and personal computers. Just as cars have had an unforeseen impact on how we design cities, where we live, and what we can do with our leisure time, personal computers are having a major impact on how we structure organizations and how we do our jobs. The changes caused by the car are relatively mature. The changes caused by the personal computer are just beginning. Many of them are still dimly understood.

Figure 1-13
Coexistence
of utilities
and personal
vehicles.

An Architectural Approach

Zachman[8] argues that there are three main participants in the development of any major system. These are the client, the designer, and the builder. These three can be identified in any major construction enterprise, whether it is a building, an airplane, or an information system. In constructing an office building, these three parties are the client, the architect, and the construction contractor. In building an airplane, the three parties are combined within a single organization, but divided into marketing, engineering, and manufacturing divisions. In the Information Systems area, these three groups have traditionally been called the users, the systems analysts, and the programmers.

Information Systems people borrowed names from architecture and engineering by referring to Information Systems Architects or Software Engineers. The subtle differences in viewpoint have also been transferred. Zachman[8], in an article on Information Systems Architecture, sees it as the methods of designing and specifying a complete system. He pays very little attention to the problems of construction.

Goldberg[3], in an article on the history of Software Engineering, sees engineering as a "discipline whose goal is to produce reliable software products in a cost-effective manner." He dwells on ways to make the process more efficient, but never mentions methods—such as Entity-Relationship Models or Business Systems Planning—which are used to identify the framework and context of the system. He takes the architecture and requirements as given and concentrates on satisfying those externally specified requirements.

The architect acts as an intermediary between the client (user) and the builder (programmer) as shown in Figure 1-14. The Systems Engineer focuses on the construction of the system, acting as the transformer of specifications into a final product.

This book is about the job of the Information Systems Architect. This is the person who acts as intermediary between the users who have needs and the programmers who have the skills to construct the system. This person is usually known as an analyst. The book focuses on the process of analysis and design and leaves construction details to the System Engineer. This is done deliberately to:

Figure 1-14

The relationship between Information Systems Architecture and Software Engineering.

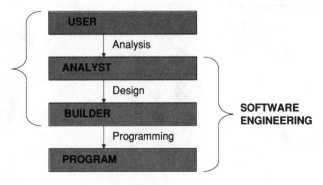

- **Focus** on analyzing users' needs and translating them into requirements.
- **Identify** analysis and design as a discipline separate from programming.
- **Separate** the design phase from the construction phase so logical requirements determine technological choices. Otherwise a selected technology determines how users' problems are viewed. Thus the logical essence of the system is separated from the implementation details.

The distinction between architect and engineer is more one of emphasis than of substance. Both viewpoints share at least half of the concepts and techniques needed for the completion of a system. In the process that begins with a concept and ends with a completed system, the architect concentrates on the concept and the engineer concentrates on the construction. The architect concentrates on effectiveness (doing the right thing) and the engineer concentrates on efficiency (doing things right).

The work of the architect must precede the work of the engineer. The architect defines the scope, framework, and logical structure of the system. The engineer then has a clear objective and clear boundaries within which to work. Many problems in the development of information systems can be traced to application of software engineering without first developing a software architecture.

Without an architecture, the engineer is not a builder but a handyman. The handyman builder continually adds a room here, a stairway there, and a new roof elsewhere without a coordinated plan. The result is usually a patchwork of expedient solutions that solve day-to-day problems. Unfortunately the result is an architectural monstrosity with no coherent plan, no cohesive structure, no continuity, and no coordination, like the structure in Figure 1-15. Additions that solve one problem are continually being torn down or bypassed because they create new problems or get in the way of solutions to other problems.

Figure 1-15
The added value of architecture is coordination, integration, and consistency.

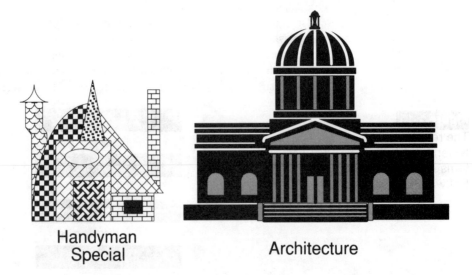

Handyman
Special

Architecture

Without an architectural design phase, the Systems Engineer—or programmer—is cast in the role of a handyman. The programmer is asked to produce programs that are expedient solutions to day-to-day problems with no coherent plan, no cohesive structure, no coordination, and no continuity. During the maintenance phase, sections of code are added, eliminated, or bypassed because they get in the way of solutions to other problems. Often new problems are introduced during this maintenance phase.

The System Engineer does not like to be cast in the role of handyman. System Engineers thrust into this situation continually demand a set of clear requirements which define the scope of the project. Unfortunately, the users cannot provide such requirements since they are not fully aware of what is possible or which problems will confront them next. Both need the help of an architect.

The engineer and architect also share a reliance on prefabricated components to complete their design. In a building, the elevator, heating system, windows, and most other components are not invented by the architect. They come "off the shelf" from a supplier. Analysts have not used prefabricated components very much in the past. This is sometimes called the NIH (Not Invented Here) syndrome. They have preferred to reinvent a wheel whenever they needed one. This satisfies a creative urge, but has occasionally resulted in some unusual wheels.

There are now a variety of components available: Data Base Management Systems, Networks, Decision Support Systems, screen painters, report generators, graphics packages, etc. Analysts have an opportunity to decrease costs and increase quality by using more prefabricated components.

The Roles of the Analyst

The relationship with the user is called *analysis*. Analysis is the identification and modeling of user requirements. This often consists of identifying the information components of an existing manual or computerized system. This is to be replaced by a new, more efficient or more functional system. Occasionally it consists of designing a system to perform a function for which there is no current system of any kind. Usually, a functioning organization already has some system in place and is interested in improving it.

Analysis is a top-down approach that works down from the general to the particular. As each level of the problem is understood, it is expanded into more detail. This can be contrasted with synthesis which is essentially a bottom-up approach. It gathers a lot of detail and then tries to organize it into a general structure. 3GL methodologies concentrate on synthesis, not analysis. The traditional system analyst really behaves more as a system synthesizer.

After the analysis stage, analysts create a conceptual model of the system to aid their own understanding of the problem and the eventual solution. This model is primarily for internal use by the analyst. It is an intermediate model that facilitates the transition between the users' and the programmer's model.

Finally the analyst transforms this conceptual model into a *design* that is communicated to CASE tools, which may in turn be communicated to the programmer. To do this the analyst needs to know what the CASE tools and programmers can accomplish with current technology, but does not need to know how to operate the technology. Thus the analyst must:

- **Analyze** the needs of the user.
- **Design** a conceptual model of user requirements.
- **Specify** these requirements using CASE tools.
- **Generate** specifications or programs with the CASE tool.

In the information systems field, the distinction between users, designers, and builders has often been blurred. Advertisements often appear for "Programmer-Analysts with two to five years of COBOL experience to design systems." We never see advertisements for "steel workers with two to five years of steel welding experience to design skyscrapers" or "mechanics with two to five years of bodywork experience to design cars." The skills needed to design a skyscraper or a car are not the same as the skills needed to build one and everyone recognizes that. The skills needed for design are much more complex and comprehensive than the skills needed for construction. The background and the education of architects and engineers is very different from that of builders and mechanics.

This confusion has resulted because the information systems field is so new that it has not had time to establish clear roles. Such roles require a body of professional skills that are used to perform the functions of each role. Architects and engineers know what their roles are and they have had centuries to establish methods and procedures for performing their respective functions. Both disciplines design large systems. They may even work on the same building.

However, the architect concentrates on identifying the needs of the user and designing a coherent edifice that satisfies those needs. The engineer typically takes the requirements specified by the architect and turns them into detailed plans for components such as elevators and air-conditioning systems. They both have the same objective—to construct a building. The architect concentrates primarily on the users' needs and the engineer concentrates on the builder's capabilities and constraints.

Technology continues to blur the distinction between architecture and engineering. The Mechanical Engineer can now design a part at a computer terminal. A Computer Aided Design system then produces instructions for numerically controlled machine tools. The tools make the dies needed to manufacture the part or they manufacture the part itself. The Design Engineer can eliminate the skilled craftsman from part of the production cycle. Similarly the analyst can use CASE tools to design a complete database structure and screens more easily than the analyst can define unambiguous specifications for a programmer.

Recently there have been references to End-User Computing which imply that the users can perform the analysis, design, and construction phases themselves. While this is not yet practical for any but the most trivial systems, it may be possible in the future with expert systems that guide the user. However, the user must learn something about the principles of good design to avoid repeating the mistakes of the past.

Successive Refinement

The building architect begins with a sketch of a building, then a layout for each floor, and finally a detailed plan for each room. Similarly the analyst first develops an overview model of the system to see what components must be included. Components are broken into pieces and finally pieces are detailed.

This successive refinement lets the analyst successively concentrate on the overall concept of the system and then on the details of each component. This refinement process may have an arbitrary number of stages depending on the complexity of the system. It always has at least two levels called the *concept* level and the *detail* level. The concept level defines the parts of the whole system. The detail level defines the properties of a single part.

Successive refinement is a process of examining systems from the top down. The analysis process begins with broad outlines of the system, then reveals new levels of detail in successive stages like using a zoom lens. First the overall scene is shown with context but no detail. The analyst then successively zooms in to examine more detailed views until the system is shown in understandable detail.

The structure of a textbook is an example of successive refinement. Sections contain chapters that treat topics in the same general theme. Chapters contain divisions that discuss specific aspects of a topic. Divisions may contain subdivisions that expand points of each aspect.

The analyst's first view of a data model concentrates on entities and relationships between them. The next refinement documents the properties—usually called attributes—that are recorded about each entity. The last refinement documents the format of each attribute. The systems are similarly refined into subsystems, activities, and program specifications.

This process preserves the context of each stage of understanding of our systems. It allows the complete system to be broken into smaller subsystems and still smaller subsystems. The boundaries between subsystems are chosen to give maximum similarity of components within the subsystems and minimum coupling between the subsystems.

Multiple Notations

The job of the analyst is primarily one of communication. Analysts need to communicate with users to determine what is needed. Analysts need to communicate with themselves to conceptualize and integrate this information to produce an integrated coherent model. Finally they need to communicate this model to the programmer. For each of these communication roles they have developed different graphic methods of presenting the information because each role communicates different information.

Different methods are needed for each role because each participant is concerned about different things. The owner of a building, such as a school, is interested in offices, classrooms, and laboratories. In addition to these, the architect has to consider such things as access routes, safety features, and how to create multiple-use spaces. The builder is concerned with the sequence of construction, the tools to be used, and the precise specification of materials.

In the same way, the user of a database is concerned with the contents of the database. The analyst is concerned with content, structure and safety features. The structure permits access by users with different needs. The safety features preserve the integrity of the data. The programmer is concerned with the language to be used and the precise definition of functions.

The Building Architect produces sketches and floor plans for the client and architectural plans for the builder. The builder finally produces contractor's plans and shop plans. In the same way the analyst produces different documents for the user, the analyst, and the programmer. Figure 1-16 illustrates two of these notations. The Data Flow Diagram is used when the analyst communicates with the user about functions to be performed. The Structure Chart is used when the analyst communicates with the programmer about the hierarchical control structure that connects the functions. Both refer to different aspects of the same functions.

Most of the documentation is in graphic form as suggested by the old adage that "a picture is worth 1024 bytes." Much of the documentation records relationships between things or processes. Entity-Relationship Models show which entities contain related data. Data Flow Diagrams show the sequence of processes and data flowing between processes. A diagram is much better than a "Victorian Novel" of text at illustrating such relationships unambiguously. Related subgroups are also easier to identify in a diagram than in text.

The Revised System Development Life Cycle

The System Development Life Cycle must change when a CASE environment is used. The BC (Before CASE) life cycle shown in Figure 1-17 is a sequential process that progresses through requirements, analysis, design, specification, coding, testing, and implementation. There are several feedback loops in the process to correct errors. When a problem is detected, the process returns to an earlier stage and all the remaining processes must be repeated.

Figure 1-16

The analyst uses two notations for the same information to communicate different aspects of a system to different people.

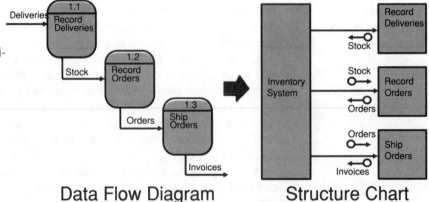

Data Flow Diagram   Structure Chart

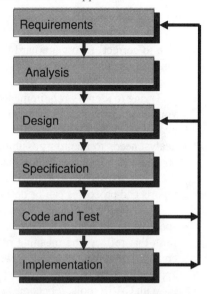

Figure 1-17

The traditional System
Development Life
Cycle used with 3GL
tools.

Figure 1-18

The modern Systems
Development Life
Cycle used with CASE
and 4GL tools.

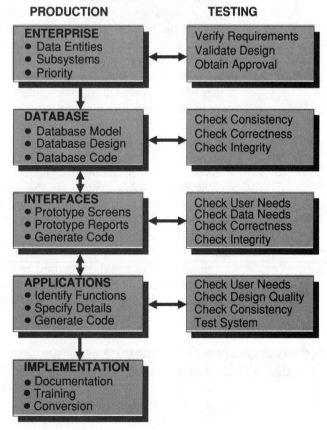

Errors detected in the early stages of the BC life cycle can be corrected inexpensively. However, errors detected at the testing stage can be very expensive to correct. Errors are hard to detect at the early stages without an architectural design phase and without CASE tools to keep track of the details of the analysis process.

Trying to identify requirements first is like trying to chase a mirage. You think you see it, but you can never get a firm grip on it. User requirements change and evolve, even as the analyst tries to identify them. Instead of requirements, the analyst needs to identify possibilities. By starting with identification of data, the analyst lays a firm foundation that makes many different applications possible. If the basic transactions of the enterprise are properly recorded, then all derived reports and processes can be defined later.

There are techniques that can identify available and useful data without specifying application requirements. If data are captured once and stored in a form that reflects the meaning of the data, then all required applications can be constructed as needed. That is why this book focusses on data before analyzing application requirements.

With CASE tools, it becomes possible to change the order of the phases of the life cycle, as shown in Figure 1-18. In this revised cycle, an architecture phase is inserted at the beginning. The architectural stage defines an Enterprise Model that consists of an Entity-Relationship Diagram to model the database and an Activity-Entity Diagram to show how the database is related to the organizational activities. The Activity-Entity Diagram is used to divide the system of activities into subsystems that can be implemented separately over a period of time according to organizational priorities.

Each subsystem is factored into database, interface, and application program components. These three components are designed in close cooperation with the users and can be delivered separately in phases. Each phase is tested at all stages of development to ensure that user needs are satisfied and that the principles of good design have been followed. The testing occurs concurrently with each stage. This reduces the chance that errors go undetected until delivery. Those that are detected in later stages usually have a limited impact on the earlier stages. Automatic consistency checks by the CASE tools prevent most errors of omission.

The adoption of CASE tools must be accompanied by a change in the life cycle to get the full benefit of the new tools. Otherwise the tools only create error-filled systems faster. The most important changes are continual close interaction with users and greater independence of the database, interfaces, and applications.

The Components of a Model

Before saying what the analyst must model, we need an idea of the analyst's function. Weber[7] suggests that the function of the Information Systems discipline is to describe the behavior of discrete things and events whose description is valid for some period.

The discrete things and events that Weber refers to are the entities, processes, and rules that describe the functions of an organization. Entities are described by storing their descriptions in data files. Processes are described with programs and documentation that recreate them. Rules specify relationships between data items, between processes, and between data and processes.

These entities, processes, and rules are the basic building blocks of our Information Systems universe. They are analogous to the particles and forces that physicists use to describe our physical universe. Physicists have struggled to produce a unified field theory that relates all of the different particles and forces into a coherent framework that describes our physical universe. We must struggle to relate entities, processes, and rules into a coherent framework that describes our information systems.

Modeling is a process of extracting the essential features of the system. The analyst must develop a model that contains all the important information and ignores unnecessary information that would clutter and confuse the design.

The important information is the information that any good reporter tries to assemble in a news story. The reporter tries to answer six basic questions: what, how, why, where, when, and who. The analyst also tries to answer these questions for each of the three parties in the design at both the conceptual and the detail level. The answers model the system and its implementation context. The analyst gives the following answers to these questions.

- **What** does the system process? Data.
- **How** does it process data? Programs.
- **Why** build the system? Benefit-Cost analysis.
- **Where** are functions done? Network structure.
- **When** must functions be done? Real-Time systems.
- **Who** builds the system? Organized people.

The matrix in Figure 1-19 shows the permutations of the six questions, the three parties to the design, and the two levels of analysis—conceptual and detail. The cell labels identify the most common concepts used in each case. Potentially each cell in the matrix could require a different analysis method and a different corresponding notation. In practice some cells are combined to simplify the problems of analysis and notation and to provide a common vehicle for the analyst to communicate with others.

Each of the six questions are now examined in more detail. The concepts in Figure 1-19 are italicized in the following descriptions.

What? Data

Data are the substance of an information system. The analyst designs a system that stores data about things and how they are related to each other. The analyst calls these *entities* and *relationships*. Refinement identifies the properties of entities and relationships. These become attributes in files. The user sees the

Figure 1-19
Questions, users, and levels of detail in a design.

	DATABASE (WHAT)	PROGRAMS (HOW)	BENEFITS (WHY)	NETWORK (WHERE)	REAL TIME (WHEN)	SKILLS (WHO)
USER CONCEPT	Entity Relationship	Activity	Intangible Benefit	Map		Organization Design
DESIGNER CONCEPT	E-R Diagram	A-E Diagram	AHP	Network		Skills Responsibility
USER DETAIL	Forms Screens	Processes Data	Tangible Benefit	Work Volume	Discrete Events	Transition Training
DESIGNER DETAIL	EER Diagram	Data Flow Diagrams	Benefit-Cost	Partition	Transition Diagrams	Methodology Tools
BUILDER CONCEPT	Normal Form Relations	Structure Chart	Function Points	System Architecture	Specifications	Learning
BUILDER DETAIL	Files	Screens Specifications	Costs	Network Specs	Interfaces	4GL CASE

concept as a set of entities and relationships which the analyst converts into an *Entity-Relationship Diagram*. The user sees the detail as a set of *forms* and terminal input *screens*. The analyst models these with the *Extended Entity-Relationship Model*. The analyst transforms this model into a *Normal Form* and specifies a set of *relational* files and screens which the programmer implements. All of these terms and models are explained in later chapters.

How? Programs

Programs manipulate information and produce outputs. At the concept level, the user sees *activities* that need to be performed. The analyst organizes these into cohesive groups or subsystems that belong together by using *Activity-Entity Diagrams*. At the detail level the user thinks of *processes* that manipulate *data*. The analyst transforms these into a *Data Flow Diagram*. This is further transformed into a *Structure Chart* which tells the programmer how the programs are connected at the conceptual level. Each program is specified at the detail level using a notation such as *Structured English*.

Why? Benefit-Cost analysis

The analyst has to identify why a system is being built so the project can be justified to the client who is paying for it. At the users' conceptual level, justification is often in terms of *intangible benefits* that increase effectiveness. The analyst may use techniques such as the *Analytic Hierarchy Process* to identify these benefits. At the user detail level, the justification is often in terms of *tangible benefits* such as reduced costs and increased efficiency. The analyst uses *Benefit-Cost* analysis to identify these tangible benefits. The builder uses *Function Point Analysis* to estimate the amount of work to be done and to estimate development *costs*.

Where? Network structure

This question asks whether the system functions are performed centrally or distributed in a network. The problem of where data are located and where computations are performed arises when the system is distributed over several machines. Systems have to be distributed when one machine is not capable of performing all of the work or when machines are located near users to reduce communication costs.

If the system is distributed, then the analyst at the strategic level has to identify where the components are on the users' *map* and how these locations are connected in a *network*. At the user detail level, the analyst has to identify what *work* occurs at each location and what *volume* of work needs to be done. The analyst then partitions work among the sites. The builder needs a conceptual *system architecture* and detailed *system specifications*.

When? Real-Time systems

The analyst needs to identify when events happen in a system if timing is an important consideration in the design of a system. This is the case whenever capacity is a binding constraint or whenever there is a need to synchronize the system with some external events.

Capacity is a concern when processing takes longer than the time available on the existing equipment. Capacity problems can often be alleviated by using larger computers or by dividing the work among parts of a distributed system.

Synchronizing a system with external events usually occurs when systems are designed to control physical processes. The physical process could be a rocket launching, a chemical reactor, or a manufacturing process. A computer system that tries to control such processes must operate faster than the physical processes. Otherwise, the physical process runs out of control and the computer system is useless.

These systems are known as Real-Time systems because they must function in the same time frame as real events and processes. A weather forecasting program is an example of such a system. It is useless for any purpose—other than retrospective research—if it takes more than 24 hours to gather data and compute the forecast for tomorrow.

Special design methods have been developed to deal with designs that interact with real-time processes. These methods are similar to the ones used for business systems, but they have extensions to document and specify the time-critical events at the detail level. The user thinks of *discrete events* which the analyst records on *Transition Diagrams*. The builder needs *specifications* and details of *interfaces* between the system and the external world.

Who? Organized people

Systems analysis must be done by people with appropriate skills for the job. The analyst needs technical knowledge to understand the technology constraints, business knowledge to comprehend the users' needs, and communications skills to get information from users and give it to programmers.

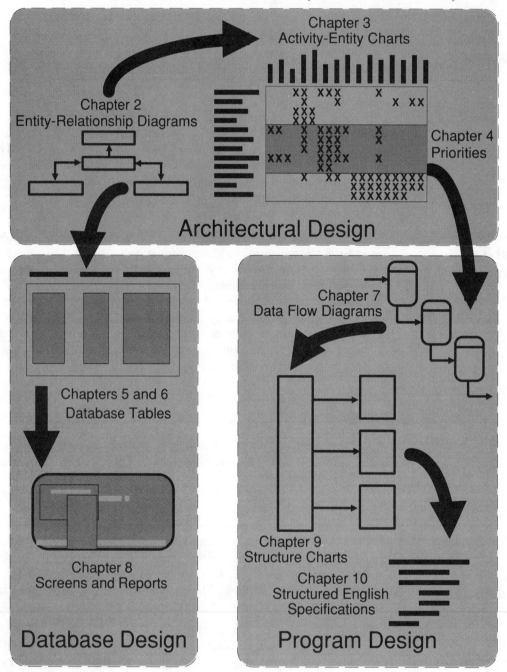

Figure 1-20
The relationships among the systems analysis tools.

At the conceptual level, the user's problem is one of *organizational design* to produce an organization that can solve the system development problem. The designer must translate this design into a set of *skills* and *responsibilities*. At the detail level, users require *training* to accomplish the *transition* from a 3GL to a CASE environment. The analyst must select appropriate analysis and design *methodologies* and *tools* for the task. The builders must learn new methods based on *CASE* techniques.

The Complete Process

The analysis and design process is a list of activities that may not always appear to be connected. Figure 1-20 shows how these activities are related. The Enterprise Model consists of an Entity-Relationship Model of the database and an Activity-Entity Model that shows how the database is used by the organizational activities. The Entity-Relationship Model serves as an input to both the Activity-Entity Model and the Database Model. The Database Model, in turn, is a prerequisite for screen and report definitions. The Activity-Entity Model provides the definition of subsystems that can be prioritized for implementation. The highest priority subsystem is then refined by using Data Flow Diagrams to describe the activities to be performed. The Data Flow Diagrams are reorganized to form Structure Charts that describe the logical system structure to programmers. Finally each module in the Structure Chart is specified using a notation that programmers can understand, such as Structured English.

The different techniques described briefly in this chapter are shown in the order that they would normally be used. Each technique is described in much more detail in the following chapters. The chapters deal with the techniques in roughly the order that they should be used. In practice, the process is somewhat iterative. An analysis may reveal an error in a previous stage that has to be corrected before the process can continue. However, the process is designed to move forward with a minimum of back-tracking.

The coverage of the chapters can be mapped into the classification system shown in Figure 1-19 as illustrated in Figure 1-21. The material in Chapter 8 is often used right after the material of Chapter 6. It is placed after Chapter 7 on Data Flow Diagrams to show the relationship between the different components to be implemented.

This book describes a generic method, rather than the mechanics of any specific CASE tool. It works with many commercial tools that enable and facilitate the use of the method. However, the method is difficult to use without computer support. The computer is needed to store and organize the detailed information gathered and to perform many of the checks and transformations that are required during the process.

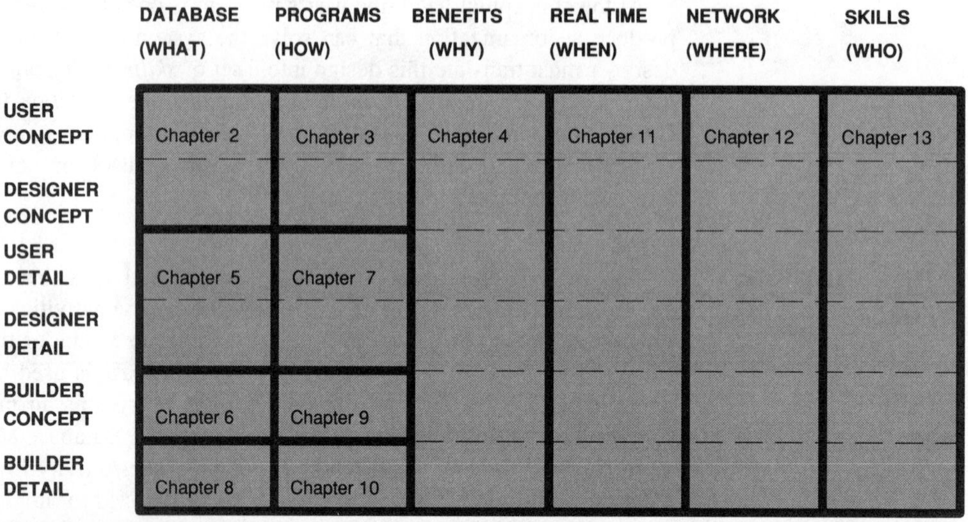

Figure 1-21
Coverage of questions, users, and level of detail by chapters.

	DATABASE (WHAT)	PROGRAMS (HOW)	BENEFITS (WHY)	REAL TIME (WHEN)	NETWORK (WHERE)	SKILLS (WHO)
USER CONCEPT	Chapter 2	Chapter 3	Chapter 4	Chapter 11	Chapter 12	Chapter 13
DESIGNER CONCEPT						
USER DETAIL	Chapter 5	Chapter 7				
DESIGNER DETAIL						
BUILDER CONCEPT	Chapter 6	Chapter 9				
BUILDER DETAIL	Chapter 8	Chapter 10				

Limitations of CASE tools

Not all computer systems can be designed using the methods described in this book. There are tradeoffs that must be considered when selecting a method and technology for development. These relate to whether the binding constraint in a good design is technical or conceptual; whether the main concern is efficiency or flexibility; whether the system must support operational or management needs; and whether the users or the information systems department control the system.

Technical vs. Conceptual Constraints

New technologies progress through a series of phases. In the initial phase the technology is poorly developed. It is easy to envision new uses for the technology, but the technology is unable to perform all the envisioned tasks because it is not yet fully developed. In the early days of the airplane, people could imagine rapid flights across great distances carrying many passengers. Unfortunately, engineers did not yet know how to build such airplanes. Actual flights were constrained by the available technology. Now the technology is mature. You can fly almost anywhere and carry almost anything if you have the desire and the payment. The problem now is whether and where to go.

Computing is undergoing a transition from the early to the mature stage. There are still problems that are constrained by technology. An airline reservation system pushes current technology to its limits. The problems are well understood, but there may be only one feasible technical solution to such problems. Designers must modify the problem to fit the technical constraints.

On the other hand, there are computers and languages powerful enough to solve many of the problems that organizations face. They have power to spare and there are many ways in which these problems can be solved technically. The constraint for these problems is not the technology, but our ability to understand the problem we are trying to solve. The constraint is our ability to conceptualize the problem, understand all the pieces, and fit them together.

CASE tools address the conceptual problem by organizing and structuring the information that the analyst uses in producing a design. They often do it at some technical cost. Larger machines may be needed to run programs produced with CASE tools. This is partly because CASE tools are still in their infancy and have not reached peak efficiency. It is also because we expect them to do more. We expect flexible data access, more integrity checks, and more access to data through on-line screens and user-friendly query languages.

The constraint also depends on the choice of technology. A problem may be technically constrained if the designer decides to solve it with a microcomputer, but would be conceptually constrained on a minicomputer. It is often necessary to make compromises in the capabilities of a system so it can fit into a smaller machine. Some of the features that the designer can conceive of are eliminated so the system can fit within the limitations of a selected technology.

Efficiency vs. Flexibility Objectives

The choice of technology depends on whether the decision-maker emphasizes efficiency or flexibility. Minimization of equipment cost may dictate that a system is implemented on a microcomputer. All of the desired features may not fit in the memory of the computer or the computer may not give satisfactory response times when some features are implemented. This makes the solution technically constrained. As a result, development costs increase and flexibility is reduced. Inflexible solutions may be satisfactory for some very structured problems, but they are usually not appropriate for unstructured problems.

There is a spectrum of methods for solving information systems problems. At one end there are traditional 3GL methods for constructing efficient, but often inflexible, systems for heavy duty applications that process many transactions. These may also be appropriate for constructing compact and efficient code that is installed on many small machines such as microcomputers. At the other end there are 4GL and CASE tools that can implement systems quickly and provide many features that might be neglected in 3GL systems. These solutions are applicable in situations where the requirements are not easily specified or where managers or other end-users are responsible for part of the implementation.

Operational vs. Management Applications

Operational applications, like payment systems, usually involve large numbers of standardized transactions. Efficient and inflexible solutions may be satisfactory for these industrial strength problems. Data entry clerks can be trained to overcome awkward features that are needed to achieve efficiency. Management applications usually involve unstructured problems, so they need maximum flexibility. Managers cannot afford much time for training and they cannot predict all of the things that the system will be used for. Compromises for the sake of efficiency are usually ill-advised in such cases.

Specialist vs. End-User Control

The professional information systems specialist usually has the technical ability to live with awkward conditions imposed by technical constraints. End-Users are much less tolerant of technical constraints. They need flexible and powerful systems if they are to make effective use of them. Many of them do not have the time to learn how to use difficult languages or unhelpful screens. They need systems that are user-friendly and easy to install, learn, and use.

Summary

The advent of CASE and Fourth Generation Languages leads to a change in the way systems are designed and implemented. The design process can become a true top-down process starting with a broad view of the complete organization. It is no longer necessary to start with the output requirements of a single project and limit analysis to those things that support a particular output. The analyst can now assume that the whole system will eventually be integrated. The data currently gathered are almost certainly required in many future systems. One starts by organizing that data into a coherent database.

The process is data-driven so inputs, processes, and outputs are identified in that order. In this overall view, the major entities and their relationships to each other are identified. Then the major activities are identified. The entities and activities are grouped into subsystems and a priority is established for the implementation of each subsystem. This method provides a strategic master plan and architecture for the development of an integrated database with integrated application programs. It avoids redundant data and redundant programs.

This is followed by successive refinement to identify the detailed structure of each subsystem in priority order. Again, the analyst analyzes and implements the inputs, the processes, and the outputs of the subsystem in that order. During the analysis, the analyst extracts the essence of the system into a logical model which is then used to specify the physical implementation.

The result of this approach is that information becomes a managed resource available to the whole organization. It is integrated so any information that exists in the organization is available for analysis if it is required. Fragmentation and duplication of data are reduced. So is a significant part of the maintenance effort required to keep the current fragmented system functional.

This approach to systems design does not always work for very large systems that are constrained by the available technology rather than by the conceptual limitations of the people involved. However, it works for a very large number of systems. It is particularly useful in situations where requirements are unclear or changing and flexibility is very important.

Keywords and Phrases

Computer Aided Software Engineering
Fourth Generation Language
Information Systems Architecture
Software Engineering
Systems Analysis
System Development Life Cycle

Review Questions

1. Define the keywords listed in the previous section.
2. Identify and describe the stages of the System Development Life Cycle. How does the cycle change when it is used in a CASE environment?
3. Identify the problems with the traditional System Development Life Cycle.
4. Identify the different classes of CASE tools. What changes do you expect in CASE tools as they mature?
5. Under what circumstances is it inappropriate to use CASE tools?
6. Compare Information Systems Architecture and Software Engineering.
7. Identify the components of a complete model of an information system.

Problems

1. Bits N. Bytes, a programmer in charge of the Accounts Receivable System is looking over a printout of the Customer Master File listing the name, address, purchases during the last year, and amount owed by each customer. The Vice President of Sales happens to stroll in and sees the listing. The following dialog ensues.

   VP: That printout of total purchases by customer would be very useful to our sales staff. It would help them to concentrate their efforts on the most profitable customers. Could you provide me with a monthly copy?

   BITS: (confidently) No problem!

   VP: (Pleased) Good! I don't need to know how much the customer owes. Can you leave that part off?

   BITS: (Still confident) I guess I can.

   VP: (Getting really interested) But I do need the customer's phone number. Can you add that in for me?

   BITS: (After some thought) I'm sorry, the phone number will take a year to get and will cost an extra $100,000.

   VP: (Angrily) Why should adding a simple phone number be so expensive? I know you already have it in the Customer Order File.

   BITS: (Patiently, as if explaining astronomy to a child) There are two ways I can provide this extra information. The first way is to add an extra field for phone numbers to the Accounts Receivable Master File. If I do that, I have to search through all of our 1400 programs to find the 45, or so, other ones that use the file. These have to be recoded to read the new record size and then they have to be recompiled and tested. That will cost about $100,000 and cannot be fitted into our schedule for at least a year. In any case, I am not sure that the Accounts Receivable staff would bother to update a field that they do not use regularly.

VP: (Sadly) And the other way?

BITS: I can create yet another file just for this application. However, that would be difficult because the files have no common identification, like a Customer Number. The names may not be identical because of the way different people enter data. There would be a complex manual matching required. It could be as costly as the first solution.

Even if I do that, we will have several problems. With the Sales Department maintaining one file and Receivables maintaining the other, we would soon have inconsistencies. Customers would get added to one file and not the other. New customers might get different Customer Numbers from each department, or different customers might get the same numbers.

VP: (Disappointedly) As usual, you bit-fiddlers turn the simplest request into a career project.

What is wrong in this situation and what can be done about it?

2. Polly Nezia is the chief analyst in an organization that plans to change their System Development Life Cycle to use CASE tools and 4GL development. Polly wants a method that will use CASE tools to greatest advantage and will provide for integration of applications and flexibility in future development.

Polly has just had a meeting with a representative from a consulting firm that sells and supports the MAZE Method of controlling system development. The method is advertised as a complete method for controlling development projects. The method is available for a license fee of $50,000. It is documented in seventeen large ringbinders. The documentation describes 4 phases which consist of 37 stages, which consist of 140 activities, which consist of 650 tasks, which consist of 2500 steps. The method includes 58 check lists and 210 standard forms that ensure adherence to the method. The lists and forms are integrated directly into a popular CASE tool that the consulting firm also distributes. The documentation explains how to use the CASE tool to collect data required by the lists and forms.

The documentation includes a decision tree for choosing stages and activities depending on whether the project is small or large; narrow or comprehensive; safe or risky; civilian or military; and manual or CASE-oriented. The four phases of the method are described in the vendor's brochure as:

- **Planning** specifies the business requirements of the information systems project, determines the enabling technology required to support the project, and identifies the role the project plays in meeting the information needs of the senior executives and operations managers. The plan creates a strategy to leverage available information to address current business issues.

- **Analysis** models the business area including processes, data, strategy, and organization. This phase produces a conceptual system design to address physical databases, application technology, and organization issues. Analysts work with users in group sessions to develop a conceptual system design. Analysts then perform a "build-or-buy" analysis to create a business solution to realize a higher rate of return than traditional methods.

- **Design** addresses business systems, technical systems, the IS environment, and testing. Design of the business system includes screens, reports, forms, and procedures. Design of technical systems defines the programs, modules, and data files required. Design of the Information Systems environment includes documentation, procedures, technology, and organization. Design of testing produces a formal test design.

- **Implementation** uses the rigorous specifications from the design stage to produce a working application. The application is tested at each stage of implementation to ensure functional and technical accuracy by adherence to the design. The method ensures that construction and implementation proceed smoothly. A full range of procedure manuals is created. Users and information system staff conduct acceptance tests.

Evaluate the MAZE Method. Pay attention to how well the method addresses Polly's concerns about CASE tools, integration, and flexibility.

References

1. Canning Publications, EDP In-Depth Reports, Vol. 12, No. 4, p 11.
2. Fisher, Alan S., *CASE: Using Software Development Tools,* John Wiley & Sons, 1988.
3. Goldberg, R., "Software Engineering: An Emerging Discipline", *IBM Systems Journal,* Vol. 25, No. 3/4, 1986, pp. 334-353.
4. McClure, Carma, "The CASE Experience", *Byte*, April 1989, pp. 235-246.
5. McClure, Carma, *CASE is Software Automation,* Prentice-Hall, 1989.
6. Meador, C.L., M.J. Guyote and P.G.W. Keen, "Setting Priorities for DSS Development," *MIS Quarterly,* Vol. 8, No. 2, June 1984, pp. 117-129.
7. Weber, Ron, "Toward a Theory of Artifacts: A Paradigmatic Base For Information Systems Research," *The Journal of Information Systems,* Vol. 1, No. 2, Spring 1987, pp. 3-19.
8. Zachman, J. A., "A Framework for Information Systems Architecture", *IBM Systems Journal,* Vol. 26, No. 3, 1987, pp. 276-292.

1
Introduction

Section I

The Enterprise Model

	DATABASE (WHAT)	PROGRAMS (HOW)	BENEFITS (WHY)	NETWORK (WHERE)	REAL TIME (WHEN)	SKILLS (WHO)
USER CONCEPT	Entity Relationship	Activity	Intangible Benefit	Map		Organization Design
DESIGNER CONCEPT	E-R Diagram	A-E Diagram	AHP	Network		Skills Responsibility
USER DETAIL	Forms Screens	Processes Data	Tangible Benefit	Work Volume	Discrete Events	Transition Training
DESIGNER DETAIL	EER Diagram	Data Flow Diagrams	Benefit-Cost	Partition	Transition Diagrams	Methodology Tools
BUILDER CONCEPT	Normal Form Relations	Structure Chart	Function Points	System Architecture	Specifications	Learning
BUILDER DETAIL	Files	Screens Specifications	Costs	Network Specs	Interfaces	4GL CASE

The objective of this section is to derive a common view of the organization. It serves as a framework for identifying subsystems and for gathering further detailed data when implementing components of the resulting model. Design is an iterative process of successive refinement. This phase of the design is a first step to be refined later by the techniques described in Section II. The techniques in this section are needed for the design of enterprise-wide systems. They usually are not required for the design of single small projects.

The chapters in this section are concerned with a very aggregated treatment of the inputs, processes, and outputs that form the architecture of an information system. The client can then see if the integrated system is justified. Later chapters specify how to design the detailed records and program modules that make up the final system.

The system plan has three parts corresponding to the inputs, processes, and outputs of the system. The inputs are the data files or database for the system. The processes are the activities that the organization engages in that transform data. The outputs are the added values that come to the organization with use of the system. This section of the book has a chapter for each of these three components. Taken together, these components are known as an Enterprise Model.

Chapter 2 uses the Entity-Relationship Data Model to identify the broad outlines of the corporate data model. The outline is in terms of the things about which data must be recorded and the relationships between them. It also identifies ways to divide the database into subject databases for use in distributed systems. Chapters 5 and 6 explain how to perform the detailed database design.

Chapter 3 broadly identifies the activities—the processes of the organization—that must be performed. It links them to the data requirements identified in Chapter 2. It also explains how to group the activities into clusters that share common data requirements. These clusters of activities form the basis of integrated development projects. Chapters 7, 8, 9, and 10 document the details of these activities.

Chapter 4 identifies the financial and non-financial benefits or outputs that result from the use of the system. It presents a method of weighting the different benefits so that aggregate benefits can be assigned to each of the projects identified in chapter 3. This allows the client to assign priorities and implementation order to the projects. This chapter is not concerned with information outputs. Chapter 8 examines these.

Chapter 2

Entity-Relationship Data Models

	DATABASE (WHAT)	PROGRAMS (HOW)	BENEFITS (WHY)	NETWORK (WHERE)	REAL TIME (WHEN)	SKILLS (WHO)
USER CONCEPT	Entity Relationship	Activity	Intangible Benefit	Map		Organization Design
DESIGNER CONCEPT	E-R Diagram	A-E Diagram	AHP	Network		Skills Responsibility
USER DETAIL	Forms Screens	Processes Data	Tangible Benefit	Work Volume	Discrete Events	Transition Training
DESIGNER DETAIL	EER Diagram	Data Flow Diagrams	Benefit-Cost	Partition	Transition Diagrams	Methodology Tools
BUILDER CONCEPT	Normal Form Relations	Structure Chart	Function Points	System Architecture	Specifications	Learning
BUILDER DETAIL	Files	Screens Specifications	Costs	Network Specs	Interfaces	4GL CASE

Objectives

This chapter shows how to develop the data component of a high-level Enterprise Model. This model serves as a high-level architectural view of the database which can be elaborated in more detail later.

At this level, the analyst focuses on the things that the organization needs to record data about. This high-level model does not consider the details that need to be recorded about each thing of interest.

Entities is the generic name for the different kinds of things that the organization needs to record information about. When information about a pair of entities is used together in an application, the pair is said to have a relationship. These relationships also need to be recorded since they place certain requirements on the kind of information that needs to be recorded.

Cardinality is a characteristic of relationships between entity types. Cardinality indicates the relative number of entity occurrences in each entity type that are related to occurrences in the other related entity type.

In this chapter you:

- Learn how to identify the entities that an organization needs to record information about.

- Learn how to identify relationships between entities.

- Learn how to identify the cardinality of a relationship.

- Learn where to obtain information about the organization that is required for a system analysis.

- Learn how to summarize information about entities, relationships, and cardinality in an Entity-Relationship Diagram.

- Learn how to test the Entity-Relationship Diagram for errors in analysis.

- Learn how to divide the Entity-Relationship Diagram into subject databases that can be implemented as smaller projects or that can fit smaller machines in a distributed network.

The Entity-Relationship Model

A strategic architecture needs a model of the database. It is translated later into the detailed definitions of files, records, and fields that go into a physical database. Unfortunately, at the time that the strategic plan is being prepared, nobody knows the detailed data requirements for the organization. Furthermore, there usually is not the time or resources to identify all of these data requirements at this stage. Therefore a model is needed that starts the analyst with a good approximation of the final structure of the business database without requiring an enormous amount of work. Note that when this book refers to a business, it should be taken to mean any organization including a club, a church, a hospital, or a government department.

The Enterprise Model concentrates on the "Big Picture" rather than on details of a design. This stage of the modeling process is designed to identify the basic structure of the enterprise, identify the data requirements, identify the activities that need to be supported, and set priorities for implementation.

At this stage a model is needed that gives us three things. It should give us the names of the necessary data groups in the database. It should give us an indication of which data groups are used together. It should give us some idea of the relative number of occurrences that can be expected in each data group. The Entity-Relationship Model developed by Chen[2] provides this starting point.

When we examine actual databases we find that they consist of records that either describe entities or describe linkages between entities. These entities are the primary things that an organization collects and records information about. Each entity has a name which is a noun. Examples of entities are persons, jobs, tasks, places, objects, customers, products, vendors, materials, resources, agents, events and other things that are the fundamental items of the business.

Some of these entities are linked by relationships. The relationships are identified by a verb. Persons *perform* jobs. Jobs *consist_of* tasks. Vendors *provide* materials. Persons *serve* customers. Customers *order* products. Perform, consists_of, provide, serve, and order are the names of relationships in the preceding examples.

These relationships have a cardinality. Cardinality identifies how many instances of one entity are related to how many instances of another entity. Thus one person holds one job in a 1:1 relationship. A job may consist of N tasks in a 1:N relationship. This means that a job has N tasks, but each task can belong to only one job. M persons serve N different customers in an M:N relationship. This means that any one person can serve any of N customers and any one customer can be served by any of M persons. M and N are made symbolically different to show that the maximum number of persons and the maximum number of customers does not have to be the same. The three types of cardinality are illustrated in Figure 2-1.

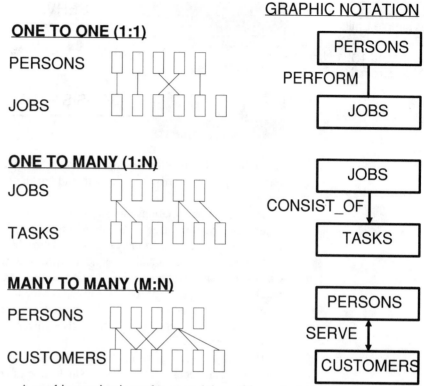

2
ER Model

Figure 2-1
Illustrations of car-
dinality.

A graphic notation is used to record the entities and relationships in a database model. Graphic notation is used because it packs so much information into a succinct, easily understood form. A few figures sketched on a pad can replace many long tedious explanations that are often misunderstood. Diagrams can provide an integrated view that is very difficult to produce with words alone. Diagrams can be tested for consistency. Alternatives can be examined easily before spending time building an actual system. Furthermore, these symbols can be manipulated and then transformed into computer code by some CASE products.

A rectangular box on an Entity-Relationship Diagram identifies an entity. The relationship is shown by a line connecting the related rectangles with the name of the relationship typed on the line, when needed for clarity. In 1:N relation-ships, the cardinality 1 entity is read first. If it is not clear in M:N relationships which direction the action occurs in, then an arrow is added to the relationship name pointing to the object of the action. Thus **JOBS CONSIST_OF TASKS** could have a small arrow after CONSISTS_OF which points toward the TASKS entity.

Cardinality is indicated by an arrowhead at the end of the line corresponding to more than one instance of an entity. Thus a 1:1 relationship has no arrowheads

Figure 2-2
A simple Entity-
Relationship Diagram il-
lustrating 1:1, 1:N, and
M:N cardinality.

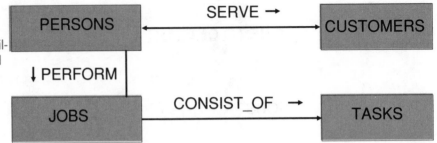

on the line. A 1:N relationship has an arrowhead at the N end of the line. An M:N relationship has an arrowhead at both ends of the line. These are illustrated in Figure 2-2.

There are other notations that are sometimes used in the literature as shown in Figure 2-3. Martin[7] uses a crowfoot—others use a trident—instead of an arrowhead to identify the M or N end of a relationship. Some authors use a single arrowhead at the 1 end and a double arrowhead at the N end of a relationship. Chen's[2] original notation used a diamond-shaped box between entities to show a relationship. A typed 1, M, or N at the ends of the lines shows cardinality. Chen's diamond notation is not used because it produces very cluttered diagrams when dealing with large numbers of entities. The choice among the other notations is somewhat arbitrary.

The analyst needs to define the basic elements of a data file which contains a number of data records. Data about a single type of entity are normally stored in rectangular tables as shown in Figure 2-4. The table contains data about the STUDENTS entity type. A single row or occurrence of the table is called an entity occurrence. Each row consists of a number of columns—called at-

Figure 2-3
Illustration of Entity-
Relationship notations.

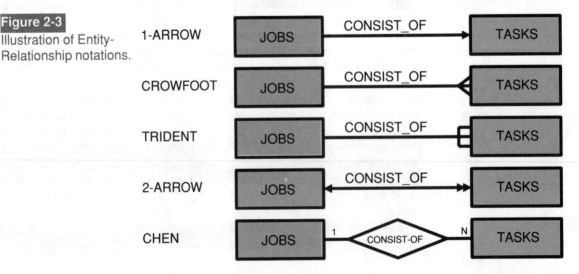

Figure 2-4
Illustration of actual data corresponding to the STUDENTS entity.

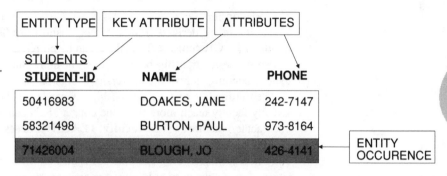

tributes—that describe the entity, such as STUDENT_ID, NAME, and PHONE number. Each row is uniquely identified by one or more key attributes. The names of key attributes are underlined to distinguish them from other attributes.

The notation used to identify parts of a database is not very consistent. The following table shows a number of synonyms often used for each of the terms defined above.

TERM	SYNONYMS
Entity type	Entity, object, table, relation, file, data store
Entity occurrence	Instance, record, row, tuple
Attribute	Property, column, field
Key attribute	Determinant, identifier, key

Three of the entities that are important in a university are STUDENTS, COURSES, and FACULTY. There are relationships between some of these entities. These relationships are shown in Figure 2-5 with directional arrows to clarify the object of each relationship. **Students TAKE courses. Faculty TEACH courses.** There may or may not be a recordable relationship between faculty and students depending on the organization of the university. In some universities each student has a faculty advisor. The relationship **faculty ADVISES students** records this. In some universities students may act as research assistants to faculty. The relationship **students ASSIST faculty** records this.

Some faculty may go to parties with some students. This is a relationship that is not normally recorded because it is not part of the business of the university.

Figure 2-5
Relationships between STUDENTS, FACULTY, and COURSES.

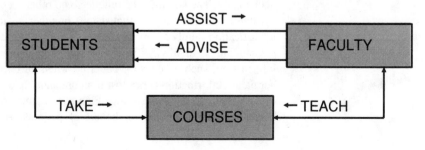

The relationship **faculty TEACHES students** does not need to be recorded either. It can be derived from the relationships **students TAKE courses** and **faculty TEACH courses**. Thus there can be no relationship between faculty and students, one relationship between them or more than one relationship between them depending on how the university is organized.

The cardinality of the relationships depends on the rules at the university. Usually faculty teach more than one course and a course is taught by more than one faculty member. Thus **faculty TEACH courses** is an M:N relationship. Similarly, students take more than one course and a course is taken by more than one student. **Students TAKE courses** is also an M:N relationship. Some universities allow a student to hold only one assistant position and a faculty member to have more than one assistant so **students ASSIST faculty** is an N:1 relationship. In other universities it may be an M:N relationship.

This shows that it is impossible to define a generic database for an organization without knowing how it is organized. All possible relationships could be included in case they might be used and make all relationships M:N, to allow for the most complex relationships. This is the most general case. At this stage, if there is a doubt, potential relationships should be included in the design. Similarly, if the cardinality is in doubt, it should be set to M:N.

However, later chapters show that extra relationships—particularly M:N relationships—imply extra files, computing, documentation, and training. Including the most general case is a good strategy if a system is being designed to be sold to all universities, regardless of their operating rules. It is not a good strategy if the system is being designed for a single university that has simpler operating rules and does not use all possible relationships.

Entities can be thought of as molecules or building blocks out of which we construct the organization and all that it contains and supports. The relationships are like intermolecular attractions that bind the entities into an organized unit.

The descriptive attributes in each record are the atoms of data which are combined to form the molecular entities. One or more of these attributes must be a unique identifier that characterizes the specific entity. This unique identifier is known as a key attribute. Such a unique identifier is needed because we often have to retrieve a single entity occurrence for, say, a particular faculty member. Employee number is a key that identifies a unique faculty occurrence.

The key does not have to be a number, but it does have to be unique and unchanging. The key must be unique so no other record has the same identifier. It is often difficult to ensure that names or other attributes are unique, so unique identification numbers are frequently assigned to entities. The identifier must be unchanging so it always refers to the same thing. It is easy to lose related information, such as pension benefits, when an employee marries and changes her name. Information is not lost if an unchanging employee number is used.

The Ontario Health Insurance Plan used names instead of identification numbers to record payments on behalf of patients. Auditors found that the files contained records for 24.6 million patients even though there are only 9.2 million people in Ontario. The extra patients resulted from having the same patient listed with incorrect spelling and various combinations of names and initials. Thus L. Fertuck, Len Fertuck, and Leonard Fertuck were treated as different patients even though they are the same person.

Some entities have a single unique key. A student number identifies students and a course number identifies courses. Relationships are made unique by using the unique key of each of the entities that they relate.

Some entities have compound keys made up of a number of different subkeys which taken together produce a unique identifier. The course number, the section number, and the term in which it is offered uniquely identify a section of a course. Anything less could identify multiple records for more than one course, more than one section, or more than one term. The subkeys should be identified as separate attributes since they each provide different information. An attribute should always record only one fact.

The key does not have to be selected or defined at this time. The analyst must merely make sure that a unique identifier exists or can be created. The exact key and its characteristics are specified later during the detailed design of the database. Inability to identify a key is an indication that the entity is not understood by the analyst.

Identifying Entities and Relationships

The major problem in preparing an Entity-Relationship Diagram is identifying the entities and relationships in an organization. The analyst needs to know what to look for so that it is recognized when it is seen. The analyst also needs to know where to look for information. A formal definition of entities and relationships makes it easier to recognize them.

Identifying Entities

Entities are the PRIMARY THINGS of a business about which users need to record data. They fall into six classes:

- **People** who carry out some function. Examples are employees, customers, and students.
- **Things** are tangible physical objects or groups of objects like equipment, products, or buildings.
- **Places** that are set aside for use by people or things. Examples are cities, offices, and routes.
- **Organizations** are formally organized collections of people, places, or things having a defined mission. The existence of the organization is independent of the existence of any individual member of the organization. Examples are teams, departments, or suppliers.
- **Events** are things that happen to some other entity at a given date and time or as steps in an ordered sequence. The events occur at discrete times and the timing is important. Examples are employee promotions, project phases, or

account payments. The occurrence of an event is identified by at least two keys. One is the time or date when the event occurs and the other is the identifier of the entity to which the event happens. Thus payment of an invoice is identified by the invoice number and the date on which it was paid.

- **Concepts** are intangible principles or ideas that an organization uses and keeps track of. Examples are projects, accounts, and complaints. Concepts may have start and stop times, but the time is not a primary concern as it is with an event.

Since entities are things, they must have names that are NOUNS and should have the properties of a noun. Sometimes the names are followed by a qualifier that limits their scope. For instance, SUPPLIERS is an entity and SUP-PLIER_ORDERS is another entity. An entity must have an identifying key and it must have some attributes or characteristics that someone wishes to record about it.

As with all models, entity types are an abstraction of the real-world entities that they represent. By giving the entity type a name, the analyst and user commit themselves to using a particular classification scheme to represent the real world. For instance, many banks in the past did not distinguish between accounts and customers. This made it impossible to identify all of the business that a customer generated under different accounts. Seeing that they really have two entities instead of one, has allowed them to focus on the profitability of each customer as well as on each product. Thus it is important that the entity types used in the model are carefully chosen to provide all the information that is needed. The entities must represent fundamental concepts, rather than combinations, exceptions, or special cases.

The analyst can identify entities by asking people in the organization questions like:

- What things do we need to keep data about?
- What things are essential to the organization?
- What things do we talk about in the organization?
- How can an occurrence of a candidate entity be distinguished from another?
- Are there subcategories of the candidate entity type for which entirely different kinds of information are collected?

Naming Entities

It is convenient to use the plural form of the noun to name the entity. The singular form can be used to refer to a single occurrence of the entity. Thus the STUDENTS entity contains records for all students and a student occurrence contains data about a single student. Some authors call the entity an entity type and each individual record an entity occurrence. When the word entity is used alone, it is a shorthand for entity type.

It is not a good idea to use encoded names for entities, relationships, or data fields. Programmers may be used to using a name like STENROL3 where ST means that it is in the student records database, ENROL means that it is an enrollment record, and 3 means that it is the third version. End users find such terminology confusing and require documentation to translate it into something meaningful. This increases the need for documentation, increases the time needed to learn the system, increases the chances of confusion, and increases the likelihood of programming errors when the name is eventually used as the name of a data file. The name should be simple, clear, unambiguous, and free of jargon.

The name of the identification key for an entity is usually derived from the entity name. The key of the STUDENTS entity can be STUDENT_ID. Entity and relationship names are specified in capitals with blanks replaced by under-scores. This makes it clearer that a specific entity is being discussed. It also conforms with the notation used by many computer programs.

An entity in one situation is not necessarily an entity in other situations. Phone number is clearly an attribute of the STUDENTS entity. However, to the phone company, phone number is an entity. It is the thing to which many other attributes are attached such as location, number of extensions, and type of ser-vice. In fact, one telephone company found that phone number was defined in over 70 ways in different parts of the organization depending on its purpose and type of use. The difference between an attribute and an entity is that attributes are atomic. They have no further attributes that describe them. Entities can be further described by their attributes.

Kernel and Characteristic Entities

Frequently entities are described by other subsidiary entities in a hierarchical fashion. In such a case, some data is stored about an entity occurrence and some other data is stored about each subsidiary entity occurrence that describes it, as illustrated in Figure 2-6. This situation can be recognized when we see that we have to store repeated values of one of the attributes of an entity.

For example, COURSES is an entity about which a university stores informa-tion such as the COURSE_ID, NAME, and CREDITS. Each course may have

Figure 2-6
Hierarchical structure of kernel and charac-teristic entities.

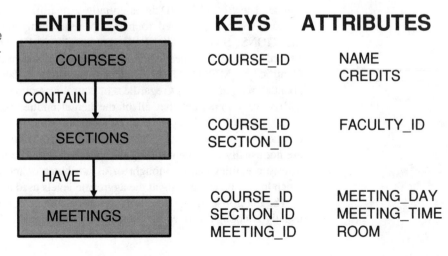

ENTITIES	KEYS	ATTRIBUTES
COURSES	COURSE_ID	NAME CREDITS
CONTAIN		
SECTIONS	COURSE_ID SECTION_ID	FACULTY_ID
HAVE		
MEETINGS	COURSE_ID SECTION_ID MEETING_ID	MEETING_DAY MEETING_TIME ROOM

several SECTIONS for each of which they must store the FACULTY_ID of the instructor. This is done by creating another entity called SECTIONS which is identified by the COURSE_ID of the course being taught and a SECTION_ID to distinguish each of the different sections of that course. If courses can be taught more than once a week, then similarly, each of the SECTIONS has a MEETINGS entity identified by the COURSE_ID and SECTION_ID plus a distinguishing MEETING_ID. Each occurrence of SECTIONS also has attributes like MEETING_DAY, MEETING_TIME, and ROOM.

COURSES has a 1:N relationship with SECTIONS and SECTIONS has a 1:N relationship with MEETINGS. An occurrence of MEETINGS inherits all of the attributes of the occurrence of SECTIONS with the same keys. The occurrence of SECTIONS in turn inherits all of the attributes of the corresponding occurrence of COURSES.

The highest entity type in such a hierarchy is called a **kernel entity**. It has a unique identity that does not depend on the existence of any other entity type. The other entities are called **characteristic entities** because they record the repeated characteristics of the kernel entity. COURSES is a kernel entity. SECTIONS and MEETINGS are characteristic entities that describe the characteristics of COURSES.

MEETINGS are the most elementary parts of a course. The SECTIONS and COURSES entities exist to store aggregate information about the more elementary parts. Thus a faculty member identified by FACULTY_ID instructs all meetings for a single section. The NAME of the course is the same for all sections and for all meetings. NAME is inherited by SECTIONS and MEETINGS.

The unique identifier for the characteristic entities is a multiple key. Both COURSE_ID and SECTION_ID are needed to uniquely identify a section. COURSE_ID is also the key for the COURSES entity which stores data about a course regardless of section. SECTION_ID is not the key for any entity. There are no common data that should be stored about section 1 regardless of the course. The SECTION_ID is essentially a qualifier to tell us which of the N sections are being referred to in a 1:N relationship between COURSES and SECTIONS. Similarly COURSE_ID, SECTION_ID, and MEETING_ID are needed to identify a meeting uniquely. There is no entity occurrence uniquely identified by MEETING_ID. There are no common data that should be stored about all second meetings regardless of course or section.

It is very important that all of the kernel entities be identified during this initial stage of the design. Other methods are used to identify missing characteristic entities during later phases of the design. Missing characteristic entities are not usually a problem during the initial design. The information in the characteristic entities can be thought of as attributes of the kernel entities without much loss of understanding at the aggregate levels used during the initial design.

The Enterprise Model does not have to be complete. For planning purposes, it usually is enough to have it 60 to 80 percent complete. This is a good starting point for the identification of subsystems. The model evolves during the design of each subsystem. Checks for accuracy and completeness are added then.

The 80/20 rule should govern the completeness of the design. Eighty percent of the accuracy and benefit can be achieved during the first 20 percent of the effort needed to generate a complete model. At the planning stage further effort usually is not justified. At this stage, it is more important to complete the plan. Then some development work can begin before the organization concludes that planning is an expensive exercise that never produces anything useful. In any case, the model could never be 100 percent correct because the organization changes gradually.

Summary Entities

A special kind of entity occurs when summary data must be recorded about an entity. Summary data about individual items are frequently needed. Examples are the number of students enrolled in each course or the total sales of a product each month by region. These are most commonly needed for current reports, for validation checks, or for inquiries and research studies such as sales forecasts. If they are needed only once for reports, users can usually generate them as needed.

If summaries are needed for validation of data, they may have to be made into an attribute of the corresponding entity occurrence in the next higher level entity in a hierarchy. For instance, there may be a quota on the number of students in each section of a course. Then an enrollment field should be maintained in the SECTIONS entity and updated with each new enrollment or withdrawal from the course. This can present an operational complication because the data entry programs have to be sure to update the count whenever a change occurs. The alternative of counting all previous enrollments before each new enrollment can be very costly in courses with large sections.

Researchers often need a series of summary data items collected over a period of time, from which they can extrapolate a trend or equation. This usually means that a separate entity must be created. It stores the time series using the time period as part of the identifying key. A monthly sales summary cannot be stored as part of the PRODUCTS record because there are many months to be matched to a single product record. The usual solution is to create a SALES_SUMMARY entity that contains records keyed by product, month, and year. Such a file can be thought of as recording the characteristics of the MONTH entity.

This summary entity can be updated automatically at the end of the month. Since all of the basic data exists in the transaction files, these summaries can be generated at a later time. There is no serious damage done to the model if all of these summary files are not identified at this time since they can easily be created later from data in the previously identified files.

Identifying Relationships

After the entities have been identified, the relationships between them need to be identified. A relationship is a business action between two associated entity types. The relationship represents some interaction between the corresponding entities in the real world. The interaction can always be defined by a simple English sentence with a subject, a verb, and an object of that verb such as **STUDENTS** *TAKE* **COURSES**. The verb—*TAKE* in this example—is the name of the relationship.

Relationships are identified by examining the entities in all possible pairs to see if there is any relationship between each pair that is worth recording. The relationship describes how entities interact. It tells us what we need to know to associate one entity with another. The relationships can be identified by asking the following questions:

- **What sentences can be constructed** of the form ENTITY *VERB* ENTITY?
- **What entities are subtypes** of other entities?
- **Which entities are different types of things,** but are associated with each other by being characteristics of some kernel entity?

The minimum data needed about a relationship is the key attribute of each entity involved in the relationship. This information records the fact that a relationship exists and allows us to link to the related entities. In addition, when the detailed design stage begins, it may be necessary to record other facts about the relationship. The users may want the date when the relationship began or ended, the quantity of something linked or transferred by the relationship such as number of units ordered, or the strength or quality of a relationship such as a grade received. These other attributes need not concern us now because they are identified during the detailed design of the database.

There are two common conventions for naming relationships. One is to use verbs such as ORDERED, ENROLLED, or IS_PARENT_OF. This method emphasizes the semantic purpose of the relationship. The other convention is to create a compound of the entities that are being related such as FACULTY_STUDENTS. This method emphasizes the entities that are being related, but does not give an indication of the purpose of the relationship. Sometimes there may be more than one relationship between two entities such as the ASSIST and the ADVISE relationship between FACULTY and STUDENTS in Figure 2-6. The compound name FACULTY_STUDENTS would be the same for both relationships. It is usually better to use a verb that identifies the purpose of the relationship.

All relationships are bi-directional. In the example **STUDENTS** *TAKE* **COURSES,** the reverse relationship is **COURSES** *ARE_TAKEN_BY* **STUDENTS**. Logically, it does not matter which way the relationship is stated, although some people might find the first one easier to understand.

Relationships are documented as lines between entities as illustrated in Figure 2-6. Sometimes the name of the relationship is left off the diagram if it is obvious. The first relationship in the figure is CONTAIN in COURSES CONTAIN SECTIONS. The second is HAVE in SECTIONS HAVE MEETINGS.

Recursive Relationships

Occasionally a special relationship occurs called a recursive relationship. In a recursive relationship, an entity is related to itself. For instance, COURSES is related to itself by the IS_PREREQUISITE_OF relationship. This relationship records the fact that course occurrences in the entity type may be prerequisites for other course occurrences in the entity type. Similar recursive relationships occur between PARTS, EMPLOYEES, or COMPUTER_SUBROUTINES. Parts in an inventory can be components of another assembled part. Employees are subordinates of other employees. Computer subroutines call other subroutines.

The PERSONS entity in a file designed to record family trees has three recursive relationships shown in Figure 2-7. IS_PARENT_OF, IS_CHILD_OF, and IS_MARRIED_TO are the minimum set for retrieving all family relationships. For instance, my brothers and sisters can be located by finding each person who IS_PARENT_OF me and then finding each person who IS_CHILD_OF those two persons. My grandparent is any person who IS_PARENT_OF a person who IS_PARENT_OF me. One entity and three recursive relationships are enough to describe all family relationships.

N-ary Relationships

Some authors suggest that there can be a single relationship between more than two entities at the same time. Such a relationship is called an N-ary relationship for the N participating entities. Such relationships indicate an incomplete analysis. A trinary relationship such as the relationship between FACULTY, COURSES, and BOOKS, is really two or more binary relationships. In this example, the relationships are actually that **COURSES HAVE SECTIONS, FACULTY TEACH SECTIONS** of a COURSE and **COURSES REQUIRE BOOKS**. SECTIONS is an entity that was omitted from the original analysis. This omission led to the false conclusion that a trinary relationship was required.

Identifying Cardinality

Cardinality is an important property of relationships that must be identified. Cardinality tells us how many occurrences of one entity type are linked to occurrences of the other entity type.

Cardinality is usually relatively easy to determine. All you have to do is select one instance from the first entity in the relationship and ask "What is the maximum number of instances in the second entity that this first entity can be related to?" Then repeat the process for the reverse order.

Figure 2-7

Recursive relationships between family members.

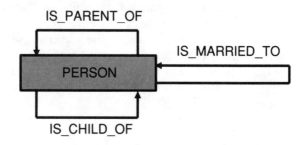

Figure 2-8
Sample Entity-Relation-
ship Diagram for part of
a university.

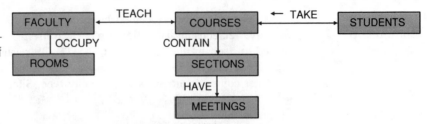

In the case of the relationship CONTAIN between COURSES and SEC-
TIONS, the maximum number of SECTIONS that a course can contain is some
number N. The maximum number of COURSES that a section can be contained
in is 1. Therefore the relationship between COURSES and SECTIONS has a
cardinality of 1:N as shown in Figure 2-8.

In the case of the relationship TAKE between STUDENTS and COURSES,
the maximum number of COURSES that a student can take is some number N.
The maximum number of STUDENTS that can be taking a course is some other
number M. Therefore the relationship TAKE between STUDENTS and COUR-
SES has a cardinality of M:N.

Cardinality depends on the rules of the organization or environment being
modeled. A good example of this is the recursive relationship IS_MARRIED_TO
between PERSON and PERSON where the first person is male and the second is
female. Where monogamy is the rule, the cardinality is 1:1. Where polygamy—a
husband with many wives—is allowed, the cardinality is 1:N. Where polyandry-
—a wife with many husbands—is allowed, the cardinality is N:1. Where both
polygamy and polyandry are allowed, the cardinality is M:N.

Finding Information

There are five main sources of information about entities and relationships:
existing forms, existing file structures, published examples, strategic plans, and
interviews. This section considers each of these sources and illustrates them with
an example for a hypothetical university. The university has been chosen as an
example because most aspects of it are familiar to students.

It is also somewhat easier to build a university example. A university is
usually a very decentralized organization with many of the functions left up to
individual departments. The library looks after its own circulation system. The
chemistry department maintains an inventory of supplies. The medical faculty
operates a receiving system for experimental animals that has many of the characteristics of a hotel. The university often operates as a bunch of fiefdoms
connected only by a central heating system. Some of the detail of parts of the
organization are ignored so that the illustration does not get too complex to
follow. The example is reasonably realistic for a small university.

Existing Forms

Forms are the most common method of data collection. An organization uses forms whenever important data of a repetitive nature must be collected in order to run the business. The forms organize the data and remind the users what to collect. They also simplify the input and retrieval of repetitive information. Databases and input screens are a newer way of accomplishing the same purpose. The forms currently used by the organization serve as a good source of information for the data model designer. If the organization has not yet computerized any of its applications, then forms may be the main source of information.

The simplified scholarship application form in Figure 2-9 illustrates the study of forms. This form is fairly typical having a heading consisting of separate blanks and one or more repeating groups. The repeating groups are **Scholarships Applied For** and **References Requested**. Some forms also have a summary portion after the repeating groups that counts or sums the items in the repeating group. Such a summary is a property of the entity described in the heading.

It is tempting to think about the form as a single record about a single entity, an application. However, whenever there is a repeating group, suspect a relationship between the kernel entity described by the form and a characteristic entity that is the repeating group. In this case, the kernel entity is STUDENTS keyed by the student number and SCHOLARSHIPS and REFEREES are the charac-

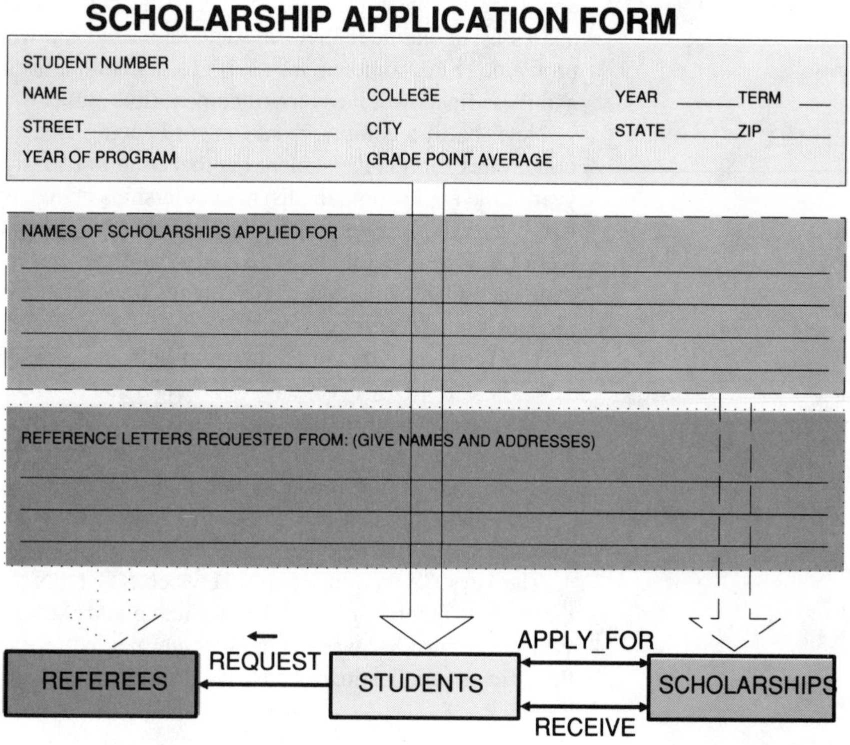

Figure 2-9

Example of a simplified Scholarship Application Form and the Entity-Relationship Diagram derived from it.

SCHOLARSHIP APPLICATION FORM

STUDENT NUMBER _____

NAME _____   COLLEGE _____   YEAR _____ TERM ___

STREET_____   CITY _____   STATE _____ ZIP _____

YEAR OF PROGRAM _____   GRADE POINT AVERAGE _____

NAMES OF SCHOLARSHIPS APPLIED FOR

REFERENCE LETTERS REQUESTED FROM: (GIVE NAMES AND ADDRESSES)

REFEREES ← REQUEST STUDENTS APPLY_FOR SCHOLARSHIPS

RECEIVE

teristic entities. SCHOLARSHIPS is likely to be another kernel entity because it is not an obvious component of any more general entity type. The name may be a sufficient key since there is very little danger of duplicating scholarship names within a single university.

If there is some rule in the university that makes it necessary to record something about the application itself, such as when it was received or who processed it, then an APPLICATIONS entity might be necessary. Assume that that is not necessary in this case.

REFEREES is not likely to be a kernel entity. A university is unlikely to maintain a separate file of referees if they are not linked to a particular application. This field is probably in the form only so that the person assembling the information can determine who to check with if a reference letter is not received. Thus REFEREES is likely a characteristic entity much like LINE_ITEMS on an order. REFEREES would probably be keyed by the student number and an arbitrary line number to distinguish them.

Since the form provides only three lines for referees, we might assume that that is the maximum number that could exist. There is a temptation to include three REFEREE_NAME fields in the STUDENTS entity and avoid the need for another entity. However, this is dangerous for three reasons. First, this field occupies storage space on the records of the many students who do not bother to apply for scholarships. Second, users may wish to add more information, like addresses, about the referees at some later time and would compound the storage problem. Third, someone may wish to maintain a historic record of applications and these fields will be overwritten next time students apply for scholarships.

Note that if a computerized system is being created the only useful information on this form is the student number used to identify the student, the term and year of the application, the list of scholarships being applied for, and the referees. All of the other information should exist within the system as part of the student record. It is very common in manual systems to provide large amounts of redundant data. One of the major advantages of automation is that these data are no longer requested or processed.

The cardinality of the relationship between STUDENTS and REFEREES is 1:N. The cardinality between STUDENTS and SCHOLARSHIPS appears to also be 1:N, but remember that other students may also be applying for the same scholarships so it is really M:N. Referees may also be sending letters for more than one student, but this does not matter if nobody intends to keep permanent separate data on each referee. In this case it may be best to duplicate the occasional REFEREE record.

The keys for the relationship between STUDENTS and SCHOLARSHIPS is the student number, the scholarship name and the term and year. The term and year are needed because the application may be repeated in following years and the different applications need to be distinguished.

From this form three entities are identified: STUDENTS, SCHOLARSHIPS, and REFEREES. Two relationships are also identified: an M:N relationship, APPLY_FOR, between STUDENTS and SCHOLARSHIPS and a 1:N relationship, REQUEST, between STUDENTS and REFEREES. Presumably there is another hidden relationship, RECEIVE, between those students who receive scholarships and the ones that they receive. The cardinality depends on whether a student can hold more than one scholarship and whether a scholarship can be received by more than one student. In general it is likely to be M:N since both conditions may apply.

Existing File Structures

Examining forms can be a tedious and complicated job prone to errors if the analyst does not understand all of the rules of the organization. It would be preferable to build on the work of others who have gone through this exercise. Existing file structures provide such an opportunity.

Most organizations have computerized at least part of their systems. However, few have developed a comprehensive model of all parts of the system. Frequently organizations have a collection of application programs that do not link to each other. They may require complex programs to transform data used by one application into a form used by another one. There are often batch oriented systems that do not permit on-line entry or inquiry. Some applications may have been purchased from vendors who provide inadequate descriptions of file structures. The files in the system may not have been broken down into entities. They may contain repeating groups like the referees seen in the forms example.

Despite all of these problems, the existing system is still the best source for identifying the entities and relationships of the data model. This section looks at the existing student records system of the example university. If there is no existing system, the analyst might be able to examine the system used by another university or a commercial package that does some of the same things that need to be done. The following notation is used to describe the sample record below:

STUDENTS: <u>STUDENT_ID</u>, NAME, ADDRESS, BIRTHDATE, (COURSE,) ...

- **STUDENTS** before the colon is the name of the record or file.
- The underlined <u>name(s)</u> are the key attribute(s).
- The other names are example attributes.
- (...) means a repeating group of attributes.
- ... means that there are more attributes not shown here.

The full set of files in alphabetical order for the Student Records System is:

ACCOUNTS: <u>ACCOUNT_ID</u>, LABEL
BUILDINGS: <u>BUILDING_ID</u>, NAME, ADDRESS, ...
COURSES: <u>COURSE_ID</u>, COURSE_NAME, CREDITS

COURSE_PROGRAM: <u>COURSE_ID</u>, <u>PROGRAM_ID</u>
DEPARTMENTS: <u>DEPARTMENT_ID</u>, DEPARTMENT_NAME, ...
ENROLLED: <u>STUDENT_ID</u>, <u>COURSE_ID</u>, <u>SECTION_ID</u>,
                       <u>YEAR</u>, <u>TERM</u>, GRADE
FACULTY: <u>FACULTY_ID</u>, NAME, ADDRESS, BIRTHDATE, ...
FEE_PAYMENTS: <u>STUDENT_ID</u>, <u>ACCOUNT_ID</u>, ...
PREREQUISITES: <u>COURSE_ID</u>, PREREQ1, PREREQ2, PREREQ3
PROGRAMS: <u>PROGRAM_ID</u>, PROGRAM_NAME
ROOMS: <u>BUILDING_ID</u>, <u>ROOM_ID</u>, SIZE, TYPE, ...
SECTIONS: <u>COURSE_ID</u>, <u>SECTION_ID</u>, <u>YEAR</u>, <u>TERM</u>,
                       FACULTY_ID, (MEETING_ID, BUILDING_ID,
                       ROOM_ID, DAY, TIME), ...
STUDENTS: <u>STUDENT_ID</u>, NAME, ADDRESS, BIRTHDATE, ...

The objective of this analysis is to draw the Entity-Relationship Diagram in Figure 2-10 to see what the results of the analysis look like so far. The remainder of the section explains the logic used to identify the entities, relationships, and cardinality. STUDENTS, REFEREES, and SCHOLARSHIPS are included from the previous section. An examination of the files and their keys provides the following information:

Figure 2-10
Entities and relationships identified from forms and files.

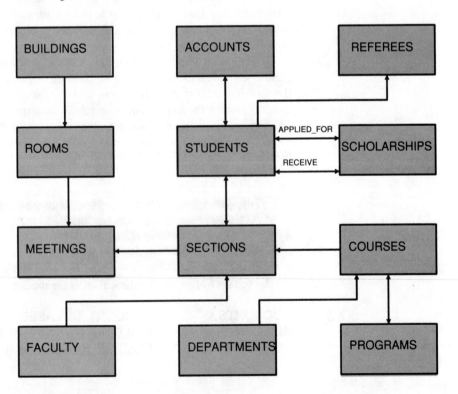

- ACCOUNTS, BUILDINGS, COURSES, DEPARTMENTS, FACULTY, PREREQUISITES, PROGRAMS, and STUDENTS can be identified immediately as kernel entities because they have single keys.
- Suspect that FEE_PAYMENTS, ROOMS, and SECTIONS are entities because their names are nouns. Check by seeing how the keys are related to the keys of other entities. If part of the key is the key of a kernel entity or characteristic entity and the remainder is not part of the key of any entity, then the file is a characteristic entity. If the multiple keys are combinations of keys for other entities, this would make them M:N relationships instead.

  First check FEE_PAYMENTS and ROOMS which each have two keys. FEE_PAYMENTS has a compound key made of the keys of STUDENTS and ACCOUNTS. It is the record of a relationship between STUDENTS and ACCOUNTS. Its name should be changed to a verb like PAYS to reflect the relationship. ROOMS does not have keys made up of the keys from the single key entities previously identified, so it must be a characteristic entity. Similarly, check SECTIONS and determine that it is also a characteristic entity.

- SECTIONS contains a repeating group of fields. This implies that each record contains multiple instances of another subsidiary entity, because an entity should not contain attributes that have multiple values for the same entity occurrence. Each occurrence of the multiple values becomes an entity occurrence in its own right. MEETING_ID, BUILDING_ID, ROOM_ID, DAY, and TIME are properties of each meeting of the section. Each meeting is identified by the MEETING_ID combined with the key of the containing entity. The complete key of the new MEETING subsidiary entity is **COURSE_ID, SECTION_ID, YEAR, TERM, MEETING_ID.**
- COURSE_PROGRAM, and ENROLLED still need to be identified. From the names, suspect that they are relationships. An examination of the keys should tell what they relate. COURSE_PROGRAM has the key from PROGRAMS combined with the key from COURSES so it must relate them. ENROLLED has the keys from STUDENTS and COURSES so it relates them. Thinking about these relationships, and the PAYS relationship identified above, leads to the conclusion that they each have M:N cardinality.
- None of the relationships have a cardinality of 1:1 or 1:N. This is because such relationships are implied by existing keys and fields. A 1:1 relationship exists whenever entities have the same identical keys. In this example, COURSES and PREREQUISITES both have the same key which implies a 1:1 relationship between them. In this example, each course can have—at most—one set of prerequisites and each set of prerequisites can apply to—at most—one course.

  Note that in this implementation the developer chose to store prerequisites in a separate record with a maximum of three prerequisites allowed rather than to design a general recursive relationship. This could be a severe problem if ever a course requires more than three prerequisites, but it may simplify the development of applications in a 3GL. A 3GL routine may be necessary because many 4GL systems are not equipped to handle the necessary logic for checking prerequisites. If this feature had been implemented as a recursive relationship, the cardinality would be M:N. If it is to be implemented this way, then there is no need for a second PREREQUISITES entity. The three data fields can just as easily be included in the COURSES entity. Thus one entity can be eliminated from the list.

- 1:N relationships are implied whenever the key of the 1 end of the relationship is also part of the record at the N end of the relationship. Thus there is a 1:N relationship between BUILDINGS and ROOMS, COURSES and SECTIONS, DEPARTMENTS and COURSES, SECTIONS and MEETINGS, ROOMS and MEETINGS, and FACULTY and SECTIONS. Note that FACULTY and SECTIONS are related even if FACULTY_ID is not part of the key of SECTIONS. It does not matter where the information to link the records is. It only has to be logically available in the model, although it may be necessary to create physical links in the physical implementation.

Published Examples

Published examples in texts or journals provide another source of information. Professional journals occasionally contain generic models of parts of databases. Scheer[9] has written a book that provides a generic model of the database for a whole organization. Barker[1] has a chapter of classical structures and generic patterns. The accounting part of the data model for the university example is illustrated by using a General Ledger Model developed by Parrello, Overbeek, and Lusk[8]. Figure 2-11 illustrates the model. This generic model may

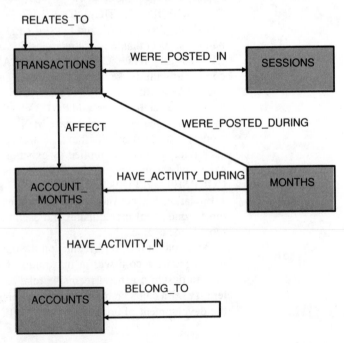

Figure 2-11

An Entity-Relationship Model of an accounting system.

not be identical to the model used in a given university, but it provides a good starting point for the design of a system. If the real system is different, it is usually because additional entities are needed to cover details not included in this model. This basic model is adequate for an initial strategic plan.

The model contains five entities and seven relationships. The most important entities are ACCOUNTS and TRANSACTIONS. Account records describe the characteristics of an account such as its label. The transactions identify the source of the transaction such as a sale or a purchase of goods. The ACCOUNT_MONTHS entity is an entity which maintains a total balance for each account for each month. This summary account makes it much easier to generate current account balances when needed. The relationship AFFECTS stores the debit or credit amount for each detail line of a transaction. The SESSIONS and MONTHS entities are needed for audit purposes so that each transaction can be traced to the time and the operator who entered it. The BELONGS_TO relationship records the grouping of the accounts into classes of accounts. The RELATES_TO relationship provides a link between transactions such as a refund of a previous payment.

Kerner[4] developed the Business Information Control Structure (BICS) method of designing information systems. He says every business has a generic set of entities that it records data about. He also says each business has a generic set of activities that it must perform depending on the answers to seven questions about how orders are processed. Recasting his model in an Entity-Relationship format, gives the Entity-Relationship Diagram in Figure 2-12.

Kerner's model has six basic entities: employees, facilities, money, vendors, products, and customers. He has eight relationships between these entities. The entities and relationships are described below.

Figure 2-12

A generic model of a transaction-based organization.

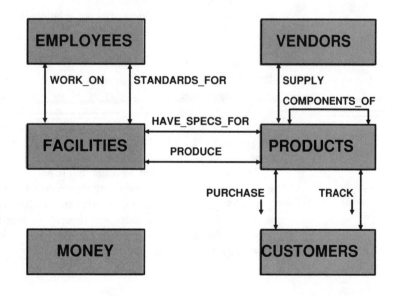

- **Employees.** This is all data about all past, present, and future employees.
- **Facilities.** These are all land, buildings, and equipment owned or leased.
- **Money.** All cash and securities owned by the organization.
- **Vendors.** All people or organizations that provide goods or services to the business. Areas in the business, but outside the scope of the study can also be considered to be vendors.
- **Products.** All goods and services that the business sells including raw materials, parts, and work in process.
- **Customers.** All people and organizations who have ordered or will order goods and services.

- **Supply.** All data about orders for products, materials, and vendor services.
- **Purchase.** All data about sales of products and services to customers who are either internal or external to the business.
- **Work_on.** This relates the employees to the equipment that they do identifiable work on while producing a product or service.
- **Produce.** This records the identifiable work done by facilities and equipment on the products that they produce.
- **Have_Specs_for.** This stores the specifications and procedures used to produce a product with some facility or equipment.
- **Standards_for.** This identifies the standards that employees must follow in using facilities or equipment to produce a product.
- **Track.** This contains all data about the relationship between a product and a customer after the product is sold. This may include warranty work, service, or other after sales relationships.
- **Component_of.** This describes the relationship between parts or components needed to assemble a product.

Kerner[4] says that each of these entities and relationships may have up to four different versions to store data about the combinations of actual, planned, descriptive, and value data. These serve the following purposes:

- **Actual Descriptive.** This category stores the properties of the entity or relationship such as name, description, color, quality, or other specifications.
- **Actual Value.** This category stores the cost or value of the entity or relationship for accounting valuation. This category usually has records for each time period, batch, or order that is being separately accounted for.
- **Planned Descriptive.** This category records data about planned changes to products, policies, training, or other future changes.
- **Planned Value.** This category records planned, forecasted, or budgeted values that are expected to occur in the future. These are used for comparison with actual values for control of costs and processes.

Some of these entities and relationships may have to be split further when the detailed contents of the records are identified. This happens when EMPLOYEES is split into FACULTY and STAFF in the university example. Some may get renamed to better reflect common use in the organization. Thus the major university CUSTOMERS are called STUDENTS. Some may not be necessary in a particular organization. In the simplified example many of these entities and relationships are ignored. This model acts as a check list of entities and relationships that are likely to be needed. The analyst should be satisfied that all of the areas in the model are either covered or can be justifiably ignored.

This model does not show the relationships between MONEY and the other entities. It would be more realistic if money in this model were replaced with the accounting model in the previous example. Relationships between TRANSACTIONS and VENDORS, CUSTOMERS, and EMPLOYEES would then provide an accounting system for this model.

Strategic Plans

Another way to identify entities is to examine the organization's strategic plan or mission statement. This plan identifies the things that are important to the organization. The nouns in the plan are good candidates for entities in a data model. Examine them carefully to eliminate synonyms and entities which do not need to be included in the model. Examples are external groups that management may wish to impress, but not want to record the characteristics of.

Strategic plans tend to ignore the more mundane aspects of an organization such as accounts and parts. They concentrate on the more global and glamorous topics such as markets and mergers. As a result, they do not identify all of the entities in an organization.

Strategic plans do serve to highlight the entities that are strategically most important. They also help to identify major changes planned in the future such as new products or markets. They identify changes in operating policy such as a change to a decentralized organizational structure. These changes can have a major impact on the structure of the information system. These possible shifts could change definitions, relationships between, or usage of the data. If such changes are planned, the scope of the study should be expanded to include the impact of these expected changes on the database model.

In the simplified example of a strategic plan in Figure 2-13 the nouns have been underlined. These are the candidate entity names. The ones in the first paragraph are the kind that are often included for outside audiences and do not likely correspond to data files that are required. Some of them (STUDENTS, FACULTY, PROGRAMS, BUILDINGS, DEPARTMENTS) have already been identified. Classrooms and offices are synonyms for ROOMS. STAFF, EQUIPMENT, SUPPLIES, VENDORS, and TASKS are new entities. Materials is likely a synonym for SUPPLIES, but managers should be questioned to see if there is a difference. Similarly, researchers may be a synonym for FACULTY.

Figure 2-13

Example of a
strategic plan
for a univer-
sity.

STRATEGIC PLAN

The university will establish new relationships with governments to harmonize our mutual goals. At the same time we will make it clear that a condition of this relationship is that the university will maintain the balance and diversity of scholarship to which we are committed.

The university and all of its parts should aspire to the highest possible level of intellectual achievement. The most able and highly motivated students should encounter the most able and highly motivated faculty and researchers supported by the most able and highly motivated staff. In particular the university will:

- Maintain and improve the undergraduate programs.

- Develop new masters and doctoral level programs.

- Maintain the quality of buildings, classrooms, offices, and equipment.

- Centralize purchasing to obtain materials and supplies from lowest cost vendors.

- Start a human resources department to insure that staff are appropriately trained and rewarded for their tasks.

Interviews

Interviews should be conducted to determine the relationships between these newly discovered entities and to identify any remaining entities that have not yet been uncovered. The interviews have been deliberately left to the end of the data-gathering process for several reasons.

- **Diagnosis** of the organization is required. The analyst needs to assess the type of information that is available. The initial examination of documentation gives a good idea of the quality of documentation, the degree of planning, and the amount of executive commitment that the analyst can depend on.

- **Preparation** is required before a user interview. The analyst needs to do homework to understand how the organization operates. If the homework hasn't been done, the analyst looks naive to the users and is not taken seriously. This preparation is also needed to be able to ask the right questions.

Figure 2-14

Example of
an interview
agenda.

2
ER Model

Interview Agenda:

30 Minute interview with Otto Maichon

- Explain current Entity-Relationship diagram. (10 min.)

- Relationships and cardinality between STAFF, EQUIP-MENT, SUPPLIES, VENDORS, TASKS and other entities. (5 min.)

- Is MATERIALS a synonym for SUPPLIES and RE-SEARCHERS a synonym for FACULTY? (2 min.)

- How are students related to ACCOUNTS? (2 min.)

- Are there any other entities or relationships left out of the Entity-Relationship diagram? (3 min.)

- Are there any plans to add new entities and relationships to the database? (5 min.)

- Possible followup questions from the interview. (3 min.)

- **Efficient** use of user time is important. Scarce executive time is needed to get the high level view needed for the strategic analysis process. This valuable time should be used only for information that cannot be obtained in other ways.
- **Clarification** of confusing issues is required. Some of the data obtained by examination of the documentation is ambiguous or conflicting. Some plans about the future are missing. Some policy decisions are required. If these cannot be resolved during the interview, then the interviewee can often at least identify the person who can clear up the problems.

You need to prepare for an interview. You should prepare an agenda outlining the topics you need to cover during the interview and the expected time that it takes to get the information. In the example, an interview is conducted with Otto Maichon. He is the new Director of Human Resources who has the job on the basis of an impressive record in the accounting department. Use his knowledge of both areas to clarify a number of points that are unclear. First draw up an agenda as shown in Figure 2-14. The diagram in Figure 2-10 is used in explaining what has already been done.

Figure 2-15 provides selected transcripts from the interview to give an indication of the kinds of information that is obtained. Known entities are shown in capital letters. New entities are underlined.

ANALYST: I have explained the Entity-Relationship diagram as it currently stands. There are a number of other entities that have been identified in the strategic plan. Could you explain how STAFF, EQUIPMENT, SUPPLIES, VENDORS, and TASKS are related to the entities in the diagram?

OTTO: VENDORS sell EQUIPMENT and SUPPLIES to us. EQUIPMENT is individual items like computers, desks, or laboratory instruments that we keep a separate inventory tag on. Each piece of equipment is kept in a designated location and assigned to a particular DEPARTMENT. When the location changes, we update our inventory records. SUPPLIES are disposable items like paper, chemicals, or lumber that we keep in stock. We only record the value and the quantity on hand, but do not track its location through its life. When they are used, a transaction is created to record the research, teaching, or administrative account that is being charged.

ANALYST: What is the relationship between STAFF and TASKS?

OTTO: They are not directly related. STAFF are people who currently fill authorized positions. TASKS are jobs that the STAFF who occupy those positions are required to do. To perform each of these tasks they will require certain skills.

ANALYST: Do FACULTY also have positions?

OTTO: Yes, but their tasks and skills are defined much more generally because they change as their research interests and teaching assignments change. The Human Resources area does not administer FACULTY hiring or supervision. The academic administration of the university does that.

ANALYST: Let me paraphrase what I think you said to see if I understood correctly. A position has a number of TASKS and TASKS each require a number of skills. For each STAFF member there is a single position.

OTTO: That is almost correct. Positions each have a job description and are funded by a DEPARTMENT. It is the job description that identifies the TASKS to be performed and the skills required to perform each TASK. There may be many positions with the same job description. Each position has a single STAFF member as-

---

Figure 2-15

Example interview to clarify E-R data. (Continued on next 2 pages.)

sociated with it. <u>Skills</u> like typing may be useful in performing a number of TASKS. TASKS like data entry may also be part of many different <u>job</u> <u>descriptions</u>.

ANALYST: Let me try that again to see if I have it right now. A <u>job description</u> has many <u>positions</u>, but a <u>position</u> has only one <u>job description</u>. Using the notation that I explained at the beginning of the interview, there is an M:N relationship between TASKS and <u>job descriptions</u> and an M:N relationship between <u>skills</u> and TASKS. Each DEPARTMENT has a 1:N relationship with <u>positions</u>. A FACULTY position requires that different information be recorded than for a STAFF position.

OTTO: I think you've got it!

ANALYST: Can I turn to some other items. Is there a difference between materials and SUPPLIES?

OTTO: No, we use the terms interchangeably.

ANALYST: Are researchers and FACULTY different?

OTTO: Effectively no. All faculty are expected to do research. Many of them have funding from one or more outside grants to support their research. When this happens, we have to provide an accounting system to administer the <u>grants</u> so that they will only be spent for authorized purposes.

ANALYST: So a faculty member can have many <u>grants</u>. Can a grant have many faculty members?

OTTO: Not really. <u>Grants</u> are normally given in the name of a single researcher who authorizes payments from the grant. We will set up one or more ACCOUNTS to record payments from each grant. The other researchers have no direct link with the grant even if their research is being supported by it. ... Let me modify that. Even if they have no administrative authority, we would like to record their relationship so that we can tell which FACULTY have been instrumental in obtaining research grants and how many they have participated in.

ANALYST: How are students related to ACCOUNTS?

OTTO: They really are not. When staff speak of STUDENTS having a relationship with ACCOUNTS, they really mean that there is some relationship with the accounting function which they find rather nebulous. STUDENTS participate in TRANSACTIONS such as fee payments which are charged to particular ACCOUNTS. You may be confused by a tendency for STAFF in the DEPARTMENTS to concentrate on which account the money comes out of, or goes into, rather than to focus on the TRANSACTIONS which is what we really record.

ANALYST: Are there any other entities or relationships that I have left out of my preliminary diagram?

OTTO: Let me see your diagram again. ... I do not see any mention of customers here. In addition to dealing with students, we provide a number of goods and services to the community. We rent rooms and provide meals for academic conventions. We sell computer time. We sometimes supply chemicals that are hard to obtain elsewhere and we perform tests and analyses for businesses and government. These customers, and SUPPLIERS for that matter, generate a great number of transactions in our accounting system and quite a bit of revenue for the university.

ANALYST: Are there any plans to add new entities or relationships to the database?

OTTO: The only concern that I have at the moment is trying to organize the Human Resources Department. This means that I want to get a good handle on what everyone does, how well they do it, and how they are being compensated for it. In addition, I have to plan for retirements and new staffing. I will need a history of how long people have worked in each position so that we can develop promotion plans. I will need to know when they will retire so that I can develop new staffing plans. I will ...

ANALYST: It looks as if we are getting into more detail than I need at this time. I will undoubtedly be coming back to you for more information when we start to design the system in detail. Let me thank you for the time that you have taken in helping to design the plan for an integrated information system. I would like to come back once more to verify that I have got all of this right when I have incorporated all of this information into a revised Entity-Relationship diagram.

OTTO: Certainly.

Drawing Entity-Relationship Diagrams

Now that all of the information has been assembled it has to be put into a presentable and understandable form. The first task is to make the data consistent by eliminating synonyms and homonyms. Synonyms occur when different people use different names for the same entity. One way of identifying synonyms is to look for entities with the same key. These often, but not always, are synonyms. In the example, STUDENTS, STAFF, and FACULTY may all be identified by a key like Social Security Number. Nevertheless, they are conceptually different enough that they should not be treated as synonyms. In the interview phase it was discovered that materials and supplies are synonyms and that researchers and faculty are synonyms. It is important to check for synonyms again before consolidating all of the information. At this stage the analyst is often dealing with information obtained from a number of different sources, each of whom use different terminology.

Homonyms occur when users use the same word for more than one entity. In the example, the examination of files showed a relationship between STUDENTS and ACCOUNTS. However, the accounting model broke the information into ACCOUNTS which is used to store the names of accounts, and TRANSACTIONS which is used to store the information about such things as fee payments. The relationship is really between STUDENTS and TRANSACTIONS. The designers of the old system did not use the same terminology as that being used in the model taken from the literature. Homonyms are often difficult to detect. They may not be noticed until the detailed design stage. At that time the analyst is likely to realize that the relationship is illogical.

It is now time to draw the Entity-Relationship Diagram. The manual method used in Figure 2-10 is satisfactory for diagrams with only a few entities. However, it becomes very messy when there are many entities. It is not unusual to have 200 entities in the complete data model of a large organization. Laying all of the entities out in a grid and try to draw all of the relationships between them usually leads to what Martin6 refers to as a COW (Can Of Worms) Chart. COW Charts may look complex and impressive. They are rarely informative as can be seen from the example in Figure 2-16.

The diagram is usually used in parts by different departments to illustrate their own special domain. A good diagram makes it easy to separate cohesive parts for this purpose. It also makes it easy to separate entities into groups that can be distributed over a network of different computers. A structured method for drawing clear diagrams is needed. The method involves:

- Organizing the data.
- Laying out the kernel entities of the diagram.
- Drawing all major relationships.
- Drawing all minor relationships.

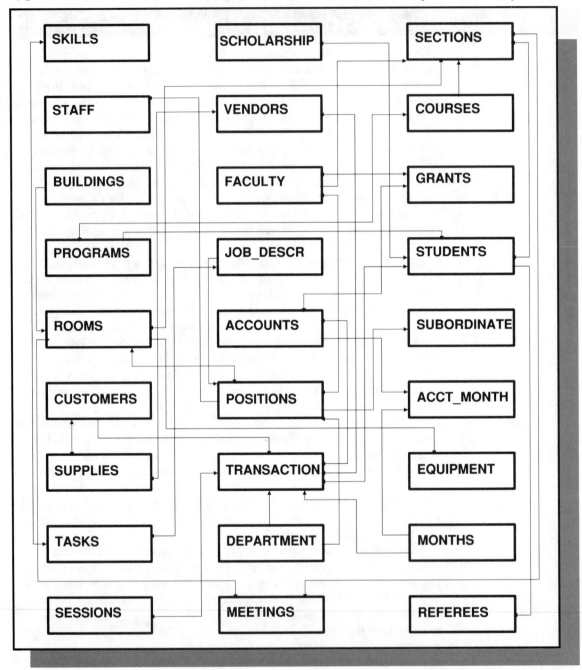

A Can Of Worms (COW) Chart of the university entities.

Organizing the Data

The analyst needs to identify the kernel entities, the characteristic entities with 1:N relationships, and the M:N relationships. Figure 2-17 records the data for the university example. The first column lists the names of all kernel entities alphabetically. They are entities that are never at the N end of a 1:N relationship.

The second column contains the names of all of the characteristic entities for the respective entity in the first column. These are the ones that are at the N end of a 1:N relationship. Characteristic entities that are 1:N subsidiaries of another characteristic entity are indented to clarify the relationship. When an entity is a characteristic of more than one other entity, the least important links are marked with an asterisk (*). The most important link is the one that has the greatest volume of transactions (insertions, updates, deletions, and reads).

The third column lists the M:N relationships between the kernel or characteristic entity on the same line and some other entity. Thus this table records all of the entities and relationships.

Kernel Entities

Figure 2-18 shows the kernel entities and all of their directly related characteristic entities. The 1:N relationships between kernel entities and the relationships marked with asterisks are temporarily left out of the figure. The M:N relationships are also omitted. This figure gives a set of building blocks from which the complete Entity-Relationship Diagram can be assembled. These blocks have strong relationships between their entities.

Major Relationships

The major relationships now have to be added. A subjective classification scheme can be used for the relationships. A relationship is more major if it is involved in frequent transactions, needs frequent checks to make sure that integrity is maintained, is used as part of the day-to-day operations, and participates in applications that demand rapid response times. The following classification is usually sufficient.

- **Type 1.** Between entities that must be in the same group.
- **Type 2.** Between entities that probably should be in the same group.
- **Type 3.** Between entities that may or may not be in the same group.
- **Type 4.** Between entities that should likely be in separate groups.
- **Type 5.** Between entities that must be in separate groups.

The 1:N relationships are usually type 1 or 2 because the kernel entity almost always has to be referred to whenever the characteristic entity is used. The kernel entity usually contains some essential identifying information, such as a name. Any reference to the characteristic entity uses the identifier, so the kernel entity should stay with the characteristic entity. The other major relationships are the most frequently used M:N relationships. These relationships typically link the building blocks that were identified in the previous step. The type 1 and 2 relationships are added in Figure 2-19. The building blocks are rearranged to place building blocks with major relationships next to each other.

KERNEL ENTITIES	CHARACTERISTIC ENTITIES (1:N)	RELATIONSHIPS (M:N)
Accounts		Are_part_of Accounts
	*Account_Months	
Buildings	Rooms	
	Equipment	
	*Meetings	
Courses	Sections	
	Meetings	
Customers		Purchase Supplies
	*Transactions	
Departments		Generate Transactions
		Have Positions
Faculty	*Sections	Participate_in Grants
Grants		Paid_into Accounts
		Administered_by Faculty
Job_Descriptions		Have Tasks
	Faculty	
	Staff	
	Positions	Occupy Rooms
	Subordinates	
Months	Account_Months	
	Transactions	Were_posted_in Sessions
		Affect Account_Months
Programs		Have Courses
Scholarships		Received_by Students
Sessions	*Transactions	
Skills		
Students		Attend Sections
		Apply_for Scholarships
		Get Scholarships
		Enrolled_in Programs
		Generate Transactions
	Referees	
Supplies		
Tasks		Need Skills
Vendors		Provide Supplies

Figure 2-17

List of kernel entities and their characteristic entities and relationships.

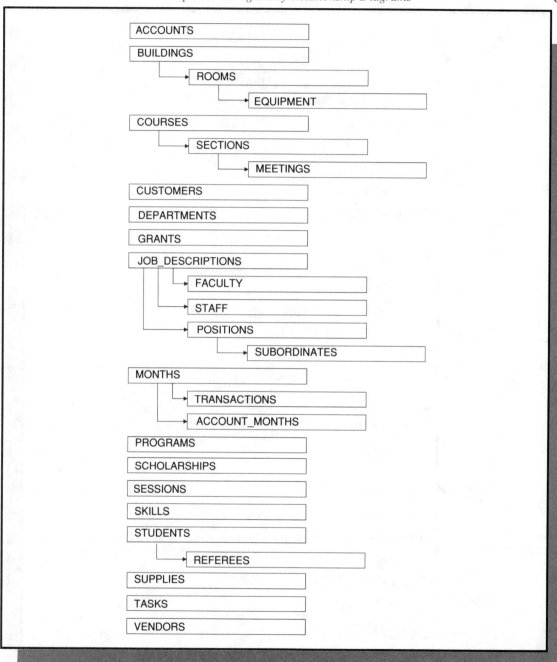

Figure 2-18

Kernel entities and their characteristic entities in the university example.

2
ER Model

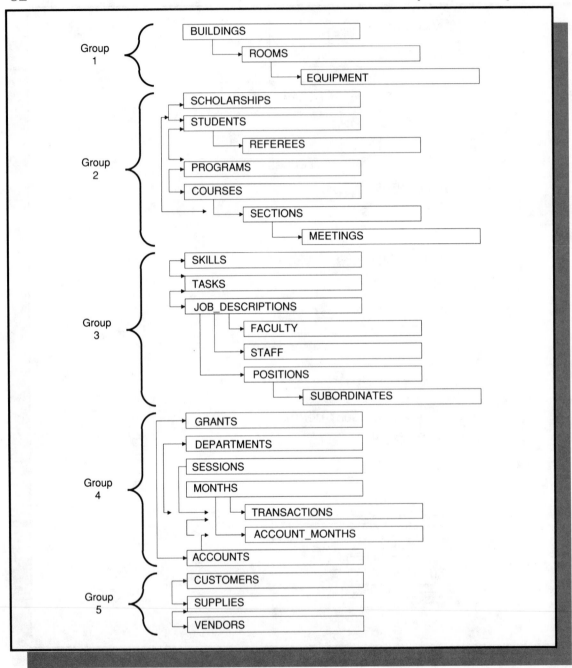

Figure 2-19
Kernel entities re-organized in groups according to major relationships in the university example.

At this stage subject databases can be identified. These are groups of entity types that belong together because they record information about the same fundamental subject. Note that in Figure 2-19 there are five groups of entities that are not related to each other. They could be implemented easily as separate databases if this were a complete description of the situation. It is not, but it is a good approximation. These five groups contain entity types that are strongly related to each other and only weakly related by minor relationships to entity types outside their own group.

An alternate approach is to add relationships in order of decreasing importance until there are only five unlinked blocks. The number five is arbitrarily chosen on the assumption that the finished system is implemented in one of two ways. It may be implemented as five related systems on different machines in a connected network. It may also be implemented as five separate systems that are each the responsibility of different department heads. Such implementations are discussed in more detail in Chapter 11.

If there is no need to distribute the database or the responsibility for it, then this distinction does not have to be made and you can go directly to the next stage. If there is a need to distribute the database, then this method organizes the database so that the least used relationships can be suppressed. This minimizes the volume of communication between databases.

Minor
Relationships

The remaining relationships can now be filled in using the relationships of types 3, 4, and 5 (shown with dotted lines in Figure 2-20). This provides a complete map of all relationships in the data model. The minor relationships are drawn to the left of the diagram to ease connection of distant groups of data. These dotted lines represent the relationships that likely have to be supported by communicating over a network if the database is distributed eventually among several machines. A computer algorithm can generate this diagram if categories are established for all of the relationships. The method works satisfactorily if there are dozens or even hundreds of entities.

Testing the Entity-Relationship Model

Several diagnostics can be used to give a clue about whether entities and relationships have been identified correctly.

CLUE #1: **The entity name is not a noun.**
CAUSE: The identified item is likely a relationship.
CURE: Examine the neighboring entities to see if they are being related by the identified item. If not, change the name to a noun.

Names like TAKES or ENROLLED in Figure 2-21, that are verbs often indicate that a relationship rather than an entity has been identified. If they contain the keys of the adjacent entities—STUDENT_ID and COURSE_ID in

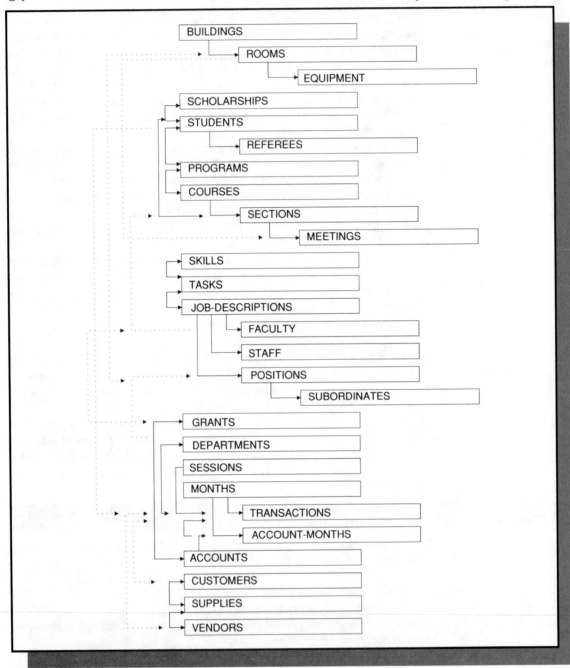

Figure 2-20
Minor (dotted) relationships added to the five groups in the university example.

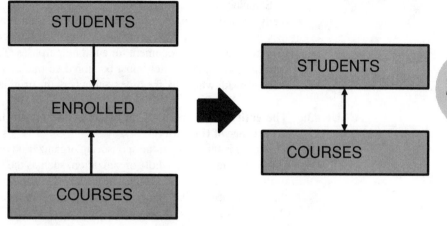

Figure 2-21
An example of a
relationship mistaken
for an entity.

2
ER Model

the example—then the relationship is M:N. In Chapter 5, it is shown that M:N relationships must be replaced by an intersection entity like ENROLLED. During the strategic design, the intersection entity is not needed.

CLUE #2:	**The entity name is the name of a document.**
CAUSE:	The entities on the document have not been identified.
CURE:	Identify the fundamental entities in the document.

Documents typically are not entities about which users want to record facts. They are objects that convey information about other entities and relationships. The application form in Figure 2-22 contains information about a student in the STUDENTS entity. It may also contain information about the relationship between the student and the schools that the student has attended. A transcript contains information about grades received at previous schools. Letters contain recommendations from referees. Similarly, an order contains information about a customer, such as name and address, and information about the relationship between the customer and the products, such as quantity ordered.

Figure 2-22
An example of a
relationship mistaken
for an entity.

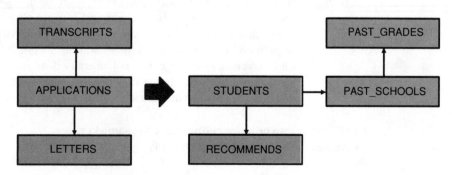

Examine entities with document names carefully to determine if they are really needed, or whether they are actually relationships. They may be entities if they represent a discrete event whose time must be recorded or if there is a need to identify the paper document for auditing purposes. Thus, ORDERS is likely an entity because information must be stored so that auditors can trace the time it was received, who took the order, and where the original document is.

CLUE #3:	**The entity is the name of an organization or job title or there is only one occurrence of the entity.**
CAUSE:	The entity is the name of the sponsoring organization or of one person or officer.
CURE:	Delete the entity. The whole organization, such as the university, usually is not a useful entity since there is only one instance of it and it is related to everything in the organization. The same is true of a single person, such as the University President or Director of Personnel.
CLUE #4:	**No identification key for entity.**
CAUSE:	Either a key has not been assigned yet, this is really an attribute of another entity, or the concept is too vague to be an entity.
CURE:	If a key is available, there is no problem. If there are no recordable details about this item, then it is an attribute of a higher entity and should be combined with the higher entity. If the concept is too vague to have a unique identifier, delete it from the model.

If there is no identification key for the entity, then consider whether this item is too vague to be an entity or really describes some other entity in the model. If it does not, then select a unique attribute of the entity as an identifier or else invent an identification code.

Each occurrence of an entity must be identifiable by a unique key. If we cannot determine the unique characteristics of an entity that distinguish each occurrence, then we probably do not have an entity. If we can't tell when we've found one, then we don't know what we're looking for.

Entities like building, customer, sale, or investment are relatively easy to identify by a name, number, or code. It is easy to envision many of the properties of them that should be recorded. On the other hand, legislation, problems, plans, and policies are less likely to be entities. It is not clear how occurrences can be identified and it is not always clear what could be recorded about such subjects. Legislation could be an entity if we want to record the number of the bill, its name, and date of passage. It is not an entity if we mean to refer to all the safety legislation that applies to the organization, but do not know how to organize it into files with distinct attributes.

CLUE #5:	**Two or more entities have the same key.**
CAUSE:	They may be the same entity.

2

ER Model

CURE: Combine them into a single entity if they have essentially the same attributes.

This situation usually arises when different subgroups of a broadly defined entity perform different roles in an organization. Thus FACULTY and STAFF may both be entities in a university identified by EMPLOYEE_ID. There are two options in this case. They can either be kept as two separate entities or amalgamated into a single entity, EMPLOYEES. The reason that two entities arose initially is often that the two entities are perceived as different in the organization. However, sometimes they arise because of different naming conventions in different parts of the organization.

There are two tests that can be applied to determine if amalgamation is appropriate. The first test is to see if the entities have substantially the same attributes. They may differ in one or two attributes and still be substantially the same. If they differ in most attributes, they are probably different entities. FACULTY and STAFF both have names, addresses, phone numbers, and a host of other common attributes. This leads us to think that amalgamation is in order.

The second test is whether the entities participate in the same relationships. FACULTY are related to COURSES, PUBLICATIONS, RESEARCH_GRANTS, and RESEARCH_PROJECTS. STAFF are usually not related to these other entities. This shows that the entities fill different roles in the organization and must be separated even if they share attributes. A similar argument can be made for not amalgamating EMPLOYEES and STUDENTS into PERSONS even though all of them are keyed on their Social Security Number.

This generalization example can be carried one step further. EMPLOYEES and VENDORS could be amalgamated into PAYEES since both of them receive payments from the organization. However, this is the only characteristic that they share. Most of the data about them would be very different. Even the nature of the payments is very different. Vendors simply receive a payment triggered by an invoice while employees receive regular payments based on complex tax, bonus, and deduction calculations. Vendors typically provide materials which go into inventory and employees provide labor which is not inventoriable. As a result, it is not likely that amalgamation of these entities achieves much simplification. It is more likely to introduce a great deal of complexity.

The decision to amalgamate entities is a tradeoff decision. If the entities are not amalgamated, then programs which operate on both of them may have to be duplicated. If FACULTY and STAFF are kept separate then the payroll program, which applies to both of them, becomes more complex or has to be duplicated. If they are amalgamated, then programs which apply only to single subgroups become more complex. If FACULTY and STAFF are amalgamated, then a number of fields, such as tenure or union membership, apply to only one subgroup. This makes input validation, reports, and queries very complex and may significantly increase machine time in searches that apply to only one subgroup.

This problem is dealt with in more detail in Chapter 5.

Figure 2-23
An example of 1:1
relationships that
should be eliminated.

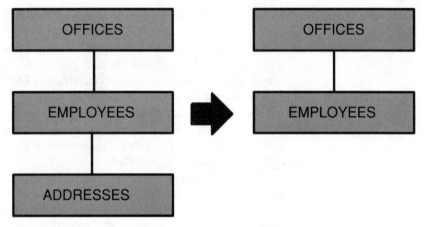

CLUE #6:	1:1 relationships.
CAUSE:	The attributes of an entity have been arbitrarily divided.
CURE:	Combine the entities. 1:1 relationships often mean that the related entities should be amalgamated. If they have the same key—as in EMPLOYEES and ADDRESSES in Figure 2-23—then the attributes can be combined into one entity. They should be kept separate if they need different keys or if they can exist without each other as in OFFICES and EMPLOYEES.

CLUE #7:	Many relationships to a single entity.
CAUSE:	The entity is too general.
CURE:	Split the entity into more specific entities.

Many relationships with a single entity suggests the entity may be an amalgamation of two or more entities that should be separated. This should trigger us to question whether each relationship involves substantially all of the occurrences and attributes in the entity. If subgroups can be identified that reduce the number of relationships with each subgroup, then consider splitting the entity.

If PERSONS is identified as an entity in Figure 2-24, it has relationships with SECTIONS, PROGRAMS, SCHOLARSHIPS, OFFICES, POSITIONS, PAY_PERIODS, and DEDUCTIONS. If PERSONS is split into FACULTY, STAFF, and STUDENTS, then STUDENTS has relationships with PROGRAMS, SECTIONS, and SCHOLARSHIPS while FACULTY has relationships with SECTIONS, OFFICES, PAY_PERIODS, and DEDUCTIONS. STAFF has relationships with OFFICES, PAY_PERIODS, and DEDUCTIONS. This provides a structure that more accurately portrays the real environment.

CLUE #8:	Two or more relationships between the same entities.
CAUSE:	Redundant relationships.
CURE:	Combine relationships if the roles are the same.

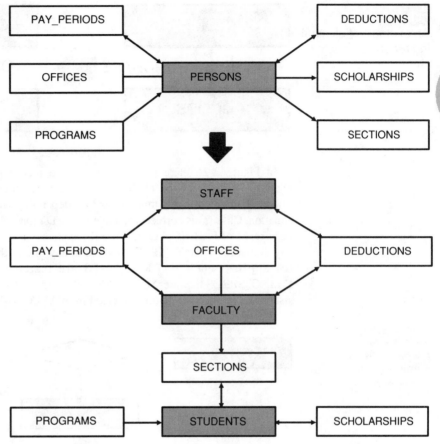

Figure 2-24
An example of a
relationship mistaken
for an entity.

It is possible to have more than one relationship between the same entities if
each relationship describes a different role. IS_PARENT_OF, IS_CHILD_OF,
and IS_MARRIED_TO are examples of such multiple relationships between
PERSONS. Here they clearly describe different relationships. Similarly, STU-
DENTS can be ENROLLED in COURSES or they can GRADE COURSES.

Customers ORDER goods and customers PURCHASE goods in Figure 2-25
are likely to be the same relationship under two different names. If so, they
should be combined into a single relationship. Examine multiple relationships
carefully to make sure that they are recording a different role and do not just
have different names with the same meaning.

CLUE #9:   N-ary relationship among 3 or more entities.
CAUSE: Incomplete analysis.
CURE: Find the missing event or transaction that records the relationship.

Figure 2-25

An example of eliminating redundant relationships.

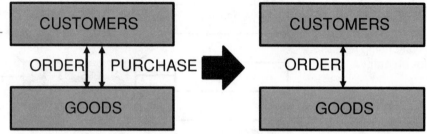

In Figure 2-26 there has to be a way to record the FABRIC_LOTS, the DYING_RUNS, and the DYING_SPECS that go together to make up a run. There are three ways that this can be done depending on the rules that govern the situation. Case (a) is correct when one of the DYING_SPECS applies to a whole occurrence of FABRIC_LOTS. Case (b) applies when DYING_RUNS consist of any one of the DYING_SPECS applied to any one of the FABRIC_LOTS. Case (c) applies when FABRIC_LOTS are tested to determine a list of DYING_SPECS that are ALLOWABLES for that lot. DYING_RUNS then consist of one of the combinations selected from ALLOWABLES.

Figure 2-26

An example of the elimination of an N-ary relationship.

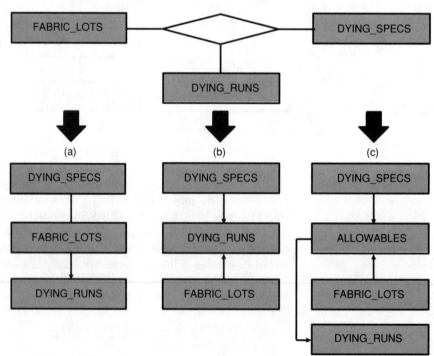

CLUE #10:   **An entity has no relationships.**
CAUSE: A relationship has been omitted or the entity is not needed.
CURE: Check for relationships with each of the other entities. If any are found, record them. If none are found, delete the entity.

CASE Tools for Entity-Relationship Models

2
ER Model

There are a number of CASE (Computer Aided Software Engineering) tools that help the analyst to produce an Enterprise Model. Comprehensive CASE tools like Excelerator provide facilities for drawing Entity-Relationship Diagrams quickly and easily. The packages take care of most of the formatting and drawing detail at the computer screen, thus relieving the analyst of a lot of burdensome detail. The results are then stored in a computer file. They can be easily modified to reflect changes during the design phase. The diagrams can be printed easily for use in paper documentation.

CASE tools also provide facilities to record other related information, such as the attributes of the entities, the cardinality of the relationships, and textual descriptions of the meaning and purpose of each entity, relationship, and attribute. This extra information can be added in stages as the analysis progresses from a broad outline to a detailed analysis. The information can also be integrated with other information that is collected during later stages of the analysis and design. For this reason, it is a good idea to start using the tools as early in the design as possible.

Some of the CASE tools provide ways of checking the integrity of the model. Some packages, like Excelerator from Index Technology Corp.[3], produce tables of diagnostics to identify possible violations of good design principles. Others, like Information Engineering Workbench (IEW) from KnowledgeWare, Inc.[5], have some intelligence built into the tools to prevent the entry of illogical diagrams. Many of the Clue/Cause/Cure problems in the previous section can be detected automatically. These facilities reduce errors and reduce development costs by catching errors early when they are easy to correct.

Figure 2-27 is a screen from the IEW planning module. It illustrates part of the Entiry-Relationship Diagram in Figure 2-20. IEW is able to display different parts of the design in multiple windows. The upper left window shows a part of the Entity-Relationship Diagram. The lower left window shows details about the Students entity. IEW uses the term fundamental for kernel entities and attributive for characteristic entities. The right hand window describes the relationship between Students and Sections. It contains names of relationships in both directions and cardinality data. M is the maximum and 0 is the minimum number of occurrences of the entity at each end of the relationship.

Excelerator has similar screens for entering Entity-Relationship data. It is a little more flexible in graphic design, but does not have multiple windows and is not as good at checking input data.

Figure 2-27

The planning module of IEW being used to enter the Entity-Relationship Model of Figure 2-20.

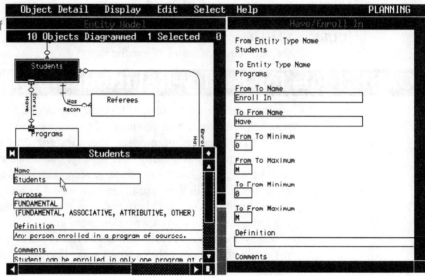

CASE tools usually have several ways of presenting the same information. The entities and relationships on the diagrams can be converted automatically into tabular reports that list all the entities and relationships in the design along with selected characteristics. Some can even use a complete design to produce computer code to implement a database in a number of selected languages.

Summary

The Entity-Relationship Model uses logical file names to model the entities in an organization that an analyst records data about and the relationships between those entities. The concept of cardinality indicates the maximum number of instances of each entity that can participate in a relationship. Cardinality is either 1:1, 1:N or M:N in data models. Kernel entities are those entities that are never at the N end of a 1:N relationship. All of the other entities are characteristic entities.

Unique identifying keys provide information for identifying entities and relationships. Information about entities and relationships can be obtained from existing forms, existing computer files, published designs, strategic plans and mission statements, and interviews.

The kernel entities and their hierarchy of characteristic entities are used as building blocks to produce an Entity-Relationship Diagram. Major relationships are added to the building blocks to produce subject databases or clusters of entities that belong together in a distributed database. Minor relationships are added to complete the model. The resulting model is used for identifying projects to implement and for setting the scope for detailed database design.

The names of entities, the number and kind of relationships, and their cardinality can be used as clues to help identify incorrect designs.

CASE tools reduce the amount of work required to produce Entity-Relationship Diagrams, help to identify errors in the diagrams, and capture the information in the diagrams for later use.

Keywords and Phrases

Attribute	Cardinality
Characteristic Entity	Entity Occurrence
Entity-Relationship Diagram	Entity Type
Homonym	Kernel Entity
Key Attribute	N-ary Relationship
Recursive Relationship	Relationship
Synonym	

Review Questions

1. Define each of the items in the list of keywords and phrases.
2. Name and define the six classes into which entities fall.
3. How can entities be identified in an organization?
4. Distinguish between a kernel entity and a characteristic entity.
5. How can relationships be identified in an organization?
6. How does a recursive relationship differ from an ordinary relationship?
7. Name the three kinds of cardinality that a relationship can have and specify how each can be identified.
8. Name the five main sources of information about entities and relationships?
9. Why does a repeating group of attributes in a file or form imply a new entity?
10. Explain how to organize a large Entity-Relationship Diagram so that it does not look like a Can Of Worms.
11. List the clues that indicate errors in constructing an Entity-Relationship Diagram.

Problems

1. Build an Entity-Relationship Model for a factory that represents the following situation:
   • A component can be used to make any of several other components.
   • A component can be made of several other components.
   • A component can be constructed from several raw materials.
   • A raw material is used in several components.
   • Each component is produced by a single worker.
   • A worker can produce many kinds of components.

2. Build an Entity-Relationship Model of a database dictionary that represents the following situation:
   • An entity type can contain many attributes.
   • An attribute can appear in many entity types.

- A database contains many entity types.
- An entity type can appear in only one database.
- A DBMS can manage many databases.
- A database can be managed by only one DBMS.
- An entity type can be part of many relationships.
- A relationship always relates two entity types.

3. Build an Entity-Relationship Model of a database that catalogs recordings for a radio station. The disk jockeys need to be able to locate selections by record-name, artist, role, and composition. This information is obtained from typical album covers like the simplified excerpt shown below.

THE PACHELBEL CANON
and Other Baroque Favorites
Jean Francois Paillard Chamber Orchestra;
I Solisti Veneti; Others
RCA AGL1/AGK1-5211

SIDE A
Handel -XERXES:LARGO (6:20)
   Hugette Fernandez,Violin
   Pierre Pierlot, Oboe
   Pro Arte Chamber Orchestra of Munich
   Kurt Redel, Conductor
Pachelbel-CANON IN D FOR STRINGS
AND CONTINUO (7:05)
   Jean Francois Paillard Chamber Orchestra;
   Jean Francois Paillard, Conductor
   .
   .

SIDE B
Handel-JUDAS MACCABAEUS:
SEE THE CONQUERING HERO COMES
   Arranged by Kurt Reidel (2:08)
   Hugette Fernandez,Violin
   Pierre Pierlot, Oboe
   Pro Arte Chamber Orchestra of Munich
   Kurt Redel, Conductor
   .
   .
   .

---

4. The following Entity-Relationship Diagram models the structure of a small organization that uses parts, obtained from suppliers, in construction projects. Answer the following business questions using the model.
   a. Do different warehouses sometimes store the same kind of part?
   b. Can an employee work on more than one project?
   c. Can an employee manage more than one project?
   d. Can a project have more than one manager?
   e. Does a project manager always work on a project?
   f. How many departments can an employee be assigned to?
   g. Can a part be provided by more than one supplier?
   h. Can parts of a single order be shipped to more than one project?
   i. Is it possible to identify the manager responsible for ordering a part for a project?

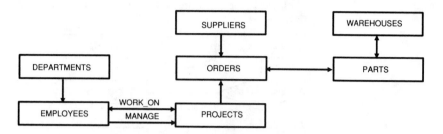

5. The following files are used by a wholesale hardware vendor. Construct the Entity-Relationship Diagram that corresponds to the files.

TERRITORY:	TERRITORY_ID, MARKET_SIZE, ...
SALESMAN:	SALESMAN_ID, NAME, ADDRESS, TERRITORY_ID, ...
CUSTOMER:	CUSTOMER_ID, SALESMAN_ID, NAME, ADDRESS, PHONE, ...
ORDER:	<u>ORDER_ID</u>, CUSTOMER_ID, WAREHOUSE_ID, PAYMENT, ...
LINE_ITEM:	<u>ORDER_ID, LINE_NUM</u>, PRODUCT_ID, QUANTITY
PRODUCT:	PRODUCT_ID, DESCRIPTION, PRICE
SHIPMENT:	SHIPMENT_ID, ORDER_ID, WAREHOUSE_ID, CUSTOMER_ID, DATE
WAREHOUSE:	WAREHOUSE_ID, ADDRESS, CAPACITY
STORAGE:	PRODUCT_ID, WAREHOUSE_ID, COUNT
INVOICE:	<u>SHIPMENT_ID, CUSTOMER_ID</u>, AMOUNT, DATE

6. The university information system example in this chapter is to be modified to include a computer lab reservation system for students. Identify the changes in the Entity-Relationship Diagram that are required to accommodate this system. The following rules apply to the use of the computer lab.
   - A student must be enrolled in certain courses before being allowed to use the lab.
   - Each computer is equipped with a specific combination of features such as printer, mouse, color screen, memory size, and hard disk.
   - Students are allowed to reserve a specific computer for a specific time so that they can get access to specific peripherals.

7. Identify the errors in the following Entity-Relationship Diagram.

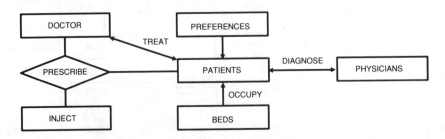

Project

Locate an organization with an Information Systems project that you can work on during this course. The organization can be a business, a public body like a school or hospital, or a charity like a church or scout group. The project should involve the analysis, design, and possibly the implementation of a computer program to solve some problem involving the gathering and use of data. The system to be selected must have the following characteristics:

- **4 to 8 entities** in the Entity-Relationship model. Projects with less than 4 entities are rarely complicated enough to make interesting projects. Projects with more than 7 or 8 entities are usually so complicated that it is impossible to complete the project during a course. Sometimes it is possible to select a subset of a larger project or share a larger project with another person or group.

- **Several reports and data entry screens.** Reports and screens tend to multiply faster than entities. You will not learn much after implementing two or three of each, but they will require a lot of work if you do not have access to tools that create default reports from the database design specifications. If there are many screens and reports required, you may be able to limit the number that must be implemented in this project.

- **A calculation or transformation problem.** This is often the most difficult thing to find in a small project. Many small projects involve only simple data entry and simple reports with simple calculation, like multiplying quantity by price to get cost. This component requires a transformation with several stages. Examples of suitable calculations are accounting reports, financial calculations, statistical calculations, summary reports, schedules, and searches for specific subsets of information.

The project will be done in stages so that you can get feedback from your instructor, grader, or project supervisor before proceeding with the next stages. The person who receives your project materials and provides feedback will be called your project supervisor in all following phases of this project. The first thing that you hand in is designed to ensure that you have been able to locate a suitable project. Provide the following information on no more than two pages:

a. The name of the organization and name, address, and phone number of your contact in the organization.

b. A brief description of the problem and a proposal stating what you intend to include as deliverables in your solution of the problem.

c. An Entity-Relationship Diagram of the data that will be needed to implement the project.

References

1. Barker, Richard, CASE*METHOD Entity Relationship Modelling, Addison-Wesley Publishing Co., 1989.

2. Chen, Peter, "The Entity-Relationship Model—Towards a Unified View of Data", ACM Transactions on Database Systems, Vol. 1 no. 1, March 1976, pp. 9-36.

3. Index Technology Corporation, 101 Main Street, Cambridge, MA 02142.

4. Kerner, David V., "Business Information Control Study Methodology" in The Economics of Information Processing, Volume 1, Management Perspectives, edited by Robert C. Goldberg and Harold Lorin, John Wiley & Sons, 1982, pp. 71-83.

5. KnowledgeWare, Inc., 3340 Peachtree Road, NE, Suite 1100, Atlanta GA 30026.

6. Martin, James, Strategic Data-Planning Methodologies, Prentice-Hall Inc., 1982.

7. Martin, James and Carma McLure, Diagramming Techniques for Analysts and Programmers, Prentice-Hall Inc., 1985.

8. Parrello, Bruce, Ross Overbeek and Ewing Lusk, "The Design of Entity-Relationship Models for General Ledger Systems", Data and Knowledge Engineering, Vol. 1, 1985, pp. 155-180.

9. Scheer, A.-W., Enterprise-Wide Data Modelling, Springer-Verlag, 1989.

2
ER Model

Chapter 3

Modeling Organization Activities

	DATABASE (WHAT)	PROGRAMS (HOW)	BENEFITS (WHY)	NETWORK (WHERE)	REAL TIME (WHEN)	SKILLS (WHO)
USER CONCEPT	Entity Relationship	Activity	Intangible Benefit	Map		Organization Design
DESIGNER CONCEPT	E-R Diagram	A-E Diagram	AHP	Network		Skills Responsibility
USER DETAIL	Forms Screens	Processes Data	Tangible Benefit	Work Volume	Discrete Events	Transition Training
DESIGNER DETAIL	EER Diagram	Data Flow Diagrams	Benefit- Cost	Partition	Transition Diagrams	Methodology Tools
BUILDER CONCEPT	Normal Form Relations	Structure Chart	Function Points	System Architecture	Specifications	Learning
BUILDER DETAIL	Files	Screens Specifications	Costs	Network Specs	Interfaces	4GL CASE

Objectives

Chapter 2 used an Entity-Relationship Diagram to create a high-level model of the data used by an organization. This chapter develops a model of the high-level activities that have to be performed by an organization. Then the activity model and the data model are combined to show how they interact. These pieces together provide a high-level model of the enterprise that can be used to identify major components of the enterprise's information system and set priorities on their implementation.

The enterprise model serves as an idealized model of the organization that can be used for planning purposes. It is like a road map. It shows the major features of the terrain to guide future progress. Yet it does not burden the reader with so much detail that the overall picture might be lost. Just as road maps often have detailed inserts to illustrate the streets of a city, this modeling process will later develop detailed models of the entities and activities. At this initial planning stage, a model of the major components is still sufficient.

A road map deliberately leaves out many details that are subject to frequent change. It leaves out details that change with weather, seasons, or maintenance activities. It concentrates on those underlying features that are relatively stable. The enterprise model similarly concentrates on the fundamental activities of the organization that remain stable while individual employees, products, or customers come and go.

This chapter will show you how to model the activities of an organization and group them to form stable subsystems. When you have finished this chapter you will be able to:

- Classify kinds of information used at different levels of an organization.

- Identify activities and structure them into a hierarchy.

- Identify which entities each activity uses.

- Compute measures of similarity to identify activities that belong together.

- Cluster activities into subsystems of high similarity.

- Identify groups of activities that constitute a development project.

Introduction and Overview

An organization is groups of individuals engaged in performing coordinated activities. The coordination is provided by a hierarchy of formal responsibility, a network of informal relationships, and a network of information. An Organization Chart is a model of the hierarchy of responsibility. The chart is an attempt to simplify the complex informal network of relationships in the organization. It reduces the organization into a simpler hierarchy that people can understand and use for assigning responsibility. Like any simplification, it is often inadequate to deal with new circumstances. So the organization structure is frequently changed in an attempt to produce a better compromise with organizational needs.

The Entity-Relationship Diagram models the network of information. Information does not need to be mapped into a hierarchy that corresponds to the administrative hierarchy. The computer allows us to organize information in complex ways that were impossible manually. The data needs are relatively stable, but the organizational structure changes frequently. It is not uncommon to find that by the time a project is completed, the requesting department has been reorganized and the original specifications no longer satisfy their needs. The information system designer's problem is that application development projects are requested by one part of the organizational hierarchy. Yet they require data from different parts of the information network provided by different parts of the hierarchy.

A method of identifying development projects is needed that is less sensitive to this continually changing organizational structure. It must be based on factors that are less subject to change. These factors are the information needs of the organization and the activities performed by the organization. The Entity-Relationship Diagram was developed without reference to the organization's structure. A model of the basic organizational activities must be developed that is independent of the current organizational structure.

An Enterprise Model consists of a model of the data used by the organization and a model of the activities which enter, use, or transform those data. This chapter explains how to model the activities at the highest level of aggregation and how to relate these activities to the data that they process. This information is used to develop a systems model that organizes the activities into groups of related activities. The information system can support them in a way that is relatively insensitive to the structure of the organization. This allows the identification of projects that can be developed independently with minimal concern about interactions between projects and changes in organizational structure. The modeling process consists of:

- **Structuring** activities in a hierarchy.
- **Identifying** activities in each level.
- **Relating** activities to data.
- **Grouping** activities into subsystems.

A top down process of identifying aggregate activities and refining them into detailed activities is used. The process is then reversed to reaggregate the detailed activities into subsystems that do not necessarily relate to the existing organizational hierarchy. This new set of aggregated activities forms the basis for defining independent subsystems that can be implemented in detail.

Structuring a Hierarchy of Activities

Hierarchical structures are a natural way of simplifying problems. A hierarchy permits a complicated structure to be expressed as a set of successively more detailed levels. The highest level provides a very general summary of the situation. Each successive lower level reveals more detail about the previous level. This hierarchical approach is used by organizations to simplify their management structure. The same approach is used in modeling the activities that an organization performs.

3
Activities

The Levels of an Organization

Most enterprises can be viewed as a pyramidal structure as illustrated in Figure 3-1. The top level consists of the president and the vice-presidents who concern themselves with a strategic view of the organization. This strategic view involves planning for the future of the enterprise and organizing the resources of the enterprise—manpower, money, and machinery—to achieve that planned future. The main concerns of this layer are broad, long-term, unstructured, and externally oriented. Their information needs are volatile and unpredictable.

Below the strategic level is the tactical layer which concerns itself with managing the specific departments of the enterprise. These middle managers try to

Figure 3-1
The three vertical management levels of an organization.

ORGANIZATION
LEVEL

INFORMATION
CHARACTERISTICS

STRATEGIC

Broad
Long-term
Unstructured
Externally-oriented
Volatile
Unpredictable

TACTICAL

OPERATIONAL

Narrow
Short-term
Structured
Internally-oriented
Stable
Predictable

organize the tasks of the enterprise as efficiently as possible. They try to convert the broad goals that are defined at the strategic level into tactics that can be implemented to achieve these goals. The viewpoint and information needs of this layer are intermediate between those of the strategic level above and the operational level below.

The operational level of the organization has specific tasks that need to be performed to achieve the goals of the enterprise. These tasks are relatively narrow, short-term, structured, and internally oriented. The information needs at this level are stable and predictable provided that the strategic goals of the enterprise do not change.

The actual number of administrative layers in an enterprise varies with size and organizational structure. Each of the three levels may actually have more than one layer of management in it.

Some people suggest that the different levels of the enterprise need entirely different information systems because of their different characteristics. The operational level relies on Data Base Management Systems (DBMS) with rigid standards and rules to determine the contents of the database. The tactical level relies on a Management Information System (MIS) that provides summary reports to monitor and control the level below. The strategic level uses Decision Support Systems (DSS) and Executive Support Systems (ESS) to help with planning, budgeting, and coordinating activities.

In practice, it is not possible to separate the systems easily. The operational level needs to have budget data passed down from above and needs to pass detailed data up to be used in monitoring and forecasting. The strategic level also must communicate with the tactical level. Information and proposals move up for analysis and approval and goals and plans move down for interpretation and implementation.

Figure 3-2

The horizontal management divisions of a typical organization.

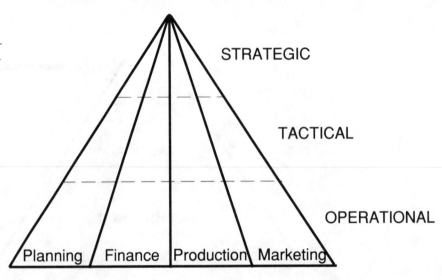

The Enterprise Diagram in Figure 3-1 also has a horizontal dimension as shown in Figure 3-2. Horizontally the enterprise structure is divided into functional areas that are each responsible for specific functions in the organization such as financing, production, and marketing. Each functional area has its own strategic, tactical, and operational level. The tasks get more specific and detailed as one progresses from the top of the pyramid to the bottom. A model of the activities of an organization needs to reflect this hierarchical structure and the progression from broad goals to specific tasks.

Figure 3-3 illustrates the upper levels of an Organization Chart for a university. It consists of a president with five vice-presidents. Under each vice-president are listed the major activities that they are responsible for as identified during interviews. There are many more layers that are not shown on the diagram. If each of these activities were to be analyzed, the number of activities would increase by a factor of five to ten. Applications processing would become: Recording Applications, Recording Test Scores, Evaluating Applicants, Mailing Acceptances/Rejections, and Recording Admissions.

The Organization Chart provides a high level view of the activities of the organization. It also identifies the individuals who should be seen for detailed information. The high level activities are named with action oriented nouns frequently ending with the suffixes -ing, -ion, or -ment. Typical names are marketing, production, accounting, budgeting, and product development. The description of lower level activities normally begins with a verb and describes the operation being performed. Typical examples are record sales, analyze costs, or process applicant.

Since each functional area can be viewed as a separate pyramid, it may sometimes be possible to analyze the structure of each functional area separately, thus narrowing the size, scope, and complexity of the architectural design. Usually there is enough information exchange between functional areas, that it is not practical to separate the architectures. The areas frequently share an interest in major resources such as personnel, customers, and products.

Figure 3-3

Example Organization Chart and activities for a university.

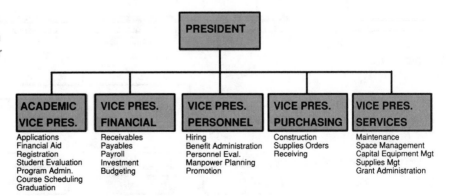

In practice, separate architectural plans should be produced only for autonomous companies or divisions which have their own distinct product line and customer base. Integrated companies need an integrated information architecture that permits coordination and sharing of information about the common elements. A decentralized company with a number of autonomous divisions needs an architectural plan for each autonomous division and one for the head office.

The Levels of Organizational Activities

The analyst's objective is to model the activities of an organization that has to be supported eventually by databases and computer application programs. The analyst's model is not identical to the enterprise's Organization Chart. However, it includes all of the activities that are shown on the Organization Chart. The Organization Chart often contains many duplicated activities.

Figure 3-4 gives two examples of duplicated activities. In the first example, the budgeting activity is repeated in each of the functional areas. From the analyst's point of view, budgeting is an activity that needs to be supported. It should be possible to design a single budgeting system that can be used by all of the functional areas. In the second example, manufacturing and sales are repeated in each of the regional divisions. If they are manufacturing and selling the same products, then the same information system should be able to support both regions.

Just as the enterprise has three levels of activities—strategic, tactical, and operational—the analyst's model has three levels of activities. However, they do not necessarily correspond to the enterprise levels. The three levels correspond instead to resources, life-cycle stages, and functions. These generic categories provide a modeling framework that is independent of the organizational struc-

Figure 3-4

Two Organization Charts with duplicated activities. The top one has duplicate Budgeting activities for each functional area. The bottom one has duplicate Production and Sales activities for each region.

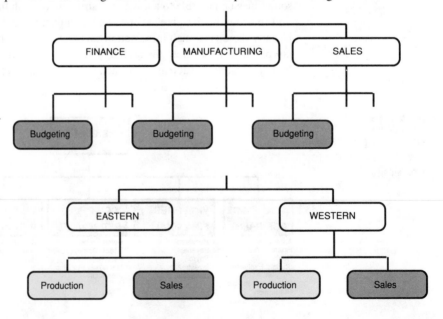

ture. As a result, the framework encourages a design that is more fundamental than the current organizational structure which is subject to frequent changes.

Resources

The first level of activity analysis identifies resources. Resources are the different things that an enterprise requires to operate successfully. The major resources of the organization frequently correspond to the kernel entities identified in the Entity-Relationship Diagram in Chapter 2. Not all kernel entities are important enough to be considered major resources, but they provide a good list of potential candidates.

The following list is typical, but not all apply in every organization and others may apply in some organizations. Each example includes illustrations of some of the special information needs that are required for proper management of the resource. These special needs have to be considered when functions are identified at the third level of analysis.

- **Money.** Money is usually such a critical resource that it is managed centrally for the whole organization. It is usually so easy to convert to unauthorized purposes that it must be managed and controlled separately from other resources. Organizations frequently have a finance department to manage this resource.
- **Materials.** Special activities may exist for certain materials that require special attention because of their value or their special properties. Valuable materials are more carefully controlled than inexpensive commodities. Dangerous materials that are toxic, radioactive, or explosive may require special controls. Materials may be managed by various departments in an enterprise, such as manufacturing, purchasing, and inventory.
- **Equipment and Facilities.** Equipment and facilities may be recorded and tracked differently depending on expected lifetime, value, hazards, or sources. Accounting for land is usually different from accounting for equipment. These resources are managed by the finance department or the manufacturing department in most organizations.
- **Personnel.** Not all activities apply to all personnel. Different activities may be needed depending on whether the employees are unionized, tenured, salaried, or on contract. The human resources department or some similar name is usually responsible for many aspects of managing personnel. Other aspects, such as hiring, may be scattered throughout the organization.
- **Suppliers.** There is a need to identify, record the characteristics of, and record the performance of principal suppliers of the resources an organization uses. This is particularly true of suppliers who are either scarce or have a continuing relationship with the organization. Purchasing and manufacturing departments are most involved with managing the relationship with suppliers.
- **Customers or clients.** In organizations that have a continuing relationship with customers or clients there is a need to maintain extensive records to identify or to serve them better. The marketing department usually does most of the work in managing customers.

3
Activities

- **Intangibles.** There are a variety of intangible resources such as patents, company image, or reputation for quality that need to be identified and tracked. These are typically handled by a number of different departments such as finance, legal services, and marketing.
- **Information.** Information is beginning to be recognized as a resource that must be inventoried and tracked like any other resource. Information can take many forms. It may consist of designs, specifications, reports, procedures, computer programs, data banks, or employee expertise. Information is rarely managed as a resource in most companies.

Sometimes a class of resources, like materials, may actually consist of more than one type because the different types are used in a different line of business. For instance, in the oil industry, there is a great difference between crude oil which is the end product of the producing division and fuels which are the end product of the refining division. These resources are handled so differently that they are treated as separate resources in the activity model.

A large organization typically has ten to twenty major resources that have to be tracked. If there are more than seven resources, this level should be split into two levels with no more than seven members under a heading. For instance, in the oil company example just given, the major resource level would include the product resource. Under product there would be two specific resources: crude and fuels.

An enterprise is often organized so that separate parts of the organization manage different resources. Thus production manages materials and marketing manages customers.

In the university example, the main resources are courses, students, staff, money, and things such as buildings and supplies. These resources are shown as the beginning of a Decomposition Diagram in Figure 3-5.

Figure 3-5

A first level Decomposition Diagram for a university.

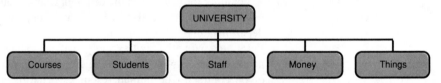

Life Cycle Stages

The second level of activity analysis identifies Life Cycle Stages. Each of the resources has a life cycle during which the resource is planned, acquired, maintained, and disposed of. These activities are described in more detail below.

- **Requirements, planning, measurement, and control.** This category has activities that determine how much of a product or resource to acquire, prepare the plan for getting it, measure the amount obtained or produced, and compare the results to the plan. Head office groups usually perform the strategic planning activities. They have broad responsibility for developing plans for the long term future of the organization. Typical examples of such activities are economic forecasting, research and development, identifying acquisitions and divestitures, corporate cash planning, and corporate budget preparation. The management control activities measure performance and compare it to some established norm such as a budget. Cost analysis, labor efficiency studies, and profitability analysis are examples.

- **Acquisition and production.** These activities involve the acquisition of resources and the conversion of these resources into a useful product or service. The most common resources are money, materials, facilities, and people. Typical activities are purchasing, fabrication, creation, engineering, recruitment, or enrollment of students.

- **Stewardship.** These activities modify or maintain the supporting resources and store or track the product or services. Stewardship involves tasks like maintenance, inventory control, storage, or warranty service. In a financial service company this could mean payment notices and dividend statements. In a school it could mean taking attendance.

- **Disposal and retirement.** These activities end an organization's responsibility for a product, service, or resource. They signal the final use of a resource. Disposal includes product sales, service delivery, payment, employee retirement, and waste disposal.

These life cycle stages can be applied to each of the products, services, and resources that the organization produces or uses. The stages of the life cycle can usually be ordered sequentially in time. The order may be different for different organizations. For instance one organization may manufacture products to keep in stock, then find customers who want them. Another organization may find customers first and then make products to order. Some companies do both with different products.

These life cycle stage activities should have the following characteristics:

- **Name.** The name should be action-oriented. It should be made by combining a verb with a noun that is the object of the verb. *Purchase materials* and *sell products* are good names because they describe what is being done and what the receiver of the action is. *Finance* is a bad name because it is not clear whether it is a noun or a verb and it is not clear what is being financed if it is a verb. Furthermore, it could be confused with the name of a department. This would carry connotations about the existing organization rather than the generic activities that the analyst is trying to define.

- **Objective.** The analyst should focus on **what** activity is performed and not on **how** the activity is performed. Procedures may change during the course of the analysis, but the objective of the activity is not likely to change. *Evaporate crude in a distillation tower* is a description of how an activity is performed. *Refine crude* is a description of what is being done.

- **Time frame.** The second level activities are ongoing and continuous. They do not have a definable starting and stopping time.

- **Data.** A life cycle stage does not have to be automated or use a database to qualify as a legitimate activity. However, the stage must create some type of information that it uses itself.

- **Quantity.** There should usually be four to seven stages for each resource. Some of these stages are very complicated for certain resources and may have to be split to obtain a reasonable balance between the components of a model. For instance, acquisition in a manufacturing organization consists of purchasing materials and manufacturing products. Each may be quite complex and deserve a separate second level stage. On the other hand, if too many stages have been identified for a particular resource, then some should be combined to get down to a limit of seven. People find it difficult to comprehend more than seven concepts at one time.

The life cycle of a resource is sometimes coupled to the life cycle of another resource. In the oil industry, the life cycle for crude oil must precede the life cycle for refined products. In the banking industry, the life cycle of each product should conceptually include the same customer so that it is possible to identify all of the business that is done with each customer. Whenever, the resources interact in this way, the analysis should start with the earliest resource in the chain.

The activities for the university Organization Chart in Figure 3-3 are recast into a life cycle framework in Figure 3-6. The five resources are recorded in the rows: courses, students, staff, money, and things. Things refers to all tangible resources such as buildings, equipment, and supplies. The activities shown in boldface type were not identified in the original interviews. They were added after examination of the original table followed by more interviews. Examination of the original table in Figure 3-6, ignoring the boldface activities, reveals a number of vacancies. There is apparently no planning stage for students or things and there is no acquisition or disposal stage for courses. There is also no disposal stage for staff or things.

Further interviews reveal that the Academic Vice-president does perform demand analysis. Up to now he has done this manually in a rather ad hoc manner, but he expects to formalize the process soon. Courses are quite stable. Departmental committees perform the process of adding and deleting courses

Figure 3-6

Activities categorized by the five resources of the university and the four stages of the resource life cycle. New activities are shown in bold type.

	PLANNING	ACQUISITION	STEWARDSHIP	DISPOSAL
COURSE	Schedule Courses		Administer Program	
STUDENT	**Analyse Demand**	Enter Applications Aid Financially Register Students	Evaluate Students	Graduate Students
STAFF	Plan Manpower	Hire Staff	Evaluate Personnel Administer Benefits Promote Employees	**Retire Staff**
MONEY	Budget Expenses	Receive Payments **Apply for Grants**	Administer Grants Invest Funds	Pay Suppliers Pay Employees
THINGS	**Budget Capital**	Order Supplies Receive Orders	Construct Facilities Maintain Facilities Manage Equipment Manage Supplies Manage Space	**Control Waste**

and do not require central support. Thus these phases are treated as simple file editing tasks that do not have to appear in this Figure 3-6. There are retirement procedures in place, but they were not mentioned during the previous interviews. The Capital Budget is part of the budgeting process. Yet it is different enough from normal budgets that it should be removed as a separate activity that plans for capital equipment.

The university requires a new system for controlling the disposal of hazardous wastes to satisfy new government regulations. Other things are scrapped or sold through the normal accounting system. The university requires no formal sales program since it is not in the business of selling things. The last item identified in further interviews was a system for generating and evaluating Grant Applications. This is another system for acquisition of money. Thus the life cycle analysis has alerted us to five other activities that were missed in the original examination of the organizational structure.

Functions

The third level of analysis identifies the specific functions that must be performed to accomplish the activities in each life cycle stage for each resource. For instance, student applications must be recorded, evaluated, and accepted or rejected. These third level activities are repeatedly executed in the enterprise. A good information activity definition can be recognized by six characteristics:

- **Processes Information.** An organization has many activities that do not process information. Operating a drill press, getting coffee for a meeting, or shelving books in a library are all useful activities. Yet they are not interesting to the analyst unless they process information. The analyst might be interested if the drill press operators get their instructions from a computer. He might be interested if the coffee fetcher has to consult an attendance list to find out how many people want coffee. She might be interested if the librarian has to catalog a book before shelving it. We confine our interest to those activities that create, update, or use information stored in a database. The database can currently reside in a computer or a file cabinet, but must be amenable to computerization at some time. The activity might be manual or might be subject to automation.
- **Identifiable Result.** A coherent activity produces a clear identifiable result. That result may be an order, a product, a decision, an analysis, an idea, or other definable output. A poorly defined activity produces no identifiable result or a collection of unrelated results, such as management reports.
- **Clear Boundaries.** A well defined activity has a clearly defined starting and ending time. It happens at a clearly defined place. It is clear when one activity stops and the next one begins. Poorly defined activities overlap and blend into one another. It is unclear who is performing the activity or where. Strategic planning is supposed to be one of the responsibilities of top management. However, in some organizations it is not clear that anyone is developing a strategic plan. If there is a planning process, it may appear to have no beginning and no end.

- **Identifiable Workers.** A single person or identifiable group perform a coherent activity. If a group performs it, they communicate, cooperate, or interact to produce their result. A clearly identified person or persons manages the activity. By contrast a poorly defined activity is carried out by a poorly defined group or by a group who do not interact or work as a team. If all term papers in a university are graded for grammar by the English department, then it is clear what is being done and who is doing it. If all faculty are supposed to help students improve their English, it is not clear who, if anyone, is performing this activity.

- **Self Contained.** A coherent activity is performed independently of other activities. The interactions between members of a team are much stronger than their interactions with other people performing different activities. If an activity requires strong interaction with another activity, then the two alleged activities are likely only one single combined activity. In many organizations, vendor selection and ordering are really a single combined activity performed by the same group or person.

- **Single Step Automation.** If the activity is automated, it is done in one stage as a single procedure. If it must be implemented in phases, the analysis should be refined to identify the single phases.

These guidelines help to identify activities, but there is no perfect definition of an activity. The objective of the exercise is to produce a model of the activities that has four properties:

- **Completeness.** The model should cover all of the activities in all of the functional areas in the organization being studied. It is not necessary to study the entire company to do a useful study, but the part that is studied must be studied thoroughly. In many organizations it is necessary to divide this task and study a single division such as human resources or marketing. This misses some of the interactions with other divisions, but is still a great improvement over the existing situation. The objective is to identify all of the activities which are sufficient to execute the mission of the organization.

- **Necessity.** The model should identify only those activities that are necessary to perform the functions of the organization regardless of reorganization or automation in the future. An activity analysis often finds that some of the activities currently being performed are not really necessary. They may be procedures that were instituted in the past to deal with a transient problem. They may be procedures that are required only to provide coordination in a particular organizational structure. A useful by-product of this analysis is that it identifies activities that can be eliminated.

- **Understandability.** The model should help the people in the organization to understand the enterprise. The activities identified at each level should seem natural and correct to the people involved.

- **Permanence.** The model should be independent of changes in the organizational structure as long as the mission or purpose of the organization does not change. Organizations frequently change their Organization Chart and their reporting hierarchy. The basic functions of an organization change only when the mission of the organization changes. A company that sells industrial equipment must take orders, ship goods, and send bills. This happens regardless of whether they organize by product, region, or industry. They must add activities if they decide to go into design or manufacturing of their products. They change activities if they subcontract product-servicing. Activities are independent of whether data are on paper, files, or databases.

Other Activity Levels

Functions can be subdivided into subfunctions and these can be subdivided again until the functions are specific enough to describe individual blocks of computer code. The first level of a function is an aggregated view such as Materials Acquisition. The next might include a detailed function such as Requisitioning Materials and the last level might include entering a line in a requisition. These examples are arranged hierarchically. Requisitioning materials is part of the process of materials acquisition. Entering a single line of a requisition is part of the requisitioning process.

The analysis is never entirely completed. New activities are discovered during detailed systems analysis and some are discarded as they become obsolete.

If this approach of hierarchical breakdown is taken, the subfunctions identified have to duplicate many subfunctions also found in other functions. The materials acquisition system may contain an accounting system to pay for the materials. This system is similar to other accounting activities in the organization. Performing the analysis at the level of basic activities allows the analyst to identify such similar activities. Application systems can then be produced that perform the same activity consistently everywhere in the organization.

Identifying the functions required by each life cycle stage permits identification of functions that are repeated in more than one of the life cycles. However, this is not always true when resources are significantly different. In the university example, courses, students, staff, money, and things are acquired in different ways. These different acquisitions need different functions to support them.

The functions level provides more detail and helps to clarify the specific activities that are included in a development project. This is accomplished at the cost of an increase in the amount of analysis required. Figure 3-7 shows how the number of functions to be identified increases with each level of analysis.

During the architectural design stage, it is usually sufficient to identify the resources and the life cycle stages. This is usually enough to identify the activities that should be implemented together as a development project.

The cost of stopping the analysis early is that some opportunities to avoid duplication are missed. The benefit is that **Analysis Paralysis** is avoided. The next level of analysis could add a year to the architectural design phase of an information system design. On balance, it is usually wiser to stop at the life cycle stage of analysis.

The functions still must be identified during the detailed design stage. However, this is part of the implementation of a specific project rather than part of a planning exercise that is often seen by management as unproductive overhead.

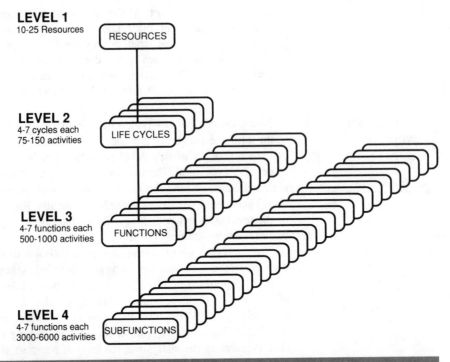

Figure 3-7
The number of functions to be identified grows exponentially with each level of analysis.

LEVEL 1
10-25 Resources
RESOURCES

LEVEL 2
4-7 cycles each
75-150 activities
LIFE CYCLES

LEVEL 3
4-7 functions each
500-1000 activities
FUNCTIONS

LEVEL 4
4-7 functions each
3000-6000 activities
SUBFUNCTIONS

Identifying Activities with the BICS Model

The functions that have to be performed to support the life cycle of a resource depend on a number of factors. It is difficult to determine whether all functions have been identified. The analyst needs a check-list that identifies generic functions that have to be performed during the life cycle of a resource.

The Business Information Control Study (BICS) Model by Kerner[5], described in Chapter 2, provides such a check-list. In Chapter 2 the model was used to describe six entities and eight relationships needed in a generic database. The model also identifies generic activities needed to maintain the information about the database and about transactions with the database. The model identifies 23 functions that must be performed to maintain data about the generic entities. It also identifies 35 functions that may have to be performed to record transactions. The approach has been validated in a number of studies.

The generic activities associated with each entity and relationship are:

EMPLOYEES
- Administer Salary
- Plan Personnel
- Account for Personnel
- Record Personnel

FACILITIES
- Plan Capital
- Specify Facilities
- Account for Facilities
- Maintain Facility

VENDORS
- Forecast Payables
- Plan Vendor Requirements
- Account for Vendors
- Manage Vendor

PRODUCTS
- Account for Product Revenue

MONEY
- Plan Funds Flow
- Plan Portfolio
- Control Cash
- Manage Portfolio

SUPPLY
- Manage Supplies
- Manage Supply Records

WORK_ON and PRODUCE
- Budgeting
- Plan Organization
- Account for Projects
- Control Organization

The next stage of the BICS Model focuses on the orders that an organization receives for each resource type. The method asks seven questions about these orders. The answers determine which of a set of 35 generic activities are required.

The orders can be for things, space, or skills. Equipment, buildings, reports, and land are things. Airline seats, rented apartments, and grave sites are spaces. Any kind of labor or service is a skill. Each of these categories may be repeated if orders for some members of the category are processed differently than others. The answers to the following questions identify the related contingent activities.

Does the supplier bill the customer? If the customer pays cash, check, credit card, or equivalent then there are no related activities. If the supplier has to send a bill later, then the supplier must:
- Approve Credit
- Account for Customer

Does the supplier deliver the service or product in the future? If the customer takes the product with him then there are no related activities. If the supplier delivers in the future, then the supplier must:
- Communicate with Customer
- Account for Orders
- Ship Product
- Backlog Orders
- Manage Orders

3
Activities

Does the supplier keep records about the prior transactions of individual customers for purposes other than billing? If every customer is a surprise then no related activities are performed. If a customer profile is kept, then the supplier must:

- Plan Accounts
- Analyze Sales
- Maintain Account History
- Record Customers
- Forecast Customers

Do the customer and supplier negotiate price? If price is negotiated, then the supplier must:

- Negotiate Contracts

If the price is fixed, then the supplier must:

- Forecast Production
- Forecast Price

Does the supplier rent the product to the customer and retain title? If the buyer takes title, then there are no related activities. If the customer rents, then the supplier must:

- Manage Rentals

Does the supplier track the product for subsequent recall or change? If the supplier does not track the product, then there are no related activities. If the supplier tracks the product then the supplier must:

- Engineer Field Changes
- Account for Field Service
- Manage Field Inventory

Does the supplier make to order? If the supplier makes the product to stock, then the supplier must:

- Plan Inventory
- Account for Inventory
- Record Inventory

If the supplier makes the product to the customer's specifications or assembles product on demand from existing specifications, then the supplier must:

- Engineer Manufacturing
- Plan Requirements
- Manage Production
- Plan Product
- Production Cost
- Plan Performance
- Estimate Product Cost
- Manage Engineering Bill of Materials
- Make Manufacturing Bill of Materials
- Manage Manufacturing Inventory
- Control Production
- Plan Production Cost Accounting
- Control Performance

Orders for things, space, and skill likely require different kinds of information and different definitions of functions. If some members of a product class are ordered differently from others, then all related functions must be implemented for both kinds of orders. Thus if some products are sold on credit and others are sold only for cash, the *account for customer* function is implemented to serve those sold on credit. Other functions may be the same for both product groups.

This method provides a check list to see if any functions have been forgotten. It is not mandatory that all indicated functions be included in the system design. It is expected that all indicated functions must be performed, but some, like forecasting, may be performed manually or intuitively. Others, like inventory management and inventory accounting may be combined into one function.

In the example, STUDENTS order COURSES is the major order to be analyzed. The courses are delivered in the future, the university maintains a student profile, and tracks the enrollments for issuing transcripts later. The university does not bill after delivery, does not negotiate prices, does not rent, and does not make courses to order.

The only aspect of future delivery that is important is the grades to be assigned and the grade report to be issued. These can be handled with existing functions. The profile data is contained in the attributes of the STUDENTS and ENROLL entity types. Products are not tracked to identify changes to the product so none of the field functions are required. The other services provided by the university are done as a public service and do not require the elaborate data systems required for a marketing and production oriented organization.

Relating Activities to Data

The activities performed by the organization and the entities about which the organization gathers data have now been identified. Next these are related to each other. The analyst needs data that specifies which entities are used by each activity. The data consists of a table with activities in the rows and entities in the columns. Each intersection of a row and a column indicates whether the activity in the row makes use of data about the entity in the corresponding column.

There are three kinds of data that could be gathered at that intersection: use, type of use, and volume of use. The simplest item to get is whether the activity uses the entity or not. This is a binary item that is coded with a 0 for no and a 1 for yes. This is called a binary Activity-Entity Incidence Matrix.

The cases where data are used can be refined into four types of use: Create, Read, Update, and Delete (CRUD). A matrix with C, R, U, or D at each intersection is called an Activity-Entity Usage Matrix.

The frequency of access for each entity could also be specified. This would give an indication of how strong or important the relationship between activities and entities is. This matrix is called the Activity-Entity Frequency Matrix.

The binary data are relatively easy to get. Once the table is created, managers or users can usually identify whether they need particular entities to perform the activity. It may be a bit tedious to fill in a large table but it is not particularly difficult. Figure 3-8 shows the data for the university example with an **X** when-

		Buildings	Rooms	Equipment	Scholarships	Students	Referees	Programs	Courses	Sections	Meetings	Skills	Tasks	Job-Descriptions	Faculty	Staff	Positions	Subordinates	Grants	Departments	Sessions	Months	Transactions	Account-Months	Accounts	Customers	Supplies	Vendors
COURSE	Schedule Courses	X	X	X				X	X	X	X				X													
	Administer Program							X	X																			
STUDENT	Analyse Demand				X	X		X	X	X					X													
	Enter Applications				X	X	X																					
	Aid Financially				X	X	X																					
	Register Students	X	X			X		X	X	X	X				X													
	Evaluate Students					X		X	X	X					X													
	Graduate Students					X		X	X	X																		
STAFF	Plan Manpower					X				X	X	X	X	X	X	X	X	X	X	X								
	Hire Staff													X	X	X		X										
	Evaluate Personnel											X	X	X	X	X	X	X	X	X								
	Administer Benefits														X	X		X							X			
	Promote Employees											X	X	X	X	X	X	X										
	Retire Staff	X	X												X	X	X	X		X	X	X	X	X	X			
MONEY	Budget Expenses					X					X				X		X	X						X	X		X	
	Receive Payments																		X	X	X	X	X	X	X	X		
	Apply for Grants														X		X	X										
	Administer Grants				X										X	X	X		X	X	X	X	X	X	X		X	X
	Invest Funds																				X	X	X	X	X			
	Pay Suppliers																		X	X	X	X	X	X	X			X
	Pay Employees														X	X	X		X	X	X	X	X	X	X			
THINGS	Budget Capital			X				X	X						X	X	X							X				
	Order Supplies																		X	X	X	X	X	X	X		X	X
	Receive Orders																			X							X	X
	Construct Facilities	X	X	X															X	X	X	X	X	X	X		X	
	Maintain Facilities	X	X	X															X	X	X	X	X	X	X		X	
	Manage Equipment	X	X	X																X								
	Manage Supplies																			X	X	X	X	X	X		X	
	Manage Space	X	X	X																X								
	Control Waste	X	X	X											X	X				X								X

Figure 3-8

Activity-Entity Matrix for the university example.

ever an activity uses an entity and a blank otherwise. This coding makes it easier to distinguish data uses just by looking at Figure 3-8. **X** is converted to 1 and blanks to 0 for analysis.

The Usage Matrix is slightly harder to generate because users have to think about whether an activity creates, reads, updates, or deletes a record. If it does more than one of these, then the highest one is recorded. Usually creation is considered to be the most important kind of use and deletion is considered to be the least important, with reading and updating being somewhere in between.

The Frequency Matrix is more difficult because it needs more data. The analyst needs to know how often the activity is performed, how many occurrences of the entity are expected to be on the file, and the probability that each occurrence is used in performing the activity.

Consider PROCESSING APPLICATIONS as the activity and STUDENTS as the entity. The student entity probably has to be accessed at different times to enter the original application, enter transcripts, enter admission test scores, record receipt of two reference letters, prepare a summary for an admissions committee, enter the decision of the committee, and send an acceptance/rejection letter. These eight accesses per student occur with certainty (a probability of 1.0). Assuming 7,500 applications, then the expected number of accesses per year for that activity-entity combination is 8x7,500x1=60,000.

Similar estimates are needed for each intersection that is used. A typical analysis may involve 50 entities and 200 activities for a total of 10,000 cells. About fifteen percent of the intersections may contain relationships that need frequency estimates for a total of 1,500 estimates. This is a significant amount of information to gather. The benefit of gathering it is that a better model of the relationships between the entities and activities can be produced. It is necessary to examine the way these data are used before deciding whether the benefits are worth the effort. For the university example, frequency data are used but the data are not illustrated.

The data can be checked to see if any of the activities have the same pattern of data use. The same pattern of use may indicate that the activities are identical or closely related. In the example, Construct Facilities and Maintain Facilities, Enter Applications and Aid Financially, and Manage Equipment and Manage Space are each pairs that have the same pattern of data use. These activities could be grouped together to simplify the analysis. They are kept separate because they do not have the same frequencies. This test is a good way of identifying similar work done in different departments.

Grouping Activities into Subsystems

The information needs of an organization change as the environment and the tasks performed by the organization change. This is one of the most difficult problems that a Systems Architect has to deal with. Somehow the architect must design a database structure and a set of computer applications that are relatively insensitive to these changes in the organization. The advent of databases that are distributed over several computers and integrated applications that share a single database makes it very costly to reorganize and move data. Many applications and people may be affected and communication costs may change in unpredictable ways.

The Systems Architect must decide how to group the components into manageable subsets, and decide who is responsible for the data in each subset. To accomplish this, the architect must start with an understanding of the changes that an organization might make and the impacts that these can have on the information system.

Organizational Theory

Galbraith[2] has developed a framework that links the structure of an organization to its information needs. The links can be best understood by considering the relationship between information processing needs and task uncertainty. Galbraith says, "The greater the task uncertainty, the greater the amount of information that must be processed amongst decision makers during task execution in order to achieve a given level of performance." Uncertainty is defined as "the difference between the amount of information required to perform the task and the amount of information already possessed by the organization."

There are three basic methods of coordination that can be used to facilitate this information processing: rules, hierarchical referral, and goal setting. Rules and procedures specify how to handle previously encountered situations. New situations are referred up the hierarchy until they reach a person who can perceive the interactions of all involved subunits. By setting goals for the subunits, the managers can force decisions to be made at lower levels. They thus reduce their own communication overload at the cost of some suboptimization.

As environmental uncertainty increases, the number of exceptions that must be referred up the hierarchy increases. So does the information overload in the communication channels. The channel overload can be reduced by increasing the information processing capability or by reducing the need for information processing. Information processing capability can be increased by developing vertical information processing systems or by creating lateral relationships. Information processing needs can be reduced by designing self-contained tasks or by introducing slack resources.

A vertical system links hierarchical levels of the organization. It increases the processing capacity by supporting frequent planning, increasing the capacity of the decision mechanism, increasing the scope of the database, or increasing the formalization of the system. Decision support systems, corporate databases, and group decision making are the main tools for accomplishing these objectives.

Lateral relationships can be created by using committees or matrix organizations and by providing integrated databases. These relationships permit various specialists to share information and decision-making authority in complex problems at the cost of increased organizational complexity.

Designing self-contained tasks requires that the analyst understand the boundaries of a task. Then related activities can be grouped into a single task that involves as few other people as possible.

Ideally, the group performing the task should be as small as possible, should be as low in the organizational hierarchy as possible, and should have all of the resources and data necessary to perform the task. A larger group requires more coordination. Putting the group higher in the organization increases the length of the communication channels to the support staff and overloads the channels. Having insufficient resources reduces the effectiveness of the decisions. Having insufficient data leads to suboptimization.

Designing a self-contained task in information processing terms means identifying activities and data items that belong together in a self-contained system.

The strategy of providing slack resources as a buffer to handle overloads may be cost effective in certain circumstances. Nevertheless, it tends to be impractical in organizations where minimizing cost is crucial to survival.

Galbraith hypothesized that these four strategies—vertical systems, lateral relationships, self-contained tasks, and slack resources—are all-inclusive. Every organization chooses some combination of them that minimizes costs in their environment. As the environment changes, the combination may have to change.

All strategies, except the slack resource strategy, are facilitated by an integrated database and an understanding of how activities should be grouped together. The slack resource strategy can be implemented by duplicating databases. The vertical processing and lateral relationship strategies essentially try to provide a technical fix. They increase the ability to manage complexity while preserving the basic structure of the organization. An integrated database and Decision Support Systems are technical changes that do this. Modifications to the organization to simplify it or to let people in different hierarchies communicate with each other are organizational methods to accomplish this. Designing a self-contained task requires a redefinition of the organizational structure.

The Information Architect must create a design flexible enough to cope with any of these strategies. It is not possible to redesign the system every time the environment changes. It is better to design it to respond easily to change. This is done by designing subsystems with components that are frequently used together and that have a minimal requirement for communication with other systems.

Activities are grouped into cohesive clusters. This reduces the complex—and possibly unsolvable—problem of designing a system for a large organization into a series of smaller problems. Each of these can then be solved in a reasonable time frame. Clusters of activities must be defined that can be grouped into subsystems to implement. If the database is in a distributed environment, then clusters of data must be defined that are stored at each node. This does not mean that these clusters are to be isolated and any communication between subsystems is to be prevented. It only means that boundaries are desired that minimize the number of communication links that must cross the boundaries between clusters.

3 Activities

What is needed is an objective criterion for determining which activities belong together. Galbraith's theory can be used to argue that organizations should organize themselves into groups that maximize communications within a group and minimize the need for communications between groups. Communications are implied whenever two or more knowledge workers have a mutual interest in a subject.

The Activity-Entity Matrix provides a proxy for the communication paths in the organization. Often there are two or more activities that need access to data about the same entity. The people who perform these activities have to communicate occasionally about some mutual concern about that entity. Even people who are just users of the data may want changes in the nature of the data to make it more useful. In the university example, the people who perform course scheduling, registration, and manpower planning are each interested in courses. They have to coordinate periodically to make sure that courses are scheduled, that students want to take them, and that faculty are available to teach them.

The amount of communication is roughly proportional to the number of times that both parties use the data. Some proportion of those communications involve conflicting interests. A few of these may escalate into conflicts that require a higher authority to resolve.

The cost of conflict is reduced if the individuals with conflicting interests work within the same administrative unit. Their immediate and shared superior can resolve disputes relatively easily. The superior understands the implications for the whole unit and can change policies for the unit. If they work in different organizational units, a more complex resolution process is often required. Two different unit interests are at stake and two unit policies may have to change.

If patterns of data use are a proxy for communications, then activities using the same data should be grouped into the same system. The system should be controlled by a single administrative unit responsible for both the data and the activities that use it. Inevitably, other administrative units also use some of the data. An organizational structure is needed that minimizes the amount of data they must share. This minimizes the number of situations leading conflict with other departments. This in turn minimizes the nededed amount of administration. This is consistent with Galbraith's idea of developing self-contained tasks.

Major system developments are often accompanied by changes in job definition and organizational structure. The Galbraith theory identifies desirable changes. Even if no changes are presently contemplated, the theory suggests that such changes occur eventually. The analyst can prepare for them by designing the system so groups of tasks use the same data and are as self-contained as possible. These groups become separate implementation projects of a manageable size containing related activities. Designing a system for a complete organization is an unmanageable project. This approach also minimizes the difficulties encountered in building interfaces between subsystems.

There is seldom a perfect matching of data used by pairs of activities. The best that can be hoped for is to identify those activities that have "similar" data requirements. Clustering is used to organize activities into subsystems of similar activities. This means that a measure of similarity for activities is needed.

There are many different methods of measuring the similarity of activities. Each method produces a square matrix in which each cell gives the similarity between the activity on the row and the activity on the column analogous to a statistical Correlation Matrix. Similarity values always range between zero and one. Ones on the diagonal mean that something is always perfectly similar to itself. Zeros mean that the two activities have nothing in common.

Appendix 3-A provides one way of calculating a Similarity Matrix. Martin[6] has another method to calcualate an Affinity Matrix. It is harder to calculate and affinities are not symmetric. It is not clear what it means when A has a high affinity with B, but B does not have a high affinity with A.

A random list of activities is not very useful to the analyst. It is desirable to order the activities in such a way that activities which are most similar to each other are adjacent to each other. They are thus most likely to be included in the same subsystem. This is a clustering problem. The Similarity Matrix is used to cluster the activities into groups that have a need for similar data.

There are many different ways of clustering things when you have a Similarity Matrix for them. Hierarchical clustering is used here because it is much easier to change the number of clusters for alternate analyses. Hierarchical clustering begins with N groups of 1 each. The two most similar groups are combined. Then the next most similar, and so on until all items are grouped into a single cluster. If you want M clusters, you can stop M-1 steps before the end of the process. Appendix 3-B describes a clustering algorithm.

Clustering accomplishes two things. It reorders the activities so that similar activities are beside each other. It also determines break points between groups of relatively dissimilar activities. The recursive clustering process can be stopped when there are M unmerged clusters. This leaves M groups that each contain activities that are very similar to each other. These M groups are as dissimilar from each other as possible. The boundaries between the groups are break points used to separate activities into separate subsystems for implementation.

If M=2 in the example, then the process is stopped when there are two clusters with activities a, b, and c in one of them and activity d in the other.

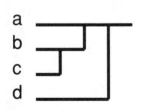

The result of the clustering process is summarized in a graph, called a dendrogram, which shows when each group joined the hierarchy. It looks like a tree in which branches successively join to form a single trunk. The graph in the margin is the dendrogram that results from the simple four activity example. The dendrogram shows when the clusters joined together. This shows the user how near activities are to each other and when they clustered. The dendrogram can be used to identify different numbers of clusters without needing to repeat the clustering calculations.

The length of the horizontal line indicates the stage at which the group formed. The shortest horizontal lines merged first. The vertical line connects the upper row of the bottom group to the upper row of the top group in each merger. Since the clustering process is hierarchical, there are N-1 vertical lines joining the N rows until they become one group like the trunk of a tree.

In the figure, the shortest horizontal line belongs to activity **c** which merged with **b** above it according to the leftmost vertical line. The next shortest horizontal line belongs to **b** (and the other activity **c** in its cluster). Activity **b** then merged with activity **a**. Finally, activity **d** merged with the cluster headed by **a** as shown by the right-most vertical line.

Figure 3-9 shows the dendrogram resulting from clustering the activities in the Activity-Entity Incidence Matrix for the university example.

Figure 3-9

Dendrogram for the university example. The dashed lines show the dividing lines between the five most independent clusters. The five clusters are obtained by cutting the last four vertical lines on the right when they start to go up.

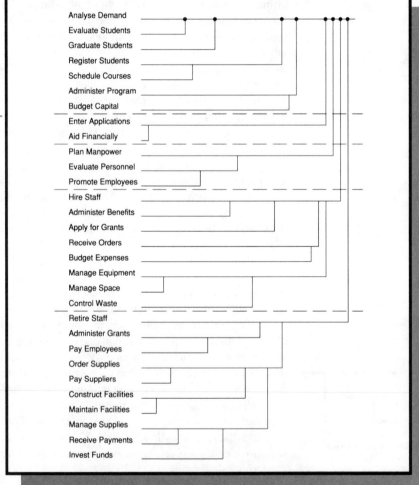

In the example, *Aid Financially* and *Enter Applications* were the first ones to merge because the vertical line joining them is the leftmost one. The next merger was between *Maintain Facilities* and *Construct Facilities*. The third merger was between *Manage Equipment* and *Manage Space*. These are the three pairs of identical activities that were identified in the Activity-Entity Matrix. Mergers continued until the last merger which joined *Retire Staff* and all of the activities below it to the cluster of all activities above *Retire Staff*. Horizontal dashed lines are drawn to separate the last M=5 clusters formed. The number five was chosen somewhat arbitrarily for comparison with the original five resources and the original five entity clusters in the analysis.

A good rule of thumb is to choose a final number of clusters equal to the square root of the number of activities being analyzed. This rule corresponds quite well with the number of clusters chosen intuitively by experienced analysts. It represents a reasonable compromise between having many small clusters with many interactions between them and having a few large clusters that are hard to implement.

There is a need for a measure of how good the clustering result is. Ideally, the clustering method should produce M clusters of roughly equal size. The worst case is when there are M-1 clusters of one each, with the rest of the activities in the remaining cluster. This does not help very much in reducing the problem to manageable pieces. Murtagh's[7] longest path is used to calculate a measure of the clustering efficiency. This measure is simple to calculate and produces a result similar to other measures that he identifies.

The measure uses LPATH, the longest path through the hierarchical tree that the clustering process generates. In the university example, LPATH=8, shown by dots on the dendrogram. The longest path successively joins Analyze Demand to Evaluate Students then to Graduate Students, then successively to Register Students, Administer Program, Enter Applications, Plan Manpower, Hire Staff, and Retire Staff. They are not always in a line. The maximum possible path length for an N item clustering is N-1. This occurs when the items are successively attached to one element in a chained fashion. The most balanced hierarchy has a path length that is the least integer greater than $\log_2 N$,—the base 2 logarithm of N—denoted by $[\log_2 N]$. $[\log_2 N]$ is the power of 2 that is just bigger than N. Thus $[\log_2 7]$ is 3 because $2^3 = 8$ is bigger than 7. Alternately, calculate $[\log_2 N] = [\log_{10} N]/[\log_{10} 2]$. Murtagh's structure coefficient is then defined as:

$$K = (LPATH-[\log_2 N])/(N-1-[\log_2 N])$$

K can take values between 0 and 1. The most symmetric case has a value of 0 and the most asymmetric case has a value of 1. The example in Figure 3-9 has a value of 0.125 which is reasonably good.

Dendrograms tell what happens if the clustering process stops at any stage. To see the last M clusters to join, just cover up the last M-1 vertical lines on the right. This leaves M separate clusters unjoined. The dashed lines in Figure 3-9 show where the breaks would be if the last four vertical lines were eliminated.

Activity	Buildings	Rooms	Equipment	Scholarships	Students	Referees	Programs	Courses	Sections	Meetings	Skills	Tasks	Job-Descriptions	Faculty	Staff	Positions	Subordinates	Grants	Departments	Sessions	Months	Transactions	Account-Months	Accounts	Customers	Supplies	Vendors
Analyse Demand				X	X		X	X	X					X													
Evaluate Students					X		X	X	X					X													
Graduate Students					X		X	X	X																		
Register Students	X	X			X		X	X	X	X				X													
Schedule Courses	X	X	X		X		X	X	X	X				X													
Administer Program							X	X																			
Budget Capital			X				X	X						X	X				X					X			
Enter Applications				X	X	X																					
Aid Financially				X	X	X																					
Plan Manpower					X		X	X			X	X	X	X	X	X	X	X	X	X							
Evaluate Personnel											X	X	X	X	X	X	X	X	X	X	X						
Promote Employees											X	X	X	X	X	X	X										
Hire Staff														X	X	X			X								
Administer Benefits														X	X				X					X			
Apply for Grants														X				X	X								
Receive Orders																			X							X	X
Budget Expenses				X				X							X	X	X				X	X	X				
Manage Equipment	X	X	X																X								
Manage Space	X	X	X																X								
Control Waste	X	X	X											X	X				X							X	
Retire Staff	X	X												X	X	X	X	X	X	X	X	X	X				
Administer Grants			X											X	X	X		X	X	X	X	X	X	X		X	X
Pay Employees														X	X	X		X	X	X	X	X	X	X			
Order Supplies																		X	X	X	X	X	X	X		X	X
Pay Suppliers																		X	X	X	X	X	X	X			X
Construct Facilities	X	X	X															X	X	X	X	X	X	X		X	
Maintain Facilities	X	X	X															X	X	X	X	X	X	X		X	
Manage Supplies																			X	X	X	X	X	X		X	
Receive Payments																			X	X	X	X	X	X	X	X	
Invest Funds																			X	X	X	X	X				

Figure 3-10

Activity-Entity Incidence Matrix with the rows rearranged by clustering on binary data.

3 Activities

Subsystem	Activity	Buildings	Rooms	Equipment	Scholarships	Students	Referees	Programs	Courses	Sections	Meetings	Skills	Tasks	Job-Descriptions	Faculty	Staff	Positions	Subordinates	Grants	Departments	Sessions	Months	Transactions	Account-Months	Accounts	Customers	Supplies	Vendors
Planning	Analyse Demand				X	X		X	X	X					X													
	Budget Expenses					X		X								X			X	X				X	X		X	
	Enter Applications				X	X	X																					
	Aid Financially				X	X	X																					
Student	Register Students	X	X			X		X	X	X	X				X													
	Evaluate Students					X		X	X	X					X													
	Graduate Students					X		X	X	X																		
	Schedule Courses	X	X	X				X	X	X	X				X													
	Administer Program							X	X																			
Staff	Plan Manpower					X			X	X	X	X	X	X	X	X	X	X	X	X								
	Evaluate Personnel										X	X	X	X	X	X	X	X	X	X								
	Promote Employees										X	X	X	X	X	X	X	X										
Admin	Hire Staff														X	X	X			X								
	Apply for Grants														X				X	X								
	Manage Equipment	X	X	X																X								
	Manage Space	X	X	X																X								
	Control Waste	X	X	X											X	X				X							X	
	Administer Benefits														X	X				X					X			
	Retire Staff	X	X												X	X	X	X	X	X	X	X	X	X				
	Pay Suppliers																		X	X	X	X	X	X	X			X
	Budget Capital				X			X	X						X	X				X					X			
	Receive Orders																			X							X	X
Accounts	Order Supplies																		X	X	X	X	X	X	X		X	X
	Receive Payments																		X	X	X	X	X	X	X	X		
	Pay Employees													X	X	X			X	X	X	X	X	X	X			
	Construct Facilities	X	X	X															X	X	X	X	X	X	X		X	
	Invest Funds																				X	X	X	X	X			
	Maintain Facilities	X	X	X															X	X	X	X	X	X	X		X	
	Manage Supplies																		X	X	X	X	X	X	X		X	
	Administer Grants				X										X	X	X		X	X	X	X	X	X	X		X	X

Figure 3-11

Activity-Entity Incidence Matrix with the rows rearranged by clustering on frequency data.

The rows of the Activity-Entity Incidence Matrix can be rearranged to see how the activities have been regrouped. Figure 3-10 shows the result of rearranging rows in the same order as the activities in the dendrogram. Note how the X's in the figure are arranged into groups or blocks. This is a graphic demonstration of how the pattern of data use identifies similar activities. A horizontal line is drawn to separate the five clusters identified in the analysis.

The clustering process groups most of the activities that we would expect to see together. The first seven activities were grouped together because they all use data about Programs and Courses. *Enter Applications* and *Aid Financially* stayed together because they both use data about Scholarships, Students, and Referees. *Plan Manpower*, *Evaluate Personnel*, and *Promote Employees* stayed together because of their common use of seven different personnel-related entities. The next eight activities only have Departments data in common. The last ten activities share data about five different accounting entities.

Figure 3-11 illustrates the rearrangement that results when similarities are based on frequency data. The groups are named to help in identifying them when they are used to set development priorities. In this particular case the differences between using incidence and frequency data are not very large. Sometimes the differences may be much larger.

This method identifies subsystems of activities that are candidates for implementation. The ideal number of subsystems depends on a number of factors. These include the degree of mutual similarity within the subsystems, the size of development project that available staff can implement, and the structure of the organization. It is sometimes desirable to make manual rearrangements of the clusters to reflect particular needs. However, this is not done here. The clusters based on frequency data are used for setting priorities in the next chapter.

Other Association Matrices

The Activity-Entity Matrix is only one of a number of tables that can be useful for cross-referencing information. It is often necessary to gather data about one or more of the following things while developing an Enterprise Model.

- **Organization.** It is often useful to know which existing division, department, or group is responsible for each activity.
- **Projects.** Projects implement systems to support a number of activities. It is helpful to record which projects support each activity.
- **Objectives.** The enterprise has a number of goals or objectives which it wants to achieve. When justifying projects, it may be useful to identify which activities or which projects support each of the objectives. This can help in setting priorities for project implementation.
- **Systems.** When determining the order in which the new system are to be developed, it is useful to know which existing systems perform each activity and provide data about each entity. It may also be desirable to record which part of the organization is responsible for each system.

The information recorded in the cells of each matrix will depend on the purpose of the matrix. All of these matrices may not be needed in a particular Enterprise Model. However, a number of them can be useful in organizing supporting information.

Extension to Organizational Design

The results of this method are also useful as an organizational design tool. The subsystems identified by the clustering method are candidate departments that form self-contained work groups in the Galbraith sense. These candidate groups may have to be modified to reflect other factors such as geography or politics. For instance, a professional group like accountants may not want to be dispersed into the various user groups that they serve.

Note that this method of grouping brings activities together along functional and resource lines. It is not likely to group activities in a manner that corresponds to regional, product, or customer lines. This is because regions are all likely to have parallel requirements and products or customers are all likely to be the same.

This approach to division of organizational activities suggests that it would be wise to have the systems design group work closely with the organizational development staff in the organization. The two groups have complementary interests. The systems people are usually more interested in technology. The organizational development people are usually more interested in organizations and people. They typically come from a psychology or sociology background and are often not particularly interested in technology. They have different backgrounds, personalities, and paradigms for development. It may be difficult for them to work together with the technology-oriented analysts.

However, the need to adopt computer technology drives a large proportion of current organizational changes. The changes are implemented by analysts and designers who frequently do not understand the organizational implications of the new systems that they are proposing and implementing. They need to work together with specialists who know how to implement organizational change smoothly with minimal organizational friction. Since the skills of the two groups are so complementary, they need to learn to work together.

Organizations have a strong incentive to bring these two groups together. A large proportion of changes in organizational structure are the direct or indirect result of changes in information technology. The development of a new information system is usually accompanied by significant changes in the way users perform their jobs. This frequently leads to accompanying changes in organizational structure. The transition is a lot smoother if the information systems group works with the organizational development group.

3
Activities

Testing the Activity Model

Several diagnostics can be used to give a clue about whether activities have been identified correctly.

CLUE #1: Activity name is the name of a department in the organization.

CAUSE: Activities were identified directly from an Organization Chart. Names such as *Administrative Services* do not convey the activity that is being performed. They may also cover a number of unrelated activities.

CURE: Reconsider the analysis to see if the activity needs to be broken into more specific activities such as *Manage Personnel* and *Manage Facilities*.

CLUE #2: Activity names are not in the form of a verb followed by an object.

CAUSE: The analyst used incorrect notation. The name does not state the function done.

CURE: Rename the activity. A name like *Work* in Figure 3-12 does not indicate whether the activity is to obtain work, schedule work, start work, finish work, or check work. Change it to *Schedule Work* to reflect its true function in this example.

CLUE #3: The Activity-Entity Matrix has columns with no entries.

CAUSE: None of the activities use the entity in the column. Either an activity is missing or the entity is useless.

CURE: Identify the activity or activities that create and use the entity. If none can be identified, then remove the entity. In Figure 3-12 the *Employees* entity is not used by any of the activities. It is deleted to correct the model.

CLUE #4: The Activity-Entity Matrix has rows with no entries.

CAUSE: The activity does not create or use any data. Either the entity that it creates and uses is missing or the activity is not an information processing activity.

CURE: Identify the entity or entities that the activity uses and add them to the matrix. If none can be identified, then delete the activity from the matrix. In Figure 3-12, the *Forecast Sales* activity does not use any entities. In this case, it is not part of the activities of the subsystem being analyzed. It is removed or moved to another Activity-Entity Matrix that deals with the subsystem that does the forecasting.

CLUE #5: Two or more activities in the Activity-Entity Matrix use all of the same entities.

CAUSE: The activities perform the same function. They have probably been identified in different parts of the organization. One department may call a function Purchasing while another may call it Materials Acquisition. Yet both are doing the same thing.

CURE: Combine the activities to form a single activity. In Figure 3-12 the activities *Control Inventory* and *Secure Materials* use the same three entities. Further investigation reveals that the two activities are synonyms for the same activity, so *Secure Materials* is removed from the diagram.

CLUE #6: **Some clusters of activities are much larger than the rest.**
CAUSE: This indicates that some parts of the organization have been decomposed into more detail than others. The decomposed activities still cluster together because they still share a need for the same data.
CURE: Aggregate some of the decomposed activities or decompose some of the other activities to achieve a better balance in the size of the clusters.

Figure 3-12

Example of errors in an Activity-Entity Matrix.

	Vendors	Raw_Materials	Finished_Goods	Equipment	Work_in_Process	Schedule	Requirements	Routing	**Employees**
Purchase Materials	X								
Receive Goods	X	X							
Control Inventory		X	X		X				
Secure Materials	**X**	**X**		**X**					
Layout Workflow				X					
Work	X		X	X	X				
Plan Capacity	X		X			X	X	X	
Plan Materials	X						X		
Forecast Sales									
Operate Plant					X	X	X	X	

	Vendors	Raw_Materials	Finished_Goods	Equipment	Work_in_Process	Schedule	Requirements	Routing
Purchase Materials	X							
Receive Goods	X	X						
Control Inventory		X	X		X			
Layout Workflow				X				
Schedule Work	X		X	X	X			
Plan Capacity	X		X			X	X	X
Plan Materials	X						X	
Operate Plant					X	X	X	X

CASE Tools

There are a number of CASE tools that help the analyst to produce an Activity Model and an Activity-Entity Matrix. IEW (Information Engineering Workbench) from KnowledgeWare, Inc., has a planning module that generates hierarchical Decomposition Diagrams, Entity-Relationship Diagrams, and Activity-Entity Matrices. It can do activity clustering using a technique called affinity analysis. Many other matrices can also be recorded and used in later stages of the design. Many diagnostics are provided to prevent the entry of illogical data.

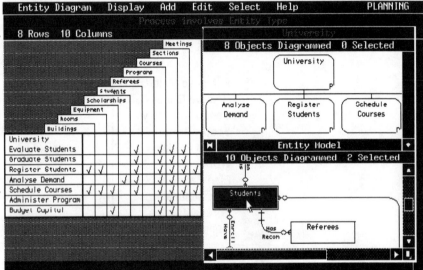

Figure 3-13

A screen from the planning module of IEW. A Decomposition Diagram is shown in the upper right window. An Entity-Relationship Model is shown in the lower right window. Any change to either will be immediately reflected in the Activity-Entity Diagram in the left window.

Index Technology Corp. has a planning product called PC Prism that produces Activity-Entity Matrices and other tables. The entries in the tables can be organized into hierarchies. It has no way of clustering activities. However, the rows of a matrix can be sorted and reported in various ways. The activities and entities can be transferred to Excelerator to serve as the beginning of a detailed design.

Summary

A model of an information system consists of a model of the data used by the organization and a model of the activities which create, read, update, or delete those data. The ideal model is insensitive to changes in organizational structure.

Activity analysis is a top down process that identifies aggregate activities that manage resources, breaks them down into life cycle stages, and breaks these into functions that must be performed at each stage. Typical resources are money, materials, equipment, personnel, suppliers, customers, intangibles, and information. The basic life cycle stages are planning, acquisition, stewardship, and disposal. Functions have identifiable results, identifiable workers, and clear boundaries. They are self-contained, they process information, and they can be automated in a single step.

The Business Information Control Study (BICS) Model provides a check-list of activities that an organization must perform depending on the answers to seven questions about transactions. The questions are:

- Does the supplier **bill** the customer?
- Does the supplier deliver the service or product in the **future**?
- Does the supplier **keep records** about the prior transactions of individual customers for purposes other than billing?
- Do the customer and supplier **negotiate price**?
- Does the supplier **rent** the product to the customer and retain title?
- Does the supplier **track** the product for subsequent recall or change?
- Does the supplier **make to order**?

Activities can be related to data entities by using an Activity-Entity Matrix. Each intersection of a row and a column indicates whether the activity in the row makes use of data about the entity in the corresponding column. This matrix can be used to cluster activities into groups that have similar patterns of data use. The results are used for identifying software systems and potentially for organizational design. The clustering method consists of the following steps:

- **Create an Activity-Entity Matrix** with a 1 wherever an activity creates or uses data from a corresponding entity and a 0 when it does not. This matrix could alternately contain the frequency with which each activity uses each entity in some base period.
- **Calculate similarities** by the matching method for binary data or the fuzzy set method for frequencies.
- **Cluster the activities** using farthest neighbor hierarchical clustering.
- **Divide the clustered activities into n groups** where n is about the square root of the number of activities. The next chapter sets priorities on which of these clusters is to be implemented first as a new computer system.
- **Check the clusters for balance** using the structure coefficient $K = (LPATH-[\log_2 N])/(N-1-[\log_2 N])$ where LPATH is the longest path through the hierarchical tree that the clustering process generates. N is the number of activities being clustered. $[\log_2 N]$ is the power of 2 that includes N.

Keywords and Phrases

Activities	Hierarchy
Activity-Entity Matrix	Life Cycle Stages
BICS	MIS
Clustering	Operational Level
DBMS	Organization Chart
DSS	Resources
Dendrogram	Similarity
ESS	Strategic Level
Functions	Tactical Level

3
Activities

Appendix 3-A: Measuring Similarity

There are different methods of measuring similarity for binary incidence data and for frequency data.

Binary Data Similarity

For binary data like the activity-entity incidence matrix, similarities can be measured by considering whether corresponding zeros and ones for two activities match. Consider a small matrix with four rows of ones and zeros labelled a, b, c, and d:

```
(a)  1  0  1  0
(b)  1  0  1  0
(c)  0  1  0  1
(d)  1  0  0  1
```

Row (a) is a perfect match for (b), but it does not match (c) at all and only partly matches (d). The similarity between (a) and (b) is 1.0 because they have the same pattern of zeros and ones. The similarity between (a) or (b) and (c) is 0.0 because they have exactly the opposite pattern of zeros and ones. The similarity between (a) and (d) is somewhere in between. The numeric value of the similarity between (a) and (d) depends on how one chooses to handle the mismatches where a 1 in (a) corresponds to a 0 in (d) or vice versa. To calculate a numeric value for similarity, the following definitions are needed:

- A is a match of two ones.
- B is a match between a one and a zero.
- C is a match between a zero and a one.
- D is a match between two zeros.

So the matches in rows (c) and (d) of the example are in order, C, B, D, and A. It is possible to compute a similarity, $S = \Sigma A/(\Sigma A + \Sigma B + \Sigma C)$ where ΣA is the total number of A type matches, etc. S for rows (c) and (d) is $1/(1+1+1)=1/3$. S for rows (a) and (b) is $2/(2+0+0)=1$.

This method of computing a similarity does not include matching zeros (D) in the numerator or the denominator. It assumes that not having things in common should not even be considered as part of the list of possibilities. This is because there are an infinite number of characteristics which two things do not share. Enumerating all of these unrelated things should not influence the measure of what they have in common. The similarity is the proportion of matches out of the cases where at least one of the activities uses the entity.

Now a matrix of similarities, like a correlation matrix, can be calculated for all possible pairs of activities. The similarity matrix for rows a, b, c, and d is:

```
        a    b    c    d
(a)     1    1    0   .3
(b)     1    1    0   .3
(c)     0    0    1   .3
(d)    .3   .3   .3    1
```

Note that the similarity on the diagonal from upper left to lower right is always 1 because any row is perfectly similar to itself. The matrix is also symmetric about the diagonal because the definition does not depend on which row is considered to be the top row in a pair of rows. Activity a has the same similarity to b as b has to a.

Frequency Data Similarity

Frequency data gives more information about the pattern of use of data. The frequency data can always be reduced to incidence data by replacing each non-zero frequency with a one. The more complicated frequency data requires a complicated formula for computing similarity. Buckles and Hardin (quoted by Palmer[8]) provide a formula based on a mathematical discipline called fuzzy set theory. The formula for the similarity S_{ij} between activities i and j is:

$$S_{ij} = \frac{\sum_{k \in K} [MIN(A_{ik}, A_{jk})]}{\sum_{k \in K} [A_{ik} + A_{jk}]/2}$$

where k is an index that ranges over the set of all entities K and A_{ik} is the total number of accesses of activity i to entity k. $MIN(A_{ik}, A_{jk})$ is the minimum of the two values in the parentheses.

This formula relates the commonality of usage of entities by determining the set intersection between pairs of entities. If an activity accesses an entity m times and another accesses the same entity n times where m<n, then it is assumed that both access the entity concurrently m times. The remaining n-m accesses are independent or concurrent with another activity. This seems to be a valid approximation to the real situation. Activities should tend to access one main entity, then others as required by the data. The denominator normalizes the similarity by the average number of accesses to the entity by the two activities.

This similarity measure on frequency data provides a better result than the matching method on binary data. It clusters activities and entities with high common usage and will give little weight to activities which seldom access data. The emphasis is on finding the pairs with the most frequent common usage.

The calculations will be illustrated with another four row matrix which has three entity columns as shown below.

```
        x    y    z
(a)    10   20   30
(b)    30   20   10
(c)     5   10   15
(d)     0   10    0
```

This matrix means that application (c) uses entity x about 5 times per hour, etc. S_{bc} = [MIN(30, 5)+MIN(20, 10)+MIN(10, 15)]/ [(30+5)/2+(20+10)/2+ (10+15)/2] = (5+10+10)/(17.5+15+12.5) = 25/45 = 0.56. The complete similarity matrix is shown below.

```
        a     b     c     d
(a)     1   .33   .33   .29
(b)   .33     1   .56   .29
(c)   .33   .56     1   .33
(d)   .29   .29   .33     1
```

Again, the similarity matrix is square, has ones on the diagonal, and it is symmetric about the diagonal. Note that the original frequency matrix is not necessarily square.

Appendix 3-B: Clustering Activities

Jackson[4] provides a good introduction to the concepts of clustering and Anderberg[1] provides detailed methods.

There are many different ways of clustering things when you have a Similarity Matrix for them. Hierarchical clustering is used because it is much easier to change the number of clusters for alternate analyses. Hierarchical clustering begins with N groups of 1 each. The two most similar groups are combined. Then the next most similar, and so on until all items are grouped into a single cluster. If you want M clusters, you can stop M-1 steps before the end of the process. There are different methods of determining how similar two groups are if each has more than one member. The farthest neighbor method is used here.

The farthest neighbor method is also called the complete linkage method[1]. It pools groups using the lowest similarity between any pairs constructed with one element selected from each group. It merges the two groups with the highest of these low pair-wise similarities. This produces more homogeneous groups with roughly equal sizes. This is usually the aim in forming manageable groups. The algorithm is iterative and consists of the following steps:

1. **Compute the Similarity Matrix,** S, defined in the previous subsection. It can be based on incidence, frequency, or some other measure.
2. **Find the highest similarity** in the matrix and merge the two activities with this similarity. If more than one pair has the same similarity, arbitrarily choose one of the pairs, such as the first.
3. **Recalculate the similarity** between each of the remaining activities and this new merged cluster. This updates the row and column of the matrix that corresponds to the new cluster (and to the two rows and columns that were merged to form the cluster). After each merger, the matrix gets smaller by one row and one column.
4. **Return to step 2** and repeat until all activities are merged into one cluster.

The only part that is difficult to understand is how to compute the new similarity between two clusters each containing several activities. Mathematically, consider the general case where clusters p and q of activities have been merged to form a new cluster t. The similarity between t and some other cluster r is determined by:

$$S_{tr} = MIN(S_{pr}, S_{qr})$$

where S_{tr} is the similarity between the two most dissimilar activities in the combined clusters t and r. MIN is an operator that chooses the smallest value from the list that follows it. This equation means that all possible pairs of activities do not have to be considered each time clusters are merged. Only the lowest similarity for each merged cluster is stored. As the number of remaining clusters is reduced, the task keeps getting easier. The algorithm is illustrated with the Similarity Matrix based on frequencies used in the example in Chapter 3.

Step 1 is to calculate the Similarity Matrix as shown below. The four rows and columns correspond to four clusters of activities each containing a single activity: a, b, c, or d.

```
        a     b     c     d
(a)     1    .33   .33   .29
(b)    .33    1    .56   .29
(c)    .33   .56    1    .33
(d)    .29   .29   .33    1
```

Step 2 is to select the pair of rows with the highest similarity not including the ones on the diagonal. The highest off-diagonal value is .56, the similarity between activities b and c. These are merged into a new cluster called b'.

Step 3 is to compute the similarity between b' and the remaining clusters a and d. The similarity between b' and d is:

$S_{b'd} = MIN(S_{bd}, S_{cd}) = MIN(.29, .33) = .29$

Similarly, $S_{b'a} = .33$. All other similarities remain as they were. The revised Similarity Matrix then becomes:

```
        a     b'    d
(a)     1    .33   .29
(b')   .33    1    .29
(d)    .29   .29    1
```

Step 4 is to repeat steps 2 and 3 with the reduced matrix. Now the highest similarity is .33 between a and b' so these two clusters are combined to form a new cluster a'. The new Similarity Matrix is:

```
        a'    d
(a')    1    .29
(d)    .29    1
```

The matrix represents two clusters. Cluster a' contains activities a, b, and c. Cluster d contains activity d. The last iteration combines these two clusters into a single cluster that contains all of the activities.

Review Questions

1. Define each of the items in the list of keywords and phrases.
2. Compare the characteristics of the information needed at different levels of the organizational pyramid.
3. Identify the three levels of activities in an information systems architecture. Illustrate them with an example from an organization of your own choosing.
4. Identify the eight kinds of generic resources that an organization typically needs to manage. Illustrate them with an example from an organization of your own choosing.
5. Identify the generic life cycle stages that a resource goes through. Illustrate them with an example for a single resource from an organization of your own choosing. Indicate which stages, if any, need to be subdivided into more than one stage.
6. List the characteristics of a good activity at the life cycle stages level.
7. What is the main difference between activities at the life cycle stages level and activities at the functions level?
8. Identify the six characteristics of a good function definition.
9. List the seven questions used to identify the generic activities that are needed to support an order in the Business Information Control Study (BICS) Model.
10. What are the advantages and disadvantages of using incidence versus frequency data in an Activity-Entity Matrix?
11. Identify the four generic strategies that Galbraith suggests for reducing communication overload in organizations. Which of the strategies does an information architecture address?
12. List the six clues that indicate problems with an Activity Model.

Problems

1. For the following Activity-Entity Incidence Matrix:

	Budget	Financial	Product	Parts	Materials
Plan Business	1	1	1	0	0
Design Product	0	0	1	1	1
Acquire Capital	0	1	0	0	0
Analyse Org'n	1	0	0	0	0
Forecast Market	1	0	1	0	0
Review Results	1	1	0	0	0

a. Compute a Similarity Matrix.
b. Cluster the activities using farthest neighbor hierarchical clustering.
c. Draw a dendrogram for the clusters.
d. Based on the dendrogram in part c, divide the activities into the two clusters that are most internally similar.

2. For the following Activity-Entity Frequency Matrix:

	Budget	Financial	Product	Parts	Materials
Plan Business	10	50	100	0	0
Design Product	0	0	30	150	200
Acquire Capital	0	30	0	0	0
Analyse Org'n	40	0	0	0	0
Forecast Market	30	0	120	0	0
Review Results	50	100	0	0	0

a. Compute a Similarity Matrix.
b. Cluster the activities using farthest neighbor hierarchical clustering.
c. Draw a dendrogram for the clusters.
d. Based on the dendrogram in part c, divide the activities into the two clusters that are most internally similar.

3. Jenny Nagy administers a Suzuki Music School. She hires violin, cello, and piano teachers on an hourly basis to teach the children how to play their chosen instrument. She is responsible for hiring and paying teachers, recruiting and billing students, scheduling lessons, and scheduling occasional concerts in which students can display their progress.

Jenny rents the school building with classrooms and offices. Students and teachers provide their own instruments. The teachers follow a program of lessons recommended by Suzuki Method International of Princeton New Jersey. Each teacher is assigned to teach in a separate practice room. The teachers modify the lessons for each student depending on the needs of the student, the preferences of the parents, and the teaching style of the instructor. Parents attend all lessons in the Suzuki method, so there is no need for written progress reports or lesson plans. Teachers make oral arrangements with parents about practicing and progress reports.

Parents hear about the school mostly by word-of-mouth from other parents. They enroll their children at the beginning of any one of three terms in the year. They pay an inclusive fee based on the length of the individual weekly lesson and whether the child is taking a biweekly group lesson. Parents are billed each term and teachers are paid monthly for the number of scheduled hours that they teach. Most students return for several years.

Jenny finds the scheduling of lesson times, billing of parents, and payment of teachers to be tedious repetitive tasks. She thinks that the tasks could be automated using a microcomputer and a database system like the one her husband uses at his office. Then she could devote more time to promoting the school and attracting more students.

a. Identify the major resources and the major life cycle processes that should form the foundation of a design for such a computer system. Are there any life cycle stages missing for any of the resources? If there are missing stages, are they needed in the design?

b. Use the 7 questions of the BICS Model to identify the activities needed to support the transaction which sells lessons to the parents of students.

4. The following dendrogram has been prepared for the activities in a manufacturing organization. Divide the activities into the three, five, and seven best clusters. Compute the structure coefficient for the dendrogram. Is the dendrogram well-balanced?

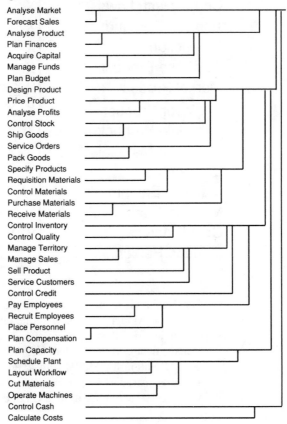

5. Identify any problems in the following Activity-Entity Incidence Matrix. Explain the nature of the problems and suggest ways of correcting the problems.

	Products	Raw Materials	Employees	Equipment	Real Estate	Accounts	Capital	Purchases	Sales	Goods	Customers	Suppliers
Forecast Sales	X					X					X	
Forecast Real Estate	X				X	X						
Forecast Finances						X	X					
Forecast Personnel			X	X	X	X			X			
Comply with Laws	X			X	X	X			X			
Analyse Demand	X					X					X	
Production	X										X	X
Advertise Product	X					X				X		
Market Product	X								X	X	X	
Engineer Product	X	X		X								X
Schedule Production	X	X	X	X					X			
Purchase Materials		X				X						
Equipment				X								
Maintain Equipment			X	X								
Manage Cash						X	X		X	X	X	X
Cost Products	X	X	X	X	X	X				X		
Manage Personnel			X									

6. Tim Burr and Seymour Wood of the Lofty Lumber Co. are developing an Enterprise Model of their manufacturing operations in preparation for the conversion of all systems to a new integrated system using a Data Base Management System and CASE tools. They have produced an Entity-Relationship Model with 43 entities. They now want you to identify the **activities** that must be performed by the new system. They estimate that there are 60 to 100 activities at the level of detail that they are looking for.

The president of the company is very supportive, but the other executives are uneasy about the process because they have never participated in such an exercise. The president has asked you to prepare a concise explanation of the process you will follow. The president will use this explanation to help convince the executives that they should cooperate in this worthwhile exercise. Include in your explanation:

a. The method you will use to gather data.

b. The kind of information you will need from them.

c. The use that will be made of the information.

References

1. Anderberg, Michael R., *Cluster Analysis for Applications,* Academic Press, 1973.

2. Galbraith, J., *Designing Complex Organizations,* Addison-Wesley Publishing Co., 1977.

3. IBM Corp., *Business Systems Planning: Information Systems Planning Guide, Third Edition, Publication GE20-0527-3,* IBM Corporation, Technical Publications, 1981.

4. Jackson, Barbara Bund, Chapter 8: *Cluster Analysis, Multivariate Data Analysis,* Irwin Publishing Co., 1983.

5. Kerner, David V., "Business Information Control Study Methodology" in *The Economics of Information Processing, Volume 1, Management Perspectives,* edited by Robert C. Goldberg and Harold Lorin, John Wiley & Sons, 1982, pp. 71-83.

6. Martin, James, *Strategic Data-Planning Methodologies,* Prentice-Hall Inc., 1982.

7. Murtagh, F., "Structure of Hierarchic Clusterings: Implications for Information Retrieval and Multivariate Data Analysis," *Information Processing and Management,* Vol. 20, pp. 611-17, 1984.

8. Palmer, D.F., "Distributed Computing System Design at the Subsystem/Network Level," *Proc. 1st Int. Conf. on Distributed Computing Systems,* pp. 22-30, Oct. 1979.

3 Activities

Chapter 4

Setting Implementation Priorities

	DATABASE (WHAT)	PROGRAMS (HOW)	BENEFITS (WHY)	NETWORK (WHERE)	REAL TIME (WHEN)	SKILLS (WHO)
USER CONCEPT	Entity Relationship	Activity	Intangible Benefit	Map		Organization Design
DESIGNER CONCEPT	E-R Diagram	A-E Diagram	AHP	Network		Skills Responsibility
USER DETAIL	Forms Screens	Processes Data	Tangible Benefit	Work Volume	Discrete Events	Transition Training
DESIGNER DETAIL	EER Diagram	Data Flow Diagrams	Benefit-Cost	Partition	Transition Diagrams	Methodology Tools
BUILDER CONCEPT	Normal Form Relations	Structure Chart	Function Points	System Architecture	Specifications	Learning
BUILDER DETAIL	Files	Screens Specifications	Costs	Network Specs	Interfaces	4GL CASE

Objectives

The previous two chapters identified the entities and activities that go into an Enterprise Model. The Enterprise Model was then divided into groups of activities, called subsystems, that belong together as separate projects.

This chapter describes the technical, organizational, and financial constraints that have to be considered before a subsystem can be implemented. The technical constraints are related to the availability and capability of hardware, software, and people. The organizational constraints are related to the organization, the department, and individuals. Technical and organizational constraints must be overcome or they will make it impossible to complete the subsystems successfully.

The main constraint on the development of a system is usually financial. Any system whose costs are higher than its benefits should not be developed. This chapter explains how to estimate the tangible and intangible costs and benefits of each subsystem. A set of evaluation criteria are identified and used to identify the development projects with highest priority. The objectives of this chapter are to:

- Determine the technical feasibility of each subsystem.

- Determine organizational feasibility.

- Estimate the cost of a project.

- Estimate the tangible financial benefits of a project net of costs.

- Estimate intangible benefits and costs.

- Identify evaluation criteria for comparing the subsystem development projects.

- Compare the projects using the evaluation criteria and the tangible and intangible benefits.

- Identify the development projects with the highest priority.

Implementation Options

In the university example in the last chapter, five clusters of activities were identified that could be considered for implementation as development projects. These clusters were Planning, Student, Staff, Administration, and Accounting related activities. The next task is to determine how these systems are implemented so their feasibility and their priority can be determined. This chapter defines a plan to "get there from here."

The following analysis assumes that the analysis and design of the new systems is done using CASE tools. A significant part of the implementation is done using either 4GL tools or code generators that are part of the CASE tools. Data are managed by a Data Base Management System (DBMS). Many of the principles of this chapter also apply to traditional environments without a DBMS. However, it is more difficult to achieve integration of the systems in a traditional environment.

There are several ways in which the clusters of activities identified in the previous chapter can be implemented as new computer systems. These ways are usually combinations of existing systems, new systems, purchased systems, and manual systems. Systems are programs or collections of programs designed to accomplish a set of related tasks.

Existing Systems

Some of the required systems may already exist. If they do, there is a need to determine whether they can be left in their existing form, converted to DBMS applications, or rebuilt entirely. They can be left in their existing form if they are already satisfactory and if their data is in a form that can be accessed by a database system. Occasionally, there are systems that can be separated from the rest relatively easily by periodically producing a copy of their data for use in a 4GL environment. These would be cases where the data needed by other systems rarely changes or where other systems do not need up-to-date data.

In general, existing systems need at least some modification to conform to a DBMS environment. If they are operating satisfactorily, this modification can usually be delayed while other systems are implemented or converted. The exception would be systems that act as a foundation for many other systems. For instance, the inventory system is likely to be a critical part of all other manufacturing operations. Even if it is satisfactorily performing the functions for which it was designed, it may have to be converted. The conversion is performed so all inventory and cost data are accessible to other systems using the database.

Purchased Systems

New systems have to be either purchased or implemented by the organization. Purchase is usually cheaper, better, and faster if packages can be found that perform the required functions.

- **Cheaper** because a vendor can spread the development cost over several users and reduce the cost to each. However, the package may be difficult to customize to fit local conditions. For instance, it may cost almost as much to modify an American banking package to fit the Canadian environment as to build a new one for Canadian use. A small organization may find that it is easier to change the organization to fit an available package than to build a new application to fit their organization.

- **Better** because a vendor usually spends more time on design and testing. The vendor has to satisfy a wide variety of users, so more time is spent on designing a flexible system that can adapt to many environments and serve most needs. The vendor also has the benefit of the experience of many clients who have previously used the system. For these reasons, a commercial package may be much better than any custom-built one that a small organization could design or could afford to build.

- **Faster** because the vendor can usually install a package on short notice without requiring a major design effort. Furthermore, maintenance is reduced because the vendor does most of the work needed to keep the system "evergreen." However, the testing of available packages and selection of the best one can also be a time-consuming exercise.

A major concern with using packages in a DBMS environment is that most commercial packages have not been designed to work in a database environment. They typically have custom designed files arranged to implement efficiently the functions that the package performs. The files may be virtually inaccessible to any other applications. One of the major benefits of a DBMS is that data from different applications can be integrated. If a purchased package prevents this integration, then it reduces the value of the whole system. The implication is that an important selection criterion for purchased packages is whether the database in the package is compatible with the target environment.

A bank provides an example of the problems that can arise with commercial packages. One found that it had fourteen different commercial packages to process loans, deposits, foreign currency, and so on. It wanted to develop an integrated customer file that could tell the bank how much and what kind of business it did with each customer. However, it was virtually impossible to integrate the incompatible information in all of the different packages.

New Systems

If a part of the system has to be implemented as a new application, another level of detail must be added to the system design. This allows estimation of the labor cost involved in building the system. Information is needed about how many files, reports, and screens are required in the new system.

All of the feasible systems cannot be implemented at once so the most valuable ones must be identified. Some may be sufficiently well implemented now that they do not need to be redone. Some may not be worth implementing at all.

Technical Feasibility

There are three kinds of feasibility: technical, organizational, and financial. Technical feasibility is concerned with the availability and capability of hardware, software, and people. Organizational feasibility is concerned with the need for leadership and the acceptance of changes that accompany the development project. Financial feasibility means that the benefits of the project are greater than the costs. Technical feasibility can be examined in terms of hardware, software, and human skills.

Hardware

The main hardware concern in a DBMS environment is whether a computer is available that is powerful enough to handle the proposed load. DBMS and 4GL systems usually consume more computer power than the equivalent 3GL systems. They need more power for three reasons.

- **File structures** designed for flexibility may make each file access less efficient than in a special purpose system. File access is one of the most time-consuming activities in a computer system. A system may be able to obtain all information about a course in a single access from a special-purpose file. It may take three accesses in a system with a file for each of the course, section, and meeting entities.

- **More data validation and security checking** is usually performed with a DBMS than is common in traditional systems. These take more machine processing time.

- **Demands for application programs** and reports increase with flexible and coordinated access to data. New applications become possible that were not considered before the DBMS was implemented.

Together these factors can easily double the requirement for machine resources even if no new functions are added to the converted system. This almost certainly requires a commitment to new hardware purchases. However, this cost must be balanced against the greater flexibility, accuracy, and accessibility of the new system.

In some cases the load is larger than any existing machine can possibly handle. This means that it is necessary to distribute the load on more than one machine. This is relatively easy in some decentralized organizations. However, it may not be practical in some large centralized organizations. Applications that require that all data be available at any point in the system are particularly difficult to distribute. Airline reservation systems and bank teller systems are examples of such systems.

In these cases, it may be necessary to compromise by leaving the high transaction-volume applications on one machine, coded in a 3GL. Management reporting needs can be serviced by copying summaries of the transaction data periodically to a 4GL system on another computer used for that purpose. The alternative is to develop a multi-machine network that can share data. This is still a very complex and difficult task that significantly increases the machine resources, the software complexity, and the operating difficulty of the system.

In principle, almost any system is now technically feasible. Distributed network systems can be constructed to split even the largest systems into subsystems that can be integrated on several machines. However, some large systems are so complicated that they are not practical with current technology.

Most hardware constraints are actually financial or political constraints. A constraint that says an application must work on a particular size of computer usually means the user cannot afford a larger computer. If an application must work on a particular brand of computer it means that a policy decision has been made to limit choices for some reason, such as simplifying maintenance.

Software

The heart of a CASE environment is the Data Base Management System software that validates the data, stores it, and retrieves it when needed by an application program. The DBMS maintains a Data Dictionary that describes the characteristics of the database. This Data Dictionary can be accessed by other programs that use the database. Thus they do not need to contain a description of the data that they use.

A large integrated system is often technically infeasible in a 3GL environment. The design of a large system becomes so complex, with so many components, that mere humans are not able to comprehend and organize all the details needed to implement such a system. They have to resort to dividing the system into separate uncoordinated components. This strategy leads to duplication of data and programs, redundant effort, and inaccessible data.

CASE tools can overcome this coordination problem by providing a structure for the acquisition, maintaining, and cross-referencing of design data. They can automate many of the analysis, design, and coding tasks. This allows designers and programmers to function at a higher level where they can comprehend the relationships in a larger integrated system.

There are now several vendors of DBMS and other 4GL software. The software that is used to implement the system must be chosen carefully. It is a choice that commits the organization to a particular vendor for the life of the system, which usually is many years. There are several criteria to be considered.

- **Vendor Stability.** It is usually difficult to convert applications from one DBMS to another. The organization needs to be confident that the vendor will be in business for the life of the system. If the vendor fails, the organization can keep the software, but will not get updates and upgrades to new machines.
- **Portability.** It is desirable to have a DBMS that is implemented on more than one vendor's hardware. This provides the flexibility to change hardware vendors without having to completely reprogram applications. In the DBMS environment, organizations become more committed to software vendors than to hardware vendors. Portability and the ability to link applications on different machines becomes very important.

- **Efficiency.** The DBMS will be used for a large proportion of all computer applications in the future. The efficiency of the software has a significant impact on the cost of the hardware needed to run applications. It may also determine whether some large applications are feasible on even the largest available hardware.

- **Distributed Database.** In large systems, it is desirable to have a DBMS that can access a database that is distributed over several different computers. This allows one to build applications that use data from more than one machine. This feature is currently rare, but will become important in the future. The vendor should at least have a commitment to develop this feature. This feature is less important in smaller organizations that can expect to get their entire database and applications on a single computer.

- **Productivity Features.** There are many packages on the market that offer some 4GL features. However, they differ greatly in capability and ease of use. A true 4GL needs four main components: screen generator, application generator, query language, and relational database.

  - **Screen Generator.** A screen generator is a program that takes a simple description of what a screen should look like and converts it into a program that implements the desired screen. This feature is very important because it reduces greatly the labor of generating input screens and it simplifies and encourages comprehensive integrity checks of the input data. Usually the same screen can be used for inserting, updating, and deleting data.

  - **Query language.** A query language allows users to define ad hoc queries without using a programmer. This releases programming resources and also leads to better reports. The reports are better because they are designed by the people who actually use them.

  - **Application Generator.** An application generator creates batch processing application programs using a high-level specification language. An interface that allows one to write COBOL applications that get data from the DBMS is not an application generator. Such an interface is occasionally needed so special applications can be written to do things not available in the application generator. This should not be the normal method of programming.

    The generator must have a complete high level language that uses the Data Dictionary in the DBMS to obtain data descriptions. It should use commands similar to those in a query language for processing. It should have a report specification and generation capability that can generate any report format.

  - **Relational Database.** The relational database facility makes it easier to design databases and applications. The next chapters show that there are a variety of features in a relational file structure that make it easier to maintain a consistent, flexible, and logical view of the data.

People

People who intend to build information systems in a CASE environment need a new set of skills. The skills needed in a traditional environment are related to COBOL programming, file structures, operating systems, and the System Development Life Cycle. In the 4GL environment the SDLC changes significantly. COBOL is seldom used, and most of the features of the file structures and operating system are hidden from the developer. This results in several changes in the way programming is done.

- **New skills.** Programmers and analysts must learn a new set of skills. These include a new language for building applications; a new System Development Life Cycle; and new ways of interacting with users through prototyping and group design sessions. Each involves changes that are more than trivial.

- **Broader view.** The new language requires that programmers learn to think at a broader level. 3GL languages require that the programmer specify the steps that the computer follows in performing a task. 3GL programmers had to learn to think like a computer. The 4GL languages are nonprocedural. Programming them involves specifying the required outputs and letting the computer determine how to provide them. Programmers have to learn to think in terms of outputs instead of in terms of procedures. In a CASE and 4GL environment they have to stop thinking like a computer and start thinking like a user.

- **New development life cycle.** The CASE System Development Life Cycle reverses many elements of the traditional SDLC. The database is developed before all the applications are defined. The users are involved at a much earlier stage. The process is more continuous with fewer discrete stages.

- **More user contact.** CASE systems require much more contact with the users. Group design sessions and prototyping sessions with the users are a key feature of such projects. There is evidence to indicate that the kind of people who go into computer science prefer machines to people. They have a high need to achieve technical proficiency and a low need to interact with other people. Such people may not be very good at the kind of interaction that is needed in group design and prototyping sessions.

Development of CASE systems requires some combination of retraining existing staff and hiring new staff with the special skills required to operate in a CASE environment.

Organizational Feasibility

A system can be technically feasible and still not be implementable. The organization also has to have the will to implement it. This willingness must come from both management and employees.

Management must *actively* support development of the system. There are a host of problems that result from attempts to introduce technology into the organization. Organizational structure and responsibilities may have to change. Information systems people and users both have to learn new methods of operating. There may be major resistance from employees who may perceive the freedom, authority, or just plain fun being taken out of their jobs. Management may be unwilling to undertake the risk entailed by all these changes.

The users also have to be willing to change and accept new methods. If the work climate exhibits resistant to change, it may not be possible to introduce significantly different systems successfully. The likelihood of success depends on such factors as the age and education of the employees, the history of new introductions, and the incentive that is provided for adopting new methods.

New systems not only have to *be* feasible and economically beneficial, they also have to be *perceived to be* feasible and beneficial. There are organizations in which the employees are resistant to the introduction of new methods for various reasons. If the new system has a low priority, it may not be organizationally feasible to overcome the resistance.

Chapter 13 deals at greater length with the changes that are required in an organization when CASE systems are implemented. These changes are at the organizational, departmental, and personal levels. They apply to management, Information Systems professionals, and end-users.

Financial Feasibility

Technical and organizational factors either allow or prevent the implementation of a new system. If they prevent the implementation, then steps can be taken to overcome the technical or organizational constraints.

Financial considerations are somewhat different in that they determine a ranking of projects. A project that has costs greater than benefits is only infeasible in the sense that it is not profitable to undertake such a project. Money might be found to implement the project, but it should not be implemented if costs are greater than benefits. The projects with the highest ratio of benefits to costs should be the first to be completed. A procedure is required to determine the order in which projects should be started. That procedure consists of the following steps:

- **Costs and benefits** are estimated.
- **Evaluation criteria** are identified.
- **Criterion weights** are specified.
- **Rankings** are calculated for the projects.

This section examines each of these stages of the evaluation procedure.

There are two components to financial feasibility: costs and benefits. The costs consist of tangible hardware, software, and people costs and some intangible costs, such as the cost of organizational change. The benefits consist of tangible cost savings and intangible quality improvements. The tangible savings lead to increased efficiency (**doing things right**). The intangible quality improvements usually lead to increased effectiveness (**doing the right things**). If a choice must be made between efficiency and effectiveness, it is better to do the right thing inefficiently than to do the wrong thing efficiently.

Improvements in efficiency lead to increased speed and productivity. Improvements in effectiveness lead to doing things that might not have been attempted without computerized help. Systems that improve effectiveness might help to locate things that are needed, alert people to problems that need attention, or categorize information so informed choices can be made. Some improvements can increase both efficiency and effectiveness. A significant increase in efficiency can release time for doing things that increase effectiveness.

This section examines ways of estimating the tangible and intangible costs and benefits that can increase efficiency and effectiveness.

Tangible Costs

The tangible costs can be divided into hardware, software, and people costs. In a 3GL environment hardware costs decrease and people costs increase as more people are needed to build increasingly complex systems. This trend is reversed in the CASE and 4GL environment by using more sophisticated software and more powerful hardware to make the people more productive so their number can be contained or reduced.

Hardware Costs

Hardware costs in business usually depend primarily on the number of transactions to be processed, the size of the files to be stored, and the number of users to be served at terminals. Exact requirements are difficult to specify, but it is not always necessary to make a commitment at the beginning. It takes several years to develop all the new systems. Computers must be upgraded or replaced about every four years because new technology makes them obsolete. There is often an opportunity to gain some experience with existing equipment before committing to a new or expanded machine. As a very rough estimate, it takes twice as much hardware to operate a 4GL as to operate the equivalent 3GL programs.

Software Costs

The cost of purchased software is the easiest item to estimate. Vendors have a price that depends on the size and number of machines on which it is installed. They provide quotations for licenses and maintenance.

People Costs

These consist primarily of the cost of time spent in analysis, programming, documentation, and testing. The first application of CASE methods may also incur some significant training costs as all the people involved with the system learn new methods of design and implementation.

People costs are quite difficult to estimate. A common method is to estimate the number of executable Source Lines Of Code (SLOC) that are needed. SLOC is then multiplied by a cost factor calibrated for the organization. This factor is surprisingly constant regardless of language. It usually ranges from 10 to 50 dollars per line depending on the complexity of the problem. Cost also depends on whether it is to be used on a single machine by one organization or on many machines by many organizations. As the number of machines and kinds of users increases, the need for generalized design, documentation, and testing increases.

Unfortunately, it is difficult to estimate the number of lines of code needed unless you have significant experience with the type of application being considered and the language and equipment being used. Furthermore, many of the 4GL environments do not use direct code. Instead, they rely on input screens with fill-in-the-blank menus to define many aspects of the system. Function Point Analysis can be used to estimate the labor to develop such systems.

Function Point Analysis

Function Point Analysis, developed by Albrecht[1] and described in more detail by Dreger,[8] takes a user's view of the system. It identifies five types of functions that link an application program to the rest of the world as illustrated in Figure 4-1. The functions are described below.

- **External inputs** are transaction data that come from keyboards, communication lines, tape, or other applications. Every entity occurrence entered as a transaction with a different format or different processing logic counts as an external input. In interactive systems, the input screens are the major external inputs. Their complexity can be classified as:
  - **Simple:** The transaction contains few data element types and references few internal files. Human factors are not a major design consideration.
  - **Average:** Neither simple or complex.
  - **Complex:** The transaction contains many data element types, uses many internal files, and human factors are a major design consideration.
- **External outputs** are reports and messages that go out to the user or to another application such as a file of reports and messages. The reports may go out to screens, printers, communications lines, or other applications. External outputs do not include responses to inquiries, output files, or reports that are

Figure 4-1
Generic Function Points in a Function Point Analysis.

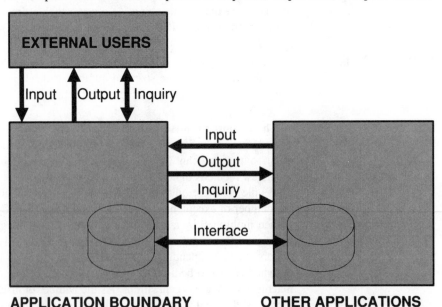

required only because of the technology used. These are covered by other types of outputs. External outputs can be classified by complexity using the same criteria as for external input. For reports use the following guides:
  - **Simple:** One or two columns with simple data transformations.
  - **Average:** Multiple column with subtotals. Multiple data transformations.
  - **Complex:** Intricate data element transformations. Multiple and complex file references to be coordinated. Significant performance considerations.

- **External inquiries** are queries from users or applications that result in a report to the user or application. They read files in a database, but do not add, change, or delete records. Count a separate type for each inquiry with a different processing logic or a different input or output format. A generalized query facility is not an external inquiry. It consists of several external inputs, outputs, and inquiries. The complexity of an external inquiry is the greater of the input and output complexity as measured by the criteria for external input and output respectively. 4GL systems often do not have code for external inquiries because the external inquiries are handled by users making inquiries with the query language provided by the package. Many inquiries can be handled by the same screens used for data input.

- **Logical internal files** are logical data files that store information for an application that generates, uses, and maintains the data. Each entity and each M:N relationship in an Entity-Relationship Model is a logical file. They can be classified by complexity as:
  - **Simple:** Few data element types. No significant performance, validation, or recovery considerations.
  - **Average:** Neither simple or complex.
  - **Complex:** Many data element types. Performance, validation, and recovery are significant considerations.

- **External interface files** contain data or control information passed from, passed to, or shared by another application. Their complexity can be evaluated using the same criteria as those used for logical internal files.

With the above description and criteria, we can count the number of each kind of function of each complexity level. The function counts are weighted as shown in Figure 4-2 to get total unadjusted function points.

DESCRIPTION	SIMPLE	AVERAGE	COMPLEX	TOTAL
External Input	___ x 3 = ___	___ x 4 = ___	___ x 6 = ___	_____
External Output	___ x 4 = ___	___ x 5 = ___	___ x 7 = ___	_____
External Inquiry	___ x 3 = ___	___ x 4 = ___	___ x 6 = ___	_____
Internal File	___ x 7 = ___	___ x10= ___	___ x15= ___	_____
External Interface	___ x 5 = ___	___ x 7 = ___	___ x10= ___	_____

Function Count (unadjusted) = FC = _____

Figure 4-2

Weights for computing the Unadjusted Function Count in a Function Point Analysis.

This count has to be adjusted to allow for the overall complexity of the application. This is done by adding the weights of the 14 application factors shown in Figure 4-3. The weighting used for each factor is:

- 0 = Not present or no influence if present.
- 1 = Insignificant influence.
- 2 = Moderate influence.
- 3 = Average influence.
- 4 = Significant influence.
- 5 = Strong influence through entire project.

PC, the sum of these factors, is used to calculate the Process Complexity Adjustment, $PCA = 0.65 \times (0.01 \times PC)$. This gives an adjustment factor that ranges between .65 and 1.35. FC, the unadjusted Function Count from Figure 4-2, is multiplied by PCA to get an adjusted Function Points measure, FP.

The application characteristics in Figure 4-3 are present when the corresponding conditions—identified below—are satisfied.

- **Data Communications** are needed to send data or control information over facilities, including terminals, connected to a local controller. This increases the number of interfaces that have to be designed and tested.
- **Distributed Functions** are used to manage data or perform processes in the application. This increases the complexity of the design.
- **Performance** in response or throughput influences the design, development, installation, or support of the application because more design effort is needed to achieve better performance.
- **Heavily Used Configurations** of equipment runs the application. Extra effort is needed to design very efficient code.
- **Transaction Rate** has to be high. It influences the design, development, installation, or support of the application. High transaction rates require more efficient code.

CHARACTERISTIC	INFLUENCE	CHARACTERISTIC	INFLUENCE
Data Communications	_____	Online Update	_____
Distributed Functions	_____	Complex Processing	_____
Performance	_____	Reuseability	_____
Heavily Used Configuration	_____	Installation Ease	_____
Transaction Rate	_____	Operational Ease	_____
Online Data Entry	_____	Multiple Sites	_____
End User Efficiency	_____	Facilitation of Change	_____

Total Processing Complexity = PC =   _____

Processing Complexity Adjustment = PCA   = 0.65 + (0.01 x PC) =   _____

Total Adjusted Function Points = FP = FCxPCA =   _____

Figure 4-3

Form for calculating the Total Adjusted Function Points in a Function Point Analysis.

- **On-line Data Entry** requires interfaces of higher complexity.
- **End User Efficiency** may be an important consideration in designing the on-line functions. If it is, then more effort is needed to test different possible designs to identify the most efficient one.
- **On-line Update** of files in the database requires more integrity checks and more controls to prevent unintended interactions between users.
- **Complex Processing** increases the complexity and cost of the design. Extensive logic, many mathematical equations, many control points, and heavy exception processing are examples of complex processing.
- **Reusability** of code in other applications or other sites can be an important part of the design, development, and support of the application. More design effort is needed to identify opportunities for reusability and to test that the code serves all of the intended purposes.
- **Installation Ease** or conversion ease are required. It costs more to develop and test a conversion and installation plan.
- **Operational Ease** is important. Simple startup, backup, and recovery procedures are provided and tested. Tape mounts, paper handling, and other manual interventions are minimized. All of these require more design effort to make sure that the simplest possible method has been chosen.
- **Multiple Sites** and multiple organizations can use the application. The system must be designed to work in several environments. It must be tested in each kind of environment.
- **Facilitation of Change** has been designed into the application. Flexible query facilities and user-modified tables are provided. These take extra time.

If an existing application is being modified, the user functions being added, changed, and deleted each count toward the total number of function points.

The final adjusted total is used for estimating programming time. A function point is equivalent to about 120 lines of COBOL code and about a tenth as many lines in a 4GL. The time required to code a function point requires calibration in each organization that uses the method. It has been estimated[2] that, in a typical organization, it takes about 1 hour to code a function point in a 4GL and about 20 hours in COBOL. The number of hours per function point is almost independent of project size in a 4GL but increases significantly with project size in a 3GL. This is because projects get broken down into smaller modules in a 4GL environment. The 4GL automatically coordinates and integrates the components.

A 4GL can reduce coding times if four conditions are satisfied.

- **Experienced end-users participate.** They make sure that requirements are satisfied as the system is built. This eliminates expensive recoding and redevelopment that results when what the programmer thought he built is not what the user thought he asked for.
- **A single language is used.** This eliminates a lot of documentation, specification, interfacing, and testing. These factors grow exponentially as the size of the project grows linearly.

- **Development teams are small.** This eliminates a large part of the coordination, system integration, and design reviews that are needed to keep a large group of programmers working toward the same result. CASE and 4GLs permit 2 or 3 people to develop systems that have the equivalent of 100,000 lines of COBOL code in as little as three months.
- **The CASE tool integrates the system.** Much of the work in a large development project consists of integrating the individual components produced by different programmers into a complete system. Another large job is testing to make sure that the components work together. A CASE tool does most of this automatically by requiring that all data, file accesses, and reports conform to the specifications in the Data Dictionary.

Jones[10] has a comprehensive analysis of the factors which influence the cost of developing software. Function Point Analysis may not apply well to projects that take less than about three months. On such short projects, administrative factors, such as organizing the work group, may dominate the development time.

In summary, the benefits of a CASE and 4GL environment are available only if the large isolated project teams and sequential steps of the traditional Systems Development Life Cycle are abandoned. They must be replaced by small project teams using prototyping methods to interact closely with users.

Function Point Example

The STUDENT cluster of activities from the activities identified in Chapter 3 is used to illustrate a Function Point Analysis. The applications are examined to identify the input documents that have to be entered into the system and the output reports that must be generated. Each is followed by a complexity rating and sometimes an explanation of why the item is expected to be complex.

- **External inputs**
  - ☐ Academic Programs - Average
  - ☐ Class Schedules - Simple
  - ☐ Teaching Requests - Simple
  - ☐ Applicants - Complex (many data elements)
  - ☐ Test Scores - Average
  - ☐ Transcripts - Complex (many formats)
  - ☐ Enrollment Forms - Average
  - ☐ Grades - Average
- **External outputs**
  - ☐ Teaching Schedule - Complex (complex format)
  - ☐ Acceptance Letters - Complex (link to word processing)
  - ☐ Enrollment Report - Complex (complex format)
  - ☐ Class Lists - Simple
  - ☐ Grade Report - Average
  - ☐ Graduation List - Simple
  - ☐ Grade Distribution - Complex (Complex calculations)

- **External Inquiries - None**
- **Logical internal files**
  - ☐ Buildings - Simple
  - ☐ Rooms - Simple
  - ☐ Equipment - Simple
  - ☐ Students - Average
  - ☐ Programs - Simple
  - ☐ Courses - Simple
  - ☐ Sections - Simple
  - ☐ Meetings - Simple
  - ☐ Faculty - Simple
- **External interface files**
  - ☐ Registrar's enrollment list. This is a complex tape file that summarizes enrollments so fees can be calculated by the registrar.

The results of the Function Point Analysis are summarized in Figure 4-4.

The adjustment factors are shown in Figure 4-5. An on-line system at a single site with minimal operator intervention has been assumed. The Function Count of 151 is multiplied by the adjustment factor of 0.97 to get a total of 146 function points. Assume a programming time of one hour per function point for a programmer experienced in the use of a 4GL Data Base Management System product, like Oracle. Then the expected development time is about 146 hours. This is about a month which is reasonable for the assumed environment.

Inexperienced programmers, or those working in a more adverse environment would take longer. The time per function point needs to be calibrated by doing projects in the actual environment to determine the productivity of programmers in the target environment.

The expected cost of programming is obtained by multiplying the expected number of hours by the hourly average cost of programmers. This cost should

DESCRIPTION	SIMPLE	AVERAGE	COMPLEX	TOTAL
External Input	2 x 3 = 6	4 x 4 = 16	2 x 6 = 12	34
External Output	2 x 4 = 8	1 x 5 = 5	4 x 7 = 28	41
External Inquiry	__ x 3 = __	__ x 4 = __	__ x 6 = __	__
Internal File	8 x 7 = 56	1 x10= 10	__ x15= __	66
External Interface	__ x 5 = __	__ x 7 = __	1 x10= 10	10
		Function Count (unadjusted) = FC =		151

Figure 4-4

Function Count for the university example.

include allowances for benefits, holidays, and unproductive time spent on education, department meetings, or other activities. If a cost of sixty dollars per hour is assumed, then the cost is expected to be 146x60=$8,760. This should be rounded to $9,000 since such estimates are only accurate to within about 20 percent.

Tangible Benefits

Tangible benefits are the ones for which a cash value can be identified. They usually involve reducing labor, inventory, defects, or other factors that cost money. This reduction contributes directly to improved efficiency.

The simplest way of estimating them is to identify the annual costs with the current system, then identify the annual expected costs with the proposed system. The difference is the annual savings due to the proposed system. In some cases it is only possible to identify a percentage change such as a 20 percent reduction in inventory and associated carrying costs.

The integration of several systems can sometimes lead to savings that could not be achieved by redesign of the individual systems. Multiple systems often have redundant components that have to be paid for again in each system.

An oil company found that it had a set of 40 related programs that repeatedly gathered the same data an average of ten times. Integration eliminated all the duplication and reduced clerical data-gathering and input costs considerably. However, the major saving was that it eliminated a need for several dozen accountants and clerks. They spent their time preparing reconciliation reports to explain why the numbers from the different programs disagreed. This single saving easily paid for the redesign and implementation of the whole new system.

One of the major savings expected from automation projects is a reduction in labor costs. This is particularly true of office automation projects. Unfortunately,

CHARACTERISTIC	INFLUENCE	CHARACTERISTIC	INFLUENCE
Data Communications	0	Online Update	3
Distributed Functions	0	Complex Processing	2
Performance	3	Reuseability	1
Heavily Used Configuration	3	Installation Ease	4
Transaction Rate	2	Operational Ease	4
Online Data Entry	3	Multiple Sites	0
End User Efficiency	3	Facilitate Change	4

Total Processing Complexity = PC =   32

Processing Complexity Adjustment = PCA   = 0.65 + (0.01 x PC) =   .97

Total Adjusted Function Points = F CxPCA = 151x .97 =   146

Figure 4-5

Complexity adjustment for the university example.

it is hard to estimate savings because it is hard to define what most white collar workers do. One method is the Time Savings Times Salary (TSTS) Method.

TSTS Method

Use the following notation in describing the TSTS method:

T_{ca} = Average fraction of time spent by employee of category **c** on activity of type **a**.

E_a = Average fraction of time employees spend on activity **a** that can be eliminated by automation.

N_c = Number of employees in category **c**.

P_c = Average annual payment to each employee in category **c** for wages and fringe benefits.

S_c = Fraction of time saved by an employee of category **c** by automation support of all activities.

We can calculate S_c from:

$$S_c = \sum T_{ca}E_a$$

We can then calculate total savings, S, from:

$$S = \sum N_c P_c S_c$$

N_c and P_c can be obtained from personnel records. T_{ca} and E_a are available from survey data obtained by the consulting firm of Booz, Allen & Hamilton in a study for Data General Corporation[6]. Values of T_{ca} are listed in Figure 4-6 for 3 categories of employees: managers, professionals, and support staff. The electronic aids that produce the savings and the corresponding E_a are also listed. The average savings per category of employee are listed below the columns for each category. If some of the electronic aids are not being used, their savings can be eliminated from the total.

It probably takes about 2 years before the full level of savings are achieved[3]. The level also depends on the receptivity of the employees to the new technology. For instance, employees who lack keyboard skills are slower to adopt computer technology. Individuals may not always achieve the calculated levels of productivity improvement, but the group should.

The TSTS method assumes that workers are worth exactly what they are paid and that the previous distribution of activities will prevail after the new system is installed. They are worth their salary in a competitive market in which managers are allowed to hire all the workers that they can justify. They are worth more than their salary if there is a budget constraint that prevents managers from hiring as many workers as they are willing to pay for.

TSTS Example

The same Student Records System is used to illustrate the TSTS method of estimating savings. The department using the new system consists of a manager and seven clerical staff providing support services. The proportion of time spent on each activity is assumed to be the same as that given in Figure 4-6. The time that can be eliminated is sometimes reduced to reflect incomplete implementation of all of the features in Figure 4-6. Only the activities impacted by the

ACTIVITIES	MANAGERS	PROFESSIONAL	SUPPORT	E_a	REASONS
DOCUMENT					
Writing/Revising	10	15	5	20	WP
Typing	0	0	25	40	WP
ADMINISTRATION					
Seeking Info	6	9	10	50	DSS, Files
Seeking People	2	2	5	25	E-mail, Calendar
Scheduling	2	4	2	30	Calendar
Filing/Copying	1	2	10	50	Files, WP
Waiting for Work	1	1	10	20	Files, E-mail
Traveling/Other	4	4	10	10	Files, E-mail
COMMUNICATIONS					
Face-to-Face	49	32	5	5	E-mail, Graphics
Telephone	9	8	10	20	E-mail
Reading	7	7	5	10	DSS, Searches
ANALYSIS					
Calculating	5	11	3	25	DSS
Planning	4	5	0	20	DSS
AVERAGE	14.20	18.45	29.35		

DSS=Decision Support Systems, E-mail=Electronic Mail, WP=Word Processing

Figure 4-6

Expected percent time savings for classes of office tasks.

proposed project are included in Figure 4-7, which illustrates the computations. Percentages are converted to decimal fractions to simplify calculations.

The calculations project that 6 percent of the manager's time and 26 percent of the average support person's time can be saved by implementing the system. Assume that the annual cost of the manager is $100,000 with benefits and the cost of seven support personnel averages $50,000 per year with benefits. Each works for 2000 hours per year. The potential savings are $(1\times.06\times100,000) + (7\times.26\times50,000) = \$97,000$. Not all of these savings can be realized in cash. It is not possible to lay off six percent of a manager. However, the six percent of the manager's time that is freed by the system may be used to perform other equally valuable tasks.

ACTIVITIES	MANAGERS	SUPPORT	E_a	REASONS
DOCUMENT				
Typing	.00	.25	.40	WP
ADMINISTRATION				
Seeking Info	.06	.10	.50	DSS, Files
Filing/Copying	.01	.10	.50	Files, WP
Waiting for Work	.01	.10	.20	Files, E-mail
COMMUNICATIONS				
Reading	.07	.05	.10	DSS, Searches
ANALYSIS				
Calculating	.05	.03	.25	DSS
Planning	.04	.00	.20	DSS
AVERAGE	.06	.26		

DSS=Decision Support Systems,   E-mail=Electronic Mail,   WP=Word Processing

Figure 4-7

Expected time savings for the Student Records example.

Similarly, it may not be possible to lay off 7×.26=1.82 support staff. However, it may be possible to reduce staff by 1.5 by eliminating one position and converting another one to a half-time position. Even if the savings in management time are ignored, this leads to a saving of at least $75,000 per year.

The previous activity distribution does not always prevail. When automated systems are installed, office workers readjust their work patterns to optimize their activities. This often has unexpected consequences. For instance, one might expect that the main effect of installing word processors would be to increase the typing efficiency of clerical staff. In fact, there is often a displacement of typing to professional staff. They find that it is faster to compose technical documents on the screen and edit them themselves. Writing a report, instructing secretaries, and proofreading the result may take longer than doing it yourself. For this reason, there is sometimes a need for a model that adjusts the time spent on each activity after the installation of new methods.

The Hedonic Method, described in Appendix 4-A, does allow readjustment of times. It assumes that time saved is used for new kinds of work with a similar value to the work currently being done. The result is not directly comparable to the TSTS method, since it assumes new work instead of work reduction. Since the amount of work in the example is expected to stay fixed, the savings calculated from the TSTS method are used in further examples.

Intangible Benefits

The tangible costs and benefits that result from increased hardware and software and reduced labor are relatively easy to calculate. There are frequently several intangible benefits that result from conversion of applications to a 4GL environment. More accurate and more current data, better decisions, more competitive customer service, and better planning are worthwhile results.

An emphasis on financial benefits alone often leads to a short-sighted investment strategy. Most investment criteria, such as Discounted Cash Flow, Payback, or Internal Rate of Return, reject projects that take more than two or three years to pay for themselves. Such criteria nearly always reject major integration projects that may take five to ten years to complete. As a result, the organization is doomed to continue indefinitely with old, fragmented systems that do not support the need for integrated information.

Unfortunately it is very hard to put a monetary value on these factors. Many organizations are very uncomfortable with estimates of the monetary value of such benefits as "faster response to customer requests." The way to break out of this cycle is to show that information systems are critical to the long-term strategy of the organization. The analyst must show that the intangible benefits are also important. The next section illustrates how this is done.

Evaluating and Ranking Subsystems

A new information system has several different impacts in different parts of the organization. Different parts of the organization see the costs and benefits in different ways because they all have their own criteria for evaluation. Net financial benefits may not be as important as better access to information for decision making or greater collaboration between different parts of the organization.

There is a need for an evaluation process that can combine objective financial benefits and subjective intangible benefits to produce a ranking of all the subsystems[15]. The ranking determines which subsystems should be implemented first and which should be left until later, or possibly not be implemented at all.

Each organization has different criteria, depending on its problems, possibilities, and objectives. There are several ways of identifying the evaluation criteria that should be used in a given organization. There are three steps in the evaluation process.

- **Identify** all of the criteria and intangible benefits. Intangible costs can also be included as negative benefits. Critical Success Factors, Brainstorming, and Nominal Group Process are used for this step.
- **Compare** the relative importance of each benefit. The most common method of making this comparison is to use the Criterion Function. The Criterion

Function requires weights for each benefit. These are sometimes difficult to agree on. This chapter uses the Nominal Group Process to provide weights. Appendix 4-B, at the end of this chapter, explains how the Analytic Hierarchy Process can also be used to achieve consensus and improve the estimates of relative weights in the Criterion Function.

- **Evaluate** each subsystem on the weighted criteria and produce a ranked list of implementation projects in priority order.

Identifying Evaluation Criteria

There are three techniques that can help in identifying the criteria that should be used in evaluating the subsystems to determine which ones should be implemented first. Critical Success Factors is a technique used to identify the most important activities that need to be supported. Brainstorming is a technique for generating new ideas and viewpoints. The Nominal Group Process is a way of building consensus about the actions that have to be taken.

4
Priorities

Critical Success Factors

One way to elicit criteria is to ask the group to identify the Critical Success Factors[9] (CSF) of the organization. These are those few things that must be done well if the organization is to survive and prosper. The Critical Success Factors are usually related to the important strategic issues with which a corporate plan must deal. Examples of strategic issues are:

- **Competitive position.** An organization can compete in different sectors of a market such as a quality sector or a low-priced high-volume sector.
- **Geographic position.** An organization can often choose to compete in selected geographic areas.
- **Redeployment of personnel.** Processes can be made more efficient so the same people can produce more or people can be retrained to perform higher level jobs.
- **Redeployment of capital.** An organization may want to invest in different lines of business.
- **Redesign of the organization.** The responsibilities and reporting structures of the organization may have to be changed to cope effectively with a changing environment. Mechanisms may be needed to facilitate collaboration between different parts of an organization.
- **Standardization of information architecture.** Standardized information systems make it possible to integrate data, exchange information, and communicate facts between different parts of the organization.

The Critical Success Factor approach has been criticized for overemphasizing current concerns and crises instead of addressing the whole range of organizational needs. The Accounts Receivable system would seldom be considered to be a critical system. However, if it ceased to function, it would become very critical. It is the system that makes sure that revenues—the life-blood of the organization—are collected from customers.

Systems that support Critical Success Factors may have prerequisites for implementation. Some things may be desirable, but not yet feasible. A marketing

Decision Support System may be desirable and even critical to success, but it cannot be implemented until all of the basic sales data have been computerized. It may be necessary to computerize the order processing first.

Systems that support delivery of goods to customers are often considered most critical. Sponsors and project dollars are easiest to find for these systems. However, such systems can never be any better than the precursor systems that provide the data they depend on. Systems that capture production and inventory must often be built before the delivery systems can be built.

The Critical Success Factors become the criteria for identifying the subsystems identified in the previous chapter which are most important to the enterprise. The important ones are the ones that contribute most to the support of the Critical Success Factors. These are the ones that convert computing power into competing power.

The Critical Success Factors approach is most helpful in selecting support systems for isolated senior executives and less helpful in identifying company-wide priorities for integrated information systems. Since the Critical Success Factor approach may ignore many other important factors, a broader approach, called brainstorming, is sometimes used.

Brainstorming

The brainstorming method gets together the group of people who are most likely to know the impacts of the new systems. They are charged with providing a list of criteria, but not an evaluation of them. The basic rule is that no idea is irrelevant or silly at this stage. The objective is to elicit a free flow of ideas, so suggestions are encouraged. No criticism of any factors is permitted at this stage.

A second stage is used to critique and consolidate the ideas generated in the first stage. This second stage permits discussion of ideas and improvement of the initial suggestions.

Brainstorming is very good at providing a list of possible candidates for goals, objectives, and criteria. However, it is not very good at consolidating and weighting the different concepts. The Nominal Group Process is a way of building consensus about the weights that should be applied to each factor.

Nominal Group Process

The Nominal Group Process has two basic phases: generation and prioritization. The generation phase is used to generate a list of important factors or goals. The prioritization phase consolidates the factors and specifies the importance of each factor.

Generation is performed in a single group if there are up to seven or eight people involved. It is performed in multiple groups of five to eight if more people are involved. Each group has a moderator who records and summarizes the ideas of the group.

The group session is begun like a brainstorming session, where every success factor suggested by the group is listed as valid for later discussion. When a list of factors has been generated, individuals can suggest reasons why factors should be dropped, added, or combined.

When the factors have been identified, they have to be refined. The refinement stage identifies the critical information, critical assumptions, and critical decisions needed to deal with each strategic issue. The critical information has been identified by the Entity-Relationship Model within the Enterprise Model.

The critical assumptions and the critical decisions serve as different ways of viewing the success factors. Critical assumptions are identified by asking a question like "What are the assumptions about your company, business, competitors, or industry that make you think that each of these success factors is valid?" Another way to think about the question is to consider what features of the industry, business, or competitors would have to change to make you change or delete a success factor.

The success factors can be further refined by examining the critical decisions. Each person in the group is asked to identify the crucial decision or decisions that directly effect the success or failure of each success factor.

The preliminary list must then be consolidated into a shorter list of factors that are relatively independent of each other. If they are not independent, then the same factor is effectively counted more than once. In addition, the number of factors needs to be reduced to a manageable number to simplify the problem of identifying their importance. Thus, factors like faster order processing and more information to customers might be combined into customer satisfaction.

One or two hours of discussion usually produces acceptable consensus within the group about which factors are important enough to consider.

If there are multiple groups involved, then the groups meet as a single body to consolidate their lists. The moderator from each group presents the factors generated by the group. The combined group can again discuss the factors and try to consolidate them.

The factors are usually combined into a hierarchy of two or three levels. The top level corresponds to the goal to be optimized. The next level is usually the objectives that contribute to the overall goal. The third level is the criteria that satisfy each objective. It is not always easy to identify GOAL, OBJECTIVES, and CRITERIA. Different people have different goals, objectives, and criteria and it is not clear which are the important ones. It is sometimes unclear whether a particular factor is an objective or a criterion. When in doubt it is better to leave extra factors in the model. Some are later identified as unimportant and can be removed then.

The objective of this process is to achieve consensus among the group members about what the future direction of the organization should be. There is no right or wrong result that must be achieved. Many different objectives are possible for any given organization. Each may lead to success if expertly implemented. None lead to success if members of the organization cannot reach an agreement to work together.

It is not important that all possible factors be identified and weighted correctly. It is important that all members feel that they have had their say and that they agree to work toward the commonly identified goals and objectives. This works best when all participants have similar goals. If the process leads to identifying winners and losers, then the participants are unlikely to achieve consensus.

In the university example, the appropriate group would be the university President, Vice-Presidents, and Deans. They are the ones who are responsible for the administrative decisions in the university. If the university already has a clear set of goals and objectives, then it may take only a day to define the goals and objectives for an information system. If they do not have a clear set of goals and objectives, then a 2 or 3 day retreat may be required to establish them, since many other issues must be considered in arriving at objectives. A retreat is usually held at some location away from the participants' offices so they can give their whole attention to the problem without interruption from current problems.

Figure 4-8 identifies factors that were identified during this process. They influence the priority order in which systems are constructed. The goals are improved administration, improved image, and net cost savings. Net Cost Savings—a summation of tangible factors—has been included as a goal so tangible and intangible factors can be compared. The other factors in the figure are objectives which contribute to the achievement of the goals. In this example, the criteria level has not been included.

Criterion Function

Weights must be assigned to each of the identified criteria. With this set of weights a criterion function can be constructed. Begin by assigning weights, W_j, to the J objectives. The weights should be fractions that total to 1. Thus all objectives make up the total value (100%) of the system. In the example, J=3 for administration, image, and cost.

Next take each of the criteria, C_i, within a particular objective and assign fractional weights that total to 1 within the objective. These tell what fraction of a particular objective is accounted for by the individual criteria. $W_j \times C_i$, the weight of the objective times the weight of the criterion, gives the contribution of each criterion toward the overall goal. Figure 4-9 illustrates a set of weights applied to the objectives and criteria identified in Figure 4-8.

Finally assign a score, V_i, to each project for each criterion. This score is the fraction that the project scores over the maximum possible score for that criterion. Dividing by the maximum normalizes the scores so the measurement scale does not effect the weight for the criteria. As an example, if the criterion is savings and the maximum savings for any of the pro-

---

Improved Administration
  Effective use of information
  Better quality information
  Improved productivity
  Better coordination
Improved Image
  Faster response
  Better students
  Better public service
  Employee morale
Net Cost Savings

Figure 4-8

Goals and objectives for the university example.

jects is a million dollars, then a project with savings of $750,000 has a score of 750,000/1,000,000=.75 for V_i. This division by the maximum score makes all units comparable when the weights are summed.

Now evaluate the Criterion Function, CF, which is:

$CF = \sum W_j \sum C_i V_i$

The process is illustrated in Figure 4-10 using a set of scores for the student records system.

If more than one person or group are providing weights, the data can be combined by computing the geometric mean of each person's importance estimates. The geometric mean is the nth root of the product of the estimates. Thus if three estimates are 0.1, 0.2, and 0.4, then the product is 0.1×0.2×0.4=0.008 and the geometric mean is the cube root of 0.008 which is 0.2. When a group is providing estimates, a good method is to vote on whether a suggested weight should be increased or decreased. The weight is satisfactory when an equal number of people want to raise and lower the value. This value is the median.

It is difficult for people to assign consistent weights to many factors. If asked to repeat the process, they may assign quite different weights each time. The Analytic Hierarchy Process, described in Appendix 4-B, provides a method for dealing with this problem. It breaks the evaluation process into a set of pairwise

Criteria	j	i	W_j	C_i	Student V_2	$W_j \sum C_i V_i$
Improved Administration	1		.30			
Effective use of info		1		.40	.90	.30x.40x.90=.108
Better quality info		2		.30	.90	.30x.30x.90=.081
Improved productivity		3		.10	.90	.30x.10x.90=.027
Better coordination		4		.20	.80	.30x.20x.80=.048
Improved Image	2		.50			
Faster response		1		.10	.95	.50x.10x.95=.048
Better students		2		.40	.90	.50x.40x.90=.180
Better public service		3		.25	.60	.50x.25x.60=.075
Employee morale		4		.25	.70	.50x.25x.70=.087
Net Cost Savings	3		.20	1.00	.60	.20x1.0x.60=.120
CF= $\sum W_j \sum C_i V_i$						.774

Figure 4-9

Criterion Function weights for the Student Records subsystem of the university example.

comparisons between factors to be weighted. These pairwise comparisons are then checked for consistency. Mathematical tools are provided for converting the pairwise comparisons into consistent weights.

Comparing Projects

The value of CF for each project gives a set of values that can be used to compare projects and identify the priority of each project. As the value of CF increases, the priority of the project increases.

Figure 4-10 illustrates a set of weights for the example problem. The sums at the bottom of each column are the relative weights for the project represented by the respective column. They are obtained by performing the computations of Figure 4-9 for each column. The results depend on the quality of the current system and the perceived needs of the users. A different university could use the same criteria and come up with a different ranking because of their different circumstances. Since the student records project in column V_2 has the highest weight of 0.774, it is the most important project and should be started first. It is used to generate the examples of detailed procedures in the rest of the text.

The Enterprise Modelling exercise is performed relatively infrequently. Now that it has been done for the university example, the results will be useful for a number of years. The model may need occasional revisions to reflect new operating procedures, but most of it will be true many years from now. The priorities specify the order in which major new systems will have to be implemented over the next few years. The priority list will be correct unless there is a major change in criteria or a major change in operating procedures.

Criteria	j	i	W_j	C_i	Planning V_1	Student V_2	Staff V_3	Admin V_4	Accounts V_5
Improved Administration	1		.30						
Effective use of info		1		.40	.70	.90	.70	.65	.35
Better quality info		2		.30	.80	.90	.70	.40	.20
Improved productivity		3		.10	.10	.90	.50	.30	.10
Better coordination		4		.20	.90	.80	.70	.40	.20
Improved Image	2		.50						
Faster response		1		.10	.60	.95	.20	.40	.10
Better students		2		.40	.40	.90	.30	.40	.10
Better public service		3		.25	.60	.60	.50	.90	.30
Employee morale		4		.25	.65	.70	.80	.75	.40
Net Cost Savings	3		.20	1.00	.30	.60	.80	.50	.10
CF= $\Sigma W_j \Sigma C_i V_i$					.539	.774	.597	.553	.208

Figure 4-10

Criterion Function for all projects in the university example.

		Buildings	Rooms	Equipment	Scholarships	Students	Referees	Programs	Courses	Sections	Meetings	Skills	Tasks	Job-Descriptions	Faculty	Staff	Positions	Subordinates	Grants	Departments	Sessions	Months	Transactions	Account-Months	Accounts	Customers	Supplies	Vendors
Planning	Analyse Demand				X	X		X	X	X					X													
	Budget Expenses					X			X							X			X	X					X	X	X	
	Enter Applications				X	X	X																					
	Aid Financially				X	X	X																					
Student	Register Students	X	X			X		X	X	X	X				X													
	Evaluate Students					X		X	X	X					X													
	Graduate Students					X		X	X	X																		
	Schedule Courses	X	X	X				X	X	X	X				X													
	Administer Program							X	X																			
Staff	Plan Manpower					X			X	X		X	X	X	X	X	X	X	X	X								
	Evaluate Personnel											X	X	X	X	X	X	X	X	X								
	Promote Employees											X	X	X	X	X	X	X										
Admin	Hire Staff													X	X	X		X										
	Apply for Grants														X			X	X									
	Manage Equipment	X	X	X														X										
	Manage Space	X	X	X														X										
	Control Waste	X	X	X											X	X		X								X		
	Administer Benefits														X	X		X							X			
	Retire Staff	X	X											X	X	X	X	X	X	X	X	X	X					
	Pay Suppliers																	X	X	X	X	X	X	X				X
	Budget Capital				X			X	X						X	X		X							X			
	Receive Orders																	X									X	X
Accounts	Order Supplies																	X	X	X	X	X	X	X			X	X
	Receive Payments																	X	X	X	X	X	X	X	X			
	Pay Employees													X	X	X		X	X	X	X	X	X	X	X			
	Construct Facilities	X	X	X														X	X	X	X	X	X	X			X	
	Invest Funds																	X	X	X	X	X						
	Maintain Facilities	X	X	X														X	X	X	X	X	X	X			X	
	Manage Supplies																	X	X	X	X	X	X				X	
	Administer Grants					X								X	X	X		X	X	X	X	X	X	X			X	X

Figure 4-11

The Student Subsystem has the highest priority in the university example.

The original Enterprise Model of Figure 3-11 has been narrowed down to a single project that can be implemented first. Figure 4-11 highlights the portion of the original model that has been selected for initial implementation. The other parts are implemented later in priority order. The analyst can now focus in more detail on the selected activities and data entities without having to consider the other activities. This converts an overwhelmingly complex system into a subsystem that is small enough to implement.

It will be easier to implement the next subsystems because some of the data analysis will have been completed for them. When the Staff subsystem is implemented, the Building, Courses, Sections, and Faculty entities will have been defined and will need little or no modification. By the time the Accounts subsystem is implemented, all the entities will be defined and only the activities and their related application programs will need to be defined.

CASE Tools for Setting Priorities

Most CASE tools do not address the issue of feasibility. Feasibility studies deal primarily with economic and organizational issues. The most common tool for economic analysis is a spreadsheet. Spreadsheets can summarize costs and benefits easily. They can easily recalculate an analysis to determine the effect of changing an assumption or a parameter.

Packages that perform the estimates and calculations needed in a Function Point Analysis are available from consultants, such as Software Productivity Research Inc., which sells a package called SPQR/20.[10]

Decision Support Software Inc. sells a program called *Expert Choice* to gather the data and perform Analytic Hierarchy Process calculations[7]. A number of consultants specialize in conducting studies and group process sessions to identify goals, objectives, and priorities.

The IEW Planning Workstation and Index Technology's Prism product both provide association matrices that can record the links between different characteristics of a system. These are useful for recording relationships between Critical Success Factors, critical assumptions, organizational responsibilities, projects, and sources of information. The matrices can be sorted by the properties recorded in them, such as priority.

Summary

This chapter showed how to evaluate the technical, economic, and organizational feasibility of a system design. The system can consist of existing subsystems, purchased packages, and newly developed programs. The major problem that arises with existing and purchased systems is that they have to be integrated into the architecture.

Technical feasibility involves hardware, software, and personnel. Hardware availability may make it difficult to implement some large systems on a single machine. In such a case a distributed system must be designed. Software selection involves evaluation of vendor stability, productivity features, portability, efficiency, and distributed database capabilities.

Personnel have to acquire new design skills and the ability to work in the new CASE environment. These skills are not that difficult to acquire, but people may resist change. They often prefer to continue doing what they have previously learned to do, rather than risk using new methods.

Financial feasibility involves tangible and intangible factors. The tangible costs for hardware and software are relatively easy to evaluate. The costs related to writing programs are harder to identify. Function Point Analysis can be helpful in estimating the cost of coding programs. CASE and DBMS environments can reduce costs significantly if experienced users participate, a single language is used, development teams are small, and the DBMS integrates the system. An alternate method of cost justification is to estimate overall savings based on either estimated Time Savings Times Salary (TSTS) or the Hedonic Method of estimating the value of the time released by the new system.

Intangible benefits and evaluation criteria can be identified by using Critical Success Factors (CSF), brainstorming, or the Nominal Group Process. The group method is usually easiest if the group shares common goals. If goals diverge significantly or if the group tends to be dominated by a few individuals, it may be more difficult to identify a consistent set of factors.

The factors can then be evaluated and ranked by using the Criterion Function or the Analytic Hierarchy Process (AHP). These methods assign weights to each factor and values to each project for each factor. The weighted sum of all the values determines the rank of each project.

All of this analysis is worthwhile only if the people in the organization have a desire to make the new system work. Without commitment by management and cooperation by staff, the system does not get implemented satisfactorily.

This chapter has focused on how to cost-justify the development of information systems. Some organizations are beginning to realize that information systems are so essential that their existence is mandatory in the same way that most people see a telephone in the office as mandatory. As with the telephone, the question is not whether the system should exist, but how to minimize the cost of the system. The emphasis is shifting from cost-justification to cost-management.

Keywords and Phrases

Analytic Hierarchy Process	Intangible Benefits
Brainstorming	Nominal Group Process
Criteria	Objectives
Criterion Function	Software
Critical Success Factors	SLOC
Goals	Tangible Benefits
Hardware	TSTS

Appendix 4-A: The Hedonic Method

Sassone's Hedonic Method[3,13,14] tries to determine the value of each kind of activity that an office worker performs. It assumes there is a hierarchy in the categories of work based on salary levels. Managers are paid more than professionals because they can do certain jobs that professionals cannot. Similarly professionals get paid more than support staff because they have additional skills. Everyone performs some mix of activities in their own category and the categories below them in the hierarchy. Their salary is some weighted average of the high value of professional work and the lower value of support functions.

When professionals perform support work like typing, their time is only worth as much as support staff doing the same work. The time spent doing purely professional activities must then be worth more than their average salary to compensate for the below average value of the clerical components. It is possible to calculate the value of each kind of activity implied by the hierarchy of tasks and the salary structure.

The first step in the analysis is to identify the categories of employees. Typically four to six categories are identified. Examples are management, specialized professional, routine professional, administrative, and clerical. We will use four in our example: managers, professionals, support staff, and non-productive. The non-productive category is used to identify time spent waiting for work, traveling, or searching for things.

The next step is to log the time spent on each category of activity by a sample of workers drawn from each category. The survey is performed for two day periods at staggered intervals so some unnoticed event does not bias the results. Participants are asked to record the category of work that they are doing every two hours during the study.

The activities identified in the TSTS method are not easy to translate into management, professional, and support tasks. For instance a manager can delegate some information-seeking tasks to support staff. Others cannot be delegated because clerical staff may not understand what to look for when very technical information is sought.

The aggregated results are summarized in Figure 4-12 along with the average hourly salary—including fringe benefits and direct overhead—of each category. The 29 in the first row tells us that managers spend an average of 29 percent of their time on professional tasks. We can use this table to construct a set of simultaneous equations that we can solve for V_c, the hourly value of each category of work. V_4, the value of non-productive time, is zero.

The equations to be solved are:

$$.30V_1 + .29V_2 + .23V_3 = 50$$
$$.02V_1 + .62V_2 + .24V_3 = 40$$
$$.00V_1 + .00V_2 + .86V_3 = 25$$

CATEGORY	MANAGER	PROFESSION	SUPPORT	NON-PROD	WAGE
	%	%	%	%	$/HR
BEFORE					
MANAGER	30	29	23	18	50
PROFESSIONAL	2	62	24	12	40
SUPPORT	0	0	86	14	25
AFTER					
MANAGER	35	35	20	10	
PROFESSIONAL	2	70	20	8	
SUPPORT	0	0	90	10	

4 Priorities

Figure 4-12

Allocation of percent of time spent in classes of office tasks.

They can be solved to get V_1 = \$95.88/Hr., V_2 = \$50.17/Hr., and V_3 = \$29.07/Hr. This tells us that managers are worth \$95.88 per hour when they are doing work that only managers can do. They are worth only \$29.07 per hour when doing work that support staff can do.

We can now compute the hourly benefit, B_c, of adjusting the work profile of an employee in category c. If we use T_{caa} and T_{cab} to refer to the fraction of time spent by employees of category c on work of category **a** **a**fter and **b**efore the new system, then the benefit due to the new system is:

$$B_c = \sum V_c(T_{caa} - T_{cab})$$

Thus $B_1 = 95.88(.35-.30) + 50.17(.35-.29) + 29.07(.20-.23) = 6.93$.

In the example, B_1 = \$6.93/Hr., B_2 = \$2.85/Hr., and B_3 = \$1.16/Hr.

If N_c employees of category **c** work H_c hours per year, then the total annual savings for all employees is:

$$S = \sum N_c H_c B_c$$

In the student records example, with one manager and seven support staff each working 2,000 hours per year, S = 1×2000×6.93 + 0×2000×2.85 + 7×2000×1.16 = \$30,100.

The value of \$30,100 means that if nobody is laid off, if the work reallocations occur as planned, and if there is new work available to be done of similar value to the work currently being done, then this new work done will have a value of \$30,100. This figure is not directly comparable to the figure obtained by the TSTS method since it is based on different assumptions.

Appendix 4-B: The Analytic Hierarchy Process

The Analytic Hierarchy Process (AHP) simplifies the estimation process by confining the estimates to pairwise comparisons. Participants find it easier to compare two things than to compare all members of a list. The rows of pairwise comparisons required for the example are illustrated in Figure 4-13. The first column of each matrix will have the same label as the first row, etc.

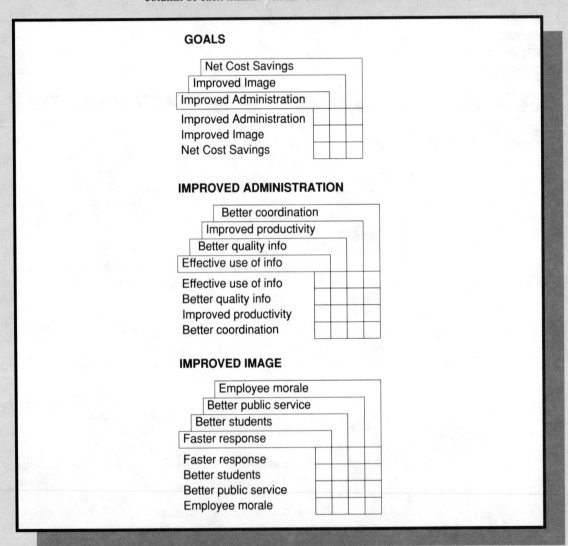

Figure 4-13

AHP matrices to be filled in for the university problem.

Participants are asked to rate each pair on the comparison scale shown in Figure 4-14. Either the verbal or the numeric comparison scales can be used. If the verbal scale on the left is used, it must be translated into the corresponding numeric scale on the right. The numeric value is placed into the corresponding cell of the comparison matrix in Figure 4-13. If the numeric scale is used, it is interpreted as a multiplier.

Thus, for the third matrix in the example, *better public service is moderately more important than faster response* means that *better public service is 3 times as important as faster response*. Thus a 3 is placed in the cell in row 3, column 1. Conversely, faster response is 1/3 as important as better public service. Thus 1/3 is placed in the cell in row 1, column 3.

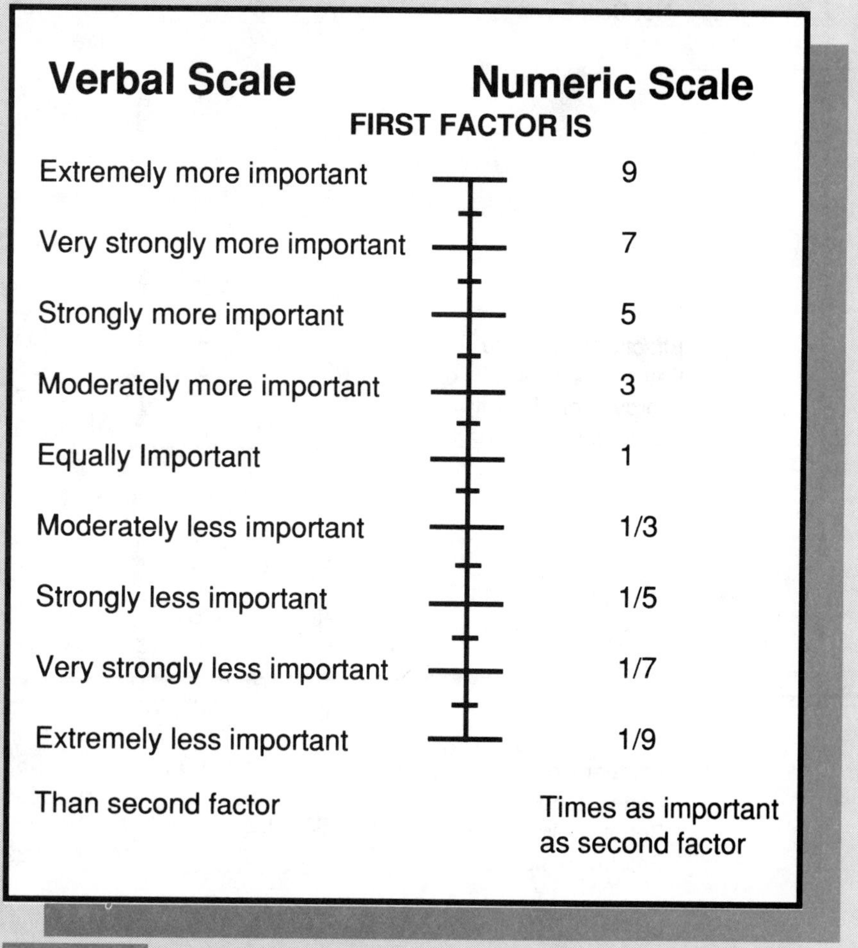

Verbal Scale   Numeric Scale
FIRST FACTOR IS

Verbal	Numeric
Extremely more important	9
Very strongly more important	7
Strongly more important	5
Moderately more important	3
Equally Important	1
Moderately less important	1/3
Strongly less important	1/5
Very strongly less important	1/7
Extremely less important	1/9
Than second factor	Times as important as second factor

Figure 4-14

Verbal and corresponding numeric scales for comparing criteria in an AHP evaluation.

	Improved Administration	Improved Image	Net Cost Savings	WEIGHTS	I.R.
Improved Administration	1	1/2	2	.297	.008
Improved Image	2	1	3	.539	
Net Cost Savings	1/2	1/3	1	.164	

	Effective use of info	Better quality info	Improved productivity	Better coordination		
Effective use of info	1	2	4	2	.435	.017
Better quality info	1/2	1	3	2	.286	
Improved productivity	1/4	1/3	1	1/2	.097	
Better coordination	1/2	1/2	2	1	.182	

	Faster response	Better students	Better public service	Employee morale		
Faster response	1	1/4	1/3	1/3	.089	.008
Better students	4	1	2	2	.434	
Better public service	3	1/2	1	1	.239	
Employee morale	3	1/2	1	1	.239	

Figure 4-15

Relative importances, criterion weights, and inconsistency ratios for the matrices in the university example.

Compute Column Sums

Improved Administration	1	1/2	2
Improved Image	2	1	3
Net Cost Savings	1/2	1/3	1
Column Sum	7/2	11/6	6

Divide by Column Sum

				Row Sum	Row Sum/3
Improved Administration	2/7	6/22	1/3	0.892	0.297
Improved Image	4/7	6/11	1/2	1.617	0.539
Net Cost Savings	1/7	6/33	1/6	0.491	0.164

To compute Inconsistency Ratio, multiply data by column weights

	.297x	.539x	.164x					Row Total
Improved Administration	1	1/2	2		.297	.270	.328	0.895
Improved Image	2	1	3	=	.594	.539	.492	1.625
Net Cost Savings	1/2	1/3	1		.149	.179	.164	0.492

Divide row sum by weights, subtract N, and compute 1/2 of average

0.895/0.297=3.013
1.625/0.539=3.015
0.492/0.164=3.000

$$\frac{(3.013-3)+(3.015-3)+(3-3)}{3} \times \frac{1}{2} = 0.00467$$

Divide by F that Corresponds to N in table below

N	1	2	3	4	5	6	7	8	9	10
F	0	0	.58	.90	1.12	1.24	1.32	1.41	1.45	1.49

Inconsistency Ratio=IR=0.00467/.58=0.008

Figure 4-16

Calculating criterion weights and inconsistency ratio for the goals matrix in the university example.

Only half of the cells in the comparison matrix, M, have to be evaluated since it is a reciprocal matrix. When $M_{i,j}$ is evaluated, we know that $M_{j,i}$ is $1/M_{i,j}$. The diagonal values, $M_{i,i}$, are all 1 because something is always 1 times as important as itself. The results of all comparisons are shown in Figure 4-15.

Each comparison matrix, M, is converted into a set of corresponding weights by computing the eigenvector of the matrix. This is a very complex calculation that requires a computer. Programs have been written in BASIC, FORTRAN, and APL to perform this calculation.[11] A microcomputer package called EX-PERT CHOICE[7] is available to perform all the AHP calculations. The details of the calculations are explained by Saaty.[11,12]

An approximate solution can be obtained by normalizing the matrix and standardizing the row sums. The calculation is performed for the objectives matrix in Figure 4-16. The procedure consists of:

● Compute the sum of each column.
● Divide each element by its column sum.
● Compute the sum of each row in the new matrix.
● Compute the average value in each row. This gives the weight, or priority vector, corresponding to the factor in each row.
● Compute IR, the Inconsistency Ratio by:
  • Multiply each value in a column by its corresponding weight.

Improved Administration	.297x	
Effective use of info	.435	= .129
Better quality info	.286	= .085
Improved productivity	.097	= .029
Better coordination	.182	= .054
Improved Image	.539x	
Faster response	.089	= .048
Better students	.433	= .233
Better public service	.239	= .129
Employee morale	.239	= .129
Net Cost Savings	.164x1.000	= .164
Total	1.000	1.000

Figure 4-17
Products of the weights for the objectives and the criteria identified by AHP in the university example.

- Compute the total of each row and divide this row total by the corresponding weight.
- Subtract N, the number of rows in the matrix, from this answer, compute the average of the remainders, and divide by 2. Divide this result by a factor obtained from the table in Figure 4-16. This adjusts for the ratio that would be expected if priorities were assigned randomly.

If IR<0.10 then the matrix is consistent and the weights computed from it can be used. If IR>0.10 then the matrix should be examined for inconsistent priorities. If B is 2 times as important as A and C is 3 times as important as B, then C should be 2x3=6 times as important as A. Significant deviations from this relationship produce a high value of IR and indicate that some of the evaluations are in error. One of the strengths of the AHP method is that such inconsistencies can be detected.

The weights for each matrix can be combined in the same way that they were combined in the Criterion Function. Figure 4-17 shows the product of the weights for each factor. Small products indicate unimportant factors that could be eliminated from consideration. Eliminating them will reduce the number of comparisons needed in the next stage of analysis. In this example, Improved Productivity has a combined weight of only 0.029 so it contributes only 2.9 percent to the final total and can safely be eliminated. It may also be possible to eliminate better coordination and faster response from the analysis.

The next stage is to compare each of the 5 projects. This is done once for each of the factors in the analysis. If we eliminate improved productivity, better coordination, and faster response, there will still be six factors to evaluate. These are effective use, better quality, better students, better service, employee morale, and net cost savings. Note that net cost savings is considered at this level because it was not subdivided into other factors.

At this final stage, six 5x5 tables of priorities have to be generated and the calculations of Figure 4-16 must be repeated for each table. The weights on each of the six criteria assigned to each of the five projects are summed to obtain the priorities of each project.

An alternative is to use the weights derived from this process in the Criterion Function in Figure 4-13 instead of the intuitively derived weights. The Criterion Function can then be used for the final evaluation. The methods are interchangeable in that both work hierarchically and both produce weights at several levels. Both methods can be extended to more levels of refinement. The weights from the two methods are not necessarily the same.

The AHP method is superior in that it provides a measure of inconsistency and it requires that only 2 factors be compared at any time. On the other hand it involves many calculations. The AHP method is relatively easy if a computer program is available to do the calculations[7].

4
Priorities

Review Questions

1. Define each of the items in the list of keywords and phrases.
2. Compare the benefits and problems of implementing new systems using existing systems, new systems, and purchased systems.
3. What are the three kinds of feasibility that need to be considered in implementing a new system?
4. What factors should be considered in choosing a software vendor for a purchased system?
5. What changes impact employees when a 4GL system is constructed to replace a 3GL system?
6. Identify the steps in selecting the highest priority project for implementation.
7. Identify the main tangible costs that must be accounted for in the implementation of a new system.
8. What conditions must occur if the expected efficiencies of 4GL techniques are to be achieved in the development process?
9. Name three ways of identifying the criteria for evaluation of new projects.

Problems

1. Bud Furd is planning to build a computerized General Ledger System that operates on a microcomputer. He expects to sell it to small consulting firms who need specialized features to account for payroll and accounts receivable. The system must have a main menu that gives access to three submenus for General Ledger, Accounts Receivable, and Payroll commands. Each of these has commands that lead to the final screens listed below.

General Ledger

Enter Ledger Entries
Enter Journal Entries
Print Balance Sheet
Print Income Statement
Print Trial Balance
Export Spreadsheet

Accounts Receivable

Enter Ledger Entries
Enter Journal Entries
Print Invoices

Payroll

Enter Ledger Entries
Enter Journal Entries
Print Payroll Checks
Print Tax Statements

In addition, the system must produce printed balance sheets, income statements, trial balances, customer lists, invoices, employee lists, payroll checks, tax payments, and tax statements. An export command transfers balance sheet and income statement data in a format suitable for use by spreadsheet programs.

The four menu screens and all screens that initiate reports are expected to be simple to design. Each report is initiated by a screen that asks the user for various parameters. The balance sheet, income statement, and trial balance reports and all journal and ledger entry screens require complex calculations and formats.

All of the data for the accounts, transactions, customers, sales, payments, and employees are to be stored in six files of average complexity.

Bud expects to sell the package on the basis of speed, end-user efficiency, and the ease and convenience of on-line data entry. The projected market is heavy users of a single stand-alone microcomputer. The users are technically unsophisticated in both accounting and computer technology. The package must be easy to install, operate, and update whenever new tax laws are implemented.

Bud has worked for a software development firm that uses Function Point Analysis to evaluate programmer efficiency. He estimates that it takes 20 hours of programing for each function point on this project, using the 3GL language that he is familiar with.

Calculate the number of function points in this project and estimate the number of hours needed to complete programming of the system.

2. Jean E. Alogy has designed a program to keep track of family trees. She wants to program it and license it to Brother Bond, a software distributor, that specializes in home computer applications such as games, financial programs, and recipe organizers.

Jean has identified the following functions that must be performed by the package. Each is selected from the main menu and each requires a number of inputs to enter data or define report parameters.

- **Enter Data.** This is a very complex screen because it has to record parent, child, and marriage relationships to other entries. It is used to insert, update, delete and view all records.
- **Print Ancestor Tree.** This report has a complex tree diagram format and requires a difficult recursive search algorithm.
- **Print Descendant Report.** This report has a simple format, but requires a complex recursive search algorithm.
- **Print Descendant Tree.** This report has a complex tree diagram format and requires a difficult recursive search algorithm.
- **Print Verification Forms.** These forms are used to request data verification from family members. They are simple in format, but

individual forms have to be organized into family groups for convenient mailing.

- **Print Customized Report.** This command allows users to select individual data fields so that they can generate special reports such as lists of birthdays or mailing labels. The options are simple and the report is of average complexity.
- **Import GEDCOM Standard Files.** This command gets data from other programs that follow the GEDCOM standard. The translation to and from the GEDCOM standard is quite simple.
- **Export GEDCOM Standard Files.** This command exports data to other programs that follow the GEDCOM standard.
- **Set Program Parameters.** This is a simple screen that sets several parameters that govern the format and data fields that are used by other screens and reports.

The program must run on two different kinds of microcomputers. Since it is intended for home use on isolated machines with relatively small files, performance is not a serious concern. However, the screens must be simple to use and have an appealing format. The three files have complex validation rules to ensure that relationships are properly maintained.

Assuming that Jean can program one function point every ten hours, how long will it take Jean to develop this package?

3. Ace Brokerage Co. (ABC) is an insurance broker specializing in home and auto insurance in a large city. Much of the work in the office consists of processing claims and sending out quotations, bills, and policies. Most of these tasks are quite standardized, but the current manual system involves a great deal of typing and filing.

Ivan Titall, the office manager, has been approached by a vendor from a computer software company that produces a program designed to support the sale and processing of home, auto, and fire insurance. Ivan has asked for a quotation on a system that would serve the needs of the sales manager, the claims manager, the office manager, the 8 sales staff and the 9 support staff in the company. The quoted price was as follows:

Minicomputer	$100,000
Terminals 20×2,000=	40,000
Software	50,000
Software maintenance	10,000/year
Hardware maintenance	12,000/year
Staff and operator training	10,000

Ivan thinks that the system would save about 10 percent of the managers' time, 15 percent of the sales staff time and 35 percent of the support staff time. Managers are paid an average of $70,000 per year including benefits, sales staff average $50,000 per year, and support staff average $25,000 per year. The president of ABC will not consider projects in which savings are less than costs over the first two years.

a. Assuming that ABC is not able to increase business significantly, but it is able to release full-time personnel in whole positions, should ABC install the computer system?

b. Assume that ABC is unable to increase their staff because of office space limitations. It is able to earn a net profit of $100,000 per year for each extra sales person, or equivalent, available through improved procedures or new technology. This is the same net revenue as that generated by current sales staff. The extra sales require support staff in the same proportion as previous sales. Should ABC invest in the computer system?

c. What intangible benefits would you expect the new computer system to produce?

4. Hugh R. Rich, the Director of Information Services for the Fantastic Financial Future Corp. is considering phasing in the replacement of the existing computer programs with new applications based on a 4GL Data Base Management System over the next five years. There are three possible options: no change, a DBMS from the hardware vendor, and a DBMS from an independent vendor.

Hugh and his staff have identified three major goals that any new system must achieve. These are Net Savings, Rapid Development, and Service. Service consists of Rapid Access to data, Better Decisions from management, and Fewer Complaints from users. Net Savings are as important as Rapid Development and Service combined. Rapid Development is two-thirds as important as Service. Among the service factors: Rapid Access and Better Decisions are equally important, and Fewer Complaints is twice as important as Rapid Access.

The three options were rated on each of the criteria as shown in the following table. Net Savings are present values in millions of dollars over the life of the project. The non-financial factors are rated on a ten point scale ranging from 0=no improvement to 10=best possible.

Option	No Change	Hardware Vendor	Independent Vendor
Net Savings	2	1	0
Rapid Development	0	5	10
Better Decisions	0	7	10
Rapid Access	0	5	10
Fewer Complaints	0	10	10

Use the Criterion Function to determine the option that is most preferred. Show your calculations.

5. In addition to the information in Question 4, the following information is available about the importance of the criteria. Fewer Complaints are 3 times as important as Better Decisions. Net Savings are twice as important as Better Service. Net Savings are twice as important as Rapid Development.

    Calculate the weights using the AHP method. Are the estimates consistent?

6. Annie Bodie is trying to determine the optimal order in which to attempt the questions in a Systems Analysis examination. Annie has the following three criteria for determining the priority of a question:
   • **Value** in marks.
   • **Time** it will take to answer the question.
   • **Certainty** about getting the correct answer.

    The following information applies to the four questions in the examination.

Question	Value	Time	Certainty
1	30	30	.65
2	10	5	.90
3	20	25	.80
4	40	30	.70

Annie thinks that the value of the question is as important as time and certainty combined. She thinks that time and certainty are of equal importance. Develop a criterion Function to determine the order in which the questions should be answered.

References

1. Albrecht, A. and John Gaffney Jr., "Software Function, Source Lines of Code, and Development Effort Prediction: A Software Science Validation", *IEEE Transactions on Software Engineering,* Nov. 1983, pp. 639-648.

2. Canning Publications Inc., "A Programmer Productivity Controversy", *EDP Analyzer,* Vol. 24, No. 1, Jan. 1986.

3. Canning Publications Inc., "The New Economics of Computing", *EDP Analyzer,* Vol. 25, No. 9, Sept. 1987.

4. Clark, Jon D. and Arnold Reisman, *Computer System Selection: An Integrated Approach,* Praeger, 1981, 221 pp.

5. Codd, E. F., "Is Your DBMS Really Relational?", *Computerworld*, October 14, 1985 and "Does your DBMS Run by the Rules?", *Computerworld*, October 21, 1985, pp. 49-60.

6. Data General Corporation, *Executive Guide to Estimating Office Automation Benefits,* Data General Corporation, Westboro, MA, 1984.

7. Decision Support Software Inc., *Expert Choice,* 1300 Vincent Place, McLean, Virginia, 22101.

8. Dreger, J. B., *Function Point Analysis,* Prentice-Hall, Inc., 1989.

9. Henderson, John C., John E. Rockart, and John G. Sifonis, "Integrating Management Support Systems into Strategic Information Systems Planning", *Journal of Management Information Systems,* Vol. 4 No. 1, Summer 1987, pp. 6-23.

10. Jones, Capers, *Programming Productivity,* McGraw-Hill, 1986, 280 pp.

11. Saaty, Thomas L., *The Analytic Hierarchy Process,* McGraw-Hill, 1980, 287 pp.

12. Saaty, Thomas L., *Decision Making for Leaders, Lifetime Learning Publications, 1982, 291 pp.*

13. Sassone, Peter G., "Cost-Benefit Methodology for Office Systems", *ACM Transactions on Office Information Systems,* Vol. 5, No. 3, July 1987, pp. 273-289.

14. Sassone, Peter G. and A. Perry Schwartz, "Cost-Justifying OA", *Datamation,* February 15, 1986, pp. 83-88.

15. Shoval, Peretz and Yaacov Lugasi, "Models for Computer System Evaluation and Selection", *Information and Management*, Vol. 12, No. 3, March 1987, pp. 117-129.

4
Priorities

Section II

Detailed Database Design

	DATABASE (WHAT)	PROGRAMS (HOW)	BENEFITS (WHY)	NETWORK (WHERE)	REAL TIME (WHEN)	SKILLS (WHO)
USER CONCEPT	Entity Relationship	Activity	Intangible Benefit	Map		Organization Design
DESIGNER CONCEPT	E-R Diagram	A-E Diagram	AHP	Network		Skills Responsibility
USER DETAIL	Forms Screens	Processes Data	Tangible Benefit	Work Volume	Discrete Events	Transition Training
DESIGNER DETAIL	EER Diagram	Data Flow Diagrams	Benefit-Cost	Partition	Transition Diagrams	Methodology Tools
BUILDER CONCEPT	Normal Form Relations	Structure Chart	Function Points	System Architecture	Specifications	Learning
BUILDER DETAIL	Files	Screens Specifications	Costs	Network Specs	Interfaces	4GL CASE

The enterprise model has been completed. The model has been divided into major modules and the order in which these modules should be converted, or implemented, has been identified. Now the database and the applications in each module must be implemented. This section concentrates on the design of the data inputs to the system. Section III deals with the design of the processes performed by the system.

The Entity-Relationship model provides a rough framework for the database. Now the detailed design of each entity is elaborated. This involves identifying the attributes of each entity and the integrity constraints that must be applied to all transaction records about the entities.

The entities and attributes are used to define files which are immediately entered into the chosen DBMS. These can be used to define screens for inserts, updates, and deletions of records. After screens are developed, it is possible to enter data and perform ad hoc queries. This allows analysts to test the screens and data using a prototyping methodology. Thus all input and file maintenance will be defined before concentrating on building the batch applications which modify the database.

This section on the design of the database is divided into two chapters. They deal with the user's view of the data and the designer's transformation of the information obtained from the user's view.

Chapter 5 uses the Extended Entity-Relationship model to determine what analysts need to know about the semantic and structural properties of the data. This allows them to design appropriate integrity controls that insure that the data are correct and meaningful. This model is then transformed into a relational data model for implementation. The analyst uses existing forms and files to get a preliminary design for the database. Group processes, like Joint Application Design, are used to identify the detailed data elements that are required in each file.

Chapter 6 shows how to convert the Extended Entity-Relationship model into a relational file structure and implement it in the SQL language. The normalization process is used as a check on the design to make sure that the database does not have redundant data, update anomalies, or incorrect implied meanings. If the previous work was done well, this should be relatively simple and should reveal few errors. The data model has three levels: conceptual, logical, and physical.

Chapter 5

Data Requirements

	DATABASE (WHAT)	PROGRAMS (HOW)	BENEFITS (WHY)	NETWORK (WHERE)	REAL TIME (WHEN)	SKILLS (WHO)
USER CONCEPT	Entity Relationship	Activity	Intangible Benefit	Map		Organization Design
DESIGNER CONCEPT	E-R Diagram	A-E Diagram	AHP	Network		Skills Responsibility
USER DETAIL	Forms Screens	Processes Data	Tangible Benefit	Work Volume	Discrete Events	Transition Training
DESIGNER DETAIL	EER Diagram	Data Flow Diagrams	Benefit-Cost	Partition	Transition Diagrams	Methodology Tools
BUILDER CONCEPT	Normal Form Relations	Structure Chart	Function Points	System Architecture	Specifications	Learning
BUILDER DETAIL	Files	Screens Specifications	Costs	Network Specs	Interfaces	4GL CASE

Objectives

The previous chapters generated an enterprise model that provides a high level view of all the data and activities in the organization. Methods were developed to subdivide the data entities into clusters and to subdivide the activities into projects. Tangible and intangible benefits were used to set priorities and identify the order in which projects will be implemented.

The next six chapters focus on the single project that was identified as having the highest priority for implementation. The methods in these chapters can be applied to each of the projects as they become the top priority for implementation. Only a single project is considered at a time so a project can be implemented within a reasonable time. It will not be confused with the largely unrelated details of other projects.

Previous chapters determined the best way of splitting a large system into smaller projects. Small systems may begin at this stage without going through the enterprise analysis of the previous chapters. The Entity-Relationship Model is still the starting point for a data centered system that stores data needed by all projects.

A magnifying glass is now applied to the selected project to produce a detailed design of the part of the total database that is needed by this project. When the magnifying glass is applied to the Entity-Relationship Model, it reveals more detail about both the entities and the relationships. The difference between the previous chapters and the next chapters is like the difference between a budget estimate for a construction project and a detailed bill of materials.

In this chapter you will learn how to:

- **Model** a database to include all necessary information in a form that can later be mapped into a physical database. The model precedes identification so the analyst will know what questions to ask.

- **Identify** data from forms, files, and text that are available and used in the organization. These data will serve the current project and any other projects that need the same data.

- **Verify** that the model is complete and correct using interviews, group design sessions, and tests.

The Extended Entity-Relationship Model

Up to now simple definitions of entities and relationships have been used. These definitions have been adequate for developing an Enterprise Model. Now they are extended to provide analysts with ways to document the attributes of each entity and the semantic meaning of the relationships.

With these extensions, organizational rules about the structure of the data can be documented. These rules, in turn, document constraints on the database. The constraints provide integrity rules that can be enforced to prevent the introduction of incorrect data into the files. In the next chapter, these detailed attributes and organizational rules are used to implement a database that contains all necessary data. It has no duplication and minimal chances of entering erroneous data.

Entities and relationships are now reviewed and extended to include the details that are needed before a full database definition can be created. This chapter defines the logical content of the database. The next chapter establishes the physical form of that information.

Entities

The following characteristics of entities have been used.
- They are the **primary things** about which an organization records data.
- They have unique **names** that are nouns.
- They have a **primary key** that uniquely identifies each entity occurrence.
- They have some **attributes** that need to be recorded.
- They must have **at least one relationship**.
- They can be divided into independent **kernel** entities and **characteristic** entities that describe kernel entities.
- The model must represent **every entity** used in the organization.

Up to now, only the name and key of each entity have been used in analysis. A detailed design needs a rigorous definition of an attribute, a primary key, alternate keys, foreign keys, attribute types, attribute widths, and identification of whether an attribute is allowed to have a null value.

Now these details are recorded for each entity. It is not practical to use a graphic technique for this task. The number of properties that must be recorded makes the results very complex and confusing. Instead, the required information is recorded in a table. Think of the table as the contents of the entity box that can be seen if the box is magnified enough to see what is inside.

Figure 5-1 shows part of the description of the STUDENTS entity. Each row describes a single attribute of the entity. Each column describes a specific property of the attribute. The columns describe meta-attributes—attributes of the attributes of the entity. Two of the properties, type and width, are not needed until physical file design begins. They are defined here for convenience.
- **Attribute.** An attribute is an elementary item of recordable data that cannot be further subdivided into meaningful data items. This column contains the name

of the attribute. It is also sometimes called a field or a descriptor. STUDENT_ID, SURNAME, and CITY are some names of attributes in the STUDENTS entity in Figure 5-1.

Some people find it difficult to distinguish an attribute from an entity. An attribute has two distinguishing features:

- **Atomic fact.** An attribute cannot have attributes of its own. It cannot be broken down and described further by other descriptors. The distinction is that an entity can be analyzed into several attributes or characteristic entities, but an attribute cannot be analyzed into any finer details.
- **Single value.** An attribute cannot have more than one value for any single entity occurrence. Anytime something has more than one value for the same entity occurrence, a new characteristic entity must be created to contain the multiple values. Thus, Highest Degree is an attribute of a Person, but Degrees is a characteristic entity because a person can have more than one degree.

The distinction between an attribute and an entity sometimes depends on the circumstances and nature of the database. In most systems, Persons is an entity with an Address, a Phone_No, and several other attributes. At the telephone company, Phone_No may be an entity with an Address, a Person (client), and several other attributes. Whether Persons or Phone_No is the entity depends on the point of view of the users. Most organizations are more interested in people than in phone numbers, so they make Persons the entity. At a telephone company, the phone numbers are the unique things at the core of their business, so they relate all other information to them. If they are equally important, two entities may be created with a 1:1 relationship between them, provided that each has other attributes.

- **Primary Key.** This attribute is used to identify uniquely each occurrence of an entity. This is often an identification number or code. The key or keys are identified by an X in the Primary Key column. STUDENT_ID is the primary key for the STUDENTS entity. A primary key has the following properties:

Figure 5-1

Decomposition of the STUDENTS entity.

ENTITY_____STUDENTS_____

ATTRIBUTE	PRIMARY KEY	FOREIGN KEY	NULL OK	TYPE	WIDTH
STUDENT_ID	X			ID	9
SURNAME<1>				CHARACTER	20
FIRSTNAME<1>				CHARACTER	20
STREET			X	CHARACTER	30
CITY			X	CHARACTER	20
PHONE_NO			X	PHONE	15
PROGRAM_ID		X		ID	9

5

EER Model

- **It uniquely identifies** one occurrence of an entity.
- **It never changes** after being assigned to an entity occurrence.
- **Never has a null** or missing value. A null value is not unique and cannot be used to cross-reference to other entities.
- **Sometimes more than one attribute** is needed to create a unique key. If the key is a single attribute, it is called an **atomic key**. Multiple attributes used as a primary key are called a **compound key** or also a **concatenated key**. No subset of the compound key is sufficient to identify every entity occurrence uniquely. If there is a choice of more than one compound key, then the one with fewest attributes is usually the best choice, unless the longer one is more commonly used in other entities or more easily remembered by the users.
- **Dataless** keys, like a student number, are preferred. Dataless keys are not subject to change in the way that keys made up of data items often do. For instance, a name may change due to marriage, legal name change, or use of a stage name or alias.

- **Alternate Key.** Sometimes there is a choice of identifiers. A student might be identified by STUDENT_ID or by name if all names can be guaranteed to be unique. Often the alternate key is used because the requestor may not know the student's identification code. Also the analyst may not have decided, at this early stage, which of several possible keys to use as an identifier. The alternate keys are identified by a number, in brackets, after the attribute name. All attributes with the same number are part of the same compound key. Thus SURNAME and FIRSTNAME together form the first alternate key in the example.

- **Foreign Key.** A foreign key is used to create a link with another entity. The primary key of one entity is also used as a foreign key in another entity to provide a logical link between the two entities. They are identified by an X in the Foreign Key column. PROGRAM_ID is a foreign key that links STUDENTS to PROGRAMS in the example.

- **Null OK.** This property is used to indicate whether this attribute can ever have a null value. A null value occurs if the attribute does not exist for some occurrences of an entity or if it exists but is not known at the time the entity occurrence is recorded. Primary keys cannot have a null value because the entity occurrence would be unidentified, and therefore unlocatable. Alternate keys should not have a null value for the same reason. Foreign keys can have a null value if the relationship that they map is optional (optionality is defined in the next section). In the example, STREET, CITY, and PHONE can have null values, but the other attributes cannot.

- **Type.** Many attributes, such as dates, are of the same generic type. If all dates are given the same form and structure, it is much easier to calculate time intervals or compare dates in different files. Examples of generic data types are: Date, Character, IDentification Code, Money, Name, Percent, Phone Number, Postal Code, and Time. This item is not required until the physical design stage. However, it is convenient to gather the information while the other items above are being gathered. In the example, SURNAME is of type Character and STUDENT_ID is of type ID.

- **Width.** Many of the data types have a width associated with them. This is the maximum number of characters recorded for alphabetic attributes or the maximum number of digits recorded for numeric attributes. Space is usually included for decimal points, plus or minus signs, dashes in phone numbers, and other special characters. Again this item is not required until the physical design stage, but may be conveniently available during the logical analysis. STUDENT_ID, in the example, has a width of 9 characters.

Kernel and Characteristic Entities

Entities can be arranged into hierarchies. The highest one in a hierarchy is called a kernel entity. It has a unique identity that does not depend on the existence of any other entity. It usually has a single atomic key to identify it.

A characteristic entity is one that is below a kernel entity in the hierarchy. It records one or more repeating characteristics of the kernel entity. Thus it cannot exist without the corresponding kernel entity. Without the kernel, it has nothing to describe. It inherits the attributes of the kernel entity. Thus the attributes of the kernel entity COURSES are also the attributes of its characteristic entity SECTIONS. The key attribute of the kernel is normally part of the key of the characteristic entity type. Thus COURSE_ID is part of the key of SECTIONS.

Naming Attributes

There are several guidelines that should be followed in naming entities and attributes. These guidelines cover length, capitalization, compound names, abbreviations, and blanks.

- **Length.** The maximum length of a name is usually determined by the target implementation environment or the CASE tool being used. The name used in analysis and design must be translated into an implementation language eventually. Many CASE tools automatically generate database definitions and code from design specifications. It is best to use the same name in design, database definitions, and programs to prevent confusion.
- **Capitalization.** Capital letters should be used for all names, unless prohibited in the target implementation language. Capital letters stand out in documentation, so names are easy to locate. Many languages require capital letters in names. A mixture of capital and lower case letters confuses people and leads to errors in programs or database queries.
- **Compound names.** The name should reflect the meaning of the entity or attribute. Often a compound name such as ADDRESS_STUDENT is required to distinguish the attribute from ADDRESS_FACULTY. The words should appear in hierarchical order, from most important to least important. This is the same convention that is used in preparing an index for a book. The general form of such a name is Noun_Qualifier, where the noun is the broadest category and the qualifier narrows its scope. The name of the entity is often the qualifier. Thus the STUDENTS entity would contain NAME_STUDENT and ADDRESS_STUDENT. If the names have to be truncated, they are still

different, rather than all being truncated to STUDENT. If they are sorted, then all attributes of the same type, like ADDRESS, appear together. The entity name is often included as part of the key name, as in STUDENT_ID.

- **Abbreviations.** Abbreviations allow more descriptive names within the limited length of a name. Abbreviations also make it harder for users to remember the name of the attribute when they are using a query language. If abbreviations are used, they should come from a standard table of abbreviations for consistency and they should follow standard rules. A common rule is to use the first three non-vowels of a word as the abbreviation, as in MRK for MARKETING. Avoid including codes for projects and programs in the name. These become meaningless when the data are shared with other applications.
- **Blanks.** Most implementation languages do not allow blanks within a name. Most languages do allow an underscore in a name, so blanks can be replaced by underscores using the convention in this book. Some code generators automatically replace blanks with underscores when they generate code. Periods and dashes should be avoided since they often have special meanings.

Relationships

Up to now, the following characteristics of relationships have been used.
- They record the **linkages** between entities.
- They have **names** that are verbs.
- They have **cardinalities** of 1:1, 1:N, or M:N.
- They have **no attributes.**

These properties make it possible to make simple semantic statements about the linkage between two entities. An extended definition of relationships allows richer statements about the relationship between two entities. The Entity-Relationship Model allows statements about *which* entities are related. The Extended Entity-Relationship Model also allows statements about *how* these entities are related. Later these statements are translated into rules that can be enforced in the database.

The definition of a relationship needs to be extended to allow for optionality, existence dependency, and abstractions.[5,7] Optionality determines whether the linked entities must always be linked. Existence dependency determines whether the existence of an entity occurrence depends on the existence of an occurrence of another entity. Abstractions permit the definition of a hierarchy of entities with rules about how the levels of the hierarchy are related. These extensions define the Extended Entity-Relationship (EER) Model. The STUDENTS application of the university example is used for most of the illustrations. The notation is illustrated in Figure 5-2.

Optionality

A relationship may be mandatory or optional. If the relationship between entities A and B is mandatory, then each instance of A must correspond to an

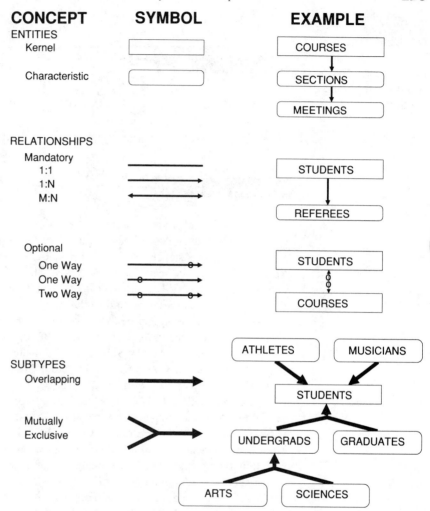

Figure 5-2
Notation for the Extended Entity-Relationship Model.

instance of B. If it is optional, then some instance of A can be recorded that has no relationship to any instance of B.

As an example, the relationship between STUDENTS and COURSES in Figure 5-2 is optional in both directions. When a student is first accepted by a university, the student is not yet enrolled in any courses. Similarly, a proposed new course exists before any students have had a chance to enroll in it. On the other hand the relationship between STUDENTS and REFEREES is mandatory. A student is not accepted without letters from referees and a referee is of no interest unless related to a student. They must come together as a set. Optional relationships are symbolized by a letter O across the relationship arrow at the end nearest to the entity which does not need to have a relationship.

Figure 5-3

Translating Entity-
Relationship Diagrams
into English sentences
about the meaning of
the data.

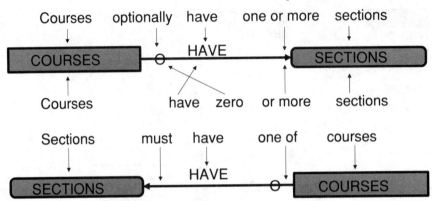

Optionality is a property defined at each end of the relationship line. Optionality can occur in both directions, in either direction, or in neither direction. For example, an instance of COURSES can exist without any corresponding SECTIONS being defined for it. However, SECTIONS cannot exist without corresponding COURSES to belong to. This is symbolized by placing the optional O at the COURSES end of the relationship arrow.

The graphic notation can be translated into an English sentence as shown in Figure 5-3. When read in the forward direction, the example means "COURSES optionally HAVE one or many SECTIONS." An alternate way of interpreting the diagram is to read the O as a zero in the cardinality. Then the English equivalent is "COURSES HAVE zero or many SECTIONS."

The graphic notation can also be read in reverse. The diagram in the bottom part of Figure 5-3 is flipped to make it easier to read. Then the English statement is "SECTIONS must HAVE one of COURSES." The absence of an O is translated as the mandatory *must*. The O does not change the cardinality of one in this direction. It only applies to the cardinality diagram at the opposite end.

Another way of thinking of optionality is to think of it as a new kind of cardinality where both the lower and upper limit are specified. Thus a cardinality of 0,1:1,N implies that the left entity is optional because it can have 0 or 1 instances, but the right entity is mandatory because it must have at least 1 instance. Similarly, 0,1:0,1 implies that 0 or 1 occurrences on the left can be related to 0 or 1 occurrence on the right. Thus both entities are optional.

Existence
Dependency

Existence dependency is a way of describing the relationship between characteristic entities and kernel entities. It occurs when three conditions are satisfied.

● The existence of an entity depends on the existence of a parent entity.
● The relationship of the characteristic entity to its kernel entity is mandatory.
● The characteristic entity inherits the identification keys of its kernel entity.

In Figure 5-2, SECTIONS is existence dependent on COURSES. A section cannot exist without first having a course to belong to. However, a course can exist for which no sections have yet been scheduled. In the same way, MEET-INGS is also existence dependent on SECTIONS.

The relationship is optional, but the optionality has a direction. Courses can exist without sections but sections cannot exist without corresponding courses. This relationship is symbolized by drawing COURSES, the kernel entity, in a rectangular box. SECTIONS and MEETINGS, the characteristic entities, are drawn in rectangular boxes with rounded corners. These characteristic entities usually store repeating details about the kernel entity.

The optionality notation could be used to describe this situation. However, it is convenient to add a notation for characteristic entities.

Abstractions

An entity can be viewed at different levels of abstraction. Undergraduates and graduates both are kinds of students. Students and employees both are kinds of people. People and companies both are kinds of payees to the payment system. Different kinds of data are usually stored about these entities when different levels of abstraction are appropriate. For instance, every student belongs to a college, but not all persons necessarily belong to a college.

The more specific entities inherit the properties of the more abstract entities. Undergraduate students have the same name as they would have if they were any other kind of student. Students have the same name as they would have if they were employees. Thus, name is a property of a person and is inherited by the more specific entities, like student or undergraduate.

Specific entities can be collected into **subtypes** that share common properties with the more general entity, which is called a **supertype**. There are two kinds of subtypes: **overlapping subtypes** and **mutually exclusive subtypes**. The supertype and the subtype entities are usually identified by the same primary key.

Overlapping Subtypes

Overlapping subtypes occur when the supertype entity can describe more than one of the specific entities at the same time. Students can be musicians or athletes or both or neither. In all cases they still have the same name and college. Different data may be recorded depending on whether they are musicians or athletes. Musicians have an instrument that they play. Athletes have a sport and maybe a position. All data are required for students who are both musicians and athletes. The example in Figure 5-2 illustrates these relationships.

The relationship between the entities is that the subtype entity IS_PART_OF the supertype. Thus, musicians IS_PART_OF students. There may be other parts to the description of the students. It is also possible that musician IS_PART_OF orchestra or that athlete IS_PART_OF team. In this case, the individuals are generalized into a supertype called an orchestra or a team. This is why an overlapping subtype is sometimes called an aggregation abstraction.

Subtype relationships are symbolized with thick arrows pointing to the supertype object. Overlapping subtypes have separate arrows with the arrowhead pointing to their supertype entity. It does not symbolize a 1:N relationship be-

5
EER Model

cause the relationships are all 1:1. Overlapping subtypes all have an optional relationship to the supertype because it is not known how many of the subtype entities, if any, the supertype entity occurrence participates in. Subtypes often exhibit existence dependency on the supertype entity.

Mutually exclusive subtypes occur when the supertype entity must be one, and only one, of the subtype entities. STUDENTS must be either UNDER-GRADUATES or GRADUATES. They cannot be both, so these subtypes are mutually exclusive. If they are UNDERGRADUATES, they may be either ARTS majors or SCIENCES majors, assuming that only one major is allowed. Again these subtypes are mutually exclusive. The example in Figure 5-2 illustrates these relationships.

A mutually exclusive subtype is sometimes called a generalization abstraction. The relationship between the entities is that the subtype entity IS_A supertype entity. Thus, undergraduate IS_A student. The mutually exclusive subtypes can co-exist with the overlapping subtypes. Thus, a student can be a musician, athlete, undergraduate, and sciences major at the same time.

Mutually exclusive subtypes have thick arrows that join before entering the supertype entity. Mutually exclusive subtypes have a mandatory relationship because the subtype entity occurrence must belong to one, and only one, of the supertype occurrences.

The subtypes inherit all the attributes of the supertype entity. Thus students have the name, address, and phone number recorded in their occurrence of the STUDENTS entity. This happens regardless of whether they are musicians, athletes, undergraduates, graduates, arts majors, or sciences majors. The subtypes are existence dependent on the supertype entity. The subtypes do not correspond to different objects. They correspond to different aspects of the same object.

The subtype structure is a convenient way of identifying specialized entities that store attributes that are common to only a subset of the occurrences in an entity. This saves storage that would be needed in corresponding files to allow for unused attributes in a single entity. It also simplifies both understanding of the system and the processing of subtypes. Other examples are EMPLOYEES who may be either FACULTY or STAFF and STAFF who may be either SALARIED or HOURLY. ROOMS may be OFFICES, LABORATORIES, or CLASSROOMS. PARTS may be PRODUCTS or COMPONENTS.

Converting M:N Relationships

M:N relationships have been used as a convenient way of recording the fact that there is a many to many mapping between two entities. This is a convenient representation for enterprise modeling. However, it is not specific enough for the detailed modeling of entities.

The M:N relationship between STUDENTS and SECTIONS says that each student can be enrolled in many different sections and that each section can have many different students enrolled in it. However, it does not provide a way of

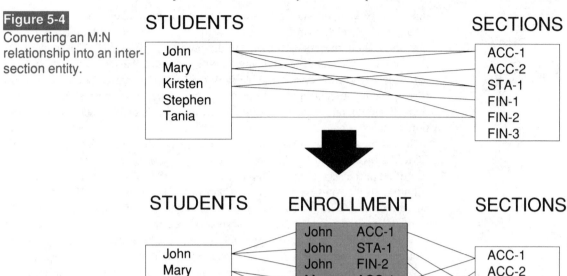

Figure 5-4

Converting an M:N relationship into an intersection entity.

telling which of the many possible sections a particular student is actually enrolled in. Nor does it provide a way of telling which of the many actual students are enrolled in a particular section.

The top part of Figure 5-4 illustrates the logical paths that have to be drawn between the STUDENTS and the corresponding SECTIONS that they are enrolled in. Unfortunately, analysts do not have a convenient notation—or implementation mechanism—for making these connections in both directions in the relational databases that are usually used to implement the design.

An M:N relationship usually represents a transaction that links the related entities. Many combinations of the entity occurrences could result, but only a few actually occur. Therefore there has to be some real-world event or transaction that determines which combinations actually occur. This event or transaction has to be recorded in another entity called an intersection entity, or sometimes an association entity. The intersection entity can be identified by asking "What event or transaction causes the M:N relationship to occur." Another way of asking the question is "At what specific time or event does one entity become related to the other?"

The intersection entity is inserted between the entities that have an M:N relationship. The intersection entity, called ENROLLMENT in the example, contains the identifier keys of each Student-Section pair that must be logically linked. In general, an intersection entity has a compound key that is made up of the keys of the related entities.

This method appears to complicate the problem even further. The number of linking lines is not reduced, and another entity is added. However, the ENROLL-MENT entity is now a simple table with two columns that can be used to link corresponding students and sections using logical selection and matching operations. Selection and matching are the main tools available for locating information in tables.

It is easy to find out which sections John enrolled in. Select all rows of ENROLLMENT with the first part of the key equal to **John**. The sections are identified in the second part of the key as ACC-1, STA-1, and FIN-2. Similarly, counting all the rows with the second part of the key equal to **ACC-1** gives the enrollment in ACC-1, which is two in this example. It is also possible to count all students enrolled in course ACC regardless of section.

A more complicated query might require that the birth dates of all students in section ACC-1 be identified. First, all occurrences of ACC-1 in ENROLLMENT are selected. Then the names beside these are matched with corresponding names in the STUDENTS file. The birth dates (not shown) are found beside the names in the STUDENTS file. This method can be used to perform any data selection. It only needs a simple tabular structure to implement it. In the next chapter, all entities and data files are implemented using such simple tables.

When files are designed to contain occurrences of the entities and relationships, entities map into files. An M:N relationship maps into an intersection entity, and corresponding file, to record the link between the entities. This intersection entity always has a compound key consisting of the keys of the related entities.

An M:N relationship is always more costly to implement than a 1:N relationship because it involves an extra table and an extra match to link desired data. There are times when it is not clear whether a relationship is 1:N or M:N as in the relationship between salesperson and customer. In some organizations each customer has a single salesperson; in others a customer may have several salespersons. An organization may change from one rule to the other.

The M:N relationship includes the 1:N relationship as a proper subset. Thus, if there is any doubt about which cardinality applies, implement the M:N relationship. It may be slightly more costly, but it is much more flexible. It is also very costly to change from 1:N to M:N at a later time. Since an extra file must be added, the logic of all applications using the file must be changed. This can be a very costly maintenance job.

The analyst can diagnose the proper cardinality by asking "Could A have an M:N relationship with B in the future?" A and B are usually locations, transactions, persons, positions, or organizations. If competitors follow an M:N rule, there is a strong likelihood that competitive pressures will force an organization to use an M:N rule someday, even if they do not do so now.

The occurrences of ENROLLMENT capture all pairs of students and sections in which a valid enrollment has occurred. Thus each occurrence of enrollment identifies a student enrolled in a section of a course. If a student is enrolled in five sections of courses, then there are five occurrences for this student in the ENROLLMENT entity. If there are 30 students in a section, then there are 30 occurrences for this section. This way it is possible to identify all the sections that a particular student is enrolled in or all the students enrolled in a particular section. The ENROLLMENT entity acts as a bridge between STUDENTS and SECTIONS. It can also be used to store other information about the relationship between STUDENTS and SECTIONS, such as grades.

The Entity-Relationship Diagram for STUDENTS, SECTIONS, and EN-ROLLMENT is shown in Figure 5-5. Note that the M:N relationship has been broken into two 1:N relationships and a new entity. The arrows pointing toward STUDENTS and SECTIONS in the M:N relationship are always converted to point toward the intersection entity in the 1:N relationships. Each student has M enrollments and each section has N enrolled students. This is the way to deal with all M:N relationships.

Figure 5-6 shows the part of the university Entity-Relationship Diagram that relates to the student records system that is being designed. M:N relationships have been converted to 1:N relationships by adding entities for ENROLL-MENTS, REGISTRATIONS, and OFFERINGS.

Analysis Techniques

The concepts needed to define the logical structure of the database have been identified. The analyst can now turn to identifying the data attributes that are needed in the new database. There are four main sources of information: forms, computer files, text, and people. Forms, files, and text are examined first. Then

Figure 5-5

Converting an M:N relationship into two 1:N relationships by creating an intersection entity.

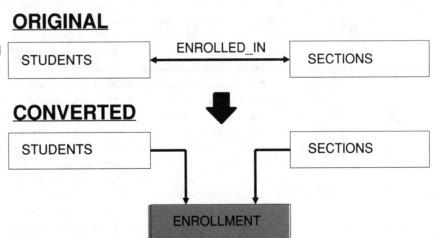

Figure 5-6
EER Model of the Student Subsystem.

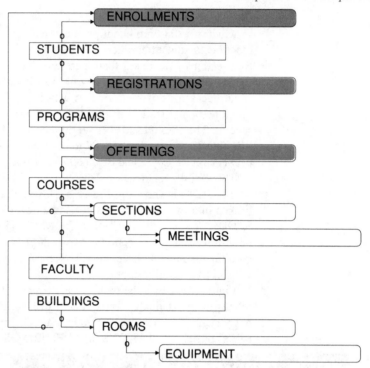

individual interview methods are used to obtain undocumented information. Finally, a group process called Joint Application Design (JAD) is used to find out any remaining information that people can provide.

Forms Analysis

Forms were used in Chapter 2 to identify entities and relationships. They are used again here to identify the attributes of each entity. The detailed analysis stage likely looks at many more forms than were examined at the enterprise level in Chapter 2. It is possible that some new entities and relationships are discovered in these extra forms. For this reason, the process of deriving entities from forms is reviewed here.

One of the best sources of information about the data that an organization uses is the forms used by the organization. Most frequently-used data get entered on forms before being processed further. Since the forms are used for all input that can be entered on the form, they are usually designed to handle most situations that are likely to arise. A careful analysis of the content and structure of the forms provides a fine introduction to the data requirements of the organization.

Batini, Demo, and Di Leva[1] have developed a procedure for analyzing forms to produce a logical Entity-Relationship Model. It consists of:

● **Identify** parts. Certification, extensional, intentional, and descriptive parts correspond to identifications, blanks, labels, and descriptions.

- **Locate** data areas. Areas are blocks, boxes, windows, or pages of the form that usually refer to a specific subject or entity.
- **Extract** elements from each area. Blanks correspond to attributes of entities.
- **Assign** each element to an attribute in an entity of the Entity-Relationship Diagram. The labels of the blanks are candidate attribute names.

Structural Parts

A form can contain four kinds of elements: certification, extensional, intentional, and descriptive information. Examples of each of these are identified in the application form in Figure 5-7. The form is typical of many university application forms and it contains many elements found in most office forms.

- **Certification Information** consists of such items as date of issue, signatures, sequential form numbers, and stamps, seals, or marks. These elements certify

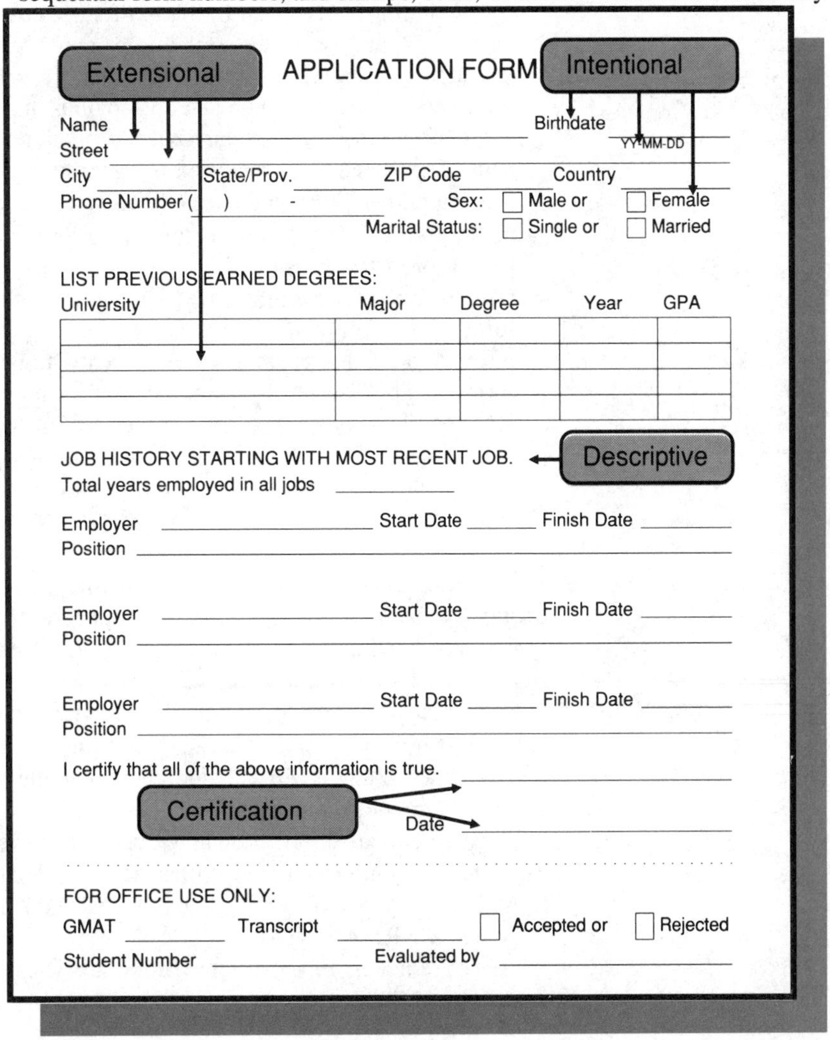

Figure 5-7

An example of a Student Application Form illustrating the parts of the form.

the existence, correctness, or authenticity of a form. They do not convey any semantic information and so they can usually be ignored. The signature and date near the bottom of the Application Form are examples of this kind of element. We can usually ignore them. However, sometimes they may be needed for auditing or control purposes.

● **Extensional Information** is the part of the form that is to be filled in. It usually consists of blanks to be written in or boxes to be checked. This part corresponds to the attributes of some entity. It can sometimes provide information about the type or width of an attribute.

● **Intentional Information** is the description of the extensional information. It consists of all the labels or descriptions for each field on the form. Some of the fields may have explicit instructions on how to fill in the form. YY-MM-DD below the birth date is an example of such information. Others, such as the name field, may assume that the user knows how to fill the form in without instructions. Some, like the field after "I certify that all of the above information is true" assume that it is obvious that a signature is needed there.

The intentional and extensional information are usually very close physically. They need to be analyzed together to obtain the meaning of the field. The intentional information usually corresponds to the names of the attributes of an entity. Some of the intentional information may correspond to constraints or instructions.

● **Descriptive Information** provides directions and constraints on the use of the form. The "**For Office Use Only**" part is an example of this kind of information. Other examples are any written instructions that accompany the form to explain when it should be used or how it should be filled out. For instance, there could be a part on the back of the form that explains that the *major* field in the table of university degrees must be filled in with one of a set of listed codes. The descriptive information may be explicit or implicit. It can be another source of constraints and business rules.

Data Areas

Forms contain separate areas for separate kinds of data. These areas may contain other areas within them. The application is divided into four areas in Figure 5-8. Each area is outlined with a dashed line and numbered in the upper right corner for easy identification.

In well-designed forms, an area is usually devoted to information about one entity. It can contain data about a single entity occurrence, several entity occurrences, or a mixture of information about a single occurrence of one entity and several occurrences of another entity.

Area 1 contains information about one occurrence of the STUDENTS entity. The intentional information identifies the following candidate attributes: NAME, STREET, CITY, STATE, ZIP_CODE, COUNTRY, PHONE_NO, BIRTHDATE, SEX, and MARITAL_STATUS.

Area 2 contains repeated information about the universities that the student has attended. Whenever there is repeated or plural information, then another entity is involved. The repeated information about universities is not stored in a single occurrence of the student entity because it is not known how many fields are needed. So another entity called UNIVERSITIES is created to store the repeating information. The intentional information identifies the following candidate attributes: UNIVERSITY_NAME, MAJOR, DEGREE, YEAR, and GPA. Repeating data almost always implies an entity for the repeating block.

Area 3 contains one piece of information about the student—the total number of years employed. The rest of the information is a repeating group. Each section contains the candidate attributes: EMPLOYER, START_DATE, FINISH_DATE, and POSITION, which must be recorded in another entity called EMPLOYERS. Summary information, such as totals, is commonly placed next to the detail from

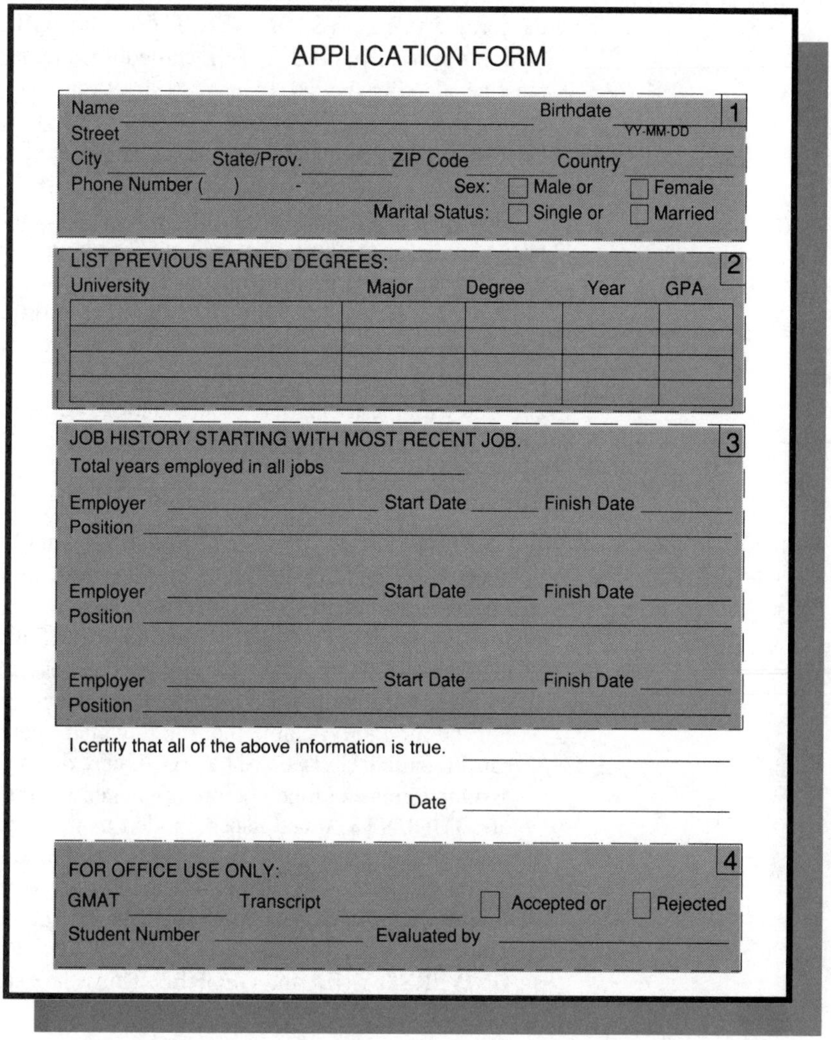

Figure 5-8

The Student Application Form with areas corresponding to entities outlined in four boxes.

5 EER Model

APPLICATION FORM

Name _____ Birthdate _____ 1
Street _____ YY-MM-DD
City _____ State/Prov. _____ ZIP Code _____ Country _____
Phone Number ( ) - Sex: ☐ Male or ☐ Female
Marital Status: ☐ Single or ☐ Married

LIST PREVIOUS EARNED DEGREES: 2
University | Major | Degree | Year | GPA

JOB HISTORY STARTING WITH MOST RECENT JOB. 3
Total years employed in all jobs _____

Employer _____ Start Date _____ Finish Date _____
Position _____

Employer _____ Start Date _____ Finish Date _____
Position _____

Employer _____ Start Date _____ Finish Date _____
Position _____

I certify that all of the above information is true. _____

Date _____

FOR OFFICE USE ONLY: 4
GMAT _____ Transcript _____ ☐ Accepted or ☐ Rejected
Student Number _____ Evaluated by _____

which it is calculated. It is easier for the form filler to concentrate on one topic while all of the information is available. YEARS_EMPLOYED is an attribute of STUDENTS, not of EMPLOYERS.

Area 4 contains more information about the student entity. It has been segregated on the form because it is filled in by a different person. It is easier for both people who fill in the form if they work in separate areas. Nevertheless, it is about the same STUDENTS entity as the data in Area 1. New candidate attributes GMAT, ACCEPTANCE, and STUDENT_ID are identified. For this analysis, assume that the transcript and the evaluated attributes have been identified, but are not included in the new system.

Identifying Entities

The previous section identified three entities about which data are recorded in the form: STUDENTS, UNIVERSITIES, and EMPLOYERS. If all of the information on the form needs to be recorded in computer files, then two new entities must be added to the list. Figure 5-9 superimposes the discovered entities on the areas of the form to illustrate where they come from. STUDENTS appears twice because it is derived from two areas. In the design the attributes from the two areas will be combined in one STUDENTS entity.

Since this is an application form, it is possible that some of the information is needed only for preliminary screening. The biographical data in Area 1 are likely to be needed in the permanent file. The university data in Area 2 are also likely to be needed for evaluation or for alumni records. The employer information in Area 3 is less likely to be useful after the student is admitted. If it is only confirmatory information, then it can be omitted from the files. This should be checked with the users, but assume that this entity can be left out of the analysis. The information in Area 4 is likely to be needed in the future so it should be included in the files.

Extracting Data Elements

Each field in the form is potentially a data element to be recorded in a computer file. Three guidelines should be followed in identifying the attributes that become data elements.

- **Identifying key.** Each entity needs an identifying key. The **Student Number** in Area 4 is apparently the unique key assigned to each student who is accepted into the program. No key has been identified for UNIVERSITIES. For the moment, assume that the university name is a suitable identifier and can be called UNIVERSITY_ID. Later, during file and screen design, that assumption is examined before implementing the file. STUDENT_ID, the key of STUDENTS, must also be added to the key. It distinguishes among the many students who may have come from the same university. Finally, add the degree to the key to distinguish among occurrences of UNIVERSITIES for students who have received more than one degree from the same university. Thus the unique identifier of UNIVERSITIES is the STUDENT_ID, UNIVERSITY_ID, and DEGREE. This is an example of a compound key.

- **Single fact.** Each attribute should contain only a single atomic fact. An atomic fact cannot be divided into smaller pieces of meaningful information. Some fields on the form may contain multiple facts. The NAME field usually contains a surname and a first name. NAME is separated into two separate attributes: SURNAME and FIRSTNAME. Then they can be treated individually for sorting, sending form letters, and other purposes.

  BIRTHDATE and PHONE_NO could also be broken down into smaller components. BIRTHDATE could be broken down into year, month, and day, but it is not clear that the parts are ever needed separately. Likewise it is not clear that the area code of a phone number are ever needed separately. BIRTHDATE and PHONE_NO are left as single attributes.

  Some fields are a single field when they appear to be more than one. Any

Figure 5-9
Student Application Form with an Entity-Relationship Diagram superimposed to show the source of data for each entity.

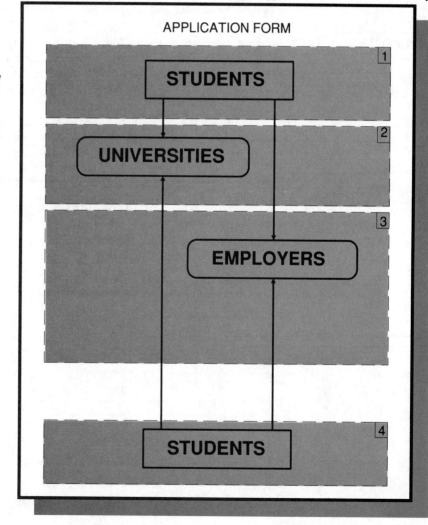

multiple choice or mutually exclusive list selection can be reduced to a code that states which item was selected. Thus fields for male and female do not have to be separated. Instead there is a single field for SEX with two possible entries: male or female. The same analysis applies to MARITAL_STATUS and to accepted or rejected in Area 4.

- **Single value.** Each occurrence must have only a single value for each attribute. There are potentially several universities identified in Area 2. The four rows for up to four universities could be treated as four attributes of the student entity called UNIVERSITY1, UNIVERSITY2, UNIVERSITY3, and UNIVERSITY4. However, they should not be treated as separate attributes. Each university is actually a separate occurrence of the same attribute in the UNIVERSITIES entity. This way attributes only have to be defined once and they can be selected and compared more easily by most database software.

Multiple Data Sources

It is common to have several forms or data files with overlapping information. The overlapping information is not always consistent. The enrollment form in Figure 5-10 illustrates several complications in data analysis that result from having multiple sources. These complications are due to synonyms, incomplete data, overlapping data, structural differences, field width, different keys, different encoding, different resolution, and manual computations.

- **Synonyms.** The Student-ID, Surname, and First Name in the Enrollment Form are obviously the same as the name and Student Number in the

Figure 5-10
Example of a university Enrollment Form.

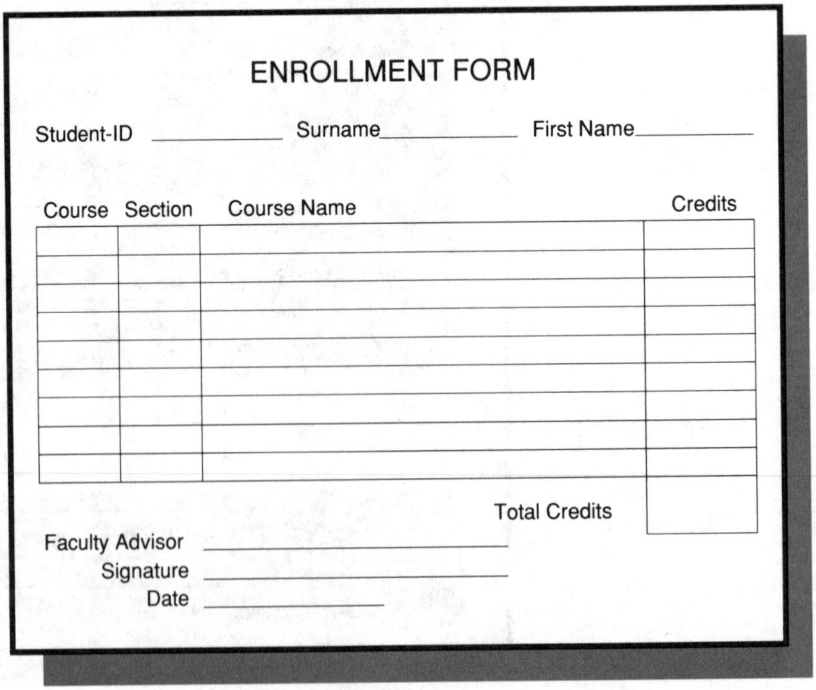
ENROLLMENT FORM

Student-ID ________ Surname________ First Name________

Course	Section	Course Name	Credits

Total Credits

Faculty Advisor ________
Signature ________
Date ________

Application Form. Note that the names are synonyms and that NAME has been split into two parts. It is common to have different labels for the same thing on different forms designed by different people.

- **Incomplete Data.** A form may contain only some of the data about an entity. It may take several forms to identify all the attributes of an entity. The Application Form did not specifically identify the surname and first name of the student. The Enrollment Form adds this information. All of the forms taken together usually identify all of the attributes that are needed. Some forms may even include attributes that are no longer useful. For instance, the credit card sale form used in most service stations contains a blank for license plate number so non-payments can be traced. Now that a large proportion of service stations are self-serve, the cashiers usually cannot see the license plate number from the cashier's booth. So they ask the customer for the plate number. If the customer is honest, the number is provided, but not needed. If the customer is dishonest, a false number is provided when the correct one is needed. In either case, the data are useless.

- **Overlapping Data.** The Enrollment Form is set up as if there is a single entity with these attributes: Course, Section, Course Name, and Credits. Course and Credits are properties of the Section. However, the Name and Credits should be the same for all Sections of a Course. Therefore these attributes should be attached to the Course, not the Section. This is an example of inheritance of attributes in which the inherited attributes have been explicitly included on the form to provide redundant information. The Course and Course Name are redundant. However, together they reduce the possibility of a Student being enrolled in the wrong Course because of an error in writing down the Course.

- **Structural Differences.** The two forms have different field widths for the Name and have a different way of specifying the Name. These are examples of differences in information structure. Structural differences include:

  - **Different field widths.** The widest field width should be used to make it easy to include all available data.

  - **Different keys.** These may both have to be included if both are used by different user groups. Sometimes it is convenient to search for a student by name and at other times it is convenient to search by STUDENT_ID. If both are not included in the new system, then all existing applications must be converted to use the chosen key.

  - **Different encoding.** Names, services, properties, or measurements may be recorded differently on different forms. The names on the Application and Enrollment forms are an example of this. Recording measurements in barrels on one form and metric tons on another or use of abbreviations on some forms are other examples. The same color may be recorded as blue, BL, or 03 on different forms. All records should be recorded in a consistent notation and converted in reports to the user, if necessary.

  - **Different resolution.** Different users often collect information at different levels of detail. Products may be weighed to different accuracies in production and shipping departments. In this case the most accurate

5
EER Model

measure should be preserved. Sometimes numbers are converted to ranges as when numeric grades are converted to letter grades. Again the most accurate measure should be preserved and converted automatically if ranges or codes are needed. Sometimes the concepts are related, but not convertible, as in interest rate and bond rating. If they are not convertible, they are different concepts and both should be preserved.

- **Manual computations.** The total credits are computed on the form, but do not have to be stored in the database. Once the courses have been related to the student, the computer can be used to compute the total credits. The general rule is that one should not enter manual calculations if they can be computed from entered data.

- **Implicit relationships.** It is not obvious from this form that a relationship between the STUDENTS entity and the SECTIONS entity is recorded. The Student-ID applies to all of the data on the form so it is related to each line of the form. Thus it must be appended to each line to record the relationship. Section and Student_ID together are the key of the Enrollment entity. Enrollment is a characteristic of Students because it tells more about the student on the form. It is also a characteristic of Sections because it tells which students are in each section. There is actually information about three entities on this form. They are STUDENTS, COURSES, and ENROLLMENT.

- **Surplus information.** The signature and date fields are certification information. For a document like this—which people have no incentive to falsify—the signature and date do not have to be recorded.

- **Obsolete information.** Forms may contain information that is no longer used. Designing a database without questioning the current and future need for each item may perpetuate useless items. Faculty Advisor on the Enrollment Form is an example of a field that applied to the example university at one time, but is no longer used. The university eliminated Faculty Advisors several years ago.

The attributes that have been identified are now tabulated. Figure 5-11 and 5-12 show the same information for the UNIVERSITIES, ENROLLMENT, COURSES, and STUDENTS entities.

Files Analysis

Existing computer files are another excellent source of information about the data that an organization uses. These files contain the data needed to operate existing computer programs. They are not always organized to reflect the entity and relationship structure that is wanted in the new file system. However, a careful analysis can convert them into the desired form.

The process is illustrated with the DATA DIVISION of a COBOL program designed to record and process all the data needed to manage teaching assignments. The data description is illustrated in Figure 5-13.

Each line of the description contains a hierarchical level number, a field name, and a picture of the data. The field name is the name of an attribute or descriptive characteristic of one of the entities previously identified. The level numbers (01, 02, 03, 04, and 05 in the example) indicate successive levels of

ENTITY_____UNIVERSITIES_____

ATTRIBUTE	PRIMARY KEY	FOREIGN KEY	NULL OK	TYPE	WIDTH
STUDENT_ID	X	X			
UNIVERSITY_ID	X				
DEGREE	X				
MAJOR			X		
YEAR			X		
GPA			X		

ENTITY_____ENROLLMENT_____

ATTRIBUTE	PRIMARY KEY	FOREIGN KEY	NULL OK	TYPE	WIDTH
STUDENT_ID	X	X			
COURSE_ID	X	X			
SECTION_ID	X	X			

ENTITY_____COURSES_____

ATTRIBUTE	PRIMARY KEY	FOREIGN KEY	NULL OK	TYPE	WIDTH
COURSE_ID	X				
COURSE_NAME			X		
CREDITS			X		

5 EER Model

Figure 5-11
Detailed attributes of the UNIVERSITIES, ENROLLMENT, and COURSES entities.

ENTITY_____STUDENTS_____

ATTRIBUTE	PRIMARY KEY	FOREIGN KEY	NULL OK	TYPE	WIDTH
STUDENT_ID	X				
SURNAME<1>					
FIRSTNAME<1>					
STREET			X		
CITY			X		
STATE			X		
ZIP_CODE			X		
COUNTRY			X		
PHONE_NO			X		
BIRTHDATE			X		
SEX			X		
MARITAL_STAT			X		
GMAT			X		
ACCEPTANCE			X		

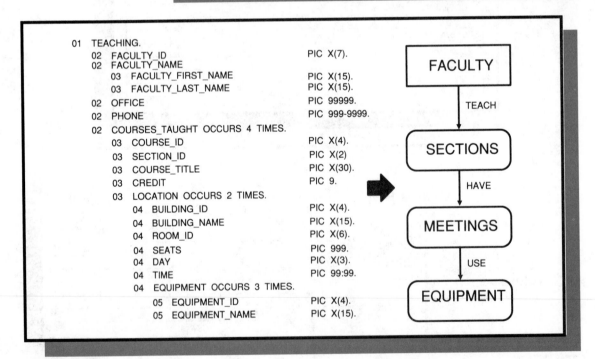

```
01   TEACHING.
     02   FACULTY_ID                        PIC X(7).
     02   FACULTY_NAME
          03   FACULTY_FIRST_NAME           PIC X(15).
          03   FACULTY_LAST_NAME            PIC X(15).
     02   OFFICE                            PIC 99999.
     02   PHONE                             PIC 999-9999.
     02   COURSES_TAUGHT OCCURS 4 TIMES.
          03   COURSE_ID                    PIC X(4).
          03   SECTION_ID                   PIC X(2)
          03   COURSE_TITLE                 PIC X(30).
          03   CREDIT                       PIC 9.
          03   LOCATION OCCURS 2 TIMES.
               04   BUILDING_ID             PIC X(4).
               04   BUILDING_NAME           PIC X(15).
               04   ROOM_ID                 PIC X(6).
               04   SEATS                   PIC 999.
               04   DAY                     PIC X(3).
               04   TIME                    PIC 99:99.
               04   EQUIPMENT OCCURS 3 TIMES.
                    05   EQUIPMENT_ID        PIC X(4).
                    05   EQUIPMENT_NAME      PIC X(15).
```

FACULTY

TEACH

SECTIONS

HAVE

MEETINGS

USE

EQUIPMENT

detail or repetition. The PICture part of the file description provides information about data type and width.

FACULTY_NAME at level 02 contains two detailed fields—FACULTY_FIRST_NAME and FACULTY_LAST_NAME—at level 03. In this case, FACULTY_NAME is just a name for the group of items at level 03 below it. Such structures are used for convenience in some languages. They allow a programmer to refer to a group of elements by a single name like FACULTY_NAME. Since attributes should be identified at the most detailed level, ignore such structures and treat FACULTY_FIRST_NAME and FACULTY_LAST_NAME as if they were at level 02. FACULTY_NAME can be ignored completely since the information is all contained in the other two attributes.

The PIC field at the end of each line describes the format of the data on the file. Thus X(7) indicates that it is a seven character field. 999-9999 indicates that the field contains three numbers followed by a dash followed by four numbers. This is information about the type and width of the element. It is not used now. However, it is useful when the design of new data files begins and the format of the data must be specified.

5 EER Model

Identifying Entities

The group name can be followed by the phrase "OCCURS n TIMES." This indicates that the whole group of items is repeated n times. Thus COURSES_TAUGHT OCCURS 4 TIMES tells us that each faculty member may teach up to four courses. Each of the courses has a COURSE_ID, SECTION_ID, COURSE_TITLE, CREDIT, and two LOCATIONs. Similarly each location has up to three pieces of equipment.

Just as forms could be broken down into sections for analysis, files can be divided into sections for analysis. The file is divided at the different hierarchical levels with an OCCURS n TIMES phrase. Repeated values are a strong signal that occurrences of another entity have been identified. If there are no repeated values, the file is likely to describe only one entity.

Compare the hierarchical structure to the Entity-Relationship Diagram in Figure 5-6. Level 02 contains data about FACULTY, level 03 contains data about COURSES, level 04 contains data about BUILDINGS, and level 05 contains data about EQUIPMENT. The name of a level number is often the name of the entity described below it. Thus 02 COURSES_TAUGHT is the hint that level 03 is about COURSES. Similarly 04 EQUIPMENT is the hint that level 05 is about EQUIPMENT.

Sometimes the names may be different from the ones used in the Entity-Relationship Diagram. 03 LOCATION is not the same as BUILDINGS, but the names below indicate that this part of the file describes BUILDINGS and ROOMS. Note that this level combines information about BUILDINGS and ROOMS even though they are two different entities. This sometimes occurs in files designed hierarchically in a language like COBOL.

ENTITY_____SECTIONS_____

ATTRIBUTE	PRIMARY KEY	FOREIGN KEY	NULL OK	TYPE	WIDTH
COURSE_ID	X				
SECTION_ID	X				
FACULTY_ID		X			

ENTITY_____MEETINGS_____

ATTRIBUTE	PRIMARY KEY	FOREIGN KEY	NULL OK	TYPE	WIDTH
COURSE_ID	X				
SECTION_ID	X				
MEETING_ID	X				
BUILDING_ID		X	X		
ROOM_ID		X	X		
DAY			X		
TIME			X		

ENTITY_____FACULTY_____

ATTRIBUTE	PRIMARY KEY	FOREIGN KEY	NULL OK	TYPE	WIDTH
FACULTY_ID	X				
FAC_FIRSTNAME					
FAC_SURNAME					
OFFICE					
PHONE			X		

Figure 5-14
Detailed attributes of the SECTIONS, MEETINGS, and FACULTY entities.

ENTITY_____BUILDINGS_____

ATTRIBUTE	PRIMARY KEY	FOREIGN KEY	NULL OK	TYPE	WIDTH
BUILDING_ID	X				
BUILDING_NAME					

ENTITY_____ROOMS_____

ATTRIBUTE	PRIMARY KEY	FOREIGN KEY	NULL OK	TYPE	WIDTH
BUILDING_ID	X				
ROOM_ID	X				
SEATS			X		

ENTITY_____EQUIPMENT_____

ATTRIBUTE	PRIMARY KEY	FOREIGN KEY	NULL OK	TYPE	WIDTH
BUILDING_ID	X				
ROOM_ID	X				
EQUIPMENT_ID	X				
EQUIP_NAME					

Figure 5-15
Detailed attributes of the BUILDINGS, ROOMS, and EQUIPMENT entities.

5
EER Model

There is an implicit 1:N relationship between a level and the level below it. Thus, the relationship between level 02 and the course information at level 03 is the TEACHES relationship. The courses at level 03 are TAUGHT_AT the building, room, and time at level 04. The ROOM at level 04 CONTAINS the equipment at level 05. 1:N relationships do not need an entity of their own to store the relationship information. Thus each of these relationships does not need to be translated into an entity or a file.

Extracting Data Elements

Often these relationships in a COBOL data definition are hierarchical with a kernel entity at the smaller level number and characteristic entities at the higher level numbers. When this happens, the characteristic entities inherit the keys from the entities above them. Thus the equipment entity inherits the BUILD-ING_ID and ROOM_ID keys from the level above. The time information at level 04 inherits the COURSE_ID and SECTION_ID information from level 03. This information is actually the information about the MEETINGS entity.

Level 04 contains information about several entities in the model. The field names give a hint of this. When a name like ROOM_ID is found, suspect that you are dealing with some attribute of ROOMS. You can be fooled when foreign keys are used to identify relationships. BUILDING_NAME is an attribute of the BUILDINGS entity. SEATS is an attribute of ROOMS. DAY and TIME are attributes of MEETINGS. BUILDING_ID and ROOM_ID are foreign keys that link MEETINGS to ROOMS.

The attributes of each of the newly identified entities are described in Figures 5-14 and 5-15. This information, combined with the information in Figures 5-11 and 5-12, covers most of the entities that were identified in Figure 5-6. REGISTRATIONS, PROGRAMS, and OFFERINGS have not yet been covered. Likely further examination of other forms and files gives information about these entities or identifies more information about the entities already studied. However, another technique is used to gather data about the missing entities.

Text Analysis

The text of a strategic plan was analyzed in Chapter 2 to identify entities by locating the important nouns in the text. A similar operation can be performed on written or verbal descriptions of processes and data requirements. These can be obtained from procedure manuals, interviews, or other sources.

Again, the nouns are important identifiers. However, in detailed descriptions, the nouns are more likely to identify attributes instead of entities. In this respect, attributes are just like entities, except they provide more detailed information.

Figure 5-16 is a verbal description of university programs in the example university. Examining it shows that PROGRAMS have a NAME, a DEGREE, and a COURSE_COUNT associated with them. They also need a PRO-GRAM_ID to identify them. REGISTRATIONS are a relationship between PROGRAMS and STUDENTS. Only the respective keys of programs and stu-

Figure 5-16
Description of
the programs
offered by the
university.

UNIVERSITY PROGRAMS

The university has a number of academic programs. Each of them leads to a different degree. Students register in a program when they enter the university. Some students may register in multiple programs such as Engineering and Business. They will get two degrees when they complete both programs.

A program consists of a number of courses that must be completed. Some courses are required and others are elective. Thus the Business program consists of 20 courses. Eight of them are required and any 12 others can be chosen from the remaining courses in the program. Some courses, like Statistics, may be approved as an offering in several programs.

---

dents are needed to establish the relationship. It may also be desirable to record the date when the student registered in the program.

The relationship between COURSES and PROGRAMS could be treated in two ways. One way is to define two subtypes of courses in each program: required courses and elective courses. This is appropriate if the attributes to be recorded for each subtype are different. The other way is to define an attribute for the relationship that indicates the type of relationship. In this example, the REQUIRED attribute is defined to indicate whether the course is required in the program. If it is not then it is an elective course. Figure 5-17 describes the data files that result from this analysis.

Individual Interviews

Forms, files, and text analysis are useful techniques for extracting information about requirements from existing documentation. Unfortunately, existing documentation is often incomplete, outdated, or conflicting. The actual operation of the organization is performed by people who modify, augment, or ignore written procedures while doing their jobs. They do this because the procedures do not completely reflect the job that has to be done. To understand what is really happening, the analyst needs to talk to these people.

Interviews can be used to gather information that has not been documented. Interviews are particularly useful in determining what problems exist with the present system or are anticipated with the future system. It is an excellent source of information about problems that the analyst is unable to anticipate from documented information. The main problem in successful interviewing is putting the

ENTITY_____PROGRAMS_____

ATTRIBUTE	PRIMARY KEY	FOREIGN KEY	NULL OK	TYPE	WIDTH
PROGRAM_ID	X				
PROGRAM_NAME					
DEGREE					
COURSE_COUNT					

ENTITY_____OFFERINGS_____

ATTRIBUTE	PRIMARY KEY	FOREIGN KEY	NULL OK	TYPE	WIDTH
PROGRAM_ID	X	X			
COURSE_ID	X	X			
REQUIRED			X		

ENTITY_____REGISTRATIONS_____

ATTRIBUTE	PRIMARY KEY	FOREIGN KEY	NULL OK	TYPE	WIDTH
PROGRAM_ID	X	X			
STUDENT_ID	X	X			
REG_DATE					

Figure 5-17
Detailed attributes of the PROGRAMS, OFFERINGS, and REGISTRATIONS entities.

interviewees at ease and building confidence so they confide in the interviewer. This can be accomplished by active listening and by participation.

Active Listening

Active listening is used to emphasize that the analyst is there to learn about the user's needs rather than to sell a preconceived idea or structure. The analyst uses open-ended questions, acceptance cues, restated responses, appropriate words, and silences to convey interest and concern about the user's needs.

- **Open-ended Questions** are questions that cannot be answered with a simple answer like yes or no. They usually begin with *what, how,* or *tell me* to encourage the users to describe the data that they use and the activities they perform. This encourages them to describe their environment from their perspective. Some questions must have simple clear answers, but these are likely to be in the minority at this stage of data-gathering.
- **Acceptance Cues** are provided mainly by nonverbal body language. Eye contact, nodding the head affirmatively, and leaning slightly forward are positive cues. Leaning back, slouching, folding the arms, looking away from the interviewee, sitting too far away, and concentrating on note-taking are negative cues. The positive cues show interest and understanding, but not always agreement. The analyst is an impartial data gatherer, not an advocate.
- **Restated Responses** help to ensure that the analyst understands the user. If you restate, in your own words, what someone has said and they still agree with you, then you have understood them. Avoid echoing the user's exact words, altering the user's meaning, or turning their statement into a question.
- **Appropriate words** help to avoid misunderstanding, emotion, and value-judgements. Colloquialisms, slang, acronyms, and computer jargon can be easily misunderstood. The analyst is there to learn, not to judge, so emotional and judgmental words should be avoided. When the interviewee describes a particularly convoluted and apparently inefficient procedure, the proper comment is "that's fascinating" rather than "that's stupid."
- **Silence** is an effective way of encouraging the interviewee to continue and elaborate on an answer. The interviewee may need time to compose an answer. If the silence is too long, the interviewer should resume speaking.

Participation

There is an old saying that you cannot understand how people feel until you have walked a mile in their shoes. One of the best ways of understanding the problems of a job is to try to do it yourself for a while. This shows the users that you really care about their job and their problems. It also exposes you to the exceptional problems that are not usually documented.

If you are designing a computerized taxi dispatching system, take a few days to drive around with one or more cab drivers. This gives you an understanding of the real problems from the point of view of the user. You learn about allegations of favoritism on the part of the dispatcher, the desire to monitor other dispatches to see how busy things are, the need for help in case of an accident or attempted robbery, and the need to book off for a while to get a coffee. These are the kinds

5
EER Model

of things that are not likely to be learned from documentation or mentioned in interviews. Addressing such issues makes the difference between a desirable system and an unattractive one.

Participation is particularly useful in situations where documentation is scarce, where procedures are complex and many informal rules have developed, or where there are significant problems with existing procedures imposed by management. It is important to take enough time to give the users confidence that you care about their job. Only then do they confide in you, particularly if they see many of the difficulties as the result of management directives.

Joint Application Design

The analyst who talks to the people actually doing the work in the organization may find inconsistencies in what they say. Supervisors do not understand all the things that their subordinates are doing. Subordinates are not aware of all of the organization's policies. Different departments interpret procedures in different ways. The analyst should not try to referee these differences. Instead, the analyst tries to create an environment where differences can be identified and resolved. The group design session is such an environment.

The Joint Application Design (JAD) method assumes that the right decisions are made only by involving the right people, with the right preparation, in the right setting, with the right guidance. It facilitates the creation of a rapid and accurate design in several ways:

- **Management commitment.** Executives show their commitment to the project by freeing up the time to attend the Joint Application Design Sessions. As a result, most issues get resolved during the sessions. This reduces the time for completion of the design by up to 40 percent.
- **Users do the designing.** The users understand the process and the results. Design flaws are detected during the design stage so there are fewer requests for changes and program maintenance and enhancement. This leads to higher user satisfaction with the system.
- **Contagious thinking.** Users are unable to individually think of everything that is relevant or even know all of their own information needs. In a group the ideas of others remind them of their own needs. Each representative in the group identifies some of the needs. Together they identify most of them. Some members of the group will also identify other relevant parties that are not represented in the group. As a result, the analysis is more complete.
- **Problem-solving style.** Most people are unable to determine their needs analytically. They need a trial-and-error approach in which suggestions and counter-suggestions are used to home in on the best solution. They are better at recognizing a good solution and improving it than at developing a good solution independently.
- **Integrated approval.** Decision makers attend the group design session. Their attendance at the sessions provides automatic approval so there are no delays for later approval. The resulting system is more responsive to management goals.

JAD sessions are an alternative to individual interviews. Not all designs benefit from JAD sessions. Standard systems that are well understood by the designers may not be improved very much by the methodology. Organizations that have difficulty in releasing all the people involved in the design at one time also have difficulty with this method. Decision Support Systems or other systems with nebulous and changing requirements are unlikely to benefit from JAD. The systems most likely to benefit are systems that:

- **Affect multiple user groups** with different interests and priorities.
- **Change the rules** by which a business operates.
- **Serve a new business activity** for which no previous experience exists upon which to base requirements.

In a JAD session, representatives of the various interested constituencies meet to make sure that they all have the same understanding of the problem. The two main constituencies are the organization representatives and the data processing representatives. The organization representatives should include people from all relevant levels. This usually means both supervisory and clerical people involved with the system under study.

The organizational representatives should also include members of all horizontally related groups. For instance, production and marketing may both be interested in the same product data. Similarly, representatives from different legal, regulatory, or cultural environments should be present if these are a factor in the design. Occasionally other special interests such as auditors, project managers, unions, lawyers, or consultants may be included to provide a perspective on specific problems. The group members have three main roles:

- **Consultative.** Participants provide expertise about the functions and data requirements of the organization.
- **Representative.** Participants represent the interests of the group from which they were chosen.
- **Consensual.** Participants make decisions about the refinements and changes that have to be made to the system.

The size of the group should be limited to about fifteen people[3]. If more people are involved, it is usually very difficult for all of them to participate effectively and some of them become passive. If a larger group is needed, then the project should be split into more than one part and separate sessions should be held for each part. A group can cover a maximum of 10 or 12 entities in a three day session. This is about the optimal size of task for a group.

The group meeting is an expensive way to acquire data.[4] It involves two to four days of time from between 10 and 20 people. Therefore a lot of homework must be done to make sure that it is productive. Business people may need to be briefed on the objectives and expected benefits of the new system. Technical people may need a better understanding of how the business operates. Some people may have to attend classes or demonstrations before the group session.

It is often useful to prepare visual materials to help participants understand the system being studied. Projection foils or icons on magnetic boards can be used to illustrate how people, machines, documents, and other components of the system interact. Some session leaders recommend that pictures of the work area be projected so participants can orient themselves to the normal workplace.

Another aspect of homework is the preparation of a data model. The techniques of forms, files, and text analysis should precede the group analysis if possible. They produce a preliminary design in a much more cost effective manner than a JAD session does. The JAD session needs a preliminary design to react to. Without such a design the group flounders looking for a structure.

In addition to the interested participants, the group design session typically needs a session leader and two scribes. The session leader conducts the session in an impartial manner and leads discussions with questions to invite information and summaries to consolidate established decisions.

Impartiality can be very important because some of the decisions may involve changes to operating policies or procedures. Some parts of the organization may see themselves as losing control or influence under the new system. The Information Systems department should avoid taking sides in such disputes since it could lose them the goodwill that they need to perform effectively. The session leader must act primarily as a therapist, eliciting information and trying to promote consensus on issues. There are several organizations that specialize in conducting group design sessions or training in-house leaders.[2,3,6]

The session leader needs to create an atmosphere for solving problems rather than just taking orders. The difference is in the way questions are asked. An order taker asks questions that identify the order taker's product. A problem solver asks questions that identify the customer's needs. Thus a car seller who is an order taker asks "Do you want a sports car, sedan, or minivan?" to solve the seller's problem of finding a product to sell. The problem solver asks "How many children do you have and do you haul cargo?" to solve the customer's problem of finding the most suitable vehicle for the customer's needs.

The problem solving approach requires a knowledge of what each available product can do and a commitment to help the customer as much as possible. The order taking approach puts the onus on the customer to know what each available product can do and makes no commitment that the product will be suitable for the customer's needs. The difference is one of attitude and responsibility. The problem solving approach requires professionalism on the part of the provider. That professionalism distinguishes the true analyst from the technojerques who sometimes masquerade as analysts.

The two scribes document the decisions taken at the meeting. One should be chosen from the business side of the organization and the other should be chosen from the Information Systems side of the organization. The first records business and policy issues that have been agreed to or that need further decisions. The second records technical information about new entities and attributes discovered, new constraints identified, and new design issues addressed.

Part of the information obtained during the sessions identifies the items of information needed at different stages in the work flow. These should be recorded carefully because they are needed later during the design of reports and the design of screens for data entry and access as described in Chapter 8. Some of the information obtained during the JAD sessions describes the processes that transform information. This information is recorded for use during the analysis and design of processes as described in Chapters 7, 9, and 10. Thus the JAD process is a powerful tool for analysis of several aspects of a system. It is described once in this chapter, but can be used again in several others. One JAD session can serve several purposes.

The objective of the sessions is to get as complete a specification as possible for the new information system. Operationally, this means getting it right, getting it once, getting it all, and getting it up-to-date. Getting it right means making sure that analysts have not misunderstood the actual operation of the organization while developing their specifications for a database. Getting it once means capturing data only once and eliminating overlapping terminology from the design. Getting it all means making sure that no entities, relationships, or attributes have been left out of the analysis. Getting it up-to-date means being able to track the history of a thing as it changes over time.

Getting it Right

The main reason for mis-specification of systems is that business people and systems people often speak different languages. The business people are interested in doing their jobs and producing their product or service. They often see an information system as peripheral to their needs. They also see it as a very technical system that they cannot hope to master. The systems people are interested in producing an information system. They are seldom interested in the details of how the business operates. They often see the business as a very technical system that they cannot hope to master either.

The result is that these two solitudes seldom speak to each other. When they do, it often occurs that "What I thought I heard is not what you thought you said." The solution to the communication problem is to restate the information systems model as a set of business rules. This restatement serves two functions. It helps to eliminate misperceptions and it explains the modeling process that the designers have used in modeling the organization. This can serve as an introduction to the group so they understand what the analysts are trying to create.

Each of the constructs in the Extended Entity-Relationship Model with keys and attributes has a business counterpart. The following example illustrates the translation of the analysts terminology **"mandatory 1:1 relationship R between entities E_1 and E_2."** R is a generic label that stands for any relationship name and E_1 and E_2 are generic entity names that stand for any two entities. The illustration is divided into three parts. There is a generic business statement of a part of an Extended Entity-Relationship Model. There is an example with real names substituted for the generic parameters. There is a business interpretation of the meaning of the statement. In the following example, Students is the example of generic entity E_1, SPONSORS is the example of E_2, and SPONSOR is the example of generic relationship R.

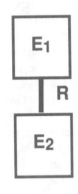

- **Mandatory 1:1 relationship R between entities E_1 and E_2.**
  - **Statement:** E_1 and E_2 can only exist if one E_1 R one E_2. Otherwise neither can exist.
  - **Example:** STUDENTS and SPONSORS can only exist if one SPONSOR SPONSORS one STUDENT. Otherwise neither can exist.
  - **Interpretation:** If a student can be recorded without a sponsor or a sponsor can be recorded without a student, then the relationship is optional. If one sponsor can sponsor more than one student or one student can have more than one sponsor, then the relationship is 1:N or M:N.

Analysts check model correctness by using terminology, like the one after **Example**, to state their understanding of the model to the users. The statement is discussed to determine whether any of the alternate interpretations are true. A complete list of statements, examples, and interpretations for all the EER concepts is found in Appendix 5-A.

Getting it Once

Data redundancy is a major hidden cost in information systems. Each time that an item of data is redundantly recorded, an extra design process occurs, an extra program is written, users key in extra data, and extra storage space is used. Together these can add up to large costs.

Data redundancy is a very common problem. A bank found that they had 15 different application programs that processed data about customer accounts. On average each of the data items used by the programs was recorded three times. A large effort was required to reconcile the different values that resulted from incorrect recording, differences in timing, or differences in definition. They were able to cost justify a project to combine the systems in a newly redesigned 4GL system solely on the basis of eliminating redundant recording costs.

Redundancy occurs either through the design of separate systems or through the use of different terminology for the same things. When separate systems are designed, the designers very likely choose different names for the same things. One department's product may be the next department's raw material. One department's cost of production is the next department's inventory cost. These synonyms are very difficult to detect.

The JAD group design process can be used to detect synonyms. The group traces the business process of acquiring materials, processing them, storing them, selling them, shipping them, and receiving payment for them. If all of the interested parties are in the same room, they can identify their own names for the various things that happen along the way. Once the different names are identified, one common name can be selected that all of them can use.

Selecting a common name is not always easy. Different groups inevitably develop a different jargon for the same concept. They feel more comfortable using their own terminology and resist an imposed change. Sometimes one must provide aliases in the database so different groups can continue to use different names for the same thing. However, this results in some organizational confusion when the groups have to communicate with each other about the same thing. It is usually better if all users can accept the same name for a data item.

Another problem occurs when the same name is used for different concepts. This same name is called a homonym because it sounds the same but has different meanings. Many different groups use the word cost. However, they may mean the purchase price, the purchase price plus shipping, the landed price plus installation, the depreciated cost, the replacement cost, the cost of repairing the machine, or the cost of operating the machine.

During the group design session, the session leader must be very sensitive to the different meanings that might be used. If there really are different meanings, they need to be identified and separately recorded. Some of them can be derived by manipulation of more basic data. For instance purchase price and shipping can be added together as needed by those who see cost as the sum of those parts.

Getting it All

An important purpose of group design sessions is to make sure that all relevant entities, relationships, and attributes have been identified. This is accomplished by tracing through the business work flow to identify all the things that must be recorded about the entities in the model. This process is based on the Joint Application Design (JAD)[2,3] Model. This can be done at the same time as the previously described process for eliminating redundancy.

There are three aspects to the work flow that need to be considered. These are management, work flow, and processing. Figure 5-18 illustrates the sequence of tasks that are involved. Each task is defined. The task is followed by questions that identify data that must be recorded to help accomplish each task.

- **Monitor Environment.** Prioritized information and controls about future work are used to manage the organization. They guide the operators or workers in receiving, scheduling, and completing work.

Figure 5-18

The stages of work flow in a generic organization.

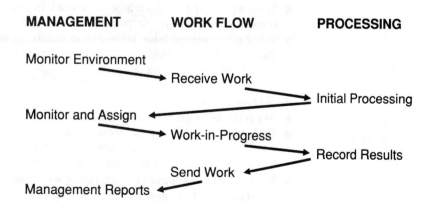

MANAGEMENT	WORK FLOW	PROCESSING

Monitor Environment → Receive Work → Initial Processing → Monitor and Assign → Work-in-Progress → Record Results → Send Work → Management Reports

- **Receive Work.** Work and resources come into the organization. Guidance, control, and identification information are needed. This is equivalent to the In-Basket on a desk.
- **Initial Processing.** Data are entered to record the time and work being performed and the status at different times for tracking the work.
- **Monitor and Assign.** Managers regularly monitor planned and received work to re-establish priorities and assign resources.
- **Work-In-Progress.** Guidance and control information is needed as work is done. Work status is periodically reported to give administrative feedback and enable administrative planning. This is like the Pending Basket on a desk.
- **Record Results.** Changes in status and final results are recorded and other interested parties are notified.
- **Send Work.** Documents and labels are prepared to authorize disposition, route the work to other locations and record the completion. This is equivalent to the Out Basket on a desk.
- **Management Reports.** Reports are prepared for management analysis of performance and comparison with budgets, schedules, and norms.

As the session leader steps the group through the different stages of the work flow, there are several questions that can be used to elicit information about how each stage operates. The answers to these questions identify information that must be in the system.

Monitor Environment

- **What information do you need about the work coming into your area?** This leads to information about work forecasts, pending tasks, pending orders, resource assignment, and work allocation.
- **What guidelines and controls are applied to the work?** This identifies operating parameters, business formulas, authorizations, security controls, and help screens.

Receive Work

- **What events or changes trigger new work in your area and what must be recorded about them?** Responses identify data that is entered or updated.
- **What other information is needed in receiving work?** Answers identify inquiry and help screens, summaries and lists of options, and messages from other members of the organization.

Initial Processing

- **Are codes assigned to identify and track work?** This gets keys for the work.
- **What checks and formulas are needed to validate information about the work?** This identifies validity checks and derivations that can be applied to the data and helps that can be provided.
- **What processes should be triggered or which people should be informed when new work is begun?** This leads to discussion of auditing, logging work, and messages or reports to acknowledge or advise about work receipt.

Monitor and Assign
- **Does anyone monitor work, check for backlogs, assign or reassign resources, or adjust priorities?** This identifies status codes, summary reports, and screens of summary or detail information needed by supervisors.

Work-In-Progress
- **What information must be recorded about changes in status or stages of completion of the work?** This identifies entry, update, and inquiry screens required to record parameters and costs that change as the work progresses.

Record Results
- **What information must be recorded when a piece of work is completed and how is it checked?** This information identifies updating and closing information, calculations, formulas, validation checks, edits, and constraints that are needed to complete a piece of work.
- **What processes should be triggered or which people should be informed when work is completed?** This identifies auditing, statistical, archiving, notification, and acknowledgement information about work completion.

Send Work
- **What information is needed to label, address, or document work as it is distributed to its destination?** This identifies routing, addressing, labeling, notification, and acknowledgement information needed to ship work.

Management Reports
- **What reports are needed to evaluate operations, project trends, and report to government or other parts of the organization?** This identifies summary data, time series, and data needed for reporting purposes but not needed in the performance of the work.

It is questions like these that allow the group to consider and identify problems that are not obvious from the existing forms and files. For instance, STUDENTS may enroll in COURSES more than once to improve their marks or make up for a failure. This means that the ENROLLMENT entity needs another key to distinguish multiple enrollments. The academic term of enrollment would be a suitable key, since a student would never enroll for the same course twice in the same term. Enrollment records should also have grades attached to them to record the result of enrolling in the course.

Getting it Up-To-Date

It is often necessary to maintain a history of transactions as they progress through different stages of processing or as the organization changes. There is sometimes a need to record planned transactions or events as well as historic ones. This applies to things that have a stack, queue, or history. Their complete structure often resembles the outline of Figure 5-19. Each thing being tracked

5 EER Model

Figure 5-19
Typical entities that are required for an inventoriable item.

may have a historic input, a historic output, a planned input, and a planned output. The thing may be inventory, employees, tasks, or any situation where there is a stock or store of the thing. If the input and output can occur spontaneously at different times and apply to groups of the item—as in the purchase of materials—then there is usually a need for two separate records. This permits calculation of materials on hand, materials on order, and materials to be ordered.

If the items are unique and separately tracked—as in enrollment in a section of a course—then a single record might suffice. In SECTIONS and MEETINGS there is a need for a term identifier. This allows sections and teaching loads to be scheduled for a future term while students enroll for the current term. The input is assumed to occur at the beginning of the term and the output is assumed to occur at the end of the term. The actual dates are usually not recorded for courses because they are not important.

The example assumes that sections of courses may be filled to capacity so students may have to request enrollment and be selected on a priority basis. This means that a new entity must be created called ENROLLMENT_REQUEST to record STUDENT_ID, COURSE_ID, and PRIORITY. This file is used by a program that actually assigns students to sections of courses. SECTIONS also requires the attributes CAPACITY and ENROLLED to record the number of positions available and the number used.

For many transactions the date is important. The dates of financial transactions need to be recorded so they can be used to prepare periodic financial statements, calculate interest charges, or generate an audit trail. In such cases, the date of the transaction may be attached automatically. For valuable items, the identity of the person entering the transaction might also be attached to facilitate auditing and identifying responsibility.

In the example, the only valuable item being recorded is the grade obtained when taking a course. The integrity of the university could be compromised if a data entry clerk were bribed to enter an incorrect grade. Thus it would be desirable to identify the operator who enters the grades. The ENROLLMENT entity needs TERM, GRADE, and OPERATOR attributes. The SECTIONS and MEETINGS entities need to have the TERM attribute added.

A similar problem frequently occurs with prices. A product may have a standard price that is an attribute of the PRODUCTS entity. This price can then be inherited by the SALES entity. However, this means that a price can never be changed without retroactively changing the price for all previous sales that inherit it. As a result, it is necessary to record the actual selling price with each sale by copying the standard price to each sales occurrence. When the price is changed in the PRODUCTS entity, the new price is copied to all future sales, but the past ones do not get changed. This arrangement also makes it possible to give a special price on some units by adjusting the recorded selling price. An alternate approach is to have a PRICES entity which stores the different prices and their valid dates for each product.

Testing the EER Model

All the tests used for the Enterprise ER Model in Chapter 2 also apply to the EER Model. In addition there are a number that apply to the EER Model and the attributes associated with it. Again there are clues that help to identify problems.

CLUE #1: **An entity has no attributes or only an atomic key.**

CAUSE: The entity is actually an attribute of some other entity.

CURE: Eliminate the entity and make it the attribute of the related entity. If the attribute is a compound key, the entity may be a legitimate intersection entity.

CLUE #2: **An attribute can be derived from other attributes.**

CAUSE: A calculated value has been included as an attribute.

CURE: Delete the attribute since it is redundant. There is no need to store a value that can be calculated, unless the calculation would be very expensive. Summary data, such as monthly sales totals, should be stored because the result is costly to derive and is needed frequently for analysis and forecasting. The cost of a line item does not need to be stored because it can be calculated easily by multiplying price by quantity. Some database languages allow calculated attributes to be defined by the required calculation without storing actual values. The result is generated whenever the attribute is used. Such attributes can sometimes be defined as a matter of convenience to users and programmers

CLUE #3: **An attribute has a plural name or repeating values or an entity has 2 or more attributes with repeating names.**

CAUSE: The attribute is really a characteristic entity.

CURE: Convert the attribute or repeating attributes to another entity. For example, if STUDENTS can have an attribute ADDRESSES or attributes ADDRESS_CAMPUS, ADDRESS_HOME, and ADDRESS_BUSINESS, the three addresses should be stored in a new ADDRESSES entity with the compound key STUDENT_ID+ADDRESS_TYPE. The same thing must be done if STUDENTS has one address attribute, but it is discovered that address can have more than one value. Note that Address is used here to illustrate an attribute, but a real address would be split into attributes Street, City, State, and Postal Code.

CLUE #4: **An attribute has a name ending in _NUMBER, _CODE, or _ID with no corresponding entity to reference.**

CAUSE: The attribute is a foreign key being used to relate to an omitted entity. The next chapter explains how foreign keys are used to record relationships.

CURE: Create a new entity having the attribute as its key and define a relationship between the old and new entities. In general, an attribute must describe the entity in which it is shown.

CLUE #5: **A foreign key or an attribute with a name ending in _NUMBER, _CODE, or _ID appears in two unrelated entities.**

CAUSE: The key is the physical implementation of a relationship between the entities.

CURE: Insert the relationship and temporarily delete the keys as in Clue #4. The next chapter shows how the keys are used to implement the relationship in a database. At this stage, physical implementation considerations should be ignored so the logical model will be correct.

CLUE #6: **Non-key attributes appear in two or more entities.**

CAUSE: The entities are one of the following:
  a. Parts of a single entity.
  b. Two levels of a generalization in which the subtype contains attributes inherited from the supertype.
  c. Subtypes of a supertype that has not yet been documented.

CURE: Depending on what caused the problem, do one of the following:
  a. Combine the attributes into a single entity.
  b. Delete attributes from the subtype and attach them only to the supertype.
  c. Define a supertype and attach the common attributes to it. Delete the common attributes from the subtypes.

CLUE #7: **Relationship can be derived from other relationships.**

CAUSE: The relationship is redundant.

CURE: Delete the relationship. The relationship between COURSES and MEETINGS in Figure 5-20 is redundant. MEETINGS contains COURSE_ID and SECTION_ID as part of its own key. Therefore, the relationship is already implied.

Figure 5-20

An example of a redundant relationship.

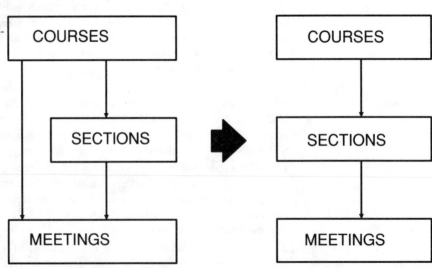

Figure 5-21
Examples of impossible
relationships.

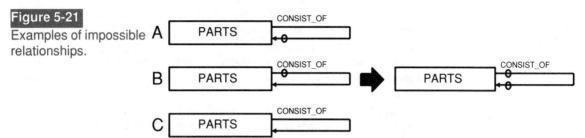

CLUE #8: **Recursive relationships cannot be mandatory.**

CAUSE: Any recursive relationship builds a chain or tree. If either end of the relationship is mandatory, the chain can never end in that direction.

CURE: Make the relationship optional. In Figure 5-21, the recursive relationships between PARTS are impossible. Example A is impossible because it says that Parts must have one or more Parts. This builds a tree that never ends. The Parts at the bottom of the tree must have further Parts which means that they are not really at the bottom of the tree. Example B suffers from the opposite problem and never has a top. Example C suffers from both problems. The same rule applies to 1:1 relationships and M:N relationships. Recursive relationships can only be optional in both directions. M:N relationships between two different entities cannot be mandatory in both directions.

The most important kinds of errors in the Extended Entity-Relationship Model cannot be tested by direct examination of the model. The principal errors result from the analyst not understanding the needs of the user organization to be supported by the new system. A model can be syntactically correct and internally consistent, but completely misrepresent the operations of the organization.

Interviews and Joint Application Design sessions are designed to detect these errors. The translation of EER concepts into Business English, as described in Appendix 5-A, is designed to make sure that analysts and users have the same understanding of the problem. Group discussion of the model is designed to make sure that all interested users have the same understanding of the problem. Tracing the work flow is designed to make sure that all aspects of the system have been covered and that no crucial stages of the process have been ignored.

The JAD session, or some equivalent process, is a crucial stage in the analysis and design process. It should not be skipped or down-graded. It is usually the best source of feed-back from the clients of the system.

CASE Tools for EER Diagrams

There are several tools used to aid this stage of the design process. Packages, like Excelerator from Index Technology Corp. and IEW from KnowledgeWare, Inc., record and produce Entity-Relationship Diagrams. IEW is illustrated in Figure 5-22 below. They also record other related information, such as the cardinality of the relationships, the attributes of the entities, and textual descriptions of the meaning and purpose of each entity, relationship, and attribute. They can expand an entity into a table that records attribute labels, keys, integrity constraints, data types, and field lengths.

Most CASE tools are able to produce diagrams using a variety of different notations. This allows the notation to be compatible with existing documentation in the organization.

Some analysts have found that a CASE tool can be useful during JAD sessions. Entity-Relationship Diagrams and attribute tables can be updated immediately and displayed to the group using a screen projector. This provides immediate feed-back about interpretation errors that the analyst or scribe may have made during the session.

Other analysts are concerned about the potential for technical failures in front of a large and important audience. Programs, computers, projectors, and other display devices must work flawlessly. Worried analysts use the CASE packages to produce printed diagrams and tables to be displayed with overhead projectors. Scribes then take notes in the usual manner.

Excelerator and many other packages allow file descriptions to be imported from existing programs. This reduces the time needed to prepare an initial Entity-Relationship Diagram from existing files.

Excelerator can then analyze the imported files to identify attributes with the same name in multiple files. This is a powerful tool for identifying redundancy. This same facility can be used to flag names that could be homonyms.

Storey and Goldstein[8] have developed an expert system, called the *View Creation System*, that guides analysts and users with questions about the database being designed. It then applies logical rules to suggest design improvements.

Figure 5-22

Illustration of attribute definition in the IEW Analysis tool. The left window shows part of the example Entity-Relationship Diagram. The right window shows the attributes of the highlighted STUDENTS entity. The key is coded by ID in the left column. Optionality is coded by a 0 in the lower limit to the left of the attribute name.

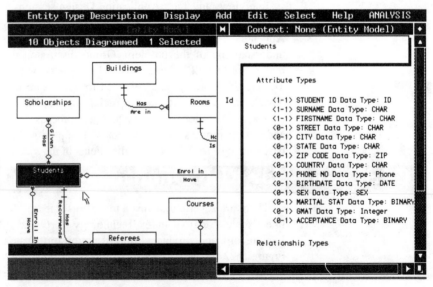

One of the benefits of these tools is that all this information is automatically transferred into the next stage of the design, where program code is generated.

Summary

This chapter extended the Entity-Relationship Model to include optional relationships, existence dependency, and mutually exclusive or overlapping subtypes of entities. M:N relationships are converted into two 1:N relationships. These concepts help to convert the data model into relational files.

Information about detailed data requirements can be obtained from forms, files, and interviews. The hierarchical structure of typical forms and files can be broken down into the entity and attribute structure of the data model. Information about primary keys, alternate keys, foreign keys, and null values must be recorded about each attribute. A typical form consists of certification, extensional, intentional, and descriptive information. These are arranged in data areas from which detailed data fields can be extracted.

Individuals and groups are a good source of information about the data that must be recorded in a system. JAD group design sessions have the advantage that overlaps and misunderstandings can be identified quickly and often resolved during the session.

Group design sessions are used to ensure that designers have understood the actual entities and relationships of the organization, have captured them without duplication, and have captured all entities, relationships, and attributes needed to do the work in a selected segment of the organization.

5 EER Model

Keywords and Phrases

Abstraction	Forms Analysis
Alternate Key	Intentional Information
Attribute	Intersection Entity
Certification Information	Joint Application Design
Descriptive Information	Mutually Exclusive Subtypes
Existence Dependency	Optionality
Extensional Information	Overlapping Subtypes
Foreign Key	Primary Key

Appendix 5-A: Business Equivalent of EER Rules

- ● **Principal Entity E₁**
  - • **Statement:** E_1 has an identity of its own and its existence does not depend on the existence of any other thing.
  - • **Example:** COURSES have an identity of their own and their existence does not depend on any other thing.
  - • **Interpretation:** If existence does depend on another entity, then the entity is a characteristic entity.

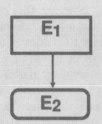

- ● **Characteristic Entity E₂ with kernel entity E₁.**
  - • **Statement:** E_2 is a more detailed description of E_1 and E_2 can only exist if E_1 exists.
  - • **Example:** SECTIONS is a more detailed description of COURSES and SECTIONS can only exist if COURSES exist.
  - • **Interpretation:** If E_2 is not a more detailed description, then it is a kernel entity.

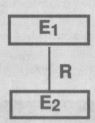

- ● **Mandatory 1:1 relationship R between entities E₁ and E₂.**
  - • **Statement:** E_1 and E_2 can only exist if one E_1 R one E_2. Otherwise neither can exist.
  - • **Example:** STUDENTS and SPONSORS can only exist if one SPONSOR SPONSORS one STUDENT. Otherwise neither one is recorded.
  - • **Interpretation:** If a student can be recorded without a sponsor or a sponsor can be recorded without a student, then the relationship is optional. If one sponsor can sponsor more than one student or one student can have more than one sponsor, then the relationship is 1:N or M:N.

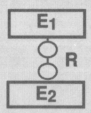

- ● **Optional 1:1 relationship R between entities E₁ and E₂.**
  - • **Statement:** E_1 and E_2 can exist separately. If they both exist, then one E_1 may R one and only one E_2.
  - • **Example:** EMPLOYEES and DEPARTMENTS can exist separately. If they both exist, then one EMPLOYEE may MANAGE one and only one DEPARTMENT.
  - • **Interpretation:** If a department cannot exist without a manager, then the relationship is mandatory. If an employee can manage more than one department, then the relationship is 1:N.

- ● **Mandatory 1:N relationship R between entities E₁ and E₂.**
  - • **Statement:** An E_1 can R many E_2. Each E_2 can R' only one E_1. If an E_1 exists, it must R at least one E_2. If an E_2 exists, it must R' with one and only one E_1.
  - • **Example:** BUILDINGS can CONTAIN many ROOMS. Each ROOM can be CONTAINED_IN only one BUILDING. If a BUILDING exists, it must

CONTAIN at least one ROOM. If a ROOM exists, it must be CONTAINED_IN one and only one BUILDING.

- **Interpretation:** If a building could exist without rooms, as it might at the planning stages, then the relationship is optional. If a building cannot have more than one room, then the relationship is 1:1.

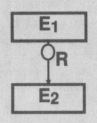

- **Optional 1:N relationship R between entities E_1 and E_2.**
  - **Statement:** An E_1 can R many E_2. Each E_2 can R' only one E_1. If an E_1 exists, it may or may not R one or more E_2, but it does not have to. If an E_2 exists, it must R' one and only one E_1.
  - **Example:** A COURSE can HAVE many SECTIONS. Each SECTION can BELONG_TO only one COURSE. If a COURSE exists, it may or may not have one or more SECTIONS, but it does not have to. If a SECTION exists, it must BELONG_TO one and only one COURSE.
  - **Interpretation:** If a course can have only one section, then the relationship is 1:1. If a course must have sections, then the relationship is mandatory.

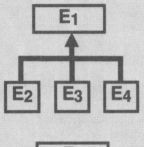

- **Mutually exclusive subtypes E_2, E_3, and E_4 of supertype entity E_1.**
  - **Statement:** An E_1 can be one and only one of E_2 or E_3 or E_4.
  - **Example:** A STUDENT can be one and only one of UNDERGRADUATE or GRADUATE.
  - **Interpretation:** If a student can be both undergraduate and graduate at the same time, then undergraduate and graduate are overlapping subtypes instead of mutually exclusive subtypes.

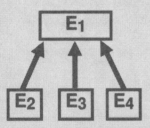

- **Overlapping subtypes E_2, E_3, and E_4 of entity E_1.**
  - **Statement:** An E_1 can be any combination of E_2, E_3, and E_4 including none of them or all of them.
  - **Example:** A STUDENT can be any combination of ATHLETES, MUSICIANS, and DEBATERS including none of them or all of them.
  - **Interpretation:** If a student can be only one of athletes, musicians and debaters, then these are mutually exclusive subtypes. If a student can be an athlete and one of musicians or debaters, then a new hierarchy has to be defined. Athletes and performers become overlapping subtypes of students. Musicians and debaters become mutually exclusive subtypes of performers.

- **Key(s) of entity E_1.**
  - **Statement:** Key K of entity E_1 uniquely identifies every occurrence of E_1.
  - **Example:** COURSE_ID of COURSES uniquely identifies every occurrence of COURSES.
  - **Interpretation:** If courses in different departments can have the same COURSE_ID, then a compound key such as DEPARTMENT_ID + COURSE_ID is needed to identify each occurrence of a course.

- **Compound key of entity E₁.**
  - **Statement:** Every part of the compound key of E_1 is either the key of another entity or is a unique subkey that identifies repeating occurrences of this entity.
  - **Example:** COURSE_ID and STUDENT_ID are the compound key of entity ENROLLMENT.
  - **Interpretation:** COURSE_ID is the key of entity COURSES and STUDENT_ID is the key of entity STUDENTS. If they identify an entity that is not defined, then this newly discovered entity should be added to the model. If the same student can enroll in the same course more than once, then a unique subkey, like ENROLLMENT_DATE, should be added to the key. This key distinguishes different enrollments in the same course.

- **Mandatory attribute A of entity E₁ with key K.**
  - **Statement:** Attribute A of E_1 has exactly one value for each value of the key K.
  - **Example:** Attribute ADDRESS of STUDENTS has exactly one value for each value of STUDENT_ID.
  - **Interpretation:** If a student can have more than one address, then address must be a new characteristic entity.

- **Optionally null-valued attribute A of entity E₁.**
  - **Statement:** An occurrence of E_1 can be recorded without having any value for attribute A.
  - **Example:** An occurrence of STUDENTS can be recorded without having any value for GMAT.
  - **Interpretation:** If an occurrence of students cannot be recorded without a value of GMAT then null-values are not allowed.

Review Questions

1. Define each of the items in the list of keywords and phrases.
2. Name the characteristics of attributes that need to be recorded during a system analysis.
3. What factors must be considered in choosing names for entities and attributes?
4. How does the Extended Entity-Relationship Model differ from the Entity-Relationship Model?
5. Why do M:N relationships have to be eliminated from a design? How are they eliminated?
6. Name the stages of Forms Analysis.
7. Name the types of elements that can be found in a typical form.
8. Which elements of a form identify entities, attributes, and data types?
9. How does JAD help to create rapid and accurate designs?
10. What kinds of projects are most likely to benefit by using JAD sessions?
11. Which people should be involved in a JAD session?
12. What are the stages of work flow that occur during management, transmission, and processing of data?

5 EER Model

Problems

1. Jenny Nagy administers a Suzuki Music School. She hires violin, cello, and piano teachers on an hourly basis to teach children how to play their chosen instrument. She is responsible for hiring and paying teachers, recruiting and billing students, scheduling lessons, and scheduling occasional concerts in which students can display their progress.

   In the past she has recorded students by typing lists for each class. Parents were recorded in a log book as they enrolled their children. She prepared paychecks for the teachers by counting the classes that they taught each month and multiplying by a table of standard rates for each kind of class.

   This system worked fine while the school was small. However, it now has over 300 students and it is getting hard to remember all of the details. She has decided that she wants to automate the system using a popular microcomputer database package. She plans to start by developing a system that produces class lists, bills for parents, and payments to teachers. The following rules and situations apply to the system.

   Bills are sent to the head of the family. Frequently, more than one child in the family is taking lessons. Sometimes, in the case of divorced parents, the parent paying the bill is not the parent accompanying the children to the lessons.

   The amount of the bill depends on the instrument studied (flute, piano, violin, or cello), the length of the lesson (15, 30, 45, or 60 minutes), the frequency of lessons (every 1, 2, or 4 weeks), and whether lessons are private or group lessons. The most common package is a weekly 30 minute private lesson combined with a 60 minute group lesson every two weeks.

Most bills are paid every three months. Some parents need special payment terms and some pay for a whole year in advance.

Teachers are paid a standard rate for private lessons and a different rate for group lessons, regardless of the instrument. They also get the group rate for supervising a one hour concert at the end of every term.

Timetables are prepared to inform parents about the room, time, and day of the week for each kind of lesson. Group lessons are given for each instrument at several levels of advancement. There may be more than one group at the same level of advancement.

Class lists of participating pupils have to be prepared for the group lesson teachers. Timetables are prepared for the teachers to tell them when they teach their private and group lessons.

Using this information, prepare an Extended Entity-Relationship Diagram and a list of attributes for each entity. Identify keys for each entity.

2. Anna Liszt has determined that there is an M:N relationship between the CUSTOMER entity and the INVENTORY_ITEM entity. Use the following Purchase Order form to detail the attributes of the entities involved. Prepare the Extended Entity-Relationship Diagram including new entities, if any, discovered during the analysis.

PURCHASE ORDER   P.O.# _____

ACME CORP.

1234 Main Street, Key East, FL 33136

Order From: Ship to:

Name _____   Name _____
Address _____   Address _____
_____   _____

DATE: _____   REQUISITION NO. _____   TERMS _____
DELIVERY DATE: _____   F.O.B. DESTINATION _____   SHIP VIA _____

ITEM #	QUANTITY	UNITS	DESCRIPTION	UNIT PRICE	AMOUNT

This order is subject to the conditions on the reverse side.
No changes may be made without written permission.
                                                    _____
                                                    PURCHASING MANAGER

3. Larson S. Hacker is designing a small system to record the characteristics of the 150 microcomputers that he supervises on the network used by the faculty and students of the Dravrah Business School. The following form has been used to collect data in the past. The new system will be used by consultants to help diagnose user problems. It will also be used to monitor the performance of components from various manufactures and to determine which components and cards should be kept in stock for spare parts. The most common cards are hard disk controllers, tape controllers, memory expansion boards, modems, display adapters, and turbo cards.

Draw an Extended Entity-Relationship Diagram for the system and identify the attributes of each entity. Be sure to specify keys and whether null values are allowed.

PC CONFIGURATION CHECK LIST

COMPUTER PROCESSOR INFORMATION

MAKER _____	MODEL _____	SERIAL NO. _____
PROCESSOR _____	ROM BIOS VERSION _____	CLOCK SPEED _____ KHz
MATH COPROCESSOR _____		RAM _____ KB
KEYBOARD MODEL _____	MOUSE BRAND AND MODEL _____	

STORAGE DEVICES

FLOPPY DISK

	DRIVE	MAKER	MODEL	SERIAL NO.	SIZE (KB)
	A:				
	B:				
	___				

HARD DISK

	C:				
	___				
	___				

TAPE

| | ___ | | | | |
| | ___ | | | | |

ADAPTER CARDS

SLOT	MAKER	MODEL	SERIAL NO.	TYPE
1				
2				
3				
4				
5				
6				
7				
8				

4. The following COBOL data definition describes the file used to record data about loan applications at a small bank. Bank references and credit card records, if any, are used to evaluate the credit worthiness of customers. Depending on the evaluation, customers may be required to pledge valuable assets as security.

Draw an Extended Entity-Relationship Diagram for the system and identify the attributes of each entity. Be sure to specify keys and whether null values are allowed.

```
01    CREDIT_APPLICATION
      02    APPLICANT_ID              PIC X(7).
      02    SURNAME                   PIC A(20).
      02    FIRSTNAME                 PIC A(20).
      02    DATE
            03    YEAR                PIC 99.
            03    MONTH               PIC 99.
            03    DAY                 PIC 99.
      02    ADDRESS
            03    STREET              PIC X(30).
            03    CITY                PIC X(20).
            03    STATE               PIX A(2).
            03    ZIP                 PIC 99999-9999.
      02    PHONE                     PIC (999)999-9999.
      02    PURPOSE_OF_LOAN           PIC A(60).
      02    SECURITY OCCURS n TIMES
            03    KIND                PIC A(20).
            03    APPRAISAL           PIC 999,999.
      02    BANKERS OCCURS N TIMES
            03    NAME                PIC A(20).
            03    STREET              PIC A(30).
            03    MANAGER             PIC A(30).
            03    PHONE               PIC (999)999-9999.
      02    CREDIT_CARD OCCURS n TIMES
            03    NAME                PIC A(15).
            03    NUMBER              PIC X(15).
            03    EXPIRY              PIC 99/99.
```

5. A professor at Drofnats U. is the treasurer of a small academic organization in an obscure discipline. It has 500 members in 40 universities across the country and abroad. The organization is divided into 8 disciplines and each member may belong to up to 3 disciplines. Membership costs $40.00 per year plus $10.00 per discipline chosen. Student members are charged half of the regular membership. Bills are sent out every October to cover membership fees for the following calendar year. Anyone in arrears is billed for the previous year also. Anyone more than one year in arrears is deleted from the membership list. The bills are normally sent to the member's university address which is usually the same for all members at a university.

The information in the membership file is used to generate:

☐ **bills**;

☐ **mailing labels** for a quarterly publication that goes to all members;

☐ **mailing labels** for journals that go to members of selected disciplines;

☐ **membership directory** which is sorted alphabetically by name and again by university.

Samples of a mailing label, an alphabetic listing of members, and a listing of members at one university follow:

Leonard Draneol
Department of Cognitive Dissonance
Rook University
246 Sweepdee St.
Happy Valley CA 90909

Faculty Directory

Draneol, Leonard, Department of Cognitive Dissonance, Rook University, 246 Sweepdee St. Happy Valley CA 90909, (805)555-7734.

Ment, Tor, Department of Dynamic Inertia, Downnsala University, R-3000 Downnsala, Sweden, 01-46-18-382-436

Pong, Ping, Department of Psychopaleontology, Dravrah University, Notsob MA 10401, (617)555-2121.

University Directory
UNIVERSITY: Dravrah University

Last Name	First Name	Phone
Pong,	Ping	(617)555-2121
Right	Wrichard	(617)555-2433
Wright	Richard	(617)555-4442

The professor employs a part-time secretary to enter data, keep the membership records up to date, produce listings, and answer correspondence. The professor does all file deletions to guard against accidental data loss.

a. Draw an Extended Entity-Relationship Diagram of the database.

b. Specify the attributes and keys of each entity.

6. The following Extended Entity-Relationship Diagram describes the data for a personnel system. Use the diagram to answer the following questions.
   a. Does every job description have a related position?
   b. Can a task exist without a related job description?
   c. Can a task be part of more than one job description?
   d. Can a skill exist without a related task?
   e. Can an employee be both staff and management at the same time?
   f. How many staff can a manager supervise?
   g. Which employees get employee benefits?
   h. Can a manager get both a pension and stock options?
   i. Do all managers get both pensions and stock options?
   j. Does every recorded position have an employee in it?

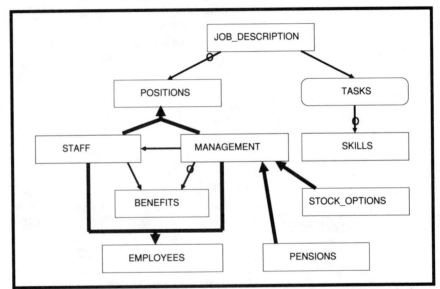

7. You have been hired by one of the five largest banks in the country to design a system for commercial loans. Currently these loans are handled manually by commercial loan officers at local branches who gather data about prospective clients on a set of standard forms. Loans under $100,000 are approved or rejected by the local branch manager. Larger loans are shipped by courier to headquarters for approval. All paperwork and control is done by the branches if the loan is approved. Headquarters gets a quarterly printed summary report about the loans at each branch. There is no central file that permits easy comparison of branches, industries, regions, or other groupings. Research on past performance is very difficult because of lack of centralized data.

   There is a commercial package designed for use by banks in another country. The systems analysis group has an evaluation copy of this package for a period of 60 days. The package does most of the things that the users at the branches and at headquarters require. However, the files and reports are designed for the foreign environment which has different laws, reporting requirements, and commercial environment. A preliminary analysis indicates that buying and modifying this package would be about as costly and nearly as time-consuming as developing a new system.

You have just joined the bank's system group. Your initial assignment is to identify the data and features the new Commercial Loans System should have, so detailed design can begin. A senior manager is sponsoring the project. The manager has announced the project to all interested groups in the bank and has agreed to introduce you to anyone whose cooperation you will need during the design project. The manager has asked you to minimize the amount of time you take with other staff since they are very busy. Your first step in planning the project is to identify the sources of information you will use in the design.

a. List the sources of information that you will use, in the order that you will approach them, from first to last.

b. For each source, specify the reason that you are going to that source, the method that you will use to gather information from that source, and the kind of information that you expect to get from that source.

8. A meta model is a model of a model. When someone has to design the Data Dictionary used in a CASE tool, they have to create a meta model of the Extended Entity-Relationship Model. This meta model identifies the entities and relationships needed to describe the data needed to construct an EER Model. Prepare a meta model of the EER Model.

9. Ivan Tobewelloff is planning to provide a computerized hotel information database over a videotex service operated by a large regional telephone company. Ivan has found that there are many different kinds of information that are published for travellers. The problem is similar to the problem of multiple (and sometimes incompatible) forms and files in computer systems in a single organization. The following excerpts come from four different sources that describe the same hotel in Ottawa, Canada. The descriptions in brackets are labels or descriptions that correspond to codes, symbols, or checked columns in the publications.

From the *American Automobile Association TourBook*:

Clarion Hotel Roxborough, * (=... very comfortable and attractive accommodations) $84.00-120.00, F(amily Rate), Senior Discount, 146 units, 123 Metcalfe St., K1P 5L9 (613)237-5171. A/C (Air Conditioning) C/CATV (Color Cable TV; movies; radios; phones; suites; pay valet parking lot. No Pets. AE, DI, ER, MC, VI (American Express, Diners, En Route, Master Charge, Visa card) (Non-Smokers rooms) (Smoke Detectors).

From an advertisement in the *American Automobile Association TourBook*:

Ottawa Hotel Roxborough, A Clarion Hotel, 123 Metcalfe Street, Ottawa, Ontario K1P 5L9 (613)237-5171. 145 Deluxe Guestrooms; Gourmet Restaurant; Room Service; Valet Parking; Complementary Continental Breakfast, Newspaper, and Shoe Shine; Children under 18 years stay free in parents room; Vacation Packages available; CAA/AAA Members 20% discount off published rates; Senior Citizens Rates. For reservations call in Toronto (416) 364-2667 or toll free Canada/U.S.A. 1-800-263-8967 or 1-800-221-2222.

From *Accommodations Ontario Canada* by Ontario Ministry of Tourism:

Hotel Roxborough **** (=High Quality) (Small Hotel) CAA OHMA (member of Canadian Automobile Association and Ontario Hotel Motel Association) 123 Metcalfe St. K1P 5L9 (613)237-5171. $90/175, 146 rooms, (Meeting Rooms) (Private Baths) (Air Conditioning) (Television) (Dining Room) (No Pool) (No Sauna) (Liquor License) (Babysitting) (No Pets Allowed).

From *Ottawa & Hull Visitor Guide 1990*:

Hotel Roxborough 123 Metcalfe (613)237-5171 1-800-263-8967 FAX 237-0733. 145 rooms $94-130 single room $104-140 double room. (continental breakfast) (no air conditioning) (no pool) (fitness gymnasium) (no kitchen en-suite) (laundry/valet) (room service) (no coffee shop) (dining room) (no tobacco shop) (non-smoking rooms) (no wheelchair access) (no children's rates) (family/weekend rates).

a. Identify the complete list of information that is available about hotels from the listed sources.

b. List the problems that you would encounter in converting the available information if it is being entered manually into the new database.

c. List any additional problems that you would encounter in converting the available information if it is being done by a computer program processing machine readable text.

10. Which of the following things are likely to be entities in a typical business system? If they are not entities, indicate why.

a. Product	**f.** Employee
b. Color	**g.** Address
c. Red	**h.** Date
d. Part Number	**i.** Buys
e. ASCII Character	**j.** Enter Order

11. Which of the following are likely to be relationships in an Entity-Relationship Diagram? If they are not, explain why.

a. Client
b. Buys
c. Compute Price
d. Works On
e. Contains

f. Spouse
g. Is A
h. Project Number
i. Payment
j. Is Part Of

12. Classify each of the following as entity, entity occurrence, attribute, attribute occurrence, or relationship.

a. Employee
b. Birth Date
c. Charles Darwin
d. Is Married To
e. Part Number
f. Contains
g. Hot Dog
h. Children
i. Supervises
j. Supervisor

Project

Using the project definition handed in after Chapter 2, as amended by your project supervisor, prepare the following items:

a. **An Extended Entity-Relationship Model** of the database for the project.
b. **A table of detailed attributes** for each entity identifying the primary key, any foreign keys, the type and width of the attributes, and whether null values are allowed.
c. **An appendix** containing samples of forms, file descriptions, and a list of other sources used in identifying the components of the data model.

This, and every project submission, should also include the following standard items:

● **A cover page** with the project title, your name, the course identification, and the date of submission.
● **A table of contents** that lists in order all the items being submitted.
● **A letter of transmittal** to explain the purpose of each component and any special features of the components that are not obvious from the submitted material.

Do not hand your database design in at this time. You will have an opportunity to check and revise your model after Chapter 6. Complete this part of the project before Chapter 6 so you will have time to complete the next phase in Chapter 6.

5 EER Model

Cooking with Cal Oreez Case

Cal Oreez is a broadcaster, actor, and an amateur gourmet chef who hosts a lot of dinners for his friends, among whom I count myself as one. He has good taste, but a bad memory. He often finds himself searching through recipe books for recipes that were tried many months ago. At the last minute he may be rushing to the local purveyor of gourmet goodies for that special essential forgotten ingredient that spells the difference between exquisite and merely palatable. Sometimes he suffers the embarrassment of serving the same recipe twice to the same person, implying that he has run out of good recipes.

I persuaded him that a computerized database is the solution to his problems. It would keep track of where the recipes are, what ingredients they need, how much of each ingredient is needed to serve a group of, say, 24 intimate friends, and to whom the recipes have been served. I have also persuaded him that you are the best person to design the database. One late evening, after a long and heated discussion about the relative merits of Dijon and Cajun mustard, he volunteered the following design information.

Each Recipe book has a unique name, like *Mrs. Beeton's Cookery in Color*. Each recipe has a unique name, such as *Fillets Florentine with Sesame Butter*, a number of servings that the recipe makes, and a classification to indicate whether it is a soup, appetizer, main course, vegetable, dessert, or drink. The ingredients can be multiplied to serve more people. Each recipe has a list of unique ingredients with an associated quantity and measuring unit like, *2 teaspoons sesame oil*. Each recipe has a unique name and starting page number within each book, but different books may have recipes with the same name and possibly different ingredients or different quantities of the same ingredient. An ingredient can appear in many recipes.

A meal is a collection of recipes that go well together. For instance, *Amish Dutch Dinner* consists of *Chicken Corn Soup, Scalloped Oysters, Sauerbraten, Potato Dumplings, Pepper Slaw, Cucumbers in Cream Dressing,* and *Pineapple Bavarian Cream*. Some of these recipes may also appear in other meals.

An event is a meal served on a particular date to a particular guest list. With all the preparation required, Cal is never able to stage more than one event per day. A meal may be used in other events. Cal wants to keep track of which recipes he has served to each of his friends because he wants to make sure that they do not get the same recipe twice. He will relax this restriction for appetizers, desserts, and drinks which may be served to the same person at more than one event. His aversion to duplication also extends to the names of his friends. He never has two friends with the same name. He needs to record the current address and home telephone number of each friend so he can prepare invitations.

Please prepare an Extended Entity-Relationship Diagram of the database that Cal would need to serve his information needs. Then prepare tables of detailed attributes for each entity identifying the primary key, any foreign keys, the type and width of the attributes, and whether null values are allowed. Cal has promised that if he likes the job you do, he will invite you to his next *Chinese Banquet.*

All project submissions should also include the following standard items:

- **A cover page** with the project title, your name, the course identification, and the date of submission.
- **A table of contents** that lists in order all the items being submitted.
- **A letter of transmittal** to explain the purpose of each component and any special features of the components that are not obvious from the submitted material.

References

1. Batini, C., B. Demo and A. Di Leva, "A Methodology for Conceptual Design of Office Data Bases," *Information Systems,* Vol. 9, No., 3/4, pp. 251-263, 1984.

2. Crawford, Anthony, *System Excellence by Design,* JAtec Designer Systems Ltd., 461 Lakeshore Road West, Oakville, Ontario L6K 1G4.

3. IBM Corporation, *Joint Application Design,* Publication G509-2019-0, IBM Corporation, 1981.

4. Kull, David, "Software Development: The Consensus Approach," *Computer and Communications Decisions,* August 1987, pp. 63-67.

5. Loomis, Mary E. S., *The Database Book,* Macmillan Publishing Co., New York, 1987.

6. M. G. Rush Systems Inc., Bloomfield Hills, MI

7. Smith, J. M., and D. C. P. Smith, "Database Abstractions: Aggregation and Generalization," *ACM Transactions on Database Systems,* Vol. 2, No. 2, June 1977, pp. 105-133.

8. Storey, Veda C. and Robert C. Goldstein, "A Methodology for Creating User Views in Database Design," *ACM Transactions on Database Systems*, Vol. 13, No. 3, Sept. 1988, pp. 305-338.

5 EER Model

Chapter 6

Database Definition

	DATABASE (WHAT)	PROGRAMS (HOW)	BENEFITS (WHY)	NETWORK (WHERE)	REAL TIME (WHEN)	SKILLS (WHO)
USER CONCEPT	Entity Relationship	Activity	Intangible Benefit	Map		Organization Design
DESIGNER CONCEPT	E-R Diagram	A-E Diagram	AHP	Network		Skills Responsibility
USER DETAIL	Forms Screens	Processes Data	Tangible Benefit	Work Volume	Discrete Events	Transition Training
DESIGNER DETAIL	EER Diagram	Data Flow Diagrams	Benefit- Cost	Partition	Transition Diagrams	Methodology Tools
BUILDER CONCEPT	Normal Form Relations	Structure Chart	Function Points	System Architecture	Specifications	Learning
BUILDER DETAIL	Files	Screens Specifications	Costs	Network Specs	Interfaces	4GL CASE

Objectives

Chapter 5 provided a detailed statement of all the entities needed in the logical data model, all the keys and attributes needed for each entity, and all the relationships between the entities. This process completed the analysis phase of the database design. The next step is the design phase, in which the logical specifications are converted into physical specifications that can be programmed using the language of some Data Base Management System. The product of this last stage is a physical file structure that can be used to store data and answer queries.

The implementation will be illustrated with an example using the SQL language. The objective of this chapter is to learn how to perform the steps in the implementation process. You will learn how to:

- **Convert** the Extended Entity Relationship Model into a Relational Data Model.

- **Normalize** the Relational Model to make sure that all data redundancies and update and insertion anomalies have been eliminated.

- **Format** the attributes with generic data types.

- **Program** the specifications in a database language like SQL.

- **Index and Cluster** data for efficient access.

- **Restructure** the database into logical views that are more convenient for use in specific programs.

Introduction

The Extended Entity-Relationship Model provides a database definition that has been derived by a largely intuitive process. Some clues have been provided to identify good and bad models, but they are based more on rules-of-thumb than on rigorous theory. The Relational Model and its concept of normalization provide a rigorous theory about the construction of a database. Normalization will be used in this chapter to test the EER Model and make sure that all the entities are associated with their correct attributes.

If the Entity-Relationship Model has been developed carefully, then the tables in the design should be normal or nearly normal. In that case, the normalization process should be a simple check of previous work. If errors have been made in the Entity-Relationship Model, then normalization reveals them before any further effort is expended to implement the model. Normalization reveals any redundancies and ambiguities that may be left in the model.

The check for normality is the last stage of logical analysis and design. The logical model can be converted into a physical specification that can be implemented using a Data Base Management System. This will be illustrated using a language called SQL (pronounced sequel). The physical specification contains features to specify the form and content of each attribute and guarantee the integrity of the database.

Normalization

The normalization process is designed to eliminate several pathological problems that can creep into a database design. The problems are redundant data, lost data, and implied spurious connections. Before seeing how the normalization process accomplishes this task, a relational notation must be defined and the concepts of projection, joining, and dependency must be defined.

Notation

Files have a very simple structure in the Relational Model. Each file consists of a rectangular table called a relation. The term relation has nothing to do with the relationships that have been used in the logical model. The term comes from the mathematical origins of the Relational Model. To prevent confusion, the relational file is referred to as a table.

Each entity in the model becomes a table. Each row of the table corresponds to one occurrence of an entity. Rows are sometimes called tuples, but are referred to as rows in this book. The rows can be in any order. Sorting is not a part of the Relational Model. The model treats sorting as something that is done to data to prepare a report.

The columns of the table correspond to the attributes of the entity. Each column stores all of the data about a single attribute. The columns are conceptually all the same. They differ only in the width and type of data that can be

| MEETINGS | | | | | | |
COURSE_ID	SECTION_ID	MEETING_ID	BUILDING_ID	ROOM_ID	DAY	*TIME*
1021	01	1	19	212	MON	0900
1021	01	2	19	212	WED	0900
1021	02	1	19	214	TUE	1400
1021	02	2	19	214	THU	1400
2202	01	1	21	107	MON	1100
2202	01	2	21	109	WED	1100

Figure 6-1

Notation for relational database tables.

stored in them. The columns are not in any specific order. Figure 6-1 illustrates a simple Relational Table and illustrates all the notation.

Three kinds of columns are particularly interesting. These three kinds are the columns that store keys, foreign keys, and optional attributes. A short-hand notation distinguishes each kind. A typical table description has the following form:

NAME (<u>KEY</u>, **FOREIGN_KEY**, **ATTRIBUTE**, *OPTIONAL_ATTRIBUTE*)

where

- **NAME** = the name of the entity being recorded.
- <u>KEY</u> = The unique identification key or compound key for the entity. These are identified by an underline. A key with a single attribute is called an atomic key. A key with multiple attributes is called a compound key.
- **FOREIGN_KEY** = The key of a related table. The foreign key is used to provide a logical link to the related table. These are identified by recording the name in **boldface** type.
- **ATTRIBUTE** = Any of the mandatory attributes of the entity being recorded. In the examples of the conversion process, the ordinary descriptive attributes are often left out and replaced by three dots as follows ...
- *OPTIONAL_ATTRIBUTE* = An attribute or foreign key that can have a null or missing value. Identifying keys can never have null values because the row could not be identified if the key was missing. Optional attributes are identified by recording the name in *ITALIC* type.

Normalization Concepts

The normalization process uses the concepts of projection, joining, and dependency.

Projection and joining are table operations to eliminate columns from a table or to join the columns of two tables. Both are illustrated in Figure 6-2.

Figure 6-2
Example of relational
projections and a rela-
tional join to reverse
the projections.

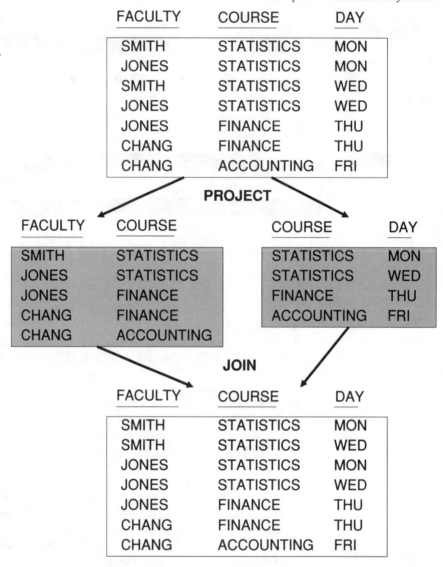

Projection is the elimination of columns of a Relational Table. In Figure 6-2 there is a table with three attributes: FACULTY, COURSE, and DAY. Two projections have been performed. The first one projects the FACULTY and COURSE attributes into a new table. The second one projects the COURSES and DAY attributes into a new table. In each case, duplicate rows have been removed. This removal of duplicates is a powerful feature of the projection operation because it reduces data duplication.

Figure 6-3

Illustration of spurious records resulting from a join.

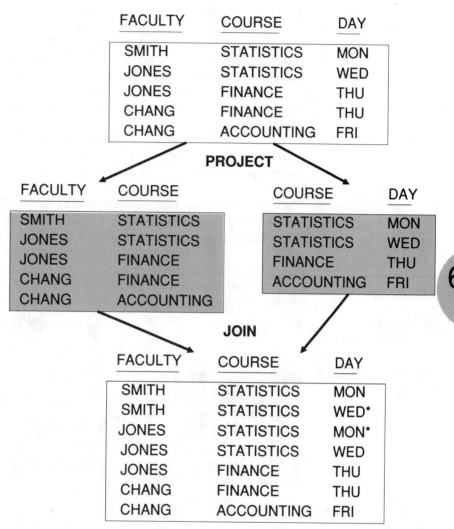

* Spurious joins

Joining is the inverse operation of projection. The two projections of the table in Figure 6-2 can be joined to recreate the original table. This is done by matching rows with a common identifying key. In the example, COURSE is the common key for the tables. Thus, every FACULTY who teaches STATISTICS is matched with a DAY on which STATISTICS is taught.

A projection and a subsequent join on the same data do not always recreate the original data. The original table at the top of Figure 6-3 is the same as the one at the top of Figure 6-2, except that the first two rows have been removed in

Figure 6-3. The projections and subsequent join give the same result as in Figure 6-2. This is because the join produces all possible combinations of the FACULTY and DAYS associated with the STATISTICS course. In Figure 6-2 all possible combinations were in the original table. In Figure 6-3 only some were in the original table. Later, ways of eliminating this ambiguity are examined.

Dependency is based on the mathematical concept of a dependent variable. Figure 6-4 illustrates a dependency between two mathematical variables and between two database attributes.

In the first case, y depends on x because it is determined by the formula $y=x^2$ Each value of x maps into a corresponding value of y. Thus x determines y with the notation $x \rightarrow y$. In the same way, there is a correspondence between NAME and STUDENT_ID in the second table of Figure 6-4. Each value of STUDENT_ID maps into a corresponding value of NAME. STUDENT_ID→NAME and NAME is dependent on STUDENT_ID for a value. In each case there is a 1:1 correspondence between the values of the independent attributes x or STUDENT_ID and their corresponding dependent attributes, y or NAME. This is called **single value dependency**.

Sometimes there is a 1:N correspondence between the independent and the dependent attributes. In Figure 6-5 there is a mathematical relationship $y=x^{0.5}$

Figure 6-4
Mathematical and database examples of single valued dependency.

$y=f(x^2)$

x	y
1	1
2	4
3	9
4	16
5	25

NAME=f(STUDENT_ID)

STUDENT_ID	NAME
601513	GREEN
602476	SETHI
613181	O'GRADY
625417	DOMSKI
629537	VAN SMA

Figure 6-5
Mathematical and database examples of multi-valued dependency.

$y=f(x^{0.5})$

x	y
1	+1
1	- 1
4	+2
4	- 2
9	+3
9	- 3

COURSE=f(STUDENT_ID)

STUDENT_ID	COURSE
601513	ACCOUNTING
601513	FINANCE
601513	STATISTICS
602476	ACCOUNTING
602476	STATISTICS
613181	FINANCE

which says that y is the square root of x. Each value of x can have two values of y, a positive one and a negative one. In the database relationship, COURSE is dependent on STUDENT_ID. Each STUDENT_ID can have several courses associated with it. This is called **multivalue dependency** which is symbolized with a double arrow as in STUDENT_ID→→COURSE.

After understanding the concepts of projecting tables, joining tables, single valued dependency, and multivalued dependency, the successive stages of the normalization process are examined.

The Normalization Process

Normalization is a test of whether the analyst has a clear understanding of the meaning of each entity. It applies to one entity at a time. It is just as necessary, whether you have one entity or many.

The normalization process consists of a series of stages which produce tables with different properties called normal forms. The first stage of the process produces tables in First Normal Form (1NF), the second stage produces tables in Second Normal Form (2NF), and so on up to Domain-Key Normal Form (DKNF). Each of these stages is examined in more detail by looking at tables which are not yet in the corresponding normal form. These are called tables in abnormal form. They are then converted into the corresponding normal form.

If the Entity-Relationship Model has been developed carefully, then the tables in the design should be normal or nearly normal. In that case, the normalization process should be a simple check of previous work. It is easier to understand the process if it starts with a table that is clearly not in normal form. It can then be seen how normalization eliminates design problems.

Each abnormal form is treated as an error with a clue to the error, a cause of the error, and a cure for the error.

6
Database

First Normal Form

CLUE: **The table has nested groups of attributes.**
CAUSE: Nested groups have not been made into characteristic entities.
CURE: Project the table into multiple tables, one for each level of nesting. Each level inherits the keys from the level above.

1NF is the least restrictive form of a table. The only restriction on it is that it must be a simple rectangular table with no nested subgroups. Figure 6-6 illustrates a table that is derived from part of the COBOL file in Figure 5-14. The nested subgroup corresponds to the OCCURS option in COBOL.

The table is in First Abnormal Form because it has nested subgroups in it. The blank fields repeat all of the values above them. For a particular faculty member, there are nested courses. For courses there are nested sections of courses. For sections there are nested days on which the sections are taught.

The nested groups can be eliminated in either of two ways. The table can be filled in by replicating the repeated values of FACULTY_ID, FIRSTNAME, LASTNAME, etc. Alternately the table can be split into smaller tables that factor

FACULTY_ID	FIRST NAME	LAST NAME	OFFICE_ID	PHONE	COURSE_ID	SECTION_ID	COURSE_TITLE	CREDIT	BUILDING_ID	BUILDING_NAME	ROOM_ID	DAY
4167	LEO	WHITE	17411	4443171	1072	01	MIS	3	19	ROSS	107	MON
									19	ROSS	107	WED
						02	MIS	3	17	HAYE	219	TUE
									19	ROSS	115	THU
					1082	01	STATS	3	19	ROSS	109	MON
									19	ROSS	109	WED
1702	KEN	BLACK	17411	4443171	2301	01	FINANCE	2	17	HAYE	130	THU
					2304	01	CAP MKTS	2	19	ROSS	111	WED
3112	JAN	GREEN	17420	2853122	1041	01	O.M.	3	19	ROSS	108	MON
									19	ROSS	108	WED
						02	O.M.	3	19	ROSS	108	TUE
									19	ROSS	108	THU

Figure 6-6

A table in First Abnormal Form. It contains nested groups.

FACULTY_ID	FIRST NAME	LAST NAME	OFFICE_ID	PHONE	COURSE_ID	SECTION_ID	COURSE_TITLE	CREDIT	BUILDING_ID	BUILDING_NAME	ROOM_ID	DAY
4167	LEO	WHITE	17411	4443171	1072	01	MIS	3	19	ROSS	107	MON
									19	ROSS	107	WED
						02	MIS	3	17	HAYE	219	TUE
									19	ROSS	115	THU
					1082	01	STATS	3	19	ROSS	109	MON
									19	ROSS	109	WED
1702	KEN	BLACK	17411	4443171	2301	01	FINANCE	2	17	HAYE	130	THU
					2304	01	CAP MKTS	2	19	ROSS	111	WED
3112	JAN	GREEN	17420	2853122	1041	01	O.M.	3	19	ROSS	108	MON
									19	ROSS	108	WED
						02	O.M.	3	19	ROSS	108	TUE
									19	ROSS	108	THU

FACULTY

FACULTY_ID	FIRST NAME	LAST NAME	OFFICE	PHONE
4167	LEO	WHITE	17411	4443171
1702	KEN	BLACK	17411	4443171
3112	JAN	GREEN	17420	2853122

CLASSES

FACULTY ID	COURSE ID	SECTION ID	COURSE TITLE	CREDIT
4167	1072	01	MIS	3
4167	1072	02	MIS	3
4167	1082	01	STATS	3
1702	2301	01	FINANCE	2
1702	2304	01	CAP MKTS	2
3112	1041	01	O.M.	3
3112	1041	02	O.M.	3

ASSEMBLIES

FACULTY ID	COURSE ID	SECTION ID	BUILDING ID	BUILDG NAME	ROOM ID	DAY
4167	1072	01	19	ROSS	107	MON
4167	1072	01	19	ROSS	107	WED
4167	1072	02	17	HAYE	219	TUE
4167	1072	02	19	ROSS	115	THU
4167	1082	01	19	ROSS	109	MON
4167	1082	01	19	ROSS	109	WED
1702	2301	01	17	HAYE	130	THU
1702	2304	01	19	ROSS	111	WED
3112	1041	01	19	ROSS	108	MON
3112	1041	01	19	ROSS	108	WED
3112	1041	02	19	ROSS	108	TUE
3112	1041	02	19	ROSS	108	THU

Figure 6-7

Conversion of a First Abnormal Form table to First Normal Form by projecting it.

out the nested groups. The first method is valid, but creates a great deal of work in the later normalization process. Later stages of normalization factor out the nested groups anyway. The second method simplifies the normalization process greatly. Figure 6-7 illustrates how this second method is used.

The original table has been split into three tables. The tables are:

FACULTY (<u>FACULTY_ID</u>, FIRSTNAME, LASTNAME, OFFICE, PHONE)
CLASSES (**FACULTY_ID**, <u>COURSE_ID</u>, <u>SECTION_ID</u>,
      COURSE_TITLE, CREDIT)
ASSEMBLIES (**FACULTY_ID,** <u>COURSE_ID</u>, <u>SECTION_ID</u>,
      BUILDING_ID, BUILDING_NAME, **ROOM_ID**, <u>DAY</u>)

Note that FACULTY_ID has been copied into all of the tables and COURSE_ID and SECTION_ID have been copied into the CLASSES and AS-SEMBLIES table. This is necessary when converting a hierarchical file, like the example file, because the earlier keys are inherited as an implicit part of the nested levels of the hierarchy. Later normalization may remove some of these inherited keys.

There are now three tables in 1NF. In each case, the underlined keys are sufficient to identify each row uniquely. The next thing to do is to check each table for 2NF and 3NF.

Second Normal Form

CLUE: One or more non-key attributes is single value dependent on only part of a compound key.

CAUSE: The attributes are attributes of a higher entity identified by the partial key.

CURE: Project the table into tables in which all attributes depend on the whole key.

The 1NF CLASSES table from the previous example is used to illustrate the Second Abnormal Form in Figure 6-8. The arrows above the table show the dependency relationships in the table. The leftmost arrows mean that FACUL-TY_ID is dependent on COURSE_ID and SECTION_ID. Thus, if you know the COURSE_ID and SECTION_ID, you can determine the ID of the FACULTY that teaches this section of the course. Similarly COURSE_TITLE depends only on the COURSE_ID and CREDIT depends only on the COURSE_ID.

The problem with this form of table is that some of the information is repeated. The COURSE_TITLE and CREDIT information are repeated each time that COURSE_ID appears in the table. This leads to three problems.

- **Multiple values.** It is possible to enter the data in more than one way. MIS might appear as *MIS* in one place, *Information Systems* in another, and *Mgt Info Sys* in a third. It becomes very difficult to search for data if they can appear in more than one way.

- **Extra storage.** The data are duplicated so they take up extra storage space in each copy.

6
Database

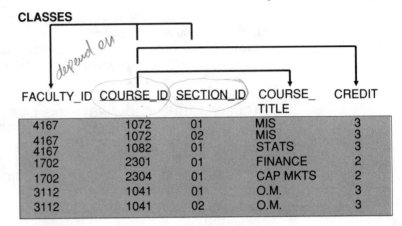

Figure 6-8
The CLASSES table in
Second Abnormal Form.

- **Lost data.** The data is associated with FACULTY_ID and SECTION_ID. If a course has not yet been divided into sections and has not yet had a faculty member assigned to teach it, then it cannot have a name or credit value assigned to it. This is called an **insertion anomaly** because it is not possible to insert this information. If it is decided that the course will not be offered this year, then the information in the row is deleted. However, that means that the name and credits are deleted also. This is called a **deletion anomaly** because desired information is deleted along with undesired information.

The Second Abnormal Form is converted into 2NF by taking projections in which all attributes in the projection are dependent on the same keys. The results are illustrated in Figure 6-9. In this example the projections are:

COURSES (<u>COURSE_ID</u>, COURSE_TITLE, CREDIT)
SECTIONS (<u>COURSE_ID</u>, <u>SECTION_ID</u>, **FACULTY_ID**)

The COURSES and SECTIONS tables contain the same information as the tables identified from the same file by the Entity-Relationship approach. The underlined keys uniquely identify each row. The same process can be applied to the 1NF ASSEMBLIES table developed in Figure 6-7. Figure 6-10 shows the dependencies and the resulting 2NF tables.

The same dependency of FACULTY on COURSE_ID and SECTION_ID is found in this table. The result is the same as the one in Figure 6-9 so it does not have to be duplicated. The SECTIONS table developed in Figure 6-9 is the only one that is needed. The other tables are:

BUILDINGS (<u>BUILDING_ID</u>, BUILDING_NAME)
MEETINGS (<u>COURSE_ID</u>, <u>SECTION_ID</u>, **BUILDING_ID**, **ROOM_ID**,
   <u>DAY</u>)

Again these tables contain almost the same information as the ones developed using the Entity-Relationship Model. The only difference is that MEETING_ID,

Figure 6-9
Converting the CLAS-
SES table to Second
Normal Form.

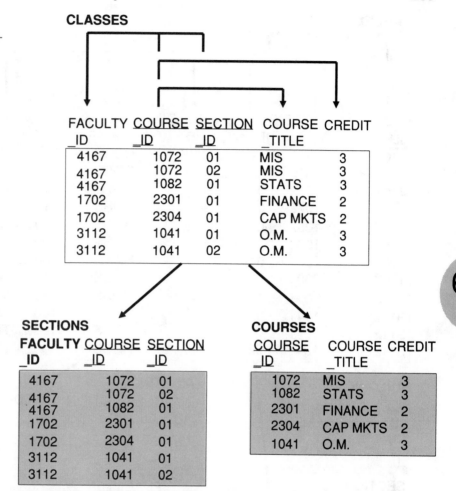

from the Entity-Relationship version, never existed in the original file in this example. DAY serves the same function in this table. It would be better to add MEETING_ID to the table as a subkey and let DAY be a dependent attribute. This result is identical to the version in Chapter 5.

Third Normal
Form

    CLUE: A non-key attribute has a single valued dependency on an attribute that is not part of the key.

    CAUSE: The attribute is dependent on a foreign key and should be an attribute of the corresponding foreign entity.

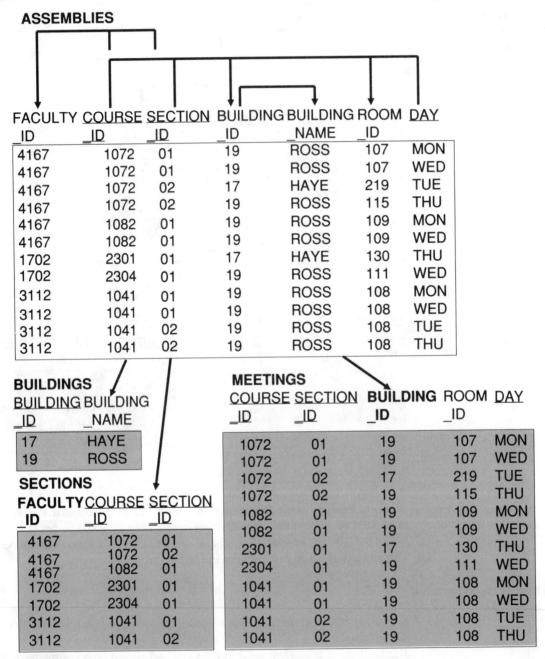

Figure 6-10
Converting the ASSEMBLIES table to Second Normal Form.

Figure 6-11

The FACULTY table in
Third Abnormal Form.

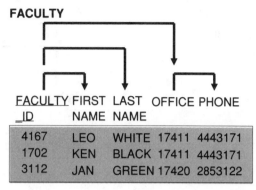

FACULTY

FACULTY_ID	FIRST NAME	LAST NAME	OFFICE	PHONE
4167	LEO	WHITE	17411	4443171
1702	KEN	BLACK	17411	4443171
3112	JAN	GREEN	17420	2853122

CURE: Split the attribute(s) and the independent attribute they depend on into a separate table. If the independent attribute is the key of an existing entity, then add the dependent attributes to that entity.

The FACULTY table in Figure 6-11 is used to illustrate this problem. The table was converted to 1NF in Figure 6-7. It is also in 2NF because it has an atomic key. Therefore, attributes cannot depend on part of the key.

All of the attributes in the FACULTY table are dependent on FACULTY_ID except PHONE which is dependent on OFFICE. In the example university, the PHONE number is a property of the office. When faculty members change offices, they also change phone numbers. Thus the primary key of the FACULTY table is FACULTY_ID, but the PHONE attribute does not depend on the primary key or any part of it. This indicates that the table is not in 3NF. Note that if PHONE depended on FACULTY_ID, there would not be a 3NF problem.

The problems that result from not having a 3NF table are the same as the problems in the Second Abnormal Form.

- **Multiple values.** If two faculty members share the same office, it is possible to enter two different phone numbers in the table even if that is not physically possible in the offices. This is an update anomaly because it is possible to create errors when updating data.
- **Extra storage.** Duplicate copies of the same data take extra storage space.
- **Lost data.** If there is nobody assigned to an office, there is an insertion anomaly because there is no way of storing the phone number associated with that office. If a person is deleted from the table, then there is a deletion anomaly because the phone number of the office is deleted with the person row, even though the phone is still associated with the office.

The problems are the same as in Second Abnormal Form and they are solved in the same way. The table is split by taking projections as shown in Figure 6-12 to get the following tables:

FACULTY (<u>FACULTY_ID</u>, FIRSTNAME, LASTNAME, **OFFICE**)
OFFICES (<u>OFFICE</u>, PHONE)

6

Database

Figure 6-12
Converting the FACUL-
TY table to Third Nor-
mal Form.

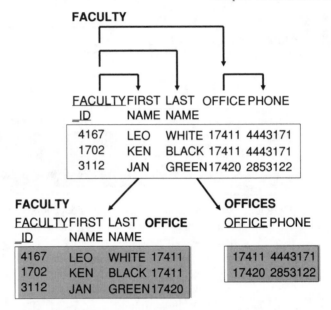

The keys are the attributes which determine all the other attributes. Thus OFFICE is a key because it determines the PHONE number. The result of converting a table into Second and then Third Normal Form is that all attributes in the table—as in the FACULTY table—depend on:

● **The key** (1NF).
● **The whole key** (2NF).
● **Nothing but the key** (3NF).

Boyce-Codd Normal Form

CLUE: **A table is in 3NF with two or more compound candidate keys that overlap.**
CAUSE: Part of the key is dependent on a non-key attribute.
CURE: Perform a relational project to split the table to remove the dependency.

The problems and the solutions are illustrated using the data from Figure 6-2. The following rules apply to the data in Figure 6-13.

● FACULTY and DAY are the compound key.
● FACULTY and COURSE are a candidate compound key that could have been selected instead. FACULTY is the overlapping attribute in the two keys.
● A COURSE can be taught on only one DAY of the week.

The data, the dependency relationships, and the correct projection are shown in Figure 6-13. The table is clearly 3NF because the non-key attribute depends on the whole key and nothing but the key.

Boyce-Codd Normal Form (BCNF) is an intermediate normal form between Third and Fourth Normal Form. The problems that result from not having a BCNF table are insertion and deletion anomalies.

Figure 6-13
Converting a table to
Boyce-Codd Normal
Form.

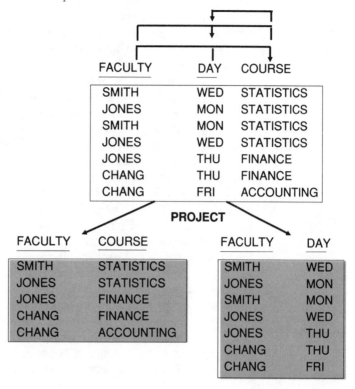

● **Insertion Anomaly.** It is impossible to insert the information that Marketing is taught on Tuesday unless a faculty member is assigned to teach it.

● **Deletion Anomaly.** If Chang changes from teaching Accounting to teaching Statistics, then the information that Accounting is taught on Friday is lost.

The problem can be eliminated by projections that split the table to separate the key and the single attribute dependency as illustrated in Figure 6-13.

Boyce-Codd Normal Form eliminates all the problems that can result from single valued dependencies. BCNF is sufficient for most database design problems. However, BCNF does not guarantee that all anomalies have been removed. The rest of the normalization problems can only result if multivalued dependencies exist. These problems are rare and often difficult to detect.

Fourth Normal Form

CLUE:	There are two multivalued dependencies that depend on the same subkey attribute.
CAUSE:	Two or more intersection entities have been combined.
CURE:	Project the table to split it into the separate intersection entities.

Problems that can be corrected by converting to Fourth or Fifth Normal Form do not exist unless the table has two properties. The table must have:

- a compound key consisting of at least three subkeys.
- at least two multivalued dependency relationships among the keys.

Third Normal Form tables with fewer keys or fewer multivalued dependencies are automatically in Fourth and Fifth Normal Form.

The problems and the solutions are illustrated again using the data from Figure 6-2. The data, the dependency relationships, and the correct projection are shown in Figure 6-14. In Figure 6-2 the dependencies were not stated. There are several possible dependency rules that could apply to the table. Each would model a different situation in the real world and each could result in a different normalized data structure. One possible rule has already been used to illustrate Boyce-Codd Normal Form.

The structure in Figure 6-14 has the following dependency rules.

$$FACULTY \rightarrow\rightarrow COURSE$$
$$FACULTY \rightarrow\rightarrow DAY$$

This structure says there is no dependency relationship between COURSE and DAY. It means that each faculty member can teach certain courses and that each faculty member is available on certain days. There is no implication that a faculty member teaches any particular course on any particular day. Thus the table tells us the availability of faculty members for courses and the days on which they are available. The fact that the courses and days are entered beside each other seduces us into believing that more is intended, but it really is not. This situation is the result of a **connection trap** in which we conclude that common keys imply a connection when there really is none.

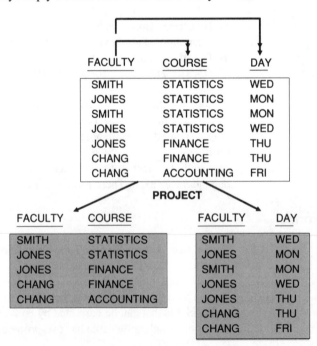

Figure 6-14
The AVAILABILITY table converted to Fourth Normal Form.

The three column table has the same possible problems that were encountered with Second and Third Abnormal Form tables.

- **Multiple values.** The facts that Smith teaches Statistics and that Jones teaches Statistics are recorded twice.
- **Extra storage.** It takes extra storage to record the multiple values. It may not appear to be as much extra space as that taken by the multiple tables resulting from projecting into two tables. However, any practical table has many combinations of such records and consumes large quantities of space recording all possible combinations of two multivalued attributes.
- **Lost data.** If Chang is unable to teach Accounting, the fact that Chang is available Friday gets deleted. Alternatively a very complex update routine is needed to replace the Accounting value with a value, such as Finance, that Chang does teach.

These problems are all solved by projecting the table into two other tables that each record only a single multivalued dependency. Neither of these tables creates any confusion about update or deletion of the data. A join can be performed to reconstruct the table. It must be understood that the meaning of the resulting table is that it lists all possible combinations of courses and days that the faculty member is **available** to teach.

Another possible dependency structure for this table is shown in Figure 6-15 where:

FACULTY→→COURSE
COURSE→→DAY

Figure 6-15
The REQUIREMENTS table converted to Fourth Normal Form.

FACULTY	COURSE	DAY
SMITH	STATISTICS	WED
JONES	STATISTICS	MON
SMITH	STATISTICS	MON
JONES	STATISTICS	WED
JONES	FINANCE	THU
CHANG	FINANCE	THU
CHANG	ACCOUNTING	FRI

PROJECT

FACULTY	COURSE
SMITH	STATISTICS
JONES	STATISTICS
JONES	FINANCE
CHANG	FINANCE
CHANG	ACCOUNTING

COURSE	DAY
STATISTICS	WED
STATISTICS	MON
FINANCE	THU
ACCOUNTING	FRI

6
Database

This one means that each faculty member teaches many courses and that each course needs to be taught on many days. This structure contains an implied dependency:

FACULTY→→DAY

The meaning of this implied dependency is that a faculty member may be required to teach the courses that the faculty member can teach, on certain days when the courses are required. Thus the original table can be referred to as a REQUIREMENTS table. Again the table can be projected into two tables that each record only a single multivalued dependency. Note that these two tables are not the same as the ones obtained in Figure 6-14. Again, a join can be used to reconstruct the information in the original table.

Another possible dependency structure for the same attributes is found in Figure 6-16. The notation A←←→→B means that each A can determine many B and each B can determine many A. The dependencies are:

FACULTY←←→→COURSE

COURSE←←→→DAY

FACULTY←←→→DAY

Since everything can be multivalue dependent on everything else, the table cannot be simplified or decomposed into simpler tables that preserve all of the information. The table is a SCHEDULE table that tells what courses a particular faculty member teaches and when that faculty member teaches each course. The table cannot be simplified because the three pieces of information are linked in a particular combination and no other combination is legitimate.

Fifth Normal Form

CLUE: **There are no obvious clues for detecting this problem.**

CAUSE: The table can be decomposed into two tables and cannot be recomposed into the original table, but can be decomposed into three tables and can be recomposed by joining all three tables.

CURE: Split the table into three tables.

Figure 6-16

The SCHEDULE table is in Fourth Normal Form and cannot be decomposed.

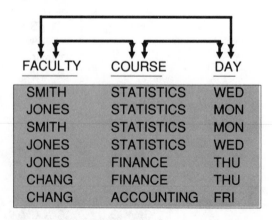

FACULTY	COURSE	DAY
SMITH	STATISTICS	WED
JONES	STATISTICS	MON
SMITH	STATISTICS	MON
JONES	STATISTICS	WED
JONES	FINANCE	THU
CHANG	FINANCE	THU
CHANG	ACCOUNTING	FRI

It has been shown that it is possible to have tables of three, or more, keys and two, or more, multivalued dependencies that cannot be decomposed. It has been shown that others can be decomposed into two tables so they can be reconstructed by joining the two projected tables. There are cases where the table can be decomposed into two tables and cannot be recomposed into the same table, but can be decomposed into three tables and can be recomposed by joining all three tables. This occurs when there is a special dependency relationship that leads to Fifth Normal Form tables. An example is shown in Figure 6-17.

Figure 6-17

The CON-STRAINED table converted to Fifth Normal Form.

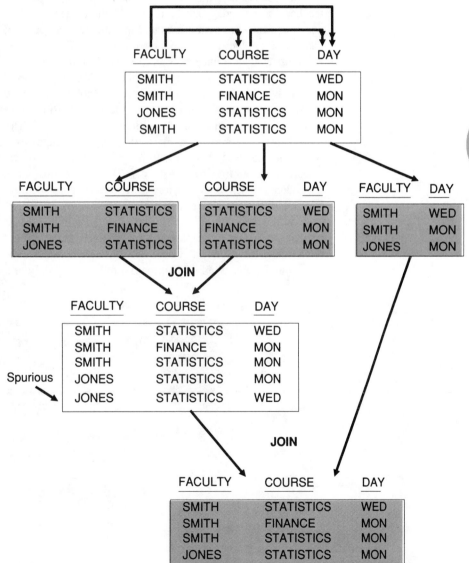

The Fifth Normal Form occurs only if there is a very special kind of constraint that goes along with the dependency structure. This constraint is:

IF

> a FACULTY member teaches a particular COURSE, and
> that COURSE is taught on a particular DAY, and
> the FACULTY member teaches on that day,

THEN

> that FACULTY member teaches that COURSE on that DAY.

This constraint requires that a faculty member teach every course that he teaches on every day that he teaches if the course is offered on that day. This constraint does not permit a faculty member to teach one course on one day and another on another day if the course is being offered on the day that he teaches. If Smith teaches Finance, Smith teaches on Monday and Finance is offered Monday, then Smith must teach Finance on Monday. Jones cannot teach Finance for Smith while Smith teaches Statistics on Monday and Finance on Wednesday.

Another way to visualize the dependency is to think of the three attributes as being at the points of a triangle as shown in Figure 6-18. The constraint says that if the three rows corresponding to the shaded triangles exist, then the enclosed white triangle must also exist. In other words, all combinations that result from joining the three triangles must exist. This is why this is called a triangular join dependency. There are other join dependencies corresponding to other geometric forms, but they are very rare in practice.

This is a very complex constraint to understand and to detect. In practice, it is unlikely that such a complex and specific constraint would occur in actual systems or that most analysts would notice such a complex constraint if it did exist. As a consequence, the Fifth Normal Form is usually only of theoretical interest.

Figure 6-18

Illustration of a triangular join dependency.

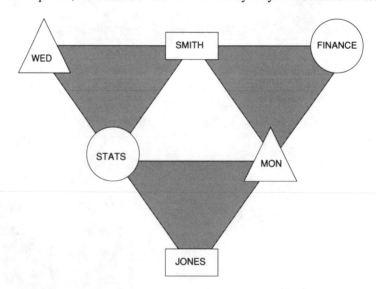

Domain-Key
Normal Form

Fagin[7] has proposed the Domain-Key Normal Form (DKNF) which does not use the concepts of dependency. It relies instead on constraints on the domains and keys of the relation. A relation in DKNF is in 5NF and thus in all other normal forms. However, DKNF cannot always be achieved. Nor is it always clear when it can be achieved. As a result, it is also only of theoretical interest. Those who want a deeper understanding of normalization should consult a text such as Date.[6]

The Normalization
Process

Now that each normal form has been defined, a process is needed to convert any Relational Table into at least Fourth Normal Form. The steps in a practical normalization process are the reverse of the steps used in explaining normalization. The steps are illustrated in Figure 6-19 using an inventory problem. The new tables created at each step are shown in list format. The steps are:

● **Specify all dependencies.** These are the single valued and multivalued dependencies that reflect the actual relationships in the organization.

● **Separate multivalued dependencies.** This eliminates nested groups of attributes that prevent First Normal Form. It also eliminates the problem that Product_ID, Production_Order_ID, and Spec_Change_ID would not be in Fourth Normal Form. Note that Product_ID, the independent attribute, is part of the compound key and the multivalued dependent attribute is the other part of the key in each case. Each multivalued dependency goes into a separate table unless the combination of attribute values is meaningful. The Schedule Table in Figure 6-16 is an example of multivalued attributes that must remain in the same table.

● **Group all attributes that depend on the same attribute.** All attributes that depend on the same attribute or attributes are part of the same relational table. The independent attributes they depend on are the keys of the respective tables. In this example, all remaining attributes depend on four keys. These are Product_ID, Supplier_ID, Postal_Code, and Product_ID+Supplier_ID. Note that Delivery_Route depends on Postal_Code which in turn depends on Supplier_ID. This transitive dependency prevents the table from being in Third Normal Form. Third Normal Form is achieved by removing Delivery_Route into a separate table with Postal_Code as a key. Postal_Code remains as a foreign key in the Supplier table.

Modified Normal
Forms

When the normalization process has been completed, there are two more things that need to be done. Tables with common keys need to be aggregated, and some tables may need to be denormalized for performance reasons.

During the normalization process, the same new tables may be created from more than one original table. An example occurred in Figures 6-9 and 6-10 where FACULTY, COURSE, and SECTION were derived from two different tables. Of course there is no need to keep these as separate tables. In general, any tables with the same keys can be amalgamated. The attributes of all these tables depend on the same keys and so they can be included in the same table.

INVENTORY(Production_Order, Spec_Change_ID, Price, Description, Product_ID,
Supplier_ID, Shipping_Date, Phone_No, Address, Postal_Code, Delivery_Route)

Identify dependencies.

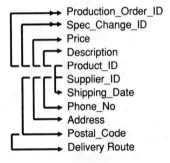

Production_Order_ID
Spec_Change_ID
Price
Description
Product_ID
Supplier_ID
Shipping_Date
Phone_No
Address
Postal_Code
Delivery Route

**Separate multivalued dependencies and
a copy of the independent attribute as a key.**

PRODUCTION (Product_ID, Production_Order_ID)
SPECS (Product_ID, Spec_Change_ID)

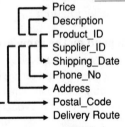

Price
Description
Product_ID
Supplier_ID
Shipping_Date
Phone_No
Address
Postal_Code
Delivery Route

**Group all attributes that depend on the same attribute.
The independent attribute(s) they depend on is the key.**

PRODUCTION (Product_ID, Production_Order_ID)
SPECS (Product_ID, Spec_Change_ID)
PRODUCTS (Product_ID, Description, Price)
SUPPLIERS (Supplier_ID, Phone_No, Address, Postal_Code)
SHIPMENTS (Product_ID, Supplier_ID, Shipping_Date)
ROUTES (Postal_Code, Delivery_Route)

Figure 6-19

The steps of the normalization process illustrated with an inventory problem.

The only exception to this rule is tables where the role or semantic meaning of the tables is different. For instance, the tables in Figures 6-14 and 6-15 may both have to exist because they have different meanings. A typical example of different roles for the same data occurs with the relationship between company names and their addresses. It is common for a company to have one address for shipping and another for billing. Two tables are needed. The keys are the same, but the data in each table have a different meaning.

Usually tables should be normalized to at least 4NF. Sometimes it is desirable to denormalize a table or leave it in a form that is not 4NF. This usually occurs for performance reasons. Every time another table is needed to fill an information request, another physical disk access is required. Thus most accesses to the SECTIONS table require a simultaneous access to the COURSES table to access the name of the course. This doubles the workload for the disk drives and halves the capacity of the system, since disk access is usually the bottleneck in most heavily loaded systems.

Copying the course name into the SECTIONS table would eliminate the need for the second access at the cost of some data duplication and some possible update problems. However, the data duplication might be an acceptable price to pay if this data is accessed very frequently. The update anomalies may not be a problem if course names rarely or never change.

A common example of data that is left unnormalized is found in addresses. The postal code depends on the city and street attributes, so the address is in 2NF. Yet the parts of an address are virtually never separated to convert these attributes to true 3NF. The street address has the characteristics of an entity with its own attributes, but it is not one about which most people wish to record data, so it is bundled as an attribute of the person. The city taxation department might take a different view since they probably do want to record information—like assessment—about the address.

Updating the Entity-Relationship Model

Normalization may reveal that some entities were not in Fourth Normal Form. The Entity-Relationship Diagram should be revised to reflect the changes resulting from normalization. Any tables that change due to normalization are replaced by the new tables. There are four cases to consider based on the keys.

- **Single atomic keys** indicate kernel entities. Thus PRODUCTS and SUPPLIERS are kernel entities.
- **Compound keys made up of keys of other tables** indicate intersection entities that result from M:N relationships. Thus SHIPMENTS records the M:N relationship between PRODUCTS and SUPPLIERS.
- **Keys of existing tables plus a qualifier attribute** indicate characteristic entities. There is a 1:N relationship between the existing table and the table whose key has a qualifying attribute. Thus, PRODUCTION and SPECS are characteristic entities of the kernel entity PRODUCTS.

- **Keys that are attributes of another table** indicate a 1:N relationship with the other table. Thus ROUTES, whose key is an attribute of SUPPLIERS, has a 1:N relationship with SUPPLIERS.

The Entity-Relationship Diagram that corresponds to the normalized tables in Figure 6-19 is shown in Figure 6-20.

Summary of
Normal Forms

There are seven normal forms including BCNF and DKNF. Each form hierarchically includes the previous one. If a table is in 4NF, then it is also in BCNF, 3NF, 2NF, and 1NF. A table is in 4NF if all attributes are functionally dependent only on the primary atomic or primary compound key. Such a table does not contain redundant data, does not consume storage space needlessly, and is not subject to update, insertion, and deletion anomalies.

Normalization up to Boyce-Codd Normal Form is based on single valued dependency relationships. 4NF and 5NF are based on multivalued dependencies.

Figure 6-20

Illustration of how relational tables are converted to an Entity-Relationship Model

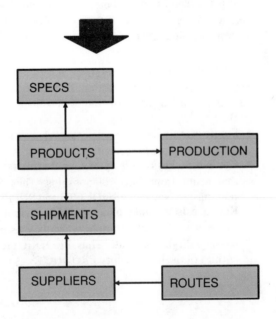

PRODUCTION (Product_ID, Production_Order_ID)

SPECS (Product_ID, Spec_Change_ID)

PRODUCTS (Product_ID, Description, Price)

SHIPMENTS (Product_ID, Supplier_ID, Shipping_Date)

SUPPLIERS (Supplier_ID, Phone_No, Address, Postal_Code)

ROUTES (Postal_Code, Delivery_Route)

The outcome of normalization depends on the structure of the business model. The same data can lead to several different designs depending on the semantic meaning of the relationships between the attributes.

The sequence of normalization processes is a useful way of understanding the stages of the process. In practice, several stages may not apply in a particular case. If the table has a single key, then only the 3NF check is required. If the table has less than three parts in a compound key and less than two multivalued dependencies among the keys, then 4NF and 5NF problems cannot occur.

The normalization process is a check to make sure that the entities have been identified correctly. The definition of normal forms in which the attributes depend on the key, the whole key, and nothing but the key are consistent with the definitions of entities as things that have an identifying key and about which people want to record data.

The normalization process uses single and multivalued dependencies as another method of revealing the existence of entities that may not have been obvious in the initial design. If the initial design of entities was good, then normalization becomes a trivial exercise in checking the design. If the initial design was not good, then normalization makes it good. Sometimes it is necessary to denormalize tables to obtain better hardware performance in the system.

Normalized tables are another way of modeling a database. The two methods are equivalent ways of representing the data. An Entity-Relationship Model identifies the tables. Normalization checks that all attributes in a table belong there. Arrows record relationships in an Entity-Relationship Model. Keys record the same relationships in normalized tables.

Converting to a Relational Model

The existing logical model identifies the keys and attributes that describe all the logical entities needed in the system that is being designed. A symbolic notation has been used to indicate relationships between the entities. Up to this stage, the analysis has been strictly at the logical level. No consideration has been given to the physical form that the data take when stored in files.

This separation of logical and physical characteristics was deliberate. By avoiding physical details until the last possible moment, all the logical relationships are preserved and none of them are neglected because of some constraint in the target physical DBMS. If sacrifices must be made in the logical structure for physical reasons, they should be made with full knowledge of the implications to the logical model. This makes clear exactly what logical properties cannot be supported by the implementation.

Fortunately, it is not usually necessary to sacrifice the logical integrity of the model. Virtually all modern Data Base Management Systems (DBMS) are implemented using a Relational Model. Most of these are implemented using a language called SQL which stands for Structured Query Language. The next stage of design is to map the logical EER Model into the Relational Model. Chen[3] also shows how to map the EER Model into a network database structure, but this procedure will not be illustrated here.

Conversion Rules

The EER Model has been checked to make sure that no design errors remain. The next step is to convert the EER Model into a Relational Model that can be implemented using a Relational DBMS. There is a set of rules[13] for conversion of the EER Model to a Relational Model.

- **Entities become Relational Tables.** Every entity that has been defined in the model becomes a table in the Relational Model. Thus the MEETINGS entity becomes the table:

  MEETINGS (<u>COURSE_ID</u>, <u>SECTION_ID</u>, <u>MEETING_ID</u>, BUILDING_ID, **<u>ROOM_ID</u>**, DAY, TIME)

- **Kernel Entities have atomic keys.** Each kernel entity should have a single atomic key. If it has a compound key, it is either not a kernel entity or the key has been developed from several attributes that are not suitable as unique identifiers. STUDENTS is a kernel entity with the atomic key STUDENT_ID. The combination of SURNAME, FIRSTNAME, and BIRTHDATE might uniquely identify a student, but it would be a very complicated key and very difficult to use as a foreign key in other tables.

- **Characteristic Entities have a compound key.** The compound key consists of the atomic key of the entity that it is a characteristic of, and a subkey that identifies each occurrence of the characteristic entity. The entities COURSES, SECTIONS, and MEETINGS are shown below with their keys.

  COURSES (<u>COURSE_ID</u>, ...)
  SECTIONS (<u>COURSE_ID</u>, <u>SECTION_ID</u>, ...)
  MEETINGS (<u>COURSE_ID</u>, <u>SECTION_ID</u>, <u>MEETING_ID</u>, ...)

  MEETINGS is a characteristic entity with the compound key COURSE_ID, SECTION_ID, and MEETING_ID. COURSE_ID and SECTION_ID are the key of the SECTIONS entity of which MEETINGS is a characteristic. MEETING_ID is the subkey that distinguishes occurrences of MEETINGS. COURSE_ID is the atomic key of the COURSES entity of which SECTIONS is a characteristic. SECTION_ID is the subkey that distinguishes each occurrence of a section of a course. The characteristic relationships can be seen from the hierarchy of keys.

- **Subtype Entities have the same key.** If the STUDENTS entity is divided into mutually exclusive subtypes GRADUATES and UNDERGRADUATES, then STUDENTS, GRADUATES and UNDERGRADUATES all have the key STUDENT_ID. In addition, the STUDENTS entity needs a new attribute STUDENT_TYPE that indicates which of the mutually exclusive subtypes the student belongs to. Occurrences of STUDENT_TYPE would contain a distinguishing code such as U for undergraduate or G for graduate.

  Overlapping subtypes also have the same key. If STUDENTS can also be either or both of ATHLETES or MUSICIANS, then the entities STUDENTS,

ATHLETES, and MUSICIANS all have the key STUDENT_ID. If it is necessary to be able to identify which of the overlapping subtypes students belong to, then STUDENTS needs an attribute for each possible subtype. Each of these attributes has a binary code such as Y for yes and N for no to indicate whether the student belongs to the corresponding subtype. The STUDENTS table needs the following attributes to identify the subtypes discussed above:

STUDENTS (<u>STUDENT_ID</u>, STUDENT_TYPE, ATHLETE, MUSICIAN, ...)

- **M:N Relationships are not allowed.** In the previous chapter M:N relationships were converted into two 1:N relationships and a new intersection entity. This process must be performed before any models are converted to relational form.

- **Relationships are represented by a foreign key.** The key of the entity at the 1 end of a 1:N relationship is a foreign key in the entity at the N end of the relationship. The 1:N relationship between ROOMS and MEETINGS is recorded by letting the key of ROOMS (BUILDING_ID and ROOM_ID) be a foreign key of MEETINGS as shown below:

MEETINGS (**<u>COURSE_ID</u>**, **<u>SECTION_ID</u>**, <u>MEETING_ID</u>,
    BUILDING_ID, ROOM_ID, ...)

Note that COURSE_ID and SECTION_ID are part of the key of MEETINGS and are also foreign keys that maintain the 1:N relationships with COURSES and SECTIONS.

1:1 relationships are represented by a foreign key in either of the entities that participate in the relationship. If STUDENTS have 1:1 relationships with SPONSORS this means that each student has 1 sponsor and each sponsor has 1 student. The relationship can be recorded with the following structure:

    STUDENTS (<u>STUDENT_ID</u>, **SPONSOR_ID,** ...)
    SPONSOR (<u>SPONSOR_ID</u>, ...)

It also can be recorded as:

    STUDENTS (<u>STUDENT_ID</u>, ...)
    SPONSORS (<u>SPONSOR_ID</u>, **STUDENT_ID,** ...)

The first structure is likely the better one since it is more likely that users would need to determine who a student's sponsor is than who a sponsor's student is. In the first structure, the student's sponsor can be found directly from an occurrence of the STUDENTS table. Sometimes 1:1 relationships are not recorded in separate entities. In the above example, it is possible that there is no need for the sponsor to have a separate existence apart from that of the student. If there is no interest in sponsors individually, then the sponsor information can be stored in the STUDENTS entity. However, the information about the sponsor would get deleted if the student record is deleted.

- **Optional relationships may have null foreign keys.** If a relationship is optional, then the foreign key at the N end of the relationship can have a null value that indicates that this occurrence of the entity does not participate in the relationship. Thus if rooms have not yet been assigned to meetings of a course, then BUILDING_ID and ROOM_ID would have null values in the MEETINGS entity.

When the optional relationship is between a kernel and a characteristic entity, then the foreign key is also part of the compound key of the entity. The key of an entity can never be null so the entity occurrence is not created when there is no relationship. SECTIONS have an optional relationship with MEETINGS because at some point sections may be created so faculty can be assigned to teach them, but MEETINGS may not yet have been scheduled. If they have not been scheduled, then MEETINGS occurrences need not exist.

● **Multiple relationships are independent.** When there are two or more relationships between two entities, they cannot always be consolidated into a single relationship. While they may appear to have the same keys and semantic content, they may be different because they may involve different occurrences of the entities and have different meanings. There may be several kinds of relationships between PERSONS and other PERSONS, such as PARENT, CHILD, SPOUSE, and EMPLOYEE. These would be recorded in three entities as follows:

PERSONS (<u>PERSON_ID</u>, **MOTHER_ID**, **FATHER_ID**, SEX, ...)
SPOUSES (<u>HUSBAND_ID</u>, <u>WIFE_ID</u>, MARRIAGE_DATE, ...)
EMPLOYEE (<u>EMPLOYER_ID</u>, <u>EMPLOYEE_ID</u>, SALARY, ...)

EMPLOYER_ID, EMPLOYEE_ID, MOTHER_ID, FATHER_ID, WIFE_ID, and HUSBAND_ID are all foreign keys that are identical to some PERSON_ID in the PERSONS table. They are given different names to distinguish their roles clearly. The separate 1:1 relationships that children have with their mother and father are recorded by the foreign keys MOTHER_ID and FATHER_ID. The SPOUSES entity is an intersection entity that records an M:N relationship between two kinds of persons. It is M:N because a man may have more than one wife and a woman may have more than one husband during their lifetimes.

The EMPLOYEE relationship is identical in form to the SPOUSES relationship. Each relates two persons using a synonym for PERSON_ID. However, they cannot be consolidated into a single relationship because the two tables record different relationships. The different relationships require different attributes like MARRIAGE_DATE and SALARY.

Note that information about both children and parents is recorded in the PERSONS table. Parents can be identified directly by the foreign keys MOTHER_ID and FATHER_ID. A woman's children can be identified by searching the table for persons who have a MOTHER_ID that is her PERSON_ID. In this case, parent and child relationships are effectively consolidated because of the reciprocal nature of the relationship. You cannot be your mother's child without her being your parent.

All other family relationships can be identified by appropriate searches of the PERSONS and SPOUSES tables. My grandparents are those with PERSON_ID equal to my parents' MOTHER_ID and FATHER_ID. My cousins are any who have the same grandparents as I have. My uncles are any males whose parents are any of my grandparents.

PERSON_ID, or its synonyms, is used as an atomic key, a foreign key, and part of a compound key in this example. In the case of the PERSONS entity, it is both an atomic key and a foreign key in the same table. Thus, the same key can serve different purposes in different tables, depending on the kind of relationship in which it is involved.

These transformation rules transform any EER Model into a corresponding set of Relational Tables that preserve all the information embodied in the EER Model. The addition of foreign keys, as specified by the conversion rules, does not cause any normalization problems. Each foreign key is dependent on the whole key which uniquely identifies the row of the table. If the design has been carefully done, the model can now be implemented in a physical database. The implementation must also enforce some rules to guarantee the consistency and integrity of the database.

Assigning Data Types

In a database of any significant size, there are usually many elements that are of the same generic type. Dates are an example. They appear in many places and in many contexts. Furthermore, it is often desirable to associate records related to the same date or compare them to determine which one has the earlier date. For instance, it might be desirable to identify, for special treatment, all the students whose enrollment date is before the date of a rule change in another table.

These comparisons are much easier if all dates in the system are stored in the same format regardless of the table that contains them. Thus it is desirable to assign a standard data type to all attributes that are of the same generic type. Examples of generic types are date, identification code, money, name, percent, phone number, postal code, and time. Even large organizations with hundreds of attributes in their tables seldom require more than 30 or 40 types of data.

Defining a type means defining the internal storage form and width, the external representation, and the checks that must be performed on the data to be sure that only valid values are entered. The form can be either character or numeric. On many computers numeric data can be further subdivided into integer, decimal, fixed decimal, and zoned decimal. The width of character fields is measured in characters. The width of numeric fields is normally measured in digits, possibly with several decimal places.

The internal physical representation and the external logical representation do not have to be the same. Coding schemes may be used to compress data and reduce storage. Dates may be stored internally as the number of days since some base period, such as the beginning of the Gregorian calendar. This makes them easy to sort. When required, they can be converted to an external format such as MM–DD–YY.

Each type generally has a set of validity checks that can be performed to make sure that input is correct. The following examples illustrate some common validity checks.

- **Names** must be entirely alphabetic.
- **Numbers** may have a valid range and they may have to be integer.
- **Dates** must be checked to make sure that such dates exist. February 30 or June 31 must not be allowed. February 29 cannot happen in 1993.
- **Phone numbers** must be either 10 or 7 digits long. If extensions or worldwide calls are allowed, the rules get more complex.
- **Codes** may have to be one of a list of valid codes.
- **New keys** must not be one of the list of existing keys.

If the database language being used does not have facilities for checking for such patterns, then standard routines must be written. These must be called whenever a type is being inserted or updated in the database. Many database systems have facilities for defining and enforcing type checks.

Identification Keys

Identification keys require some special design because they are so important in identifying things. Make sure that the key is not only a valid number, but that it is also the correct number. It can cause many problems if, say, a bank deposit is deposited to the wrong account number because of a keying error by the teller. Such problems are greatly reduced by the use of check digits.[2]

A check digit is an extra digit at the end of an identification number which is calculated from the other digits in the number. There are also ways to calculate check digits from letters. This digit is a redundant piece of information that can identify common errors such as:

- **Transcription errors** that occur when an incorrect digit is copied such as a 7 instead of a 1.
- **Transposition errors** that occur when correct numbers are entered, but their positions are reversed. An example is entering 4576 instead of 4567.
- **Double transposition errors** that occur when numbers are transposed between non-adjacent columns. as in 143256 instead of 123456.
- **Multiple errors** that involve some combination of the above errors.

Figure 6-21 illustrates a common way in which the check digit can be calculated for the identification number 12345. It uses modulus 11 arithmetic to generate the check digit. This means that some calculated number is divided by

Figure 6-21

Computing a check digit for a five digit STUDENT_ID using prime number weighting and modulus 11 arithmetic.

PRIME NUMBER WEIGHTING

STUDENT-ID	1	2	3	4	5
	x	x	x	x	x
Prime Weights	11	7	5	3	2
Multiples	11+	14+	15+	12+	10=62

Subtract 62 from next highest multiple of 11
Check digit =66-62=4
STUDENT_ID with check digit = 123454

11 and the remainder is used as a check digit. In the example, 11 minus the remainder is used as a check digit.

The number used to compute the remainder can be computed in several ways. Usually each digit of the identification is multiplied by a different number in a series and the products are summed. The series may be arithmetic which grows at a constant rate as in 2, 3, 4, ... It may be geometric which grows in a multiplicative (exponential) series like 2, 4, 8, 16, ... The series could consist of the series of prime numbers 2, 3, 5, 7, 11 ... The modulus 11 method with prime number weighting detects all transposition and transcription errors. This is the method used in the example.

If modulus 11 arithmetic is used, some numbers have 10 as the remainder for a check digit. When this occurs, a letter, like X, can be used instead of the normal check digit. Alternately, the value can be rejected as an illegal code. That way the field is always numeric.

The check digit is usually placed at the end of the identification number, but could be placed in any consistent location. It can also be applied to a compound key in which several numeric keys are combined. If the combined keys are normally used together, then the one check digit serves to check the validity of the combined key.

The International Standard Book Number (ISBN) is an example of a compound numeric key with a check digit. The first digit identifies an international group of publishers. The next three digits identify a particular publisher within the group. The next five digits identify a particular title or edition by the publisher. The last digit is a check digit.

Not every identification needs a check digit. COURSE_ID, SECTION_ID, AND MEETING_ID in the example do not need a check digit because users are likely to know the meaning. Also the consequences of an error in entering these codes are not severe since errors will likely be detected later by users.

Guidelines for Keys

An identification code needs to be easy to write, easy to read, and easy to hear since people frequently copy it, read it, or say it over the telephone. There are several rules used to ensure this when designing an identification code.

- Avoid the letters O, I, Z, S, and V because they can be easily confused with 0, 1, 2, 5, and U when hand written.
- Avoid letters that sound similar like M and N or B, C, D, G, P, T, and V.
- Break codes of more than four alphabetic or five numeric characters into chunks to make them easier to recall. The phone number 416-555-1212 is easier to recall than 4165551212. It is more likely to be accurately recorded.
- Record time on a 24 hour clock to avoid confusion between AM and PM.
- Avoid using the codes of participating entities to record a relationship if the relationship is liable to change. For instance, a truck shipment from Toronto to New York could be recorded using the code 317-215-891121. 317 is the code for Toronto, 215 is the code for New York, and the rest is the scheduled departure date. However, the departure date might change or the shipment

may get rerouted to another city. A customer or expediter who knows only the original shipment code would not be able to trace the shipment once the new information was entered. The shipment should have its own identification number that users can refer to consistently.

- Avoid using letters if codes might need to be transmitted over touch tone phones. Letter codes make it almost impossible to implement automated catalog orders over the telephone since many letters have the same code.
- Use codes that are as intuitive as possible. It is clear that Room C617 is on the sixth floor of Building C or Wing C. It is less clear that Room 3617 is on the sixth floor of Building 3. It might also be on the 36th floor of a building.

In many designs, identification codes have already been defined. In fact, too many identifications may exist. A system can get unnecessarily complicated when different departments have different identification codes for raw materials, subassemblies, products, and catalog numbers. The organization may have a mixture of raw materials, subassemblies, and products in its catalog. This would be an ideal situation for the design of a unified identification code that can be used in all applications. Similar situations often exist with employee or customer identification codes.

Integrity Rules

The Extended Entity-Relationship Model has been treated as a static model that describes the database at an instant in time. It also implies some dynamic constraints that must be enforced when rows of a table are created and deleted. Integrity rules are divided into domain integrity rules and referential integrity rules. Domain integrity rules ensure that the value stored in an occurrence of an attribute is of the proper data type and contains a value from the domain of possible values.

There are three integrity rules that must be enforced to make sure that rows in related tables are still correctly related after insertion, update, or deletion. These rules apply to intersection entities that implement M:N associations, kernel to characteristic existence dependencies, and subtype relationships.

- **Domain Integrity.** All input characters must belong to those allowed for the attribute's data type. Most DBMS have data types that allow only integers, decimal numbers, characters or dates. Some allow the Data Base Administrator to define other data types. Some also allow table lookups to make sure that an entry is one of an allowable list of values. A key must always be non-null and unique. This is sometimes called the entity integrity rule. SQL has commands to enforce entity integrity. It has very limited facilities for enforcing other domain integrity rules.
- **Intersection Rules.** These rules apply to the intersection entity used to connect entities that are linked by an M:N relationship in the basic Entity-Relationship Model. The rules are:

- **Creation.** A row in the intersection table can only be created if the corresponding rows in the tables being related already exist.
- **Deletion.** If a row of either of the entities being intersected is deleted, the corresponding rows of the intersection table must be deleted.

● **Dependency Rules.** These rules apply to pairs of kernel and characteristic entities. They also apply to the relationship between characteristic entities and other characteristic entities below them in the hierarchy, such as the relationship between SECTIONS and MEETINGS. The rules are:

- **Creation.** A row in the characteristic entity cannot be created unless the corresponding row of the kernel entity exists.
- **Deletion.** If a row of the kernel entity is deleted, all corresponding rows of the characteristic entity must be deleted.

● **Subtype Rules.** These rules apply to entities that have either mutually exclusive or overlapping subtype entities related to them. The rules are:

- **Creation.** A row in the subtype entity cannot be created unless the corresponding row of the supertype entity exists.
- **Deletion.** If a row of the supertype entity is deleted, all corresponding rows of the subtype entity or entities must be deleted.

There are three basic strategies for dealing with integrity constraints when keys are deleted or updated. The changes can lead to cascaded effects, restricted operations, or null values.

● **Cascades** occur when a deletion or update cascades to delete or update all of the related rows in other entities.

● **Restricted operation** occurs when deletions and updates are restricted to cases where they will not impact other rows of related data.

● **Null values** replace foreign keys when a deleted or updated row removes the entity occurrence that a foreign key was pointing to AND the row with the foreign key is still valid without the referenced row.

Ideally, these rules should be enforced uniformly by the Data Base Management System. In practice, many DBMS are not able to do this, so application programs need code to enforce these rules. Some systems provide integrity enforcement features in screen or code generators. Honkanen[9] specifies routines that can be used to enforce integrity in a SQL Relational Database.

Physical Database Definition

The Extended Entity-Relationship Model has been normalized and the type has been specified for each attribute. It is now time to define the database physically in the computer. This definition resides in a component of the database called the Data Dictionary. There are three points of view from which the completed database can be viewed. These are the logical, physical, and application points of view. When the database has been implemented, security rules have to be applied to make sure users only perform allowable operations.

Appropriate parts of the SQL language are used to illustrate the definitions. SQL is gradually becoming a standard[1] and many systems are implementing the SQL interface that IBM developed.

Implementations of SQL vary in their capabilities. Codd[4] has identified the desired characteristics of a good implementation. These are outlined in Appendix 6-A at the end of the chapter.

The Data Dictionary and Design Repository

Data Dictionary is a term that means different things in different environments. In general, the term refers to a component of the system that stores the definitions of the different parts of the database. Different implementations use different methods of storing the definitions, store different amounts of information, and provide different degrees of access to the information.

Most Relational Data Base Management Systems store the Data Dictionary in the same kinds of tables that are used for ordinary data. Thus there is a table for the entity definitions, a table for the attribute definitions, a table for the key definitions, and so on. This makes it easy to use the query language of the DBMS to query the Data Dictionary in the same way as querying the database.

Using this approach also makes it easy to extend the Data Dictionary to include related information that is not part of the standard Data Dictionary provided by the vendor. This may include details about the design process or about the administrative structure of the organization.

CASE tools also contain a Data Dictionary. They have much more design information, but usually have less implementation information. Many have the ability to convert the specifications in the design directly into database definitions that can be entered into the DBMS Data Dictionary. Some can also convert the specifications of existing databases into design information such as Entity-Relationship Models.

Ideally, all information about the analysis, the design, the database, and the application programs would be stored in a single central repository. IBM[10] has announced specifications for such a repository. A number of CASE vendors have agreed to make their products compatible with it. The repository lets all analysts, designers, programmers, and users access the same store of information. In practice, there is likely to be a split for some time between the analyst's version in the CASE tool and the application version in the DBMS. It takes some time for all of the groups involved to convert to a standard repository.

Three Views of a Database

Different users have different views of a database as illustrated in Figure 6-22. The analyst/designer is primarily interested in a logical view that shows how all components of the database are logically related. This is used to locate the specific components needed by other users. It corresponds exactly to the model which has been developed in this chapter.

The application programmer is usually not interested in the logical organization of the entire database, because only certain parts of the database are relevant

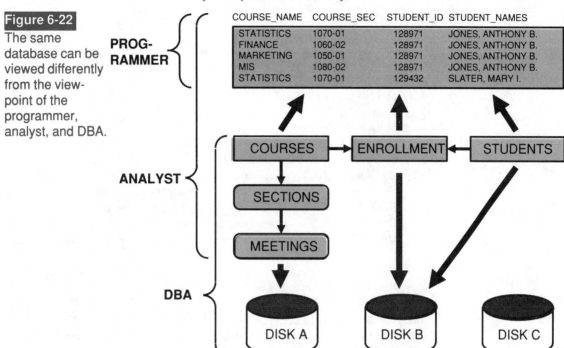

Figure 6-22
The same database can be viewed differently from the viewpoint of the programmer, analyst, and DBA.

to a given application. The programmer is not interested in the physical organization because 4GL commands do not correspond to physical access. The programmer is interested in a logical view of a subset of the database. Sometimes that view may include transformations or selections from the overall logical design.

The Data Base Administrator (DBA), who is responsible for the day-to-day management of the database, is frequently interested in the physical organization of the data on the disks that store it. Different physical organizations can lead to large improvements in the efficiency of the system when it is accessing data.

The users, programmers, and DBA have a secondary interest in how their colleagues view the database. The analyst needs some knowledge of how the programmer use the data. The programmer may need some knowledge of the logical structure of the components being used. The DBA needs some knowledge of how the programmer uses the data to be able to design an efficient physical design. The three views are illustrated with the appropriate SQL commands for part of the student record system that was developed in Chapter 5.

Logical View

The CREATE TABLE command defines the logical view of a data table. The CREATE TABLE command has the following syntax:

    CREATE TABLE table_name
    ([column_name data_type [NOT NULL]] . . .) ;

where:

- lower case names are replaced with the names of tables or columns.
- Items in square brackets [ ] are optional.
- Groups followed by three dots may be repeated.
- NOT NULL can be used to force a key, or any other attribute, to have a non-null value.
- data_type can be one of:

INTEGER	a 4 byte integer with an optional sign.
SMALLINT	a 2 byte integer with an optional sign.
DECIMAL (p,[q])	a packed decimal number of p digits with optionally q digits after the decimal and an optional sign.
FLOAT	a signed 8 byte floating point number.
CHAR (n)	a fixed length character string of n characters.
VARCHAR (n)	a varying length character string of up to n characters.

Some implementations may support other data types, such as DATE, or they may allow the designers to define their own data types.

Figure 6-23 illustrates the creation of tables for the STUDENTS, COURSES, SECTIONS, and ENROLLMENT tables defined in Chapter 5. Note that the integrity of the identification keys is enforced by specifying that the individual columns are NOT NULL and that the index on the atomic or compound key is UNIQUE. There is no way in early implementations of SQL of specifying referential integrity constraints such as "the STUDENT_ID value in ENROLL-MENT must already exist in the STUDENT_ID of STUDENTS." Because of this deficiency in the design of SQL, such constraints must be enforced by writing routines in the application programs.

Similarly, there are no features in SQL that can enforce domain integrity constraints on attributes, such as "SEX of STUDENTS must be either M or F in capital letters." Again, application code is required to enforce such constraints. Some Database Management Systems like Ingress[12] and PowerHouse[5] do store constraints as part of the database definition. Others, like Oracle[11], provide features in their forms and screen generators to enforce constraints.

Physical View

A Data Base Administrator has two main physical design parameters available. One is the creation of an index to access occurrences of a table in sorted order. The other is the creation of clusters to position occurrences physically next to each other. The index speeds the search for particular occurrences in the same way that the index of a book speeds the search for information about a topic. Clusters speed retrieval of rows by positioning rows so adjacent items can be retrieved with a minimum of slow physical movements of the disk.

Figure 6-23

Illustration of table
definitions in SQL.

```
CREATE TABLE STUDENTS (
                          STUDENT_ID        INTEGER NOT NULL,
                          SURNAME           CHAR(20),
                          FIRSTNAME         CHAR(20),
                          STREET            CHAR(30),
                          CITY              CHAR(20),
                          STATE             CHAR(5),
                          ZIP_CODE          CHAR(9),
                          COUNTRY           CHAR(20),
                          PHONE_NO          CHAR(12),
                          BIRTHDATE         CHAR(8),
                          SEX               CHAR(1),
                          MARITAL_STAT      CHAR(1),
                          GMAT              SMALLINT,
                          ACCEPTANCE        CHAR(1) );
CREATE TABLE COURSES (
                          COURSE_ID         SMALLINT NOT NULL,
                          COURSE_NAME       CHAR(20),
                          CREDITS           SMALLINT) ;
CREATE TABLE SECTIONS (
                          COURSE_ID         SMALLINT NOT NULL,
                          SECTION_ID        SMALLINT NOT NULL,
                          FACULTY_ID        INTEGER NOT NULL,
                          TERM              CHAR(3) NOT NULL) ;
CREATE TABLE ENROLLMENT (
                          STUDENT_ID        INTEGER NOT NULL,
                          COURSE_ID         SMALLINT NOT NULL,
                          SECTION_ID        SMALLINT NOT NULL
                          TERM              CHAR(3) NOT NULL,
                          GRADE             SMALLINT,
                          OPERATOR          CHAR(10) ) ;
```

6 **Database**

Keys for tables are defined by the CREATE INDEX command with syntax:

```
CREATE [UNIQUE] INDEX index_name
    ON table_name    ( column_name [ order ]
                     [, column_name [ order ] . . .] )
        [ CLUSTER] ;
```

where

- order can be ASC for ascending or DESC for descending. ASC is assumed if this parameter is not specified.
- UNIQUE indicates that duplicate values of this index are not permitted. This ensures that duplicate values of a key are never entered.

```
CREATE UNIQUE INDEX ISTUDENTS ON STUDENTS
    (STUDENT_ID ASC);
CREATE UNIQUE INDEX ICOURSES ON COURSES
    (COURSE_ID ASC);
CREATE UNIQUE INDEX ISECTIONS ON SECTIONS
    (COURSE_ID, SECTION_ID, TERM_ID);
CREATE UNIQUE INDEX IENROLLMENT ON ENROLLMENT
    (STUDENT_ID, COURSE_ID, SECTION_ID, TERM_ID) ;
CREATE UNIQUE INDEX ISTUDENT ON ENROLLMENT
    (STUDENT_ID) CLUSTER;
CREATE INDEX IINSTRUCTOR ON SECTIONS (FACULTY_ID);
```

Figure 6-24
Illustration of index definitions in SQL.

- CLUSTER indicates that new records are to be physically inserted next to identical values of this index. This can be used to make access easier for searches that are performed in groups such as all courses taken by a student. Only one index on each table can be clustered. Otherwise the physical record might have to be put in two places at once.

Figure 6-24 illustrates the physical definition of indexes for the tables in Figure 6-23. Note that all applications would function without these definitions. Their only purpose is to decrease the physical access time for some applications. The UNIQUE attribute also enforces unique values for keys.

The problems of tuning the physical design of the database to optimize performance is not discussed. Such tuning is very dependent on the features of the particular DBMS in which the design is being implemented.

Many CASE tools are able to generate the code in Figures 6-22 and 6-23 directly from the logical specifications in the Entity-Relationship Model and the tables defining the attributes of each entity.

Application View

The CREATE VIEW command allows the DBA to create a special subset of the database that is more convenient for certain users or programmers. The syntax of the SQL CREATE VIEW operation is:

```
CREATE VIEW view_name
    [( column_name[, column_name] ...)]
    AS subquery;
```
where
- view_name is the name of a view of the data. This view can be treated as the name of another entity table for programming purposes.
- column_name is the name of an attribute to be included in the view.
- subquery is the table that results from any query on the existing database.

It might be useful to have a view that combines the COURSE_NAME from COURSES with the attributes in SECTIONS. The following statement creates it.

```
CREATE VIEW COURSE_SECTION
(COURSE_ID, SECTION_ID, FACULTY_ID, TERM, COURSE_NAME)
AS SELECT COURSE_ID, SECTION_ID, FACULTY_ID, TERM,
    COURSE_NAME
FROM COURSES, SECTIONS
WHERE COURSES.COURSE_ID=SECTIONS.COURSE_ID ;
```

Such a view would not speed access to the data. The DBMS would still have to perform the query before retrieving the data. Not all views can be updated, since some involve irreversible transformations, like summations. However, such views can be a convenience to programmers who otherwise would have to define them within their programs. It can also be a convenience in maintaining security because access rules can be applied differently to different views.

Database Security

The last stage of database design is to apply security constraints to ensure that users are given access only to the information they require. The view statement can hide some tables and columns from users. It does not specify what the users are allowed to do with the ones that are visible. The GRANT and REVOKE statements perform that function. The syntax of the GRANT statement is:

```
GRANT privilege[, privilege]...
    [(column_name[, column_name] ...)]
ON TABLE table_name[, table_name]...
TO user[, user]... ;
```

where

- privilege is one of SELECT, UPDATE, DELETE, INSERT, ALL, ALTER, and INDEX.
- column_name is the name of a column.
- table_name is the name of a table or view.
- user is the account name of a user. PUBLIC is a special name for all users.

A similar syntax is available for revoking selected privileges. GRANT is replaced by REVOKE and TO is replaced by FROM.

These commands can control what each user can do to a selected table, a selected column within a table, or rows selected by a view definition.

The definition of tables, indexes, views, and privileges completes the implementation of the physical database. It is now ready to be populated with actual data occurrences. Before this can happen, screens, or other input systems, have to be designed to enter the data. Some CASE and 4GL systems provide screen generators that make this task very easy.

Once test data have been entered, it is possible to use the query language within SQL—and every other major database language—to define simple reports. The database can be used as a powerful foundation for prototyping applications with the screen generator and the query language. This approach is used in the following chapters.

6
Database

Testing the Database Model

The normalization procedure is a test of the data model. It determines whether the model contains errors that can lead to redundant data, different values for the same logical data occurrence, and insertion, update, or deletion errors. The implementation language provides minimal testing for syntax errors.

Most of the remaining testing of the model occurs during the prototyping of screens, reports, and application programs. At that time, users have another opportunity to identify problems with the design.

These later design stages may reveal some data items that have been omitted. However, it is relatively safe to construct the database now. Most Relational DBMS make it quite easy to redefine many features of the design, even after screens and application programs have been developed. It is particularly easy to add new attributes to a table as long as the key structure does not have to be changed. Thus a table can be extended to include new attributes that are discovered after the initial design is completed. This forgiveness of initial design errors is one of the things that makes a Relational DBMS so attractive.

CASE Tools for Database Implementation

Many CASE tools are able to do much of the work in this chapter. For instance, IEW from KnowledgeWare, Inc., can normalize a hierarchical file description up to 3NF. Many CASE tools are able to convert detailed specifications of entities, relationships, and attributes into SQL code as shown in Figure 6-25. Some are also able to produce data declarations for COBOL or other languages.

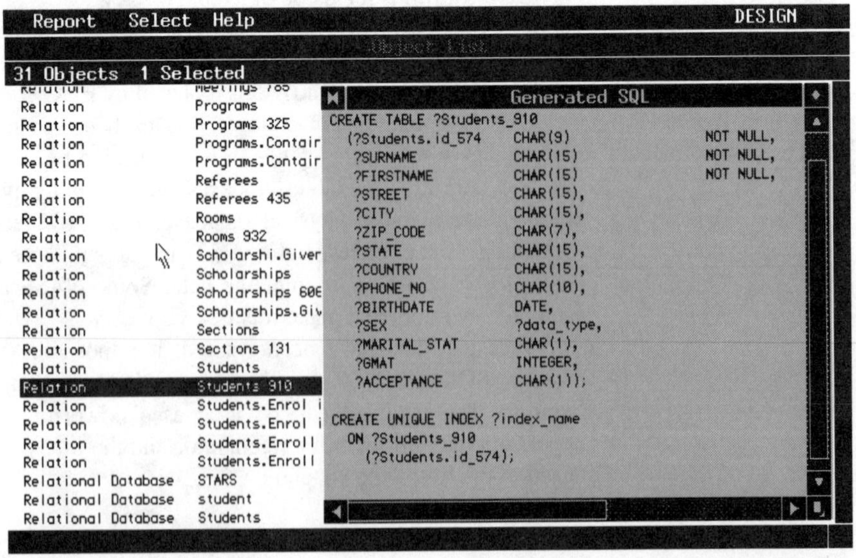

Figure 6-25

An example screen from the IEW Design Workstation in which the Students table is defined in SQL. The left side of the screen allows the user to select one or more objects. The right window illustrates a generated CREATE statement.

These features illustrate the true power of CASE tools. Effort expended in documenting the design in previous chapters pays off here. Automatic code generation is a direct product of that effort. If entity, relationship, and attribute information are entered correctly, then the generated database is also correct. The cost of programming and later error correction are largely eliminated. If errors are detected, it is relatively easy to regenerate a correct definition.

There are a number of commercial products that help in the database implementation phase. Many of them are designed to work with IBM's DB2 version of SQL. Garcia-Rose and Fosdick[8] have surveyed the use of these tools.

The implementations of SQL vary in their ability to enforce integrity constraints. The integrity of identification keys is enforced by specifying that the individual columns are NOT NULL and that the index on the atomic or compound key is UNIQUE. Vendors are working hard to provide features for referential integrity and domain integrity. Support for integrity constraints should be an important factor in selecting a DBMS. Honkanen[9] specifies routines that can be used to enforce integrity in a Relational Database until integrity constraints are part of SQL.

There are many implementations of SQL. Each of the main hardware vendors has one or more implementations that work on their own hardware. Oracle Corp. has a version that works on dozens of diferent hardware platforms. Their version has a CASE tool for defining Entity-Relationship models and converting them to database definitions. Oracle also has tools for creating screens, reports, and application programs that link directly to the database. Several microcomputer databases support SQL. Teradata Corp. sells a database machine that communicates directly in SQL over a network without the need for a separate DBMS.

Index Technology has a Design Recovery product that reads COBOL source code, screen designs, and IMS database definitions to automatically recover the structure and definitions of the database. These can then be used in a new integrated database design.

Summary

In this chapter the Extended Entity-Relationship specifications of previous chapters has been converted into a Relational Database specification. The Relational Database tables were checked for design errors by using normalization. Finally the normalized database was translated into a physical design using the SQL language.

The rules for converting the EER Model to a Relational Model are:

- **Entities** become Relational Tables.
- **Kernel entities** have atomic keys.
- **Characteristic entities** have a compound key.
- **Subtype entities** or overlapping subtypes have the same key.
- **M:N Relationships** are not allowed.
- **1:N Relationships** are represented by a foreign key.

- **Optional relationships** may have null foreign keys.
- **Multiple relationships** are independent.

Normalization avoids wasted storage, lost data, and multiple values for the same thing. The process uses single valued and multivalued dependency relationships between attributes to identify abnormal tables. All attributes in a table—containing only single valued dependencies—must depend on the key, the whole key, and nothing but the key. Tables with multivalued dependencies may need splitting depending on the semantic meaning of the relationships between the attributes.

Data types make sure that data that are semantically comparable, like dates, are also accessible in comparable forms. Key data types are often encoded with check digits to detect transcription and transposition errors during data entry.

The database implementation has features needed by the designer, the Data Base Administrator, and the programmer. In addition there are security features that prevent users from performing unauthorized operations on selected rows, columns, or tables.

Existing DBMS do not support all of the logical constructs that have been defined in the design methodology. However, there is a lot of work being done to implement all of these concepts.

Keywords and Phrases

Atomic Key	Insertion Anomaly
Check Digit	Join
Compound Key	Foreign Key
Connection Trap	Multivalue Dependency
Deletion Anomaly	Optional Attribute
First Normal Form	Project
Second Normal Form	Relation
Third Normal Form	Single Value Dependency
Boyce-Codd Normal Form	Table
Fourth Normal Form	Tuple
Fifth Normal Form	Update Anomaly

Appendix 6-A: Relational Database Features

It is hard to determine whether a database is really relational. Codd[4] identifies 12 features that are required in an ideal Relational Database. They are listed here for those who need criteria for selecting Data Base Management Systems.

1. **All information is in tables.** The logical view of all information in the database—including the Data Dictionary containing the table descriptions themselves—must be logically represented as tables. This eases the Data Base Administrator's job since all information about the data is organized. It also makes it easier for developers to produce compatible software packages since there is a way of consistently defining old and new information.

2. **Access is by table, key, and column name.** A relational system does not have logical access methods based on order, position, or file linkages. It needs some way of ensuring that all fields can be located and accessed by their value. Table name, primary key value, and column name must be sufficient to define and locate all field values if primary keys can be guaranteed to be unique.

3. **Null values are treated systematically.** Null values represent missing or inapplicable information. This allows the system to maintain the integrity of unique key values, since such a key can never be undefined. Special values—such as blanks or zeros—do not serve this purpose because they are unsystematic since the programmer must remember to define them correctly.

4. **Data Dictionary based on Relational Model.** The Data Dictionary has the same form as ordinary data. Authorized users can use the same language to learn the data structure or to extend the capabilities of the Data Dictionary.

5. **Single language for all operations.** The Data Base Administrator needs a seamless language that deals with all aspects of data definition, data changes, authorization, integrity constraints, and data recovery. This does not prevent the creation of other interfaces, such as screen windows or menus.

6. **All views are updatable.** Most database environments allow the definition of "views" which give the user access to a restricted or transformed portion of the data. It is important that the DBMS be able to update the data seen in these views if it is theoretically possible to do so. If it can be updated, then the user does not need to know whether a view or a real table is being provided. This makes it easier to manage security and access, because the programmer does not need to distinguish between views and actual table definitions. The database can be updated regardless of which way access was provided.

   Some views, such as aggregates, cannot be updated even theoretically. There is no theoretical way to update an average which is produced by calculation from raw data in the tables. Such views are not considered by this rule. A view is theoretically updatable only if there exists a time-independent algorithm that can unambiguously determine a series of changes to the database that produce the desired changes.

7. **High-level insert, update, and delete.** Retrieval, insert, update, and deletion should all work on individual rows of the table and on whole tables. This

allows the system to optimize access code and simplify operation of distributed databases. A single request can then access all required rows.

8. **Physical Data Independence.** Changes to storage or access methods must not change the logic of programs or terminal activities. This is true if the DBMS has a clear boundary between the logical view of data accessed by the programs and the physical view of data as stored by the machine.

9. **Logical Data Independence.** Information preserving changes to the data structure must not impact the logic of programs. One information preserving change is splitting a table vertically or horizontally to distribute parts of it around a network. Another example is the lossless joining of two relations. This capability allows the database administrator to modify the database structure to improve performance without modifying programs and screens.

10. **Integrity Independence.** Integrity constraints must be defined in the relational language and stored in the Data Dictionary. If they are not stored in the Data Dictionary, then they cannot be enforced for every data access. If they are in the Data Dictionary, they can be changed as the business rules change without needing to change the programs that manipulate the data. Two examples of integrity constraints are:

    • No component of a primary key is allowed to have a null value.
    • Every distinct non-null value of a foreign key must have a matching value of a primary key in some table.

11. **Distributed Independence.** The applications do not change when data are first distributed or when they are redistributed. If the data described by the Data Dictionary appear to be local, then the applications do not change, even if the actual location of the data is changed. Again this is a separation of physical and logical structure. Even if the DBMS does not currently support distributed data, it should be possible to enhance it to support distribution if the data is described to the program only at the logical level.

12. **Subversion Integrity.** A relational system may have a 2GL or 3GL language that accesses single rows at a time to remain compatible with procedural languages like COBOL. It must not be possible to subvert integrity rules by using this language. All accesses to the database must be performed by using commands that are stated in the high level relational language which enforces the integrity rules. Otherwise, programmers using 2GL or 3GL facilities could compromise the integrity of the database.

Rules 1, 2, 3, 4, and 12 are essential to maintain the integrity of the database. Rules 1 and 4 make it easy for authorized users to explore the database and its documentation. Rules 5, 6, 7, 8, 9, 10, and 11 facilitate design and maintenance. The independence rules prevent interactions that normally cause extensive maintenance whenever any part of the system changes. None of the present DBMS products satisfies all of these criteria, but it is important to select one with as many of these features as possible. As more applications are based on a DBMS, the benefits of each feature grow exponentially.

Review Questions

1. Define each of the items in the list of keywords and phrases.
2. Specify the rules for converting an Extended Entity-Relationship Model into a Relational Model.
3. Distinguish between the six different normal forms.
4. Can a table that has been projected into two smaller tables always be reconstituted by joining the smaller tables.
5. Distinguish between single valued dependency and multivalued dependency.
6. Identify the characteristics of an attribute that, together, go to define a data type.
7. What is the purpose of a check digit? Specify one way in which check digits are computed.
8. Use the modulus 11 method with prime number weighting to compute the check digit for the number 857142.
9. What is wrong with each of the following codes used to identify parts in a warehouse? ZITS125, MBC-NDT, 428571428.
10. In what ways do analysts, programmers, and Data Base Administrators look at a database system in different ways?
11. Which one of the following would be most likely to use the CLUSTER option in the SQL CREATE INDEX command: analysts, programmers, or Data Base Administrators?

6
Database

Problems

1. Check the solution of Problem 5-1 to make sure that it is in Fourth Normal Form. Write SQL code to define the logical and physical view of the entities and attributes in the checked solution.
2. Check the solution of Problem 5-2 to make sure that it is in Fourth Normal Form. Write SQL code to define the logical and physical view of the entities and attributes in the checked solution.
3. Check the solution of Problem 5-3 to make sure that it is in Fourth Normal Form. Write SQL code to define the logical and physical view of the entities and attributes in the checked solution.
4. Check the solution of Problem 5-4 to make sure that it is in Fourth Normal Form. Write SQL code to define the logical and physical view of the entities and attributes in the checked solution.
5. Check the solution of Problem 5-5 to make sure that it is in Fourth Normal Form. Write SQL code to define the logical and physical view of the entities and attributes in the checked solution.
6. The following Extended Entity-Relationship Diagram describes the database of a small contractor.
   a. Transform the EER diagram into a Relational Database Model. Specify all of the keys that are needed in the database. Identify all of the atomic keys, compound keys, foreign keys, and other attributes needed to reflect the

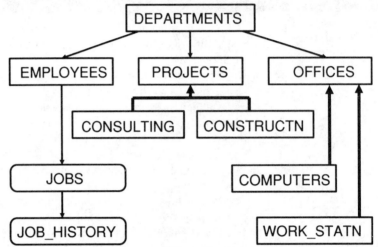

relationships in the diagram. When a key is needed, use the singular of the entity name followed by _ID. Thus DEPARTMENT_ID is the key of DEPARTMENTS.

b. Write SQL code to define the logical and physical view of the entities and key attributes in the Relational Database Model.

7. The following Extended Entity-Relationship Diagram describes the database for a small airline.

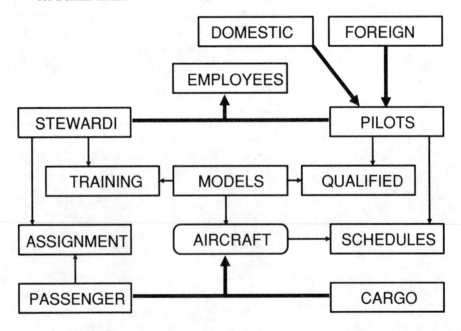

a. Transform the Extended Entity-Relationship Diagram into the tables of a Relational Database. Specify all of the keys that are needed in the database. Identify all the atomic keys, compound keys, foreign keys, and other attributes needed to reflect the relationships in the diagram. When a key is needed, use the singular of the entity name followed by _ID. Thus EMPLOYEE_ID is the key of EMPLOYEES.

b. Write SQL code to define the logical and physical view of the entities and key attributes in the Relational Database Model.

8. The following is a sample of the data in the PROGRAMS table. COMPUTER_ID is the identification number of a microcomputer. SOFTWARE is the name of a software package. MEMORY is the amount of memory required by the package. Which of the following statements are true?

PROGRAMS

COMPUTER_ID	SOFTWARE	MEMORY
101	Write-On	256K
101	Lily Pad	384K
102	Write-On	256K
103	Lily Pad	384K
103	Wide-Spread	640K
103	Polly-Graph	512K
104	Wide-Spread	640K
104	Private Ledger	128K
105	Write-On	256K

a. COMPUTER_ID → SOFTWARE
b. (COMPUTER_ID, SOFTWARE) → MEMORY
c. SOFTWARE → MEMORY
d. COMPUTER_ID →→ SOFTWARE
e. SOFTWARE → COMPUTER_ID
f. MEMORY → (COMPUTER_ID, SOFTWARE)

Answer the following questions.

g. What is the key of PROGRAMS?
h. In what normal form is PROGRAMS?
i. Give examples of any anomalies in the table.
j. Convert the table to Fourth Normal Form. Illustrate the contents of the converted tables, as derived from the existing table.

9. The following figure shows some examples from the SALES table.

SALES

SELLER	CUSTOMER	CITY	MODEL
JONES	ACME	NEW YORK	1043
JONES	ACME	NEW YORK	1041
SMITH	ACME	LONDON	4176
SMITH	APEX	LONDON	2106
SMITH	APEX	PARIS	6106
BLACK	ALPHA	TORONTO	7155
BLACK	ACME	NEW YORK	1043

6

Database

    a. Show the CLIENT table obtained by projecting SALES on the SELLER and CUSTOMER attributes.

    b. Show the PURCHASE table obtained by projecting the table on the CUSTOMER, CITY, and PART_ID attributes.

    c. Join the CLIENT and PURCHASE tables on the CUSTOMER attribute.

    d. Which attributes belong in the key of the SALES table?

10. A retail store chain is designing an inventory system. One of the Relational Tables in the initial design is:

INVENTORY(STORE_ID, STORE_NAME, STORE_STATE, INVENTORY_ID, INVENTORY_NAME, INVENTORY_QUANT, SIZE, COLOR, PRICE, TAX)

The following rules apply to the attributes of the table.
- STORE_ID and INVENTORY_ID are unique identifiers.
- Each STATE can have a different TAX.
- Each store carries only some of the possible inventory items.
- INVENTORY_QUANT and PRICE are set by each store.
- Each INVENTORY_ID has more than 1 COLOR and SIZE combination.
- The PRICE of an INVENTORY_ID does not depend on COLOR or SIZE.
- Each store has a STORE_NAME and is located in a STORE_STATE.
- An INVENTORY_NAME describes an INVENTORY_ID.

    a. Diagram the single and multivalued dependencies between the attributes.

    b. Normalize the INVENTORY table to Fourth Normal Form.

    c. Draw the E-R Diagram that corresponds to the normalized structure.

    d. Write SQL code to define the logical and physical view of the entities.

11. The CASE Software Company provides the following information about their active consulting projects. Based on the following sample data table (and any reasonable assumptions that you may require):

    a. Diagram the single and multivalued dependencies between the attributes.

    b. Normalize the table of active projects to Third Normal Form.

    c. Draw the Entity-Relationship Diagram that corresponds to the normalized structure.

    d. Write SQL code to define the logical and physical view of the entities.

PROJECT_ID	PROJECT_NAME	START_DATE	EMPLOYEE_ID	EMPLOYEE_NAME	TITLE	HOURS_WORKED
1010	TechnoJolly	Nov 05	2050	I. M. Keene	Sr. Analyst	30
1010	TechnoJolly	Nov 05	2140	U. R. Knott	Jr. Gofer	15
1020	DataMagic	Dec 11	2050	I. M. Keene	Sr. Analyst	20
1020	DataMagic	Dec 11	2140	U. R. Knott	Jr. Gofer	20
1020	DataMagic	Dec 11	2330	E. S. Kwik	Coder	40

12. A database is used to support an association of soccer referees. The association schedules referees for three youth leagues, for any high school game in the county, and for any college game at the local university. Currently, the database contains only one data table with the following information: unique game number, date of game, time of game, location of game, telephone number of referee, home team, visiting team, league in which the teams compete, and league office telephone. The database stores data on all games for several weeks in advance. In the case of youth games, a referee may be assigned to more than one game per day.

    a. Diagram the single and multivalued dependencies between the attributes.
    b. Decompose the data structure into Fourth Normal Form.
    c. Draw an Entity-Relationship Diagram that corresponds to the resulting tables.

Project

Using the Extended Entity-Relationship Model developed for the assignment in Chapter 5:
a. **Diagram the dependencies** in the tables of attributes.
b. **Convert the tables to Fourth Normal Form** by making any necessary changes.
c. **Convert the tables to a Relational Model** by adding foreign keys as needed.
d. **Specify integrity rules** for any attributes that need them.
e. **Specify data types** for the attributes.
f. **Write SQL code** to define the logical and physical view of the entities.

Cooking with Cal Oreez Case

Using the Extended Entity-Relationship Model developed for the assignment in Chapter 5:
a. **Diagram the dependencies** in the tables of attributes.
b. **Convert the tables to Fourth Normal Form** by making any needed changes.
c. **Convert the tables to a Relational Model** by adding foreign keys as needed.
d. **Specify integrity rules** for any attributes that need them.
e. **Specify data types** for the attributes.
f. **Write SQL code** to define the logical and physical view of the entities.

References

1. Baker, Jerry, "SQL: A New Standard," *Computerworld Focus,* February 19, 1986, pp. 55-58.

2. Burch, John G. and Gary Grudnitski, *Information Systems Theory and Practice, Fourth Edition,* John Wiley & Sons, 1986.

3. Chen, Peter S., "Database Design Based on Entity and Relationship" in *Principles of Database Design Vol I*, edited by S. Bing Yao, Prentice-Hall, 1985, pp. 174-210.

4. Codd, E. F., "Is Your DBMS Really Relational?", *Computerworld*, October 14, 1985 and "Does your DBMS Run by the Rules?", *Computerworld*, October 21, 1985, pp. 49-60.

5. Cognos Inc., *PowerHouse Manuals,* Cognos Inc., 275 Slater St. Ottawa, Ontario.

6. Date, C. J., *An Introduction to Database Systems, Fourth Edition, Volume I,* Addison-Wesley, 1986.

7. Fagin, R., "A Normal Form for Relational Databases that is Based on Domains and Keys," ACM TODS Vol. 6, No. 3, September 1981.

8. Garcia-Rose, Linda and Howard Fosdick, "The Maturation of DB2," *Datamation,* March 15, 1990, pp. 75-80.

9. Honkanen, Pentti A., "The Integrity Problem and What can be Done about it Using Today's DBMSs," *Data Base,* Fall 1989, pp. 21-27.

10. Mercurio, V. J., B. F. Meyers, A. M. Nisbet, and G. Radin, "AD/Cycle Strategy and Architecture," *IBM Systems Journal,* Vol. 29, No. 2, 1990, pp. 170-188.

11. Oracle Corp., *SQL*Plus Reference Guide,* Oracle Corp., Belmont, California.

12. Relational Technology Inc., *Ingress Manuals,* Relational Technology Inc., Alameda, California.

13. Yang, Dongqing, Toby J. Teory and James P. Fry, "A Practical Approach to Transforming Extended ER Diagrams into a Relational Model," *Information Sciences*, Vol. 42, 1987, pp. 167-186.

Section III

Design of Applications

	DATABASE (WHAT)	PROGRAMS (HOW)	BENEFITS (WHY)	NETWORK (WHERE)	REAL TIME (WHEN)	SKILLS (WHO)
USER CONCEPT	Entity Relationship	Activity	Intangible Benefit	Map		Organization Design
DESIGNER CONCEPT	E-R Diagram	A-E Diagram	AHP	Network		Skills Responsibility
USER DETAIL	Forms Screens	Processes Data	Tangible Benefit	Work Volume	Discrete Events	Transition Training
DESIGNER DETAIL	EER Diagram	Data Flow Diagrams	Benefit-Cost	Partition	Transition Diagrams	Methodology Tools
BUILDER CONCEPT	Normal Form Relations	Structure Chart	Function Points	System Architecture	Specifications	Learning
BUILDER DETAIL	Files	Screens Specifications	Costs	Network Specs	Interfaces	4GL CASE

This section expands the subsystems identified in Chapter 3 into detailed specifications to programmers. These subsystems process data to transform it into new data and useful information. This section addresses the basic input operations of insert, update, and delete that operators perform at a screen. It also deals with the batch operations that handle large numbers of transactions that do not need operator intervention. Payrolls and production schedules are examples of such applications.

The main focus of this section is the identification of user needs and the design of cohesive, loosely coupled modules that are easy to maintain. This section on designing the modules that perform processes in the system is divided into four chapters. These chapters address the inputs that the designer needs to design the system, the design of screens, the processes that the designer uses to transform the inputs, and the outputs that the designer produces. These outputs are usually specifications for programmers—or sometimes analysts with code generators—to implement.

Chapter 7 describes methods for documenting the existing business processes if the analyst does not already understand them. These documents serve as inputs to the design process. Data Flow Diagrams communicate from the clients to the designers. Analysis divides the system into those parts that consist of input screens, those that provide output reports, and those that require batch programs to implement.

Chapter 8 shows how to design forms and interactive screens for data input and how to generate clear reports. The chapter develops principles of good form, screen, and report design. These produce helpful user-friendly systems, minimize operator errors, and reduce the need for user training.

Chapter 9 deals with those parts of the design that are implemented as batch programs. It describes the processes the designer uses to transform the inputs from users into outputs to programmers. This chapter focuses on ways to separate the process into cohesive and loosely coupled modules.

Chapter 10 describes methods of documenting the required modules so programmers can easily convert the specifications into program code. Chapters 7 and 8 identify ways of communicating between the user and the designer. This chapter identifies ways of communicating between the designer and the programmer. The objective is to provide clear unambiguous specifications that are easy to implement without errors.

Chapter 7

Data Flow Diagrams

	DATABASE (WHAT)	PROGRAMS (HOW)	BENEFITS (WHY)	NETWORK (WHERE)	REAL TIME (WHEN)	SKILLS (WHO)
USER CONCEPT	Entity Relationship	Activity	Intangible Benefit	Map		Organization Design
DESIGNER CONCEPT	E-R Diagram	A-E Diagram	AHP	Network		Skills Responsibility
USER DETAIL	Forms Screens	Processes Data	Tangible Benefit	Work Volume	Discrete Events	Transition Training
DESIGNER DETAIL	EER Diagram	Data Flow Diagrams	Benefit-Cost	Partition	Transition Diagrams	Methodology Tools
BUILDER CONCEPT	Normal Form Relations	Structure Chart	Function Points	System Architecture	Specifications	Learning
BUILDER DETAIL	Files	Screens Specifications	Costs	Network Specs	Interfaces	4GL CASE

Objectives

This chapter describes techniques for identifying the processes that must be performed by a new application program. The application programs in this chapter assume that most of the data exists in tables in a database as described in Section II. The applications also assume that most reports that do not change data in the database are produced using a report generator or an interactive query language, like SQL. The application programs are therefore mainly entry screens to enter new data, or batch programs that transform existing data to reflect events in the real world.

The techniques used to design these applications are similar to those used in the traditional System Development Life Cycle. The difference is that the designer can start with a database and a file structure in place. Generation of most reports can be deferred to a later time since 4GL systems provide query languages that allow users to design and tailor reports to their own needs. The techniques apply equally well to 3GL and 4GL environments. The difference in the CASE and 4GL environment is that some processes are implemented automatically and less documentation is required in some cases.

Eliminating database design and report generation produces enormous simplification in the design of applications. The problem is reduced to determining how inputs are converted into required outputs. This is the manufacturing process in which raw inputs in the database are converted into useful outputs reflecting important operations in the organization.

This chapter focuses on the process of identifying how the existing system, if any, operates and what modifications are needed to convert it into the desired future system. This process is called analysis because it analyzes an existing system to identify its components. The design process in the next chapters synthesizes these components into a new system. In this chapter you learn how to:

- Identify the **bounds** of a system.

- Identify the **terminators** that interact with a system.

- Identify the **processes** carried out by a system.

- Draw **Data Flow Diagrams.**

- Refine Data Flow Diagrams into progressive **levels of detail.**

Systems Concepts

The process of systems analysis consists of mapping the components of a real system into an information model of the system. This model can then be implemented as a physical information system. The basic tool used in identifying the processes that must be performed is called the Data Flow Diagram (DFD). As data flows through the process it is transformed by various programs, machines, or people. The DFD method identifies these transformations as they physically happen in existing systems. They are then converted into a logical model that eliminates the existing physical constraints.

The logical model is partitioned into those parts that can be implemented as interactive screens, those that are implemented with a query language or a report generator, those that must be implemented as batch programs in a programming language, and those that must be performed manually. The process of designing screens and reports is described in Chapter 8. The process of designing batch programs is described in Chapters 9 and 10.

An information system is a state-tracking mechanism that tracks the state of some real system. The real system starts in a stable state. It then receives some discrete stimulus from its environment and generates a response according to some rules that the system obeys. These rules may be physical laws, legal laws, or corporate or social rules. The result of the response is a new stable state for the system.

Figure 7-1 illustrates a real system in which raw materials are delivered, by truck, to the doors of a factory. Before the truck arrives, the system is in a stable state in which the raw materials belong to the supplier. When the materials are delivered, there is a change to a new stable state in which the factory owns the materials and owes money to the supplier. The delivery is the stimulus that triggers the new state. In this example, the rules that govern the transaction are embodied in accounting and commercial law.

The information system must record the stimuli that impact the real system and change its own state to match the new stable state in the real system. The information system is a representation of the real system. It consists of data tables that record the current state of the system and programs that record the rules changing the state of the system. It processes stimuli in the form of transactions to produce responses like file updates, reports, and other transactions.

In the example of Figure 7-1, the information system begins with an order recorded in data tables. When the order is received, the information system must update the data tables to record that the order has been filled, the materials have been placed in inventory, and an account is now payable to the supplier. This new state is stable until the bill comes due, the bill is paid, or inventory is used.

The delivery of a needed material could trigger several other real events, such as the beginning of a production run. Several rules govern the relationships between the items of information in the system. For instance, the amount of

Figure 7-1
A real system that
delivers raw materials
to a factory.

money owed to a supplier equals the sum of the unit price times the quantity of
each material purchased.

The process of analysis consists of creating a model of the information system. The entities and attributes of a data model are a model of the states of the
system. The rules of the system are modeled by processes. The stimuli and
responses are modeled by data flows. All of these model components are combined into a graphic model called a Data Flow Diagram (DFD).

There are three representations of an information system: the real system, the
Data Flow Diagram Model, and the physical implementation of the information
system. Each has an environment, a current state, a stimulus, a response, and
rules for transforming one discrete state into another discrete state. The following
table shows how the parts are related and named in each representation.

REAL SYSTEM	DIAGRAM	PHYSICAL SYSTEM
Environment	Terminator	Supplier, Customer, ...
State	File	Table
Stimulus	Data Flow In	Input Transaction, Update
Response	Data Flow Out	Report, Query
Rule	Process	Program, Module, Subroutine

The Data Flow Diagram is not meant to provide a complete representation of
either the existing real system or the future physical implementation of the new
system. The DFD is there to capture only the *essential features* of both. The
easiest way to identify which features are essential is to imagine that the system
will ultimately be implemented using an ideal technology that:
- costs nothing,
- takes no time to do its job,
- has no size, and
- never makes mistakes.

If the DFD is implemented using such an ideal technology, there will be no need for error checking or for physical considerations such as file size, computation time, and how data are transported. The model ignores physical processes that store and transport data, the people and machines that perform the processes, the media on which data are stored, and any error-checking processes. The actual system will need to consider these factors, but this is a way of deferring these decisions until the implementation stage by using "constructive procrastination.".

The resulting Essential Model in the Data Flow Diagram concentrates only on *what* must be done and not on *how* it is done. Likewise, it ignores the procedures implemented in the past to cope with technological and human weakness. These will probably be changed in the new system anyway. Many technological weaknesses are eliminated by new technology. Many human weaknesses are eliminated by automating the most error-prone human activities.

Data Flow Diagram Concepts

Data Flow Diagrams have a notation for each of the components of a system. They also have a notation for representing different levels in a hierarchy of detail used to describe the system. This notation makes it possible to represent an overall view of a large complex system and a detailed view of a part of a system using the same notation. Parts of a system can be isolated into independent subsystems. These work together as a unit to perform a set of processes that must be done together at one time. There is a standard process that an analyst can follow to make sure that all components of a system are identified.

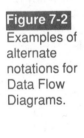

Figure 7-2

Examples of alternate notations for Data Flow Diagrams.

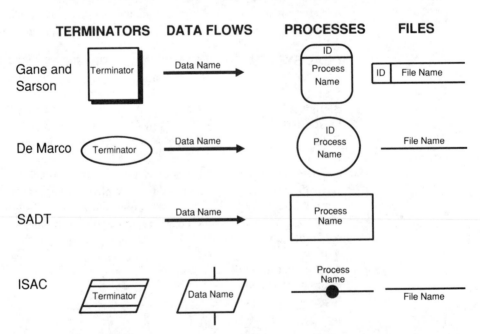

Notation for Components

Figure 7-2 summarizes all the symbols used in drawing Data Flow Diagrams. It also shows corresponding symbols that are used by various methods. This book follows the graphic conventions of the Gane and Sarson[2] Method.

Data Flow Diagrams are constructed from four basic building blocks: terminators, files, data flows, and processes. These are described below.

- **Terminators.** A terminator is an external source of information or an external sink for information. Terminators are named with a noun. All terminators must have at least one data flow entering or leaving the terminator. The terminator is symbolized by a shadowed rectangle. Some methods call a terminator an entity. This term is not used here since it can be confused with data entities.

- **Files.** Files (sometimes called stores) store data for use at a later time, by another process, or in a different place. Files normally correspond to the tables defined in Chapter 6. The tables correspond to the entities identified in Chapters 2 and 5.

- **Data Flows.** The data flow arrow carries data in the direction of the arrow. The name of the data flow is shown above the arrow. The arrow can carry data from a terminator or file to a process and from a process to a file, a terminator, or another process. Data cannot flow directly between terminators, between files, from a terminator to a file or from a file to a terminator. The data can be in any form, including forms, magnetic tapes, electronic signals, or verbal messages. The content of the data flow can be in any degree of detail or aggregation. The detailed contents of the flow are described in a Data Dictionary entry that references the name of the data flow.

  The flow is labeled with a noun and sometimes an adjective to distinguish different flows with the same name, as in Pending Application and Completed Application. The data flows to and from files are usually unlabeled because the label is assumed to be the name of the file and the contents are assumed to be all the attributes of the file.

  When data flows in both directions, as in an update, then the arrow points in the direction of net flow. An arrow pointing toward a file indicates that data in the file are updated or data are inserted. In an update, a read operation is assumed and the arrow points toward the file to show that the net effect is to change the file. An arrow coming from a file indicates that data in the file are used, but not changed. If data are both used for some calculation or decision and also updated, two arrows should be used.

- **Processes.** The process box transforms one or more incoming data flows into one or more outgoing data flows. A process without any incoming flows is a random number generator, since no incoming data determine the outcome of the process. A process without any outgoing data is like a black hole, because nothing useful ever emerges. Each process name should be a strong active verb with a single explicit terminator. The overview processes at the highest level of aggregation correspond to the activities identified in Chapter 3.

7
DFD

A process can be thought of as a machine, or transformer, that transforms input data into output data. It may also record a history of all past input. This is a record of the history of the states of the machine.

Each process has an identification number at the top of the process box. The number is used for cross referencing to other documents and diagrams. The numbers are customarily consecutive integers. Where possible, they are assigned in the order that the processes normally occur, but they do not imply sequencing because some of the processes may occur simultaneously.

Several data flow methods have been developed and each one has a different set of symbols. De Marco[1] suggests a very simple diagram that can be easily drawn with pencil and paper. The Structured Analysis and Design Technique (SADT)[7,8] has been designed to document ordinary file-based systems as discussed in this chapter, and also real-time systems as discussed in Chapter 12. SADT has another variant in which the data are in boxes and the processes are on lines. This is also the notation that has been chosen in the Information Systems work and Analysis of Change (ISAC)[3] method.

Presumably there is a limit to how many more sets of symbols can be developed. However, readers wanting to develop their own unique method still can make use of—as yet unclaimed—heart shapes and heptagons.

Figure 7-3 uses the Data Flow Diagram notation to describe the Systems Analysis and Design Process. The single Data Dictionary file is used to represent all the tables that would typically be found in a Data Dictionary. The notation allows such aggregate data files, but it is not usually good practice to use them in documenting a system. Aggregation is used here to simplify the illustration.

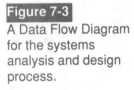

Figure 7-3

A Data Flow Diagram for the systems analysis and design process.

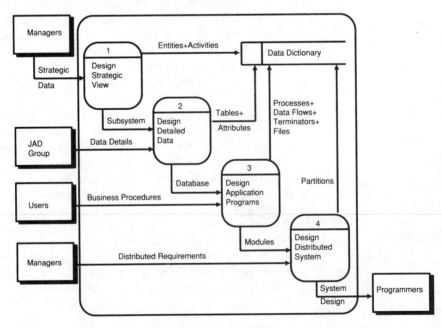

The Systems Analysis and Design Process actually has several feedback steps. These allow errors and omissions discovered at a later stage to be reflected in earlier stages. For instance, if new data requirements are discovered during Design Application Programs, then the analyst goes back to Design Detailed Data to change the database. A Data Flow Diagram does not show this feedback because it assumes an ideal technology that never makes errors. Such feedbacks, error checks, and control information are introduced to the notation in Chapter 9 when analysis has ended and detailed design begins.

The round-cornered box that encloses the processes and files, but excludes the terminators, shows the boundaries of the system. Everything inside the box is part of the system and is subject to analysis and design. Everything outside the box is part of the environment and cannot be changed.

Data Flow Diagrams combine information about the two most important parts of an information system: data and processes that transform data. The Activity-Entity Matrix in Chapter 3 performed this same function at a high level. The Data Flow Diagram adds features to distinguish terminators, data flows, and the relationships between processes.

They show at what points the world outside the system interacts with the system. They also show which processes transform data from its input form to its storage form. The description of these processes eventually becomes the description of programs or manual procedures that have to be implemented.

The Data Flow Diagram focuses on the flow of data. The diagram is drawn from the data's viewpoint. It shows what happens to the data as they progress through the organization. It does not show what happens from the user's viewpoint. The user's viewpoint only reveals parts of the system that a single user sees. Neither does it show what happens from the system's point of view. The system's viewpoint reveals the flow of control that governs the invocation of the various programs and logical components that make up the system.

The viewpoint of the data reveals all the data transformations, since the data are used in all parts of the system. All parts of the system—input screens, files, and programs—are in contact with the data. All of them are identified if the system is viewed from the viewpoint of the data.

Isolated Processes

The analyst often has a problem deciding where the boundaries between processes should be drawn. It is possible to partition a system into processes in many different ways. Some partitions are better than others. A process should have the same characteristics as the functions defined in Chapter 3. These characteristics are reviewed here:

- **Process Information.** Physical processes—however important they may be—are not part of the information system.
- **Identifiable Result.** A poorly defined process has no result or a collection of unrelated results.

- **Identifiable Time.** A properly defined process has a clear beginning time and a clear ending time.
- **Identifiable Workers.** A single person or identifiable group performs the activity.
- **Self-Contained.** The interactions within the process are much stronger than interactions between processes.
- **Single Step Automation.** The process is automated in one stage as a single procedure.

The first partitioning of a system should create **isolated processes**. These are sometimes called unit processes. A group of one or more processes is isolated if the processes in the group communicate only with themselves, files, and terminators. They may not communicate directly with other processes by a data flow. They are isolated in the sense that they do not have to be performed at the same time, in the same place, or by the same person, as the other processes. This means that they can be automated as single self-contained independent modules.

An isolated group of processes is the smallest sensible unit of work that can be performed at one time. systems composed of modules that implement isolated processes are very adaptable because the isolated modules can be used as independent building blocks from which larger systems are constructed. Like children's building blocks, they can be easily disconnected and reassembled into systems that appear to be very different.

Processes that should be isolated can be identified by examining the processes at each end of a data flow and asking three questions:

- Could the next process be performed at a **different time**?
- Could the next process be performed in a **different place**?
- Could the next process be performed by a **different person?**

If the answer to any of these questions is yes, then the processes should be isolated. They are isolated by writing data to a file after the previous process is finished and reading it from the file when the next process is executed. The file stores the data for access at a different time, by a different person, or in a different place. The file maintains the continuity of a higher-level process when there are discontinuities in time, person, or place.

Figure 7-4 illustrates two processes that are isolated as a group. However, Process 2 depends on Process 1 for earnings data. Process 2 can be isolated if Process 1 stores earnings data in the EARNINGS file. Then Process 2 can access the data independently at a different time or place, or under the control of a different person. Isolation is achieved at the cost of more file storage and processing.

The four processes in Figure 7-3 should each be isolated. They are clearly done at different times. They are often done by different people. They may even be done in different places.

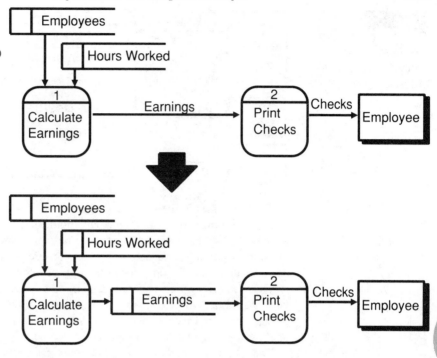

Notation for Hierarchical Structure

It is impossible to document most systems on a single sheet of paper. Even if the sheet is large enough, the Data Flow Diagram becomes too complex to understand if more than about 7 processes appear on the same sheet. Data Flow Diagrams have a notation that allows:

● progressive refinement of detail at several levels,
● linkages to ensure consistency between levels, and
● a hierarchical numbering system to identify the different levels.

Figure 7-3 illustrates a view of a system at a particular level of detail. The Systems Analysis and Design Process can be aggregated into a single process to show less detail. Each process in Figure 7-3 can also be exploded into several more detailed processes.

Figure 7-5 shows the Context Diagram that corresponds to Figure 7-3. Context Diagrams consist of a single process, all of the terminators, and data flows to represent each kind of communication between the system and the external environment. The Context Diagram is usually drawn first to identify the flows to and from the environment. A single process represents the whole system to keep from distracting the viewer with excessive detail. The process is a generalization of all the processes that occur inside the system boundaries in Figure 7-3.

The **Context Diagram** gets its name because it documents the context in which the system operates. The system interacts with the rest of the universe by passing messages to or from terminators, like machines, people, or organizations.

Figure 7-5

The Context Diagram for the systems analysis and design process.

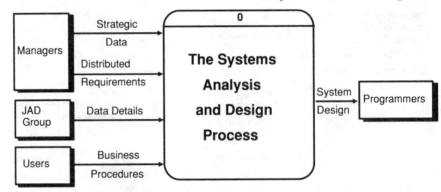

The rectangles in the Context Diagram stand for external users who interact with the system. Those that provide input to the system are usually placed on the left side. Those that receive output from the system are placed on the right side. The inputs (stimuli) and outputs (responses) are documented using a labelled arrow that points in the direction of the flow of information.

Thus *Managers* provide *Strategic Data* to the design process. They also provide *Distributed Requirements* for distributed systems. Sometimes users both provide input and receive output. In such cases two separate rectangles appear, on the left and right side, to document the two kinds of flow.

The following guidelines apply to Context Diagrams:

- **Terminators are not labelled with people's names.** Use the title or role name if the terminator is a person. Use Accountant instead of Mary Meigh.
- **A handler is not a terminator.** Distinguish between who delivers a flow and where it is coming or going. An inflow comes from a Client, not from the Mail. An outflow goes to a Customer, not to a Courier.
- **Communication between terminators is not documented.** Terminators, by definition, are outside the system. What they do between themselves in the privacy of their own boardrooms is none of the analyst's concern.
- **Every event should create a response.** Inflows are a signal from the outside world that something of interest has happened. The system usually generates a response to the event and sends it back to the outside world.

Progressive Refinement

Examining a process at a new level of detail is like removing the labeled lid from a black box to see what is inside. The label describes the contents of the box. The label and data give some idea about what transformation the black box does. However, they give no idea of how the box performs its transformations.

Alternately, think of taking a magnifying glass to reveal details that are not initially visible in the box. In this example, the details of the Context Diagram really consist of four processes. The designer designs the strategic view, the detailed data, the application programs, and the distributed system.

The DFD approach to systems analysis makes significant use of this principle of progressive refinement. It is a top down approach that first tries to get a view of the forest that corresponds to the system. It then refines the analysis to view groups of trees that correspond to subsystems. It finally documents individual trees, or single processes, that correspond to single computer modules. This process is illustrated schematically in Figure 7-6.

At the lowest level of detail, the parts are documented by techniques that are more suitable for recording procedural detail. The data tables, as described in Chapter 6, provide the detailed documentation of files. For processes, the detail is documented by one of several techniques that are described in Chapter 10. The data flows are normally documented by the forms or other documents and data records that flow along the data flow arrows. The flows to and from terminators are usually forms and screens, described in Chapter 8.

When the Context Diagram is exploded, the inputs and outputs are still the same as in the Context Diagram. The explosion makes it possible to see which of the detailed processes uses each input. Sometimes, terminators or inputs must be split or reordered to make the diagram easier to read. In Figure 7-3, Managers is split into two terminators because the two different flows are used in widely separated processes.

Figure 7-6

Successive levels of refinement for the elements in a Data Flow Diagram.

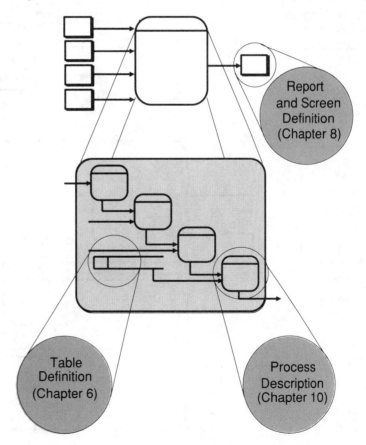

7 DFD

Linkage Between Levels

Any process can be exploded further to provide as much detail as needed. Figure 7-7 explodes Process 3 in Figure 7-3 to show the details of that process.

A border is drawn around the exploded diagram to show where the boundaries were before the explosion. This border shows which flows originate externally and which originate internally. The flows across this border must be the same as the flows into and out of the process at the higher level. The two diagrams are said to be balanced or leveled when the flows are the same.

Some authors suggest rigid rules about which level of the Data Flow Diagram should contain the first reference to each file. The main reason for these rules is so it will be easy to identify all the files that will be needed in the design of the database. It also clears up possible problems with files that are given different names at different levels of the diagram, thus potentially creating duplicate files.

These problems are not important when the database has already been designed, as it has if the method in this book is followed. As a result, it is relatively

Figure 7-7

Explosion of the Design Application Programs process to show the subprocesses contained in it.

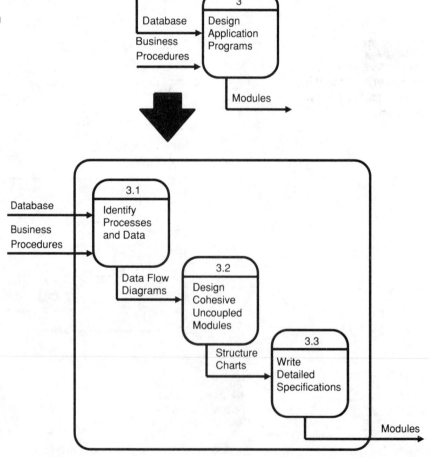

safe to introduce files in the first level at which a process actually needs them. Files may also be used in more than one process without causing problems. Multiple references to the same file make it easier to concentrate on the flow through the processes and on the isolation of the processes. Wherever the files are first introduced, the Data Flow Diagram should remain balanced. The same file should not be drawn at two different levels for the same flow. If the file is shown flowing into Process 2, only the corresponding data flow is shown flowing into Process 2.1.

Hierarchical Numbering

The processes in the exploded diagram inherit the identification number used in the higher process. A decimal extension is appended to differentiate each of the sub-processes. Thus Processes 3.1, 3.2, and 3.3 are detailed components of Process 3. Similarly there may be another level of detail showing Processes 3.1.1 and 3.1.2 which provide another level of detail for Process 3.1. The Context Diagram is always numbered with a zero and the zero is not inherited by the exploded levels. With this notation, the level of each process is obvious. Thus it is not necessary to show both levels on the same diagram, as in Figure 7-7. Both levels have been shown together only to illustrate how they are related.

Figure 7-8 shows the next level of detail in the Systems Analysis Process by exploding Process 3.1. The rest of this chapter deals with analysis at this level.

7 DFD

Figure 7-8

The systems analysis stages needed to identify processes and how they use data.

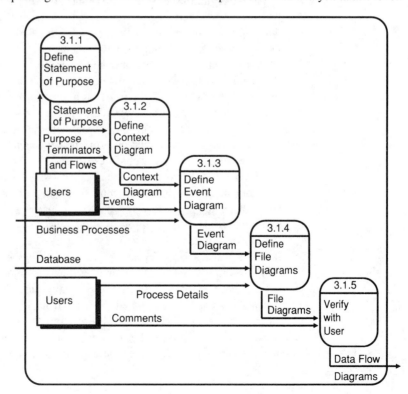

The Analysis Process

Systems analysis can be divided into five stages. These are:
- **Produce a Statement of Purpose** to identify the bounds of the system.
- **Produce a Context Diagram** to identify the context of the system.
- **Produce an Event Diagram** to partition the system into independent units.
- **Produce File Diagrams** to document processes and their use of data.
- **Verify the model** with the users.

Each stage of the analysis process has a different purpose, process, and product. Each is illustrated using the Student Records project.

The Bounds of the System

Every system has to have some boundary to distinguish the system from the rest of the world. Everything interacts with everything else in some way. However, it is not possible to model the whole universe. The analyst models some part of the universe, and ignores the rest. The system of interest is separated from the rest by a boundary.

PURPOSE: Identify the bounds of the system.
PROCESS: Directive from the project sponsor, Activity-Entity Diagram, or interviews.
PRODUCT: Statement of Purpose.

At the beginning, this boundary is usually very fuzzy. There are some things that are clearly part of the system and others that are not. Between them are things that might be part of the system if the analyst and sponsor remember to include them or are willing to change them.

A statement of purpose should be prepared to define the bounds of the system. It is a single paragraph that defines what is included and what is not included in the system being designed. It provides a reference that can be used to delineate a boundary in the gray area between the system and the rest of the universe.

The bounds of a system may be defined by the project sponsor. This is the case with many implementation projects, such as designing a word processor or implementing an inventory control system.

When a system has a very broad scope—such as an information system for a large organization—the system must be divided into smaller subsystems that can be implemented separately. In Chapter 3, clustering was used to identify subsystems that could become projects with relatively clear boundaries. Figure 7-9 repeats the Student subsystem from Figure 3-11 of the university example to illustrate how a subsystem can be used to identify the bounds of the system.

This Activity-Entity Diagram identifies the major activities in the Student Records System that is being designed. It also identifies the entities or data tables that are involved. The detailed file design in Section II has identified several other tables that are needed also. These should be included in the Activity-Entity Diagram if it is going to be used as a starting point for process analysis. The analysis can begin by going to the organizational units that perform these activi-

Figure 7-9

The Student Subsystem from the Activity-Entity Diagram of the university example.

	Buildings	Rooms	Equipment	Students	Programs	Courses	Sections	Meetings	Faculty
Register Students	x	x		x	x	x	x	x	x
Evaluate Students				x	x	x	x		x
Graduate Students				x	x	x	x		
Schedule Courses	x	x	x		x	x	x	x	x
Administer Program					x	x			

ties to verify that the revised strategic level design is an accurate reflection of the actual situation.

For the Student Records System example, the analyst goes to the university department that looks after program administration, course scheduling, student registration, evaluation, and graduation. In the example university this department is called the registrar.

An interview with the registrar reveals that the actual operations of the department are the same as those originally identified in the Activity-Entity Diagram. The office also looks after all applications from new students.

At this point the analyst must decide whether the original strategic plan has to be modified to include applications. This is the only other function performed by the registrar. Since much of the information for the student record is captured from the applications, it makes sense to include application processing as part of the new system.

The strategic design provides a framework for setting priorities and for identifying the scope of the design. However, it should not be a strait jacket that prevents sensible modifications that cope with problems identified during the detailed design stages.

On the other hand, boundaries between systems do have to be defined. Actual systems are highly interconnected. The project cannot include every activity that has some connection to the system or else the project grows to include all parts of the organization.

The statement of purpose for the Student Records System is shown below.

> *The purpose of the Student Records System is to handle all the details of course scheduling and academic interactions with students. This includes applications, selection, scholarships, registration, grading, and graduation of students. It also includes course scheduling and enrollment. It does not include alumni relations, financial transactions, and accounting.*

Now that the scope of the system has been defined, the analyst can use a Context Diagram to identify flows into and out of the system.

The Context Diagram

The Context Diagram serves as a logical starting point for designing a new system. Its components are easy to identify. The entire system is represented by a single activity box. The major terminators (the users) and the major inputs and outputs are also easy to identify.

PURPOSE:	Identify all interactions with terminators outside the system.
PROCESS:	Identify events that trigger processes.
PRODUCT:	Event List and Context Diagram.

The first task is to draw a large activity box in the middle of the page. Often, the second task is to find an acronym that can be used to identify the system. Our example system is called the Student Timetable Administration Records System (STARS). The STARS project involves many people during the design stage, so a short name is handy for communication. If it is pronounceable and meaningful, that is even better.

The next task is to identify all the terminators that use STARS. These may be people, organizations, or job titles that either provide information (stimuli) to the system or receive output (responses) from the system. The terminators that provide input to the system are lined up on the left side of the page. The terminators that receive output from the system are lined up on the right side of the page. If a terminator, like a student in STARS, both provides and receives information, then that terminator appears on both sides of the page.

Some people prefer to draw flows coming and going to the same terminator box, instead of having inputs on the left and outputs on the right. The purpose of the Data Flow Diagram is to identify the flow of information. The flow is easier to visualize if data always moves forward even if the terminators using the data have to be repeated.

The final step is to identify all of the major inputs and outputs of the system. These may be forms, reports, data tapes, electronic messages, or any other way that the system can communicate with the outside world. In Data Flow Diagrams, the medium is **not** the message (with apologies to Marshall Mc-Luhan). The only thing that matters is the logical content of the message.

The medium often changes during the design process. Paper records may get replaced by data from electronic recording devices. Mailed orders may be replaced by telephoned orders or orders placed at a terminal on the customer's premises. Printed inventory reports may get replaced by exception reports on a screen. In all these cases the information conveyed is likely to stay essentially the same. For this reason, the physical form is not a major concern at this stage. Only the logical content of the information flows needs to be recorded. Flows occur in three major cases:

- **Major inputs** like applications, orders, or payments for sales.
- **Major outputs** like class lists, reports, or payments to suppliers.
- **Time-triggered outputs** like graduations, payrolls, or monthly bills.

At this stage it is important to concentrate only on the major data flows. Minor flows such as change-of-address forms and error reports can be deferred until later. They frequently change or become unnecessary. The objective at this stage is to get "The Big Picture." At this stage, leave out details of profound insignificance that might sidetrack you away from a global understanding of the system. Progressive refinement eventually reveals the details.

Sometimes it is difficult to find one person who has a complete enough understanding of the whole system to identify the components of the Context Diagram. In such cases it may be necessary to get the information for a Context Diagram from several people and combine the result into a single diagram.

An Event List is a useful way to identify all flows. It lists all the stimuli in the environment to which the system must respond. Events are usually initiated by some person or organization, such as *student applies to program*. Alternately, events may be triggered by the passage of time, such as *monthly report is due*. The list should identify all the events to which the system must respond. All business transactions, such as orders, shipments, payments, and loans are events because they trigger some response, even if the response is only an entry in the accounting records. The Context Diagram shows the inputs and outputs triggered by each event.

Events do not correspond directly to data inflows. They are the triggers that cause inflows. When a student applies to the university, this event triggers the flow of an application, references, transcripts, and test scores. It also triggers a response in the form of an acceptance or rejection letter. References, transcripts, and test scores do not have their own event. They are a consequence of the Application event. The system may initiate some of these consequential flows by, say, calling a referee for a reference. The events in STARS are:

- Administration changes course, program, or offering.
- Administration schedules classes.
- Student applies to program.
- Student requests courses.
- Instructor submits grades.
- Graduation deadline is reached.

Figure 7-10 is the finished Context Diagram for STARS. Faculty, Applicants, and Students provide information and receive information from the system. The Administration and the Testing Center provide information but do not receive any. The Dean and the Controller receive information, but do not provide any. The various flows are labelled to indicate the kinds of information that are provided in that flow. It usually is necessary to maintain some record of the detailed contents of the flows. The name of the form or report is usually sufficient at this stage.

Once the Context Diagram has been prepared, the analyst can explode it into an Event Diagram.

Event Diagrams

The next step explodes the Context Diagram to see what isolated processes are inside the system. This is the Event Diagram. Each event on the Event List requires a separate subsystem to handle it. Inputs that change or update previous inputs are usually part of the subsystem that processed the original input.

Figure 7-10
The Context Diagram
for the STARS project.

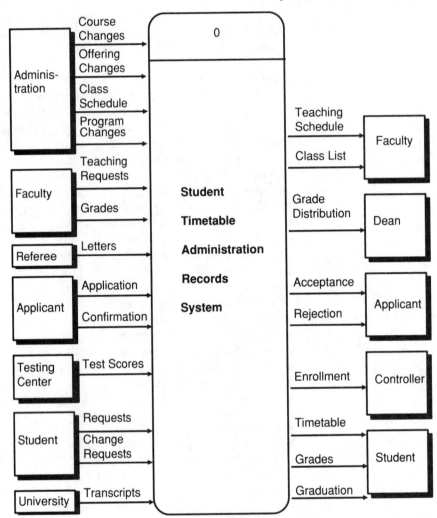

PURPOSE: Identify isolated subsystems that can be independently analyzed, designed, and implemented.

PROCESS: Use Event List to identify processes. Group processes in groups of seven or less. Connect terminators to processes.

PRODUCT: Event Diagrams.

   The Event Diagram has a process for each event in the Event List produced for the Context Diagram. The processes are arbitrarily numbered from 1 to N, where N is the number of events. For convenience in exposition, they can be arranged in the order in which they logically occur to a student (customer) passing through the process. The order has no effect on the design task.

The Event List for large systems may contain 50 or 100 events. This is much too complex to show on a single Event Diagram. Since each event can occur at a different time, the corresponding processes are isolated processes. Each process can be treated as a separate system for analysis and design purposes. In fact, each process can be taken into a separate Context Diagram with its own input and output terminators. In practice, if it is necessary to divide a large number of processes, they are divided into related groups of no more than seven processes.

It is sometimes useful to think of the logical group or unit of work for organizing events as a case—as in a case handled by a doctor or lawyer. There are many events that occur as a doctor treats a patient, such as the initial call, receipt of laboratory tests, and surgery. These belong together as a set because they are all part of the treatment of a case. Recording the progress of a student through a university and performing a database design are other examples of cases that contain many separate events.

This introduces another level of Data Flow Diagram between the Context Diagram and the detailed Event Diagrams. The extra level explodes the Context Diagram into cases and each case into individual events. This makes it easier to present them to users, even if several different Event Diagrams are produced.

The opposite extreme occurs in very simple systems when an Event List contains only one event. In this case, the Event Diagram is the same as the Context Diagram. The analyst can proceed directly to detailed analysis.

The processes in the Event Diagram are likely the same as the activities identified in the corresponding Activity-Entity Diagram, shown in Figure 7-9. They were obtained by clustering to partition the work of the system into processes that minimize the number of connections between processes. Partitioning the system into processes that handle events has a similar result. The previously identified activities serve as a check of the Event Diagram.

The steps in constructing an Event Diagram are:

- **Draw processes** for each of the events on the Event List.
- **Name the processes** to describe the *response* to the event by using a strong active verb and a single explicit object. Usually the response is to generate an output, such as a report, a payment, or a confirmation. Sometimes the response is to store data in a table until it is needed by another process.
- **Connect** the required input and output data flows to the process.
- **Split** large systems into subsystems or cases of no more than seven processes.
- **Check** the results against the Context Diagram, the Event List, and the Activity-Entity Diagram for accuracy and completeness.

Figure 7-11 illustrates the Event Diagram for the STARS project. There are six processes. Five of them correspond to the original five activities in the Activity-Entity Diagram. The sixth is the application screening process that was identified during interviews to define the scope of the project.

All the processes, except the first and last, have at least one input from a terminator, a process, and at least one output to a terminator. The first process does not produce an output because all users are able to see changes by examin-

Figure 7-11
The Event
Diagram for
the STARS
project is ob-
tained by ex-
ploding the
Context
Diagram.

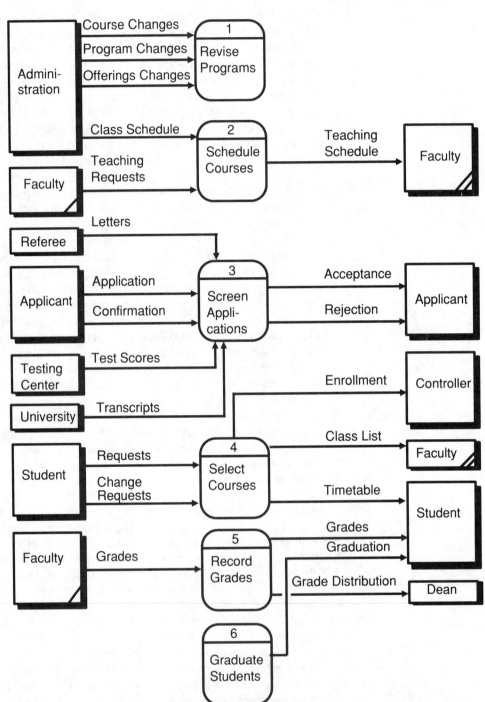

ing screens in the system. The last is triggered by an operator at graduation time, and does not have a corresponding data flow.

Sometimes it is difficult to draw the arrows that enter or leave a terminator box without having them cross over each other. Figure 7-11 illustrates two ways of dealing with this problem. One way is to break the lines that are being crossed to show that the lines do not join each other. This has been done with the arrow between the Graduate Students process and the Student entity. The line crosses over the Grade Distribution flow which is broken to provide an *overpass* in the same way that overpasses are shown on a highway map.

The other way to deal with the problem is to draw the terminator box again and mark it to indicate that it is duplicated elsewhere on the diagram. This has been done with the Faculty terminator on both the left and right sides. In the input terminators, a single diagonal bar in the lower right corner has been used to identify the duplicated terminators. In the output terminators a double diagonal bar has been used.

The processes involve some interactions with data tables. However, these interactions can be treated as internal operations of the process at this level of analysis. The purpose of the Event Diagram is to identify self-contained subsystems that can be designed separately. Any subsystems that could be used at different times, in different places, or by different people are conceptually separate. They may communicate with each other by placing information in files, but they do not communicate directly with anything other than the terminators.

Traditional analysis methods included the data stores at this stage of analysis because the stores were the first clue to the data needs of the system. With a data-driven method the stores are already known and defined in data tables. They can be safely suppressed until the next level of analysis.

File Diagrams

This level of analysis explodes each process on the Event Diagram to identify the processes and data needed to perform transformations triggered by the event.

PURPOSE: Identify all processes needed to respond to an event and link them to the data they use or produce.

PROCESS: Existing systems are analyzed by Structured Analysis or Reverse Engineering. New systems are synthesized by Disassembly of outputs or Forward Assembly of inputs.

PRODUCT: File Diagrams.

This next level of detail may take one level of explosion for simple systems or several levels for complex systems. Files are added to the components in the Event Diagrams.

There are four methods that can be used to identify the processes in a system. The appropriate method depends on whether a working system exists, or an entirely new system is being designed. A typical Data Flow Diagram will be illustrated by using an explosion of Process 1. The Structured Analysis method for redesign of existing processes is illustrated using the Screen Applications process from the Event Diagram. The synthesis method for design of new processes is illustrated using the Select Courses process. The other processes are not exploded further because they would not illustrate any new concepts.

Analysis of Revise Programs Process

Figure 7-12 illustrates the explosion of Process 1. The top version is typical of how many analysts draw Data Flow Diagrams. The diagram looks like a plate of spaghetti and meatballs. It looks nice and appears to have some different com-

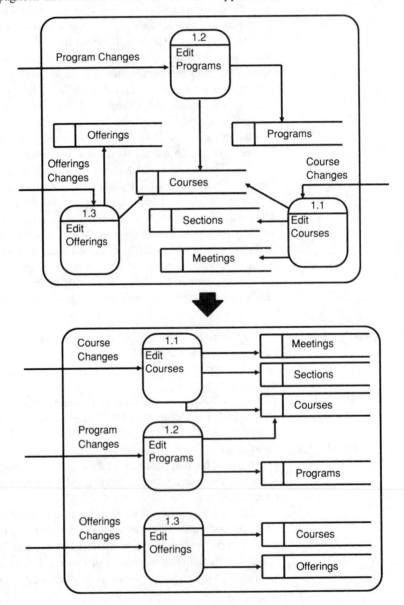

Figure 7-12

The exploded view of Process 1 in the university example. The top version shows a poorly drawn diagram. The bottom version shows good graphic placement to emphasize isolated systems.

ponents, but any underlying logic to their placement is a deep mystery. The processes are scattered around the diagram like meatballs. The data flows and files fill up the space between them to produce a pattern that would make a good wallpaper design. The result may even have a rare beauty suitable for framing, but there is no hint as to where the beginning and end are—if a beginning and end exist.

The bottom version documents the same process, but follows some rules of good graphic placement. These are:

● **Processes progress from top to bottom.** Processes may occasionally split or recombine, but the general progression from one process to the next is from top to bottom. If the progression stops because the processes are isolated—as they are here—then the isolation is very obvious.

● **Data flows from left to right.** Inputs come in from the left of the process and outputs go to the right. This rule may occasionally be violated to reuse an existing file. If in doubt, show another copy of the file to the left of the process for input or to the right for output from the process.

● **Combined flow is from upper left to lower right.** The main flow follows the diagonal like a waterfall. Tributary processes can branch to the sides or join this flow. A broken flow identifies isolated processes.

Figure 7-13 shows a further explosion of Process 1.1. This is a typical explosion of an editing process in a batch processing environment. The standard editing processes are insert, update, and delete. A separate process is usually

7 DFD

Figure 7-13

Explosion of a typical batch editing process, showing an insert, update, and delete process.

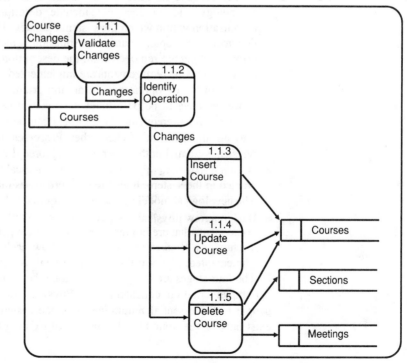

needed at the beginning to validate the changes to make sure that they are allowed. Another is needed to determine which of the three standard processes will be needed and pass data to it. Note that deletion of a course requires deletion of the corresponding sections and meetings. Insertion does not require addition of sections and meetings since the relationship is not mandatory.

If a screen is used for entry and editing, this explosion is not necessary. Prototyping—discussed in Chapter 8—is used to identify all operations. A Screen Painter automatically and invisibly generates similar processes as needed.

Analysis of Screen Applications Process

If an existing system is being automated, then Structured Analysis can analyze the physical system to determine its constituent components. The existing system is documented and transformed into a new automated system. The stages are:

- **Document the existing physical system.** This consists of following all inputs through the system until they become the outputs of the system. Existing documents, procedures, and people in the system may be included in the documentation. The existing order of the processes is also documented. The physical approach is easy for the users in the department to understand. They can describe exactly what they do without getting bogged down in the differences between forms, data flows, and files.

- **Extract the essential logical model.** The logical model describes the behavior and the interactions with terminators. It is sometimes called the Essential Model because it identifies the essence of the process. It assumes ideal technology and so does not include descriptions of the technology or organization within which the system operates. Thus all references to existing documents, people, data transmission, mechanical procedures, and error-checking are removed from the description. The logical model does not consider how the requirements are implemented.

  The order of operations is an important logical consideration. Some processes have to be performed in sequence because they rely on previous processes for prerequisite data. Others can be performed in parallel because they are independent of each other. Processes must be in some order in the physical system, but the order can be ignored if it is not logically required.

- **Design a new logical model.** The new logical model adds new features wanted in the system. It also revises processes that change in the new system. The new logical model specifies the required behavior of the new system.

- **Design a new physical system.** This last stage breaks the system up into components that are implemented by different people, programs, or machines. Technology choices are made about how each part of the system is to be implemented. The next three chapters deal with this stage.

The four stages are designed to separate the logical requirements from physical implementation considerations. Physical considerations sometimes blind people to the essential requirements of the system. Existing procedures often exist only to get around the limitations of existing technology or organizational structures. It is easier to see the implementation options if the view is not clouded by existing procedures.

Old Physical Data Flow

Screening applications involves several processes. The administrative personnel who perform the work explain that the following steps are required in processing an application manually:

- Peter, the mail clerk, sets up a file folder for each application received on an R2 form.
- Peter inserts referee letters and transcripts in the file folder and notes on the application that they have arrived. The folder is then passed to Gladys, the assistant registrar.
- Gladys calculates the Grade Point Average (GPA) from the transcripts. Different schools have different grading scales. Manual adjustment is sometimes needed to convert all GPA to a common scale before transferring them to the application form.
- Peter copies test scores to the application form when they arrive. Test scores come monthly from the Testing Center on lists arranged alphabetically by surname. It is common to receive test scores for some people who never apply and to have some people apply, but never have their test scores sent.
- Gladys performs an initial screening of applications when all transcripts, test scores, and referee letters have arrived. The initial screening consists of eliminating applicants who do not have a sufficiently high GPA or test score to be admitted. The rejections are passed to Marion, who sends rejection letters. After screening, Gladys produces lists for the Admissions Committee.
- Gladys gives the completed files of qualified applicants to the Admissions Committee for final screening. The committee considers the application, GPA, test score, and referee letters for each applicant. It then makes a final decision to accept or reject the application. The files are passed to Marion.
- Marion, the typist, sends rejection letters to rejected applicants and acceptance letters to request confirmation from accepted applicants.
- Peter passes all confirmations from applicants to Marion who files them in the applicant's file. Files for applicants who have been accepted, but decide not to come, are stored in a suspense file in case they change their minds and want to reapply at another time.

This is a typical example of the physical description of a manual process. The corresponding physical DFD is shown in Figure 7-14. The Data Flow Diagram follows the processing of the application through the various sequential stages of data gathering, analysis, and processing. The process is viewed as being continuous even though it may take many days or weeks to complete. The names of people, positions, and forms are often included to make it easier for the users to understand the diagram. The processes are arranged like a waterfall flowing from upper left to lower right to emphasize the progression of processes.

7 DFD

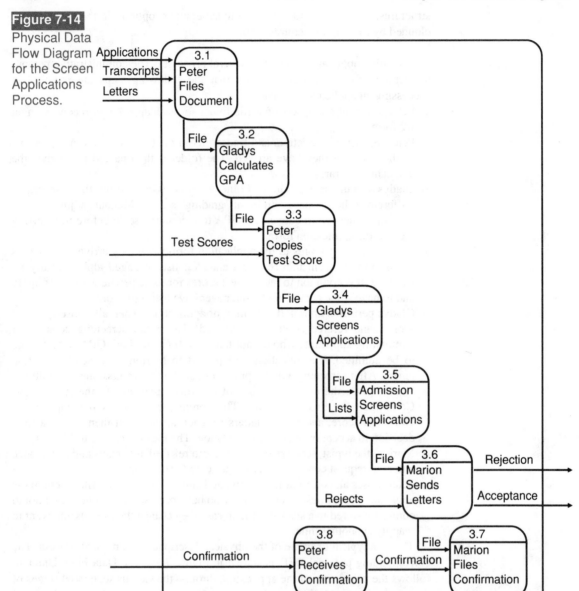

Figure 7-14
Physical Data Flow Diagram for the Screen Applications Process.

Old Logical Data Flow

The next stage is to convert the physical DFD to a logical DFD. This means removing all references to people, positions, and forms. It also means removing purely physical operations like Process 3.8, which merely passes on a document. Reference letters are not entered into the computer system, but are filed in the applicant's file folder for examination by the screening committee. Filing references is another purely physical process.

Conversion means rearranging the sequence to reflect the required order instead of the current physical order. Many things that are done in sequence physically can be done in parallel. For instance, test scores, transcripts, and reference letters can arrive in any order. Therefore they are parallel processes that can be processed in any order. The only constraint is that they must all be present before the application can be screened.

Figure 7-15 shows how the Logical Data Flow Diagram looks after physical processes have been removed, but before data files have been inserted. This is a conceptual step to illustrate the analyst's thinking process. Normally this step would never be documented on paper. The next step is to insert data files in the diagram and identify isolated processes. This step breaks a conceptually continuous process into steps that can be executed at different times.

The flows in the application process show that each one of the activities is independent. Applications, transcripts, test scores, acceptance decisions, and confirmations may all arrive at different times. Therefore a separate application program or screen is required to deal with each one. The equivalent logical DFD for Figure 7-15 is shown in Figure 7-16.

New Logical Data Flow

The next stage of analysis is to modify the Logical Data Flow Diagram to incorporate improvements to the present system. Sometimes this step requires a small incremental change. Sometimes it requires major reorientation. For instance, an insurance company wanted an incremental change to allow a 4-digit code number for the product type instead of 3 digits. Closer examination revealed that the problem was not a need to identify more than 999 kinds of policies. It was a need to reduce the number of kinds by providing a basket of standard features from which customers could select.

The desired improvements in STARS, according to the sponsor, are to simplify data recording, allow flexible assignment of staff, rank applicants by GPA and Test Scores, and automate the acceptance and rejection letters.

Some data entry stages can be combined. There are three basic ways that the process could be designed using interactive screens.

- **Data are entered as they arrive.** This could require separate processes for each entry and many file accesses on the computer. However, it would eliminate a great deal of manual scheduling and control to determine which files are complete and ready for entry.
- **All data are entered together.** The staff can wait until applications, transcripts, and test scores have all arrived before entering the application data. This

7
DFD

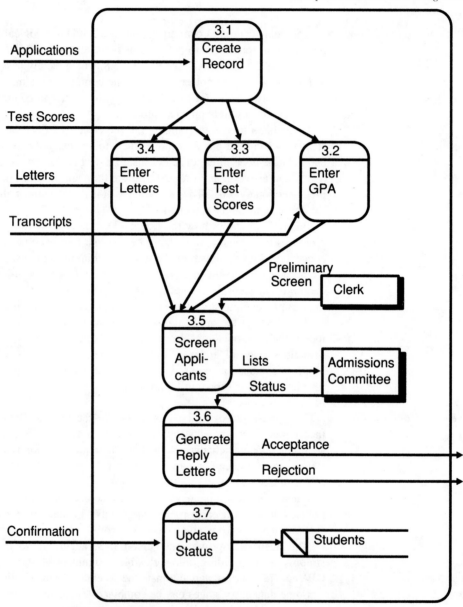

Figure 7-15

Logical conversion of the Physical Data Flow Diagram before files have been inserted between isolated processes.

would reduce the number of accesses required and possibly the number of screen designs. Then the computer could automatically perform the preliminary screening, generate lists, and generate form letter replies.

- **Only acceptable data are entered.** The staff can wait until all material has arrived, perform the initial screening manually, and enter data only for those applicants who are judged acceptable. This would reduce the data entry by

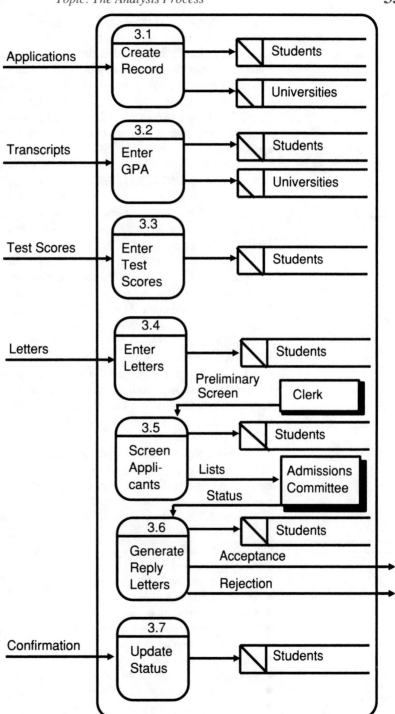

Figure 7-16
The Logical Data Flow Diagram for the current Screen Applications Process showing all files and isolated processes.

eliminating unacceptable candidates from the system. It would also prevent later studies to compare acceptable and unacceptable candidates.

In this example, assume that the first alternative is considered to be most suitable. It provides maximum flexibility because a system that supports this alternative also supports all others.

Note that Processes 3.1, 3.2, 3.3, and 3.4 all involve data entry to the STUDENTS table and two of them involve data in the UNIVERSITIES table. This suggests that the processes are closely related. In fact, all three processes enter applicant data at a screen. The different processes could possibly be implemented using a single screen. The screen inserts a new row in the STUDENTS table and new rows in the UNIVERSITIES table, as needed for applications. Most screen generators produce screens that can insert, update, and delete data on one screen.

Process 3.2 can use the same screen to update the UNIVERSITIES table by entering a GPA whenever a transcript arrives. Process 3.3 can use the screen to enter Test Scores in the STUDENTS table whenever Test Scores arrive. Process 3.4 can also use the screen to record a rating in the STUDENTS table based on reference letters. A clerk uses the same screen to perform Process 3.5 by screening candidates as GPA and test scores are entered. The unacceptable ones can be flagged with a code in the ACCEPTANCE attribute of the STUDENTS table.

It may be desirable to have a separate simpler screen that does not display universities for Processes 3.3, 3.4, and 3.5. This eliminates the need to read the UNIVERSITIES table when entering test scores or recording letters of recommendation. However, then the GPA would not be visible and the clerk would not be able to see if the record is complete. So preliminary screening could not be done during data entry. On balance, it is probably better to use the same screen for all processes. The same screen can also be used to enter the acceptance status after committee review.

Process 3.5 also produces lists of applicants for the Admissions Committee. This process has to be changed to produce ranked lists that help the committee identify the best students. A measure based on a weighted average of the GPA and Test Score can be used for ranking.

Process 3.7, which enters confirmations, can also use the same screen if the ACCEPTANCE attribute gets an expanded definition. Now it becomes clear that there are more than two possible values for the ACCEPTANCE attribute. It should be changed to a STATUS attribute. The student can have any of the following status levels during various stages of application and enrollment:

- Incomplete application.
- Complete application ready for Admissions Committee.
- Rejected application but no letter sent.
- Accepted but no letter sent.
- Rejected application with letter sent.
- Accepted application with letter sent but no confirmation.
- Accepted application declined by the applicant.
- Confirmed acceptance.

- Enrolled in first, second, etc. year.
- Withdrawn student.
- Expelled student.
- Graduated student.

It is usually convenient to mail acceptances, rejections, grades, graduations, and other notices in periodic batches. Acceptances and rejections may be updated and mailed on a weekly or biweekly basis. A separate status is needed to indicate whether a notice has been mailed. Then unnotified candidates can be selected for mailings with the next batch. The student follows a sequential process through the university with one status at a time so a single attribute can record the status.

Process 3.6 mails acceptance and rejection letters. It is a batch process that selects all students who have been accepted or rejected, but have not yet been sent a notification. The name, address, and status of each such applicant is selected into a temporary file. Then they are passed to a word processing program. The word processor merges this information into a form letter and prints mailing labels or addressed envelopes for the letters. When the applicants are selected, the status is changed to record that notifications have been mailed.

In a 4GL environment, with a query language or application generator, this process is so simple that it does not need to be exploded again. A simple specification of what is required can be given to an application programmer who can implement it in a couple hours, at most. In a 3GL environment Process 3.6 is exploded once more as shown in Figure 7-17. Then formal specifications are developed as described in Chapters 9 and 10.

If a 3GL, like COBOL, is used to define the screens, at least another level of explosion is needed for the data entry process. The extra level explains the logic of the different steps in reading a table, accepting input, checking it, and updating it. This is not necessary with a screen generator because many of these processes are generated automatically. One of the benefits of using a 4GL is that the required amount of analysis and documentation is reduced somewhat, along with the amount of programming and testing.

Figure 7-17

Explosion of the Generate Reply Letters Process.

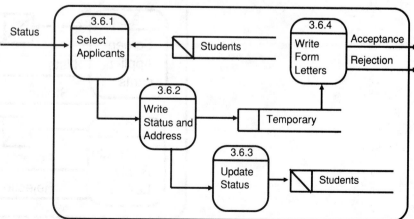

The new logical Data Flow Diagram is illustrated in Figure 7-18. Note that the terminators are no longer included in the leveled diagrams. The contents of an exploded DFD are the same as the contents of the process being exploded. The flows into and out of the DFD are the same as those into and out of the higher-level process.

Note that the process of recording and screening applications, and notifying applicants is rather complicated. Yet, it is implemented with a single screen, a program to rank candidates, and a small program to select records for a form letter. This single screen application can support any of the three suggested ways of organizing the paper flow: continuous processing, collecting all material before entry, or entry of accepted applications only.

Furthermore, staff can be organized in any of a variety of ways. Different people can look after different stages of the process or different people can look after different groups of applicants. These groups could be selected by department, by region of application, or by position in an alphabetic list.

One of the benefits of an interactive screen-based system is that it often simplifies data entry, update, and inquiry tasks. It does this while increasing the

Figure 7-18

The new Logical Data Flow Diagram of the Screen Applications Process after combining the entry of student data on one screen.

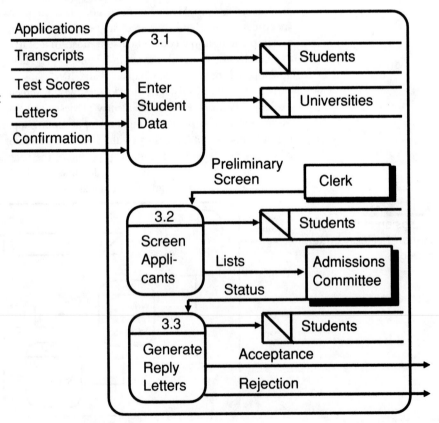

organization's flexibility. It is then possible to reorganize people's respon-sibilities in the most effective manner without having to reorganize the computer systems. This is accomplished by identifying independent modules of work. Then organizational procedures and job definitions, rather than programs, pro-vide the structure that connects the modules.

Structured Analysis designs systems by successively documenting old physi-cal, old logical, and new logical models. It allows the analyst to learn about the user's system and to communicate with users in an understandable way. How-ever, Yourdon[9] makes a convincing argument that the method needs to be modified for the following reasons:

- **Wasted effort.** Up to 75 percent of the physical model does not go into the new model because of duplicated functions, redundant data, and multiple error-checks.
- **User reluctance.** Users do not want to pay for detailed documentation of a system that will be replaced by the new system.
- **Analyst zeal.** Some analysts forget that documentation of the current system is only a means to the end of learning about it. They waste time documenting it in minute detail.

Yourdon recommends going directly to modeling the new system, if possible. The old physical and logical models should be used when necessary, but should not necessarily be used. The only time that the old system needs to be modeled is if the analyst has no understanding of the existing system and needs to document it to understand it. Even then, only the parts that are not understood need to be modeled.

The physical model can usually be avoided by translating user descriptions directly to the logical model. The analyst should concentrate on the new logical model. For the past thiirty years analysts have automated nineteenth century processes. Automating the processes of the past is no longer a satisfactory way to design systems. We must now use the power of computers to improve the proces-ses of the future.

Reverse Engineering

The premise of Reverse Engineering is that existing code can be recompiled into a logical specification. It uses the code, the internal documentation, the existing modularization, and some artificial intelligence inferences. A great deal of research has been launched in pursuit of this "Technological Fountain of Youth" that could somehow rejuvenate old tired programs with cancerous growths and terminal ailments. The search will likely have no more success than the one by Ponce de Leon in 1513. Even if it were possible to recreate the specifications, the following problems would remain in most systems.

- **Wrong data model.** Since the old code probably uses a variety of redundant hierarchical files, it will be necessary to change the data structure, eliminate redundancies, and translate attribute names.
- **Program structure follows data structure.** A different program structure is needed to navigate hierarchical files than to select data from relational tables.

7 DFD

- **Redundant data requires redundant code.** Much of the code deals with checking that should be done by the DBMS, duplication of operations done by other programs, and reconciliation of differences between different data files. All of this has to be removed.
- **Programs are based on obsolete technology.** The programs likely use hierarchical files instead of relational databases; batch updates instead of screen entry of data; and character based screens instead of Graphic User Interfaces. These cannot be modernized automatically.
- **New features are required.** When a major redesign is undertaken, there are usually new features required. The old code has to be understood before the new features can be added.

Trying to Reverse Engineer old code to bring it into a modern DBMS is like trying to Reverse Engineer a quarter horse in hopes of getting a Ferrari. They may both be expensive and designed for racing, but they are not compatible. Reverse Engineering looks like a logical extension of Code Restructuring, which is already available. However, Code Restructuring only changes the form of programs, while Reverse Engineering attempts to change the substance.

The only purpose that Reverse Engineering is likely to serve in systems analysis is to produce a specification that serves the same function as the old physical model. It quickly produces a description of how things have been done, but most of it has to be changed before a new logical model emerges. It is more useful in database design because data requirements do not change as much.

Synthesis of Select Courses Process

If an entirely new system is being designed, then it is not possible to start by documenting an existing system. The analyst must resort to either Disassembly or Forward Assembly approaches.

Disassembly of Output

The Disassembly approach starts with the output. It tries to factor the output into its components by removing the last piece that was added before completion of the single output product. This can be thought of as a kind of disassembly line. Orr[5] calls this Data-Structured Design because it builds the processes around the kinds of data needed to assemble an output.

If we were building a microcomputer, we would ask what was the last piece that was put on. The answer would likely be the case. Then we have two components: a case and the rest of the computer. For each one, the designer can ask, "Is it an existing component or is it a subassembly that must again be decomposed? If it is an existing component, do we have it, can we build it, or can we buy it?" The process is repeated until the microcomputer is disassembled into basic components that exist or can be purchased. Then an assembly line can be created to reverse the order and assemble it again.

A computer example is the calculation of a student's Grade Point Average for the courses in a specific Program. It ends with the calculation of an average. This requires the grades for the courses taken in the program. This, in turn, requires the complete list of courses taken by the student and the list of courses which are allowable in the program. Processes are needed to get a list of allowable courses, get a list of courses taken, identify the allowable courses taken, and compute an average of their grades.

This method requires a clear definition of the output of a system. It can work satisfactorily when the analyst has a good understanding of the process and does not have to rely on the user to explain the process being used currently. It also applies when the user has a reasonable understanding of the analysis process or when no system currently exists for performing the work. A new organization, department, or function does not have a current system to analyze.

This method focuses on a single output. Most information systems produce more than one output so the disassembly process has to be repeated for each output. However, this process usually leads to the identification of common modules or subassemblies at the points where a good system is divided into separate modules anyway. It is somewhat like designing a line to produce different models of microcomputers. The basic microcomputer is the same until different power supplies, disk drives, or auxiliary boards are installed to differentiate the models.

Forward Assembly of Inputs

The Forward Assembly approach starts with the input and tries to determine what must be done with it to produce the desired output. It is a creative process in which the analyst must synthesize, or invent, a way of performing the required processes. The designer is like a sculptor who starts with a block of marble and has to figure out what parts of the block must be modified to create a statue.

The analyst is designing an assembly line in which inputs are transformed into outputs. The analyst starts with raw data and identifies ways to process it into the desired outputs.

Often it is best to use both the Forward Assembly and the Disassembly methods together. The analyst works back and forth through the processes until they are understood.

The Select Courses process illustrates the analysis of a new process. In the example university, there are not always enough places available in each class to enroll every student who wants to take a given course. As a result, students have to fill out forms in which they request courses that they would like to take and assign a priority to each. A program has to match the desired courses with available spaces using several criteria. The criteria in order of importance are:

- Students must take prerequisites before they can take a selected course.
- The assignment is performed in order of decreasing number of courses passed with a grade point of 1.00 or better. This ensures that students who are about to graduate get first chance at courses, since they never get another chance. Within a group who have taken the same number of courses, assignment is performed in order of decreasing GPA to give the best students first choice.
- All students are first assigned to their highest priority course, if possible. This gets each student gets into at least one course that is strongly wanted. If the first choice is filled, the student is given the next available priority.

● Students are then assigned to the next four available courses on their priority lists. The assignment is done in order of decreasing number of courses passed with a grade point of 1.00 or better. Ties are ordered by decreasing GPA.

These rules may be too complicated for some 4GLs and Code Generators to handle. If this is true for the selected 4GL, they must be programmed in a 3GL environment. The 3GL can access records in the database using some of the features of the DBMS query language.

Unlike the previous example, there is no existing physical procedure to follow. This procedure for assigning students to sections is new. It deals with complaints about the existing system. Now, students are enrolled on a first-come-first-served basis that leads to long lineups at registration time. The analyst cannot use a process of documenting the physical process and converting it to a logical process. Instead, the logical flow must be developed directly.

Figure 7-19 illustrates the Data Flow Diagram for the Select Courses process. The diagram was generated using a combination of Forward Assembly and Disassembly approaches.

Figure 7-19

Explosion of the Select Courses Process to illustrate the use of Disassembly and Forward Assembly of a new process.

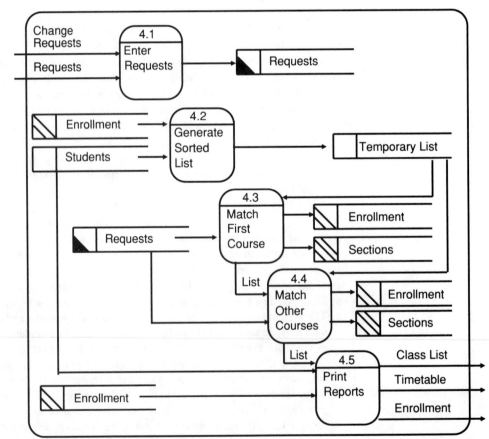

Process 4.1 is an isolated process that enters data and changes from the request forms. It should be separated into another process because data entry will likely be done at some other time. Process 4.2 is also an isolated process. However, it is likely to be performed at the same time as the rest of the processes since all it does is generate a temporary file used by the next processes. It is triggered by the same deadline that triggers the matching process. The rest of the processes are an isolated sequence of processes. They process requests to update the ENROLLMENT and SECTIONS table and they produce the three kinds of system reports.

Using forward assembly on the Request file, quickly shows that the requests cannot be processed until a list of students, in priority order, is available. Thus, this information must first be provided in the Temporary file. Then it is possible to work forward again to enroll in the first requested course for each student and then process the other requests in priority order.

The processes can be checked by Disassembly of the outputs. Working backwards from the Timetable, reveals that Enrollments are required. Enrollments require the Requests and the priority of each request. The priority of a student is established by sorting on decreasing number of courses taken. Requests are already in priority order.

Process 4.4 is like Process 4.3 except that it enrolls a student in up to four sections, instead of one. It needs a loop to call the functions in Process 4.3 several times. Process 4.5 contains three independent processes that write three kinds of reports. These are called at the end of the Select Courses process. That is a convenient time to produce reports for all of the interested parties: students, faculty, and controller's office. It may also be convenient to be able to run these reports separately to reflect later changes in enrollment. A separate screen is probably needed to enter these changes.

Note that several data tables are used many times. The SECTIONS table is used to determine the number enrolled in the section and the capacity limit of the section. The ENROLLMENT table is needed to determine how many courses the student has taken, what the student's GPA is, and whether the student has taken the prerequisites. It is also used to record enrollment in the next course. The files are shown several times to make it clear when they are used for input and output and to avoid crossover data flow arrows.

Figure 7-20 shows an explosion of Process 4.3. Note that Process 4.3.3 requires a file of prerequisite courses. This file was not identified in all of the previous database design work. This is not an uncommon occurrence, but it is not a problem either. It is relatively easy to define an extra file now. None of the other data tables or processes has to be changed to make this addition.

Verifying the Model

The analyst has produced Data Flow Diagrams to describe all processes in the system. The user input is often large at the beginning, but tapers off as the

Figure 7-20

Explosion of the Match
First Course Process.

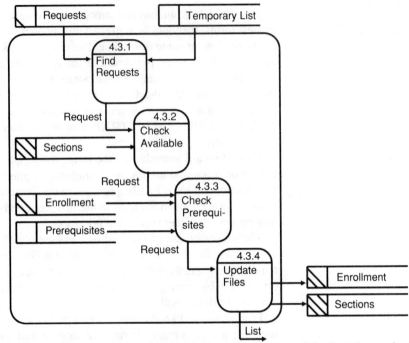

analyst begins to understand the users' needs. It is possible that the analyst's
perception of the problem will start to diverge from the user's perception.

PURPOSE: Verify that Data Flow Diagrams correctly describe the desired system.
PROCESS: Joint Application Design (JAD) or Structured Walkthrough.
PRODUCT: A verified Data Flow Diagram.

The analyst uses Data Flow Diagrams to make notes about the system during
the analysis process. Analysis is a learning process in which the analyst—who
may not understand the system requirements—tries to learn from the users—who
do understand the system requirements. The DFD echoes the user's explanation
of the system back to the user, to see if it is understood by the analyst.

As with any learning process, the analyst must be prepared to admit mistakes
and correct them when users identify errors in understanding. This correction
process is so important that it is formalized in methods like Joint Applications
Design and Structured Walkthroughs.

JAD is used in Chapter 5 to identify the detailed database requirements at the
beginning of the analysis. Most variations of JAD obtain process descriptions
with the data descriptions. The same people are needed to provide process information, and they can do it easily while they are discussing data issues. The same
advantages of management commitment, direct user contact, and integrated approval are obtained for process analysis as were obtained for the data analysis.

Data Flow Diagrams are used in the JAD session to describe the system.
Structured Analysis, Disassembly, and Forward Assembly are used as appro-

priate. The only difference is that the result is discussed with a group rather than an individual.

Structured Walkthroughs are similar to JAD sessions, but they are held after the initial analysis and are designed to check the results of the analysis. A group of users and analysts examine the Data Flow Diagrams to check for terminators, data flows, processes, and files that are missing or incorrect.

The objective of the walkthrough is to make sure that the analysis procedure has accurately captured all the data flows and processes that must be supported by the system.

Summary of DFD Steps

The process of defining Data Flow Diagrams consists of the following steps:

- **Identify all input data flows** and draw them at the left of the diagram along with the terminators that send them.
- **Identify all output data flows** and draw them at the right of the diagram along with the terminators that receive them.
- **Identify processes** by following the input flows forward, the output flows backward, or both until they meet in the middle.
- **Partition work** into processes that respond to single events and that minimize the number of required connections between processes.
- **Label all interface data flows** and make sure that the flows are the same as those for the same process in higher-level diagrams.
- **Label all of the processes** using a strong active verb and a single explicit object. Avoid weak verbs like process, handle, or administer. They do not convey any information about what is being done by the process.
- **Ignore any initialization and termination** processes, trivial error paths, or flow control information. These are added later. Now they distract the analyst and the user who should be concentrating on the main flow of the processes.
- **Be prepared to redo** parts of the Data Flow Diagram. Include corrections identified by users or improvements in the partitioning of the processes.

7 DFD

Testing the Data Flow Diagram

Previous diagrams concentrated on illustrating properly drawn Data Flow Diagrams. In this section the emphasis is on identifying poorly drawn diagrams, explaining what is wrong with them, and showing how they can be improved. The terminators, data flows, processes, and files provide clues to errors.

CLUE #1: **Terminator is the name of a person.**
CAUSE: Physical model instead of logical model.
CURE: Use role or title as a terminator name.
In Figure 7-21, Polly Morfus is replaced by her title, Purchasing Agent.

CLUE #2: **Data Flows between terminators.**
CAUSE: Documenting flows that are not part of the system.

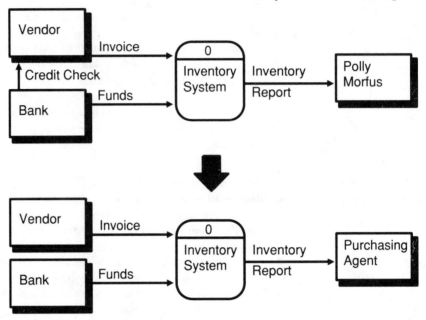

CURE: Delete the flows.

In Figure 7-21, the Bank and the Vendor may communicate. They may even communicate about the system being built. However, if it is not possible to influence what is said or how it is said, then the flow is not part of the system.

CLUE #3:   **A common carrier is a terminator.**
CAUSE: The handler has been identified instead of the terminator.
CURE: Replace the handler with the terminator.

In Figure 7-22, a request is received by FAX and sent by mail through the post office. However, the terminator is the Client in each case. FAX and post office are merely messengers. As you do not shoot the messenger who brings bad news, you do not document the messenger who carries any information. The exception is if the carrier is a part of the system to be designed, such as a videotext service that distributes the information system being designed.

CLUE #4:   **The communications medium is described.**
CAUSE: Physical characteristics have not been eliminated.
CURE: Describe the Data Flow and not the medium.

In Figure 7-22, a Change Diskette is sent to the Client. The diskette is a physical medium that unduly constrains possible implementations. The new system might communicate changes via a modem or through a bulletin board. The only essential characteristic of the system is that a change be provided. Diskettes, tapes, multipart forms, mail services, couriers, trains, planes, boats, bicycles, dog

Figure 7-22

An incorrect Context Diagram showing common carriers and communication media.

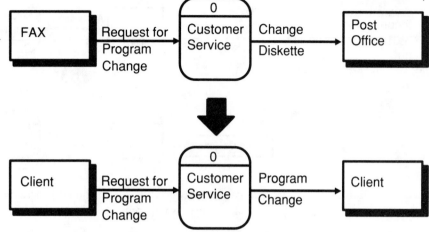

sleds, phones, FAX machines, satellites, smoke signals and meaningful gestures usually have no place on a Data Flow Diagram.

CLUE #5:	**An event does not generate a response.**
CAUSE:	A response has been omitted.
CURE:	Add the response to the Context Diagram.

In Figure 7-23, the Subscriber initiates separate events to order a magazine and pay for it. The payment generates a deposit as a response. The subscription

Figure 7-23

An incorrect Context Diagram where an event generates no response.

EVENT LIST

1. Subscriber orders a magazine
2. Subscriber pays bill.

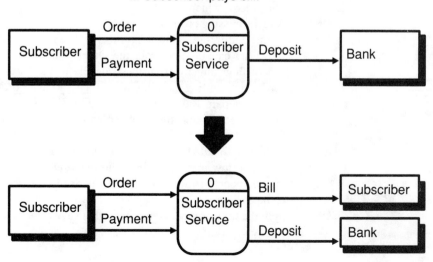

Figure 7-24
Incorrect processes
with no input or no out-
put.

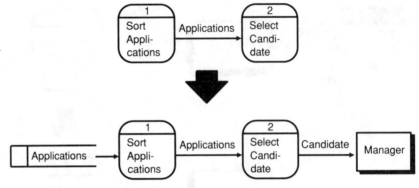

apparently generates no response. It should generate a bill so the customer will know what payment is required.

CLUE #6: **No input data flows to or output data flows from a process.**

CAUSE: An input, trigger, or output data flow has been left out. The process may also self-start by reading data from a file or screen.

CURE: Add the missing data flow.

In Figure 7-24, Process 1 has no input and Process 2 has no output. The problem is easily corrected by showing the file that provides data to Process 1 and the terminator that receives data from Process 2. Without these, Process 1 apparently has nothing to work on and Process 2 apparently produces no results. Process 1 is analogous to the cosmological "big bang" because things appear from nowhere. Process 2 is a "black hole" because nothing ever leaves it.

CLUE #7: **Data flows directly from a terminator to a file, from a file to a terminator, or between files.**

CAUSE: The process which obtains the data and passes it on has been omitted.

CURE: Add the missing process.

In Figure 7-25, there is no process to enter customer orders into the Orders file. Data cannot flow from the Orders file to the Bills file. Similarly, a bill cannot flow directly from the Bills file to the Customer. The first problem is solved by inserting the Fill Order process to enter orders into the Orders file. A second Prepare Bill process can send bills directly to customers. It should also modify the Accounts Receivable file to reflect the bill that has been sent.

CLUE #8: **Non-specific labels or unlabeled data flows.**

CAUSE: The data flow may be a composite for which there is no good name. A process may be poorly structured or poorly defined. The analyst may have forgotten to name an item.

CURE: Split the flow or process into items that have clear names.

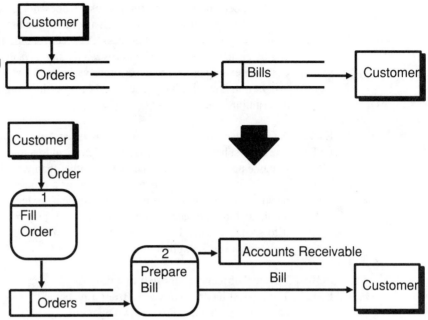

Incorrect data flows between terminators and files are fixed by putting a transforming process between the terminators or files.

Data labels like Input Data in Figure 7-26 are completely content-free. The arrow tells us that data is coming in. The label does not provide any new information about what data are flowing into the process. The second flow has no name at all. When the analyst is unable to think of a good name that describes the data flow, then the flow is usually a composite that should be broken into multiple flows. These multiple flows often go to different processes. Application and Evaluation give a much better idea of the data that are being processed.

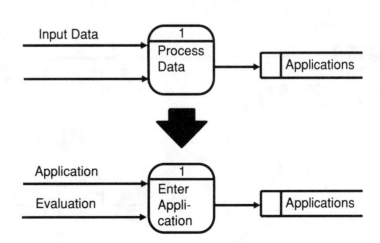

Examples of data flows with missing or meaningless labels.

The label Process Data for Process 1 does not give any indication of what Process 1 accomplishes. Again, such a content-free name often indicates a poorly defined or poorly structured process. A process should have a single purpose that can be clearly described. The verbs *administer, process* and *handle* are the most common examples of nondescriptive verbs used for naming. The objects *input* and *output* are similarly useless, because they do not provide meaningful descriptions of data.

CLUE #9:   **A noun, person, or terminator name is used as a process name.**
CAUSE: The analyst has not converted from a physical to a logical view of the system.
CURE: Rename process to show what is done rather than who does it.

In Figure 7-27, Clerk is not the name of a process. It is likely the title of the person who performs the job in the manual system. The new system may be automated to eliminate the need for a clerk. It may redefine the process to assign it to someone else. That is why process names must consist of a strong active verb with a single explicit object.

CLUE #10:   **Physical objects are named in a data flow.**
CAUSE: The analyst has not converted from a physical to a logical view. Only flows of data are recorded in a Data Flow Diagram.
CURE: Delete the flow or name the information that flows with the physical object.

In Figure 7-28, the Pack Items process does not transform the Order information and Shipment is not an information flow. There may be a process that transforms an order into an invoice that is included with the shipment and sent to the shipper. If this is the case, then the process should be renamed to reflect the data transformation that is occurring. The data flow also has to be renamed to reflect the kind of data that is flowing.

An alternate possibility is that the order goes to the packer and no further data is recorded. If this is the case, then the packer should be treated as a terminator that receives the data.

Figure 7-27

A process incorrectly labeled with a noun instead of a verb.

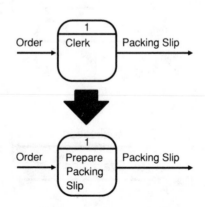

Figure 7-28

An incorrect Data Flow
Diagram with physical
objects and processes.

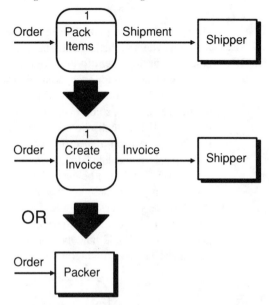

7 DFD

CLUE #11: **No file between two processes at different times.**
CAUSE: Analyst has not identified isolated processes.
CURE: Insert the file(s) required to hold data until it is needed by the next process.

In Figure 7-29 there is clearly a delay of months between the time a student enrolls and the time grades are assigned (unless this is a degree mill that sells instant degrees). The ENROLLMENT table stores the enrollment information during that period. Each process will need the STUDENTS and SECTIONS tables to verify that the enrollment is valid.

Figure 7-29

An incorrect
Data Flow
Diagram
with proces-
ses that
occur at dif-
ferent times.

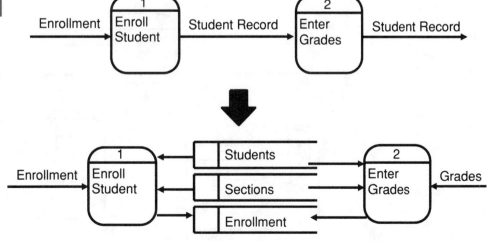

CLUE #12:   **Isolated groups of processes in Leveled Data Flow Diagrams.**

CAUSE: Missing events in the Event List.

CURE: Add the missing event to the Event List and create an event handling process in the Event Diagram for each isolated group.

If an isolated process can be performed at another time, in another place, or by another person, some event has to trigger the execution of the process. Each process will eventually be coded as a block of program code. That code will be invoked to perform a specific task triggered by the event. It should not contain code that is not needed for the task at hand. Whenever there are two isolated groups, one would not be needed whenever the other is invoked.

In Figure 7-30, there are two isolated groups of processes. Processes 1 and 2 handle orders. Processes 3 and 4 handle payments. They are not used together. Therefore the Record Sales process defined at a previous level was not properly partitioned. It should have been partitioned into Enter Order and Enter Payment processes. The Event Diagram also needs to be changed to reflect this correction.

Figure 7-30

A Data Flow Diagram with isolated groups of processes that should be combined at a different level.

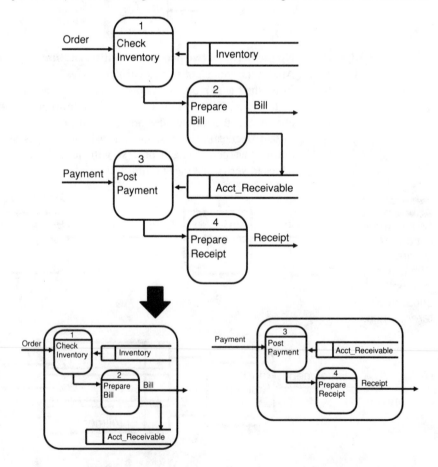

CLUE #13: **A complex interface with many data flows.**
CAUSE: Several independent processes have been combined.
CURE: Separate the independent processes.

The five data flows entering Process 6 in Figure 7-31 are going into a physical process. Routing input documents does not transform the data. Eliminate Process 6 and send the data directly to the processes that normally receive the data.

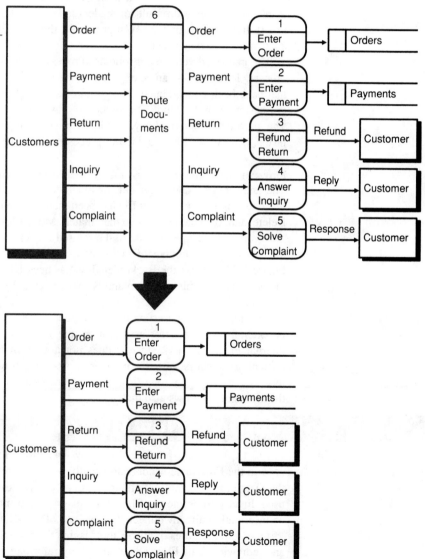

Figure 7-31

A complex interface with many data flows indicates that a process can be split into independent processes.

CLUE #14:   **More than seven processes on one diagram.**
CAUSE: The processes have not been grouped properly. The diagram looks like wallpaper design by French Cubist artists and is as difficult to understand.
CURE: Combine some processes into an aggregate process. Then use explosions to reveal the processes that have been combined.

Figure 7-32 contains ten processes. The diagram is getting very cluttered and hard to understand. A rule of thumb is that seven processes is the maximum number that should appear on a single diagram. Miller[4] has shown that more than seven makes it difficult for readers to keep track of all the different processes. If there are more than seven processes, the Data Flow Diagram should have another level to make each level simpler.

The improved version consolidates Processes 3 to 8 into the new Enter Order process. This process can be exploded at the next level to reveal the six processes that have been consolidated. This requires a second diagram, but both diagrams are easier to understand. The processes have been renumbered consecutively. The partitions should always explode to approximately the same number of levels. Otherwise, minor and major processes are being mixed.

CLUE #15:   **Flows in an exploded process do not balance flows in the parent process.**
CAUSE: The analyst has added, left out, or renamed a flow. An internal file has been made external or an external file has been made internal.
CURE: Delete, add, or rename flows so they match. Move files in or out of the process.

Figure 7-33 is an explosion of the revised Process 3 in Figure 7-32. It contains three errors. The number of inputs and outputs does not match the original in Figure 7-32 because the Backorder flow has been left out of Process 3.4. This is the result of a simple omission and is easy to detect by counting the in-going and out-going flows.

There are two other errors that are harder to detect. The Inventory file should be external to the process as it is in Figure 7-32. The Customers file should be internal to the process, since it does not appear in Figure 7-32. This error is difficult to detect because the number of out-going flows is still the same. Nevertheless, they are the wrong flows. These errors can be detected by checking that the names of the flows also match.

CASE Tools for Data Flow Diagrams

Most CASE tools produce Data Flow Diagrams. The definitions of activities used in the Enterprise Model can usually be used directly as a starting point for the Data Flow Diagrams. Similarly, the table definitions for the database can be used directly to define the files in the diagram. An integrated CASE tool builds on information already collected in the tool's Data Dictionary.

One of the features of CASE tools is that they simplify the process of drawing and redrawing Data Flow Diagrams. Many reformatting features are provided. If

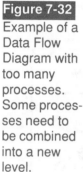

Figure 7-32
Example of a Data Flow Diagram with too many processes. Some processes need to be combined into a new level.

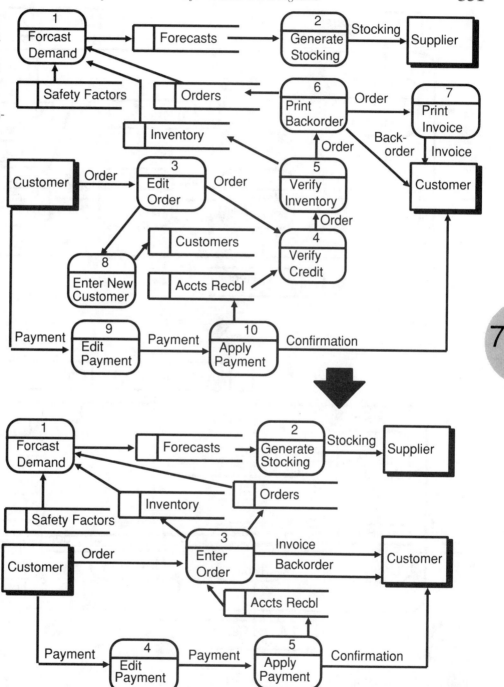

7 DFD

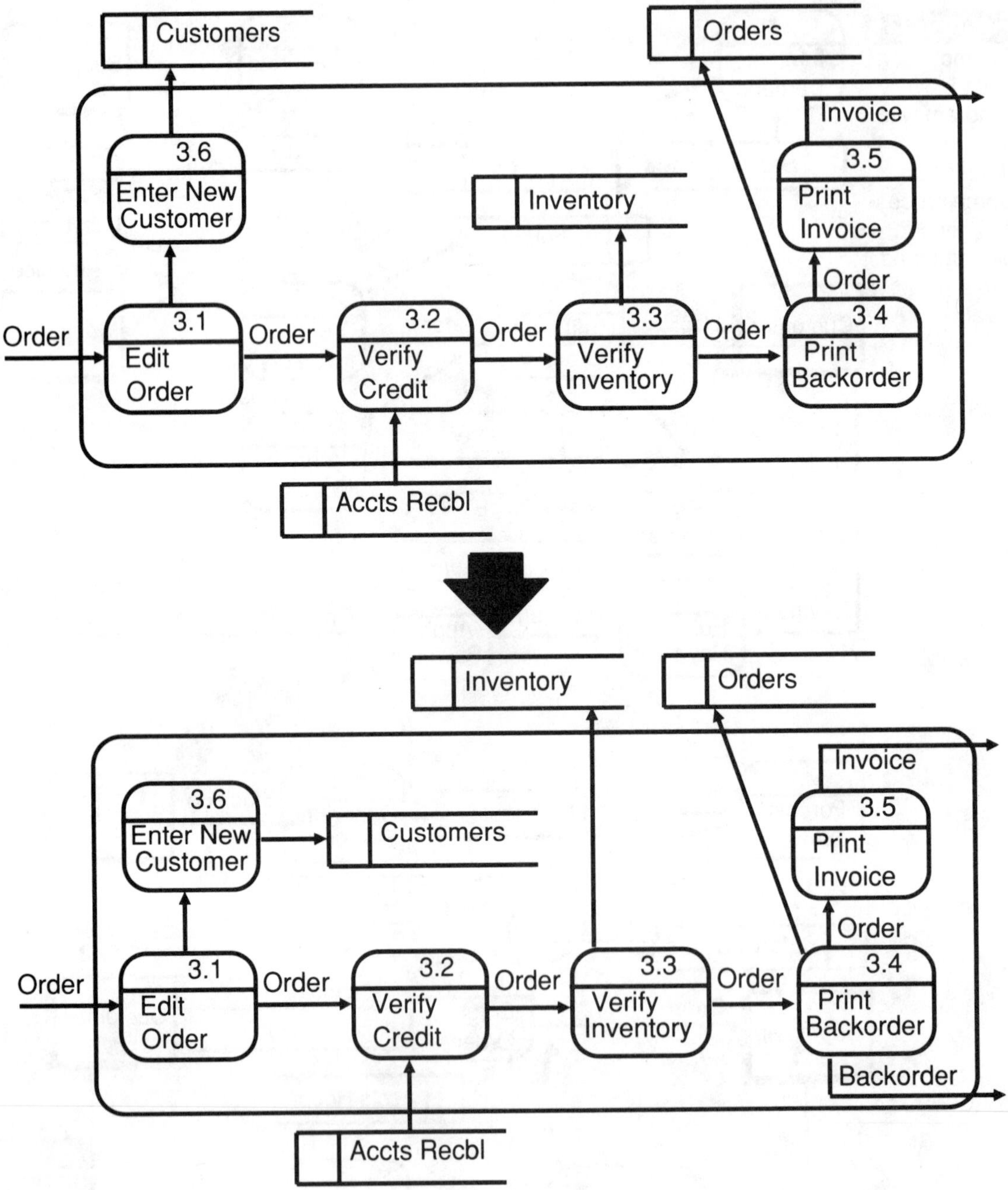

Figure 7-33
Examples of unbalanced data flows when exploding Process 3 at the bottom of Figure 7-32.

a process is moved on the diagram, the data flow lines are redrawn automatically, with connections to the new location. Some tools move process boxes to make room for a new process that is being added.

It is easy to create exploded views. Usually, a touch of a function key or a mouse button on the selected process produces an explosion of the process. This makes it very easy to go back and forth between levels.

Figure 7-34 illustrates four screens from an Excelerator session used to reproduce Figure 7-19. Excelerator uses a series of menus to select modules and tools used to enter and modify the model. An extensive documentation module can combine graphics, tables, and text into reports. Many checking features are provided to make sure that the model is internally consistent. Data flows can be exploded to display the corresponding table definition as shown in the bottom screen. Processes can be exploded into other Data Flow Diagrams or other documentation.

Most CASE tools provide extensive checking of the diagrams. Explosion levels are checked for balanced data flows. Processes without inputs or outputs can be identified. Data flows between terminators and files can be prevented. Conflicting names are identified or prevented.

Most CASE tools also allow the analyst to explode data flows to insert detailed descriptions of the data flows. These are then checked to make sure that they are consistent with data available in files.

Data Flow Diagrams can be prepared easily using built in templates for the terminators, flows, processes, and files. Most CASE tools provide templates for both the Gane and Sarson[2] and the De Marco[1] notations.

It is so easy to prepare diagrams that the tools can be used interactively while users describe their processes. This allows the analyst to verify the diagrams as they are produced. It is also easy to use interactive screens during JAD sessions or Structured Walkthroughs.

These features lift a burden of drawing that the Data Flow Diagram method imposes on the analyst. The need to draw many diagrams and redraw them to reflect new information is a main reason that analysts avoid using the method. The benefits of clarity and communications are lost if analysts do not prepare diagrams and validate them with the users. Thus a major contribution of the tools is that they facilitate economical iteration of the design until it is correct.

Once the Data Flow Diagrams have been exploded sufficiently to make them understandable, each of the isolated processes can be developed into computer programs. The isolated processes are the sets of processes that only obtain data from, or transmit data to, files or external users. Different processes are often developed using different tools. There are three main tools used for development:

- **Screen generators.** These are used to develop interactive screens that perform the four basic database functions of inquire, insert, update, and delete. The next chapter deals with how to use these tools.
- **Report generators.** These are used to generate printed reports for users. They operate on existing files and do not modify the contents of the files. Reporting

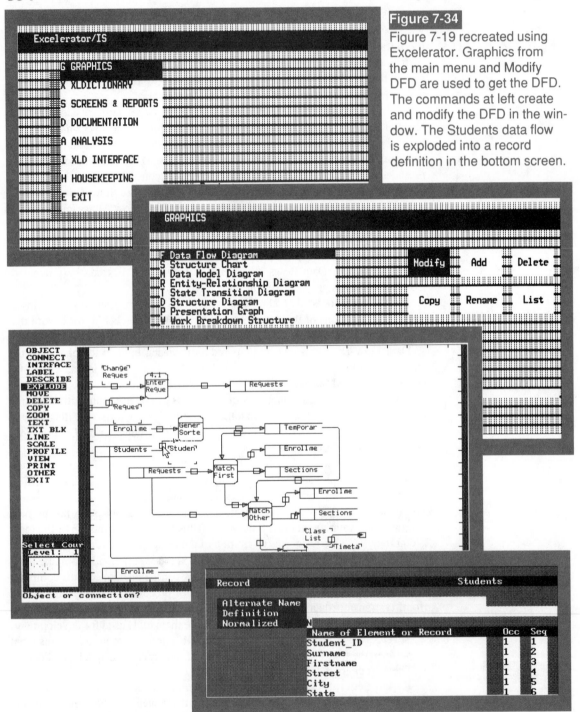

Figure 7-34
Figure 7-19 recreated using Excelerator. Graphics from the main menu and Modify DFD are used to get the DFD. The commands at left create and modify the DFD in the window. The Students data flow is exploded into a record definition in the bottom screen.

functions usually should be separated from other processing functions because the format and content of reports change frequently. It also is possible to delegate the design of some reports to users. Simple report generators are available and the users know best what they need. Security need not be compromised because users can be given read-only permission to access the required files. The next chapter also describes report generators.

- **Application generators.** Most of the remaining processes are really batch processes. They are activated periodically to perform some calendar or demand driven function like producing a payroll, sending monthly bills, scheduling a production run, or assembling orders to be shipped. They rely on information that was entered using interactive screens. They often change existing information as a by-product of performing the process. After a payroll has been run, accounts are changed to reflect changes in payments made and payments owed. After orders have been assembled, files are updated to reflect new inventory levels and bills that have been sent to customers.

Some application generators have broad capabilities that allow them to generate screens, reports, and batch programs as part of the application.

Many applications can be generated using high-level languages that interact directly with a Data Base Management System. If these generators can be used, the process diagrams can often be simplified. If a 3GL like COBOL handles the logic of the process, the Data Flow Diagrams may need another level of explosion to explain the detail required by a lower level language. Chapters 9 and 10 explain how to convert Data Flow Diagrams into functional specifications for application programs.

7 DFD

Summary

Data Flow Diagrams are used to document the processes that transform data in a system. Data Flow Diagrams document the data flows, processes, files, and terminators in a system. The processes are the organizational operations that transform data from one logical form to another. The files are the tables defined in the previous chapter. The terminators are the external users of the system.

The Data Flow Diagram is a top-down hierarchical diagram that can provide successive levels of detail that make it easy to understand the system. The details of the DFD can be determined by using Structured Analysis to trace the data flow forward through an existing system. If there is no existing system, the processes can be identified by assembling the output from the beginning or by disassembling the output back to the inputs.

Good Data Flow Diagrams have strong descriptive names for flows and processes. They have no more than seven processes at any single level. They have no physical features of the system in them. All flows at one level also appear at the next level below. A valid process must have both inputs and outputs. Every Data Flow must either begin or end at a process.

A Statement of Purpose is used to define the boundaries of the system.

There are three kinds of Data Flow Diagrams: Context Diagrams, Event Diagrams, and File Diagrams. The Context Diagram identifies the terminators and data flows that come from or go outside the boundaries of the system. It is accompanied by an Event List that identifies events that trigger processes. Event Diagrams partition the system into processes that respond to each event on the Event List. File Diagrams identify the detailed processes in the system and how they interact with files.

The DFD can be broken into isolated processes that stand alone and can be implemented separately. These isolated processes are groups of processes that interact only with files or with terminators. They represent blocks of work that could be done at different times, in different places, or by different people.

Isolated processes are implemented using screen generators, report generators, or application generators, depending on the main function of the process. Each of these types is covered in later chapters.

Keywords and Phrases

Balanced Diagram	Isolated Process
Context Diagram	Process
Data Flow	Response
Data Flow Diagram	Rules
Disassembly	State
Event Diagram	Statement of Purpose
Explosion	Stimulus
File	System
File Diagram	Terminator
Forward Assembly	

Review Questions

1. Define each of the items in the list of keywords and phrases.
2. How are a real system, a Data Flow Diagram, and physical implementation of a data processing system related?
3. What are the stages of the systems analysis process?
4. How are the boundaries of a system determined?
5. How is an existing system documented and converted into a new system?
6. How are the processes and data flows of a new non-existent system determined?
7. How can connected processes be converted into isolated processes?
8. What is the purpose of a Structured Walkthrough?

Problems

1. Prepare a Context Diagram and Event List for the Suzuki Music School described in Problem 1 of Chapter 5.

2. The following Data Flow Diagram describes the physical flow of a manually operated order processing system. Convert it to a logical Data Flow Diagram.

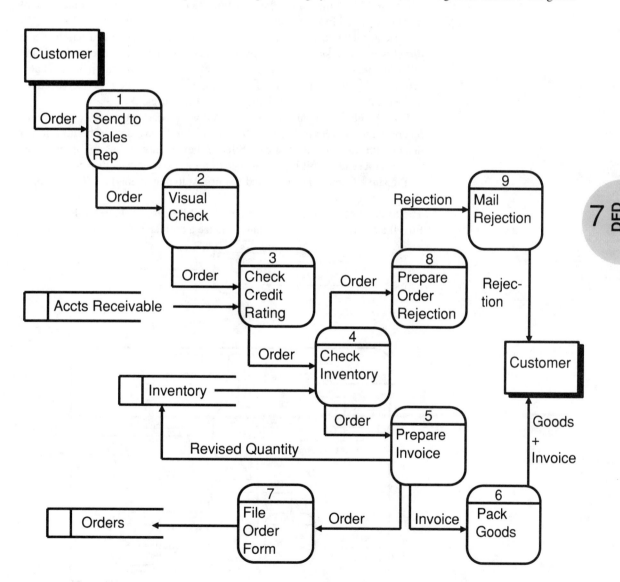

7 DFD

3. Metro Gas Utility is designing a new billing system. Meter readers go monthly to read the meter for each residential and each business customer. The readings are used to prepare a bill that is sent to the customer. Business customers get a different kind of bill than residential customers. Payments are normally received in the mail within the 20 day time limit specified on the bill. All payments are recorded and then deposited in the bank.

   Metro Gas has an arrangement with several local banks so customers can pay their bill at the bank. Participating banks send a weekly statement of money collected from customers.

   Special meter readings are required when a customer sells a building and turns over possession to the new owner. These have to be calculated and billed separately to reflect a bill for part of a month. A special reading is also provided by the maintenance department when a meter is repaired or replaced. A separate bill is not prepared in these cases.

   The accounting department is provided with a daily summary of payments received and a weekly list of bills unpaid for ninety days. The accounting department tries to collect unpaid bills. If they are not successful, they cut off service and send the billing department a notice to terminate the account.

   Prepare a Context Diagram and Event List to document the billing system.

4. The following Data Flow Diagram explodes Process 4 which sends gas bills. Find the errors in the diagrams and produce a corrected diagram.

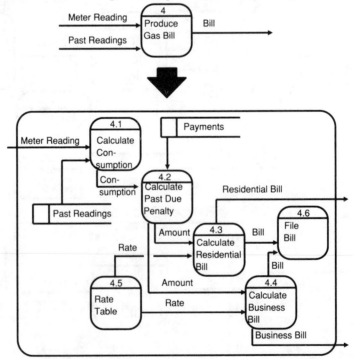

5. Identify the isolated groups of processes in the following Data Flow Diagram for a small store. Show how to convert Process 1 into an isolated process.

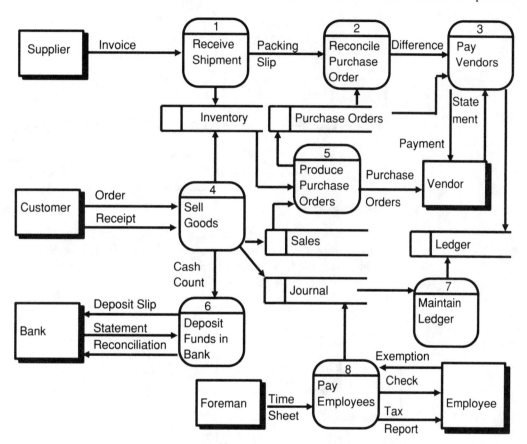

6. Sally opens the mail and checks orders for completeness. Incomplete orders are given to Nancy in Customer Relations who sends them back to the customer with an explanation of the problem. Complete orders are taken to Accounting by Pete, the messenger. Accounting checks the customer's credit rating. If it is okay, the order is sent to Sales, which checks to see that the item is in inventory. If it is not, Sales backorders the item and informs Nancy, who informs the customer. If it is, Sales prepares a three-part packing slip and sends it to Shipping. Shipping pulls the items and sends them to the customer with the first copy of the packing slip. The second copy of the packing slip goes to Accounting, which bills the customer. The third copy is used by Sales to update the inventory records.

Construct a physical Data Flow Diagram that models the Order Entry process. Derive a logical Data Flow Diagram from the physical one.

7. Identify the errors in the following Context Diagram. Redraw the Context Diagram to correct the errors.

EVENTS

1. Customers phone in orders and bills are mailed to them.
2. Suppliers send invoices which are paid by check.
3. Miss De Boat, the sales manager, requests sales summary.

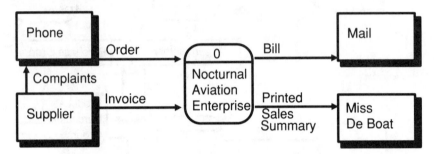

8. The followoing Logical Data Flow Diagram describes the processes performed by the clerk who serves customers in a video movie rental store. Assume that the logic of the processes is correct. Identify the structural and syntactic errors in the Data Flow Diagram.

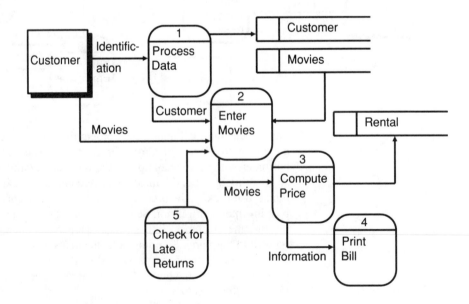

9. The following Logical Data Flow Diagram describes an Employment Agency System that enters the qualifications of a prospective employee and searches a file of jobs to identify positions for which the applicant has the qualifications. The agency charges a fee and promises to run a weekly search of its files for up to four weeks or until the candidate finds a job, whichever comes first. The candidate receives a list of jobs in the mail and is responsible for contacting employers. Identify the diagramming errors in the Data Flow Diagram.

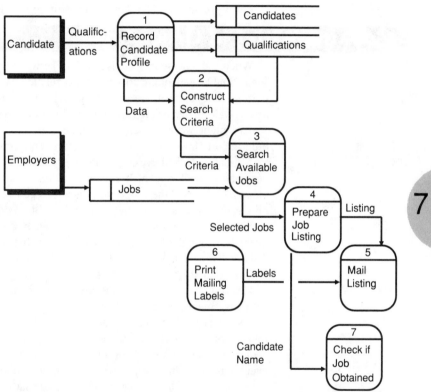

7 DFD

Project

For the next phase of your project, prepare the following:

a. **A Statement of Purpose.**
b. **A Context Diagram.**
c. **An Event List** to go with the Context Diagram.
d. **An Event Diagram** to correspond to the Event List.
e. **Leveled Data Flow Diagrams.** Many projects involve more Data Flow Diagrams than it is feasible to produce in a student project. If this is a problem, discuss with your project supervisor the possibility of producing

only some of them. Try to include more than one hierarchical level in any subset you produce (Level 2, Level 3, and maybe Level 4). Also try to include at least two screens, at least two reports, and at least two with some significant logical manipulations that require detailed documentation in a later chapter. Examples of logical manipulations are choices among several alternatives, statistical calculations, and matching of criteria.

f. **Amended database definitions** if any new data requirements are discovered. If no new data requirements are discovered, include a copy of the existing Entity-Relationship Diagram to provide context for your supervisor.

Cooking with Cal Oreez Case

When Cal saw your database design, he was very impressed. However, I had some trouble explaining to him that a relationship did not mean "a protracted liaison" to an analyst. He is starting to see many uses for the database. He can hardly wait for screens to enter data and routines to let him "delve into the data."

Last night we were sampling some cheeses Cal picked up at a fascinating little import shop that we sometimes frequent. You really should see it. It has a long counter stacked eye-high with every imaginable kind of cheese and several not quite as well known. It emanates an exotic aroma that is indescribable, but memorable. Henri, the proprietor, dispenses generous samples to make sure that his customers are satisfied before they buy. But, I digress.

Somewhere between an ambrosial French Camembert that verged on the metaphysical and a Norwegian Goat Cheese that should have stayed in the goat, Cal asked me what the next step is in implementing his computer program.

I told him you would need to know how he plans to use it.

He said that first he would need to enter the data on books, recipes, ingredients, meals, events, and friends. Whenever he gets a new recipe book, he browses it and selects recipes that he would like to try sometimes. Sometimes he invents, or otherwise acquires, a single recipe that he wants to catalog. When he decides to prepare a meal for an event, he would enter any new friends for that event. I assured him that you would know how to implement screens to do that.

He also wants to be able to find recipes that use a particular ingredient. For instance, last week he acquired some Smoked Scottish Salmon and needed a recipe that would do it justice. At other times he needs a list of possible recipes in a category, such as soups, or fish dishes. Sometimes he needs a category that uses an ingredient, such as a soup that uses calamary.

His biggest problem is producing a guest list for his intimate little soirées. He first plans a meal with a set of recipes. Some of the recipes may exist in the file and some may be newly added ones. He then has to find guests who have not had any of the recipes before. Appetizers, desserts, and drinks are exceptions that may be served to the same person more than once.

He needs a process that identifies all guests who have not had any of the unrepeatable recipes in the planned meal. Ideally, the process would provide a menu of allowable guests that Cal could select from. The selected guests would be automatically placed on a mailing list and mailing labels would be generated for their invitations.

Potential guests must satisfy several conditions. Some friends suffer from allergies and are not invited if any ingredients in the meal—like peanuts—cause allergies. People who were invited to the last event should not be invited so they won't wear out their welcome. "Close friends" can be invited even if they have had some of the recipes in the meal, because they are understanding.

Cal would appreciate it if you could produce an analysis of the things the system must do. I suggested to him that you would probably want to produce:

a. **A Statement of Purpose.**
b. **A Context Diagram.**
c. **An Event List** to go with the Context Diagram.
d. **An Event Diagram** to correspond to the Event List.
e. **Leveled Data Flow Diagrams.**
f. **Amended database definitions** if any new data requirements are discovered during the analysis. If no new data requirements are discovered, include a copy of the existing Entity-Relationship Diagram to provide the context for your analysis.

References

1. De Marco, T., *Structured Analysis and System Specification*, Yourdon Press, 1978.
2. Gane, C., and T. Sarson, *Structured Systems Analysis: Tools and Techniques,* Prentice-Hall, 1979.
3. Lundeberg, Mats, Goran Goldkuhl, and Anders Nilsson, *Information Systems Development: A Systematic Approach,* Prentice-Hall, 1981.
4. Miller, G. A., "The Magical Number Seven, Plus or Minus Two: Some Limits on our Capacity to Process Information," *Psychological Review,* Vol. 63, March 1956, pp. 81-97.
5. Orr, Ken, *Structured Requirements Definition,* Ken Orr and Associates Inc., Topeka Kansas, 1981.
6. Powers, Michael J., David R. Adams, and Harlan D. Mills, *Computer Information Systems Development: Analysis and Design,* South-Western Publishing Co., 1984.
7. Ross, D. T., and K. E. Schoman, "Structured Analysis for Requirements Definition," in *Tutorial on Software Design Techniques,* ed. P. Freeman and A. I. Wasserman, IEEE Computer Society, 1980, pp. 97-106.
8. Ross, D. T., "Structured Analysis (SA): A Language for Communicating Ideas," in Tutorial on Software Design Techniques, ed. P. Freeman and A. I. Wasserman, IEEE Computer Society, 1980, pp. 107-125.
9. Yourdon, Edward, *Modern Structured Analysis,* Yourdon Press, 1989.

7 DFD

Chapter 8

Forms, Screens, and Reports

	DATABASE (WHAT)	PROGRAMS (HOW)	BENEFITS (WHY)	NETWORK (WHERE)	REAL TIME (WHEN)	SKILLS (WHO)
USER CONCEPT	Entity Relationship	Activity	Intangible Benefit	Map		Organization Design
DESIGNER CONCEPT	E-R Diagram	A-E Diagram	AHP	Network		Skills Responsibility
USER DETAIL	Forms Screens	Processes Data	Tangible Benefit	Work Volume	Discrete Events	Transition Training
DESIGNER DETAIL	EER Diagram	Data Flow Diagrams	Benefit-Cost	Partition	Transition Diagrams	Methodology Tools
BUILDER CONCEPT	Normal Form Relations	Structure Chart	Function Points	System Architecture	Specifications	Learning
BUILDER DETAIL	Files	Screens Specifications	Costs	Network Specs	Interfaces	4GL CASE

Objectives

There is now a complete model and implementation of the database for the first subsystem. Data Flow Diagrams have identified all the processes that have to be implemented by the system. These components define what the computer application is supposed to do. This chapter deals with how the computer communicates with users and other objects in the real world. Most of this communication occurs through forms, screens, and reports that are associated with the system.

The forms will be used to collect data for the system. The screens will be used to enter data interactively at the keyboard. The reports and screens will deliver information to users. This chapter explains how to identify input transactions and how to design reports and screens for them.

When the forms, screens, and reports have been defined, a major part of the system will be complete. With the forms and screens defined, data can be entered into the database. With data entered in the database, it is possible to use a query language to generate reports about the data. The only part that will then remain is the batch processing applications—like payroll programs—that take entered data, perform calculations on it, update files, and generate outputs.

After completing this chapter, you will be able to:

- Specify the characteristics of a good form, screen, and report design.
- Identify the different components of forms, screens, and reports.
- Identify the different styles of forms, screens, and reports.
- Assess the impact of physical considerations on the design of forms, screens, and reports.
- Use prototyping to design screens.
- Adjust the design of screens for different countries and languages.

Introduction

A computer is useful only if it has some impact on activities that are of interest to people. It can have an impact only if it is able to communicate with people and machines that use the computer. **Communication** is the **exchange** of messages with some **permissible content** within some **context** to produce a **conversation**. This definition contains terms that need further explanation.

- **Exchanges** are usually commands or data sent to the computer followed by a reply from the computer. Everything sent to the computer must be acknowledged by the computer to let the sender know that it was received and that an appropriate action is being taken. The acknowledgment may be a new menu, a move to the next item, a simple OK, or other response.

- **Context** is the environment that gives meaning to the exchange. A question provides the context that gives meaning to the word YES. Without a question, there is no way of determining what has been agreed to.

- **Permissible content** is the set of messages that are allowed in a particular context. The question, "How many items do you want to buy?" has permissible answers like none, seven, or five thousand. "When all is said and done, a lot more will be said than done" is not a permissible answer in that context. It may be a permissible statement in some other context.

- **Conversation** is a series of exchanges linked together to assist in performing some process in the application's environment. The previous exchanges provide the context for following exchanges. The conversation ends when all data needed to complete the process have been provided.

This chapter identifies the elements of conversations between people and computers. The conversation between machines and computers is covered in Chapter 12. Broadly, people provide data to computers and computers provide reports to people. The most common way of getting data to computers is to enter data on forms, then key the data into a computer screen. The most common forms of output from computers are a printed report or a report on a screen. Forms, screens, and reports each have unique characteristics that are discussed.

There are two trends that are changing the relative importance of forms, screens, and reports. These are interactive data entry and interactive data inquiry.

- **Interactive data entry** allows users to enter data directly. Forms are not needed to capture data so they can be sent for keying. The forms that remain are primarily for communication with outside parties such as customers and suppliers. There is now a strong move to eliminate even these paper communications by using standardized Electronic Data Interchanges (EDI).

- **Interactive data inquiry** allows users to produce ad hoc reports whenever they need them. Query languages permit easy specification of the data that need to be retrieved. Default formats eliminate the need to specify the exact format of the report. It is no longer necessary for the analyst to specify the contents of every report that is needed by the organization. Users can specify their own reports when they need them. More important, they can stop getting them when they no longer need them.

Many reports are of a temporary nature, designed to solve a specific problem, or satisfy the needs of a particular individual. Once the problem is solved, or the individual has moved on, the report is no longer needed. Such reports are best created and managed by the user.

Many reports have been created "just in case" the information is ever needed to satisfy a customer inquiry or other information need. The reports were often designed to satisfy the needs of a number of different and sometimes conflicting users. Millions of trees have given their lives so that weekly or monthly listings of files could be printed (often in multiple copies) and put on shelves, seldom to be seen again. Most such inquiries are now dealt with by direct inquiry on a screen. As a result, no report is needed.

Form Design

Forms are not always needed. Data may be captured directly on a screen or other device such as a bar code reader. Preprinted input forms are still needed in three cases. Forms are needed for input from people who do not have access to a workstation. They are needed for legally important documents. They are needed for turnaround documents, like bills, that come back with additional information.

Ideally, the forms used to capture data and the screens used to enter data should be designed together. The data capture process is more efficient if the two components are designed to complement each other. If existing forms are not well-designed, then this is the ideal time to redesign them.

This section examines the characteristics of good forms, the components of a form, and the physical considerations in designing a good form. The detail is sufficient to present to an organization's Form Design department. The same factors are examined for screens and reports in later sections.

8
SCREEN

Form Design Criteria

A well-designed form must satisfy the criteria of consistency, completeness, flexible entry, economy, and organization.

- **Consistency.** The form must be internally consistent. It must also be consistent with related forms and with other forms and screens in the organization. Consistent forms make it easy for users to learn how to fill them in and for data entry clerks to learn how to key data from them. This reduces errors and data capture costs.
- **Completeness.** The form should gather all data at the source so there is no need to transcribe data to other forms–a major source of errors.
- **Flexible entry.** It should be possible to enter data in longhand or with a typewriter. In most cases, both kinds of entry occur.
- **Economy.** The total cost of design, printing, data entry, and data keying must be minimized. Often it is necessary to increase one cost to reduce another. Handling costs are usually many times the cost of design and printing. More

resources spent on design and printing can often reduce the cost of capture and keying. This is particularly true if the form and associated screen are similar.

- **Organization.** Arrange the parts of the form in an efficient order with visual separation between the parts. The order may be a compromise between sequence of entry, frequency of use, function, and importance of data. The first data available, the most frequently used data, and the most important data should be at the beginning of the form. All data about a single function, like enrollment, should be together. Irrelevant information must be minimized.

Components of Forms

Designing forms is the inverse of the forms analysis task discussed in Chapter 5. The basic elements of the form are listed again below.

- **Descriptive information** which provides help on how to identify, fill in, or use the form. This includes titles, section headings, and instructions.
- **Intentional information** which is the labels and headings to indicate what goes in the blanks.
- **Extensional information** which is the spaces to be filled in. The spaces can be blanks in which numbers or text are entered. They can also be check boxes that are to be selected with a checkmark or an X like a ballot.

These elements are illustrated in Figure 8-1.

In forms analysis the form is divided into data areas. An area frequently corresponds to a file which stores the data in that area. In screen design the screen is divided into areas called panels which usually correspond to files that contain data for the panel. The paper form used to capture original data should correspond as closely as possible to the screen form used for keying the data. This simplifies the operator's data keying task.

Styles of Forms

There are three common styles of forms. They differ in the relationship between the intentional captions and the extensional blanks. The captions can be within the blanks, above the blanks, or preceding the blanks.

Captions Within Blanks

Figure 8-1 is an example of captions within blanks. The caption information is found within the area reserved for the fill-in data. Different sizes of type are used to distinguish titles, headings, and captions. Sometimes the area reserved for data is left white and all other areas are printed in grey or a light shaded color. This form style provides the clearest relationship between the captions and the blanks. The shaded area reduces the visibility of irrelevant information during entry and keying.

Captions Above Blanks

Figure 8-2 repeats Figure 8-1 using captions above blanks. This style has most of the features of the previous style. It is a good style when it is not possible to shade the captions. The box serves the function of the white area in the previous form. This style does not provide quite as much separation between the captions and the extensional data. Both styles can be filled in by hand or typewriter.

Captions Precede
Blanks

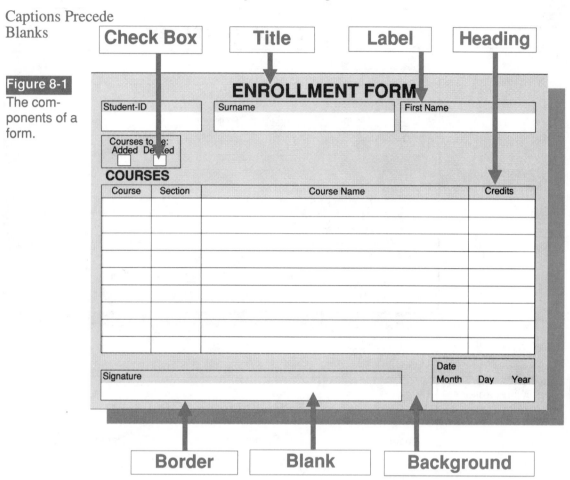

Figure 8-1

Figure 8-1

The components of a form.

Figure 8-3 repeats Figure 8-1 using captions before blanks. This style is often used when the original form is created with a typewriter or a word processor. The headings, titles, and captions are all in the same type size and style. This makes it difficult to determine the function of different parts of the form. The relationship between captions and blanks is not as clear as it was in previous forms. It is also more difficult to produce a screen that matches this style.

Physical Considerations in Form Design

There are several physical characteristics of a form that have to be specified. These are size, color, format, type, spacing, position, and preprinted sequence numbers. Most organizations have a Forms Design department that has set standards for each of these. Typical standards follow.

- **Size.** Standard pages are 8.5x11 and 8.5x14 inches. Small forms are sometimes designed to be half of these standard sizes, namely 8.5x5.5 and

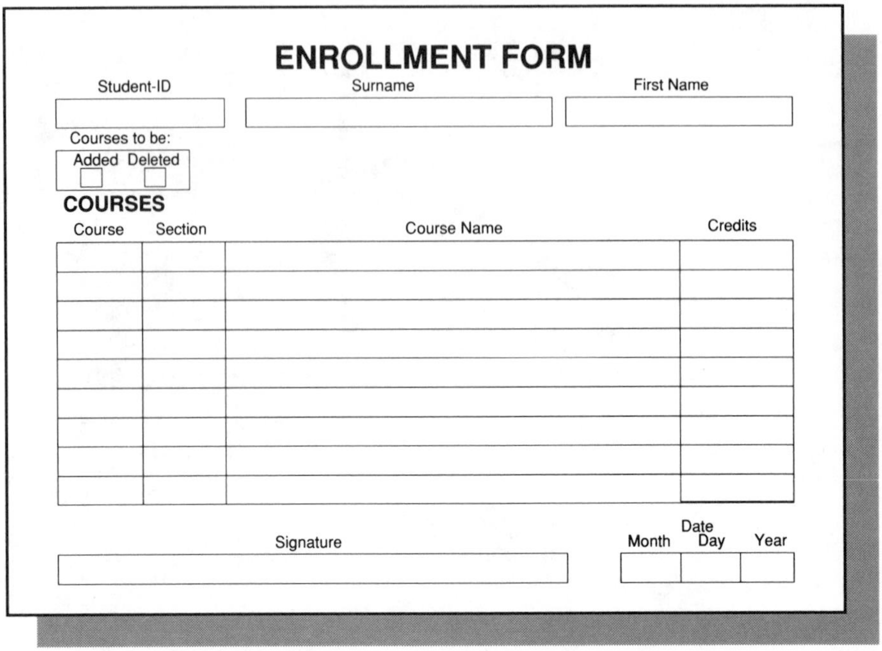

Figure 8-2
Form with captions
above blanks.

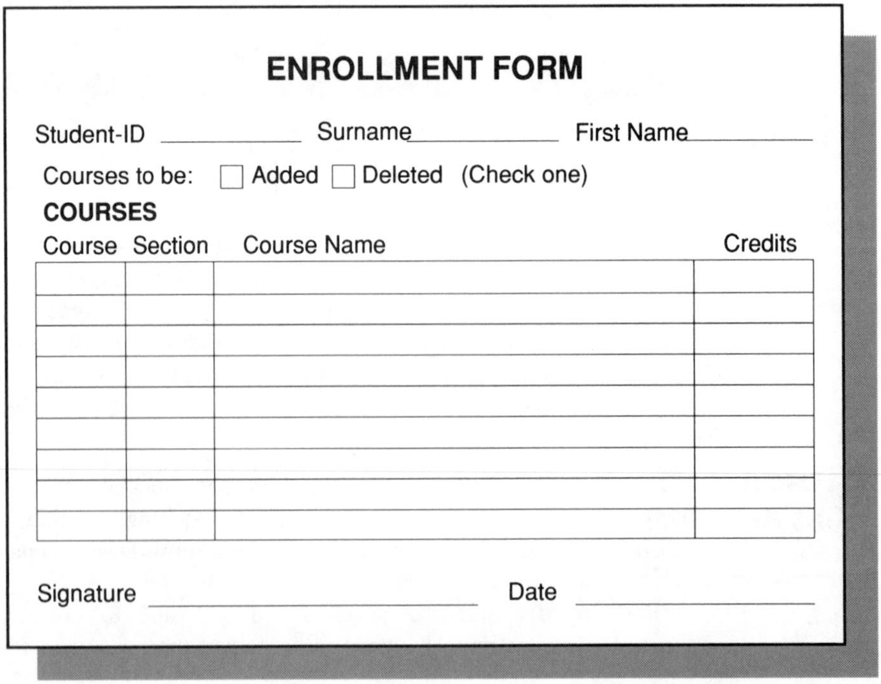

ENROLLMENT FORM

Student-ID   Surname   First Name

Courses to be:
Added Deleted

COURSES

Course	Section	Course Name	Credits

Signature

Date
Month Day Year

Figure 8-3
Form with captions
preceding blanks.

ENROLLMENT FORM

Student-ID _____ Surname_____ First Name_____

Courses to be: ☐ Added ☐ Deleted (Check one)

COURSES

Course	Section	Course Name	Credits

Signature _____ Date _____

8.5x7 inches. A margin of at least a third of an inch is needed on all sides. Sometimes an extra margin is needed on one side to allow binding or to fit in a clipboard.

- **Color.** The paper should be a light color, like white or yellow, to make the written material readable. If colored backgrounds are used, they should be about 30 percent color and 70 percent white. Type should be in black ink for maximum visibility.

- **Format.** The 8.5 inch dimension should always be horizontal. This matches the width of computer screens. It also fits standard printers, file folders, and document feeders. If the back of the form is also printed, the top should be at the same end of the sheet on both sides. This allows the pages to be turned like book pages. The tumble-turn in which the bottom of the front becomes the top of the back may confuse users.

- **Type.** The type should be a clear simple font, such as Helvetica. Ornate fonts are hard to read. Captions should be at least 5 points high (a printer's point is 1/72 of an inch). Titles and section headings should be at least 10 points high. Boldface type can be used to emphasize major headings and titles. Different widths of ruling lines can be used to identify sections, subsections, and data fields.

- **Spacing.** Vertical spacing between lines is in multiples of 1/6 inch so a standard typewriter can be used to fill in the form. The fill-in area should be 1/5 inch high for typed-only input or 1/3 inch high for handwritten input. The horizontal width should be 1/5 inch per character to allow handwritten input. Vertical tick marks should not be placed between characters. Different typewriters have different horizontal spacings. The tick marks also distract the people who have to read or key the forms. White space should be used liberally to separate areas in the form.

- **Position.** Titles are centered at the top of the form. Section headings are positioned at the top of the section starting at the left margin. Instructions should come before the section to which they apply. The start of fill-in areas are vertically aligned to simplify setting tab stops on typewriters.

- **Preprinted sequence numbers.** These are used when the forms have a monetary value and must be accounted for individually. Check blanks, airline tickets, or refund forms are examples. Sequence numbers should be avoided on other forms. A university faculty found that their graduate school would not give them application forms to send to prospective students because the preprinted numbers were accounted for. Yet the forms had no value and no use was ever made of the numbers.

Not all input comes from forms that are keyed at screens. Optical scanners, bar code scanners, Magnetic Ink Character Recognition (MICR), magnetic stripes, telephone keypads, voice, electronic instruments, operators, and files can also be used.

- **Optical scanners.** Scanners can read printed or typed characters as if they had been entered at a keyboard. Some can even read hand printed characters.

8 SCREEN

Scanners can be used to read forms automatically without the need to rekey data.

- **Bar code scanners.** Laser scanners in supermarkets read the Universal Product Code (UPC) on products and transmit it to a computer that computes prices, prints a bill, and updates inventory. The same system can be used to control inventory or track parts in a factory.

- **MICR.** Magnetic Ink Character Recognition is a simple system that reads specially shaped alphabetic characters that have been printed with magnetic ink. Reading the characters is like reading an audiotape or videotape. The most common use for this technique is sorting bank checks.

- **Magnetic stripes.** The magnetic stripe on the back of a credit card has identification data that can be read by a reader somewhat like a tape recorder. The reader can automatically call a computer, send the card identification, and receive validation of a purchase. Similar systems are used to identify people entering secure areas or using banking machines.

- **Telephone keypads.** The touch tone keypads on telephones can be used to call computers and send numeric data directly to them. Customers can transmit credit card numbers, authorization codes, catalog numbers, and desired quantities directly in response to computer generated voice instructions. This can eliminate the need for keyboard operators to enter orders or other kinds of requests.

- **Voice.** Voice recognition devices can understand a limited set of words, like numbers and letters. They are very useful for collecting spoken data when the operator is not able to write or key the data. Such devices can be used to collect the same data entered with telephone keypads when older pulse code phones are being used. They are also useful for collecting information from assembly line inspectors or mail sorters whose hands are busy.

- **Electronic instruments.** Instruments can collect data automatically and send it to computers for further processing. This technique is useful in many places ranging from factories to gasoline stations. Data are captured rapidly and accurately without transcription errors or other losses.

- **Operators.** Telephone operators, or others, can receive data from customers and key them without using intermediate forms. Sometimes customers use terminals to enter orders directly into a supplier's computer.

- **Files.** Data suppliers can create files that contain text or data. Files can be transmitted by tapes, diskettes, or over telephone lines. Such systems are frequently used by reporters to file their stories or salespeople to enter orders.

Data entry is a costly and error-prone activity. All of these technologies are designed to reduce the cost and the number of errors. Systems that capture the data at the source without human intervention are less likely to introduce errors and are more likely to eliminate delays.

Screen Design

The computer screen and its associated keyboard (and sometimes mouse) are the interface that lets the user communicate with the computer. (The author resisted the temptation to title this section "Of Mice and Menus" or "Windows of Opportunity".) The communication is in the form of an interactive dialog. The dialog has semantic and syntactic rules just like a dialog between two people. The semantics determine the meaning of the elements in the interface. The syntax determines the sequence and order of the elements.

In database systems, screens are used primarily for data input, data updating, data deletion, and data inquiries. The data input task is similar to filling in a form. In fact, data input is often done by transcribing information from a paper form to a form on the screen. Updating is similar to correcting an entry on a form. Deletion is like destroying a form. Inquiry consists of asking the computer to retrieve one or more forms for inspection. This section describes the criteria used in screen design, the components of a screen, the different styles of screens, and the physical considerations in screen design.

Not all screens correspond to forms. Some are used in direct conversations with a client over the counter or over a telephone. Examples are when a student changes a course, an airline books a seat, or a patient checks into a hospital.

Screen Design Criteria

A good screen design reduces interface complexity *as perceived by the user*. It is like an automatic car transmission that converts a complex process of gear changes to a simple process of selecting direction. The screen converts a complex navigation through data files into a simple data entry process. It may be complex internally, but it should appear to be simple externally.

Several features make an input screen easy to use. These features are embodied in many of the screen interfaces found on microcomputers such as the MacIntosh™, the GEM™ and Windows™ environment on the IBM PC™, or the X-Windows™ and Open Look™ screens found on larger computers. These screens are usually called Graphic User Interfaces (GUI). Each feature needs some elaboration.

- **Concreteness.** People find it easier to work with a concrete object than with an abstract concept. Thus, it is easier to learn to use icons than abstract commands. The icon is a picture of an object on the screen. It is mentally associated with a tool that performs a specific function. An icon of a pair of scissors may be used to initiate a command that deletes or cuts out part of a picture in a drawing program.
- **Visibility.** Users find it easier to operate an interface where they can see the commands rather than remember options from a language syntax or an invisible list. People have highly developed powers of pattern recognition, but relatively poor memories. Thus, commands, function keys, options, and helps should be visible on the screen. People have difficulty generating or creating

something new. It is easier to select from a list of options. When a user is asked to enter a vendor identification on a purchase order, a scrollable list at the side of the screen helps by identifying the vendor codes and the corresponding names of the vendors.

- **Modifiability.** It is easier to copy a template or partially completed example than to create something new. The template acts as a reminder of what needs to be done. People also find it much easier to recognize errors and fix them than to specify commands or programming steps. Where possible, a blank should be filled with a default value which can be corrected by the user. This gives the user a hint about what is wanted, and makes it easier to identify the available options. The user, specifying a file directory, is helped if the program inserts the current file directory in the blank. If it is the right one, there is no more work to do. If it is not, then the user has a hint of the format to be used for the input.

- **Interaction.** Interactive interfaces are better than batch interfaces because they provide continual feedback and make very limited demands on peoples' short-term memory. Each field can be checked as entered and the user can be notified of errors immediately. Batch interfaces often require long inputs with no feedback to the user about the status of the input. As a result, the user may continue to make errors unknowingly.

- **Familiar conceptual model.** The user finds it easier to use a familiar model than an unfamiliar model. The desktop with paper documents on it is a familiar model to most users. Thus, it is easier to use a form for filling in data than a command syntax in a programming language. The SQL language has a command syntax for inserting, updating, and deleting data, but most users would rather use a form on a screen for these tasks.

- **Consistency.** The same command should perform the same function everywhere in the system and a function should always require the same command to invoke it. Function keys should always have the same meaning on every screen and preferably every version or release of the system. People require extra time to learn every new concept and differentiate it from known concepts. Users get confused when a different command is used to, say, exit every program. The user never knows whether to use stop, quit, exit, end, logoff, bye, or terminate. One of the major advantages of the MacIntosh interface is that it constrains the originality of developers and forces some consistent interface rules.

- **Simplicity.** The best guideline for screen design is **KISS**—Keep It Simple Simon. Design elements should be used judiciously. A screen cluttered with lines, boxes, blinking characters, and characters of different color and brightness confuses users by overloading their cognitive processes. Blank space is usually the best separator. Sound should be used like a car horn—only in emergencies. The user is usually aware of an error without needing a beep to announce it. An exception occurs in touch typing applications, such as data entry and word processing where the user rarely looks at the screen. Users do not want the computer to loudly criticize every error and they do not want the whole office to know about every mistake. They should at least have a way of shutting the sound off.

- **Tailorability.** Users have different tasks, different models of the world, different degrees of expertise, and different working environments. They need ways to tailor an interface to match their needs. The ability to specify default starting points, level of expertise, terminal capabilities, preferences for output format, private mailing lists, or personal procedures eliminates the need for long starting procedures at each session.

- **Pointing.** It is easier for most people to use a mouse or finger to point at an option on the screen than to type in a command. However, skilled typists may find that function keys are faster for choosing commands or options. This is particularly true if using a pointer requires a shift from touch typing, which often happens with data entry or word processing.

- **Context sensitivity.** The options and commands that are available on a screen should depend on the current state of a screen. For instance, a help key should provide help about the current screen or the currently selected command. Commands that are inappropriate in the current mode of operation should not be made available. Alternately, they should be marked to indicate that they are unavailable. This reduces the need for the user to learn and remember rules about what is allowed.

Components of Screens

A screen is built up using several components. Each of these components has a purpose and function. The components are the semantic elements of the dialog between the user and the computer. The sequence in which they are used determines the syntax of the dialog. The components are described below. They are illustrated in Figures 8-4 and 8-5 which are examples of screens in Ventura Publisher™.

- **Panel title.** This tells the user what the panel is about. It may contain the name of the file being used. It may contain an identification that specifies where the user is in a connected series of panels or screens. This could be a form number for data entry or a page number in a word processor.

- **Action bar.** This lists the groups of actions that a user may request. The specific actions in a group are listed in a pull-down. The action can be selected by pointing, cursoring, or entering a key letter. Pointing is done with a mouse or a finger on a touch sensitive screen. Cursor keys can be used to move to a selected action and a key, such as the ENTER key, is used to select the action. Sometimes an action can be selected by entering a key letter. The letter may be underlined, brightened, or capitalized to identify it within the action label.

- **Pull-down.** This lists the specific actions that are available within a group. Actions that generate another panel are followed by three dots. The user selects the action or actions that are needed. As with the action bar, the command may be selected by pointing, cursoring, or entering a letter. Frequently-used commands can sometimes be selected directly by function keys without using the pull-down menu.

8
SCREEN

Figure 8-4

Illustration of screen components. The cursor is used to select the Footnote Settings command in a Pull-Down Menu for the Chapter command in the Action Bar. The Pull-Down Menu temporarily covers text in the window.

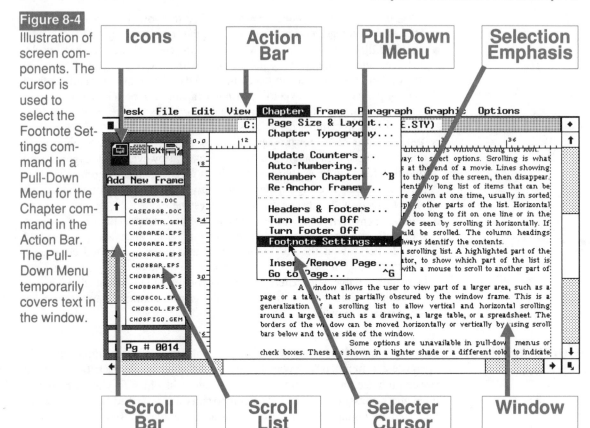

- **Check box.** This is another way to list specific options or actions that are available. The user checks the box or boxes that are needed by pointing or cursoring to the box.
- **Icon.** This is another way to specify options. It consists of an area with a picture that reminds the user of the mode or action that is selected. It has the advantage that it provides a visual reminder that even illiterate users can understand. Icons may be difficult to understand if the pictures are not chosen well. Icons are almost always selected by pointing. Frequently used options can sometimes be selected directly by function keys without using the icon.
- **Scrolling list.** This is yet another way to select options. Scrolling is what moviemakers do to display the credits at the end of a movie. Lines showing the cast start at the bottom and roll up to the top of the screen, then disappear. Scrolling is used when there is a potentially long list of items that can be selected, such as files. A few items are shown at one time, usually in sorted order. The list can be scrolled to display other parts of the list. Horizontal scrolling can be used for rows that are too long to fit on one line or in the

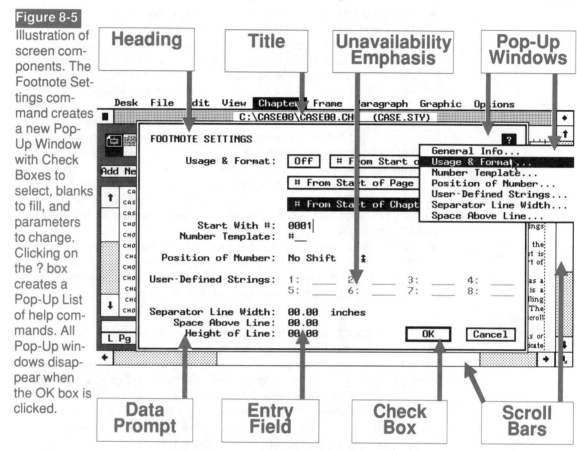

Figure 8-5
Illustration of screen components. The Footnote Settings command creates a new Pop-Up Window with Check Boxes to select, blanks to fill, and parameters to change. Clicking on the ? box creates a Pop-Up List of help commands. All Pop-Up windows disappear when the OK box is clicked.

available field. The complete line can be seen by scrolling it horizontally. If scrolling is used, only the data should be scrolled. The column headings should remain visible so the user can always identify the contents.

- **Scroll bar.** This is a bar at the side of a scrolling list. A highlighted part of the bar rides up and down, like an elevator, to show which part of the list is visible. The highlight can be moved with a mouse to scroll to another part of the list.

- **Window.** A window allows the user to view part of a larger area, such as a page or a table, that is partially obscured by the window frame. This is a generalization of a scrolling list to allow vertical and horizontal scrolling around a large area such as a drawing, a large table, or a spreadsheet. The borders of the window can be moved horizontally or vertically by using scroll bars below and to the side of the window.

- **Availability emphasis.** Some options are unavailable in pull-down menus or check boxes. These are shown in a lighter shade or a different color to indicate that this option is not currently available.

- **Selection cursor.** The option at which the cursor is currently placed is emphasized by making it brighter, a different color, or in reversed colors.
- **Selection emphasis.** Options or icons are emphasized to tell the user that they are currently in effect. This emphasis is used when an option or icon changes the mode of operation of the panel and is always kept visible. An example is a choice between text and graphics entry in a publishing package.
- **Pop-up window.** This is a portion of the screen that pops up to extend the dialog to a new level. A pop-up window is used when a specific task must be accomplished before returning to regular processing. Pop-up windows are used for error messages, confirmations, or parameter specification.
- **Heading.** This is used to identify columns or groups of related items. *Address* can identify the group of fields that go together to define an address.
- **Entry field.** This is the space in which users type data. The data may be an entry into a database, a command, text in a word processor, or any other kind of textual entry.
- **Prompt.** A prompt is a label that identifies the kind of data that must be entered into a field. The prompt must be unambiguous. For instance, it is not always clear from the context whether DATE on an order screen means the order date, today's date, or the expected shipping date.

Styles of Screens

Forms are used only for data capture. Screens are used for many other purposes. They can identify an application by presenting logo information. They can present selection menus or lists. They can be used for entering data, tables, and parameters. They can be used for presenting textual and graphic information. Each of these purposes requires a different style of screen.

A screen is divided into panels that are used for different purposes. One or more panels can be combined on a single screen to generate a screen that serves any purpose. The kinds of panels are described below.

- **Logo Panels.** A logo panel displays ownership, copyright, and login information. A logo panel usually occupies the whole screen and it is usually the first screen that a user sees in an application. It must have a command that moves the application to the next screen. Alternately, the logo screen can disappear after a timed interval, revealing the next screen.
- **Menu Panels.** Menu panels contain one or more choices that a user can select. Menus are implemented with variants of action bars, pull-down menus, and icons. A menu may take up a whole screen at the beginning of an application when a major module must be selected. It may take up only a one line menu bar at the top of a screen for commands that are available while an entry panel is being used.
- **List Panels.** A list panel is usually used as a pop-up window that allows the selection of files, customers, accounts, or other appropriate items from a list of those available. The list panel usually pops up when needed and disappears when a selection has been made.

- **Entry Panels.** Entry panels are used to enter data, parameters, text, or graphics of any kind. They are the panels where the work of the application occurs. In a database environment, they are the panels where data are inserted, updated, or deleted. The format of the panels depends on whether the panels are used for entering parameters, forms, or tables.
  - **Parameter Entry Panels.** These are used to enter parameters that are needed by the application program before it can perform a function. They are usually implemented as pop-up windows that appear when an action has been selected from a menu. For instance, if the action is to save a file, then a parameter panel appears to ask for the file name and directory where the file will be stored. The panel usually has headings, prompts, and entry fields. It needs some way of indicating that the panel has been completed and the parameters are ready to be accepted. This is often a check box that activates the function as soon as it is checked. It is sometimes a return key or function key.
  - **Form Entry Panels.** These are similar to parameter entry panels, except that they are designed to match the structure of a paper form. In some cases, such as taking telephone orders, there may be no corresponding paper form. They are usually used for repeated data entry, so they occupy all or most of the screen. They stay on the screen while a series of forms is entered and they do not pop up and disappear.
  - **Tabular Entry Panels.** Tabular panels are form entry panels that accept repeated lines of data, like the lines of an order form. They have a heading at the top of each column and several lines for data entry. Otherwise, they have the same characteristics as form entry panels.
- **Information Panels.** These panels display help information, messages, and reports. The content of the panel cannot be changed by the user. It is used only for communication from the computer to the user. If the information occupies more than one screen, the screen needs a scroll bar or function keys to move up and down through the contents. Information panels are usually implemented as pop-up windows. Some messages are designed to inform the user about the progress of long tasks by providing a count of records processed, a graph of fraction completed, or a message that tells the user that the computer is "working." These messages alleviate worries about whether an error has been made, if no output is received.
- **Combined Panels.** It is often convenient to combine several panels on a single screen. A very common case occurs when an instance of a kernel entity and the related instances of a characteristic entity have to be entered. A form entry panel is placed in the top half of the screen for the kernel entity. A tabular entry panel is placed below it for the characteristic entity. An action bar or other menu may be located across the top to select actions such as insert, update, and delete. An information panel may be placed at the bottom of the screen for error messages or help information.

8
SCREEN

A system needs standard rules for format, messages, and function keys. Standard keys for basic functions—like moving the cursor, asking for help, editing data, and exiting a screen—reduce the learning needed to master another screen or application. They also simplify programming because utility routines can be written to perform the same task for each screen. They can be copied into each screen definition without having to design and debug each new version.

Standards are also required for the placement of major elements of the screen. Headings, pop-up menus, exit commands, and help messages should always appear in a consistent place. This reduces the operator's search time to locate a desired item.

Experienced users should be provided with shortcuts to speed their use. A function key can provide an alternative to multiple menu selections for commonly used functions, like saving data. A typeahead buffer can allow experienced users to continue keying the next item while processing continues on the current item.

There have been several recent moves toward standards for screens. The MacIntosh™, the GEM™, the Windows™, the Open Look™[4], and the X-Windows™[8] interfaces are graphics interfaces that strongly resemble each other. Hayes and Baran compare them.[3] IBM has defined the Common User Access[5] standard for screens that they are recommending to all of their customers. This standard has many features in common with the other interfaces. It also suggests standard ways to implement many features on unprogrammable terminals.

Physical Considerations in Screen Design

There are two main kinds of screens: programmable and unprogrammable. Programmable screens are usually attached to a microcomputer. They can process the logic needed to implement pop-up menus, highlighted cursors, and position cursors to follow a mouse or other pointer. Unprogrammable screens can only do this by communicating with a remote computer. This communication is costly and time consuming when the computer is far from the screen. It degrades the performance of the remote computer. The terminal operator may have to wait while this communication occurs.

Additionally, screens can be divided into graphic screens and character-oriented screens. Character-oriented screens can display a limited set of alphabetic and special characters. Graphic screens can generate any object, character, or shape on the screen. Graphics increase the cost of the screen somewhat, but increase the amount of communication and computation enormously because there are many graphic points to communicate when generating each character. Communication to track a mouse pointer and update its position on a screen is prohibitively expensive if this has to be done by a computer many miles away.

It is not surprising that most of the commercially implemented graphics interfaces have been implemented on personal microcomputers. The microcomputer does not incur any communication costs because the screen is attached directly to the computer. The personal computer costs do not increase because the computer would not be performing any other useful task while waiting for input.

Experienced users, such as data entry clerks, may not need the features of a programmable graphics interface. Such an interface may even reduce their efficiency. An operator, performing repetitive tasks, quickly learns the commands and codes that apply to the task. Waiting for lists to be painted on the screen or moving a hand from the keyboard to a mouse slows the operator down. When performing repetitive tasks, a graphics interface can increase communication and computation costs while decreasing operator efficiency.

People who use computers infrequently often prefer personal computers. They may not perform a particular task often enough to get skilled at it, or they may forget what they have learned before the next use. They need helpful reminders of what to do next. Efficiency may be less important than convenience and easy access.

Some applications are used by both experienced and inexperienced operators. For these applications, the screen has to be designed to satisfy both kinds of users or else different screens are needed for different classes of users. Both users can sometimes be satisfied by providing more than one way to use the same screen. For instance, inexperienced users with poor typing skills can use a pointer while experienced users with good typing skills use function keys to activate the same function.

Report Design

The design of reports is a cross between the design of forms and the design of screens. Reports are usually printed on paper, but they may be shown on screens or stored on files to be used by other application programs. Printed reports are used when the output goes to an outside organization, is too voluminous to be browsed on-line, or is needed for control or audit purposes. Screen reports are used for inquiries about single occurrences in a database, low volume outputs, or when the inquiry is one step in an interactive process.

Many of the elements of a report correspond to elements of forms and screens. Each has titles, headings, and fields. However, reports are frequently used to summarize data or identify subsets for further examination. As a result, the criteria, components, and styles are different in several ways.

Report Design Criteria

Reports convey information from the computer file to the user. They perform this task best when they do it clearly and economically in a timely and accurate manner. Clarity requires that all of the required information be presented in a form that is understandable by the intended user. Economy requires that this be accomplished without wasting computer resources or the user's time. There are several criteria that can be used to judge the quality of a report.

- **Timeliness.** Reports must be prepared in time to be used. Most reports provide information that is used to make decisions. Information is of very little use if it arrives after the decision deadline.
- **Accuracy.** The data must be accurately recorded, accurately transmitted, and accurately transformed into summary data. The data must also be captured on time. Incomplete data are also inaccurate.
- **Relevance.** The information must be relevant to the purpose of the report. This is a selection process. All of the relevant information must be included. At the same time, all of the irrelevant data must be excluded. The result must include everything that is needed and nothing that is not.
- **Clarity.** The report must present information in a clear and understandable form. The report must be designed to present data in a logical order. Desired information must be easy to locate. Comparisons, ratios, exception flags, and graphs should be used where appropriate.
- **Cost.** Each report has two costs. The first is the cost of preparation which consists of analysis, design, computation, and distribution. The second is the cost of reading the report and locating germane parts of it. The cost of reading the report is often forgotten in the calculation of costs. The reading cost can often be reduced by careful design to select only appropriate information and present it clearly. The total cost must always be less than the expected benefits. Otherwise the report should not be prepared.

Components of Reports

Reports have many of the same components as forms and screens. They have titles, headings, captions, and fields in which data are presented. In addition they have several unique characteristics that are listed below and illustrated schematically in Figure 8-6.

- **Title page.** A report often consists of many pages. If it does, it should have a title page to identify the report and possibly to explain the source and purpose of the report.
- **Table of contents.** A report with many parts should have a table of contents to guide the user to where the different parts begin.
- **Footnotes.** Reports often contain complex coding structures that have to be explained in footnotes. The explanations sometimes appear in a separate explanatory page at the beginning of the report. In Figure 8-6, a footnote explains the special coding for audited courses.
- **Address.** If an address is included on a communication with a customer, it should be placed so it can be easily folded to show through a window envelope as shown in Figure 8-6.
- **Sorted lists.** Many reports contain lists of items such as customers or products. These lists should be sorted in an order that makes it easiest for the user to locate the desired information. Customers might be sorted alphabetically by last name. Cost of goods produced might be sorted in decreasing order of deviation from budget. In Figure 8-6, the pages are sorted by student name and the courses are sorted by COURSE_ID.

Figure 8-6
Example of a timetable report for one student. X is used to show where characters are printed on each report.

```
                              TIMETABLE

        Student Number      XXX-XXX-XXX

        Name          ┌─────────────────────────────────┐
        Address       │  XXXXXXXXXX XXXXXXXXXXXX          │
                      │  XXXXXXXXXXXXXXXXXXXXXXX          │
                      │  XXXXXXXXXXXXXXXX XX XXXXX        │
                      └─────────────────────────────────┘


        Course  Section   Term    Course Name        Credits  Room   Day   Time
        XXXXXX    XX       XXX  XXXXXXXXXXXXXXXXXXXX     X     XXXX   XXX   XX:XX
                                                              XXXX   XXX   XX:XX
        XXXXXX    XX       XXX  XXXXXXXXXXXXXXXXXXXX     X*    XXXX   XXX   XX:XX
                                                              XXXX   XXX   XX:XX
        XXXXXX    XX       XXX  XXXXXXXXXXXXXXXXXXXX     X     XXXX   XXX   XX:XX
                                                              XXXX   XXX   XX:XX
        XXXXXX    XX       XXX  XXXXXXXXXXXXXXXXXXXX     X     XXXX   XXX   XX:XX
                                                              XXXX   XXX   XX:XX
        XXXXXX    XX       XXX  XXXXXXXXXXXXXXXXXXXX     X     XXXX   XXX   XX:XX
                                                              XXXX   XXX   XX:XX
        XXXXXX    XX       XXX  XXXXXXXXXXXXXXXXXXXX     X     XXXX   XXX   XX:XX
                                                              XXXX   XXX   XX:XX

        Total     XX                                  XX

        Credits:  * means auditing only
```

- **Control breaks.** Lists of sorted items are often broken into sub-groups whenever the sorted variable changes to a new value. For instance, purchases might be sorted by customer name first and then by date of purchase within each customer. A report is simpler and clearer if each customer begins on a new page with the name at the top of the page. Such a report is said to break on customer name. This means that there is a break in the listing when the customer name changes. Different material, such as headings and totals, is usually inserted when there is a break. In Figure 8-6 there is a page break before each new name. A total is computed at each break. There is a minor break at each COURSE_ID to prevent repetition of course, section, term, and credits information.

- **Summary data.** Users often do not want to see detailed data. They want to see an aggregated summary of the data, such as total purchases by each customer. The summary data may be included in a control break between more detailed items or they may be the only data that are reported. The most common summary data are count, total, average, minimum value, and maximum value. Sometimes the summary values are summarized again to produce, say, a grand total. In Figure 8-6 the Total line counts the number of courses and totals the number of credits.

8
SCREEN

- **Exception highlights.** Some reports are designed to identify special cases, such as excessive costs or low levels of inventory. In such cases, the report should highlight the exceptions automatically by using bold type, underlining, or an asterisk beside the item. If only the exceptional items are of interest, then other items should not be listed. In Figure 8-6, an asterisk in the Credits column highlights exceptions where courses are audited without credit.
- **Confidentiality.** Multipart forms can be designed with black zones to make certain information, like value, invisible on some copies. Printing black ink on red paper makes the document readable, but almost impossible to photocopy.
- **End of report.** The end must be clearly identified so the user knows that all of a multipage report has been provided. The end may be identified by a grand total, a page count (page 15 of 15), or a message like THE END. The end of the run that prints the reports in Figure 8-6 should have a total count of the number of Timetables printed.

Styles of Reports

Information can be communicated by the computer in three general ways: files, text, and graphs. The form and use of each are discussed below.

- **Files.** Text and graphs are used when the computer is communicating with people. Files are used when the computer must communicate with another computer program. The data being communicated are stored in a file in some standard form that the receiving program can understand. That program then reads the data and does further processing. Communication files are commonly used to send data to:
  - **Statistical packages.** The packages can then analyze the data to produce summaries, correlations, forecasts, and many other statistical results.
  - **Graphic packages.** These programs can produce a wide variety of graphs to help visualize the data.
  - **Spreadsheets.** A spreadsheet program can insert the data into a mathematical model to create special reports and projections.
  - **Word processors.** These are able to format data, insert it into reports, or merge information into form letters.
- **Text.** Textual reports use words and numbers to provide information in the form of lists and tables, possibly with page breaks and summary data. Such reports are complete, precise, and difficult to understand. They are complete because the lists and tables can be made long enough to include all applicable items. They are precise because enough digits can be printed to provide an arbitrary level of precision in all numbers. They are difficult to understand because people have to compare individual numbers to determine trends or variations in the data.
- **Graphs.** Graphs convert numbers into scaled lines, areas, or positions that are easy to compare visually. Graphs are not as complete or precise as tables. Small values may be invisible. Precision is limited by the resolution of the display medium and the ability of the viewer to measure positions visually. However, graphs are very good at revealing relative size, proportion, trend,

and variation of the data. These are often important concepts because they translate into value, share, growth, and risk in a business context. Tables of data inform users, but graphs convince them.

Different kinds of graphs are used depending on how many variables must be shown and whether the variables are continuous or categorical. A continuous variable, such as sales, can take on any value within a range. A categorical variable, such as region, can take on any of a set number of values. The values do not have to be numeric and they do not necessarily have any particular order.

The most common kinds of graphs are Bar Graphs, Pie Charts, Column Graphs, Stacked Bar Graphs, Area Graphs, and Line Graphs. Each kind provides different information. They are easy to generate with many software packages on the market. The examples in Figure 8-7 were generated in less than an hour using Quattro Pro™ produced by Borland International Inc.

- **Bar Graphs** are used when a continuous variable can be divided into portions for each category of one categorical variable. An example is sales in each region. Sales is the continuous variable being divided. Region is the categorical variable. Bar Graphs provide a clearer indication of the relative importance of each category than do tables of numbers. The bars may be horizontal or vertical with a scale to measure length or height.

- **Pie Charts** serve the same function as Bar Graphs, except that they emphasize proportion rather than amount. Sometimes one sector is exploded to draw attention to that component. The actual amounts or percentages are sometimes shown with the category labels.

- **Column Graphs** serve the same function as Pie Charts. They show the proportion of a continuous variable in each category of one categorical variable.

- **Stacked Bar Graphs** are an extension of Column Graphs using a second categorical variable. The graph shows the amount of the continuous variable that is in each of the cells created by the two categorical variables. It shows the same information as a two-way cross tabulation chart. An example is share of each kind of expenses in each region. Share of expenses in one region is a Column Graph of the continuous variable, expenses, divided into expense groups. The Stacked Bar Graph is a Column Graph for each region shown side-by-side. The expenses of a single kind in a single region are shown in the areas of the bar graph. Alternately, the regions could be stacked for a single expense type. The expense categories can also have separate bars shown side-by-side. and the bars can be vertical or horizontal. The shading identifies the different expense categories.

- **Area Graphs** are similar to Stacked Bar Graphs, except that the continuous variable is categorized by a single categorical variable and is plotted against another continuous variable—usually time—on the horizontal axis. It shows how the share of each category changes over time.

8 SCREEN

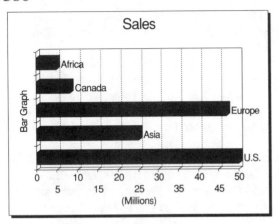

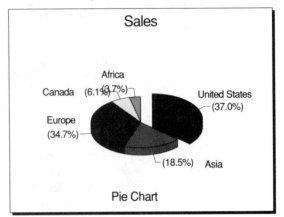

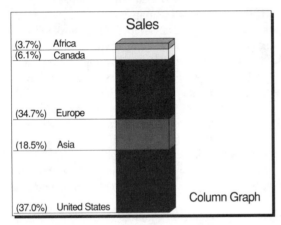

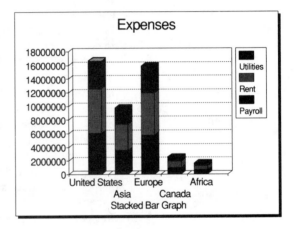

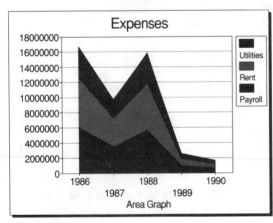

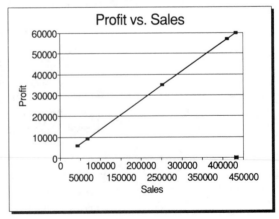

Figure 8-7

Examples of kinds of graphs.

- **Line Plots** are used when two continuous variables are being related. The plot shows the relationship between the two variables. The variable on the vertical axis is dependent on the variable on the horizontal axis. When the independent variable on the horizontal axis is time, the graph is called a Time-Series Plot. Such a plot can show the trend and variation of the vertical variable with respect to the horizontal axis. If the vertical variable is not perfectly correlated with the horizontal variable, then the plot can illustrate correlation between the variables. The data points are then scattered about a line representing the relationship between the variables and the plot is called a Scatter Plot.

Graphs can be a powerful tool for communicating information. They can also be a powerful tool for communicating misinformation. An honest graph follows a number of guidelines to make sure that the impression gained by the viewer corresponds to the reality of the situation.

- **The zero point of the dependent axis** must be shown clearly. Otherwise trivial variations may look more important than they really are.
- **The visual space** occupied by a variable should be proportional to the data being graphed. Representing labor costs by pictures of people of different heights is misleading. As costs double, the area covered by the person quadruples leading to the impression that costs have quadrupled.
- **Monetary time series** should be deflated to remove the impact of inflation and converted to common units of exchange for comparability.

Tufte[9] provides guidelines for designing graphs.

Physical Considerations in Report Design

The device used for output can influence the design of a report. Each device has advantages and disadvantages. The most important characteristics in choosing an output device are resolution, type fonts, graphics, volume, and cost as described below.

- **Resolution** refers to the amount of detail that can be printed. It is usually measured in dots per inch (dpi). Visual clarity increases as the number of dots per inch increases. 75 dpi is a minimal resolution for readable output. 300 dpi is adequate for office correspondence. 1000 dpi or more is used in high quality magazines and books.
- **Type** fonts are complete sets of print characters with the same face, size, and style. Face refers to the character shape. Size refers to the character height. Style refers to the character thickness (thin, normal, and bold) and whether the characters are slanted (italic).
- **Graphics** is the ability to draw lines and pictures. Many devices are only capable of printing alphabetic characters.
- **Volume** is the speed of output in characters per minute (**cpm**), lines per minute (**lpm**), or pages per minute (**ppm**). This can range from 1800 cpm for slow dot matrix printers to 150 ppm for large laser printers.
- **Cost** is the production expense per page for paper, ink, maintenance, operators, and equipment depreciation plus the cost incurred while users go to

8 SCREEN

collect output and wait for it. Cost increases as resolution and choice of type increase. Cost decreases as volume increases. Low volume devices are often used—in spite of their high production cost—because they can be placed near the users to reduce delivery time.

There are many kinds of output devices. The most common ones are dot matrix printers, ink jet printers, line printers, laser printers, pen plotters, computer output to microfilm, and display screens. Each of these has different characteristics which are summarized in Figure 8-8.

- **Dot matrix printers** print individual characters by the impact of a vertical row of wires through an inked ribbon. The character is constructed from an array of dots. The resolution depends on the number of dots used to construct the character. Resolution can vary between 75 and 150 dpi. Apparent resolution can be doubled by reprinting the line with dots between the first row of dots. Volume varies between 1,500 and 15,000 cpm. This is equivalent to about 20 to 200 lpm. Cost increases as resolution and volume increase. Dot matrix printers can produce graphic images and they can print multiple copies using carbon paper. Cost is as low as a few hundred dollars.

- **Ink jet printers** are similar to dot matrix printers. The image is created by droplets of ink that are directed at the paper by electrostatic charges. The resolution and volume are similar to that of dot matrix printers. Ink jet printers are somewhat costlier and much quieter than dot matrix printers. Ink jet printers can produce graphic images but they cannot print multiple copies.

- **Line printers** print a whole line at a time by the impact of hammers through an inked ribbon on a band, drum, or chain of letters that rotates past the paper. They can achieve volumes from 200 to 3600 lpm. Resolution can be very good if carbon paper ribbons are used. Usually resolution is very poor because cheaper cloth ribbons are used. The positioning of the characters can vary if the hammers are not perfectly synchronized. This can produce untidy looking output. Only one font is available with no graphics capability. Cost is relatively low. Line printers can use carbon paper to print multiple copies. These devices are often used for high volume applications such as billing.

- **Laser printers** use a mechanism that is similar to a photocopier. The time taken to print a page is relatively independent of the number of characters on the page. Times can increase greatly for documents with a lot of graphics or many fonts that have to be transferred from the computer. Volume can range between 4 ppm and 150 ppm depending on whether the printer is a desktop

Figure 8-8	DEVICE	RESOLUTION	FONTS	GRAPHICS	VOLUME	COST
Summary of the characteristics of output devices.	Line Printer	Low	One	No	High	Low
	Dot Matrix	Medium	Few	Yes	Low-Med	Low
	Ink Jet	Medium	Few	Yes	Low-Med	Low
	Laser	High	Many	Yes	Med-High	Medium
	Pen Plotter	Medium	Poor	Yes	Low	High
	Microfilm	Medium	Varies	Yes	High	Low
	Screen	Low	One	Yes	Low	Low

printer or an industrial strength printer for high volume output. This is approximately equivalent to 200 to 7500 lpm. A wide variety of fonts is available. Most laser printers can accept new fonts from the computer. Laser printers cannot make carbon copies, but they can make extra originals easily. Cost ranges from about $1000 for personal laser printers to hundreds of thousands of dollars for large systems. As costs drop, laser printers are displacing dot matrix and ink jet printers because of their quality and low cost.

● **Pen plotters** have one or more pens that are moved over a sheet of paper to draw continuous lines. Flatbed plotters have a flat sheet and pens that move vertically and horizontally across the sheet. Drum plotters wrap the paper around a cylinder. An arm moves the pen across the cylinder and the cylinder rotates to move the pen in the perpendicular direction. Resolution depends on the diameter of the pen that is used. The pens usually move in increments of 0.01 inches. Volume depends on the number and length of lines to be drawn. The fonts are limited to those that can be drawn with a pen. The drawing area can be very large on some plotters. Plotters are used primarily for scientific and engineering drawings. Laser printers are becoming competitive with pen plotters for many applications.

● **Microfilm** is used when economy, compact storage, or archival permanence are important. Microfilm costs 15 to 20 percent as much as paper, takes two percent of the space, and lasts almost forever. A laser-generated image is projected onto a piece of photographic film which is then processed like any other film. A magnifying viewer is needed to view the result. Printed copies are relatively expensive and have relatively poor resolution. Graphics and multiple fonts can be generated. Microfilm is often used for catalogs and for bank, hospital, and insurance records.

● **Screens** are used when the report does not have to be stored. The user can see a result, take action, and go on to another task. This is common when random inquiries, such as airline reservations, have to be processed. Graphics are possible. Volume is limited by the transmission speed from the computer and the rate at which the user can read the screen. Reading rate is usually the bottle-neck. Fonts and resolution usually are not important in such situations.

Design by Prototyping

Prototyping is a technique in which the analyst rapidly develops a proposed screen or report and asks the intended user to critique it. This initial design is called a prototype. On the basis of the critique, the screen or report is modified and the modifications are critiqued again. This process is repeated until a representative sample of users is unable to identify further problems with the design. Iteration allows the system to develop through a process of evolutionary discovery by users rather than omniscient revelation by the analyst.

Prototyping can be a very effective way of bridging the communication gap between designers and users. Users have difficulty in specifying exactly what they want to see on the screen. They have the same difficulty in specifying the characteristics of a good cake, wine, date, or mate. However, they can tell you whether they like an example when they taste or see it. The prototype is a way of triggering the user's memory and initiating a dialog about the design in an environment of uncertainty or ambiguity.

Prototyping was difficult or impossible in the past because available programming techniques were too slow. The user became tired, frustrated, or disinterested while a programmer coded and compiled changes to a screen. The changes on a screen could take a day or more. By that time, the user thought of further changes or forgot what changes were wanted. Then the whole costly process had to be repeated. With modern screen generators, the process is much faster and much less frustrating for all concerned.

The ease with which data files and screens can be defined using CASE and 4GL tools makes it tempting to use prototyping early in the design process as a way of finding out what the user requirements are. However, if prototyping is used before a proper analysis of data structures is completed, it can lead to very poor designs. Prototyping may identify missing data attributes to be added, but it never provides the overview needed to see how data should be organized. Prototyping without a database has sometimes been referred to as the **fire, aim, ready** method that gets all the steps backwards.

There is a correct order for prototyping steps. The analyst first needs to get **ready** by preparing a data model as described in previous chapters. The analyst then takes **aim** by identifying knowledgeable users who have an understanding of data integrity requirements. Finally the analyst is ready to **fire** screens at the user.

If a data model is in place and a screen generator is available, prototyping in front of a user can make sure that:

● **Data** are provided where necessary.
● **Format** is easy to use and understand.
● **Variations** of records or transactions are handled.
● **Input errors** are detected.
● **Help** is provided to make screens self-documenting.

Prototyping is a simple process of modifying and testing a screen design in successive stages until the user is satisfied with it. If the system is to be used by many users, it should be tested with a representative sample of users to make sure that it satisfies all of them. Users from different departments, educational levels, professions, countries, or cultural backgrounds should critique the prototype to detect new problems or requirements. They may find that features that were obvious to the designer or to one user are not obvious to them.

Prototyping is an alternate method of systems analysis and design. It has often been proposed as a general approach to analysis. However, it is not effective for system parts that a user cannot "see and feel." It is very effective for the design of paper and screen forms where the content and organization of the form is very important. It is particularly useful when the user cannot articulate a precise specification or is uncomfortable with abstract specifications.

Prototyping is not very useful for batch programs or modules with complex logic. A prototype is not of much use in determining if the logic has been correctly programmed. The users frequently cannot follow the logic in the program code. They also find it hard to determine whether the output result is correct. A complex financial or statistical calculation may look correct and yet contain errors. Only a rigorous testing procedure can detect such errors.

Prototypes can also be used for exploration and examination. Such prototypes are not intended for end-users. These prototypes are intended to test ideas rather than to trigger the memory of users. They serve a useful purpose in helping professionals to select among alternatives. Alternate formats, algorithms, or implementation methods can be tested to determine efficiency, ease of use, ease of learning, feasibility, or other design choices.

Prototyping speeds the development of a good system. The traditional System Development Life Cycle delivers a first prototype when the system is installed. Maintenance and enhancement stages slowly produce the equivalent of new prototypes. It could take years to deliver a system that is as good as the result of prototyping.

The prototyping process needs clear stages. Otherwise it goes on forever as users suggest endless changes and variations on the basic design. The design process has three phases: standard setting, design, and packaging. The standard setting phase sets standards that will be followed by all screens and reports. Within the design process there are three more stages in designing each screen and report. These are identification, formatting, and enhancing. A final packaging stage integrates all screens into a system by providing menus to access them. At the end of each stage, the user agrees to freeze the specifications identified during that stage.

These stages are illustrated with an example from the STARS system in Chapter 7. The example is a screen to enter student enrollments in courses, update enrollments, and retrieve information to answer inquiries from students. The example assumes that the paper enrollment form in Figure 8-1 is used for all data collection.

Setting Standards

This phase sets standards about the format of screens and reports and possibly about the tools or languages that will be used to generate them. The main objective of this phase is to produce consistent products. Consistency makes it easier for users to learn how to use all the screens and makes it easier for designers to specify each screen or report.

The main elements of a standard deal with the capabilities of the target equipment which will display screens, the use of function keys, capitalization, fonts, ruling lines, and color, and the positioning of different screen elements. These elements include command menus, headings, tables, and help panels. If a Graphic User Interface is being used, there should be standards for titles, icons, window size, menu commands, emphasis, and scroll bars.

8 SCREEN

Most Graphic User Interfaces have their own standards for many of these items. If they do not, the designer should test mock screens that implement the standard to ensure operator and machine efficiency. For instance, badly designed icons can confuse the user and increase errors and training costs.

Standards may also cover invisible components such as internal documentation, error checking, and testing.

Identify Data and Actions

The first stage of prototyping is the identification of the data that has to appear on the screen and the actions that have to be performed on the data. If many kinds of users are involved, a Joint Applications Design session can be used for this stage. In small projects, the data model, processes, and screens may be analyzed in a single JAD session.

The data are organized into screens, panels within screens, and fields within panels. The basic actions are reading fields from tables, entering data into fields on the screen, checking the validity of entries, and writing fields to tables.

Identifying Screens, Panels, and Fields

Most screen generators or screen painter programs make it easy to design screens that perform insertions, updates, deletions, and inquiries on the same screen. Thus a single screen can handle all interactions with enrollments.

When a screen contains attributes from more than one table, the designer needs to identify all the tables that are involved in the screen. This is done most easily by examining the Entity-Relationship Diagram that shows how all the entities and their corresponding tables are related. Figure 8-9 repeats the portion of Figure 5-6 that is used in this design. The operations to be performed on each table have been written above each corresponding entity.

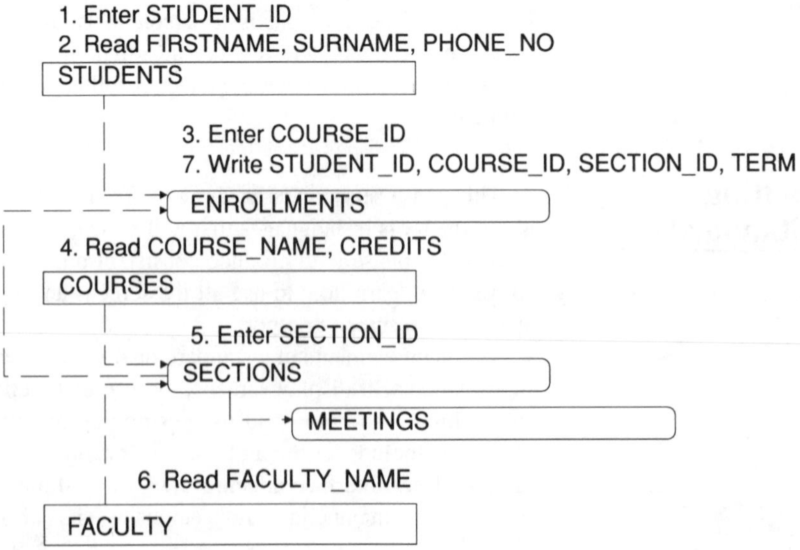

Figure 8-9

A Data Navigation Diagram for the Enrollment Screen.

1. Enter STUDENT_ID
2. Read FIRSTNAME, SURNAME, PHONE_NO
STUDENTS

3. Enter COURSE_ID
7. Write STUDENT_ID, COURSE_ID, SECTION_ID, TERM
ENROLLMENTS

4. Read COURSE_NAME, CREDITS
COURSES

5. Enter SECTION_ID
SECTIONS

MEETINGS

6. Read FACULTY_NAME
FACULTY

The enrollment activity starts with the identification of a student to be enrolled. For each student there are many enrollments. For each enrollment there is a corresponding section of a course. For each section there is a corresponding faculty member who teaches the section. All the relationships are optional so the entries for characteristic entities may not exist. However, if the characteristic entity is being created, the kernel entity must already have been created. This guides the designer in defining validity checks later.

When the Entity-Relationship Diagram is annotated to specify the order in which data tables are accessed, it is called a Data Navigation Diagram. The annotations are numbered to show the order of the actions.

The Data Navigation Diagram identifies the possible tables that are available for use on the screen and the actions that need to be performed. The attributes of each table identify the fields that can be placed on the screen. Sometimes additional fields are generated by transforming or summing existing fields. Occasionally, users identify attributes that must be added to tables. Added attributes are rare if the database has been designed carefully.

At this point, it is useful to sketch the proposed arrangement of fields on the screen. The sketch shows the user what the screen looks like. Leave the details of the format until all fields have been identified. The analyst should generate the first sketch. If the user has to work to generate a sketch, the user becomes committed to the design and the sketch becomes a requirement. This may preclude possible later improvements.

A sketch of the proposed screen is shown in Figure 8-10. This sketch is the result of discussions with one or more representative users. The sketch does not have to be neatly drafted. The actual size and position of each label and area does not have to be accurate. The attribute names in the database can be used as labels at this stage. Most screen generators look after details like centering and identifying the width of fields. Elements can be moved or resized later to improve appearance or function. At this stage the emphasis is on identifying all the data that must appear on the screen.

The only fields absolutely needed to record an enrollment are STUDENT_ID, COURSE_ID, SECTION_ID, and TERM. The user has asked for the rest of the fields on the screen to provide information for checking and for inquiries. The first and last name are included so the operator can perform a visual check to make sure that the correct student has been selected. The phone number is included in case the operator has to call the student for further information or clarification. The total credits, course name, credits, and professor are frequently used to answer questions from students. The total credits field is not in the database, but it can be computed when needed.

Identifying Actions

The actions to be performed were specified on the Data Navigation Diagram. A more formal specification is needed when the specification is implemented by programmers. An Action Diagram serves this purpose. The Action Diagram in

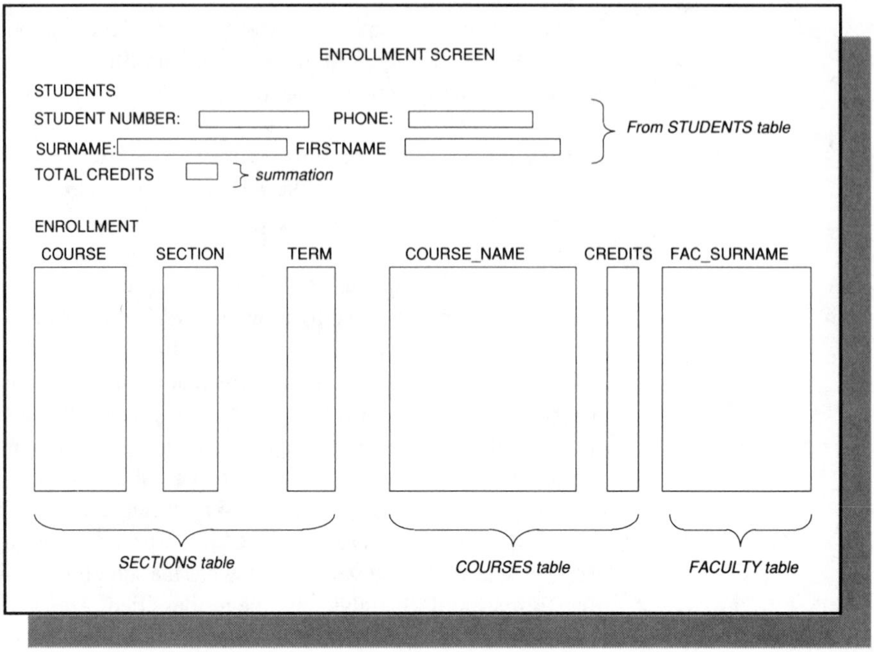

Figure 8-10

A sketch of the proposed Enrollment Screen showing the source tables for each data item. It contains an upper panel of student data and a lower panel of repeating enrollment data.

ENROLLMENT SCREEN

STUDENTS
STUDENT NUMBER: [   ]   PHONE: [   ]   } From STUDENTS table
SURNAME:[   ]   FIRSTNAME [   ]
TOTAL CREDITS [   ] } summation

ENROLLMENT

| COURSE | SECTION | TERM | COURSE_NAME | CREDITS | FAC_SURNAME |

SECTIONS table   COURSES table   FACULTY table

Figure 8-11 presents the same information as the Data Navigation Diagram in Figure 8-9. In addition, the IF statements provide some information on the conditions that need to be satisfied during the use of the screen. The brackets provide information about the hierarchical structure of the instructions. The statements have been numbered to maintain correspondence with the Navigation Diagram. Usually they are unnumbered.

Figure 8-11

Action Diagram for the Enrollment Screen showing repeating groups of operations to be performed.

1. Enter STUDENT_ID
        IF student exists in STUDENTS
2. Read FIRSTNAME, SURNAME, PHONE from STUDENTS

    3. Enter COURSE_ID
            If course exists in COURSES
        4. Read COURSE_NAME, CREDITS from COURSES
        5. Enter SECTION_ID, TERM

            If section exists in SECTIONS
        6. Read FAC_SURNAME from FACULTY
        7. Write STUDENT_ID, COURSE_ID, SECTION_ID, TERM
            to ENROLLMENTS

The vertical brackets enclose the steps that need to be performed as a unit in sequence from top to bottom. A bracket with a double line at the top, as in the one above step 3, signifies iteration. Such groups of instructions may be performed more than once. They correspond to the multiple course lines on the screen. A condition at the top line of a bracket applies to all instructions enclosed by the bracket. If the condition at the top of a bracket is not satisfied, none of the instructions within the bracket are performed.

The Action Diagram is a simple way of specifying processing logic to programmers. It can be maintained easily on many word processors. It shows the order of instructions, the blocks of instructions that go together, and the conditions that apply to them. It is relatively easy to add instructions by inserting lines between existing lines. The Action Diagram, as a specification technique, is examined further in Chapter 10.

The screen sketch in Figure 8-10 and the Action Diagram in Figure 8-11 are the outputs of the first prototype phase. The screen sketch can be drawn on paper, specified using a screen painter in a CASE tool, or implemented with a Screen Generator depending on the technology available. The user must agree at the end of this stage that all data elements have been identified.

Define Format

When the data elements have been identified, the user and the designer can turn their attention to the format of the screen. The format elements are labels, positions, and emphasis. Labels identify elements and panels on the screen. The elements should each be in a convenient position. Some elements and panels need to be emphasized for better visibility and navigation around the screen.

Position

The screen is constructed in panels. Each panel presents the elements of a single table and any items related to the table. In this example, there are two panels: one that corresponds to the STUDENTS table and one that corresponds to the ENROLLMENT table.

The first panel, called the STUDENTS panel, contains all the information needed about a single student. If enough space is available on the screen, then all fields should be positioned above one another in a column with prompts followed by corresponding fields. Prompts should be aligned on the right and fields should be aligned on the left as shown in Figure 8-12. If the screen has many elements, more than one field may have to be put on a line to conserve space.

The second panel, called the ENROLLMENT panel, contains all the information about the sections of courses that the student in the previous panel has enrolled in. Since there are many enrollments for each student, this panel is a table with each row corresponding to an enrollment.

In addition, the screen needs a screen title, an action bar, and a help area. The action bar needs commands to find, insert, update, and delete information. The panels are shown in Figure 8-13 with tentative labels.

8
SCREEN

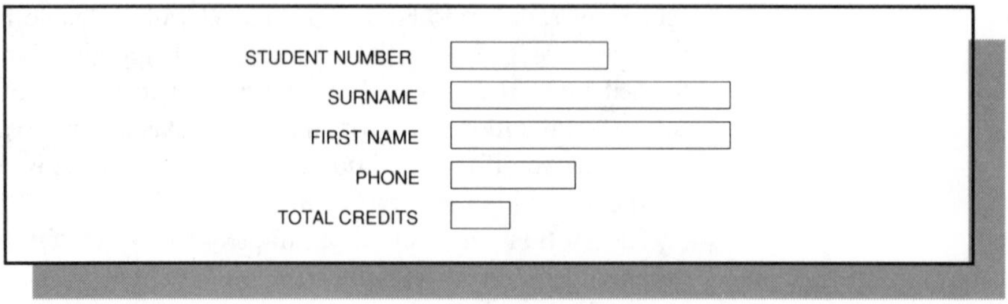

Figure 8-12

Illustration of right
alignment of
prompts and left
alignment of data
fields on a screen.

STUDENT NUMBER	
SURNAME	
FIRST NAME	
PHONE	
TOTAL CREDITS	

The panel positions are chosen to make the screen easy to use. The action bar and screen title are placed at the top as part of a standard format for all screens. Similarly, the help area is placed in the last line. This consistency makes it easy for the user to find components that are regularly needed.

The position of the fields within each panel is designed for easy entry. The STUDENT_ID is the first item in the STUDENT panel. When a STUDENT_ID is entered and the Find command is selected, the rest of the panel is filled with information from the files. When the COURSE_ID, SECTION_ID, and TERM for a new course are entered, the course name, credits, and professor name are automatically retrieved from tables.

If the screen is used to enter data from a form, the position of each blank on the screen should correspond closely to the position of the same data on the form. The order of entry should be the same. This makes it easy for the operator to key data in order, as seen on the form.

Labels

The panel title, prompts, command names, and heading names are all labels. They must be clear and readable to avoid confusion. Many screen generators automatically create prompts and headings from the attribute names in the data table. These are often unsuitable for use on screens. Attribute names may be chosen for naming consistency, easy reference, or conformity with some organizational standard. They often are not chosen for easy reference by screen users. They may have to be translated into terms that are easier for the user to understand. For this reason some Data Base Management Systems maintain both a table column name and a printable report name for each attribute.

Figure 8-14 illustrates new labels that users have suggested because they are easier to understand.

Emphasis

The elements of a screen can be emphasized by using borders, blank areas, capital letters, and brightness. In addition, many screens can use color, blinking characters, and sound. A panel can be surrounded by a border to make it clear that items belong together in a panel. Blank areas around the panel can be used to provide further separation between panels. Capital letters can be used to separate titles and headings from input data.

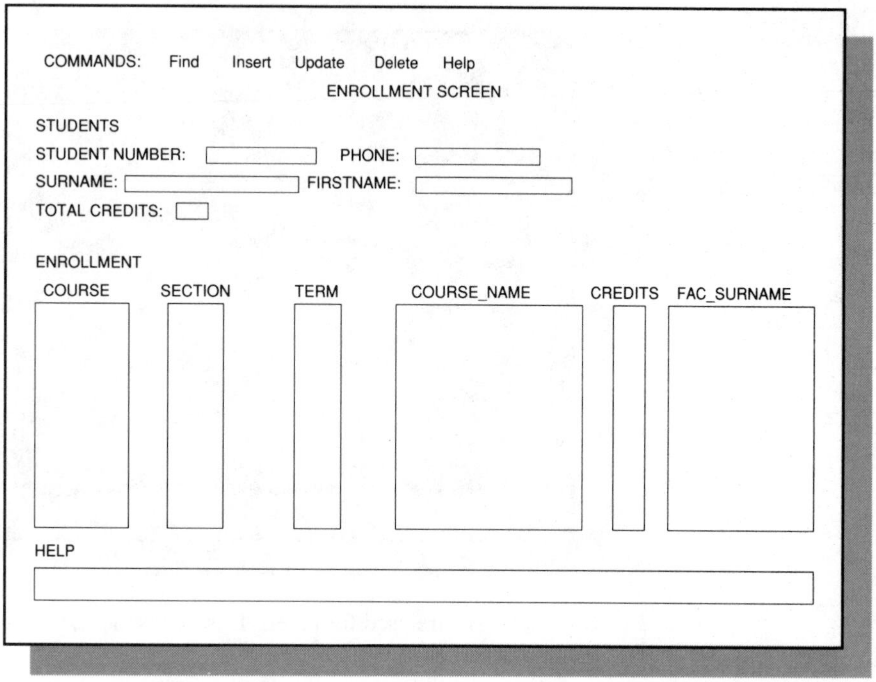

Figure 8-13

Proposed position of all panels in the Enrollment Screen before adding new labels.

```
COMMANDS:     Find    Insert    Update    Delete    Help
                        ENROLLMENT SCREEN
STUDENTS
STUDENT NUMBER: [          ]      PHONE: [              ]
SURNAME: [                ]    FIRSTNAME: [              ]
TOTAL CREDITS: [    ]


ENROLLMENT
    COURSE      SECTION       TERM        COURSE_NAME       CREDITS  FAC_SURNAME



HELP
```

If color and shading are available on a screen, they can be used to separate the intentional labels from the extensional blanks. A shaded background with clear blanks makes the screen look more like the corresponding paper form. Brightness can also be used to separate prompts from data. If data are brighter than other items on the screen, they stand out making it easy to find them for editing.

Different colors can be used to identify kinds of panels. However, colors can be dangerous if some users have screens without colors. In such cases, there must be a way of tailoring the colors or shading so users without a color screen can still access the screen. Otherwise, some colors can become invisible and data are unavailable to the user.

A color screen can be confusing to the 5 percent of the population that is color blind. The most common form is red-green color blindness in which people cannot differentiate between red and green. Blue-yellow color blindness also occurs, but is less common.

Blinking characters and sound should be reserved for severe errors and emergencies. Blinking characters can be annoying and distracting. Sound often annoys users and disturbs other workers in the office. Sound also broadcasts to everyone else in the office that the user just made a mistake.

In the example in Figure 8-14, a line border is placed around the Students and the Enrollment Panels. Shading is used to identify the blanks and the help area.

8 SCREEN

Figure 8-14

The finished Enroll-
ment Screen with bor-
der lines, emphasis
shading, and under-
standable labels.

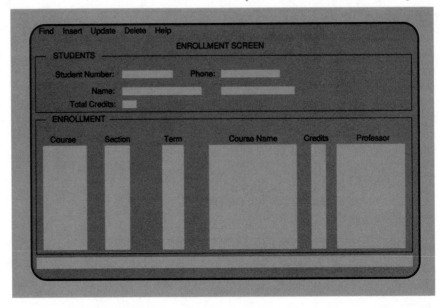

Capital letters are used for labels. Lower case letters are used for all prompts and column headings.

Screen generators usually have simple or automatic features for producing borders and emphasized areas. They can also determine the width of the field from the Data Dictionary of the database. Labels can usually be changed by typing new labels over the old ones.

At the end of the format stage, the users agree to the format of the screen that they helped to develop. They expect to get a screen that looks like the prototype. They also expect that they can enter data on the screen and have it inserted into the database.

Add Enhancements

The last stage of screen development is to turn the prototype into an "industrial strength" application screen. The finished screen needs validity checks, operator aids, help facilities, and documentation. These features can take quite a bit of time to develop and test, but they do not change the appearance of the screen. These features require some expertise to develop and the user is not involved with most of them. Since the screen appears to be finished, user may have difficulty understanding why there is still work to be done. The analyst must resist pressure to deliver the screens before this last enhancement stage.

Validity Checks

Ideally, validity checks should be performed by the Data Base Management System. If the DBMS records relationships, keys, data types, and other constraints, then it can check for mandatory relationships, unique keys, allowable values, and other constraints whenever data are inserted, updated, or deleted.

Unfortunately, many DBMS do not have such features. If they do not, then the programmer who develops the screen must design ways of performing the checks as the screen is used. The following list identifies needed checks.

- **Mandatory fields.** Some fields, particularly key fields, must have a value in them. The NOT NULL option in SQL enforces this requirement.
- **Unique values.** Keys must have unique values when new rows are entered in a table. The UNIQUE option in SQL enforces this requirement.
- **Mandatory relationships.** When the relationship between entities is mandatory, the foreign key that records the relationship must exist in both related tables. This is enforced by checking for their existence before each insert, update, and delete.
- **Unchangeable fields.** Some fields must not be changed once they have been entered. This is particularly true of fields containing accounting data and audit trails. Sometimes fields can be changed only if they are currently null. Sometimes they are provided for information only, like the name fields on the example form. It would not be reasonable to allow an operator to change the name of a course from the Enrollment Screen. The name should be changed from another screen that enters and edits new courses.
- **Hidden fields.** Some fields, such as time of transaction or operator identification are used to track a transaction. These usually do not have to appear on the screen because they can be filled in automatically by the system. If they do not appear on the screen, they cannot be updated by the operator.
- **Allowable values.** Each field must be checked for allowable values. If the DBMS has a way of enforcing data types, this is done automatically. Otherwise, separate routines have to be written to check each type of data. Checks are commonly performed for character set, values set, and range.
  - **Character set.** Characters may be restricted to numbers, letters, capital letters, or other special groups. Capital letters are often used to eliminate ambiguity between lower and upper case letters in text searches. If entry is restricted to capital letters, the screen should convert lower case letters automatically. This eliminates the need to shift to capitals at the keyboard.
  - **Value set.** Some fields are restricted to a particular set of values, such as the months of the year. Entries have to be checked against a list or against a column of a reference table. Foreign keys must be checked against the column of keys in the parent table.
  - **Range.** The range of numeric entries may be restricted to integers and to values between a lower and an upper bound. Percentages between 0 and 100 are an example.

There are five kinds of events that can trigger the various checks and aids.

- **Entry** when the cursor first enters a screen, panel, record, or field.
- **Query** before or after records are retrieved.
- **Change** after a field is changed or before or after records are inserted, updated, or deleted from the database.
- **Exit** when the cursor leaves a screen, panel, record, or field.
- **Keystrokes** when the operator presses a selected function key.

In the example screen, the STUDENT_ID must be checked for validity as soon as it is entered. The COURSE_ID, SECTION_ID, and TERM combination is checked to make sure that it exists in the SECTIONS table. It must not be duplicated in the ENROLLMENT table for this student. These checks are performed every time a course is inserted or updated. The other fields are read from files for information, so they cannot be updated. The total credits are computed when the student record is placed on the screen and again whenever course enrollments are inserted, updated, or deleted. The STUDENT_ID from the student panel is appended to the COURSE_ID, SECTION_ID, and TERM when an enrollment is inserted or updated.

Operator Aids

There are several features that can be added to a screen to improve operator efficiency. These include defaults, scroll lists, sorting, and queries.

Defaults

Some fields have predictable values that can be inserted to simplify the screen operator's task. If most clients are from the same state, the default state can be filled in automatically. In those cases where the client comes from a different state, the operator can type over the default value. If the default field is long, like country, it should be blanked as soon as anything other than a tab or carriage return is entered. On the example screen, the current term should be the default value in the TERM field.

Sometimes the default value is the value used in the same field on the previous screen. This would be the case for the surname where records are usually entered consecutively for several members of a family.

Scroll lists

Scroll lists can be used to provide the operator with a list of possible values. This may happen automatically when the field is entered or it may happen only when a help key is pressed. A selection can then be made from the list. COURSE_ID and the corresponding course name would be useful when the operator goes into an empty course field. Another list could appear to list the available sections after a course has been selected.

Sorting

Existing information is often easier to locate if lists and tables are sorted by date, key, or name. In the example screen, existing enrollments should be sorted by TERM and by COURSE_ID.

Queries

It is often helpful if the screen can be used to search for selected records. A common way of searching is to fill in the fields that are known and let the computer find all records that match. Thus the operator can enter the phone number, issue the Find command, and the student with that phone number is located. Sometimes several records might be located, and the operator would have to page through them to find the correct one. This capability is known as

Query By Example because the query is issued by providing an example of what is wanted on the screen.

SQL*Forms[7] from Oracle Corp. automatically provides a window in each screen where users can specify an SQL query to select records for display on the screen. This is handy for the few people who understand SQL and know the names of required tables and attributes in the database.

Helps

Screens are designed to be clear and easy to use. Yet users may not always know or remember what the screen is for, how to use it, what data to enter in a field, or how to recover from an error. Different levels of help are needed to overcome these problems.

Users should never be placed in a situation where they do not know what to do next. There should always be help available for them. This usually requires some layering and cross-referencing. The helps need to deal with at least the following questions.

- **How do I learn about the system?** Interactive tutorials can be very helpful in teaching new users how to use the system. It is very expensive to hold training courses for new employees. Special instructors, rooms, and equipment are often required. Employees are rarely hired in groups, so they have to wait until there is a large enough group to justify offering another course. A good interactive tutorial takes longer to design than a course, but it is available to all users whenever it is needed. It is also available whenever a user has forgotten how to perform a rarely used procedure. All large systems with users scattered in many locations, such as airline reservation systems, need a tutorial system as part of the design.

- **How do I navigate through fields and screens?** The user needs help to understand the standard commands for data entry, editing, and navigation around the screen. The user also needs to know how to delete input, cancel transactions, and log off the terminal. There should be one standard function key to provide this kind of help at any screen in the system. This is usually the F1 function key or a **?** button on a graphics screen.

  If there is a tutorial in the system, these help screens can be cross-referenced to the tutorials that cover each topic on the help screen. That way the help acts as a reminder of rules and syntax for those who have already learned the system. The tutorials act as a training vehicle and a refresher course on selected topics.

- **What does a screen do?** This requires a descriptive title and a meaningful description of each choice on the menu screen. Acronyms should be avoided because they are meaningless to the uninitiated. The UNIX™ operating system abounds with examples of meaningless acronyms. It has a command called **GREP** whose meaning is completely opaque to most new users. This leads to many errors and much wasted time. Even the full expansion of the acronym (**G**lobal **R**egular **E**xpression **P**rinter) does not enlighten most users about what the command does.

8
SCREEN

The first layer of help for a screen should be one or more screens which explain the use of the screen. The help screens should answer such questions as where data are normally obtained, when the screen is needed, what kinds of transactions are supported, and what special features must be understood.

- **What data goes in a particular field?** This layer of help explains how to enter data in a particular field on the screen. This is the kind of help that might appear in a single-line information panel at the bottom line of a screen. It should be context sensitive so the message that appears depends on the field that is currently in use. Context sensitive systems provide different help messages when a function key is pressed, depending on which screen, field, or command is being used.

- **What did I do wrong?** When an error has been identified, the user must get a clear message explaining what went wrong. Messages like "IEC071 DATA ERROR" are completely useless because they do not give the user any idea of what went wrong. A message like "Error: this field must contain a date in the form YYMMDD" tells the user what went wrong and what to do about it.

  The error message should be polite and nonthreatening. Some messages contain more violence than newscasts, crime shows, or children's cartoons. Hostile words like *abort, terminate, crash,* and *fatal* should be avoided. Such words frighten many users and make them reticent about using the system in case they bring about some disaster.

  The error message should have a standard format and it should appear in a standard place like the last line of the screen. The message should address severity, errors, and corrections. Severities range from warning, through error, to critical error. The message should not only specify what the nature of the error is, but also what the correct input is.

When validity checks, operator aids, and help facilities have been incorporated into the screen, it is ready to be tested. Each of the fields must be tested to make sure that they do not accept invalid data. Each of the commands must be tested to make sure that they perform their function.

The screen then must be tested with real users to ensure that the prompts and help messages are understandable. Ideally these are users who were not part of the specification process, so they do not bring previous knowledge to the test.

Documentation

Every system needs documentation to record the purpose and function of screens and programs for maintenance, user training, and user reference. Traditionally, the documentation has consisted of voluminous manuals that are expensive, confusing, not up-to-date, unavailable when you need them, and seldom read by the users. Because of these problems, there has been a trend toward on-line documentation.

On-line documentation has several advantages:

- **Low cost.** The documentation still has to be prepared, but does not have to be printed. It can be shipped with the software or on an update diskette. It does not require that the receiver spend time inserting update pages in a binder.

Hewlett-Packard Co.[2] calculated that if it converted to on-line documentation for 800 UNIX field engineers, it could save money on paper and distribution costs. These savings are substantial enough to buy each of them personal computers with compact disk drives to read the on-line documentation. In addition, there are savings in handling and storage of manuals.

- **Convenience.** On-line documentation is always available on the same computer that provides the software. Thus it can be used at the time that it is needed. It acts as a "cheat-sheet" for new users who have not yet learned all the commands in the system. It does not require a trip to the office or to a documentation library.
- **Intelligence.** On-line documentation can be connected to the application so help is available by using a function key or a check box. The help key can find the relevant documentation immediately. Scrolling windows can provide multiple pages. A search command can locate topics and an electronic index can jump immediately to topics. Hypertext techniques can be used to cross-reference and jump to another part of the documentation for further explanation whenever the cursor is placed on a highlighted key word. Documentation can be linked to tutorials to demonstrate difficult concepts.

Integrating Screens With Menus

The above procedure deals with the design of individual screens. Each main screen performs a specific self-contained activity. Different screens are integrated into an application by collecting groups of them in menus. This task is very simple if the screens are independent. Dependent screens are prototyped at the same time to make sure that the dependencies function properly.

The complete set of screens for an application should be designed consistently with the same format, rules, and appearance. This not only makes the system look more professional, it also makes it easier to learn and use. Selection of a single Graphic User Interface for implementation promotes such consistency.

Screens are arranged in a hierarchy. The first menu—often implemented with an action bar—selects a group of screens. In an accounting package, the action bar might contain payables, receivables, payroll, and so on. The next level of the hierarchy—usually implemented by pull-down lists—identifies individual screens like ledger, journal, and display. A menu should not contain more than about 10 items. Otherwise it gets hard to use and requires long movements with a mouse. Large systems may need a second level of pull-down menus to accommodate all the choices. Operations like insert, update, and delete are usually implemented on the selected screen by using function keys, check boxes, or another pull-down menu to select the operation.

In most business applications, the natural grouping of screens depends on the structure of the organization. Screens should be grouped so users can find most of the screens they need on the same menu. In the university example, alumni screens might be under students, external, or financial depending on which department is responsible for alumni.

8
SCREEN

The organization of the selection menu is not a crucial issue. All the menu does is select independent screens. They can be easily rearranged. Rearrangement will not impact the system in any major way, since the independent screens do not interact with each other. This makes it easy to restructure a system to respond to organizational changes and reassignment of duties. The identification of isolated processes ensures that logical units of work can be assembled in any way that is logical in the organization.

Foreign Countries and Languages

Some applications need to be accessible to users of more than one language. In Canada it is common to have to support both English and French users. International companies may have to support users in several different countries and languages. Various factors should be taken into consideration if multilingual and multinational support are required.

- **Formatting rules.** The format of common data items such as dates, numbers, and money vary from country to country.
  - **Dates and times.** There are many formats for dates. In North America it is common to use MM/DD/YY. In Europe DD/MM/YY is more common. Alphabetic forms like 25-DEC-1992 should be avoided in international applications because the alphabetic portion would have to be changed for each language. A local configuration option should be provided so that each user can specify how the internally stored date is displayed.

    Different conventions also exist for time notation. North Americans are used to seeing 9:10 am and 8:45 pm for time. This format is generally not understood outside the English-speaking community where 9.10 and 20.45 are the equivalent standard. A local configuration option can handle this.
  - **Numbers.** Numeric values are represented differently in different countries. In the United States and Canada a period is used to separate integers from fractions and a comma is used to separate the integer portion at every 3 orders of magnitude as in 1,234,567.89. In most of Europe the opposite convention is true as in 1.234.567,89. A few countries like Finland and France do not group the integers at all as in 1234567,89. A configuration option is needed to allow each user to set a preference for local display of numbers.

    Even the English words used for large numbers differ by country. In Canada, the United States, and France a billion is a thousand million. In Britain and Germany a billion is a million million. Similarly, in these countries trillion, quadrillion, etc. jump by steps of a million instead of by steps of a thousand. Written numbers of this size should be avoided.
  - **Currency.** Currency symbols are different in each country and they can consist of more than one character, either preceding or following the figures. Examples include $20 (Canada and United States), 100F (France), Fr100 (Switzerland), £10 (England), and DM25 (Germany). Again, a local configuration option is needed so the user can specify the display format. If

multiple currencies can be displayed at once, then the currency symbol must be part of the data entry.

- **Units of measure.** Different countries use different units of measure. Metric units are becoming more common, but there are still places that use feet, pounds, miles, gallons, tons, stones, and hundred weights. Even these may be different in different regions. An Imperial gallon has 160 ounces while an American gallon has 128 ounces. A British long ton is 1,016 kg, an American short ton is 907 kg, and a metric ton is 1000 kg.

  The designer of an international system must establish a standard measurement system for the whole international organization. All measurements are stored in, say, metric measures. A user configuration option can display the measures in local units by multiplying data by a conversion constant.

- **Languages.** Different languages place different requirements on the designer. The main differences have to do with word length, word order, sorting, and multilingual documents.

  - **Word length.** Text often expands in languages other than English. A label that just fits into a line in English may take two lines in French or German. Tables and screens need extra space in them to permit translation.

  - **Word order.** Command languages that are based on English syntax may become very unnatural when translated to another language. The basic order of English is Subject-Verb-Object. Arabic uses Verb-Subject-Object and Japanese uses Subject-Object-Verb. A qualifying adjective precedes the described noun in English but follows it in French and can become a part of the word in German. For this reason, menus are usually better than syntactic languages for multilingual environments. Menus also are less sensitive to keying direction than syntax based commands.

    Arabic and Hebrew[1] are keyed from right to left instead of left to right as in most other languages. This may require that tables be filled in reverse order on the screen with the identifying key on the right and other data to the left. Even in these languages, numbers are keyed from left to right. The cursor must move in the right direction depending on the kind of input.

  - **Sorting.** One would expect that a, â, ä, à, å, A, Ä, and Å would all sort before b and B. However, if the software uses the EBCDIC or ASCII internal character codes as the basis for the sort, then the result is incorrect. Unfortunately, most Data Base Management Systems perform their sorting based on the internal character codes. This problem can be solved by developing sorting algorithms based on the lexical order of the characters.

  - **Multilingual documents.** Each language presents unique problems. The problems get worse in a system that uses more than one language at a time. Several countries have more than one national language. Belgium uses Flemish and French. Canada uses French and English. India uses English and Hindi. Switzerland has four national languages, and Yugoslavia has five. Many companies have international operations that require them to communicate in more than one language. In many of these cases, applications must be able to support more than one language on a terminal.

8

SCREEN

Testing Screen Designs

The prototyping process is a continual test of the design because users are continually critiquing the design. A helpful guideline during the design is that the function of each screen element should be obvious without reading the meaning of the words. Test this by replacing all letters with a single letter, such as X. Alternately look at the screen without glasses or squint to blur the letters.

Titles, headings, command lists, panels, prompts, and entry fields should be identifiable by their position, emphasis, and relationship to other elements. Borders or white space should separate panels or major divisions of the screen.

Formal test procedures are needed to ensure that commands and validity checks work as intended. Each entry field is tested with both valid and invalid data. Check all commands and options to ensure that they work as intended.

Large complex systems may benefit from a formal human factors analysis[6] to identify cognitive problems when users utilize screens.

Testing should be done by someone who specializes in testing. The designer and builder often assume that systems will work well because they were so careful during design and implementation. The tester does not suffer from this bias because this is the tester's first contact with the product. The specialist has developed various techniques for identifying errors.

CASE Tools for Input and Output Design

Many tools are available that aid in designing forms, screens, and reports. They are found in form, screen, and report generators, and in CASE tools.

Form generators are usually specialized word processors or desktop publishing packages. They have features that make it easy to generate ruled lines, boxes, and labels in various fonts and styles. They can usually produce a master copy on a high quality printer. This can be used to reproduce many copies of the form.

Screen generators link to the Data Dictionary of the Data Base Management System. They retrieve names and attribute specifications from the DBMS and use them to generate an automatic prototype of the screen. This prototype has reasonable default characteristics for entering data into a single table. The designer must specify the tables used by the screen, the area for each table, and how many records are allowed in each table.

The generator produces a screen with labels based on attribute names and fields based on attribute types. Tables are created when more than one record is allowed on the screen. The screens usually have standard commands or function keys for inquiry, insertion, update, and deletion. Support for various kinds of hardware is usually provided automatically. Oracle's SQL*Forms Version 3.0 automatically supports several different Graphic User Interfaces. The designer can then add, modify, or delete elements of the initial prototype screen. The initial prototype can be created in about 15 minutes. The finished screen can be produced in a few hours at most.

Report generators are similar to screen generators. They also retrieve names and attribute specifications from the DBMS and use them to generate an automatic prototype of the report. They have some form of query language that selects the desired data and produces breaks and aggregates in sorted order. Report generators usually have very complex formatting facilities to deal with all possible cases of pagination, position, and printing style. They significantly reduce the work of designing a report.

Generators produce computer code that is used in the final implementation. They can usually be used to create a prototype design which then becomes part of the implementation. The implementation should not be released until it is bullet-proofed by adding enhancements to check validity, provide operator aids, and provide help messages. The computer code may be in a standard language, like COBOL, or it may be in some proprietary language or code known only to the vendor of the generator. In any case, the code should never be modified. If modifications are needed, the specifications should be changed and the code should be regenerated.

CASE tools usually have screen prototyping facilities. They can obtain information about tables, fields, and labels from the Data Dictionary in the CASE tool to produce a prototype screen. However, they usually cannot produce a finished screen so the whole process must be repeated to build the actual screen. For this reason, it is usually better to use a screen generator that is coupled to the DBMS.

Most end-users can use report generators to produce their own specialized reports with very little effort. Such reports are easy to get if the user is not interested in complex and specialized formats. The reports can be changed easily as the user's needs change. Reports can also be customized for individual users.

The system becomes sensitive to the different needs of users in different departments, different levels of management, or different stages of the learning process in their jobs. This flexibility and simplicity reduces the maintenance burden that has plagued computer systems in the past. For this reason, reports are often separated from the rest of the system and left for the user to develop.

Summary

Forms, screens, and reports are instruments of communication between people and computers. Communication is the exchange of messages with some permissible content within some context to produce a conversation.

The criteria of a well-designed form are consistency, completeness, flexible entry, economy, and organization. The basic components of a form are descriptions, intentional labels, and extensional spaces. The paper form used to capture original data should correspond as closely as possible to the screen form used for keying the data. The three main styles of forms have captions within the blanks, above the blanks, or preceding the blanks. The physical characteristics of forms are size, color, format, type, spacing, and position.

8
SCREEN

Not all input comes from forms keyed at screens. Optical scanners, bar code scanners, MICR, magnetic stripes, telephone keypads, voice, electronic instruments, operators, and files can also be used.

In database systems, screens are used primarily for data input, data updating, data deletion, and data inquiries. Screens are easiest to use when they deal with things that are concrete, visible, modifiable, interactive, familiar, consistent, simple, tailorable, selectable, and context sensitive. Menus and graphic features makes screens easier to use, but increases machine and communication costs.

Screen painters can be used to simplify the task of screen design. They create screens from basic elements. These elements are panel titles, action bars, pull-down menus, check boxes, icons, scrolling lists, scroll bars, cursors, emphasis, pop-up windows, headings, entry fields, and prompts. These components are used to construct parts of screens called panels. Panels can be categorized into logo panels, menu panels, list panels, entry panels, and information panels.

Screens can be programmable or unprogrammable. Each of these can also be graphic screens and character-oriented screens. Programmable graphic screens provide the greatest flexibility, but have the greatest cost.

Good reports should be timely, accurate, relevant, clear and economical. The components of reports are titles, headings, captions, fields, tables of contents, sorted lists, control breaks, summaries, and highlighted exceptions. Reports can be in the form of computer files, text, or graphics. The physical characteristics of printed reports are resolution, type fonts, graphics, volume, and cost. Reports can be produced on dot matrix printers, ink jet printers, line printers, laser printers, pen plotters, microfilm, and screens.

Prototyping is an effective way of communicating between designers and users. The users are able to see the results of the design and make suggestions for improvement before the design is frozen into a working system. Prototyping is done in stages of identification, formatting, and enhancing. The identification stage identifies all data elements that must be present on the screen. The formatting stage determines the position, label, and emphasis of each element. The enhancement stage adds validity checks, operator aids, and help facilities.

A Data Navigation Diagram can be used to identify the tables that are needed in a screen. The Navigation Diagram can be translated into an Action Diagram that specifies the actions to be performed by the screen. A screen may have to perform special actions that can be triggered by input to, changes in, or exits from a field, panel, or screen. These actions can consist of validating input, creating default values, filling in values from another table, performing computations, changing screens, and enabling or disabling selected commands.

Screen design can get complicated if the screens have to work in several different languages and countries. Numbers, dates, times, currencies, and units of measure are often represented differently in different countries. Different languages have different characters, word length, word order, and direction of entry. All of these can have an impact on the screen design.

When the screens have been implemented, a major part of the system has been completed. Data can now be entered into the database through the screens. Reports can be generated about the data in the database using interactive query languages like SQL. Finally batch programs can be designed to manipulate the data that has been entered in the tables.

Keywords and Phrases

Action Bar	Line Printer
Action Diagram	Menu
Bar Code Scanner	MICR
Check Box	Microfilm
Context Sensitive	Optical Scanner
Communication	Panel
Control Break	Pen Plotter
Cursor	Pop-Up Window
Data Navigation Diagram	Prototyping
Dot Matrix Printer	Pull-Down Menu
Font	Resolution
Graphics Screen	Scroll Bar
Icon	Scroll List
Ink Jet Printer	Summary
Laser Printer	Validity Check

Review Questions

1. Define each of the items in the list of keywords and phrases.
2. Specify the criteria used to identify a good form design.
3. Identify the three common styles of forms and list their advantages and disadvantages.
4. List and describe the important physical characteristics of forms.
5. List and describe technological alternatives to capturing data on forms and keying data from the forms.
6. Identify the criteria used to evaluate a good screen design.
7. List and describe the basic components used to construct screens.
8. List and describe the purpose of the different styles of screens.
9. When is a mouse an inappropriate means for selecting screen options?
10. What are the criteria for judging a good report design?
11. List and describe the purpose of components used to construct reports.
12. List and describe the different styles of reports.
13. List and describe the main features of the different classes of output devices.
14. What purpose do each of the three stages of the prototyping method serve?
15. What different functions do help messages perform?
16. What factors have to be considered when designing a screen for use in a second language, such as French or Spanish?

8
SCREEN

Problems

1. John Steele is developing a microcomputer program to record, maintain, and report data about family trees. The program must record detailed data about individual people and relationships between them. The following data about each person must be recorded. The field width is given in brackets after each field name.

   - **Name (30).** This is entered in First Middle Last order. A subroutine splits the whole name into parts as required for reports or searches. Married women always retain their maiden name for identification purposes.
   - **Number (4).** The computer assigns a sequential identification number to each new individual. A limit of 9,999 individuals is adequate for the planned market.
   - **Sex (1).** This is coded as M for male or F for female. It is a mandatory field so that marriage relationships can be validated.
   - **Birth date (12).** This allows dates like JAN 10 1942 to be displayed with a one-character code like (?) to be placed after dates to indicate questionable dates, Julian calendars, etc.
   - **Birth place (30).** This can be any optional character field.
   - **Baptism date (12).** Like birth date.
   - **Baptism place (30).** Like birth place.
   - **Death date (12).** Like birth date.
   - **Death place (30).** Like birth place.
   - **Occupation (30).** This can be any optional character field.
   - **Reference (20).** This can be any optional character field to identify the data source for later reference.

   In addition, a **marriage date** and **marriage place**, like birth date and birth place, are recorded for each marriage. The children, if any, of each marriage are treated as a separate family. The program assembles the different families later to create reports.

   Design a form for collecting information for the family tree program. The form has two possible applications. The first application is a blank form that can be printed and given to individuals who fill it in to provide data about their part of the family. The computer program prints the forms for the user. The blank forms have room for two parents and an arbitrary number of children selected by the user.

   The second application is a form that can be filled in by the computer. This form contains any data known by the computer and a blank to be filled in when no data are known. This form is a turn-around document, used to echo known information to people who can verify, correct, or add to it. It should look like the original blank form so that users are not confused by different formats. It prints only data for the actual number of children in each family.

2. Design a data entry system for the family tree program described in Question 1. Assume a microcomputer with graphics screen that can present 25 lines of 80 characters. The system must cope with the following problems.

   Data entry is performed using the form created in Question 1.

   Corrections to data entries should be simple edits or replacements of existing data on the screen. It should be possible to locate people by name or identification number. Names are frequently duplicated in the same family, so extra information like birth date or parents should be provided to identify the desired individual.

   Relationships between individuals should be easy to indicate. A person can be related to two parents, a spouse, and a number of children by that spouse. Another spouse can lead to a relationship with other children. Any of the relationships may, or may not, exist for a given individual.

   Modifications of relationships should be simple. The following are common changes that have to be made.

   - **Parents have to be added** when new data are available or deleted when data are found to be incorrect. The added parents may already exist in the database. Deleted parents may have to remain in the database because they are still related to others in the database.
   - **Spouses may have to be added, deleted, or reordered.** They may have to be added between existing spouses if the user did not know about the second of three marriages. Deleting a spouse must also delete the related children, if any. Reordering can occur if the user did not get the order right initially. The marriage date cannot be counted on to determine the order because it frequently is not known.
   - **Children may have to be added, deleted, or reordered.** The problems are the same as for spouses. Birthdates are not always available. Additionally, children often get assigned to the wrong parents. This is because sources can remember that they exist, but are not always sure which of several spouses is the parent.

3. Design a report for the family tree program in Question 1. Show the name, birth date, death date, spouse(s), and children for all descendents of one individual. Compactness is important because the report could get quite large if many generations are involved. Assume a printer with 8.5x11 inch pages and up to 132 characters per line.

4. Design a Student Application Form to be used with the STARS university system used as an example in previous chapters. The form must contain at least the information that an applicant would be expected to provide for the database as defined in Chapters 5 and 6. You may invent other information, such as deadline dates.

5. Design a screen to enter the data gathered by the Application Form designed in Question 4. Assume a non-programmable screen with 24 rows of 80 characters that the host computer can transmit in 2 seconds. The screen has the usual characters available on a typewriter, but has no special characters for drawing boxes. Characters can be underlined, blinking, or reversed.

6. Miss R. Able is responsible for inventory control in the warehouse of a large supplier of steel bars. The company stocks about 25,000 different kinds of steel bars made up of different combinations of shapes, metals, and sizes. The inventory contains everything from standard concrete reinforcing bars to special tool steels. She has to perform a delicate balancing act between running out of stock, which annoys customers, and keeping too much stock, which can be very costly. It can take up to six months to restock some of the items, since they have to be specially manufactured with a long lead time. About half of the items are manufactured by the manufacturing division of the company and the rest are purchased from about a dozen specialized manufacturers.

   Miss R. Able identified minimum stock levels that should trigger a reorder and standard order quantities that should be placed when the minimum is reached. Each week she gets a computer-printed listing of the current inventory level for each of the 25,000 stock units. She examines the list to identify those that are approaching the minimum. She then makes up an order listing the kind and quantity of steel to be purchased from each of the suppliers.

   There is a preferred supplier for many of the items. Some can be obtained from several suppliers, so she tries to call some of them to find out which one gives her the best price. She would like to check current prices for all orders, but cannot because she does not have enough time. She thinks she could save up to $100,000 per year if she had the time to check more of the items. However, it takes all of her time to get the orders placed without worrying about getting the best price. She has asked for an assistant, but has been refused because the company is trying to cut office costs.

   Half of her time is taken up reading and making calculations from the weekly stock report to identify the approximately 600 that have low inventories. The rest of her time is spent grouping the orders by manufacturer, typing the orders, and talking to suppliers.

   Suggest ways to remove some of the misery from Miss R. Able's work.

7. A mail order firm takes orders over the phone from customers with company credit cards. An operator keys the credit card number, address, phone number, catalog numbers, and quantity of each into a local microcomputer which stores them on a diskette. Each night the day's orders are transmitted to a central computer which checks the validity of the credit card number and the catalog numbers. Valid orders are transmitted to the warehouse for shipment and to accounting which makes a charge against the credit card.

Invalid orders are printed and returned to the originating office. Expediters then call the customer to determine the correct order and resubmit it. Sometimes this takes several calls because the customer may not be at home. Frequently, the customer has given an incorrect number, the telephone operator has made a keying error, or the goods are out of stock. Customers often ask whether the goods are in stock and when they will be delivered, but the operator does not have access to that information at the local microcomputer. Sometimes a keying error creates a different, but valid, catalog number and the customer receives three refrigerators instead of three pair of socks. The store takes the merchandise back, but the customer is still annoyed.

The operators use the following screen to enter orders. If more than three items are ordered, the name scrolls off the top of the screen as new lines are created for the other items. Operators have no way of scrolling the screen back if they want to see the customer's name.

Suggest ways in which the existing order entry system can be improved.

```
                    PAN WORLD DEPARTMENT STORES
                        ORDER ENTRY SYSTEM

    CUSTOMER NAME _____

    CREDIT CARD NUMBER _____

    ADDRESS LINE 1 _____
    ADDRESS LINE 2 _____
    ADDRESS LINE 3 _____

    PHONE NUMBER _____

    CATALOG NUMBER _____
    QUANTITY _____
    PRICE_____

    CATALOG NUMBER _____
    QUANTITY _____
    PRICE_____
```

8. Identify the most suitable output device for providing printed output in each of the following cases.
   a. A small business needs a printer for letters. Economy and high print quality are important. Speed and capacity are not since the business is very small.
   b. An engineering firm needs to print large computer-generated drawings with speed and accuracy.
   c. A publisher needs to print individual letters to prospects to announce that they may already be winners of a million dollars in a contest. Speed, high volume, and moderately good print quality are important.

9. You have been asked to design the user interface for a new microcomputer package that is to be sold to laboratories that have to keep track of a large number of animals. The package must produce management reports on such things as health, costs, residence duration, and kinds of experiments performed. Users are expected to range from clerks and technicians in some laboratories to administrators and scientists at other sites.

   Specify the major issues that you expect to be important in the design of this system and the major tradeoffs that must be made in selecting the most suitable kind of interface. Identify the interface features that you expect to be mandatory if this system is to be successful.

10. Gino Mozarelli is designing a computer system to take orders for a chain of pizza shops. Customers dial HOT-FOOD to reach a central switchboard that takes their order and enters it into a computer system that dispatches it to the nearest of many local shops. The chain guarantees delivery of the correct order within a half hour or the pizza will be free, so it is important that the system is fast and error-free.

    Each pizza ordered can be in one of three sizes: regular, large, and humongous. It can be topped with one or more portions of any of the following toppings: extra cheese, pepperoni, ham, peppers, pineapple, and mushrooms. Customers can order any number of the following drinks: cola, diet cola, uncola, root beer, unbeer, and coffee. The customer must provide a phone number, address, and optional directions such as "go to back door."

    Customers frequently want to know the price of each item. They often change their mind about size, quantity, toppings, and drinks.

    There are many repeat customers who order the same thing on a regular basis, so the system stores the last order and automatically displays it when the phone number is keyed in. This makes it easy for customers to order "the usual" and also makes it easy to track the status of orders if a customer calls about an order that has not arrived or needs to be changed. It also identifies multiple orders from the same address, which often signifies pranksters who do not intend to pay for the order.

    The computer checks the address and phone number against a list of places that have previously ordered food and then not been there to pay for it. The switchboard operator is warned about previous bad orders and tells the customer that the order will not be taken. The computer automatically computes the price of each item and the total price including sales tax. It also computes the required delivery deadline half an hour from order time. Using an address file, it computes the nearest shop and dispatches the order to it.

    Design an input screen to be used by the switchboard operator. Assume an alphanumeric screen with 25 lines of 80 characters. Repeat the design assuming a Graphic User Interface.

Project

a. **Design the forms, screens, and reports for your project.** If there are a large number of them, discuss with your project supervisor, the possibility of implementing a subset of them. At a minimum, there should be at least two of each. If possible, choose at least one screen that requires multiple panels.

b. **Draw a Data Navigation Diagram** for each screen and report you design.

c. **Prototype screens.** If you have prototyping tools available, work with a project user—or a classmate as a surrogate—to prototype the screens. Document the requirements agreed to by the user or surrogate at the end of the identification, formatting, and enhancement stages. Print out a sample screen.

d. **Screen and report sketches.** If you do not have prototyping tools available, sketch the screen and report designs on grid paper, being careful that all information looks neat and all labels and fields fit on the screen. Specify the dimensions of the screen you are designing in characters.

Cooking with Cal Oreez Case

Cal and I chatted last night. He was wondering how his information system is coming along. He is getting concerned that all he has seen is a lot of paperwork.

I told him that an information system, like a great meal, takes much planning.

He pointed out that even with the greatest meal, you eventually must get cooking. He says he can sometimes imagine how a recipe will taste, but the real test is when you lick the spoon. He sounded hungry for some tangible results.

I told him that he should soon have something tangible to see, if not to taste. I suggest that you relieve some of his anxiety by providing him with screens to go with the existing database. He can use the screens to enter data. That will keep him so busy that you will have some breathing room to finish the project.

He needs to enter data on books, recipes, ingredients, meals, events, and friends. I suggest that you start by providing screens to enter these data items. Find the best cook that you know and employ that person as a surrogate user to help you prototype the screens. If you do not have any friends who can cook, consult a cookbook and figure out what is needed. If you do not have a screen generator available, sketch out the screens on paper. Make sure that all of the data will fit on the screen. You should produce the following items:

a. **Data Navigation Diagram** for each screen.

b. **Requirements agreed to** by your cook at the end of the identification, formatting, and enhancement stages of the most complex screen.

c. **Sketches or implementations** of the screens and explanations of their use.

d. **Sketch of an input form** to match the recipe input screen.

e. **Sketch of a report** listing candidate guests for an event.

g. **Amended documents** for previous stages of analysis if you discover new requirements. Include a copy of the data definitions for each file used in the screens you design. These provide continuity when Cal examines your design.

8 SCREEN

References

1. Becker, Joseph D., "Arabic Word Processing", *Communications of the ACM*, July 1987, Vol. 30, No. 7, pp. 600-610.

2. Hamilton, Robert, and Dennis Hamilton, "On-Line Documentation Delivers", *Datamation*, July 1, 1990, pp. 45-50.

3. Hayes, Frank and Nick Baran, "A Guide to GUIs", *Byte*, July 1989, pp. 250-257.

4. Hoeber, Tony, "Face to Face with Open Look", *Byte*, December 1988, pp. 286-296.

5. IBM Corp., *Systems Application Architecture: Common User Access, Panel Design and User Interaction, IBM Corporation, Boca Raton, Florida, SC26-4351-0, 1987.*

6. Mantei, Marilyn M., and Toby J. Teorey, "Cost/Benefit Analysis for Incorporating Human Factors in the Software Lifecycle", *Communications of the ACM*, April 1988, Vol. 31, No. 4, pp. 428-439.

7. Oracle Corp., *SQL*Forms Designer's Reference*, Oracle Part Number: 3304-V2.0, Oracle Corporation, Belmont, California, 1986.

8. Scheifler, R. W., and J. Gettys, "The X-Window System", *Transactions on Graphics, Special Issue on User Interface Software, Part I*, ACM, 1987, Vol. 5, No. 2, pp. 78-109.

9. Tufte, Edward R., *The Visual Display of Quantitative Information*, Cheshire, Connecticut: Graphics Press, 1983.

Chapter 9

Design With Structure Charts

	DATABASE (WHAT)	PROGRAMS (HOW)	BENEFITS (WHY)	NETWORK (WHERE)	REAL TIME (WHEN)	SKILLS (WHO)
USER CONCEPT	Entity Relationship	Activity	Intangible Benefit	Map		Organization Design
DESIGNER CONCEPT	E-R Diagram	A-E Diagram	AHP	Network		Skills Responsibility
USER DETAIL	Forms Screens	Processes Data	Tangible Benefit	Work Volume	Discrete Events	Transition Training
DESIGNER DETAIL	EER Diagram	Data Flow Diagrams	Benefit-Cost	Partition	Transition Diagrams	Methodology Tools
BUILDER CONCEPT	Normal Form Relations	Structure Chart	Function Points	System Architecture	Specifications	Learning
BUILDER DETAIL	Files	Screens Specifications	Costs	Network Specs	Interfaces	4GL CASE

Objectives

Chapter 7 showed how Data Flow Diagrams can be used to identify all the processing components of an information system. The viewpoint of the data was adopted so the data could be followed as it was modified by all of the different processes involved in the system. A Data Flow Diagram is an analytical tool that provides a structured way in which the analyst can identify existing components in a system and use them to discover the components that are required in a system.

Chapter 8 showed how some of these processes are implemented using prototyping with high-level screen and report generators. This chapter deals with the design of the rest of the processes. These processes usually involve automated manipulation of stored data to transform it into new stored data. The processes are often triggered at regular time intervals, such as a monthly billing cycle. They often involve no interaction with people.

In this chapter the analytical data displayed in the Data Flow Diagram are converted to design data. The emphasis is on designing a new system that incorporates the requirements identified during the analysis phase. Since the system must be executed by a computer, the system is viewed from the point of view of the computer. The processes are viewed as a set of functions that are organized into a hierarchical command structure. This view corresponds to the way programs are written and executed.

The main problem is to identify a set of modules that are easy to design, construct, test, and maintain. The modules should be manageably small. They should be as independent of each other as possible, so they can be removed from the system, modified, and returned without affecting the rest of the system. The methods in this chapter are suitable for batch systems where prototyping is inapplicable. In this chapter the reader learns to:

- **Convert a Data Flow Diagram** into a Structure Chart that shows the command structure and data flow between program modules.

- **Design cohesive modules** that perform a single well-defined function.

- **Design independent modules** that are linked by clear simple interfaces that are not strongly coupled to each other.

- **Identify a satisfactory span of control** and size for modules.

Modular Design Criteria

The previous chapter dealt with the design of screens and reports which can be produced by prototyping with screen and report generators. This chapter and the next deal with the design of "hard-core" applications that are difficult to prototype because they do not involve much user interaction.

Common examples are batch-processing programs that periodically perform a standard function such as billing or payroll calculations. Such applications read data from the database, perform some manipulation, and write new data to the database. They do this for a large number of records, so efficiency is important. They have a long life, so maintainability is also important.

When the payroll is calculated, wage rates and hours worked are used to compute deductions and payments. Checks or bank deposits are produced and various accounting records are updated to recognize the payments and deductions. Data entry is usually not an important part of the process. Reporting is also a minor part of the process. Algorithms that perform the transformations are often a major part of the process.

There are many examples of programs that cannot be coded with application generators. These include commercial software which has to operate more flexibly or more efficiently than is possible with generated code. Programs like Data Base Management Systems and Application Generators themselves are also included.

Such applications may be coded in either a 3GL or a 4GL depending on the nature of the process, the availability of an Application Generator, and the efficiency constraints on the system. The designer of such computer applications has to keep several objectives in mind.

- **Efficient Production.** This means that systems must be completed on time and within budget.
- **Error-free Programs.** This means that the design should be as correct as possible and that if there are errors in the design, they should be easy to trace and eliminate.
- **Maintainable Programs.** This means that software has to be easy to modify or expand to incorporate changing needs and specifications.

The design of a computer application is very much like the design of an organization made up of people. Human organizations are hierarchical with a boss in charge and with several workers performing functions assigned by the boss. The hierarchy may have several levels as the task of the organization is refined into more detailed tasks. The workers at the bottom of the organization are typically very specialized and perform a very limited set of tasks. This allows them to become adept at their tasks and simplifies the organizational structure.

A computer application also needs a boss and several workers who specialize in particular tasks. The parts of an application that correspond to workers in a human organization are called programs, subroutines, functions, tasks, paragraphs or modules in different computer languages. These modules are more likely to achieve the objectives of being efficient, error-free, and maintainable if they possess the following properties:

- **Hierarchy.** The program is hierarchically structured so each module provides an overview of the program logic below it. A module controls modules after it in the hierarchy. It is controlled by other modules above it.
- **Cohesion.** Each module performs only one well-defined function that can be easily understood by anyone who has to modify it. The identification, in Chapter 7, of isolated subsystems that respond to a specific external event helps to define cohesive systems.
- **Uncoupling.** Each module has access only to the specific data that it needs to do its job. Changes to the module do not produce a HICCUP (Horribly Inconvenient Computer Crash Under Pressure) in other modules. In Chapter 7, data flows were usually into and out of normalized tables. This helps to ensure that only necessary data is accessed by the routine.
- **Autonomy.** The higher-level modules are unaffected by minor changes in specifications, data structure, or file structure.
- **Reusability.** The module makes use of utility modules to perform common standardized tasks. They are coded and tested only once but are used in many places. This concept is sometimes called reusable code.
- **Explicitness.** A good software design should be like an "X-Rated" movie. It should reveal all the structural detail and leave nothing of any importance to the imagination. This explicitness makes it easier to modify and maintain computer programs because all necessary information about data and control is visible.

This chapter explains how to incorporate these characteristics into a new system. It defines a set of symbols that can be used in designing systems, a set of rules for transforming Data Flow Diagrams into Structure Charts, and a set of guidelines for avoiding bad designs.

9
Structure

Structure Charts

Structure Charts graphically depict the architecture of a software system. They show the control relationship between modules, the data passed between them, and the control information passed between them. The architecture is shown from the point of view of the software system. This is different from the data viewpoint used in Data Flow Diagrams.

As with Data Flow Diagrams, there are specific graphic symbols for each element of the diagram. These symbols are illustrated in Figure 9-1 along with their Data Flow Diagram equivalents. Some elements have no equivalents in Data Flow Diagrams. Each element is described below.

- **Module.** A module is a set of programming instructions that can be invoked by name. It is the program or subroutine that performs the functions included in a process in a Data Flow Diagram. Files or tables are not shown on a Structure Chart because they are not part of the module. They are part of the external world from the point of view of a program module. A module may be

Translation of Data
Flow Diagram notation
into Structure Chart
notation.

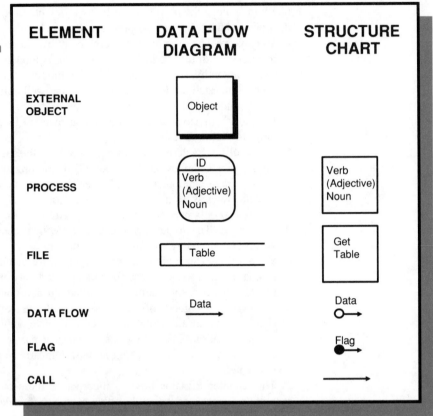

needed to read the table or write to it. Alternately, the read or write may be
performed by lines of code within the module. Specifications of the internal
structure of a module are covered in the next chapter. A module is symbolized
by a rectangular box. A module available from a library of standard programs
is distinguished by a vertical bar drawn on each side of the module.

- **Module name.** The name of the module is a statement of its job. It indicates
  what the module does each time that it is called. The name should consist of a
  strong active verb followed by a single direct object. The verb indicates what
  the module does and the object indicates the receiver of the action. Sometimes
  modifiers can be used to clarify the function of the module. These are the
  same guidelines used to name processes, so the process names on Data Flow
  Diagrams can usually be used as module names.
- **Call.** A module often calls on other modules to perform specific tasks. The
  call is symbolized by an arrow. The arrowhead points from the calling module
  to the module being called. Control of the process passes to the called module
  until the task is completed. Control returns to the calling module after
  completion of the task.

- **Data.** A calling module may pass data to a called module. It also may receive data from the called module. The data are the same data shown on the flows of a Data Flow Diagram. However, they are symbolized by a small arrow with an open circle at its tail and a name above or beside it. The arrow points in the direction of the flow. If the data flow in both directions, there is an arrowhead at both ends and an open circle in the middle of the arrow.
- **Flag.** A calling module may exchange control information with a called module. Control information is information about what the module is supposed to do or a report about what the called module did or found out. This information is called a flag. The difference between data and a flag is that data are related to the problem and flags are related to the solution method. Data are eventually received from users, stored in tables, or sent to users. Flags are used by the modules to communicate with each other about processing details. They are of no interest to users and they have no equivalent in a Data Flow Diagram. They are symbolized by arrows, like data arrows, except that the circles are solid, not hollow.

  Flags serve three purposes: reporting, controlling, and directing.
  - **Reporting flags** pass status information from the called module to the calling module. The calling module can then test the flag and take some action to deal with the situation described by the flag. Error codes and End-Of-File (EOF) codes are common examples of reporting flags.
  - **Control flags** going from the calling module to the called module tell the called module which of several options to select.
  - **Directive flags** from the called module to the calling module tell the calling module which of several options to select.

  Figure 9-2 is a Structure Chart illustrating the design process followed in this book. It is an expanded version of the Data Flow Diagram in Figure 7-3.

  The rectangular box at the extreme left is the **"Boss"** module that controls all of the other modules. Its name indicates the function of the entire program. Its only equivalent in a Data Flow Diagram is the single process in the Context Diagram. The boxes at the right are **"Worker"** modules that perform single lower-level tasks for their respective bosses. The boxes in the middle are workers for the boss on the left and bosses for the modules on the right.

  The boxes are not necessarily executed in order from top to bottom, although it is a good idea to draw them that way if possible.

  Some approaches—such as the Michael Jackson,[5] De Marco,[2] and HIPO[6] methods—draw the Structure Chart with the boss at the top and the workers arranged below. Each module has a box that is the same size. Modules are connected with curved or diagonal arrows. This resembles the format of organization charts. The horizontal format used here has several advantages.
- **Shape.** The boss module is at the top, the diagrams get very wide and hard to draw on narrow vertical pages. The horizontal format used in Figure 9-2 makes it much easier to include the data flows and their labels since both the

9 **Structure**

Figure 9-2
A Structure Chart
of the analysis and
design process
derived from Figure
7-3.

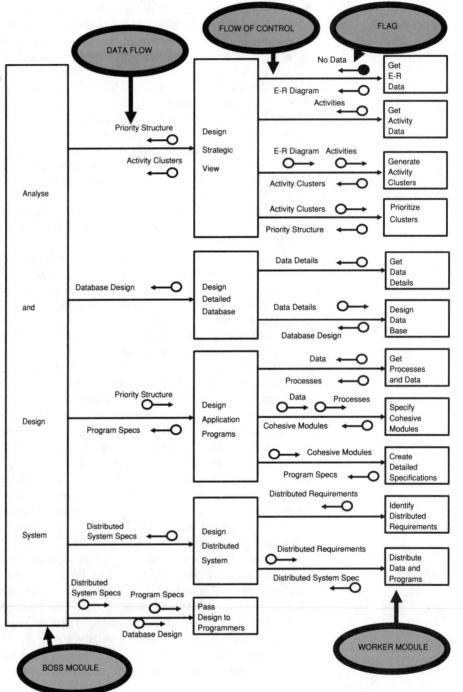

Figure 9-3
Warnier-Orr notation
for the Structure Chart
in Figure 9-2.

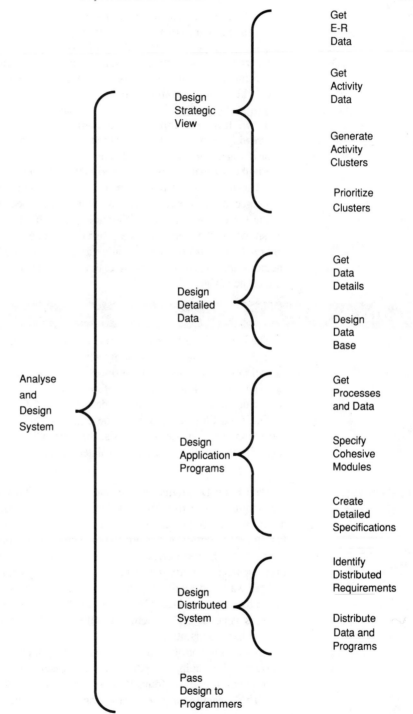

words and the arrows are horizontal. The shape of the structure chart is usually similar to that of a standard page.

- **Character set.** All elements can be produced on a standard keyboard. Only horizontal lines, vertical lines, and alphabetic characters are needed. All data and flag arrows and their labels are horizontal. This makes them easy to enter on a keyboard or graphic screen.
- **Implied meaning.** Hierarchies in organization charts traditionally have been drawn from the top down to convey the relative rank of the members. Drawing them from left to right shifts the emphasis from rank to concepts of progress and refinement of detail.

Another format that is often used is the Warnier–Orr[7] format shown in Figure 9-3. The modules are placed in the same position as in Figure 9-2. The main difference is that a brace is used at the left to connect all modules that are called by the same boss. Another difference is that the data flows and parameters are not shown on the diagram. As a result the Warnier–Orr diagram is easier to draw and read, but it is not as informative as the Structure Chart. Later in the chapter, methods are presented for using data and flag information to improve the structure of the design.

Converting a DFD to a Structure Chart

The logical Data Flow Diagram is the starting point in the process of developing a Structure Chart because it has several desirable features:

- All inputs and outputs are defined.
- All needed subfunctions are defined.
- No unneeded subfunctions are defined.

The Data Flow Diagram can be converted to a Structure Chart by using a process called Transform Analysis. Structure Charts define the command structure of programs that implement isolated modules in a Data Flow Diagram.

Transform Analysis

Data Flow Diagrams identify the processes that must be performed and the data required to perform them. They imply a processing order since the processes are drawn in a sequence. They do not provide information about iteration, error handling, or control of the processes. The design process adds these features to the system. The most critical problem in design is the identification of groups of processes that simplify the structure of the final system.

One way to design a structure is to define a worker module to correspond to each process on the Data Flow Diagram. Next define a boss module that calls the workers as needed. This method usually leads to very complicated boss modules that are hard to maintain.

Another method is to identify "natural" groupings of processes. Usually the most natural grouping is to divide the processes into an input group, a processing group, and an output group. Processes need valid data before they can do their job. They usually produce some transformed data. These data usually need further transformation to make them useful to people or other systems. The most elementary iteration is to get good data, process it, and format it for presentation.

Transform Analysis consists of identifying the major inputs, major outputs, and the central transform in the Data Flow Diagram. These are transformed into a Structure Chart that has a hierarchical organization, somewhat like a military command. Like the units of an army, each module has its own job, it performs the job only when given orders from above, and it communicates only with superiors and subordinates. The stages of analysis are:

- **Identify the main modules** on the Data Flow Diagram.
- **Rearrange the main modules** so they are called by the boss module.
- **Change graphics and names** to correspond to Structure Chart notation.
- **Add utility modules** to access files and output devices.
- **Add Flags** to provide control information.

Identify Main Modules

There are three basic kinds of main modules: input, processing, and output modules. They are identified by following the flows in the Data Flow Diagram forward and asking at each process, "Is this still input?" The output processes are similarly identified by following the outputs backward to the beginning and asking "Is this still output?" The parts between the inputs and the outputs are the processing modules. The chains of processes that are recognizable as input or output are organized into input and output modules.

The generic Data Flow Diagram in Figure 9-4 illustrates the process of identifying inputs, outputs, and processes. There are two input streams, two main processes, and two output streams. The first input stream gets A and sorts it to make it ready for processing. Transformations like sorting, summarizing, aggregating, editing, matching, or exploding data are just manipulations of the data input. They can be thought of as part of the process of getting suitable input data. As a result, they can be collected together under a single main subroutine that is responsible for getting good input data. The second process that gets B is just a simpler version of such an input routine.

Similarly the processes that aggregate and print E are really just part of a single task that outputs E. Print D is a simpler version of an output task. Transformations like aggregate, sort, format, or edit are all part of the process of generating output. The remaining processes—First Process and Second Process—are the central transforms that convert input into output. Figure 9-5 illustrates how this generic process is converted into a Structure Chart. Note that the data flows between processes have been replaced by a flow from the process to the boss and from the boss to the next process. A hierarchy of command has been superimposed on the modules to orchestrate their activities. A boss has been created and the processes have been turned into subroutines. Sometimes modules like **Output E** are created to supervise several related modules. This reduces the span of control for the boss module and simplifies the structure so it is easier to maintain.

Figure 9-6 repeats the Data Flow Diagrams developed for the Select Courses process in Figures 7-19 and 7-20. It illustrates the starting point of the conversion process. In the Select Courses example the inputs and outputs are simple single processes and do not need further refinement or aggregation.

In a 3GL environment, Generate Sorted List might be a complex module that needs several worker modules to identify priority factors, organize the data, and sort by priority. However, in a 4GL environment such tasks are often handled by a single query in a language like SQL. Thus the boss module is often quite a simple module that calls each of the other main modules, checks to see that they have done their work, and passes data to the next called module.

Figure 9-4

A generic Data Flow
Diagram illustrating the
identification of inputs,
processes, and outputs.

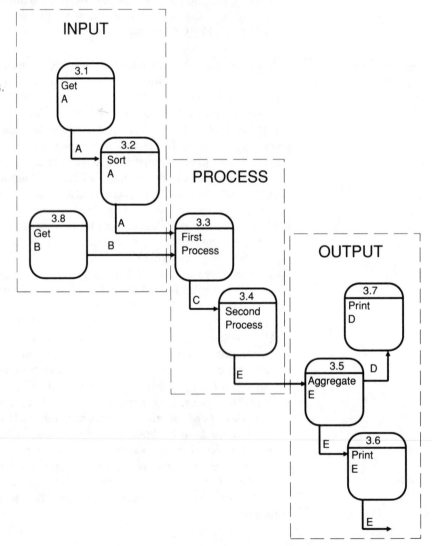

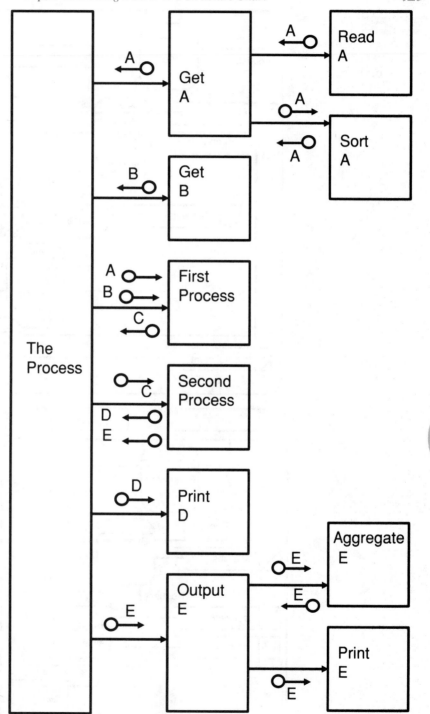

Figure 9-5
The Structure Chart derived from the Data Flow Diagram in Figure 9-4.

9
Structure

Figure 9-6
The Select Courses
Processes and an ex-
plosion of Process 4.3.

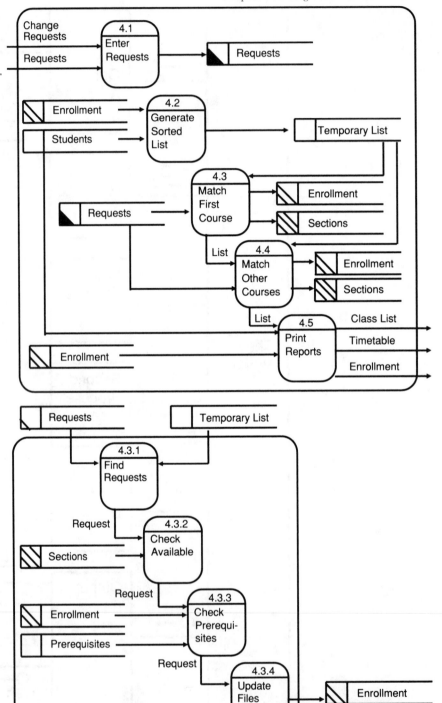

Rearrange Main Modules

When main modules have been identified, they are rearranged. The diagonal sequence used for Data Flow Diagrams becomes a vertical sequence that is used for the Structure Chart. Figure 9-7 illustrates this conversion.

Note that the flows from files have been removed during the rearrangement. In a 3GL environment, they are often replaced with modules that read the file or write to the file. Such modules are frequently quite complex because they involve editing, formatting, and validity checking. In a 4GL environment, they are usually single statements. They can be included as part of the processing inside the module that needs or produces the data. They reappear as read and write statements in program specifications in the next chapter. For the moment they can be thought of as having been swallowed up inside the process modules.

The four subprocesses in the explosion of process 4.3 are included in Figure 9-7. Note that module 4.3 acts as a boss module to supervise the operations of subordinate processes in an Explosion Diagram. Again, file flows have been suppressed. Flows between processes have been replaced by calls from 4.3, the boss module. Explosions in Data Flow Diagrams correspond to another level of modules in the Structure Chart. As with Data Flow Diagrams, each successive level of refinement of complicated structures can be shown on a separate page.

Figure 9-7

A conceptual rearrangement of the Select Courses processes.

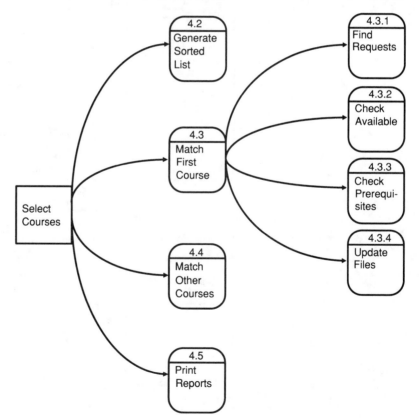

9

Structure

**Change Graphics
and Names**

The process blocks become module rectangles. The data flows become arrows with an open circle at the end. The names of the processes should be strong active verbs with an object to describe the receiver of the activity. If new boss modules are created, they need such names also. Figure 9-8 shows what happens when the graphics have been transformed. Of course, Figure 9-7 is only an intermediate conceptual step. In practice, there is no need to draw this diagram.

Figure 9-8

The Select Courses processes with revised Structure Chart graphics.

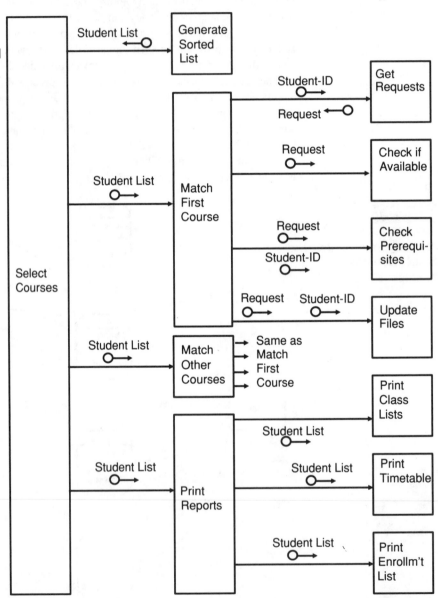

Add Utility Modules and Control Flags

The last step in transforming a Data Flow Diagram to a Structure Chart is to add the control flags and utility modules as shown in Figure 9-9. The control parameters are flags that indicate whether a module has completed its job satisfactorily. When a boss module calls a worker to do a job, it needs to know whether the job was satisfactorily completed. It could be incomplete because the worker ran out of data, found an error in the input, or found an unacceptable

Figure 9-9

The Select Courses Structure Chart with control flags added.

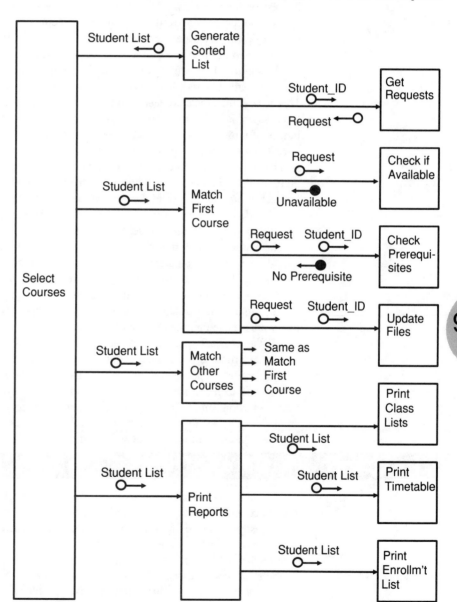

9

Structure

situation such as an insufficient balance when paying a bill. If such a problem occurs, the boss module needs to know so it can take alternate action. These control parameters are symbolized by an arrow with a solid dot on the tail.

There are certain tasks that reappear frequently in applications. These include editing input, checking for errors, posting error messages, reading files, updating files, converting data, and performing complex calculations such as computing interest or depreciation. These functions are needed in several applications if they cannot be performed directly by the implementation language. It is a good idea to design separate modules to perform each of these tasks. A 4GL can perform most of these tasks directly so separate modules may not be needed.

These reusable modules can be stored in a program library and called whenever they are required. They are coded and tested once and used many times. This makes maintenance easier and it also helps to enforce standards for such tasks as error checking, report formatting, and message presentation. Such a library of reusable code can reduce the design and coding effort in an organization. Many modules of the next program will already exist in tested form.

The finished Structure Chart can serve as an organizational map of the program to be developed. It identifies each of the modules needed in the final product. It provides job titles for each of the modules to describe briefly what the modules do. It also specifies the information needed by each module and the information that each module delivers to its boss.

The nature of the modules depends on whether they are primarily boss modules or worker modules. Boss modules perform management tasks, use low volumes of data, use many control flags, and use mainly validated data. Worker modules perform detailed tasks, use high volumes of data, use few control flags, and use mainly unvalidated data. Middle level modules that are part boss and part worker have intermediate characteristics.

All the external specifications have been provided. Now the internal details can be specified so programmers can code the logic of the modules. Before the analyst begins to specify the internal details, these external specifications should be checked to make sure that they are correct. This involves checks for maximum cohesion, minimum coupling, and span of control. If modifications result from these checks, they should be reflected in the Structure Charts and the Data Flow Diagrams from which they were derived to simplify later maintenance.

Testing the Structure Chart

The analyst's objective in designing the Structure Chart is to produce a program architecture that is easy to understand, code, and maintain. The objective is more easily achieved if the modules have the characteristics of a black box, which are information hiding, independence, and nesting.

- **Information hiding.** The internal structure of a black box can be hidden from the user, who does not have to understand how it works to use it. The user only needs to know what inputs to give the black box and what outputs to expect from it. When file structures or machine, language, and vendor specific details are hidden, then portability, maintenance, and ease of conversion are improved.

- **Independence.** Black boxes act independently, except where they are connected by standard interfaces. They can be modified to have new or different features as long as their interfaces conform to the accepted standard. This means that problems can usually be traced to a single black box which can then be repaired or replaced.

- **Nesting.** Black boxes can contain other black boxes. This hides details from the user and makes it easier for the user to concentrate on the functions of the black box instead of the contents.

A stereo sound system as illustrated in Figure 9-10 is a good example of a common system composed of black boxes. The tuner, tape player, amplifier, and speakers behave as black boxes. Few of us know how they work inside, yet we are able to use them regularly and effectively. They are connected using standard interfaces that consist of a pair of wires for each speaker, four pairs of wires for the tape player, and two more pairs for the tuner.

The components are interchangeable, so it is possible to purchase different standard components that can replace existing ones. An AM tuner can be replaced with an AM/FM tuner that provides new functions. An analogue tuner can be replaced with a digital tuner or a remote controlled tuner. The tape player and the amplifier continue to function properly.

One of the reasons for this interchangeability is that each module has been designed to be independent. For instance, each module needs a power supply and each module contains its own power supply. It would be possible to design a stereo system that relied on a single common power supply, but it would make the interfaces much more complicated. Standards would have to be set for the kind and amount of power needed by all components. The design of new or replacement components would be more difficult and the likelihood of design problems would increase.

9
Structure

A stereo sound system viewed as a set of black boxes connected by signal wires.

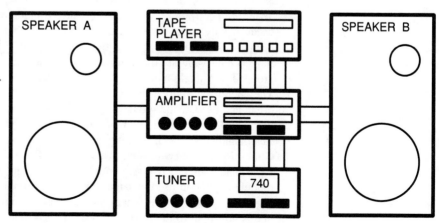

The black box principle is used in designing most mechanical devices such as cars, computers, and cameras. Nature has even designed our bodies with black box modules that process food, move our arms, or think about black boxes. The modules in the Structure Charts developed earlier in the chapter need to be tested to see if they have the characteristics of black boxes. These characteristics prevent many errors in design, specification, coding, and maintenance. The test is performed by examining cohesion, coupling, span of control, and module size.

Testing for Cohesion

Cohesion is a measure of how closely the instructions, processes, or statements within a module are related. It is the degree to which a module serves a single purpose rather than a multiplicity of purposes. In a module with high cohesion, all instructions contribute toward the complete performance of a single well-defined function. This makes the module easy to understand and easy to maintain. Therefore, high cohesion is desirable. A module with poor cohesion has multiple goals, none of which are clear-cut. This makes it difficult to modify and maintain.

Cohesion is an indication of how closely a module resembles a black box. It indicates the independence of the module. Cohesion measures the ability to hide information so users and maintainers only need to know the inputs and outputs to understand how a module is used.

One way of evaluating the cohesion of a module is to identify the type of cohesion in the module. Cohesion cannot be evaluated numerically, but types of cohesion can be ranked from best to worst as follows:[1,4,8,9]

- **Functional cohesion.** Everything in the module contributes to accomplishing the same specific, discernible, easily specified task. The task may be simple or complex, but there is a single task. This makes it easy to maintain the module because a programmer can determine what to expect inside by looking at the name of the function. A functionally cohesive module is recognized by a name that has a strong verb acting on a clear noun to perform a single task that is clearly within the scope of the system.

- **Sequential cohesion.** The functions of the module are in the same module because they must be executed in sequence. The result of one function becomes the input to the next function. Sequential cohesion occurs when a sequence of processes that follow the same path in the Data Flow Diagram are grouped in a single module. They are like the processes on an assembly line. They could be divided into separate modules, but the separate modules are often not needed individually. No extra control flags are required. If the individual processes are complex or long enough, they can be split off into functionally cohesive modules.

- **Communicational cohesion.** This occurs when subtasks in a module use the same data, but are not sequentially related. The various functions of the module happen to use the same input data or produce outputs for use by the same next module. The functions are otherwise unrelated and the output of one is not input to the next. An example is a module that computes a Grade

Point Average, counts credits earned, and checks for required prerequisites. All of these tasks require courses and grades, so they are performed at the same time. This kind of cohesion is usually not a problem. If the definition of GPA changes, then the other functions likely have to be modified. Communicational modules can be partitioned into simpler modules with functional cohesion.

- **Procedural cohesion.** This occurs when the functions in a module are grouped on the basis of the order of their occurrence. They are together because they are part of the same sequence or repetitive loop in a program. They are *not* linked by data fed from one to the other as in sequential cohesion. They do *not* work on the same data as in communicational cohesion. The problem occurs when several logically unrelated functions happen to occur in the same processing loop. An example is calculating the mean of one list followed by the standard deviation of another list. The order is arbitrary and either could be deleted without affecting the other.

  The problem with such cohesion is that the design of the module is governed by the execution sequence of the program rather than by the logical requirements of the task. If the requirements change, the sequence may change in ways that are very difficult to maintain. Procedural modules can be partitioned into simpler modules with functional cohesion.

- **Temporal cohesion.** This cohesion occurs when functions are placed in the same module only because they have to be performed at the same time. A typical example is the inclusion of all initialization or termination functions in the same module. The only thing that opening files, setting counters, and initializing constants have in common is that they must all occur before a processing loop can begin. When these functions are grouped together, the functions that read files, count data, or use constants are no longer independent. They depend on the combined function for survival. Anyone modifying any of them must also modify the initialization and closing routines. It is logically more consistent to let the processing modules look after their own initializations and terminations, if possible.

- **Logical cohesion.** Logical cohesion occurs when a module performs several functions that are logically similar but procedurally different. An example is an edit module that validates numeric inputs even though they may be integers, fractions, binary numbers, or phone numbers. Each of these requires different checks and should have different modules. Logically cohesive modules usually share some code, such as checking that all characters are numeric. The different functions should be split into separate modules and the shared code should be placed in a separate utility module.

  The problem with this kind of cohesion is that the boss needs to know how the module works. It has to pass additional parameters that specify which version of the function is required *this* time. When such a function is maintained, changes to one part of the function may inadvertently harm another part. These modules suffer from an identity crisis because they try to be all things to all people. These are usually the most difficult modules to maintain.

9 Structure

● **Coincidental cohesion.** This level of cohesion occurs when there is no clear reason for having the functions in the module together. These modules occur when unstructured programs have been arbitrarily cut into pieces to reduce module size. They may also occur when "clever" programmers place functions together because they share some small algorithm. This may save some memory or some execution time, but it complicates maintenance massively. Such illogical designs are pathological and should never be tolerated. They are very difficult to maintain. The functions should be separated into functionally cohesive modules.

It is not always possible to achieve the highest level of cohesion, functional cohesion, but that should be the aim of a good design. Cohesion problems can be identified by examining the Structure Chart. The name, the organization of the modules, the data, and the flags passed between the modules give the designer clues about possible problems with the modules. The remainder of this section is based on Dolan's[3] analysis of clues to problems, the cause of the problem, and the cure for the problem.

CLUE #1:	**Module name has connectives like *and, or, then,* or *commas.***
CAUSE:	The module performs multiple functions.
CURE:	Split the module into single-function modules.

In Figure 9-11 there are three separate functions being performed. Timetables, Class Lists, and Enrollment lists should each be in separate modules. The module has only logical cohesion because it performs three different printing tasks. Splitting it produces three modules with functional cohesion. It is very likely that the three reports are needed separately at different points in the system. For instance, individual timetables may be needed whenever a student changes course selections. If separated now, the individual modules can be used whenever needed.

Figure 9-11

A module that performs multiple functions should be split.

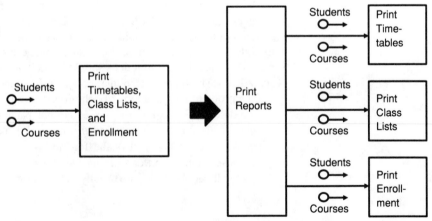

CLUE #2:	**Weak module name.**
CAUSE:	The module performs multiple functions.
CURE:	Split the module into separate functions.

A module name can have the required verb and object and still not give a clear idea of what it is doing. This happens if the name contains weak verbs like INITIALIZE, DO, PROCESS, or TERMINATE or weak objects like DATA, INFORMATION, INPUT, OUTPUT, NAMES, PARAMETERS, or WORKSPACE. Resorting to names like that often means that the module contains several unrelated functions. The analyst is unable to think of a strong name that describes all the functions.

Initialize Program in Figure 9-12 is a weak name hiding two separate functions that are being performed. The module has only temporal cohesion. Splitting it produces two modules with functional cohesion. The verbs *initialize* and *terminate* usually indicate modules with temporal cohesion. The verb *process* often indicates procedural or communicational cohesion.

CLUE #3:	**A worker's function does not help its boss function.**
CAUSE:	The worker is reporting to the wrong boss.
CURE:	Move the worker on the structure chart.

This problem is detected by asking yourself whether each module helps to perform the broader function implied by the name of the boss module. In Figure 9-13, the answer is yes for all but one module. The module, **Print List of Enrolled** does not help the module **Get Enrolled Student.** It is there only because the data happens to be available at that point in the program. **Print List of Enrolled** has functional cohesion and so it has no problems. The problem is with **Get Enrolled Student,** which has only communicational cohesion. When **Print List of Enrolled** is moved to work for **Print Reports**, then both **Get Enrolled Student** and **Print Reports** have functional cohesion.

The initial structure is likely to cause maintenance problems. First, the maintainer would not suspect that **Get Enrolled Student** is involved in printing reports, so it is harder to locate the source of problems in the report. Second, the

9
Structure

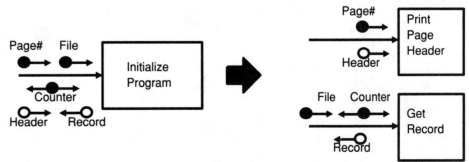

Figure 9-12
Initialize Program is a weak module name that indicates a need to split the module into more than one function.

Get Enrolled Student module may be needed again in another part of the program at some later time. The report is not likely to be needed in that location. As a result, the module would have to be recoded to exclude the report printing resulting in two modules that are almost, but not quite, the same. The alternative is to include a flag in the module that can shut the report off. The flag adds unnecessary complexity to the module and makes it harder to understand.

The analyst should always ask what each module does for its boss. If the answer is "nothing" then the module should be relocated. The motto is *"Ask not what the boss can do for the worker, but what the worker can do for the boss."*

CLUE #4:   **The module deals with too many parameters.**
CAUSE: The module is performing multiple functions.
CURE: Split the module into modules with single functions.

In Figure 9-14, the **Get Enrollment Details** module has a total of six parameters. They are not related to the performance of any single function since they are part of at least three different files. When **Get Enrollment Details** is examined, it is found to get three different records. This is the same problem that was encountered with CLUE #2. The example in Figure 9-12 had many parameters and a weak module name. The same problem is encountered here and the same

Figure 9-13

Print List of Enrolled does not help to Get Enrolled Student. It reports to the wrong boss.

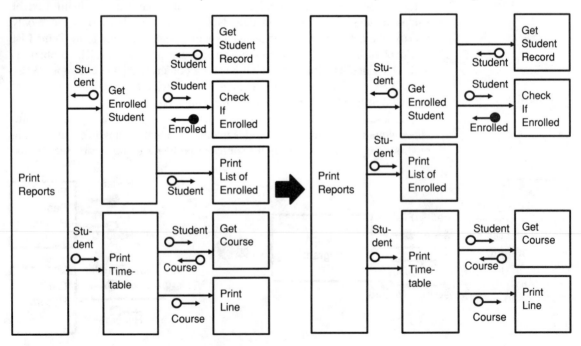

cure is appropriate. The module needs to be split to separate the multiple functions in the module.

On the other hand, note that Print Timetable in Figure 9-14 also has a lot of parameters. In this case, all the parameters are detailed fields to be printed on a single line of the timetable. In this case, the module should not be split into multiple functions. The parameters should be aggregated into a single parameter that corresponds to the output line to be printed. The choice between splitting the function and aggregating the parameters depends on the cohesion of the module. If the module has low cohesion, it should be split. Otherwise, the parameters can be aggregated.

CLUE #5: **The boss module sends a control flag.**
CAUSE: The module is performing more than one function and it is not a black box.
CURE: Split the module into separate functions.

In Figure 9-15 **Print Class List** specifies a **Record-Type** to **Get A Record.** This is a control flag going from the boss to the worker. A control flag means that there are several options from which to select, indicating that the worker module

Figure 9-14

Get Enrollment Details passes too many parameters and should be split into separate functions.

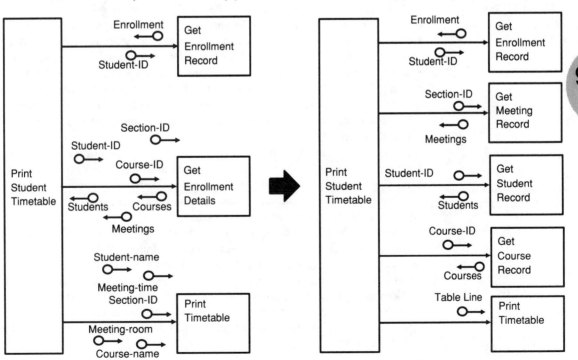

Figure 9-15

Record-Type is a control flag that can be eliminated by splitting Get A Record into two functions that can be called as needed.

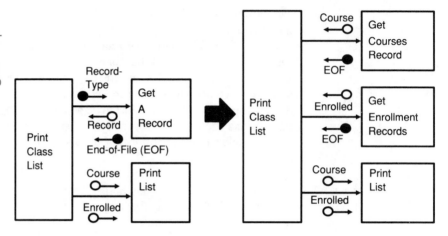

does not have functional cohesion. **Get A Record** must be able to get more than one kind of record. If each record type requires substantially separate coding, then this is an example of logical cohesion. The cohesion can be improved to functional cohesion by splitting the module into two or more modules that each gets one kind of record.

Testing for Coupling

Cohesion is a microscopic view that deals with what goes on within one module. The smallest object of interest is an instruction within the module. **Coupling** is a macroscopic view that deals with what goes on at the interface between modules. The smallest object of interest is a module. Coupling is a measure of the strength of the connections between modules. The degree of coupling is the probability that the contents of another module must be taken into account while designing, implementing, or modifying a module. The greater the interdependence between modules, the higher the coupling between them. The higher the coupling, the worse the design.

Coupling indicates the quality of the interfaces between black box modules. Interfaces are needed if the modules are to work together to perform a large task. Data, flags, memory areas, and files can act as interfaces that convey information between modules. The interfaces need to be as simple and standardized as possible so modules can be reused and maintained.

Coupling, like cohesion, can be classified into a number of qualitative categories that can be ranked from best to worst as follows:[1,4,8,9]

- **Data coupling** occurs when only required data are passed between modules and they are passed through explicit, elemental, calling parameters. An elemental parameter cannot consist of other parameters arranged in a structure. In that way, the data being passed is obvious from the name. There are no possible interactions created by data from other sources not in the parameter list.

- **Stamp coupling** occurs when structured parameters are used to pass data. The data have to be arranged in the required structure. Some parts of the structure may not be used. This happens when a complete record is passed to a module, but only part of the record is needed. The coupling is bad because the modules need to know not only the data being passed, but also the format. This can create a problem because any change to the record structure effects both the boss and the worker module. In effect, the worker module is constrained to function only with input provided by the current boss module. Other modules which have the inputs, but not the required structure, are unable to use the worker module unless the data is structured first.

- **Tramp coupling** is another version of stamp coupling. It occurs when data flows through several modules to get from where it is produced to where it is used. The intermediate modules must carry the data even though it serves no function within them. The intermediate modules cannot be used in any other place unless a dummy parameter is passed into them.

- **Control coupling** occurs when the calling module sends a control flag to the called module directing it to perform one of several possible actions. Such coupling is bad because the boss module has to know something about the internal structure of the worker module. The worker is no longer a black box. This problem is an indication of excessive coupling and poor cohesion.

- **Common coupling** occurs when modules share data by leaving it in an agreed global area of memory that is accessible to all participating modules. Sharing files does not cause common coupling. The type is named after the COMMON statement in the FORTRAN language which creates such an area. Common coupling is used when many parameters must be shared among several modules. It saves the time taken to pass long parameter lists, but it comes at a significant cost in programming and maintenance problems.

It is easy to make mistakes in the name or position of parameters in a list of common elements. Changes in the organization of the common area can propagate errors through all other modules that use the area. There is only one way to identify the modules that are affected by a change. One must examine each module to see if it has a COMMON statement or the equivalent in the implementation language. An error in one module can ripple through many other modules with no indication about the source of the problem.

Some languages, like APL, permit global data definitions as the default case. In these languages, every variable in all modules must be examined to determine whether a change in the global variable impacts any other modules. Such coupling can make maintenance very difficult and error prone.

Common coupling can be reduced or eliminated by bringing modules that produce and use common data together under a common boss that can receive and pass the needed parameters.

There are occasions when common coupling may be justified. Operating systems need to provide many modules with access to variables that indicate the status of programs, files, and communications ports. Common coupling

9
Structure

provides this information in a pervasive way without requiring the passing of many parameters.

Statistical programs are another example of justified common coupling. Many different statistical procedures may need access to the same table of raw data. Common coupling avoids the need for multiple copies of the data for each module. In this case, the data array is very standardized and it is unlikely that the data structure would have to be modified. As a result, it may be acceptable to use common coupling in this case. Usually, common coupling is not a good idea.

- **Content coupling** occurs when one module reaches into the internals of another module to deposit data or control its function. Changing either module requires a thorough examination of both to determine the impact of the change. The APL language provides an extreme case of this problem. It allows the programmer to write a program which actually modifies the code of other modules before they are executed. As a result, there may be no way of finding out what code was being executed when a problem occurred. Such insidious practices should never be tolerated, because they can create problems that are almost impossible to trace. Programmers who use such practices should be encouraged to take up another line of work.

The number of parameters, the names of the parameters, and the flags passed between modules reveal clues to coupling problems.

CLUE #6:	**Module does not get enough data to do its job.**
CAUSE:	One or more parameters are missing or data are being passed through common statements.
CURE:	Specify the missing parameters explicitly to the module.

In Figure 9-16 the **Get Student Record** module is expected to get a record to be updated. However, it does not know the Student-ID to which the record belongs. It needs the Student-ID to be able to do its job. This would not be a problem if the record were being written, or if the next sequential record were required. However, that is not likely to be the case during an update. The only other way that the information could be obtained is by common coupling or by burying the information as part of some other input parameter. Either of these strategies would obscure the information and make maintenance difficult.

CLUE #7:	**A directive flag goes up to the boss module.**
CAUSE:	Authority goes from bottom to top instead of top to bottom.
CURE:	Rename the flag or move the special activity down to the worker.

In Figure 9-16 the **Get Student Record** module directs the **Update Student Record** module to **Print Error Message.** It does not have the authority to tell the boss module what to do. The boss module may have other ways to deal with

Figure 9-16
Get Student Record
needs a Student-ID to
do its job and it should
not send a directive
flag to its boss module.

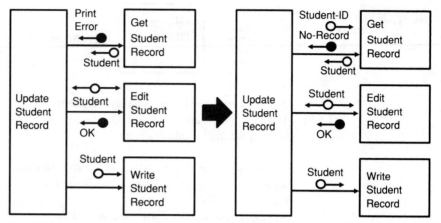

the error, such as fixing it. In any case, if the boss module were a true black box, the worker module would not know how it does its job.

The problem can be cured in one of two ways. The simplest way is to rename the flag as **No-Record** to make it a reporting flag. This may not change the content or structure of the flag, but it does change the implied relationship between the modules. Now the worker is only reporting the state of the transaction and leaving the boss module to decide how to handle it.

Another way to handle such problems is to move the function that the worker module is asking to be done, down into the worker module. The worker module could print the error message directly. It would still have to send a flag to report the status of the transaction to the boss. Then the boss could not assume that the erroneous transaction was correct and ready for further processing.

CLUE #8:	A module receives data groups containing data it does not need.
CAUSE:	A data structure is passing both necessary and unnecessary data, creating stamp coupling.
CURE:	Pass only the required data fields.

In Figure 9-17, Student-Records contains test scores and other information such as address and phone number. Only the test score is needed, so it should be extracted and passed along. All of the test scores should be extracted as a list or vector before being passed so the average can be computed in a single call. This also simplifies the calling structure.

Figure 9-17
Student-Records con-
tains more data than
the module needs.

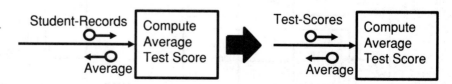

Figure 9-18
Ambiguous data names should be more specific.

CLUE #9:	**A data parameter has an ambiguous name.**
CAUSE:	The parameter is an unnatural aggregate.
CURE:	Identify the individual parameters.

Names like amounts, data, names, and parameters in Figure 9-18 are very ambiguous. They are assigned when the analyst cannot think of a natural name for the data. This often means that there is no natural name because the data aggregate is unnatural. Clarify the data contents before continuing.

Figure 9-19

Course is passed to the root module unnecessarily.

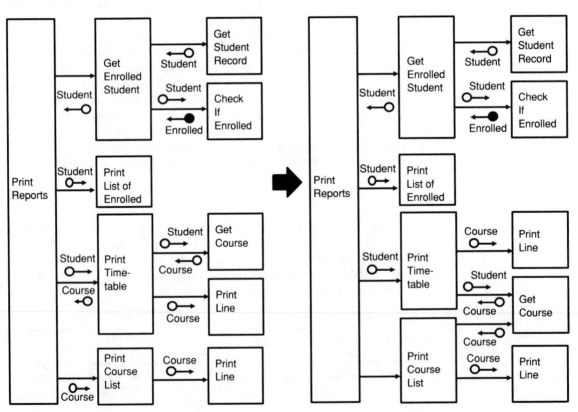

CLUE #10: **A module passes data that it does not need to another module.**
CAUSE: The module is acting as a go-between that carries data between two other modules creating tramp coupling.
CURE: Let the module that needs the data get the data itself.

In Figure 9-19 Course data is read by the **Get Course** module and is passed all the way to the root module and back down to **Print Course List** and **Print Line**. This eliminates rereading of data at the cost of creating tramp coupling. **Print Reports** has to pass the data even though it has no use for it.

The problem with passing unneeded data is that maintenance programmers have to spend time figuring out why it is there. In addition, they may change or eliminate the data, causing further maintenance problems.

The way to deal with the problem is to let the **Print Course List** module get its own copy of the data. In the revised version, **Get Course** reads the data again. This may result in some extra file reads, but the reduced maintenance cost likely more than makes up for it.

CLUE #11: **Reporting flag goes up too far.**
CAUSE: The module that should interpret the flag is passing the job to a higher module creating tramp coupling. Detection and handling of errors have been separated too much.

Figure 9-20

The Invalid flag is passed too far up the Structure Chart.

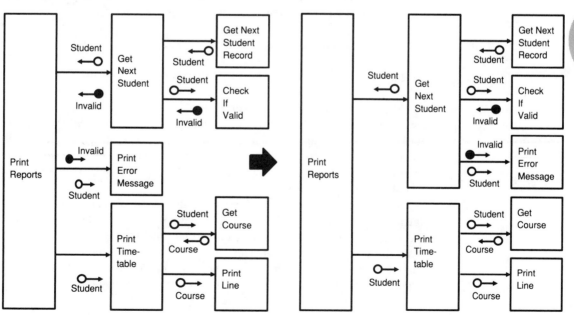

CURE: Interpret and deal with the flag in the first module that gets it.

Figure 9-20 shows the **Invalid** flag moving from **Check if Valid** through two other modules before causing the **Print Error Message** module to be executed. The **Get Next Student** module should deal with the error and print the message as is done in the corrected version of the Structure Chart.

With this correction, only one module has to concern itself with the existence of the Invalid flag. Furthermore, the boss module does not have to concern itself with invalid transactions at all. It can count on dealing with valid transactions.

Testing for Span of Control

A module is difficult to understand and maintain when it uses more than seven other modules. The human mind can only juggle about seven different chunks of information at one time.

CLUE #12:   **The boss module calls more than seven workers.**
CAUSE: The boss is too complex.
CURE: Add a level of "middle-management" between the boss and the workers.

A module normally should not have to control more than seven other modules. The logic within the boss module of a Structure Chart like the one in Figure 9-21 gets very complicated if it is doing anything more than simple menu selection. The solution to the problem is to create an intermediate level of modules between the boss and the workers. This allows designers and programmers to subdivide the problem into pieces that are easier to comprehend. Anything that is easier to comprehend is also easier to maintain.

CLUE #13:   **A 3GL worker module is called by only one boss.**
CAUSE: The module is performing a trivial task.
CURE: Include the worker code in the boss module.

In a 3GL environment, the worker modules at the right hand side of the Structure Chart should consist mainly of utility modules. These perform standard tasks such as reading data, validating data, performing standard calculations, writing records to files, and generating reports. Many of these functions are performed more than once in a program. Thus these reusable worker modules should be called more than once.

Reusable code is much less applicable to 4GL environments. A 4GL environment provides many standard capabilities automatically. Selection, aggregation, sorting, date conversion, validation, input, output, update, and deletion capabilities are part of the language. In effect, the reusable code is embedded in the 4GL language. A single line of 4GL code invokes these capabilities. As a result, many utility routines do not have to be designed or programmed.

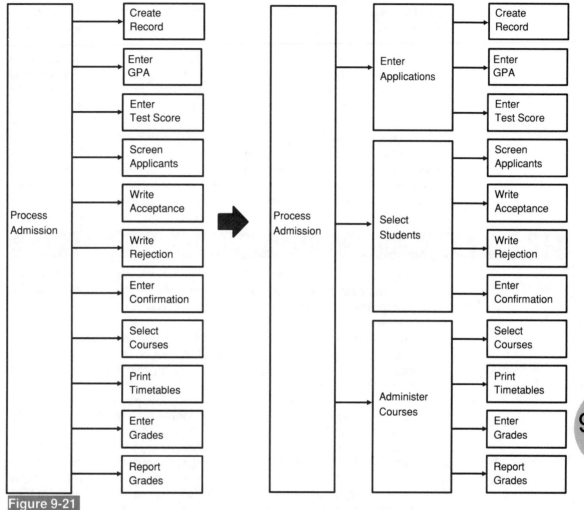

Figure 9-21

Boss modules with too many workers need a middle level of control.

Testing for Module Size

There is no ideal size for modules. There are several factors that influence the desired size of a module. The following factors should be considered in deciding when a module is the wrong size:

- **Cohesion** decreases to unsatisfactorily low levels as module size increases. This is because more functions are included in the module as it gets larger.
- **Coupling** increases as module size decreases. Small modules require more coordination so there is more coupling between many small modules than among a few large modules. Since cohesion and coupling work in opposite directions, larger programs likely need larger modules to strike a balance between these opposing forces.

9

Structure

- **Comprehension** decreases as programmers have to flip through multiple screens of code. For this reason, many analysts suggest that a module should not be longer than one screen.
- **4GL code** is much more compact than 3GL code which can take up to ten times as many lines. Fewer modules are needed in a 4GL environment. Separate 3GL modules that get data, validate it, sort it, and format it are combined into a single 4GL module that fits on one screen. Sometimes data aggregates that require many modules in a 3GL are produced by a query in a language like SQL. This often eliminates the lowest layer of detail modules.

Variations occur in individual modules. Guidelines occasionally have to be violated. A routine to calculate the hypotenuse of a triangle is naturally small and should stay that way. On the other hand, a complicated report format may be very difficult to break into smaller modules. Some judgment has to be used in identifying things that can be placed in a module.

High Cohesion and Low Coupling in Design

The concepts of high cohesion and low coupling are useful in a wide variety of systems and structures. The analyst can use these concepts in Entity-Relationship Diagrams, Normalization, Activity-Entity Diagrams, Organizational Design, Data Flow Diagrams, and Structure Charts.

- **Entity-Relationship Diagrams** illustrate high cohesion between attributes that belong together in one entity because they describe a single thing or event. They also illustrate the minimum coupling that is needed to maintain the relationships between entities.
- **Normalization** is a way to achieve high cohesion and low coupling in database design. Conversion to a higher normal form increases cohesion by eliminating attributes that are not about the same entity, as identified by the same key. The conversion reduces coupling by separating attributes that do not naturally belong together. The coupling is documented by foreign keys.
- **Activity-Entity Diagrams** are clustered to bring together highly cohesive activities which belong together in a single subsystem. Cohesion comes from performing similar functions on related data. Coupling comes from sharing the same data. The clusters are designed to share as little data as possible.
- **Organizational Design** tries to form cohesive work groups. The groups belong together because they are working toward the same objective. The groups are most cohesive when their objectives are most similar. They are coupled by a need for shared information. Coupling is minimized when the organization is structured to minimize the need for shared information.
- **Data Flow Diagrams** attempt to partition the processes in a system so each process performs a single function to make it as cohesive as possible. The concept of isolated subsystems helps to accomplish this. The processes are coupled by the minimum necessary data flowing from one process to the next.
- **Structure Charts** refine Data Flow Diagrams with flags and control structures. These give diagnostics to identify coupling and cohesion problems.

CASE Tools for Structure Charts

Most CASE tools that support Data Flow Diagrams also support Structure Charts. Figure 9-22 illustrates an Excelerator Structure Chart that corresponds to the Data Flow Diagram in Figure 7-34. Corresponding components can be mapped automatically from one diagram to the other and back. Some CASE products automatically revise the corresponding Data Flow Diagram when a Structure Chart is modified. Flags and calling relationships are the only additional information provided by a Structure Chart. These are easy to add. As a result, this stage proceeds quickly when CASE tools are used.

CASE tools can check that all data and flags passed to the module appear in the internal specification of the module to be discussed in the next chapter. These checks can diagnose stamp and tramp coupling problems. Other errors are harder to diagnose, since most kinds of coupling and cohesion are sometimes legitimate.

Design is a process of choosing among alternative ways of solving a problem. A benefit of CASE tools is that they make it easy to explore different alternative structures. If more alternatives are considered, better choices can be made.

Index Technology has a Design Recovery tool that reads COBOL code and creates a set of Structure Charts that show the hierarchy of program paragraphs and sections. This can be useful in maintenance or in redesign of systems.

CASE tools automate documentation of a design. Maintenance programmers find it easier to understand programs produced by using CASE tools. They are able to refer to the Structure Chart to see the relationship between modules. They can use the CASE tool to search for modules that use a variable that is being modified. These are usually very time-consuming tasks without CASE tools.

9
Structure

Figure 9-22

The Structure Chart from Figure 9-9 produced using Excelerator. Note that Excelerator does not support left-to-right structures.

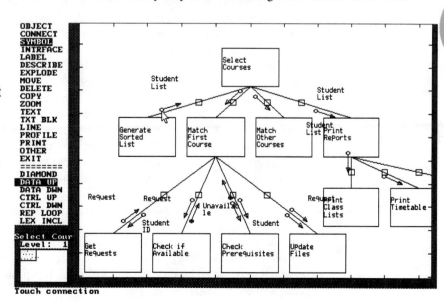

Summary

Coupling and cohesion serve the same function in module design that normalization serves in data table design. They provide guidelines for designing components that are easy to extend and modify and are not prone to duplication and errors. This chapter converts a Data Flow Diagram into a Structure Chart. The chart defines a program design with the characteristics of a black box: nesting, independence, and information hiding.

- **Nesting.** The program is hierarchically structured so each module provides an overview of the program logic it calls in the modules below it.
- **Independence.** The higher-level routines are unaffected by minor changes in specifications, data structure, or file structure.
- **Cohesion.** Each subroutine performs only one well-defined function that can be easily understood by anyone who has to modify it.
- **Coupling.** Each subroutine uses a standard interface to access only the specific data needed to do its job.
- **Reusability.** The module makes use of utility routines that perform common standard tasks. They are coded and tested once but are used by many modules.

To convert a Data Flow Diagram to a Structure Chart by Transform Analysis:

- **Identify the main modules** on the Data Flow Diagram.
- **Rearrange the modules** so they are called by the boss module.
- **Change graphics** and names to correspond to Structure Chart notation.
- **Add control flags and utility modules** to access files and output devices.
- **Test** the module names, module organization, data, and flags passing between the modules for problems of cohesion and coupling.

The cohesion of a module can be classified from best to worst as functional, sequential, communicational, procedural, temporal, logical, or coincidental. Similarly, coupling can be classified from best to worst as data, stamp, tramp, control, common, and content coupling. Other indicators of good module design are span of control and module size. Cohesion is the strength of the association between data and instructions inside a module. A cohesive module completes a single well-defined function each time it is called. Cohesive modules should be named with a strong active verb and a specific direct object. Cohesive modules should perform a part of the overall task performed by their boss function.

Coupling is interdependence between multiple modules. To minimize interdependence, a module should only have access to the data it needs to do its job. A flag should be used to report on actions and problems encountered. It should not direct the activities of higher modules and the higher modules should immediately diagnose and act on the reports from lower-level modules.

A boss module should normally not have to call more than seven worker modules. Calling more makes it difficult for maintenance programmers to understand the module. A low-level worker module should be elementary and useful enough to be called by more than one module. It is usually a utility function that can be used to build other programs.

Keywords and Phrases

Black Box	Functional Cohesion
Boss	Information Hiding
Call	Logical Cohesion
Cohesion	Module
Coincidental Cohesion	Procedural Cohesion
Common Coupling	Reporting Flag
Communicational Cohesion	Reusable Code
Content Coupling	Sequential Cohesion
Control Coupling	Span of Control
Control Flag	Stamp Coupling
Coupling	Structure Chart
Data Coupling	Temporal Cohesion
Directive Flag	Tramp Coupling
Flag	Worker

Review Questions

1. Define each of the items in the list of keywords and phrases.
2. What are the major objectives of module design?
3. What are the criteria by which a good module design can be identified?
4. What are the advantages of using a horizontal format instead of a vertical format for drawing a Structure Chart?
5. What are the steps in converting a Data Flow Diagram to a Structure Chart?
6. Explain the difference between cohesion and coupling.
7. List the levels of cohesion and explain the problems associated with each.
8. List the levels of coupling and explain the problems associated with each.
9. What factors have to be considered in determining the size of a module?
10. How do coupling and cohesion relate to other areas of analysis and design?

9
Structure

Problems

1. The following Data Flow Diagram is an explosion of Process 5 in Figure 7-11. It is a batch process to be implemented in a 4GL environment. Convert it into a Structure Chart. Add any necessary flags.

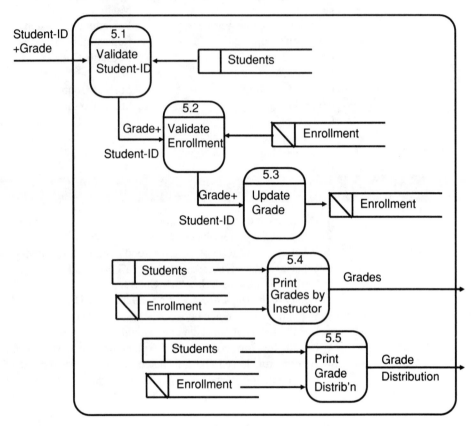

2. The following Data Flow Diagram documents a simple order processing activity with an explosion of one of the processes. Convert it into a Structure Chart. Add any necessary flags. Assume that it is a batch process to be implemented in a 4GL environment.

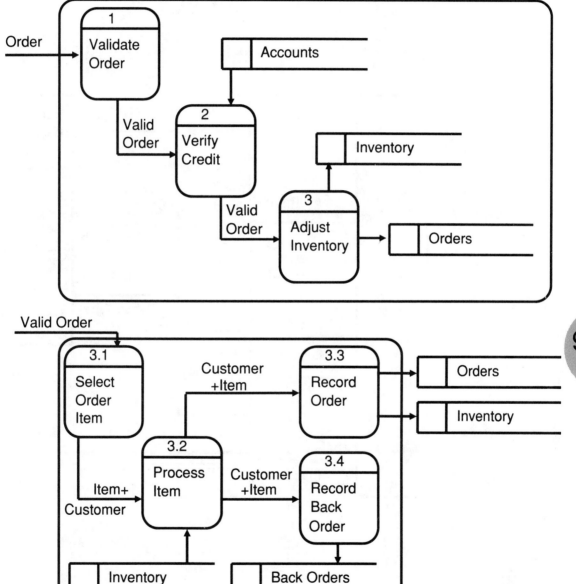

3. Find all of the design errors in the following Structure Chart. Explain the problems that each error can cause. Redraw the Structure Chart, correcting the errors.

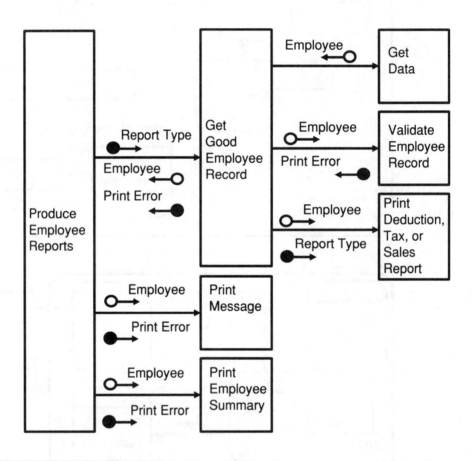

4. Find all of the design errors in the following Structure Chart. Explain the problems that each error can cause. Redraw the Structure Chart, correcting the errors.

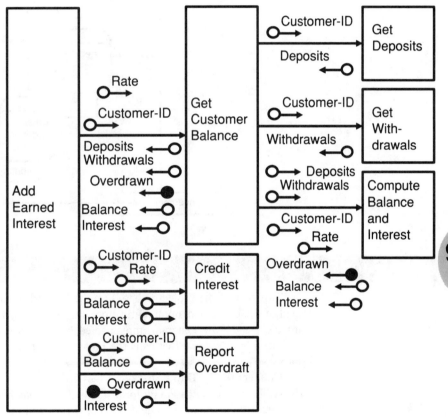

5. The following Data Flow Diagram describes an Order Entry Process for a manufacturing firm. The Edit Order process enters orders using a screen. The other processes are executed automatically when the order has been entered. Convert the diagram to a Structure Chart. Add any necessary flags.

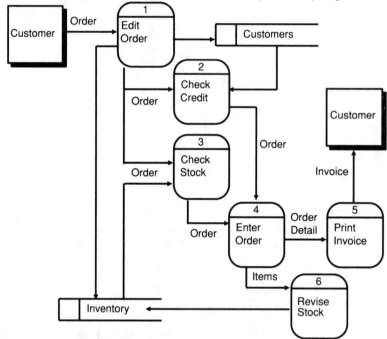

Project

This part of the project is based on the Data Flow Diagram produced at the end of Chapter 7 and any modifications suggested by your supervisor. Any parts of the Data Flow Diagram implemented by prototyping in Chapter 8 can be replaced by a module that calls the prototype systems. Complete the following tasks:

a. **Convert the DFD** to a Structure Chart.

b. **Add utility modules** to perform standard tasks, such as financial or statistical calculations. Include modules to access files and output devices only if your supervisor has specified a 3GL target language.

c. **Add flags** to provide control information on the Structure Chart.

d. **Check the Structure Chart** for coupling, cohesion, span of control, and module size.

e. **Include a copy of the Data Flow Diagram** to show the source of the Structure Chart information. Revise the Data Flow Diagram to reflect any changes that result from the design of the Structure Chart.

Cooking with Cal Oreez Case

Cal and I looked at the Data Flow Diagrams you produced at the end of Chapter 7. I took the liberty of making a few notes on them. I would suggest that you proceed to convert them into Structure Charts, complete with utility modules, and control flags. I don't need to remind you to check for coupling, cohesion, span of control, and module size. Include a copy of the Data Flow Diagrams to make it eassier for me to see how you derived the Structure Charts. Revise the Data Flow Diagrams to correspond to the Structure Charts if you make significant changes in the design. Structure Charts are unnecessary for the parts of the system that are implemented by screens. I expect that the most interesting chart will show the logic used to generate a guest list in which guests do not get duplicate meals or foods to which they are allergic.

References

1. Adams, David R., Michael J. Powers and V. Arthur Owles, *Computer Information Systems Development: Design and Implementation,* South-Western Publishing Co., 1985.
2. De Marco, Tom, *Structured Analysis and System Specification,* Yourdon Press, 1979.
3. Dolan, Kathleen A., *Business Computer Systems Design,* Mitchell Publishing Inc., 1984.
4. Gane, Chris and Trish Sarson, *Structured Systems Analysis: Tools and Techniques,* Prentice-Hall, 1979.
5. Jackson, Michael A., *System Development,* Prentice-Hall, 1983.
6. Martin, James, and Carma McClure, *Diagraming Techniques for Analysts and Programmers,* Prentice-Hall, 1985.
7. Orr, Ken, *Structured Requirements Definition,* Ken Orr and Associates, Inc., 1981.
8. Peters, Lawrence, *Advanced Structured Analysis and Design,* Prentice-Hall, 1987.
9. Steward, Donald V., *Software Engineering with Systems Analysis and Design,* Brooks/Cole Publishing Co., 1987.

9

Structure

Chapter 10

Implementation and Installation

	DATABASE (WHAT)	PROGRAMS (HOW)	BENEFITS (WHY)	NETWORK (WHERE)	REAL TIME (WHEN)	SKILLS (WHO)
USER CONCEPT	Entity Relationship	Activity	Intangible Benefit	Map		Organization Design
DESIGNER CONCEPT	E-R Diagram	A-E Diagram	AHP	Network		Skills Responsibility
USER DETAIL	Forms Screens	Processes Data	Tangible Benefit	Work Volume	Discrete Events	Transition Training
DESIGNER DETAIL	EER Diagram	Data Flow Diagrams	Benefit-Cost	Partition	Transition Diagrams	Methodology Tools
BUILDER CONCEPT	Normal Form Relations	Structure Chart	Function Points	System Architecture	Specifications	Learning
BUILDER DETAIL	Files	Screens Specifications	Costs	Network Specs	Interfaces	4GL CASE

Objectives

Chapter 7 showed how Data Flow Diagrams can be used to identify all of the logical components of an information system in a format that the analyst can use to communicate with the users. Chapter 9 explained how the analyst can convert the Data Flow Diagram into a Structure Chart that organized the logical components into a hierarchy of modules that can perform all the functions of the system.

The Structure Chart corresponds to the hierarchical structure of common programming languages. This format can be understood easily by programmers who have to implement the system. The Structure Chart provides an overview of the control structure of the program. It treats each module as a black box that performs some function by an unspecified method. It also identifies the input and output parameter and the reporting flags that worker modules provide to their boss. It deliberately does not specify the detailed contents of the modules since this would be distracting while the designer is concentrating on the overall structure.

This chapter explains how to document the detailed contents of each module in the Structure Chart. Again, this process is like applying a magnifying glass to the module to see what is inside. This documentation must also be in a language that can be unambiguously understood by programmers since they have to convert the specifications into computer programs.

There are different ways of providing detailed documentation. This chapter explores the properties of several of them. The chapter also provides an overview of implementation and testing to show how the modules are completed. The reader learns how to:

- Specify the fundamental programming concepts of sequence, selection, and iteration.

- Write specifications using Structured English and Action Diagrams.

- Write specifications using Decision Tables and Decision Trees.

- Test modules, groups of modules, and systems.

- Select an implementation method.

- Select an installation method.

The Black Box Concept

The previous chapter stated that a black box had the following properties:

- **The user does not have to understand how a black box works** to use it.
- **Black boxes act independently,** except where they are connected by standard interfaces. They can be modified to have new or different features as long as their interfaces conform to the accepted standard. This means that problems usually can be traced to a single black box which can then be repaired or replaced.
- **Black boxes can contain other black boxes.** This hides details from the user and makes it easier for the user to concentrate on the functions of the black box instead of the contents.

The black box is called a black box because users are unable to see what goes on inside the box. They can only see the inputs or stimuli that enter the box and the outputs or responses that the box sends in response to the stimuli.

Figure 10-1 shows the correspondence between the module defined in Chapter 9 and the conceptual black box that is used to explain detailed specifications. The input data flows correspond to the input stimuli of the black box. The output data flows correspond to the output responses of the box. The main difference in notation is that the input and output streams are now connected to opposite sides of the box.

It is now time to remove the black curtain from the box to see what is inside. This is done in two stages. First, the box is opened up to see the two categories of things in the box: state information and machines. Then the machines is expanded to reveal the logic of the operations inside the box. Figure 10-2, known as a State Machine Diagram[5], looks into the box to reveal the two major kinds of components in the box: states and machines.

- **State.** The state is a record of the history of the box. This allows the box to behave differently depending on its history. Consider a black box that edits text in a word processor. It has an UNDO command that allows the user to undo the last Insert or Delete command. The black box needs to remember the last insertion or deletion to be able to undo it. Thus it must always know the current state of the document being edited and the state before the most recent Insert or Delete command. The behavior of the UNDO command depends on the previous state of the box.

  Many black boxes do not need a state history because the box always behaves in the same way. The behavior of a box that computes the square root of the input number should not depend on previous input values. Thus it does not need a state history. The most common uses for state histories are in

Figure 10-1

Converting a module to a black box.

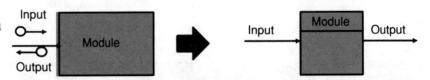

Figure 10-2

A State Machine Diagram.

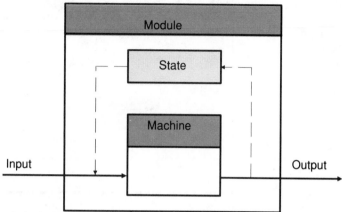

Object-Oriented Programming Systems described later in the chapter and Real-Time systems described in Chapter 12.

The state history, if needed, is usually implemented as some record stored on a file or some data stored in a common or globally available part of the computer memory. It can be thought of as a type of internal input to the process of the black box. Part of the output of the box is this internally stored history. Not every black box stores a state history, but the concept is included for generality.

- **Machine.** The machine in the black box is really another black box that responds to both the external inputs and the internal state. Just as the black box could be opened up to reveal a state machine, the machine can be opened up to reveal the contents of the machine. This is called a clear box view.

Each of the machines in the clear box view is another module at a more detailed level. It can be exploded into another state machine view and another clear box view. Thus a machine is an implementation of a module in the Structure Chart. The module, in turn, is the specification of a process in the Data Flow Diagram.

The clear box view reveals the logical operations that are performed by the machine. These logical operations fall into five basic categories: Sequence structures, Selection structures, Repeat While true structures, Repeat Until true structures, and Concurrent structures. These basic structures are illustrated in Figures 10-3 to 10-7. They can be combined into more complicated logical structures that can describe any process.

The **Sequence** structure in Figure 10-3 describes processes that are performed in a required logical sequence. There can be more than two processes in the sequence, but they must all be performed and they must be performed in the order shown.

The **Selection** structure in Figure 10-4 is used when only one of several processes is to be chosen. The process chosen depends on some logical condition symbolized by the diamond with the question mark in it. When only two options

10
Program

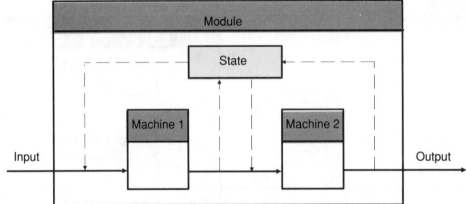

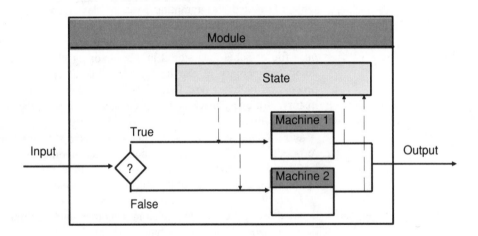

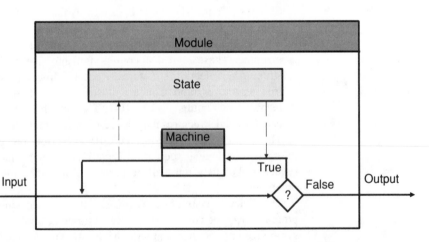

Figure 10-6

The clear box Repeat Until structure of State Machines.

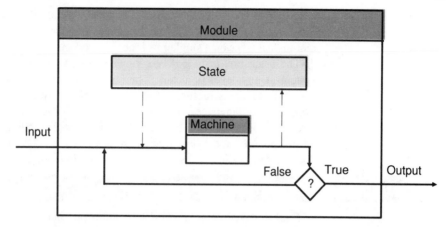

Figure 10-7

The clear box Concurrent structure of State Machines.

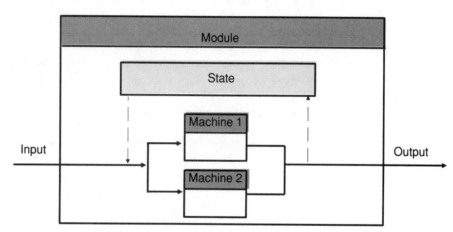

are available, this is usually called an IF ... THEN ... ELSE ... structure. In many programming languages it has the form: IF true THEN machine 1 ELSE machine 2. If more than two options are available it is usually called a CASE structure because the appropriate case must be selected from a list. There is either a code to identify each case, or a more complex logical test.

The **Repeat While** structure of Figure 10-5 and the **Repeat Until** structure of Figure 10-6 are both examples of iteration structures. They are both designed to repeat a process until some condition is met such as processing all items on a list. They differ only in when the logical test is performed. The Repeat While structure performs the logical test before the process is executed and so the process may not get executed at all. The Repeat Until structure performs the test after the process has been executed and so the process must get executed at least once.

The **Concurrent** structure of Figure 10-7 allows two processes to be performed simultaneously. This can happen physically if there is more than one

10
Program

computer in the system. It can also happen logically if the physical order of the processes is unimportant. Some languages provide support for multiple concurrent logical tasks on a single machine.

The black box and clear box views can be used to describe completely any system at any level of detail. The structures of the clear box view also corresponds to the structures that programmers use in many of the common programming languages. The boxes make it easy to visualize the control structure of a program. However, the box views are rather tedious to draw. Expanding all the modules in the Structure Chart into box views becomes a large and costly documentation exercise. Structured English provides a simpler solution.

Structured English

English has a remarkable breadth and depth that can be used to communicate ideas and stir emotions. This results from a large vocabulary with many overlapping shades of meaning that can be used to evoke a wide variety of ideas and impressions in the reader. Unfortunately, it is this same imprecision, wordiness, and redundancy with its associated implications, associations, and connotations that makes English—or any other natural language—a very poor choice for specifying programs. A specification language has to be clear, concise, and unambiguous.

An example of ambiguity is a statement like, "Students with a Grade Point Average (GPA) of more than 2 can continue to the next year of the program, while students with a GPA of less than 2 must repeat the year." It is unclear what students with a GPA of exactly 2 must do. It is also unclear how a GPA is computed. How are repeated courses treated? How are Pass/Fail courses treated?

Another example is "Accept applicants with two years of work experience and a test score of 500 or a GPA of at least 3.0." This could be interpreted as "Accept applicants with two years of work experience and *at least one of the following:* a test score of 500 or a GPA of at least 3.0." It could also be interpreted as "Accept applicants with *both* two years of work experience and a test score of 500 *or accept applicants with* a GPA of at least 3.0." Any sentence with both an *and* and an *or* in it is likely to be ambiguous unless carefully qualified to eliminate ambiguities.

Adjectives also lead to ambiguity and imprecision. A *good* student or a *regular* customer are indistinguishable from a *poor* student or an *irregular* customer without some further criteria. A quantitative definition of good and regular are required. Good may be defined as having a GPA greater than 3.0. A regular customer may be defined as one who made at least three purchases in the last month.

If English is to be used to describe program modules, it needs to be restricted to remove the features of the language that cause ambiguity and confusion. Therefore this restricted subset of English should **eliminate:**

- **Adjectives and adverbs.** They are almost always not defined with enough precision to be useful. An adjective (as in *large* order) or an adverb (as in respond *quickly*), has no meaning without some numeric reference scale.
- **Compound sentence structures.** Long, complex, compound sentences—like this one—with many subordinate clauses and explanatory phrases, are difficult to understand and often lead to confusion about which parts belong with which other parts. Sentences should be clear and short with one idea per sentence.
- **Nonimperative moods.** Commands in imperative mood are ideally suited to describe the imperative actions performed by programs.
- **Punctuation.** Most punctuation—when used at all—leaves the writer more certain than the (long-suffering,) overtaxed, and confused reader as to the intended syntactic (?) meaning!
- **Conditional and logical statements.** Only a specific subset of these is permitted.
- **Footnotes.** Any statements out of sequential order make a description harder to follow.[*] Footnotes are not permitted.

A notation cannot be defined only by what it does not contain. The definition must also state what the notation must contain. Structured English consists of the following components:[1,2,3,4]

- **Verbs** in the imperative mood.
- **Nouns** defined as tables or attributes in the database or module and flag names in the Structure Chart.
- **Logical control statements** that correspond to the kinds of logical machines identified earlier in the chapter. The following are suggested:
  - **Sequential operations** are specified as separate imperative statements, each beginning on a new line, in the order of execution. The statements may be optionally numbered to emphasize the sequential nature of the operations.
  - **IF ... THEN ... ELSE ...** conditions should be written on separate lines as follows with suitable conditions and indented imperative statements replacing the triple dots. Some people prefer that the whole structure be terminated with another line labelled END IF. The ELSE portion can be omitted if there are no alternate procedures.

```
IF ...
THEN
      ...
ELSE
      ...
END IF
```

---

*1   See what I mean?

- **Case selections** can be treated as an extension of the IF structure where ELSE IF is used for each alternative.

  IF (condition 1)

      ...

  ELSE IF (condition 2)

      ...

  ELSE IF (condition 3)

      ...

- **REPEAT WHILE and REPEAT UNTIL** iterations are shown as a command followed by indented instructions. They are optionally terminated by an END REPEAT statement to make the end clear.

  REPEAT WHILE (condition)

      ...

  END REPEAT

  Sometimes the repetition is for all occurrences of a transaction, record, or event. In these cases, it is sometimes easier to specify the iterations as FOR EACH or FOR ALL records.

  FOR EACH record

      ...

  END FOR

- **Concurrent operations** are treated as sequential operations.
- **Indentation** to indicate the hierarchical control structure. Subordinate commands are indented and all commands in a sequence with the same priority are indented the same amount.
- **Logical relationships** are specified using the keywords AND, OR, NOT, EQ (equal), LT (less than), GT (greater than), LE (less than or equal), GE (greater than or equal), and NE (not equal). Parentheses can be used to eliminate ambiguities that result from using AND and OR or other logical combinations.

- **Module references** can be made in the Structured English specification. The reference should include the input and output parameters of the module. The following example illustrates how to call the Calculate module with inputs A and B and outputs X and Y.

  CALL CALCULATE using

      INPUTS A, B

      OUTPUTS X,Y

  Module references are normally not used in Structured English when it is being used for highlevel descriptions. When used for detail descriptions of modules in a Structure Chart, module references become essential to show how the different modules are coupled. In the same way, the description of a module should indicate the input and output parameters that the module uses.

These are placed at the start of the description so readers know immediately what external data are involved. Parameters are windows through which data are passed into and out of the module. The names can be different in the calling and receiving modules, as long as the values and type are the same.

- **Capitalization** of keywords, module names, and names defined in the database is used to identify things that have already been defined. This makes it easy for programmers to distinguish what has already been defined from those things yet to be defined.

- **Comments** can be delimited with an asterisk at the start of each comment line. This allows explanatory comments, instructions, or cross references to be included in the specification. These can later be included in the actual code for the module. An example is:

* Use the interest rate equations in the Van Horne text.

- **Keywords** for such things as selection, repetition, reading, and writing should be standardized at an installation. The actual keywords used are not important if they are understood by both users and programmers. It is convenient to use the same keywords as the ones used in the installation's implementation language. Thus, an installation that normally codes in the PL/1 language would use DO WHILE instead of REPEAT WHILE as the keyword for repetition. Highly abbreviated keywords, like ITR for iteration, should be avoided. They discourage users from trying to understand the descriptions. Then validation of specifications becomes very difficult.

The advantage of using English for specifying modules is that it is understood by both users, who must validate the specifications, and programmers, who must translate the specifications into code. However, these two groups usually use the language in ways that are mutually incomprehensible. When this happens in multicultural trade and commerce, a simplified hybrid called a pidgin language is used. A pidgin language incorporates the vocabulary of both groups and a simplified grammar of one of them.

Structured English is such a pidgin language. It uses a restricted vocabulary common to programmers and users. It uses a syntax that is based on fundamental constructs of computer programming languages. It permits intelligent communication between the user and programmer groups on the limited set of things that are of mutual interest, namely module requirements.

The level of detail required in the Structured English specification depends on the assumed programming environment and on the assumed abilities of the programmers. In a bank or insurance company it is usually safe to specify a line that says "Compute the present value of X in N months discounted at an annual interest rate of Y% compounded semi-annually." This should be a familiar calculation to all programmers in a bank. On the other hand it would likely be a very unusual calculation in a social service agency. In that case it might be necessary to specify the computation algorithm or a reference to a standard text that provides the equation for calculation.

10
Program

Similarly, if a 4GL is going to be used, many selection and data arrangement problems can be specified very simply because they can be directly implemented in the 4GL. Many of the REPEAT WHILE and REPEAT UNTIL groups can be eliminated because the 4GL performs the repetition automatically and delivers a table of results.

If the project is small and the analyst understands the processes in the project, then the analyst may want to avoid Data Flow Diagrams and Structure Charts by starting directly with Structured English. Usually this is not a good design strategy because the various consistency and integrity checks identified for Data Flow Diagrams and Structure Charts are not applied to Structured English.

The "standard" Structured English sometimes may be augmented or modified with ordinary English to make it easier for users to understand. This is best done after "standard" Structured English has been used to define the module unambiguously.

Structured English Examples

The first example of Structured English is the Select Courses module from the Structure Chart in Figure 9-9 which is repeated in Figure 10-9. The logic is typical of highlevel modules. All it does is call the four lower modules and pass data between them. The Structured English specification is illustrated in Figure 10-8. The first line after the name calls the GENERATE-SORTED-LIST module which produces an output called STUDENT-LIST. This output is used within SELECT-COURSES as an input to each following module.

Figure 10-10 illustrates the Structured English specification of the Match_First_Course module. This one is somewhat more complicated. It has a sequence of modules being called. It also has several logical tests for error conditions and repeated procedures. The Match_First_Course module has an input parameter which is listed right after the module name.

The FOR EACH loop processes each STUDENT_ID in the input parameter, STUDENT LIST. The first REPEAT UNTIL loop calls GET_REQUESTS until a value of REQUESTS is found. The second REPEAT UNTIL loop encloses the

Figure 10-8

Structured English specification of the Select Courses module.

```
MODULE SELECT_COURSES
        CALL GENERATE_SORTED_LIST using
                OUTPUT STUDENT_LIST
        CALL MATCH_FIRST_COURSE using
                INPUT STUDENT_LIST
        CALL MATCH_OTHER_COURSES using
                INPUT STUDENT_LIST
        CALL PRINT_REPORTS using
                INPUT STUDENT_LIST
END MODULE
```

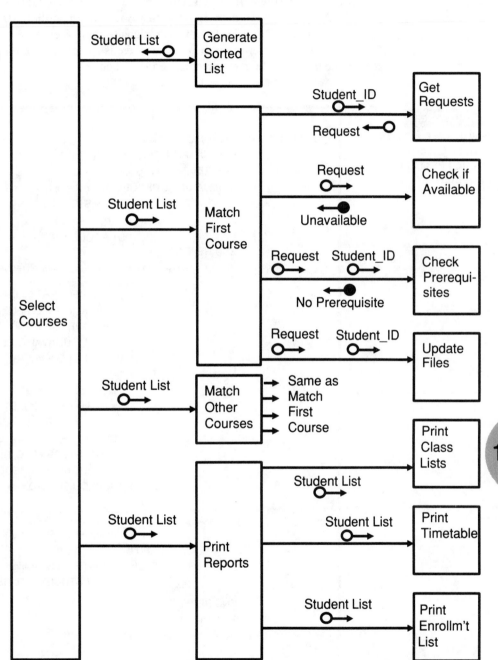

Figure 10-9
The Select Courses module repeated from Figure 9-9.

10
Program

different sequential procedures that are needed to assign a course. Three called modules (CHECK-IF-AVAILABLE, CHECK-PREREQUISITES, and UPDATE-FILES) do most of the work. The first two have output flags (UNAVAILABLE and NO-PREREQUISITE) that can signal errors. They have to be checked in case there is an error. In each case, if there is an error then a message is printed and the search for the current request is abandoned.

Figure 10-10

Structured English specifications for the Match First Course module.

```
MODULE MATCH_FIRST_COURSE with
            INPUT PARAMETER STUDENT_LIST
    FOR EACH STUDENT_ID in STUDENT_LIST
            REPEAT UNTIL REQUESTS is not empty
                    CALL   GET_REQUESTS using
                            INPUT STUDENT_ID
                            OUTPUT REQUESTS
        END REPEAT
        REPEAT UNTIL one course is assigned or all requests
                        have been processed
                        select next  of REQUESTS into REQUEST
                        CALL    CHECK_IF_AVAILABLE using
                                INPUT REQUEST
                                OUTPUT UNAVAILABLE
                        IF UNAVAILABLE EQ true
                        THEN
                                print error message
                                abandon this REQUEST
                        END IF
                        CALL    CHECK_PREREQUISITES using
                                INPUT STUDENT_ID, REQUEST
                                OUTPUT NO_PREREQUISITE
                        IF NO_PREREQUISITE EQ true
                        THEN
                                Print Error Message
                                abandon this REQUEST
                        END IF
                        CALL    UPDATE_FILES using
                                INPUT STUDENT_ID, REQUEST
            END REPEAT
        END FOR EACH
END MODULE
```

REPEAT UNTIL loops are used to deal with the possibility that empty lists or errors occur and the next student in the list or the next request must be processed.

Note that the IF statements have a THEN part, but no ELSE part. Some also require that the calculation be abandoned. This means that the following procedures within a REPEAT group are not performed until the next repetition of the loop. This structure is typical when several error checks have to be performed. Once the result of the check is known, the module decides how to handle errors.

With some modifications to keep track of how many requests have been satisfied, this same logic can be used for the Match Other Courses module.

Structured English is a useful tool for describing program logic. Users, analysts, and programmers can all understand it. It does not contain any graphics so it is easy to enter on any keyboard. However, some graphics would help to make it more understandable. Action Diagrams add graphics to Structured English.

Action Diagrams

Action Diagrams[4] were introduced briefly in Chapter 8. They contain all the programming constructs needed to describe the logic of a program. The Action Diagram shows how groups of Structured English statements belong together by enclosing modules within brackets. Figure 10-11 illustrates the symbols that are used in an Action Diagram. There are three basic kinds of brackets:

Figure 10-11
The symbols for program structures used in an Action Diagram.

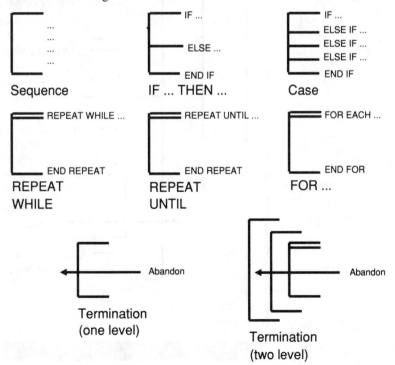

10
Program

- **Simple brackets** enclose a sequence of instructions.
- **Split brackets** show mutually exclusive actions in IF ... ELSE ... or case.
- **Double line brackets** to show repetition.

Figure 10-12 shows how the Structured English specification in Figure 10-10 is converted to Action Diagram format. Note how the left-pointing arrow is used to indicate that a repetition or other grouping is terminated. The whole group of statements is abandoned and the next statement in the group at the head of the arrow is started. In the example, either arrow abandons the processing of a request and returns to selecting a new request if available.

Figure 10-12

The Structured English specification of Figure 10-10 converted to an Action Diagram.

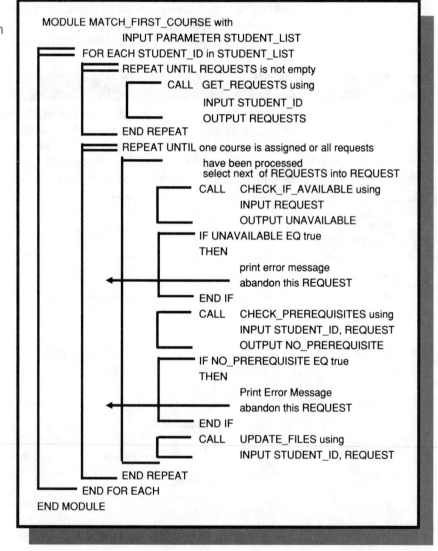

```
MODULE MATCH_FIRST_COURSE with
                INPUT PARAMETER STUDENT_LIST
        FOR EACH STUDENT_ID in STUDENT_LIST
            REPEAT UNTIL REQUESTS is not empty
                    CALL   GET_REQUESTS using
                            INPUT STUDENT_ID
                            OUTPUT REQUESTS
        END REPEAT
            REPEAT UNTIL one course is assigned or all requests
                            have been processed
                            select next  of REQUESTS into REQUEST
                        CALL    CHECK_IF_AVAILABLE using
                                INPUT REQUEST
                                OUTPUT UNAVAILABLE
                        IF UNAVAILABLE EQ true
                        THEN
                                print error message
                                abandon this REQUEST
                        END IF
                        CALL    CHECK_PREREQUISITES using
                                INPUT STUDENT_ID, REQUEST
                                OUTPUT NO_PREREQUISITE
                        IF NO_PREREQUISITE EQ true
                        THEN
                                Print Error Message
                                abandon this REQUEST
                        END IF
                        CALL    UPDATE_FILES using
                                INPUT STUDENT_ID, REQUEST
            END REPEAT
        END FOR EACH
END MODULE
```

The brackets of the Action Diagram can be expanded into a rectangle that encloses the steps in the brackets. This notation allows the designer to attach the inputs and outputs of the module to the rectangle. Inputs are listed at the top right corner and outputs are listed at the bottom right corner. Normally only input and output parameters are listed. Reports to printers or other devices are not.

Figure 10-13 shows how Figure 10-12 looks with this modification. The Check Prerequisites module is outlined in a round cornered rectangle to show that it is coded in detail elsewhere. This makes it possible to use Action Diagrams in place of Data Flow Diagrams, Structure Charts, or Structured English. This saves some effort in converting from one notation to another. However, this is done at the cost of compromising some of the best features of each notation. That is why the three different notations have been used in this book.

In summary, Action Diagrams have several advantages.

- The structure of a specification is conveyed more clearly than with Structured English.
- They can be produced manually or with a text editor and they can be printed on normal width paper.
- They graphically illustrate all of the standard programming concepts.
- They can be used to replace Data Flow Diagrams and Structure Charts.

Figure 10-13

The Action Diagram of Figure 10-12 converted to a Rectangular Action Diagram.

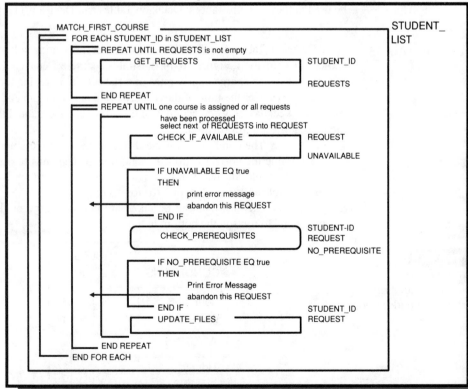

10
Program

Complex Logical Decisions

Structured English is a useful way of specifying procedural rules with a natural order. There are many situations in program specification where the rules are non-procedural without a natural order. They have a case structure with many possible cases based on values of several different criteria. These can always be described with several nested IF ... THEN ... ELSE ... structures. However, such a structure is very confusing and prone to errors.

A typical problem of this type is the decision on acceptance or rejection of an applicant to a university. A simplified example of a written rule might be:

Get the applicant's test score and grade point average (GPA). If the test score is below 575 or the GPA is below 4, reject the applicant. Applicants with a test score of more than 625 and GPA of 4 or more should be accepted. Similarly, applicants with a test score between 601 and 625 with a GPA of more than 6 should be accepted. All others should be given to the admissions officer for detailed evaluation.

This description is complicated. It is not clear how to convert it into a specification that can be coded. It is also not clear that all possible cases have been identified. There are two special supplementary descriptive tools that can be used in these circumstances: Decision Tables and Decision Trees.

Decision Tables

A Decision Table is a formal technique for presenting all of the possible choices in a situation. Figure 10-14 illustrates a simple Decision Table for determining whether to charge hourly rates or a flat rate in a parking lot. The decision depends on whether the time of day is between 8 am and 6 pm and the day of the week is a weekday between Monday and Friday. The Decision Table consists of three categories of information.

- **Conditions.** The conditions are the different decision variables that are used to determine the correct action. A condition corresponds to a row in the top half of the table. In the example the conditions are Time=8-6 and Weekday with possible answers Y(es) or N(o) for each.
- **Actions.** The actions that can be taken are hourly charge or flat rate. These correspond to rows in the bottom half of the table.

Figure 10-14

A simple Decision Table for calculating charges in a parking lot.

CONDITIONS	RULES			
	1	2	3	4
Hours 8-6	Y	N	Y	N
Weekday	Y	Y	N	N
ACTIONS				
Hourly	X			
Flat rate		X	X	X

● **Rules.** The rules correspond to columns of the table. They are particular combinations of conditions that lead to a particular set of actions. In the example, rule 3 is: if time=8-6 and weekday=No, then charge flat rate.

Now consider the original example of selecting student applications. A Decision Table is constructed using the following steps.

● **Identify the conditions.** In the example there are two conditions: *test score* and *GPA*. These are inserted as the rows in the top half of the table. Note that test score >625 is not a condition. >625 is a state of the test score condition. Similarly, male and female are not two different conditions. They are two states of the gender condition.

● **Identify the number of states for each condition.** There are 4 possible states for test score and 3 possible states for GPA. The number of states are the number of values of a condition that each require different actions. Often a range of values, like GPA of 4 to 6, have the same action. In such a case, any number in the whole range has the same state. The states in the example are shown below with identifying letters:

CONDITION	STATE
Test Score	A: >625
	B: 601-625
	C: 575-600
	D: <575
GPA	X: >6
	Y: 4-6
	Z: <4

● **Calculate the number of rules.** A rule is needed for each possible combination of conditions. This is the product of the number of states for each condition which is 4x3=12 in the example. This determines the number of columns in the Decision Table.

● **List all combinations of states under the rules.** The easiest way to generate all combinations is to start with the first condition and cycle through the states for that condition repeatedly until all rule columns in the row are filled. Thus the cycle is ABCDABCDABCD to fill the 12 columns. Then cycle through the states for the second condition, but keep the same state for one whole cycle of the previous rule. The previous rule had a cycle of ABCD so this condition should start with four copies of the same rule, XXXX. This is followed by YYYY and then by ZZZZ. Figure 10-15 illustrates this result. If

10
Program

The start of a Decision Table with all conditions and number of rules identified.

CONDITIONS	RULES											
	1	2	3	4	5	6	7	8	9	10	11	12
Test Score	A	B	C	D	A	B	C	D	A	B	C	D
GPA	X	X	X	X	Y	Y	Y	Y	Z	Z	Z	Z

there were a third condition with states P and Q, the first 12 columns would be filled with P to cover a whole cycle of the previous row and so on.

- **Identify the possible actions.** In the example there are three possible actions: *accept, evaluate,* and *reject.* These actions become the rows in the bottom half of the table. Figure 10-16 illustrates the result of this stage.
- **Mark the actions to be taken for each rule.** Place an X under the rule at each action that applies. In some problems an X appears for more than one action at some rules. Sometimes the description is incomplete and users have to be consulted to determine the correct actions. The result of this stage is shown in Figure 10-17.
- **Simplify the table by combining rules with the same action.** Sometimes a condition is irrelevant to the decision. In the example, when the test score is less than 575, then it does not matter what the GPA is because the applicant is rejected in any case. Similarly, when the GPA is less than 4, it does not matter

Figure 10-16

A Decision Table with all possible actions identified.

CONDITIONS	RULES											
	1	2	3	4	5	6	7	8	9	10	11	12
Test Score	A	B	C	D	A	B	C	D	A	B	C	D
GPA	X	X	X	X	Y	Y	Y	Y	Z	Z	Z	Z
ACTIONS												
Accept												
Evaluate												
Reject												

Figure 10-17

A Decision Table with all the correct actions identified.

CONDITIONS	RULES											
	1	2	3	4	5	6	7	8	9	10	11	12
Test Score	A	B	C	D	A	B	C	D	A	B	C	D
GPA	X	X	X	X	Y	Y	Y	Y	Z	Z	Z	Z
ACTIONS												
Accept	X	X			X							
Evaluate			X			X	X					
Reject				X				X	X	X	X	X

Figure 10-18
A simplification of the Decision Table in Figure 10-17.

		RULES							
CONDITIONS	1	2	3	4	5	6	7	8
Test Score	A	B	C	D	A	B	C	-
GPA	X	X	X	-	Y	Y	Y	Z
ACTIONS								
Accept	X	X			X			
Evaluate			X			X	X	
Reject				X				X

what the test score is because the application is rejected. This can be indicated with a dash in place of the category symbols to which the decision is indifferent. The dash acts as a "wild card" that stands for all possible values. In this example, place a dash in the GPA condition for test score category D and a dash in the test score condition for a GPA of <4. The result is illustrated in Figure 10-18.

- **Order the rules by frequency of use.** Programs will usually be more efficient if the most frequent occurrences are dealt with first. If Reject is known to occur most often and Accept occurs least often, then the best order for the rules is likely 4, 8, 3, 6, 7, 1, 2, 5.

This process for constructing a Decision Table is simple and straight forward. A Decision Table can deal with large complex problems with many conditions, states, and actions. There are always a precisely determinable number of rules for such a problem. This determinable number acts as a check to make sure that all situations have been covered.

Decision Trees

Decision Trees have been used for a long time to structure choices in fields as different as taxonomy and circuit design. A Decision Tree consists of a set of branches that lead from the root or start of the decision process to leaves which each contain a decision. The Decision Tree in Figure 10-19 is a direct transformation of the previously constructed Decision Table. In fact all Decision Tables can be transformed into Decision Trees.

Some people find it easier to understand the data in the form of a Decision Tree. Most people find it harder to draw a Decision Tree, particularly if it is complicated. Simple problems can be presented more easily as a Decision Tree and complicated problems can be presented more easily as a Decision Table. Either method of presentation can be used to supplement module specifications when complicated decision rules are involved.

10
Program

Figure 10-19

A Decision Tree ver-
sion of Figure 10-17.

TEST SCORE	GPA	
	>6	Accept
>625	4-6	Accept
	<4	Reject
	>6	Accept
601-625	4-6	Evaluate
	<4	Reject
	>6	Evaluate
575-600	4-6	Evaluate
	<4	Reject
	>6	Reject
<575	4-6	Reject
	<4	Reject

CASE Tools for Specification

Most CASE tools have features that help in the specification process. Processes in Data Flow Diagrams or modules in Structure Charts can usually be exploded to reveal a textual description. If this textual description is entered in Structured English, it can be used to produce printed specification documents to be passed to programmers. Decision Tables and Decision Trees are less common.

Some CASE tools support Action Diagrams with keywords that match specific target programming languages. IEW from KnowledgeWare is able to generate COBOL code directly from Action Diagram specifications. Telon is another product that generates code from specifications. Other vendors are working hard to provide similar facilities.

Future CASE products are certain to include further improvements. The ideal CASE tool would have the following features:

- **Enterprise Modeling Features** like Activity-Entity Diagrams and clustering of activities. Excelerator and IEW have some capability in these areas.

- **Extended Entity-Relationship Models** to define the database. This is available in many systems.

- **Importing of Data Definitions** from existing applications so they can be analyzed and used to design new databases. A few products have a limited ability to do this for applications in a limited set of languages. This capability is difficult to support because of the many implementation environments that are used for existing systems.

- **Database Dictionary Generators** that will produce code to define the data structures automatically in the desired implementation language. Excelerator, IEW, Oracle's CASE*Method, and several other products will generate data definitions in SQL, COBOL, and several other languages directly from an Entity-Relationship Diagram. As extended features are included in implementations of SQL, undoubtedly the Extended Entity-Relationship Model will also be coded directly.

- **Data Flow Diagrams** to define the processes in the system. These are also widely available to support a variety of notations. Many, but not all of them share definitions of the database developed in the Entity-Relationship Model. A few, like IEW, are able to use the activities in an Activity-Entity Model as a starting point for the Data Flow Diagram.

- **Structure Charts** for documenting the structure of a system of programs. Again it is important to be able to use the information collected in the Data Flow Diagram and convert it directly into a Structure Chart. Most systems support such a conversion.

- **Module Specifications** for each of the modules in a Structure Chart. Most systems support this at least at the level of a textual description. Some support Action Diagrams. Very few support Decision Tables or Decision Trees.

- **Screen Painters** to produce prototype screens. Oracle, Excelerator, and IEW can all produce prototype screens based on a database definition. Oracle can also produce code for the screens directly with validation and integrity checks.

- **Code Generators** to convert specifications directly into implementation code. Some products provide some kinds of code generation. For instance, Oracle can generate database definitions from an ER Diagram and screen definitions from a screen painter. Application code can be generated, but there is no support for the initial Data Flow Diagrams. IEW can generate COBOL code.

- **Testing support** to generate test data and compare test results with correct results to identify errors. Such products exist for individual languages. They are uncommon in CASE Tools and will remain uncommon until code generators are perfected. Some will be needed even if code is generated automatically, because the designer can never be sure that the specifications used to generate the code are correct.

- **Validity checking** to diagnose logical errors in the specifications. The user should be warned that a process on a Data Flow Diagram has no input or no output. Excelerator provides a number of reports that make it possible to diagnose such errors, but they are produced after the design is completed. IEW has an internal expert system that monitors such errors and warns the analyst immediately. Most products still have little or no diagnostic aid.

- **Integrated Data Dictionary** to make all data about the analysis and design available to the analyst. Most products have a Data Dictionary to store information collected by the product. A few can accept information from a DBMS Data Dictionary. Very few can let analysts share data between them from a single common dictionary. Sharing usually requires that one analyst make a copy to be given to another. There is no agreed standard by which dictionary information can be shared between products.

- **Integration of all analysis phases** so an analyst can begin with an Enterprise Model and end with a finished implementation using a single tool. This dream is still several years away for most products. IEW currently comes closest to achieving it.

10
Program

System Implementation

The complete system specifications specify the modules, the interactions between them, and the details within each module. A Structure Chart identifies the modules and the interactions between them. Structured English, Action Diagrams, Decision Tables, or Decision Trees specify detailed procedures within the modules. Once the system has been specified, it must be implemented and installed to function over an extended period. The implementation process includes phases for programming, testing, training users, installation, maintenance, and post-implementation evaluation.

Programming

Specifications are converted into useful systems by producing computer code in some computer language. The method of implementation depends on the language being used. Systems can be implemented using 2GL, 3GL, 4GL, and Object-Oriented languages.

2GL and 3GL Environments

2GL and 3GL languages are very complex and very procedural. Professional programmers are normally required to implement a system in these languages. If they are given clear and complete specifications, they know how to implement the system in an appropriate target language. The choice of language and details of the implementation are too detailed for this book.

CASE and 4GL Environments

In 4GL environments, the system may be implemented by professional programmers or it may be implemented directly by the design team. There are several tools that the designer can use to partially automate the coding process. These are 4GLs, code generators, program templates, code translators, and code re-engineering tools.

- **Fourth Generation Languages.** These are highlevel specification languages having powerful commands that can perform many tasks—such as data manipulation, editing, and formatting—with very few statements. These languages can reduce the number of lines of code by up to 90 percent compared to a 3GL.
- **Code generators.** A code generator is similar to a 4GL in that it uses a high-level specification language. However, it produces a program in a 3GL such as COBOL. Vendors of code generators claim greater machine efficiency. However, this is often at the cost of higher development and maintenance costs. Code generators do not always use a DBMS and an interactive Data Dictionary that documents the structure of the database.

Some CASE tools can translate specifications in a restricted form of Structured English directly into 3GL or 4GL code. Such tools may eliminate programmers. They also allow maintainers to make changes directly to the specifications and generate new code. This can reduce maintenance labor because the maintenance programmers work at a less detailed level.

- **Program templates.** These consist of prewritten skeleton programs that can be customized to deal with specific application problems. For instance, the skeleton of an inventory valuation program would recognize all needed commands and process them. However, it would have to be customized to access a particular file and use a particular method of inventory valuation. Templates are an intermediate between 3GL and 4GL.
- **Code translators.** These tools can translate a program written in one 3GL into another 3GL. Sometimes they translate code written in a 4GL into a 3GL language to increase efficiency. They may be used to translate tested utility modules needed in a different language. They cannot integrate separate programs into a set of programs with consistent files and user interfaces.
- **Code re-engineering.** These tools take badly written 3GL programs and reorganize them automatically to have a more maintainable structure. Sometimes they can be used to salvage code from existing applications to reduce the amount of new code that must be produced. Again, they cannot integrate separate programs into a set of programs with consistent files and user interfaces.

Object-Oriented Programming

Object-Oriented Programming Systems (OOPS) are a new approach to programming. OOPS create independent objects that perform a specific task. The objects work together by passing messages to each other to invoke specific actions. The key features of Object-Oriented Programming are message passing, encapsulation, and inheritance.

- **Message passing.** Modules are not called in a hierarchical manner as shown in a Structure Chart. Instead, they are activated by passing an appropriate message to them. Think of them as things that are always ready to do their job as soon as someone sends a message that requires some action. The message may be sent privately to a single object or publicly to all interested objects.
- **Encapsulation.** Encapsulation is another name for information hiding. An object is like a black box. It is not possible to see how the actions inside are implemented. The state of the object, the messages it can exchange, and the actions it can perform are encapsulated in the object.
- **Inheritance.** Objects can be cloned to produce new objects with the same properties. Some of these properties can be modified to produce different objects of a similar class. The remaining properties of the parent object are inherited by the clone. This simplifies implementation by permitting the sharing of code created in the parent object. As an example, a bank account object might have a number, owner, balance, and interest rate. Savings account and checking account objects inherit these properties and add some new ones, such as number of checks allowed. This makes it easy to implement overlapping and mutually exclusive subtypes.

OOPS is a new concept that is still in the experimental stage. There are not yet any Object-Oriented languages that are suitable for building complex "industrial-strength" business applications. However, the concept promises to

10 Program

simplify the design process by eliminating the rigid hierarchical relationships between modules. Objects have the same characteristics as isolated processes and cohesive loosely coupled modules.

Some people have expressed hopes that Object-Oriented Databases will simplify design and use of databases by making each database entity a self-contained system with data, validity checks, integrity checks, and semantic relationships bound together in one OOPS object. Such systems may make it simpler to manipulate complex data structures, such as statistical data matrices, graphics, or voice messages. It is not clear that it would have any significant advantage for implementing relational databases. Modern relational DBMS are beginning to support validity checks, integrity checks, and semantic relationships. A well-designed database can work in either implementation. A badly designed database will likely be even harder to modify and improve in an OOPS environment.

Testing Application Programs

As program modules are implemented, they have to be tested to make sure that they do exactly what is required and avoid anything that is not required. The purpose of testing is not to prove that the system works as specified. The purpose is to identify all the ways in which it can fail. This subtle distinction focuses the testers attention on anticipating all possible problems.

Of all things produced by humanity, only software is expected to be perfect. While this expectation can never be fully satisfied, it can be approached when good design is followed by careful testing. Testing is needed because the implementation process is very complex. It goes through many stages of translation from specification to program code and each stage is prone to errors. It also involves many complex interactions that no single human mind can keep track of. It is not uncommon for testing to take as much computer time as is used during all stages of productive use that follow.

Testing has the objectives of validation and verification.

- **Validation** asks "Am I building the right product?" This determines if the product solves the right problems. User interaction during the design process validates the system as it is being designed. This is more effective than comparing the final program to a set of requirements defined at the beginning of the design. Requirements change as users become familiar with the system features. Exposing users to the system early concentrates the "requirements creep" into the early phases of design when changes are least costly.
- **Verification** asks the question "Am I building the product right?" This determines whether the product functions correctly. Verification is a process of rigorous and relentless error detection.

Some errors are more serious than others. A formatting error may only affect the looks of a report. However, a Stock Exchange index lost 574 points in 22 months due to a rounding error in calculating the index. A mathematical error in an F16 flight simulator program made the plane flip upside down when it crossed the equator. Such errors cost money or endanger lives.

Different testing methods are needed depending on the stage of the system development and the kind of failure that is being tested. There are different testing strategies and different testing levels.

Testing Strategies

There are three strategies used in testing: clear box testing in which the logic of the program is tested, black box testing in which the results of the program are tested, and ticking box testing in which the user is left to do the testing.

Clear Box Testing

In this strategy, a module is tested by examining the code inside the module. Test methods are designed to verify that the code matches the requirements of the application. These methods are usually used before Black Box methods so that the Black Box reviews do not have to be repeated if problems are discovered. Common clear box techniques are peer review, structured walk-through, and code inspection.

- **Peer Review** occurs when programmers, who are not on the design team, examine the overall design and specifications. They provide a critique of the design to identify possible problems. They usually do not make suggestions for improvement because this would cast them in the role of designers. This is often used for a high-level review of the initial design.
- **Structured Walk-Through** is a method in which the designers step through the logic of their design to qualified peers. The peer group may include a standards enforcer, a program maintainer, an analyst, a customer, a note taker, and sometimes a representative of computer operations. The peers check for good design and correct logic by starting with the outer DO WHILE loops and ending with the inner lines of code. The note taker records any points raised and gives them to the author. The notes are not used to evaluate the programmer. They are used only to identify corrections that need to be made. The review identifies problems, but usually does not suggest solutions, since these are the programmer's problem. This method is often used as a review of the Structured English before coding begins. Reviews can usually handle 100 lines of code in a one hour session.
- **Code Inspection** is a detailed line by line inspection of code by a programmer who did not produce the code. It is like a Walk-Through with a single person and no formal meeting. This serves as a check on the quality of the code and sometimes as a check on the quality of the programmer.

Black Box Testing

This method treats the coded module as a black box. The module is run with inputs that are likely to cause errors. Then the output is checked to see if any errors occurred. For instance, a module that computes logarithms would be given a negative number to see if it could detect such a faulty value. This method cannot be used to test all errors, because some errors may depend on the code or algorithm used to implement the module.

10 Program

Ticking Box Testing

This name is facetiously chosen to indicate testing that is left undone so users have to discover errors in a product that is ticking like a time bomb. This is not a recommended method of testing. It stands for all the testing that is left undone. While it is never desirable to deliver software containing errors, it is also never possible to detect all errors. The best that can be hoped for is to estimate the number of errors remaining after testing is completed. There are two techniques for estimating the number of errors remaining: seeding and failure intensity.

- **Seeding** is implemented by deliberately introducing a number of errors into the program before testing. The proportion of introduced errors detected is assumed to equal the proportion of real errors detected. If 100 are introduced and 90 percent are detected while 450 real errors are detected, then it is estimated that (450/.90)-450 = 50 real errors remain.
- **Failure intensity** is estimated[6] by plotting the logarithm of error density (defined as errors per CPU hour of operation) on the Y-axis against cumulative hours of operation on the X-axis. Alternately cumulative errors can be plotted on the X-axis. The plot is roughly linear and can be extrapolated to estimate the number of hours of testing needed to achieve a desired level of reliability.

Testing Levels

Different tests are performed at the level of individual modules, integrated groups of modules, and whole systems.

Unit Testing

Unit tests are performed on individual modules to detect errors in interfaces, input, output, data structure, arithmetic, comparisons, and control logic.

- **Interfaces.** The interface is the part of a module that passes data and flags to and from another module. The calling and the called modules must exchange the same number, type, and size of data fields in the same order.
- **Input and output.** These tests make sure that data exchanged with external devices, such as files, printers, and metering devices are correct. As with interfaces, the number, type, size, and order of data items are checked. Also, table keys, attribute names, and file structures must be used correctly. Empty files, missing data, and end-of-file flags must be handled correctly.
- **Data structure.** These tests detect errors in formatting data, converting data types, generating arrays, handling compound keys, and initializing counters.
- **Arithmetic.** Common arithmetic problems include invalid operations, incorrect equations, mixed data types, and rounding errors. Division by zero and logarithms of negative numbers are examples of invalid operations that are not mathematically defined. Equations can be incorrect because the wrong equation was used, variables and brackets are incorrectly used, or calculations are not performed in the right order. Some languages are not able to perform arithmetic between mixed data types, such as multiplying a decimal number by an integer. Rounding and truncation errors can occur if storage fields are not long enough or if numbers are rounded or truncated.

- **Comparisons.** Compared data items must be of the same type. It is not reasonable to compare numbers with characters. The value of logical expressions using AND and OR often depends on the calculation order.
- **Control logic.** IF-THEN-ELSE, CASE, and REPEAT structures change the sequence of execution of instructions. Each part of a CASE or IF-THEN-ELSE structure must be executed under appropriate conditions. Each block of a CASE structure must have a label at the front to locate it and a termination at the end to prevent execution of the next block. REPEAT structures must be executed the correct number of times. It is very easy to have errors with empty lists or the first or last item in a list.

Unit tests are performed by calling the module with test data designed to check behavior under circumstances where errors are likely to occur. The tester can select the type, range, list, and order of data for each input variable. In each case, the outputs are examined to make sure that they are correct.

- **Type.** A module should not accept data of an incorrect type. If an input should be integer, it should not accept decimal numbers. If an input should be numeric, it should not accept alphabetic characters. An empty or missing value should be included in the test data. One representative example of each possible kind of error is enough to detect problems with data type. A module may assume correct input only if a database or edit module has previously checked for all errors.
- **Range.** Most inputs have a valid range. For example, percentages range between 0 and 100. Four data points are needed to test for range: the smallest allowable, the largest allowable, just smaller than the smallest, and just larger than the largest. If the percentages must be integer, then -1, 0, 100, and 101 test to see that all legal and illegal values are handled properly.

  Sometimes more than one variable must be tested in combination. Not only must individual percentages be between 1 and 100, but the sum of a list may have to be 100. Lists that sum to less than 100 and more than 100 are included in the test data for such a situation. Accounting Debits and Credits that must sum to zero are another example. Many mathematical functions, like exponentiation, have a theoretical range that is infinite, but a practical range beyond which the computer cannot calculate.

- **List.** CASE or IF-THEN-ELSE structures are often controlled by a list of codes that trigger the different cases. Each value in the list must be tested to make sure that each case is handled correctly. If the trigger is a combination of variables (as described by a Decision Table or Decision Tree) then all combinations must be tested. In addition, an illegal value is included to make sure that illegal values are handled properly.
- **Order.** The order of data items may be important in sequential files or sorted lists. Correct selection from ordered lists is tested by selecting the first, last, and one in the middle. In addition, error handling is tested by selecting non-existent values before the first, in the middle, and after the last. Finally, values that are out of order are included in the test.

Integration Testing   Unit tests test single modules in isolation. Integration tests test modules together to make sure that they work as a group. Integration tests are performed incrementally by adding another module to the system and testing to make sure that it functions properly before adding the next module. This makes it easier to trace errors when they are discovered.

There are two general approaches to integration testing: top-down and bottom-up. In top-down testing the boss module is produced first and the workers are integrated incrementally. In bottom-up testing, the workers are produced first and then integrated incrementally with the boss module. The modules in Figure 10-20 are used to illustrate both approaches.

Top-Down Testing

In top-down testing, Generate Report in Figure 10-20 is coded first and unit tested. It sends Key to Get Valid Data and receives lists of Names and Values that correspond to each Key. If there is No-Data for a Key, then the Key is ignored. When data for all values of Key are received, the data are reorganized, transformed, and reported. Since Generate Report calls Get Valid Data, Transform Data, and Put Report, it cannot be tested without these three worker modules.

Figure 10-20
A Structure Chart to illustrate testing order.

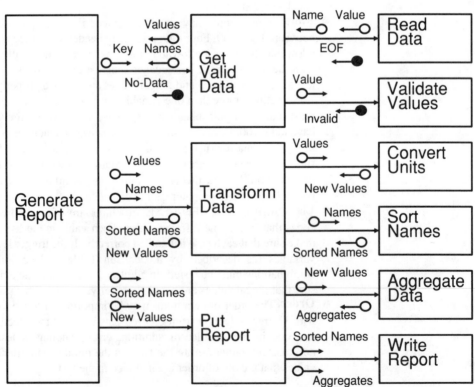

This problem is solved by coding simple modules called *stubs* that simulate the behavior of the workers. The simulation only has to be good enough to accept parameters and deliver representative data and flags. Stubs are like counterfeit money or stand-in actors. They look like the real thing, but they cost much less to obtain. The Get Valid Data stub does not have to read data or call Read Data and Validate Values. It only has to accept Key and return a Values list and a Names list. Random number and random character generators could be used to provide Values and Names for testing.

Similarly, the Transform Data stub can ignore the Values and Names passed to it. It only has to return Sorted Names and New Values of the correct type and range. The Put Report stub does not have to use the data sent to it. It can print a mockup report or a message that says that Put Report has been called.

Generate Report can be tested with the stubs to make sure that module logic is correct, flags are handled correctly, and all expected conditions can be processed. The No-Data flag is the only flag it receives. At least one test must check to make sure that Generate Report handles it correctly.

The process is repeated at the next level. For this example, the next implemented module is the Get Valid Data module with stubs to simulate the Read Data and the Validate Values modules. Get Valid Data fetches all data that corresponds to Key. It reads an individual Name and Value with Read Data, checks the values using Validate Values, and collects the names and values into lists called Names and Values until EOF (End Of File) is encountered. It sends a No-Data flag if the file contains no names at all. Invalid records are discarded. The Read Data stub does not have to read the data file. It can generate a random name and value. At some point it also generates an EOF to terminate the process. The Validate Values stub can randomly return an Invalid flag to simulate value checking. The stubs should count the number of values sent to make sure that data are not lost by Get Valid Data.

Often the input and output modules are developed first so the user can see a prototype of the system. This makes it easier to identify problems or missing features in the specifications. Sometimes modules that are critical to the system are developed first to prove that anticipated problems can be solved.

The advantage of top-down testing is that the architecture of the system is tested early to make sure that all components eventually fit together. An early prototype is available to show users that something is being produced. The prototype can also be used to validate the design specifications.

The disadvantage of top-down testing is that it may be difficult to produce stubs that generate all the situations with which the boss module must deal. There may have to be multiple versions of the stub for the different cases to be tested. Alternately, the stub may be a screen that the tester can use to enter different test cases. When the interactions between stubs are complicated, then the tester may have problems keeping all the stubs synchronized.

10
Program

Bottom-Up Testing

This approach begins by implementing the lowest level of worker modules first. Read Data and Validate Values in Figure 10-20 are implemented first. Then a driver module is coded to simulate calls by Get Valid Data. A driver is like a stub except that it acts as a boss instead of a worker. The driver that simulates Get Valid Data has to send Key to Read Data and Value to Validate Values. It accepts all values sent to it, but does not need to create lists of Values and Names or send the No-Data flag to a boss. Separate drivers can be used to test Read Data and Validate Values. The purpose of the driver is not to show that they work together. It is to show that they each do their job.

This approach tests the utility modules to make sure that they work before proceeding with the control structure. Input and output modules are often implemented first under this approach also. When a library of utility modules exists, then useful modules can be tested quickly. Validate Values, Convert Units, and Sort Names may already exist in tested form in a program library. If so, development can start with middle level modules like Transform Data. However, the overall architecture cannot be tested until all modules are complete. If there is an error in the overall design, it may have an impact on many lower modules which must be redesigned, recoded, and retested.

In practice, the best place to start coding and testing is at the most uncertain modules. These are most likely to require specification changes that cause a ripple of changes through the other modules. If the architecture is uncertain, then start at the top. If the user interface is uncertain, then begin with input and output. If the processing algorithm is expected to be a bottleneck, then start with the central transformation modules.

Function Testing

Function tests make sure that the integrated system performs all the functions defined in the specifications. The same test data used for module tests should be processed to make sure that the complete system functions properly. All screens, files, processing options, and reports should be used. Documentation and user interfaces should be tested using new users who have not worked with the system. When these tests are complete, it is assured that the system is capable of doing all the things that have been specified. It is not yet assured that they can be done efficiently or effectively.

System Testing

System testing determines whether the system can perform all of it functions in a realistic operating environment. It must be able to handle peak loads, store all required data, respond rapidly, and recover from mechanical failures.

- **Peak load.** The system must be able to handle all transactions during periods of peak load without failures or unreasonable delays. Peak loads may occur during busy seasons, such as winter holidays in a ski resort. Peak loads may occur at certain times of day, such as lunch breaks in banks, just before flight departures in airlines, or just after computer labs begin in a school. Driver programs can simulate terminals to test peak input volumes.

- **Storage.** Storage devices must be able to store the maximum number of records that the system is expected to encounter. Many file structures use extra space to provide for indexes and file expansion. Inserts, updates, and even deletions may have unexpected impacts on storage requirements and access time. Synthetic records can be generated to fill the files. Driver programs can generate suitable numbers of insertions, updates, and deletions to make sure that storage systems perform properly.

- **Response.** A system may respond quickly with a few transactions, yet be unacceptably slow under peak loads. The system must be tested to determine how long it takes to get a response to a screen query, transmit a message across a network, and run major tasks like printing a long report. These tests must be done under realistic loads because response time can rise exponentially as more users are added to the system.

- **Recovery.** Most computers fail occasionally due to power failures, lightning storms, hardware failures, or other emergencies. Data Base Management Systems usually have features that aid in recovering from such unanticipated stoppages. Procedures must be in place to recover from failures. A "fire drill" is needed to make sure that they work.

Drivers and Stubs

Drivers and stubs are important tools used for testing. They simulate the environment in which a module must operate. They provide a fake boss and fake workers to fool the module into behaving as if it were part of a complete system. A module can act as a boss, a worker, or both, depending on the nature of the module. Figure 10-21 shows the Get Valid Data Module, its boss, and its workers from Figure 10-20. A complete test of the module requires a driver to simulate the call from the Generate Report Module and stubs to simulate the behavior of the Read Data and Validate Values Modules.

A boss module typically performs three major functions:

- **Select module** to call.
- **Pass data** between modules.
- **Terminate jobs** that are impossible.

Figure 10-21

Driver and stubs for testing a module.

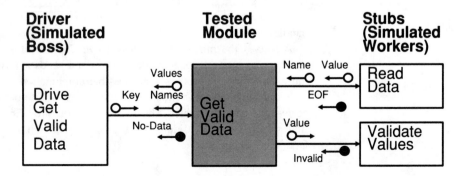

Driver (Simulated Boss)

Drive Get Valid Data

Tested Module

Get Valid Data

Stubs (Simulated Workers)

Read Data

Validate Values

A driver that simulates a boss calls only the module being tested. It does not test the selection of the correct module and it does not simulate the termination logic. However, it must be able to pass data to the module being tested and it must make sure that any data being received has the correct form and value. The most common way to obtain test data is to store all required test cases on a file along with the expected results. The test data are read by the driver, passed to the module under test, and the results are compared with the expected results. The following Structured English specifies a driver that calls Get Valid Data to test it with different test cases.

```
MODULE DRIVE_GET_VALID_DATA
   REPEAT WHILE NOT End_Of_File
      READ NEXT Key, Exp_Values, Exp_Names, Exp_No_Data from
         Driver_File
      CALL GET_VALID_DATA using
         INPUT Key
         OUTPUT Values, Names, No_Data
      IF Values NE Exp_Values
         PRINT Key, Values, Exp_Values
      ENDIF
      IF Names NE Exp_Names
         PRINT Key, Names, Exp_Names
      ENDIF
      IF No_Data NE Exp_No_Data
         PRINT Key, No_Data, Exp_No_Data
      ENDIF
   END REPEAT
END MODULE
```

Driver_File contains test data records with valid data, invalid keys, and keys for non-existent records. The expected results (variables beginning with Exp_) are stored with the test data to make comparisons easy. Only the erroneous results are printed along with the input key to make it easy to trace errors. The test cases should start with good data and end with bad data. First make sure that the module does everything it is supposed to do. Then test to see if it detects and handles errors.

A stub is the mirror image of a driver. Instead of sending parameters and receiving answers, it receives parameters and sends answers. A worker module must know how to process each possible combination of inputs and what possible errors can occur. A file is often the easiest way to obtain the right answer to correspond to a parameter. The following Structured English specifies a driver that simulates the Validate_Values Module which is a worker that serves Get_Valid_data.

```
MODULE VALIDATE_VALUES
    INPUT Value
    OUTPUT Invalid
    REPEAT UNTIL Value=File_Value
        READ File_Value, Invalid from Stub_File_2
    END REPEAT
    PRINT Value, Invalid
END MODULE
```

Stub_File_2 must contain the corresponding value of Invalid for each of the values used in the tests. This lets the module validate every test case. It does not have to be able to validate every possible value. It only validates the values used in testing. Stub_File_2 must contain test data corresponding to Stub_file_1 used by the Read_data stub and Driver_file which checks the results in the driver. Test data are usually developed as a set. When the real Validate_Values is completed, the stub and its corresponding file will not be needed. It may be worth keeping the test files for use during maintenance. Revised modules can usually be retested using the same stubs and drivers. A similar stub will be needed to simulate the Read_Data Module.

If Top-down implementation is used, only stubs will be needed. If bottom-up implementation is used, then only drivers will be needed. If individual modules are being implemented, as in the above example, then both may be needed.

Training Users

Users must be trained before they can use a new system. Training begins while the system is being completed and before it is installed. Several training methods are available. Each may be suitable for different groups of users.

Training Methods

There are four common training methods: manuals, courses, consultants, and computer-aided tutorials.

- **Manuals** are provided with most systems. They have the advantage that they are cheap, portable, and accessible. They can be used at the office, taken home, or kept beside a terminal. However, the manuals have to be well organized so the user can find needed information easily.

Two kinds of manuals are needed. The first is a tutorial manual that is used to learn a system for the first time. It takes a problem-oriented view and steps the user through a typical problem. An example is a word processing manual that shows the user how to do all things needed to prepare a business letter. The second manual is like a dictionary. It lists each feature or option and what happens if it is used. This manual is useful to experienced users who know how to do most things they need, but have to look up details occasionally.

It is difficult and costly to keep manuals up-to-date. They change frequently and new copies or update pages have to be sent to users regularly. Users may neglect to insert updates in their master copy. The manual may not be

10
Program

with the user when it is needed. Also the user must be willing to look in the manual for information. Many users are intimidated by large manuals and prefer to ask other people for help.

A trend is developing toward electronic manuals on the computer. These are cheaper and they can be placed on the same computer as the software. If the software is on a network, the manual only has to be installed once to serve all users on the network.

- **Courses** are useful when several people must be trained at the same time. Trainees can actually use the system during the course and they can ask questions of the instructor. However, they can be expensive and they are impractical for training only a few users at one time. Courses for standard software are provided by vendors and external consulting organizations.
- **Consultants** should always be available to help users who run into problems. Many organizations set up an Information Center which has people with the job of helping users with computer problems. They may also have the responsibility for offering special courses as required.
- **Computer-Aided Tutorials** can be a useful way of training new users. A well-designed tutorial can simultaneously instruct the user in how to use the system and illustrate how it operates. It is available at any time, so users can take a refresher course whenever they need it. New users can use it immediately without waiting for scheduled courses. However, good tutorials are expensive and hard to develop. Poor ones are sometimes worse than useless. So tutorials are usually justified only for systems with very many scattered users, such as commercial microcomputer packages.

Categories of Users

There are usually three broad categories of users that need separate training programs. These are operators, users, and supervisors. They can each be trained by one or more of the training methods just outlined.

- **Operators** are the people who run the computer on a daily basis. They start up the application, run batch jobs, backup data files, and restore the system if it fails. They need to know how to do each of these things, how to diagnose problems, and how to overcome them. Operators provide a service function to keep the system running.
- **Users** are the people who enter data, obtain reports, and interact with the system to obtain useful output. These are the people for whom the system was designed. They need to become very proficient in using the system.
- **Supervisors** are responsible for training and helping users, setting broad parameters of the system, and providing access for users. They need a broader knowledge of the system than most users, but they are less proficient with it.

Installation

After the users have been trained and the system has been fully tested, it is ready for installation. In most cases this means replacing an existing system and converting old files to run on the new system. If the file structure changes in a major way or if multiple files have to be merged, file conversion can be a complex exercise. The installation may be accompanied by some combination of new hardware, new procedures, new activities, and new people. There is a period of adjustment while all these components are brought together.

There are four common approaches to conversion: the plunge, the pilot, the phase-in, and the parallel. They differ in the time at which each component is installed as illustrated in Figure 10-22.

- **Plunge.** This is the "cold-turkey" method in which the old system is closed and the new one is installed all at once, often over a weekend. This method provides a clean psychological break with the past since there is no old system to fall back on. However, it can lead to disaster if the new system has problems and the old one no longer works. One company did a direct cutover of its cost accounting system and found that it did not work. They were without cost data for nearly a year before the system was fully functional.

- **Pilot.** The pilot method installs the system with a group of representative users who test the system. All other users continue with the old system. The group using the system has an opportunity to shake the system down and identify problems. When the problems are ironed out, the system is installed for everyone else.

- **Phase-in.** The phase-in method installs the system in stages. The stages may be different parts of the system or they may be different groups or regions in the organization. This method is most useful if a lot of training and installation is involved. The same group can move from one site to another to perform the same tasks as the phase-in progresses. The old system disappears by gradual withdrawal. If problems are encountered, the new system can be delayed and the old one can continue to function until the problems are resolved.

Figure 10-22

Different strategies for timing installation.

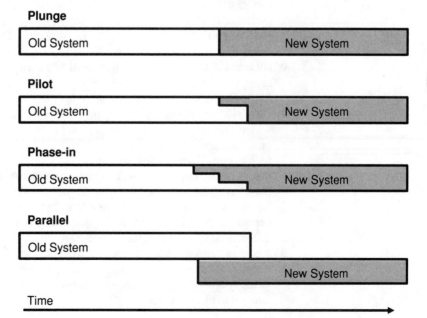

Plunge

Pilot

Phase-in

Parallel

Time

- **Parallel.** The parallel method runs both the new and the old system for a period until the new system has been proven. It is the safest method because the old system still exists in case the new one fails. It is like wearing both a belt and suspenders. However, users are less motivated to learn the new system while they still have the old one. The cost and personnel requirements of running two systems may also be prohibitive.

Maintenance and Support

A computer system is a model of some aspects of the operations of an organization. As the organization changes, the system must change to reflect the organization using it. Maintenance is the task of keeping the system "evergreen." Most Information Systems Departments devote about 75 percent of their effort to maintenance activities. There are several causes of maintenance and there are several ways of implementing revisions to a system.

Causes of Maintenance

The most common causes of maintenance are program errors, changing needs, changes in the external environment, changing technology, and aging.

- **Program errors** remain in systems even after rigorous testing. They are often called bugs, and like bugs, they must be exterminated. They are common in new systems and gradually disappear as users detect and report them.
- **Changing needs** require that systems be adapted to meet them. Users usually specify a system to deal with current problems. As the system helps to solve the current problems, it reveals other problems that have remained hidden or arise as a consequence of the solution to the initial problems. A customer information system in a bank may be installed to identify the profitability of different classes of customers. If it is successful, it will create a need for a system that helps tellers cross-sell services to groups of customers that have been identified as prospects for the service. Thus a person obtaining a mortgage may be suggested as a likely prospect for a home-furnishings loan.
- **Changes in the external environment** often require system changes. New laws, taxes, or competitive forces usually require a response in the system. These changes are often mandatory, rather than discretionary.
- **Changing technology** may require changes to the internal structure of the system. New screens, printers, language versions, telecommunication protocols, and computers may require changes in the way a program performs its functions. New screens may require different screen layouts. New printers may generate opportunities for graphic reports. A new version of a language may have incompatibilities with an old version or features that increase efficiency if the program is recoded. Telecommunications protocols may permit integration of applications that used to be separate. A conversion to a different computer often involves changes to all of the other factors.
- **Aging** systems gradually become difficult to maintain. After many patches by the maintenance staff, the original cut and fabric of the system may become virtually unrecognizable. The system becomes unwieldy and needs a complete renewal to modernize it.

Revisions

The different causes of maintenance lead to problems with different degrees of complexity and urgency. Major software organizations divide revisions into three classes: fixes, releases, and versions.

- **Fixes** are emergency corrections of errors or emergency responses to competitive pressures. They are made available as soon as possible. They may not be tested and documented as completely as a normal system.
- **Releases** are collections of periodic enhancements and corrections that are delivered every few months. They eliminate the turmoil of continual revision and eradicate minor annoyances that are not urgent enough to require fixes.
- **Versions** provide major functional or technical changes. They are released every few years and they represent a major effort with complete testing, new documentation, and possibly a need for user training.

Post-Implementation Evaluation

None of us likes to be evaluated. Evaluation has a connotation of blame and finger-pointing. However, evaluation can also be an important method of learning. If used in this way, a post-implementation audit can provide useful suggestions for future improvement. There are actually two different kinds of evaluation. These are a review and an audit. The review examines how the system was implemented. The audit examines how successful the system is.

Review

The review is designed to find out what lessons were learned from the development project that can be passed on to future projects. It consists of a one or two hour brainstorming session right after project completion. The result is a set of recommendations for changes in the way future systems are implemented. It may recommend that an experimental method be incorporated into standard operating practice. Alternately, it may recommend that some design stages be changed, reordered, or eliminated. The emphasis should be on improvements, not mistakes.

Audit

The audit evaluates the success of the system after it has been in operation for at least several months. The delay provides time to shake out initial installation problems and gives the users a chance to understand the full potential of the system. Success can be measured in terms of cost, delivery schedule, completeness, and quality.

- **Cost** is evaluated by comparing the actual cost of the system with the estimated costs used to justify the project. Similarly, the benefits should be compared to the benefits used to justify the project.
- **Delivery schedule** is evaluated by comparing the projected delivery schedule with the actual delivery schedule.
- **Completeness** is evaluated by comparing the user requirements stated during the various stages of analysis with the functions actually delivered by the system.

10 Program

- **Quality** is the most difficult factor to measure. A user survey can provide a surrogate for a quality measure. A system that is liked by the users and is heavily used by them is likely of high quality. Heavy use is a measure of quality only when the users have a choice about using it. Some systems, like the corporate accounting system, may have to be used because there is no alternative. In such a case, the satisfaction survey is a better indicator.

The audit results lead to more realistic estimates of future project costs and benefits. They will also influence the acceptance of future projects. For this reason, the audit should be performed by an impartial group that is not suspected of any bias.

Review

This completes the analysis, design, and implementation of both the database and application programs. The stages are displayed in Figure 10-23. The three major phases of a system design are architectural design, database design, and program design.

The architectural design precedes database and program design in most large systems. It lays a foundation for the other two phases. The main products are an Entity-Relationship Diagram that is a foundation for database design and a set of activities that is a foundation for program design. The two are used together to identify clusters of activities that should be implemented together. Economic and other factors can be used to determine which cluster has the highest priority and should be implemented first.

The database design begins with an Entity-Relationship Diagram. This is refined to create an Extended Entity-Relationship Diagram that includes all entities in the system and the constraints on their relationships. Forms analysis, file analysis, and interviews are used to identify the attributes of each entity. Normalization is used to make sure that the entities do not contain redundant data that can lead to insertion, update, and deletion anomalies. Then the database can be implemented using a Data Base Management System. With an implemented database, prototyping can be used to design and implement forms, screens, and reports.

The activities identified in the architectural design become the high-level processes of a Data Flow Diagram which begins the process of program design. The Data Flow Diagram identifies all the processes in the organization as the data are transformed by the processes. It can be converted to a Structure Chart which forms the skeleton and control structure of the application modules. These are checked for coupling and cohesion problems to make sure that the modules are as independent as possible. Then each module is specified in detail using Structured English, Decision Tables, or Decision Trees. Finally the design is implemented, users are trained, and the system is installed.

This is an idealized view of the analysis and design process. In actual practice, there is more interaction and iteration between the stages. The architecture

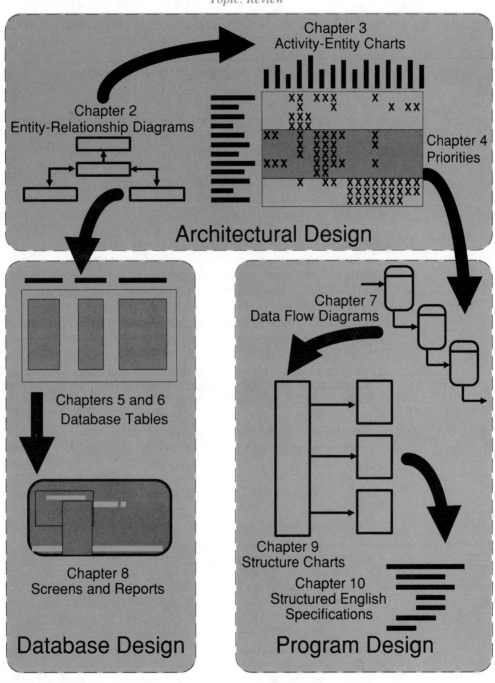

Figure 10-23

The stages of an analysis and design project.

changes as the database and applications are designed. In actual development projects there are many opportunities to reorder the development stages to speed development, reduce work, or get better coordination. The presentation of methods in a book must be sequential. In actual practice, work phases may overlap or be carried out in parallel. the following are some of the ways that analysis stages can be rearranged.

- **Joint Application Design** sessions can be used to identify data, screen, application, and report requirements at the same time. Prototype screens, Context Diagrams, and Data Flow Diagrams may be used in JAD sessions to show users what the system will look like or what it will do. Prototype screens are a good way of finding out what data the users need. Data Flow Diagrams are a good way of getting users to explain the processes they perform.

- **Attributes and data normalization** can be considered while gathering data for Entity-Relationship models. This speeds the process since the same sources are used for all data. An analyst who understands normalization will naturally design independent entities and normal tables.

- **Data Flow Diagrams, Structure Charts, and Structured English** can be combined once good habits are formed. Module specifications are often gathered when information for the Data Flow Diagram is being gathered. The Structure Chart is a good way of learning to detect coupling and cohesion problems. The experienced analyst learns to recognize these problems while producing a Data Flow Diagram. The analyst can then move directly to Structured English or Action Diagrams. On small projects, an experienced analyst may start with Structured English. This is not advisable for inexperienced analysts because they must first get practice in recognizing places where coupling and cohesion problems occur.

- **Database and application design** can be performed in parallel by coordinating teams. This can reduce total development time. This only works if there is a good Entity-Relationship Model for both groups to work from. If the data model has not been normalized, there will be many iterations as the data structure changes. Detailed design of screens, reports, and applications sometimes identifies new data requirements.

- **The Enterprise Model** may not be needed on small projects. This shortcut may be satisfactory when the project never interacts with other projects, as in a commercial software product. However, eliminating this step leads to unintegrated systems and data duplication in most organizations.

- **Standards and technology** can be selected in parallel with Enterprise Modeling or detailed analysis and design. CASE tools must be selected early, but computers will not be needed until implementation. Programming and interface standards should be set once and adhered to for all applications.

- **Training and documentation** can occur in parallel with implementation. JAD sessions and prototyping can be part of the training. User-friendly systems require less documentation because they use standard interfaces and intuitive models. Online documentation can be created from selected parts of the documentation stored in the CASE tool.

- **Report design and implementation** can be left to the end of the development cycle. Reports will not be needed until the other parts of the system are working.

The analyst must resist the temptation to take too many shortcuts. The architectural design stage is needed. Without it there is a big danger that the implemented pieces will not work together. The database should usually be implemented first. Otherwise, the needs of other applications are not considered during database design. Structure Charts should be produced until the design of cohesive and uncoupled modules is an entrenched habit. Then use Action Diagrams.

The remaining chapters of this book deal with extensions to the design process. Chapter 11 covers the design of systems distributed over several computers. Chapter 12 covers the design of systems in which computers interact with continuous processes in factories or other environments. Chapter 13 deals with the organizational problems encountered in converting to a CASE environment.

Summary

This chapter has explained how to specify the details of a module unambiguously so a programmer can correctly code and test the module.

The basic operations that a programmer can perform are:

- **Sequences** of commands.
- **Selection** of alternatives. This can be accomplished by using either an IF ... THEN ... ELSE ... structure or a CASE structure.
- **Iteration** through an arbitrary number of loops. If the test is performed before the beginning of a loop it is called a REPEAT WHILE loop. If the test is performed after the completion of a loop it is called a REPEAT UNTIL loop.

Specifications can be written in **Structured English** or Action Diagrams. Structured English is a restricted subset of English that corresponds to the operations that can be coded in a computer program. It is easy to write and it is fairly easy to understand.

Action Diagrams are similar to Structured English with some graphic features to make them easier to understand the specifications. They are still relatively easy to draw and they can be used as a substitute for Data Flow Diagrams and Structure Charts.

Decision Tables and **Decision Trees** can be used as a supplement to the previous methods when the logical choices in the module are complicated. Decision Tables are preferred for the most complex problems. Some users prefer Decision Trees for simpler problems.

The ideal method of specification must be relatively easy for both users and programmers to understand. The user is asked to verify the correctness of the specifications. The programmer is asked to implement them.

The system may be implemented in a 2GL, 3GL, or 4GL environment. 4GL environments provide languages, code generators, program templates, code translators, and code re-engineering tools.

10
Program

Programs can be tested using clear box or black box strategies. Peer review, structured walk-throughs, and code inspection are used in clear box methods. Test data that are expected to detect errors are used in the black box strategy.

Tests can be performed at the unit, integration, function, and system level. Unit tests are performed on individual modules to detect errors in interfaces, input, output, data structure, arithmetic, comparisons, and control logic. Integration tests are done incrementally by adding successive modules to the system and testing to ensure that they function properly. The additions can be in top-down or bottom-up order. Function tests are designed to ensure that the integrated system performs all the functions defined in the specifications. System tests ensure that the system can process peak loads, store all required data, respond rapidly, and recover from mechanical failures.

Users can be trained with manuals, courses, consultants, and computer-aided tutorials. Operators, users, and supervisors need different training.

There are four common approaches to conversion of applications: the plunge, the pilot, the phase-in, and the parallel. The plunge converts all at once. The pilot installs a test system. The phase-in installs the system in stages. The parallel method runs both the new and the old system for a while.

Keywords and Phrases

Action Diagram	Machine
Black Box	Object-Oriented Programming
Bottom-Up Testing	OOPS
Clear Box	Peak Load
Code Generator	Peer Review
Code Re-Engineering	Repeat Structure
Code Translator	Selection Structure
Concurrent Structure	Sequence Structure
Decision Table	State
Decision Tree	State Machine Diagram
Encapsulation	Structured English
Function Testing	Structured Walk-Through
Inheritance	System Testing
Integration Testing	Top-Down Testing
Keyword	Unit Testing

Review Questions

1. Define each of the items in the list of keywords and phrases.
2. What components are visible in a clear box but not visible in a black box?
3. Name and explain the basic structures used to document all processes.
4. In what ways is Structured English better than ordinary English for describing the detailed contents of a module?
5. How does Structured English differ from ordinary English?

6. Explain the advantages and disadvantages of using Action Diagrams instead of Structured English to document the details of modules.
7. Identify the steps in producing a Decision Table.
8. Identify the tools that a designer can use to automate the coding process. Explain what each tool does.
9. How does black box testing differ from clear box testing?
10. Identify the different kinds of unit tests and give an example of test data that would be used for each test.
11. How are integration tests performed?
12. What purpose do system tests serve?
13. Identify the different methods of training users and specify the circumstances under which each would be used.
14. What options are available for scheduling the installation of a new system? What are the advantages and disadvantages of each method?
15. What are the main reasons that a software system needs maintenance?
16. What are the different classes of revisions produced by a maintenance group and how do they differ?
17. What factors are used to measure the success of a system development project?

Problems

1. Produce a Decision Table that is equivalent to the retirement benefit policy described below in Structured English.

   IF employee has served less than 2 years
   THEN return employee contribution to employee
   ELSE
       IF employee is at least 50 years old
       THEN
           IF employee has at least 20 years service
           THEN pay pension of 2.0% per year of service
           ELSE pay pension of 1.9% per year of service
           END IF
       ELSE return employee + company contribution to employee
       END IF
   END IF

2. Design a set of data files that can be used to unit test the MATCH_FIRST_COURSE module and its submodules documented in Figure 10-10. Assume that units are developed and tested in bottom-up order.

3. Assume that the MATCH_FIRST_COURSE module documented in Figure 10-10 is being coded in top-down order. You are responsible for writing stubs to test the module. What stubs are required? What does each one do?

10
Program

4. A bank provides a special service package for a monthly fee of five dollars. It provides reduced charges for a number of services, including writing checks. The charge for checks for each type of account is computed as follows:

   Checks written on a checking account cost 50 cents per check without the service package and nothing with the service package. Checks written on a savings account are free for the first two each month and cost 40 cents for all others. Savings account customers with a service package pay half as much. Customers with a bonus savings account pay 25 cents for each check written on the account with or without the service package.

   Document the calculation of charges for checks on monthly statements using each of: Structured English, an Action Diagram, a Decision Table, and a Decision Tree.

5. The calculation of tuition fees at a university is a complicated function of program, residency, and number of courses. Undergraduates taking less than three courses are charged $200 per course or a flat charge of $1000 per term if three or more courses are taken. Graduate students are charged $1500 per term regardless of the number of courses. Foreign students are charged twice as much if they are part of an exchange program or three times as much if they are not part of an exchange program. In addition, all students pay a student fee of $100 plus an additional fee of $50 if they are living in a university residence.

   Document the calculation of the bill to students, using a Decision Table and again using a Decision Tree.

6. A program has three numeric inputs that represent the lengths of the three sides of a triangle. It returns a result that identifies the triangle as one of the three kinds of triangles: equilateral, isosceles, and scalene. As an example, if it gets the inputs 3, 3, 2, it identifies the triangle as isosceles. Design a set of black box tests to detect errors in the program.

7. A system is designed to provide automatic approval of credit card purchases using a card reader attached to the merchant's cash register. The card reader dials the credit card company's computer and transmits data once the connection has been established. The data has the following contents:

   - **MERCHANT_ID.** This is a 9 digit number of the form 999 999 999.
   - **CUSTOMER_ID.** This is a 10 digit number of the form 9999 999 999.
   - **EXPIRY_DATE.** This is a numeric date of the form MM/YY.
   - **AMOUNT.** This is the sale amount which must be a money value of the form 999999.99.

   A module checks the transaction to make sure that it has all the following properties:

- The MERCHANT_ID is in the list of valid merchants.
- The CUSTOMER_ID is in the list of valid customers.
- The EXPIRY_DATE is the same as the one recorded for the CUSTOMER_ID.
- The card has not been reported stolen on the customer record.
- The AMOUNT is above zero and no larger than the customer's recorded credit limit.

Design a set of test data to unit test the module that checks for valid transactions. Explain what each test record is testing for.

8. The following "Structured English" instructions were written by an analyst who is no longer with your organization because the analyst was difficult to understand. Identify the errors in the way Structured English has been used and convert the instructions into correct Structured English.

     READ a transaction from the file called CUSTOMERS.
     ADD the variable called SALES to TOTAL and also add it to
        GRAND-TOTAL.
     REPEAT this until a new customer has been encountered.
     PRINT the customer name and the TOTAL and then reset it to zero.*
     REPEAT this a lot of times until there are no more CUSTOMER'S
        records on the file.
     THEN print the GRAND-TOTAL.

     *Remember to set TOTAL to zero before the first customer is read.

9. Nocturnal Aviation Insurance Inc. is implementing a new sales support system that is to be used by all 1500 sales representatives. Portable terminals will be issued to representatives who can connect directly to a company computer during a sales presentation to a customer. The system will enter customer information, list available options, quote prices, and record a sale.

   The new system will replace an existing system based on paper forms and is expected to reduce entry errors and transaction delays. Each representative must attend a one week course in how to use a terminal. They also learn how to change the sales approach to the customer to capitalize on the progressive image that the terminals are expected to create. A new sales commission structure is being implemented at the same time to encourage use of the terminals.

   The system will run on the five regional computers operated by the company. The system is scheduled for completion by mid November. The Accounting Department is anxious to have the system installed by January 1 to coincide with the start of the next fiscal year. This would eliminate the need to calculate commissions by both the new and old methods in the same year.

   The Information Systems group thinks that it could install the system in all five regions if there are no delays in the completion date. They have com-

10 Program

pleted 80 percent of their projects on time over the last three years. They would have to put in some overtime during the installation period, but they are used to that.

The Marketing group expects resistance from some of the older sales representatives who have a congenital fear of computers. They also think that it would be difficult to schedule training in December because of Christmas holidays and a year-end rush to make sales that count toward annual bonuses.

Your superior wants you to propose an installation schedule that considers the needs of the different groups in the company and is best for the company as a whole.

10. The following instructions are typical of many documents designed to explain systems to users. They are taken from the Educational Deduction section of the Canadian General Tax Guide which accompanies all Canadian Income Tax forms.

"A qualifying program is one in which courses were at least three consecutive weeks duration. There must have been at least ten hours work in the program each week, at a post-secondary level. Courses at an institution certified by the Minister of Employment and Immigration need not be at the post-secondary level. They must, however, be courses that furnish a person with skills for or improve a person's skills in an occupation.

Full-time attendance at a university outside Canada in a course at least 13 weeks long and leading to a degree also qualifies. You also qualify if you lived in Canada and commuted to the United States to attend a college or university there.

You may not claim this deduction if (i) you received training allowances under the National Training Act, (ii) you were a nurse in training and received free board and lodging or other allowance from the nursing school, (iii) you were reimbursed for the cost of the courses (other than by award money), or (iv) you were receiving salary or wages while taking a job-related course.

You may not need all of this amount to reduce your taxable income to zero. In this case a supporting person may be able to claim the unused portion. If you are a supporting person claiming an "equivalent to married" or "child" exemption for someone who qualifies to claim this deduction, you may claim the deduction to which the dependent would be entitled on your own return. If you are supporting a person for whom you are prevented from claiming such an exemption only because his or her net income exceeded $4,140, you may still be able to transfer a portion of the education deduction. Only the amount not required to reduce the students **taxable income** to zero may be claimed. This applies even if no tax was payable by the student."

a. Critique the understandability of these instructions.

b. Rewrite the instructions to make them clearer using the concepts of Structured English.

11. Fill in this crossword puzzle using words defined in Chapters 5 to 10.

DOWN

1 A procedure that links two relational tables by common attributes.
2 Highest entity type in a hierarchy of entities.
3 Diagram of data structure.
5 Row in a relational table.
6 Alias.
10 Level of coupling in which modules share data stored in a global area of memory.

ACROSS

2 Attribute(s) that uniquely identify an entity occurrence.
4 Temporary module used to simulate the behavior of a boss module during testing.
7 Measure of how closely statements in a module are related.
8 A kind of key used to create links with another entity.
9 Tasks performed to achieve a mission.
11 List from which users select on a screen.
12 Software system used to create, manage, and protect data.
13 Set of programming instructions that can be invoked by name.
14 Picture on a screen representing an application or action.

10 Program

12. Saul Oman is in charge of a corporate system development group. The group consists of 75 programmers and analysts of various ages ranging from older COBOL programmers, who remember what an IBM 7040 is, to exuberant young programmers who learned and loved 3GL C programming in their recent Computer Science degrees. The normal career path is for programmers to become programmer-analysts, and then analysts, just like Saul, himself.

Saul's group is quite decentralized. Saul believes that analysis, design, and programming are creative processes. He prefers to hire bright people and give them the freedom to use their talents to best advantage. This often leads to new and creative solutions to problems. On the other hand, the users complain that the software they have is difficult to learn because each package has different commands, different rules, and different screens. Saul has allocated more of his staff's time to writing user documentation to overcome this problem. Saul believes the users like the results they have been getting because they keep coming back to ask for improvements and extensions. There is a three year backlog of new applications waiting to be done.

Since the programs may also be written in different languages, the programmers who wrote the original application usually also have to maintain it. They keep private files of their program documentation or rely on memory when maintenance becomes necessary. This sometimes leads to problems. Once an application had to be rewritten when a programmer left to join a commune in the Kootenay Mountains and nobody could find any documentation to describe what the program does or even where the source code was stored.

Managers have been asking for more and more special reports that involve more than one independent system. These have usually been produced by writing a special program that scrapes data from the required files and organizes them into a new report. This has led to a proliferation of small applications. Lately there have been many examples of users who have entered data from printed reports into their microcomputers so they could perform analyses themselves to avoid the backlog.

The development process in Saul's department uses clear specification, analysis, design, production, and testing phases. The users, with some help from an analyst, produce a requirements document that states their needs. Then Saul assigns an analyst to go through the requirements and convert them into specifications that can be understood by programmers.

A lead programmer and a team of programmers is assigned to implement the project. The lead programmer partitions the project out to individual programmers. They design the screens, reports, and application programs needed to meet the specifications. Each of the programmers codes their design, tests it, and delivers it to the lead programmer, who integrates the different parts into a complete system.

Programs are usually written in COBOL, although there has been a trend lately to use more C Language. A programmer recently tried to do the reports and screens for a project using a report writer and screen painter. However, this led to more trouble than it was worth because these components were hard to integrate with the Cobol and C programs used by the other people on the team. The time saved by the new tools was used up in integrating with the other components.

The lead programmer is the key to the success of the system, because the different parts do not always fit well together. The lead may have to make modifications under severe time and budget pressures at the end of a project.

The group is responsible for development and maintenance of all programs in their organization. About 15 percent of their time is spent on new development and the rest is spent on maintenance of existing programs. Saul has been warned by his manager that there is a plan to commission a large new application in about a year that will be critical to the future success of the business. He estimates the application will tie up 25 of his staff for a year and a half using current methods. This will not only preclude all other new development, but it will also make it very difficult to do anything more than essential maintenance. Programmers not directly involved with the new project will have to maintain the programs usually handled by project personnel, even if they are not familiar with the application or the computer language.

Saul is excited by the new project, but worried about whether his current staff can handle it. Hiring more than one or two new programmers is out of the question due to budget considerations. He has heard claims about large savings that can be obtained by using CASE tools. Yet the group's experience with report writers and screen painters suggests that these gains may be illusory. What would you suggest that Saul plan to do about the new project?

Project

This part of the project is based on the Structure Chart produced at the end of Chapter 9. Do the following things based on the Structure Chart. If the Structure Chart is very large, your supervisor may give you permission to leave out some modules. Select modules that are complex enough to show off your abilities.

1. Produce detailed specifications of the modules in the Structure Chart. At least one specification should be for a boss module and at least two should be for worker modules. Use each of the following methods at least once.
   a. Structured English.
   b. Activity Diagram.
   c. Decision Table.
   d. Decision Tree.
2. Use Structured English to specify a driver to test one worker module.
3. Use Structured English to specify stubs to test one boss module.
4. Develop tests for each of the modules you have specified. Be sure to identify the purpose of each test and the data values required to achieve the purpose.
5. Include a copy of each Structure Chart that relates to the specifications and tests produced above. These provide the context for the specifications.
6. Produce a one page Post-Implementation Review or "analysis of the analysis" to describe your experience with this project. Identify:
   a. the major things you learned from the experience,
   b. the things you liked most about the project, and
   c. the things you liked least about the project.

Cooking with Cal Oreez Case

Cal is concerned with the way this project has been going lately. He didn't realize how much paperwork was involved in developing a computer program. I tried to explain to him that the process is like preparing a meal. The consumers only see the final result, but somebody has to select the items, peel the potatoes, stir the soup, and wash the dishes. In the same way there are a lot of tasks that have to be done in the analysts workshop before the user sees the results. To keep up the momentum, you should complete the detailed specifications for the system. I suggest that you do the following things. Then we can contract the actual coding to a programmer that Cal recently invited to one of his major meals.

1. Produce detailed specifications of at least four of the modules in the Structure Chart produced in the previous chapter. Select modules that are complex enough to show off your abilities. At least one specification should be for a boss module and at least two should be for worker modules. Use each of the following specification methods at least once.
   a. Structured English.
   b. Activity Diagram.
   c. Decision Table.
   d. Decision Tree.
2. Use Structured English to specify a driver to test one worker module.
3. Use Structured English to specify stubs to test one boss module.
4. Develop tests for each of the modules you have specified. Be sure to identify the purpose of each test and the data values required to achieve the purpose.
5. Include a copy of each Structure Chart that relates to the specifications and tests produced above. These provide the context for the specifications.
6. Produce a one page Post-Implementation Review or "analysis of the analysis" to describe your experience with this project. Identify:
   a. the major things you learned from the experience,
   b. the things you liked most about the project, and
   c. the things you liked least about the project.

References

1. De Marco, Tom, *Structured Analysis and System Specification,* Yourdon Press, 1979.
2. Dolan, Kathleen A., *Business Computer Systems Design*, Mitchell Publishing Inc., 1984.
3. Gane, Chris and Trish Sarson, *Structured Systems Analysis: Tools and Techniques,* Prentice-Hall, 1979.
4. Martin, James, and Carma McClure, *Diagraming Techniques for Analysts and Programmers,* Prentice-Hall, 1985.
5. Mills, H. D., R. C. Linger and A. R. Hevner, "Box Structured Information Systems," *IBM Systems Journal,* Vol. 26, No. 4, 1987.
6. Schindler, Max, *Computer-Aided Software Design,* John Wiley & Sons, 1990.

10
Program

Section IV

Special Topics

	DATABASE (WHAT)	PROGRAMS (HOW)	BENEFITS (WHY)	NETWORK (WHERE)	REAL TIME (WHEN)	SKILLS (WHO)
USER CONCEPT	Entity Relationship	Activity	Intangible Benefit	Map		Organization Design
DESIGNER CONCEPT	E-R Diagram	A-E Diagram	AHP	Network		Skills Responsibility
USER DETAIL	Forms Screens	Processes Data	Tangible Benefit	Work Volume	Discrete Events	Transition Training
DESIGNER DETAIL	EER Diagram	Data Flow Diagrams	Benefit-Cost	Partition	Transition Diagrams	Methodology Tools
BUILDER CONCEPT	Normal Form Relations	Structure Chart	Function Points	System Architecture	Specifications	Learning
BUILDER DETAIL	Files	Screens Specifications	Costs	Network Specs	Interfaces	4GL CASE

This section covers special topics that deal with organizational change and the design of real time systems and distributed networks. The methodology discussed so far is satisfactory for typical business systems. In business systems all functions are performed on one computer and there are no real-time systems. Real-time systems must be synchronized with the operation of a physical process such as a refinery or automatic control system.

Chapter 11 explains the implications of distributing a system over a network of several computers. The main changes are that the data has to be either split into subsets appropriate for each machine or replicated so that all machines can have access to a copy of it. The Data Base Management System will normally take care of communication and update problems.

Chapter 12 explains how the design methodology is modified when real-time systems that interact with external sensors in manufacturing equipment are part of the design. There are two main modifications to the design methodology. A special notation has to be added to the data flow diagram to differentiate between data and control information. A state transition diagram has to be added to the function design to describe all of the possible cases that the system must be able to cope with.

Chapter 13 examines the organizational changes that must occur in the firm and of the Information Systems department when 4GL systems are implemented. The changes involve new authority and responsibilities for data. They also involve new skills and new organizational structures to implement the new methodology. These changes apply to the organizational, the departmental, and the individual levels.

Chapter 11

Distributed Data and Processing

	DATABASE (WHAT)	PROGRAMS (HOW)	BENEFITS (WHY)	NETWORK (WHERE)	REAL TIME (WHEN)	SKILLS (WHO)
USER CONCEPT	Entity Relationship	Activity	Intangible Benefit	Map		Organization Design
DESIGNER CONCEPT	E-R Diagram	A-E Diagram	AHP	Network		Skills Responsibility
USER DETAIL	Forms Screens	Processes Data	Tangible Benefit	Work Volume	Discrete Events	Transition Training
DESIGNER DETAIL	EER Diagram	Data Flow Diagrams	Benefit-Cost	Partition	Transition Diagrams	Methodology Tools
BUILDER CONCEPT	Normal Form Relations	Structure Chart	Function Points	System Architecture	Specifications	Learning
BUILDER DETAIL	Files	Screens Specifications	Costs	Network Specs	Interfaces	4GL CASE

Objectives

Previous chapters have treated the problem of designing a database and application programs as if they were going to exist in a single seamless processing environment. This is typically accomplished by having a single central processing unit that runs a Data Base Management System. The DBMS serves the needs of a number of applications running on terminals all connected to the same processor. In practice, the data and the application programs may be distributed over a number of processors that may or may not be connected together by a network.

This chapter examines the problems of designing a distributed system in which multiple processors—usually connected by a network—are used to store data and execute programs. The main problems in designing such a system are determining whether the system should be distributed at all, and where the management, processors, and data should be located if the system is distributed. In this chapter you learn:

- The advantages and disadvantages of a distributed system.

- How to use horizontal partitioning, vertical partitioning, and replication to split a database among nodes in a network.

- How to identify the best locations for the nodes in a network.

Defining Distributed Systems

A distributed system consists of two or more processors that are designed to work together in supporting the information needs of an organization. If the processors are not designed to work together, then they are really independent systems that can be designed separately. In that case, the techniques discussed in previous chapters apply to each system independently.

Working together implies that there is some sharing of data between the processors. The data could be on a single processor accessed by applications on the other processors. It is more likely to be distributed over more than one processor. If the data are distributed over several processors, then there are a number of design complications having to do with access and integrity control.

In the ideal distributed system, the data and processing power are located in the most efficient location. In such a system, the users and the application programs do not need to know where the data and processors are located. This simplifies the design process and makes it possible to relocate data and processing power to improve efficiency without retraining users or rewriting application programs. A very sophisticated Network Data Base Management System is needed to make such an ideal system possible.

Evaluating Distributed Systems

Distributed systems have several advantages and several disadvantages. The decision to move to a distributed system is essentially a choice between economy and complexity. Economies may result from distribution. Several design and operational complications may result from distributing a database.

Advantages of Distributed Systems

The three main reasons for distributing parts of a system are efficiency, availability, and autonomy.

Efficiency

Distributing a system can improve efficiency by reducing communication costs and by reducing processing costs.

Communication costs can be reduced by locating the data near the users. It requires less communication to access data that are near the user than to access data located on a central machine that may be far away. However, locating data near the main users sometimes increases communication costs if applications have to get data from several different geographic locations to perform their functions.

Processing costs are lower on smaller machines. The cost of a machine instruction is cheapest on microcomputers, more expensive on minicomputers, and most expensive on large mainframe computers. Small machines are cheaper for several reasons. Producing large volumes of small machines creates production economies. The sophisticated technologies needed to build powerful processors increase complexity and cost. The need to coordinate the many application programs that are using the same machine increases the complexity of the hardware and software on large machines.

The implication of these economic rules is that it is desirable to move processing down to the smallest practical machine. This leaves the large central machines with the tasks that cannot be delegated to small machines. However, nothing comes for free. The coordination eliminated in the large central machine may now have to be provided in coordinating the multiple users of a database distributed over a network.

In summary, there are potential savings to be had from eliminating the need for long distance communication and in using cheaper small processors. The savings may be reduced by the overhead required to coordinate and collect the data required at each node of a distributed system.

Availability

Availability of data for an application depends on the computer and the network being functional. It also depends on the communication being fast enough to respond to user needs quickly. A distributed system contributes to availability in five ways:

- **Less communication.** Most of the needed data are located at the users' site. Thus the delays created by the communications network are reduced.
- **Faster communication.** Communication between the computer and local disk drives or local terminals is usually faster than communication over a long-distance network. This provides faster response to user requests.
- **More machines.** A local computer is likely to have more capacity available than a central system that must serve many users.
- **Survivability.** A failure of the central machine ends service for all users. A failure of a local machine effects only the local users. Disasters lead to degraded performance rather than complete stoppage of the system.
- **Growth.** Machines can be added in smaller increments to match changes in processing demand.

Autonomy

A common argument for distributed systems is that local users have more autonomy to develop systems to serve their needs. They are independently able to develop applications that meet their own priorities. They are less subject to the stultifying bureaucracy of a central systems group.

The problem with independence is that it can also lead to incompatible systems and incompatible data structures. This makes it very difficult to integrate systems at a later time. As a result, independence is often a very temporary phenomenon.

Autonomous development can be very appropriate when the organizational unit operates independently of the rest of the organization. For example, the rest of the organization rarely cares about all the data used to control production in a

11

Network

factory or chemical plant. The data is very technical and very specific to the production task. In such a situation, autonomy can be appropriate.

On the other hand, the accounting data for a production process must be integrated with the accounting data for the rest of the organization. Independent development of accounting systems would be disastrous in most organizations.

A strong desire for independent systems is often a clue that the central Information Systems group is not providing very good service. They may have become unresponsive to user needs. They are using inflexible technology that cannot respond to changing user needs. Alternately they may be outdated and do not know how to respond. Autonomy is often a costly way to produce reform in a backward data processing group. The users get so frustrated that they would rather build and operate a system themselves than wait or beg for applications from the central service.

Autonomy needs to be balanced with central planning. Standards are required for such things as Data Base Management Systems, data formats, and identification keys. Locally needed data and applications can be added within this framework to gain both the benefits of autonomy and the services of a coordinated system.

Disadvantages of Distributed Systems

The main disadvantages of distributed systems are related to coordination problems and integrity controls.

Coordination Problems

If the authority to design and modify systems is decentralized, then the system eventually reverts to several islands of automation that cannot be coordinated. Data required to operate the business may exist in several places in the system. Yet it is not possible to bring the data together. This is because they are on different brands of computers, are on incompatible databases, or do not have consistent common keys that can be used to join the data.

These problems can be overcome by centralized management and standards. The standards require compatible hardware, compatible software, consistent names, and consistent identification keys.

Integrity Controls

Even if standards are enforced, there are still several technical problems that make it difficult to distribute a database. These problems revolve around the need to maintain integrity constraints in the database. Specifically, there is a need to make sure that insertions, updates, and deletions are performed consistently.

If customer records are stored at one processor site and orders are stored at another, then integrity problems occur. It is important to make sure that an order cannot be added if a corresponding customer record does not exist. It is equally important to make sure that a customer record cannot be deleted if the customer has an outstanding order. It is also important to make sure that two different order entry clerks do not each promise the last unit in inventory to the customers from whom they are taking orders. Data Base Management Systems have methods of dealing with these problems. The methods become much more complicated when the data are at multiple processor sites.

Another integrity problem occurs when a system fails in the middle of a transaction. The Data Base Management Systems handles this problem by using techniques called rollback and rollforward. Images of the records before and after the updates are recorded on a system log file. It is then possible to rollback the file to the image before the transaction and restart the transaction.

It is also possible to use this facility to undo an erroneous transaction. If the current files are completely destroyed, it is possible to recreate the files. A backup copy of the files taken earlier is installed and the system log is used to rollforward to the current time. The procedure becomes very complicated when parts of the transaction are on different processors, when the same files are duplicated on more than one processor, or when one of the processors in the network fails.

Designing Distributed Databases

The design of a distributed database begins just like the design of a single database. Entity-Relationship Models, Extended Entity-Relationship Models, and Normalization still apply. Once these methods have been used, then the data tables have to be assigned to processors and nodes in the distributed network.

There are four basic methods of allocating data to the different nodes. These are database partitioning, replication, horizontal table partitioning, and vertical table partitioning. These methods can be used in combinations where appropriate.

Replication

Replication means making a separate copy of each required data table for each location. This method is suitable for data which are rarely updated, such as library catalogs, airline schedules, product specifications, course lists, and directories. A telephone directory is an example of a stable table that is replicated in many locations to reduce the cost of communications. It is usually reproduced on paper instead of in a computer file, but the same logic would apply if it were in a computer file.

Often the simplest way to revise such files is to ship a new copy to replace the old file. This may be done by communication over a network. It may even be done by shipping a replacement tape or diskette by mail or courier.

Figure 11-1 illustrates the replication of a table of simple student records. The two replicated tables are identical to the original table.

Replication is unsuitable for data tables that require frequent update, because it is very difficult to keep all tables correctly updated. The communication costs

11

Network

Figure 11-1
An example of a replicated table. Both copies are identical.

can be large and there is a danger that some tables may not get updated because of communication failures.

Horizontal Table Partitioning

Horizontal partitioning means replicating the table structure at different locations, but having different instances of the rows at each location. This method applies when users at different locations need the same kind of information, but they want that information to be about different items. A typical example would be a customer file for a sales organization. Each location needs the same name, address, phone number, and credit rating information. However, each location wants to store information about a different group of customers with which that location deals.

The horizontal partition corresponds to a SQL query which selects certain rows required by a particular user group. Figure 11-2 illustrates a horizontal partitioning of the same student table illustrated in Figure 11-1. The partition is based on department names in this example. It would correspond to a decentralized system in which each department maintained the records for its own students.

This structure usually makes it easy to insert, update, and delete records. However, it may become difficult to access data if the inquirer can be at several locations. This can happen when national customers place orders at several different locations. It can also happen when customers, like bank customers,

Figure 11-2

An example of horizontal partitioning by departments. The attributes are the same, but the occurrences are different.

STUDENT-ID	DEPARTMENT	NAME	ADDRESS
514731	ARTS	ANSEL, G.	132 MAIN
518232	ARTS	GALLANT, A.	410 ELM
519465	ARTS	MORDEN, L.	151 BELMAN
519831	BUSINESS	BAUMAN, C.	261 CURLEW
519841	BUSINESS	CORRY, R.	892 DANBY
519958	BUSINESS	SILDER, P.	611 MAPLE

STUDENT-ID	DEPARTMENT	NAME	ADDRESS
514731	ARTS	ANSEL, G.	132 MAIN
518232	ARTS	GALLANT, A.	410 ELM
519465	ARTS	MORDEN, L.	151 BELMAN

STUDENT-ID	DEPARTMENT	NAME	ADDRESS
519831	BUSINESS	BAUMAN, C.	261 CURLEW
519841	BUSINESS	CORRY, R.	892 DANBY
519958	BUSINESS	SILDER, P.	611 MAPLE

travel to different locations and want access to their records at any location. Another example is students who take courses in more than one department.

The data structure and processing applications are centrally designed in this method. The local regions are usually responsible for inserting and maintaining records in the database.

Vertical Table Partitioning

Vertical table partitioning means storing some columns of a table at one location and others at another location. Each location must also store the identifying key or keys. This method is suitable when different departments in different locations need different information about the same entity. A typical example would be an employee record that is partitioned between the personnel and the payroll departments. Personnel may need access to biographic information, but does not need access to payment information. Payroll needs access to payment information, but does not need access to many of the other fields in the employee record. Both need the employee number to identify the employee. Both may also need replicates of address information.

Vertical partitioning can be done by a SQL query which selects only required columns. It is equivalent to a relational project operation. Figure 11-3 illustrates a vertical partitioning of the previous example. In this case, the department designation may be needed in a system that computes cost and budget information. The other information is needed in a different system for a variety of administrative tasks.

This structure is usually easy to update because the different fields can be updated locally. It is difficult to insert new records or delete old records since the different parts must be simultaneously inserted or deleted at all locations.

11

Network

Figure 11-3

An example of
vertical par-
titioning of a
table. The key
is the same,
but different at-
tributes are in
different tables.

STUDENT-ID	DEPARTMENT	NAME	ADDRESS
514731	ARTS	ANSEL, G.	132 MAIN
518232	ARTS	GALLANT, A.	410 ELM
519465	ARTS	MORDEN, L.	151 BELMAN
519831	BUSINESS	BAUMAN, C.	261 CURLEW
519841	BUSINESS	CORRY, R.	892 DANBY
519958	BUSINESS	SILDER, P.	611 MAPLE

STUDENT-ID	DEPARTMENT
514731	ARTS
518232	ARTS
519465	ARTS
519831	BUSINESS
519841	BUSINESS
519958	BUSINESS

STUDENT-ID	NAME	ADDRESS
514731	ANSEL, G.	132 MAIN
518232	GALLANT, A.	410 ELM
519465	MORDEN, L.	151 BELMAN
519831	BAUMAN, C.	261 CURLEW
519841	CORRY, R.	892 DANBY
519958	SILDER, P.	611 MAPLE

The data structure must be centrally designed to insure compatibility of keys and any replicated columns. Extra columns or attributes can be added locally without destroying the integrity of the database. Application programs can be developed locally because only local data are used in them.

Partitioned Database

Database partitioning is a special case of vertical partitioning in which whole tables are assigned to different locations. One group of tables is stored at one location near the main users of those tables. Another group of tables is stored at another location where it is used by a different group of users.

A typical example is the separation of production and marketing data into two different locations. The tables associated with production are located in a computer at the factory where they are near the production personnel who use the data. Marketing data are stored in computers at the sales offices.

Figure 11-4 illustrates a database partitioning based on strong and weak relationships as defined in Figure 2-20. The dashed relationships between partitions would have to be maintained by replication of some tables or by linkages over a network.

It is easy to insert, update, and delete data in partitioned databases. Each partition acts as an independent database. The main difficulty arises when data from multiple locations are needed to complete a transaction or query. An order in a sales region may need to create a record in the sales database and update a factory inventory record. Some of this processing is done locally and some of it must be done remotely. Furthermore, an order for a part cannot be taken by sales without confirming the existence of the part in the factory inventory record. In Figure 11-4, it is not possible to schedule MEETINGS without using information about the availability of ROOMS in BUILDINGS.

Figure 11-4
An example of a database partitioned into five parts. The horizontal lines separate the five partitions at the weakest relationships.

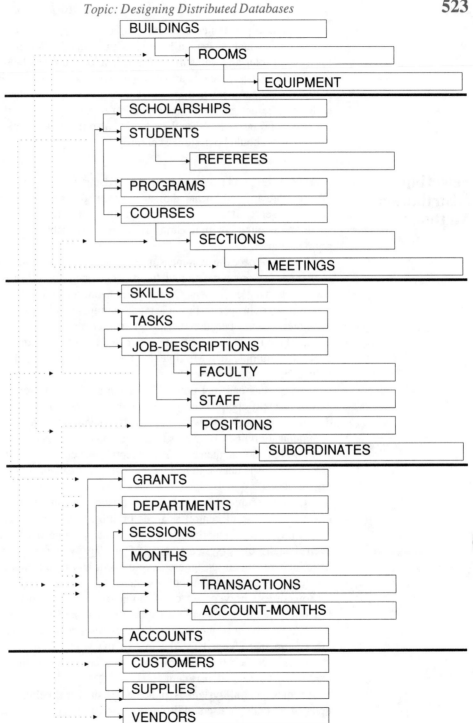

Design of a partitioned database can be partly central and partly local. There is a need to set central standards on keys and other fields that are used at multiple locations. Tables and fields that have only a local use can be designed locally. It is unlikely that any other part of the organization would want information the production department gathers on reactor pressure in a chemical plant. These tables can be designed by the production department. However, marketing, accounting, and possibly other departments also need information about products. These tables should be designed centrally.

Selecting Distribution Methods

There is no good reason to distribute a database to more than one processor if all users are located "near" the same processor and the processor is powerful enough to serve all users. "Near" means that communication costs are relatively small and enough communication capacity is available to provide satisfactorily rapid response.

Near is not necessarily a measure of distance. It could be a very long distance if there is a communication network developed for other purposes with the capacity to handle all users. On the other hand, the author knows of a university where it was cheaper to buy a separate computer than to connect to a campus computer system, because the university network did not reach across a busy street. The only other options are expensive leased lines for each user or equally expensive multiplexors. Multiplexors combine several signals on a single line to reduce the number of leased lines.

If the processor is not powerful enough to serve all users, it is usually easier and cheaper to upgrade the processor than to design and operate a distributed database. A distributed system is costly because the multiple computers need communication lines, operators, separate copies of leased database software, and more design and maintenance. An exception occurs when even the largest available processor is unable to handle the load. This can easily happen in very large organizations.

Another common problem is unrealistic costing of services which either penalizes the use of central services or subsidizes the creation and use of distributed systems. Central systems often charge large overheads to all systems even though not all systems benefit from the overhead services. On the other hand, departments often ignore development and maintenance costs in their estimates of the cost of a distributed system.

Sometimes, the very act of charging for services can be the cause of inefficiency. One university had a comprehensive system of charging for many small jobs. Forty percent of the computer cycles were devoted to running the accounting system that charged for the rest of the work. Some departments found it cheaper to get their own system which needed no accounting because it was all paid for by the same department.

A single central system is indicated if data are being constantly read and updated by multiple users in different geographic locations where the users need immediate up-to-date access to information created in other geographic regions. Typical examples are credit checking systems, airline reservation systems, and on-line banking systems. In each case it is not possible to partition the system into unrelated subsystems. An airline reservation system creates records that connect information about many geographic locations. The bank and credit checking systems have clients who need access to their own records and those of others from a variety of locations.

The pure central system and the pure unconnected distributed system are relatively easy to recognize. The difficult design choices occur when users are at several locations. Then there is a clear tradeoff between the simplicity of a centralized system and the communication savings that can result from a distributed system.

The method of partitioning depends on the design stage at which the decision must be made. If the decision to partition must be made at the time subsystems are being defined as described in Chapters 2 and 3, then an approximate partitioning method must be used. At this stage of the design only approximate information is available for making design decisions. If the database design has been completed, then detailed methods can be used.

Preliminary Design Methods

Preliminary designs can be generated either by using entity groups or by clustering entities. The choice depends on the kind of information that is available. Entity groups are based on the structure of the data in the Entity-Relationship Diagram. Clustering can be useful when the analyst has a broad knowledge of which applications need which data.

Entity Group Method

The entity group method uses the same data that were used to group entities in Figure 2-20. The method in Figure 11-4 is based only on an Entity-Relationship Diagram and a subjective evaluation of strong and weak relationships. It was used in Chapter 2 to simplify the drawing of an Entity-Relationship Diagram. However, it can also serve as a way of defining major segments of the database for distribution.

Figure 11-5 combines the same entities with activities that use information about each entity. The entities along the top of the diagram are in the same order as in Figure 11-4. This reproduction of Figure 3-11 has been modified with vertical lines to show the boundaries between potentially distributed components of the database. These are the same boundaries identified in Figure 11-4.

The shaded areas show regions where there is a high correlation between the activity group and the data group. These regions are identified visually by the high proportion of X's in the rectangle. These regions of high correlation form a natural basis for a distributed system. The corresponding activities and entities in one shaded rectangle should all be located on the same processor in a distributed network. Thus the STUDENT group of activities and the STUDENT group of entities should be together.

		Buildings	Rooms	Equipment	Scholarships	Students	Referees	Programs	Courses	Sections	Meetings	Skills	Tasks	Job-Descriptions	Faculty	Staff	Positions	Subordinates	Grants	Departments	Sessions	Months	Transactions	Account-Months	Accounts	Customers	Supplies	Vendors
Planning	Demand Analysis				X	X		X	X	X					X													
	Budgeting					X				X						X			X	X				X	X	X		
	Applications				X	X	X																					
	Financial Aid				X	X	X																					
Student	Registration	X	X		X			X	X	X	X				X													
	Student Evaluation				X			X	X	X					X													
	Graduation				X			X	X	X																		
	Course Scheduling	X	X	X	X			X	X	X	X				X													
	Program Admin.							X	X																			
Staff	Manpower Planning					X			X	X		X	X	X	X	X	X	X	X	X								
	Personnel Eval.											X	X	X	X	X	X	X	X	X								
	Promotion											X	X	X	X	X	X	X										
Admin	Hiring													X	X	X			X									
	Grant Application														X				X	X								
	Capital Equipment	X	X	X															X									
	Space Management	X	X	X															X									
	Hazardous Waste	X	X	X											X	X			X								X	
	Benefit Administration														X	X			X						X			
	Retirement	X	X												X	X	X	X	X	X	X	X	X	X				
	Payables																		X	X	X	X	X	X	X			X
	Capital Budget				X			X	X						X	X			X					X				
	Receiving																		X								X	X
Accounts	Supplies Orders																		X	X	X	X	X	X	X		X	X
	Receivables																		X	X	X	X	X	X	X	X	X	
	Payroll													X	X	X			X	X	X	X	X	X	X			
	Construction	X	X	X															X	X	X	X	X	X	X	X		
	Investment																		X	X	X	X	X					
	Maintenance	X	X	X															X	X	X	X	X	X	X	X		
	Supplies Mgt																		X	X	X	X	X	X		X		
	Grant Administration				X									X	X	X			X	X	X	X	X	X	X		X	X

Figure 11-5

Identification of distributed activities and data based on frequency clustering of activities and strong relationships between entities.

		STUDENT											STAFF						ADMIN									
		Buildings	Rooms	Faculty	Meetings	Courses	Sections	Students	Equipment	Programs	Scholarships	Referees	Skills	Tasks	Job-Descriptions	Subordinates	Staff	Positions	Grants	Sessions	Months	Vendors	Departments	Supplies	Account-Months	Transactions	Accounts	Customers
Planning	Demand Analysis			X		X	X	X		X	X																	
	Budgeting					X	X												X	X			X	X	X		X	
	Applications					X					X	X																
	Financial Aid					X					X	X																
Student	Registration	X	X	X	X	X	X	X		X																		
	Student Evaluation			X		X	X	X		X																		
	Graduation					X	X	X		X																		
	Course Scheduling	X	X	X	X	X	X		X	X																		
	Program Admin.					X				X																		
Staff	Manpower Planning			X		X	X	X					X	X	X	X	X	X	X		X							
	Personnel Eval.			X									X	X	X	X	X	X	X		X							
	Promotion			X									X	X	X	X	X	X										
Admin	Hiring			X													X	X					X					
	Grant Application			X															X				X					
	Capital Equipment	X	X						X														X					
	Space Management	X	X						X														X					
	Hazardous Waste	X	X	X					X														X	X				
	Benefit Administration			X																X				X				X
	Retirement	X	X	X																X			X				X	
	Payables																		X	X	X	X	X		X	X	X	X
	Capital Budget			X			X		X	X									X				X				X	
	Receiving																						X	X	X			
Accounts	Supplies Orders																		X	X	X	X	X	X	X	X	X	
	Receivables																			X	X		X	X	X	X	X	X
	Payroll			X													X	X	X	X	X		X		X	X	X	
	Construction	X	X						X										X	X	X		X		X	X	X	
	Investment																		X	X	X	X	X	X	X	X	X	
	Maintenance	X	X						X											X	X				X	X	X	
	Supplies Mgt																		X	X		X	X	X	X	X	X	
	Grant Administration			X					X								X	X	X	X	X	X	X	X	X	X	X	

Figure 11-6

Identification of distributed activities and data based on frequency clustering of activities and frequency clustering of entities.

Those activities also need information about Faculty and Rooms. This information must be obtained either by communication over a network or by using a replicated copy of the information at each site.

There must be no more than one shaded rectangle in each block of rows or columns. Two shaded rectangles in a vertical block of entities would mean that the entity data are stored in two locations at once. Such replication is not likely to be appropriate for major blocks of information. Two rectangles in a horizontal block would leave some other block with no local data. This is also not likely to be efficient.

The diagram should have an equal number of horizontal and vertical blocks so it is potentially possible for each activity block to "own" an entity block. When some rows or columns have no obvious rectangles of high correlation, it means that these are not good candidates for decentralization. They should be combined with some of the major blocks already identified. Thus ADMIN and ACCOUNTING should be combined into a single group because the share a lot of data. Similarly, the applications and the financial aid activities should be combined with the STUDENT group of activities. The remaining PLANNING activities should be combined with administration.

This design has been based on subjective evaluations of the importance of relationships between data. If frequency of use data are available, then the same clustering method used to group activities can be used to group entities. The result is groups that belong together on the basis of shared use.

Clustering Method

In this method, activities are grouped by clustering on the basis of their similar patterns of data use. In the same way, entities can be grouped on the basis of their similar patterns of use by activities. All one has to do is transpose the data array in Figure 11-5. One can then apply the same algorithm that was used in Chapter 3 to cluster activities. Transposing means interchanging the rows and columns in the table so rows are entities and columns are activities. Mathematically, the same result can be accomplished by interchanging all of the i and j subscripts in the equations in Chapter 3.

Figure 11-6 illustrates the result of applying the clustering procedure to entities with the frequency data used to generate Figure 3-6. The results are similar to the results in Figure 11-5. Some entities have been included in different blocks. If the frequency data are accurate, then this design is better than the previous one because it reduces communication costs. The same comments apply about combining blocks without clear correlations between activities and entities.

If the different groups of users have essentially unrelated needs, then a system can be divided into separate processors, possibly with no network connecting them. This is a common situation in universities where each of the departments have their own special needs and very few of them overlap. The ones that do overlap can usually be replicated because very few systems rely on current information. The same situation may occur in very decentralized organizations such as government departments or conglomerate corporations in which the divisions do not interact very much.

In Figure 11-6 there is much overlap between administrative and accounting activities and the entities in the student block. However, most of these overlaps are related to buildings, rooms, equipment and faculty which rarely change. Replication is an adequate way of providing data to these groups of activities.

Detailed Design Methods

If the database and application designs have been completed, then much more information is available about what activities and data are required at each processor site. The data requirements are known at the attribute or column level. With this knowledge, it is possible to make choices about replication or horizontal and vertical partitioning. A good structure can usually be selected by asking four questions about the system. The four questions are:

- **Is the system spread over a large geographic area?** A large geographic area is one where communication charges across the area become a significant part of the costs of the system. Usually a region would have to span hundreds of miles to be large. If the region is not large, then there is usually no incentive to partition the database. In a large area, it may be necessary to replicate or partition—if possible—to reduce costs of transmission.

- **Do all users need the same kinds of data?** If they need the same kinds of data, then horizontal partitioning or replication may help to reduce the cost of data transmission in a distributed system. When user groups need different data, then vertical partitioning is the right solution. When users need different data and do not need to access data held by a different user group, then a vertical partition is needed and a network may not be needed.

- **Do all users share data?** All users share data if users in any region frequently need current data about any items in the database, regardless of the region in which data originate. Data are shared if this need occurs often enough that special inquiries are very inconvenient. Data are not shared if shippers have to make occasional calls to another warehouse when they cannot fill an order themselves. Data would be shared if there is a policy that orders are always shipped immediately from the nearest warehouse that has stock.

If needs are the same and unshared, then each group of users needs the same kind of data. However, they never need data about customers, students, parts, or other items stored by a different user group. In such a case, a network may not be needed. If needs are the same and shared, then the groups need access to each other's data. Such a situation occurs in a bank where customers may come into another branch or region and need information about the account in their local bank. In this case a database can be horizontally partitioned, but a network is needed to provide access to remote data.

If the needs are different, but some information is shared with other locations, then a central system is the best choice. Sometimes the data needed from remote locations is quite stable and can be replicated. For instance, a student record system needs data about rooms and buildings for scheduling purposes. These data do not change often so they can be replicated.

● **Does data get updated frequently and do users need current data?** Data must be current if users must determine the status of a fast-changing situation. Current values are needed for data such as whether an uncommon item is available for a customer who can not wait. The data must be current if it is not sufficient to provide a value from last night or last week when the last replication of current data was provided. It is rare that aggregate data such as financial or sales summaries need to be current.

When updates are rare or can be delayed without causing significant problems, then a replicated database is the best choice. This is the case with a telephone directory. A replicated database can usually be updated overnight via a network. If weekly or monthly updates are satisfactory, then updates can be provided by mail or courier.

With the answers to these questions, a good system can be chosen from the table in Figure 11-7. The figure shows the preferred choices as a function of user needs and update requirements.

Users can need either the same kind of data at each location or they can need different kinds of data at their different locations. If the needs are the same, then horizontal partitioning is indicated. If the needs are different, then vertical partitioning is indicated, either at the table or the database level.

Practical distributed systems usually combine these methods. For instance, in a university the student records may be horizontally partitioned by department, while administrative data are vertically partitioned by administrative responsibility group. Within each, some relatively stable data—such as building records and past student grades—are replicated.

These techniques assume that the location of each processor has been decided. However, sometimes there is a need to identify the best location for the processors. This problem requires some other techniques.

Figure 11-7

Options in distributing a database and the criteria that determine selection.

USER NEEDS	UPDATES	
	FREQUENT	RARE OR DELAYED
SAME AND UNSHARED	HORIZONTAL PARTITION WITH NO NETWORK	REPLICATED
SAME AND SHARED	HORIZONTAL PARTITION WITH NETWORK	REPLICATED
DIFFERENT AND UNSHARED	VERTICAL PARTITION WITH NETWORK	REPLICATED
DIFFERENT AND SHARED	CENTRAL	CENTRAL OR REPLICATED

Locating Processors

Locating the processors is a two-part decision. First, the designer must decide what kinds of a computers should do the processing and whether software is available to support them. Second, the designer must decide where each kind of computer should be located.

Three Tier Architecture

In the past, most systems consisted of mainframes or minicomputers with communications lines connecting them to all of the users' terminals. Now the terminals are being replaced by microcomputers that are capable of doing much of the processing formerly done on larger machines.

This is leading to a three-tier architecture consisting of micros, minis, and mainframes. The microcomputers perform the screen display, menu selection, and editing tasks at the user's desk. The minicomputers often act as departmental machines to store local data and perform local tasks such as volume printing. The mainframes act as database servers for data needed by several departments.

Database machines provide a further complication. These are computers specifically designed to perform database operations. Some communicate directly in the SQL language. They are designed to accept a SQL query or update request and generate a table or reply for the requesting machine. Microcomputers are now capable of creating and accepting SQL transactions over Local Area Networks. It is conceivable that the minicomputers and mainframes will only provide network communications in future systems. Teradata of Los Angeles has developed a SQL database machine.

The main force behind the three-tiered Architecture is economics. A capacity of a million instructions per second (1 MIP) costs about $4,000 in a microcomputer. A similar capacity in a mainframe costs about $160,000.[6] This provides an incentive to move as much computing as possible down to the microcomputer.

A further incentive to concentrate computing at the microcomputer is the combination of user-friendly software and communication costs. User-friendly software usually means a lot of graphics, on-line help, and checking of input. These features require a lot of communication between the screen and the processor. sending such volumes of information between a screen and a remote mainframe many miles away is prohibitively costly. It costs practically nothing to send the same information from a micro to a screen two feet away.

These developments are leading toward a client-server architecture for distributed systems. The clients are mainly microprocessors on the desks of users. The servers perform a variety of functions. They include database servers, network gateways, high capacity printers, color printers, FAX machines, and scientific supercomputers. The clients and servers are usually not arranged in a hierarchy. The client machine can send work to any server and a server can serve any authorized machine. This is called a peer-to-peer architecture. Figure 11-8 illustrates part of a typical microcomputer network.

11 Network

The client-server model allows work to be partitioned to take advantage of the best features of different machines. A client machine usually looks after the interface screen, many preliminary integrity checks, and most local printing. The server usually looks after specialized tasks, such as maintaining a database, volume printing, scientific calculations, and connecting to a network.

Figure 11-8
Illustration of a segment of a microcomputer network.

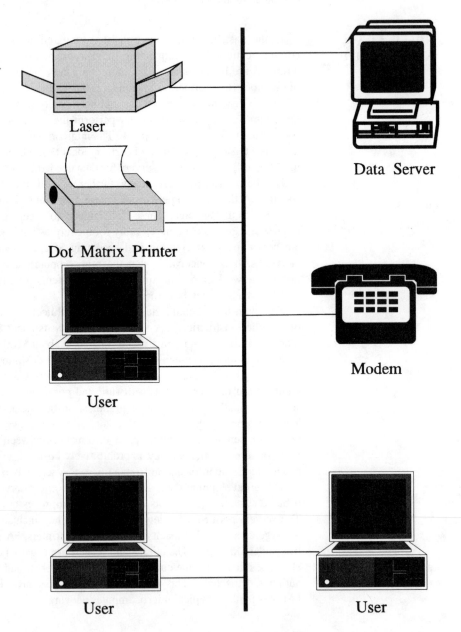

Database Software

A multi-tiered architecture requires database software components that can function together on several different machines. That way the user—and even the designer—do not have to know where the data are located and which machine is doing the work. Such software is now becoming available.

Oracle Corp. (Oracle), Relational Technology (Ingres), Cognos Inc. (Power-House), and Information Builders (Focus) all have versions of their software that run on a wide variety of brands and sizes of machines including personal computers. In most, a database can be defined on a personal computer and then the definition can be uploaded to a larger computer. All provide ways of downloading a data table to a personal computer. Some of them also provide network versions that can link data at different sites into a single application. These features are usually first provided in a form that can be used only for queries. Later versions deal with the more difficult problems of distributed updates.

Locating a Single Processor

A single processor is usually very easy to locate. It should be as near as possible to its users. An isolated microcomputer should obviously be on the desk of the user. A minicomputer typically serves a group of users who are all in the same building, or at least in nearby buildings. It should therefore be located to minimize the length of the communication lines needed to connect it to the users. The exact position does not change costs dramatically as long as it is in the same building.

Figure 11-9

Forty Canadian cities with transaction volumes.

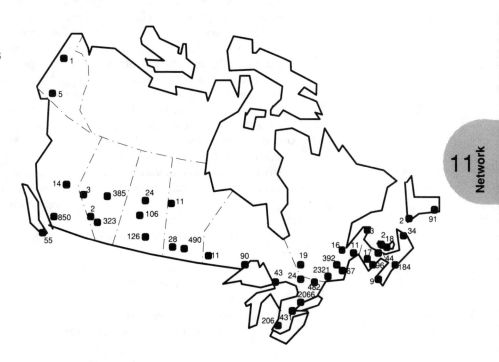

11

Network

Mainframes are often used to serve many users who are geographically scattered. Public networks are usually used to connect mainframes to users that may be many miles away. Significant savings are possible if the computer is located to minimize communications costs. Figure 11-9 illustrates an application in which an organization has offices in forty communities across Canada. The relative volume of transactions is shown beside each community on the map. It is proposed that a central system be located to minimize total communication costs.

A central or a data-replicated system needs to have a single location where the main data can be stored. Sometimes there is no choice of site. This could happen if a policy decision has been made that all data must be stored at existing sites such as head office or regional offices. If there is a choice, then the best site is usually the one which minimizes communication traffic by being near to the largest group of users. A location algorithm is available[5] to compute the optimal location under these circumstances. Two pieces of information are needed to compute this location.

- **Number of transactions** generated by each geographic location per period. The period can be of arbitrary length, such as minute, hour or day, so long as a consistent measure is used for all sites. The transactions should be measured in units, such as transmission packets, which are proportional to the network charges which they incur. We shall call the transactions per period the Volume, V. Sometimes, but not always, The number of users or customers may be a good proxy for the volume at each site.

- **Distance** between each pair of geographic locations. Again the units can be arbitrarily set to miles, kilometers, centimeters on a map, or some other measure as long as they are consistent. The distance, D, is a proxy for line lease costs, so lease costs could be used instead of distances. Adequate estimates of D can often be obtained from sources such as highway maps as long as charges are linear and they are related to highway distances rather than air distances or tariff zones. Certain pairs of points can be kept from being chosen for connection by making the distance between them artificially large. It may be desirable to connect a city to another city in a geographic region even though another network node is just across a regional boundary. This is accomplished by setting the distance between the unconnected centers to be very large compared to the distance between the connected centers.

Sometimes it is necessary to limit the maximum distance, MAX_i, between a node and the farthest user location. This may happen due to technological limitations such as signal degradation.

The objective function to be minimized is $SUM(D_{ij}V_i)$ such that $D_{ij} < MAX_i$ where:

D_{ij} = a matrix of distances where D_{ij}=the distance between nodes i and j.

i = a subscript indicating the source location.

j = a subscript for the destination location.

MAX_i = the maximum distance that node i can be from server node, j.

V_i = the number of transactions originating at location i.

The data can be simplified by letting $W_{ij} = D_{ij}V_i$. W is a matrix of distance-weighted volumes. Note that W is not a symmetric matrix. Each element of D is multiplied only by the volume at the origin and not the volume at both the origin and destination.

The location that minimizes communication costs is determined by looking for the location that corresponds to the column with the smallest sum, $W_{.j}$.

The best solution for the example in Figure 11-9 is shown in Figure 11-10. This is the best location if a single processor is to be used.

Locating Multiple Processors

A more complicated solution is needed when multiple processors are used. Suppose that the system in Figure 11-9 is to be implemented on five processors. The problem is to find the locations of five processors that minimize communication costs. This problem is sometimes known as the warehouse location problem. The solution method is commonly used to locate warehouses in a way that minimizes transportation costs.

The method for solving this problem makes several assumptions as follows:

- **Major subsystems have been previously identified.** The clustering methods in the previous sections could be used for this. A major subsystem is a set of activities and a set of entities which are the responsibility of a single administrative group. It may be located in several geographic areas. It may use data from entities that are the responsibility of other administrative groups (with their permission). Only those subsystems that are to be implemented

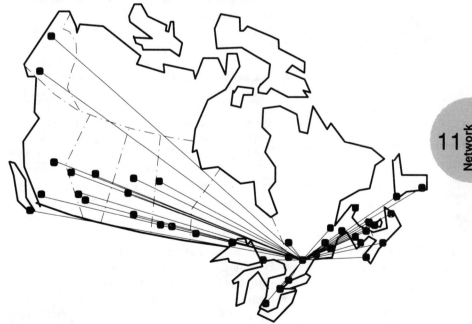

Figure 11-10

Forty cities connected to the single best node.

11
Network

within the planning horizon need to be considered. Low priority systems can be ignored for now.

- **The location of all user groups is known.** This is usually a list of all of the different physical locations from which the administrative group may want to use computers or get computer information. A physical location is any building or group of buildings that could share a Local Area Network. Local Area Networks are assumed to be connected to a large computer or a long distance network by some gateway. Thus the Local Area Network is treated as a single load on the larger network.

- **Distances between all locations are known.** If not known, they can be calculated from cartesian coordinates on a map.

- **The number of transactions originating at each location can be estimated.** For network design purposes, the subsystem is the unit of analysis. The transactions generated by all activities in the subsystem are aggregated, but they must be divided among the physical locations from which the users access them.

- **There are two kinds of network communications:** from users to database servers and from users directly to other users. The first kind requires that the databases be located at central sites which minimize the communication distance. Person to person communication requires the design of a network that connects all users to all other users with whom they may need to communicate. Redundant connections may have to be added for safety reasons. Transaction volumes of all kinds can then be added to determine the aggregate volume that the network must handle.

- **Communications volume within subsystems is much greater than between subsystems.** This is a result of the clustering approach to subsystem design. Thus subsystems can be located independently without regard to the location of other subsystems. Communication between subsystems is treated in the same way as person to person communications.

- **The network is not constrained by capacity limitations.** It is assumed that the cost of building the required network capacity is lower in the long run than the cost of moving applications and people to fit within some technical constraint. Thus work groups are placed in efficient locations, communication needs are calculated, and the necessary communication capacity is installed. The strategic design produces a global routing between sites and an estimate of relative traffic volumes. The detailed design of an efficient network is not included in this strategic design. Similarly, the choice of Local Area Network technology at each site is not considered in this analysis. The existence of some Local Area Network to connect local users is assumed.

Process Overview

There are several steps in the design of a distributed system.

- Determine for each subsystem whether it is central, replicated, horizontally partitioned, or vertically partitioned.

- Identify the optimal number of nodes and locations for each database and compute the network traffic volumes that result. If multiple databases are

involved, it may be possible to identify opportunities for amalgamation of central sites for different subsystems to reduce fixed costs.
● Link the server nodes into a connected network.
● Add redundant network links for economy and safety reasons.
● Identify communications volume between people and between subsystems. Add the communications between subsystems and between people to compute a total communications volume between all geographic locations.
● Compute the line capacity needed to handle all communications between network nodes.

Partitioning has already been discussed. The most difficult task is determining the optimal location of central processors. The method uses the same weight matrix, W, used for determining the best location for a single site. The calculations are more complex though. They involve an iterative trial and error solution. The procedure is illustrated with a simple matrix of five columns as illustrated in Figure 11-11. The network has five nodes—A, B, C, D, and E. The distances between the nodes are given in the first matrix which shows the distance from the row node to the column node. Thus the distance from node B to node C is 3. The diagonal is always 0 since the distance from any node to itself is 0.

Figure 11-11

A network example with 5 nodes—A, B, C, D, and E. The numbers at the nodes are transaction volumes from the nodes.

$$\mathbf{D_{ij}} \quad \times \quad \mathbf{V_i} \quad = \quad \mathbf{W_{ij}}$$

	A	B	C	D	E
A	0	4	5	8	7
B	4	0	3	7	7
C	5	3	0	4	5
D	8	7	4	0	3
E	7	7	5	3	0

$\mathbf{V_i}$

5
10
1
10
5

	A	B	C	D	E
A	0	20	25	40	35
B	40	0	30	70	70
C	5	3	0	4	5
D	80	70	40	0	30
E	35	35	25	15	0

	A	B	C	D	E
SUM=	160	128	120	129	140

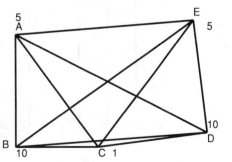

The transaction volumes originating at each node are shown on the network map and are repeated in the one row matrix. The weight, $W_{ij} = D_{ij}V_i$. is shown in the last matrix. The column sums are shown below the last matrix. The lowest value of 120 below column C shows that C is the best node to use if all computing is to be located at a single node, as illustrated in Figure 11-10.

The solution to the multiple node problem is shown in Figure 11-12. This illustrative problem uses three nodes. The steps of the solution are:

- **Select three nodes to start the solution.** Nodes A, C, and E have been chosen arbitrarily.
- **Compute the sum of row minima.** For each row in the subset columns ACE, take the minimum value. In row B, 30 is the minimum of 40, 30, and 70. Then compute the sum of the minima which is 60 for columns ACE.
- **Substitute all candidate columns for the first trial column and compute the sum of row minima for each substitution.** In this example, A is the first column to be substituted out. B and D are the only columns available to replace A. The sum of minima is 50 for BCE and 55 for DCE. Since 50 is the lowest sum and is lower than 60 for ACE, BCE is the new best solution. The

Figure 11-12
Computing the sum of row minima for each column substitution in the candidate solution matrix.

W_{ij} → **Select** → **Row Minumum**

	A	B	C	D	E
A	0	20	25	40	35
B	40	0	30	70	70
C	5	3	0	4	5
D	80	70	40	0	30
E	35	35	25	15	0

A	C	E
0	25	35
40	30	70
5	0	5
80	40	30
35	25	0

Row Minumum
0
30
0
30
0
SUM=60

	SUBSTITUTE A		SUBSTITUTE C		SUBSTITUTE E	
	BCE	DCE	BAE	BDE	BDA	BDC
	20	25	0	20	0	20
	0	30	0	0	0	0
	0	0	3	3	3	0
	30	0	30	0	0	0
	0	0	0	0	15	15
SUM=	50 *	55	33	23 *	18 *	35

process is repeated by substituting A and D for C. This shows that BDE is the new best solution with a sum of minima equaling 23. A further substitution of A and C for E gives a new lowest sum of 18 for combination BDA. Note that the highest volumes are in the solution

- **Repeat substitutions until there is no improvement.** Possible substitutions for BDA—the new best solution—are CDA, EDA, BCA, BEA, BDC, and BDE. None of them produce a sum of minima less than 18, so BDA from the previous solution is the global minimum. The procedure is repeated until a complete set of substitutions produces no improvement. Solutions are obtained quite quickly if the initial guess is good. Good guesses are nodes with high volumes and even spacing between them.

- **Assign each row to the column containing the minimum row value.** For the solution BDA, node B is obviously served from node B, D from D, and A from A. C is served from B since the minimum value in the row is 3 and it is in column B. Similarly E is served from node D because the minimum of columns B, D, and A in row E is 15 found in column D.

A more complicated example of the same solution process is illustrated in Figures 11-9, 11-10, and 11-13. Figure 11-9 illustrates 40 communities on a map of Canada with the transaction volumes shown by each node. Figure 11-10 shows how the nodes are connected if a single node is used as a server. The single best node is Ottawa with all 9102 transactions. Note that it does not produce the largest number of transactions, but is about midway between the two largest centers, Toronto and Montreal.

Figure 11-13

Forty centers connected to the five nodes that minimize communications costs.

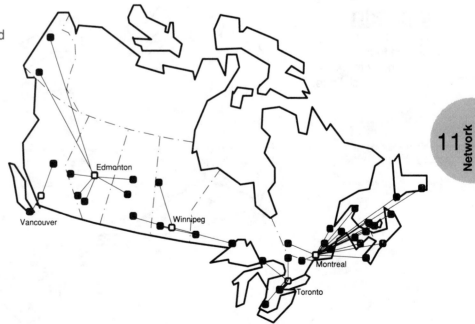

11

Network

Figure 11-13 shows how the nodes are connected if there are 5 server nodes. The 5 servers are Vancouver with 919 transactions, Edmonton with 849, Winnipeg with 756, Toronto with 2770, and Montreal with 3808. The algorithm tries to minimize distances and does not try to balance loads at each server node.

The analysis can be repeated for four and six server nodes to see if costs can be reduced by decreasing or increasing the number of nodes. The optimal solution balances the increased fixed costs of more server nodes and the decreased cost of fewer and shorter communication lines.

Once the optimal number and location of the server nodes has been computed, the server nodes can be connected into an integrated network. Figure 11-14 illustrates the connections in the example. These connections minimize the cost of the links. Usually this means minimizing the distances covered.

This problem can be solved by using a Minimum Spanning Tree algorithm to compute the minimum line length needed to connect all points in the subsystem. The algorithm is described in most Operations Research texts[3]. Sometimes it is more important to connect nodes with heavy internodal communication. In Figure 11-14 the links are obvious since there are only five nodes that need to be connected.

Note that no attempt has been made to minimize the length of the communication lines needed to connect all of the local nodes to a server. The Minimum Spanning Tree algorithm can also be used for this purpose. It may or may not be appropriate depending on the technology used to connect each node.

Figure 11-14

Five server nodes connected together in one network by trunk lines shown as thick lines.

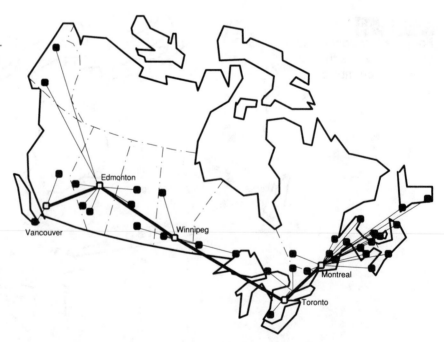

Sometimes the cost of multiplexors, or other methods needed to place multiple signals on a single line, is more than the cost of separate lines for each node.

The last physical links are those needed for redundancy. If any link in Figure 11-14 is broken, then the network is partitioned into two parts which are unable to communicate. At least the most important nodes should be connected by redundant alternate paths that can be used in case the main path is not functioning. Figure 11-15 illustrates redundant paths connecting the five server nodes. In this figure there are at least two—and sometimes more—ways of connecting each pair of server nodes. Individual user nodes can still be disconnected from the network by a single link failure. Sometimes it is also worth providing redundant paths between links.

Once the physical links have been identified, they have to be sized. This requires a good estimate of the overall traffic volume on each link. The volume consists of three kinds of traffic:

● **Transactions between a node and a server.** These are usually inquiry, insert, update, and delete activities related to the database at the server node. These volumes were used in identifying the server nodes.

● **Transactions between servers nodes.** These are usually data transfers that result from inquiries, inserts, updates, and deletes of data that are not stored on the node that serves the user initiating the transaction. Such transactions result from horizontally or vertically partitioned data tables.

● **Transactions between user nodes.** These are usually electronic mail messages or other communications that can originate at any node and be

Figure 11-15

Five server nodes with redundant connections between them.

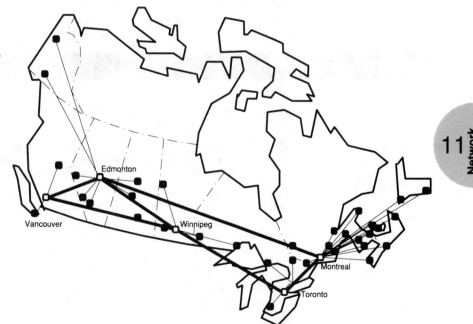

directed to any other node. Such communications normally travel from a user node to a server node, possibly to another server node, and finally to another user node. Normally the shortest route along the links in Figure 11-15 is chosen.

All of these kinds of communication must be added to identify the total communications volume expected over each link. The communication technology suitable for the volume at each link can then be selected.

This is a relatively simple design method. Much more complicated methods have been developed using Linear Programming algorithms.[2] Such formulations can take into consideration processing, storage, and communication capacity constraints; processing, storage, and communication volumes; and the fixed and variable costs of the communication system. These formulations are very difficult to solve because of their size.

Locating Programs

It is usually very simple to solve the problem of locating software and programs. Programs can be replicated in many locations. They do not need to be maintained and updated in the same way that data are. A periodic installation of a new release does not cause the same concurrency problems that result from a data update.

Sometimes different, but compatible, versions of programs must be produced to run on different kinds of hardware at different network nodes. Several Data Base Management Systems are available with versions for different hardware configurations.

Sometimes different programs on different machines need to interact. These are usually parts of Real-Time systems, which are the subject of the next chapter.

Summary

The three main reasons for distributing components of a system are efficiency, availability, and autonomy. Availability increases because there is less network communication, faster local communication, more computer power in local computers, and greater survivability when several machines are used. Autonomy can lead to improved development or to uncoordinated development.

The main disadvantages of distributed systems are related to coordination problems and integrity controls. These problems can be overcome by centralized management and standards that require compatible hardware, compatible software, consistent names, and consistent identification keys. Integrity controls are needed to make sure that insertions, updates, and deletions are performed consistently. The Data Base Management Systems handles this problem by using techniques called rollback and rollforward.

There are four basic methods of assigning data to the different nodes in a network. These are replication, horizontal table partitioning, vertical table partitioning, and database partitioning. Replication means making a separate copy of each required data table for each location. Horizontal partitioning means replicating the table structure at different locations, but having different instances of the rows at each location. Vertical table partitioning means storing some columns of a table at one location and others at another location. Database partitioning is a special case of vertical partitioning in which whole tables are assigned to different locations.

The kind of data distribution depends on the size of the geographic area, whether all users need the same kind of data, whether users share data, and whether users need updated data.

A single central system is indicated if data are being constantly read and updated by multiple users in different geographic locations where the users need immediate up-to-date access to information created in other geographic regions. When a distributed system is required, preliminary designs can be generated either by using entity groups or by clustering entities.

Some systems are using a three-tier architecture consisting of micros, minis, and mainframes. Database machines are also being used to perform database operations more efficiently.

A location algorithm can be used to locate single or multiple processors to minimize communication costs. Location algorithms minimize a weighting factor, $W_{ij} = D_{ij}V_i$ where D is distance between points and V is the volume of transactions. These processors are then connected together to provide a fully linked network with possibly some redundancy to allow for failed links.

Keywords and Phrases

Backup	Partitioned Database
Database Machine	Replicated Table
Distributed System	Rollback
Gateway	Rollforward
Horizontal Partitioning	Three Tier Architecture
Integrity Controls	Vertical Partitioning
Local Area Network	

Review Questions

1. Define each of the items in the list of keywords and phrases.
2. List the advantages and disadvantages of a distributed system.
3. Name the four generic ways in which a database can be partitioned.
4. What factors determine the method that is used to partition data in a network?
5. What characteristics of an application indicate that a single central database should be used?
6. List the available methods for producing a preliminary design for a distributed network.

11
Network

Problems

1. The following diagram shows entities, relationships, and attributes for part of a company. Parts of the data are used by three departments with three separate computer systems connected by a network. The same database is used on each computer. The Data Base Management System can read and write data stored on other computers, but this is discouraged, because it is costly and inefficient. The departments are: costing, warehousing, and project management.

   Costing computes wages and sends checks to employees at the end of each month. It also computes labor and supplies costs for the manager of each project at the end of each month. It pays suppliers for all ordered materials after they have been received at the warehouse. Costing tries to make payments within ten days of receipt to take advantage of early payment discounts. If total spending is over the project budget, payment must be approved over the phone by the project manager.

   Project managers order parts from suppliers. Each order specifies the warehouse address the supplier is supposed to ship to. Managers also record hours worked by each employee on their project.

   When parts are received at the warehouse, the receipt is recorded and the parts are stored in a bin. When all parts for an order arrive, they are shipped to the project site and the shipment is recorded on the parts record. Then the project manager is notified of the shipment.

   Each warehouse looks after its own shipments and it is very rare that shipments have to be diverted to another warehouse. A project may be supplied from more than one warehouse, but this is uncommon and has to be arranged in advance by the project manager.

   Design a database distributed among the three computers in the system. Specify which parts of the database reside on each computer. Show clearly any replication, horizontal partitioning, and vertical partitioning. For replicated data, where is the master file and how frequently and when are copies of the file sent to the sites containing replicates?

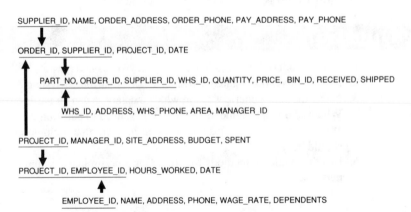

SUPPLIER_ID, NAME, ORDER_ADDRESS, ORDER_PHONE, PAY_ADDRESS, PAY_PHONE

ORDER_ID, SUPPLIER_ID, PROJECT_ID, DATE

PART_NO, ORDER_ID, SUPPLIER_ID, WHS_ID, QUANTITY, PRICE, BIN_ID, RECEIVED, SHIPPED

WHS_ID, ADDRESS, WHS_PHONE, AREA, MANAGER_ID

PROJECT_ID, MANAGER_ID, SITE_ADDRESS, BUDGET, SPENT

PROJECT_ID, EMPLOYEE_ID, HOURS_WORKED, DATE

EMPLOYEE_ID, NAME, ADDRESS, PHONE, WAGE_RATE, DEPENDENTS

2. The following figure gives the location of four nodes in a distributed network. The numbers at the nodes specify the number of transactions that must be processed at the respective node in thousands of transactions per day. The numbers on the lines specify the distance between nodes in hundreds of miles. The cost of transmitting the data for transactions is approximately proportional to the number of transactions and the distance that the data are being transmitted.

a. Find the best location for a single computer to serve all four locations.

b. Find the best locations for two computers to serve all four locations. Which locations does each computer serve?

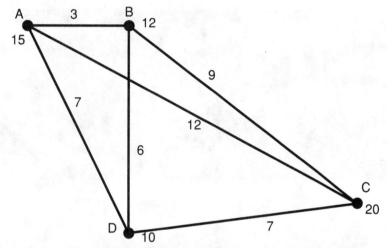

References

1. Conard, James W., Editor, *Handbook of Communications Systems Management,* Auerbach Publishers Inc., 1988.
2. Gavish, Bezalel and Hasan Pirkul, "Computer and Database Location in Distributed Computer Systems", *IEEE Transactions on Communications,* 1986.
3. Hillier, Frederick S., and Gerald J. Lieberman, *Introduction to Operations Research, Fourth Edition,* Holden-Day Inc. 1986, pp. 300-304.
4. Martin, James, *Design and Strategy for Distributed Data Processing,* Prentice-Hall, 1981.
5. Rushton, Gerard, Michael F. Goodchild and Lawrence M. Ostresh Jr., *Computer Programs for Location-Allocation Problems,* Monograph Number 6, Department of Geography, The University of Iowa, July 1973.
6. Schussel, George, "Application Development in the 5th Generation", *Datamation,* Nov. 15, 1987, pp. 94-102.

Chapter 12

Real-Time Systems

	DATABASE (WHAT)	PROGRAMS (HOW)	BENEFITS (WHY)	NETWORK (WHERE)	REAL TIME (WHEN)	SKILLS (WHO)
USER CONCEPT	Entity Relationship	Activity	Intangible Benefit	Map		Organization Design
DESIGNER CONCEPT	E-R Diagram	A-E Diagram	AHP	Network		Skills Responsibility
USER DETAIL	Forms Screens	Processes Data	Tangible Benefit	Work Volume	Discrete Events	Transition Training
DESIGNER DETAIL	EER Diagram	Data Flow Diagrams	Benefit-Cost	Partition	Transition Diagrams	Methodology Tools
BUILDER CONCEPT	Normal Form Relations	Structure Chart	Function Points	System Architecture	Specifications	Learning
BUILDER DETAIL	Files	Screens Specifications	Costs	Network Specs	Interfaces	4GL CASE

Objectives

This chapter deals with the design of real-time systems. These are systems that interact with some external process such as a chemical process or a manufacturing control system. Data processing systems are defined by their data and their processing requirements. Real-time systems require a third design dimension which deals with the control and synchronization of multiple processes. The data and process descriptions are handled in the same way as they are in ordinary data processing systems. The real-time aspects require extensions to the design methodology that will be described in this chapter.

There are two main modifications to the design methodology. A special notation has to be added to the data flow diagram to differentiate between data and control information. A state transition diagram has to be added to the function design to describe all of the possible cases that the system must be able to cope with. In this chapter you learn:

- How to identify a real-time system.

- How to extend the Data Flow Diagram to include control information.

- How to use a State Transition Diagram to describe all of the states that the system can be in.

- How to document interfaces between programs and external devices that provide information or interact with a process.

- How to split and combine State Transition Diagrams.

- How to convert control and state transition information into detailed specifications.

Characterizing Real-Time Systems

The term real-time system is sometimes used to refer to any system that operates in an on-line interactive mode with a requirement for fast response times. By this definition, most modern systems could be called real-time. However, such systems can be designed using the tools described in previous chapters. Ward and Mellor[5] identify a set of characteristics that are possessed by true real-time systems. The characteristics are:

- **Problems are formulated in scientific or engineering terms.** Real-time systems usually deal with the control of some process that is dominated by the immutable laws of physics, chemistry, or biology.

- **Real-time systems contain sensors and actuators to interact with their environment instead of with humans.** All systems interact with an external environment. A student records system interacts with students who are external to the system by sending them reports and with administrators who make decisions that change the environment. A real-time system has sensors to sense important physical parameters such as temperature, pressure, or speed directly. It does not get the information from human operators. It also has actuators such as valves and thermostats that can make direct changes to the environment without going through a human intermediary. These input and output activities are often continuous and overlapping. They thus require a degree of coordination similar to the eye-hand coordination of people.

- **Real-time systems often require concurrent processing of multiple inputs.** This is different from on-line systems which merely have to provide fast response time to several users. The problems of the different users can still be treated separately. In a real-time system the different inputs have to be coordinated. Temperature, pressure, and acidity may have to be sensed and used together to calculate how to control a chemical reaction. Valves and heaters may have to be adjusted simultaneously to maintain the desired flow rate, temperature, and reaction rate.

- **Real-time systems operate at very short time scales.** One second is a short period for responses to human operators. Yet it is often a very long time for responses in a chemical plant or a nuclear reactor. Such systems may require responses in milliseconds or even microseconds. Such rapid response times may sometimes be at the limit of the available technology. As a result, there may be several technological constraints in the design of the system.

- **Real-time systems require higher precision than ordinary systems.** An on-line system may "require" a response time of one second. However, no great harm is done if the response is shorter or occasionally even several seconds longer. Such variations in a real-time system are likely to spoil a product or even lead to dangerous and uncontrollable reactions.

- **Constraints are imposed by the task, not the user.** These constraints guarantee safety, liveness, and timeliness. Safety means that responses match specifications and the system is fault-tolerant. Liveness means that the system responds to all events. Timeliness means that the system responds within time constraints imposed by the environment. Meeting a time constraint means that the system must be "fast enough" rather than just "very fast."

This list of characteristics is not mandatory. A real-time system may contain only some of them and usually contains most of them. However, a method for designing real-time systems must be able to deal with all of them.

The distinction between an on-line system and a real-time system often depends on what components are included in the system. Consider the design of a point-of-sale terminal system using debit cards. The card identifies the purchaser and the system automatically debits the purchaser's account and credits the seller's account. Such a system contains sensors to read the debit card, coordinates the transaction between the purchaser and the seller, handles many transactions per second, and must handle each in precise order to match the buyer and the seller.

If all the components of this system must be designed from the start, this may be a real-time system. However, the system can also be viewed as a simple transaction between a purchaser and a seller with no other parties involved. The complexity only arises because many other buyers and sellers want to use the system simultaneously. If the problem is separated into a component that handles single transactions and a component that synchronizes many individual transactions, then the problem can be simplified.

The component to handle single transactions is an ordinary on-line system of the kind that has been covered in previous chapters. The component to synchronize many transactions is an operating system that is usually provided by the computer vendor. The operating system has to read debit cards, send messages, handle multiple inputs from many readers, and work precisely within a short time scale. This makes the design of the operating system a problem in real-time systems design. Given an operating system that can do all of this, the designer of the debit card system does not need to consider real-time systems as part of the design.

Thus the design of an operating system, a database management system, or a network communications facility is usually an exercise in the design of real-time systems. The design of programs that use these facilities is not always a design of real-time systems because the environments may take care of the real-time complications. Often, even with the help of all of these environmental utility programs, the designer must still take care of many real-time aspects of the system.

The need for real-time techniques usually occurs if the interface device is included in the system. If the system must deal with magnetic card readers, bar-code readers, and display hardware directly, then it probably must be treated as a real-time system. If the system can be designed using input and output messages that go to or from hardware of unknown characteristics, then the problem can be simplified greatly and does not need real-time methods. Thus the

12 **Real-Time**

need for real-time techniques often depends on the sophistication of the operating system environment and the availability of standard device interfaces.

This is the reason that General Motors proposed the Manufacturing Automation Protocol[4] (MAP) specification for communication between equipment components in automated factories. MAP specifies standard communication protocols so designers do not have to deal with how messages move between sensors, computers, and actuators. Under MAP the designer is freed to concentrate on the system logic, not the communications between components.

Scientific and engineering terminology, short time scales, and high precision do not complicate the design process. Conceptually they can be handled by the methods described previously. However, the concurrent processing of information related to many sensors and actuators does complicate the design process significantly. Since many different things can be happening at once, the designer must be able to keep track of which events currently need attention.

This need to detect events which define the state of the system and control the relationship between simultaneously active components requires a new view of the system. Up to now, the system has been viewed as consisting of two kinds of components: data and processes. Events provide a third dimension in which we can analyze a process as shown in Figure 12-1. Graphic tools are needed to document and understand the data and process dimensions of a system. Similarly, graphic tools are needed to analyze the events dimension.

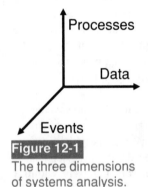

Figure 12-1
The three dimensions
of systems analysis.

Business systems in the past have rarely needed to deal with the events in real-time systems. Such problems have usually been the domain of engineers designing chemical plants, robotic assembly lines, computer hardware, or rocket control systems. However, as automated factories are integrated with materials supply, product costing, and customer orders, the factory automation systems are beginning to share the same database as the management systems. The production systems rely on data that are captured in the normal business cycle. In turn, the production systems provide information about resource consumption, quality, production levels, and costs.

Integration of the production view and the management view requires changes on both sides. The management side must understand the special problems of analyzing, designing, implementing, and operating production systems. The production side must learn to use integrated databases and structured designs that are compatible with business systems.

Event-Based Real-Time Analysis Tools

There are two main extensions that have to be made to the methods already presented. The first is a method of documenting all the controls required to activate the different processes in the system. This is accomplished by extending the notation in the Data Flow Diagram. The second extension is a method of documenting the different states in which a system can be and the transitions between these states. This is accomplished with a State Transition Diagram.

The best-known real-time extensions to Data Flow Diagrams are those of Ward and Mellor[5] and those of Hatley and Pirbhai.[2] The Hatley and Pirbhai method provides more complete documentation of complex systems, but is somewhat harder to follow and to use. The method described in this chapter is closer to that of Ward and Mellor.

Data Flow Diagram Extensions

There are three extensions that need to be added to the normal notation for Data Flow Diagrams. They are illustrated in Figure 12-2. The extensions are to document control processes, document control signals, document control files, and distinguish between discreet and continuous signals.

- **Control processes.** These are special processes that control the activity of all other processes in the system. They are similar to the boss module in a Structure Chart. In the normal method, control issues are deferred until the Structure Chart is developed. In normal designs, the process is the most important part of the diagram and control issues are unimportant. In real-time systems, control issues are very important and need to be analyzed earlier. A control process is indicated by a process box drawn with dashed lines.

    Control processes are exploded like other processes. They are numbered like ordinary processes. A process is assumed to be disabled until it is explicitly enabled. When a process is disabled, all of its subprocesses are disabled.

- **Control signals.** Control signals are data flows created by a control process to enable or disable a process. They act as switches or level settings to determine the behavior of a process. They are part of the control process, so they are also distinguished by dashed lines. The distinction is the same as the one between data and flags in a Structure Chart.

- **Continuous and discrete data flows.** Data can have a continuous value that exists at all times or a discrete value that exists only at a point in time. Temperature is an example of a continuous value. A room has a temperature at all times, even if it gradually varies. Using a remote control to turn a television set on is an example of a discrete signal. It happens at an instant in time and then stops. If the set is not plugged in at the time, the remote control

Figure 12-2
Extensions to the Data Flow Diagram.

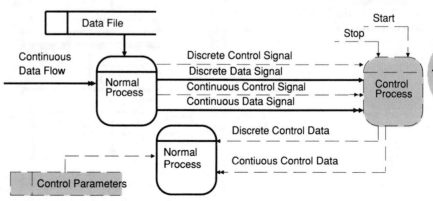

12 Real-Time

has no effect. If the set is later plugged in, the signal still has no effect because it has stopped. Discrete signals have to be identified because they can be missed if a process is not ready to receive them. Continuous signals are identified by a double arrowhead on the data flow line. Discrete signals have a single arrowhead.

● **Control files.** Special files or storage areas are often needed to store frequently used variables such as target values or set points. These are distinguished–like all control information–by file symbols in dashed lines.

State Transition Diagrams

Figure 12-3 illustrates a generic State Transition Diagram. It models the different states that a system can be in and the control signals and actions that cause the transition to another state. The four components of a State Transition Diagram are states, transitions, controls, and actions. Each is defined as follows:

● **States.** A state is an externally observable mode of behavior. It is symbolized with a rectangle and named after the behavior that the system exhibits when in that state. A strong transitive verb and an optional noun usually make good names. You can think of a state as a manager or coordinator that is waiting for something to happen so it can respond. Thus a state is a steady condition such as waiting for a command or pumping at a steady rate. Most systems start in an initial idle or waiting state.

● **Transitions.** These are symbolized by arrows which point from a previous state toward the next state. A state can have one or more transitions coming into it and one or more transitions leaving it. Each transition has a control and one or more actions associated with it.

● **Controls.** A control is a condition or event that causes a system to make a transition between states. Lifting the receiver on a telephone when it is not ringing is a condition that causes a telephone to go from a state of waiting for a call to a state of making a call. Controls are symbolized by a condition name written beside the transition line to which it is related.

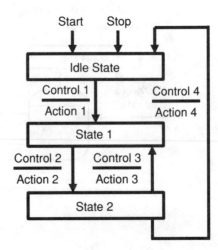

Figure 12-3
A generic State Transition Diagram.

● **Actions.** Actions are things that must be done during the transition from one state to another. When a telephone is making a call, dialing a number is the action that is performed. The action is written below a line that separates it from its related control. The two can be read together as *if condition then action*. More than one action can be associated with a control condition, but all are assumed to occur instantly during the transition to the next state.

A State Transition Diagram is needed only in situations where a memory of the system history is required. The State Transition Diagram specifies what a signal means depending on the current state of the system. If signals always have the same meaning, then the system has only one state. In that case, the system can be modeled more simply by a Decision Tree or a Decision Table.

Example State Transition Diagram

Figure 12-4 illustrates a Data Flow Diagram for a system that maintains the temperature of a reactor at a set level. CONTROL TEMPERATURE is a control process that regulates the actions of the other processes: HEAT QUICKLY, HEAT SLOWLY, and REFRIGERATE. It accepts control signals and generates new signals to enable or disable the processes that control heaters and refrigerators. HEAT QUICKLY operates a large gas heater that can raise temperature quickly, but is very difficult to regulate. HEAT SLOWLY operates a small electric heater that can be regulated accurately when the temperature is near the set point. REFRIGERATE operates a refrigeration unit that can reduce the temperature when required.

Figure 12-4
Data Flow Diagram for a temperature control system.

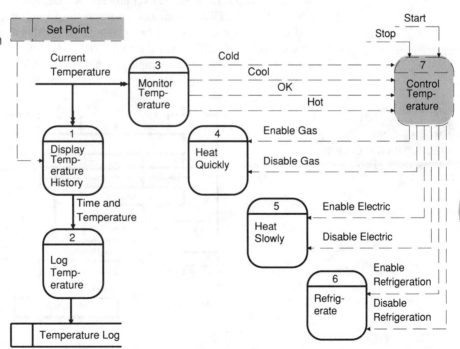

12
Real-Time

The MONITOR TEMPERATURE process does four things. It accepts continuous temperatures from a thermocouple. It compares them to a temperature stored in the SET POINT file. It breaks the temperatures into ranges corresponding to four control signals. Finally it sends one of four signals: COLD, COOL, OK, and HOT. DISPLAY TEMPERATURE HISTORY is a process that plots recent temperatures on a graphic screen. It also uses the LOG TEMPERATURE process to store temperatures periodically on the TEMPERATURE LOG file.

This diagram shows the processes that are involved in the entire system, but it does not document the logical relationships between the different processes. The Data Flow Diagram does not indicate which conditions trigger the different processes. We have to look inside the CONTROL TEMPERATURE process to find out how its inputs are related to its outputs.

Looking inside processes in normal systems, we find descriptions of the logic in Structured English, Decision Tables, or Decision Trees. Looking inside a control process, we see a State Transition Diagram which is a specialized notation for describing control structures. Figure 12-5 illustrates the State Transition Diagram inside the CONTROL TEMPERATURE process.

The process begins in the idle state. A START or STOP signal can be used to turn the system on or off. It can receive COLD, COOL, OK, or HOT control signals which activate different processes. A HOT control signal results in an ENABLE REFRIGERATION signal being sent to the REFRIGERATION process. A COOL control signal results in an ENABLE ELECTRIC signal being sent to the ELECTRIC HEATING process. A COLD control signal results in an ENABLE ELECTRIC signal being sent to the ELECTRIC HEATING process and an ENABLE GAS signal being sent to the GAS HEATING process. Note that the GAS HEATING and the ELECTRIC HEATING states can be enabled simultaneously. This is an example of simultaneous processes in action. An OK signal leaves the system in the idle state, so it is not shown.

Figure 12-5

The State Transition
Diagram for the Control
Temperature Process.

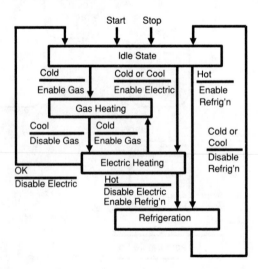

If the system is in the electric heating state, it can transfer to GAS HEATING, IDLE STATE, or REFRIGERATION depending on whether a COLD, OK, or HOT signal is received.

Another way to present the same information is to use the Action Table (sometimes called a State Transition Table) shown in Figure 12-6. It lists the possible states down the left side and the possible signals that the system can receive along the top. The entries are the actions that must be taken when a signal is received while in a particular state. Blank entries mean that no action is taken and the system remains the same.

An Action Table is somewhat like a Decision Table in that it identifies all of the possible states, signals, and outcomes. The structure of the table forces the designer to consider each possibility. In Figure 12-6 there is no entry for the REFRIGERATION state when an OK signal is received. That implies that refrigeration should continue. Yet clearly, the system should return to the IDLE STATE if an OK signal is received.

It is easier to see this omission in an Action Table than in a State Transition Diagram. Now that the error has been detected, the State Transition Diagram is modified to accept a COLD, COOL, or OK condition while in the REFRIGERATION state. The same problem does not exist for the GAS HEATING state. The COOL signal occurs before an OK signal, so the transition to electric heating state occurs before the OK signal can arrive.

A large Action table is easier to prepare than an equally complex State Transition Diagram, but may be harder to understand. A large Action Diagram usually has many empty cells. The analyst can use either notation, or both depending on circumstances.

SIGNALS STATUS	Cold	Cool	OK	Hot
Idle	Enable Gas Enable Electric	Enable Electric		Enable Refrigeration
Gas Heat		Disable Gas		
Electric Heat	Enable Gas		Disable Electric Idle	Disable Electric Enable Refrig'n
Refrigeration	Disable Refrig'n Idle	Disable Refrig'n Idle		

Figure 12-6

An Action Table equivalent to the State Transition Diagram in Figure 12-5.

12
Real-Time

Identification of System Boundaries

The boundary of the system is the first thing that needs to be defined in a real-time system design. It is relatively easy to define the functions that are to be performed by the system. It is often hard to define which parts are within the system and which parts are considered to be part of the environment.

Figure 12-7 illustrates the stages that a typical signal goes through as it passes from being a real-world event to becoming a signal in the logical system. In the real world, the system has a continuously changing temperature. This temperature can be sensed in several ways. A thermocouple produces a voltage that is proportional to its temperature. A thermistor has a resistance that is proportional to its temperature. Other devices produce other kinds of signals that are related to temperature.

Whichever device is used to detect the temperature, the signal usually has to be converted to a digital signal. That signal then has to be converted to a meaningful scale that is suitable for processing—Celsius temperature in this case. Finally the temperature may have to be translated into a meaningful event, such as entering a range that is too hot for the system to tolerate.

System signals that produce actions in the real world have to go through a similar process in reverse. A signal to raise temperature to a set point is converted to degrees of temperature, then to a gas flow rate, then to a number of steps on a stepping motor that adjusts a valve.

The system can be thought of as consisting of three layers. The first or outer layer is the real world in which physical things happen according to the laws of physics, chemistry, and biology. The last, or inner layer, is the logical system in which logical events are detected and signals are sent out to the real world to change controllable factors. Sandwiched between these two layers is a layer of interface technology that translates real-world events into logical events and action signals into adjustments of the real world.

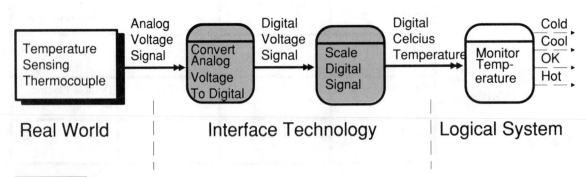

Figure 12-7

The elastic boundaries between the logical system and the real world.

The question is, "Where in this sequence do we draw the boundary between the real world and the system?" Initially the boundary is drawn as near to the logical system as possible. The reason is that many of the technical decisions about the kinds of sensors and actuators used in the interface have not been made at the initial stages of the design. Generally, several options are available and each of them can be tailored to signal the required event to the system.

When the technological decisions are made, functions supporting the interface technology are added to the design. These usually do not change the system design because they do not change the logic of the system side of the interface.

This problem is similar to the problem of defining the boundaries between a word processor and its associated printer and display screen. This problem is usually solved by keeping the logical operations of the system—inserting, editing, and deleting—in the logical system. The interface technology for the printer is kept as a separate process driven by different configuration tables for different printers. A new printer can be installed without changing the logic of the system as long as the printer has the minimal functions needed to print the document. Similarly, a new display screen can be installed by installing a new configuration table that describes the properties of the screen.

Occasionally the technology of the sensor or actuator should be included in the initial design. This is most likely to happen when the nature of the data received from or sent to the real world depends fundamentally on the choice of technology. It is also desirable when the sensor or actuator has to be controlled by the logical model and the nature of the controls depends on the sensor or actuator that is chosen. A robot is an example of such a device.

The interface should be left out of the initial design if the nature of the data being sent—such as temperature—is relatively independent of the chosen technology. This makes it easier to design standard interfaces that allow the technology to be changed easily if a new sensor is adopted.

Another component of the technological interface is the communication network that transmits the signals between the computer and its sensors or activators. The sensors and activators are often far from the computer. The signal must then be sent through some communications network. There are many possible communications protocols that can be used.

Different component vendors may support different protocols which complicates the design further. For this reason General Motors proposed the Manufacturing Automation Protocol[4] (MAP) standard to define standard communication interfaces. A standard interface simplifies the design enormously because it removes the communication interface from the detail design. The system can assume that all communications arrive and leave through a standard interface.

When the boundaries of the system have been defined, the designer can develop the database design and the process design in the usual way. When these have been designed, the designer can document the events on the State Transition Diagram.

12 Real-Time

Developing the State Transition Diagram

The State Transition Diagram is defined by the states of a system and the events that put it into those states. The main sources of information for the State Transition Diagram are the Entity-Relationship Model and the Data Flow Diagram. These resources can be used in a standard development procedure.

Development Procedures

The following procedure provides an initial State Transition Diagram which can be further refined.

- **Identify external events from the Context Diagram.** An event can only be detected if it produces some kind of a data flow or signal. These signals usually arrive from outside the system, so they are documented in the Context Diagram. An event can occur under three circumstances:
  - **A discrete data item arrives.** A discrete signal has a finite number of values with no ranking or ordering of the values. On and off, hot and cold, or red, yellow, and blue are examples of discrete signals. In this situation, data arrives intermittently and the system waits for data arrival before doing anything. This occurs when a computer waits for a keyboard command or an atomic particle counter waits for a particle to arrive.
  - **A required time passes.** This may be a time allowed for processing product or it may be a specific time, such as the time for a daily report.
  - **A recognition device signals an event.** Some device may be monitoring the environment. It signals that a certain value has occurred, a certain relationship to stored data has occurred, or a certain combination of data values has been detected.
- **Arrange the events in sequential order.** If the event can permit or prevent the system from responding to other events, then it needs a control mechanism to activate and deactivate the responses. These responses create a new state that is terminated by new events. If the event cannot affect other events, then it is only a data transformation, like the calculation or recording of data. Similarly, if other events can prevent or permit a system response to this event, then the other events must precede this one.
- **Identify states from the Data Flow Diagram.** The processes in the Data Flow Diagram are good candidates for states in the State Transition Diagram. In Figure 12-4 the HEAT QUICKLY, HEAT SLOWLY, and REFRIGERATE processes correspond to states of the system. The MONITOR, DISPLAY, and LOG processes are not controllable states. Since they operate continuously, they do not need to be controlled. They are only data manipulations and are not states of the system.
- **Add an IDLE state to the list.** Every system has a state in which nothing is happening or when the system is waiting for something to happen. Usually this is the first state in the State Transition Diagram. Sometimes, the system is waiting for commands or signals. This is the state of a system when it presents a menu on a screen and waits for a reply.

- **Combine states and events into a State Transition Diagram.** When the events have been ordered, the states can be introduced between the events to produce a preliminary State Transition Diagram. This preliminary diagram often reveals events without corresponding states or states without corresponding events. This may be due to missing information or to poor analysis that identified non-existent events or states. The diagram needs to be adjusted to reconcile the differences.
- **Identify actions that need to be performed after each event.** Clarify the relationships between the events and the states that they lead to. Then identify the actions that invoke these states and add them to the State Transition Diagram. Most of these actions send signals to enable or disable processes.
- **Identify states that split into substates.** Just as a Data Flow Diagram can have processes that contain subprocesses, a State Transition Diagram can have states that contain substates. These substates need to be identified if they exist. Sometimes a complicated diagram needs to be simplified by grouping several states into a new higher state. The criterion for grouping states is the same as for grouping processes: minimize the number of data and control connections between groups.
- **Use an Action Table to check for missing states and events.** An Action Table forces the designer to consider the relationship between all pairs of states and events. This sometimes reveals new actions or even new states and events. Particular attention should be paid to starting and stopping the process. Often special procedures are required to ensure that the process does not stop in a dangerous state or that it can restart after problems such as power failures.
- **Walk through the State Transition Diagram with the users to verify it.** When a process has been fully defined, check it with the user to ensure that all requirements are covered and all events are accounted for. The "user" of a real-time system is often an engineer or other technical specialist who understands all the technical requirements of the system and its environment. The walk through consists of following the typical—and sometimes atypical—series of events through the system to make sure that the system behaves properly.

Testing the State Transition Diagram

There are several common errors that are made in constructing State Transition Diagrams. The states, events, actions and transitions are examined for clues to these errors.

CLUE #1:   **No transition out of a state.**

CAUSE: An event and transition line have been omitted.

CURE: Identify the event and add the transition.

In Figure 12-8 the Cooling state has no exit. This is because the OK event and its corresponding Disable Cooling action have been omitted. The diagram is corrected by adding them back.

12

Real-Time

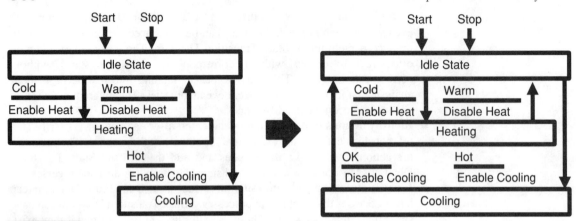

Figure 12-8
Figure 12-8
A State Transition Diagram in which the Cooling state has no exit.

CLUE #2:	**No transition into a state.**
CAUSE:	An event and transition line have been omitted.
CURE:	Identify the event and add the transition.

In Figure 12-9 the Cooling state has no transition entering it. This is because the Hot event and its corresponding Enable Cooling action have been omitted. The diagram is corrected by adding them back.

CLUE #3:	**The State Transition Diagram is too complicated.**
CAUSE:	The diagram should be redrawn in multiple levels.
CURE:	Identify independent groups of states and give them a group name. Each group can then be redrawn in detail on separate diagrams. Such leveling reduces the complexity of the diagrams and makes it easier for the reader to identify the different processes that are being controlled.

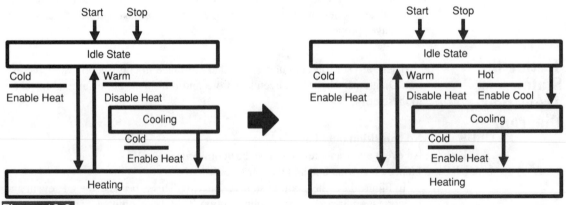

Figure 12-9
A State Transition Diagram with no way to get into the Cooling state.

In Figure 12-10, there are two separate control functions for temperature and pH. These control functions can be identified as major functions that are called. The detailed contents can then be documented in the two functions: Control Temperature and Control pH. Such a separation makes it clear that there are two separate functions that are unconnected. It also makes it easier to understand each of the lower functions, since the diagrams are not cluttered with documentation of unrelated functions.

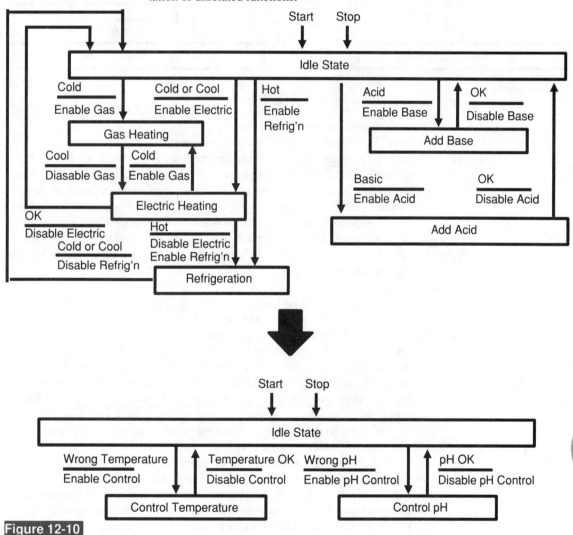

Figure 12-10

This State Transition Diagram combines two control functions that should be separated and leveled. Control Temperature and Control pH can then be exploded separately.

12
Real-Time

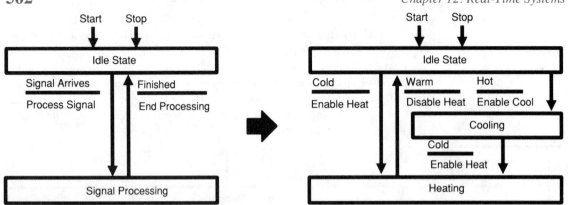

Figure 12-11

Signal Arrives and Finished are not clearly defined events.

CLUE #4:   **Ambiguous or unclear event names.**
CAUSE: The analyst has not identified all of the events and relationships.
CURE: Identify all the events and include them in the State Transition Diagram.

In Figure 12-11 the Signal Arrives and Finished events are very unclear. They do not say anything about the basic discipline of the system (unless it is a signal processing system). Signal Processing is also a poorly defined state. The analyst needs to understand the domain of knowledge of the system and must clearly identify the events, actions, and states that describe the system. Fuzzy definitions lead to poorly chosen system boundaries and systems that are incorrect or hard to implement and maintain.

CLUE #5:   **Events with continuous instead of discrete signals.**
CAUSE: The signal is not an event. It is a raw data stream.
CURE: Extract the events triggered by special data values.

An event has to occur in the external environment of the system, elicit a planned response from the system, and occur at a specific point in time. In Figure 12-12, temperature and pH are not events because they do not occur at specific points in time. They occur continuously. Specific events are reaching 0 degrees Celsius, remaining constant for five minutes, reversing the direction of change, or going outside an acceptable range. Each of these can be pinpointed to a specific time at which they occurred.

An analyst who mistakes a continuous signal for an event often finds there is no corresponding action or the action is a vague and ambiguous one like "control" or "process" something. As always, vagueness is a sign of ignorance and the analyst should go back and understand the system before proceeding.

The State Transition Diagram can be corrected by identifying the specific temperature or pH condition(s) which invoke a state that controls or changes the current values.

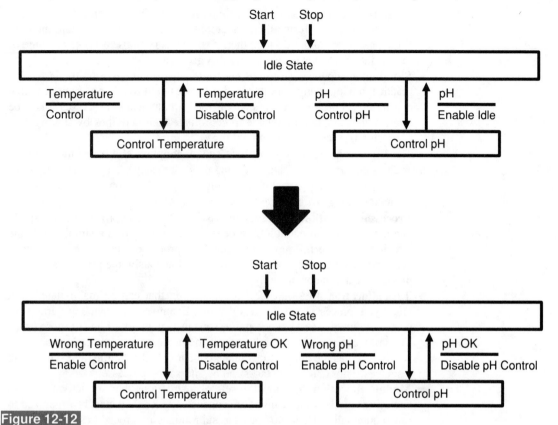

Figure 12-12

Temperature and pH are not events. They are continuous data streams.

Converting Logical Designs to Physical Designs

The logical model documented in the State Transition Diagram has assumed a rather idealized world. It does not deal with physical constraints such as processor power, message arrival rates, or required response times. This has been done to simplify the problem and allow the designer to concentrate on the essential problem. Once the essential properties have been captured in the logical model, the designer can turn to the problem of implementing the model in a real hardware environment.

The idealized logical system assumed that:

● **All processing can be done by a single processor.** This means there are no constraints on processor power, memory availability, data storage, or data transmission capacity. If a single processor cannot handle the load, either functionality must be reduced or multiple processors must be used. If multiple processors are used, then there is a need for extra processes that coordinate the activities of the different processors.

12
Real-Time

- **All state transitions occur instantaneously.** This implies that the processor is fast enough to perform all computations within an arbitrarily small interval. If the processor cannot do this, then it is necessary to use a faster machine or to schedule processes in a sequence that gives satisfactory performance.
- **Simultaneous processes can be continuously and independently active.** In practice, having many simultaneous processes could violate various resource constraints. Furthermore, many of the simultaneous processes may be interdependent. They may have to coordinate their activities by sharing data or passing messages to each other.

The ideal technology is error-free. This assumption eliminates the need for error-checking and safety features during the design stage. This assumption must be relaxed during implementation. A logical model is converted into an implementation model in six stages. These are:

- **Processor allocation.** Processes are assigned to several processors if a single one is not powerful enough. A processor may range from a simple analogue circuit to a powerful supercomputer. The processors are connected into a network. Since each processor can run simultaneously, the processes on each processor can run concurrently.
- **Task allocation.** Tasks are sets of instruction that can be manipulated as a unit by a processor's system software. Examples are batch programs or on-line interactive tasks. Each processor runs a network of one or more tasks. The tasks can run concurrently only if the processor has multiple processors within it or has the ability to simulate concurrency by sharing and scheduling resources. Thus concurrent tasks can be interacting processes.
- **Module allocation.** Modules are sets of instructions that are activated as an exclusive unit. Modules cannot run concurrently, so they must be organized to run sequentially. Thus modules are subroutines or procedures that perform non-interacting processes.
- **Interface design.** Interfaces to the input sources, the output processors, and the user must be added to the system to connect the outside world to the logical system.
- **Self-testing, redundancy, and maintenance.** Real systems suffer from mechanical failures. Self-testing detects these failures. Redundancy provides a way to bypass failed components. Systems can be designed to warn when maintenance is needed.
- **Detailed specification of control modules.** A State Transition Diagram specifies the control logic of the system. The system is implemented by coding the logic in an implementation language using tools like Structured English to specify the requirements.

Processor Allocation

A single processor is nearly always the simplest configuration to build. It eliminates the need for interfaces, coordination, and communication between processors. If a single processor is unable to do all the work, then work must be allocated to multiple processors on the basis of required capabilities such as:

- **Capacity.** Processing speed, memory, and data storage capabilities are the main measures of capacity.
- **Features.** Many special features are available. These include floating point arithmetic, double precision arithmetic, array processing, or the ability to interface with special hardware.
- **Physical features.** Real-time systems often go into harsh environments such as factories or space satellites. Such systems must meet special criteria such as extreme temperatures, low weight, special packaging, or military standards.
- **Redundancy.** It may be necessary to duplicate processors to be sure that a critical function can be performed even when there is a hardware failure.
- **Packaging.** It is sometimes convenient to package a processor within a sensor or actuator. Thus an analogue to digital converter may be packaged as part of a sensing device. A processor may be included as part of a robot controlled by a central computer. Communications networks commonly have processors as part of the network hardware. Then these components do not have to be duplicated by a new system.

The part of a logical model that is allocated to a particular processor is then responsible for receiving data, sending data to other processors, processing data, and recording when appropriate.

Splitting data between processors is handled in the same way as described in the previous chapter for distributed databases. Splitting a State Transition Diagram is equivalent to splitting the processes in a Data Flow Diagram into multiple processes at a new level. The following algorithm splits the events on a State Transition Diagram.

- Duplicate the State Transition Diagram for each processor involved.
- For each condition and action pair, perform the correct case below:
  - **Same processor senses condition and takes action.** Add an action at the performing processor to signal to other processors that the condition has been sensed. Remove the condition and action from other processors and replace with receipt of the signal from the performer.
  - **One processor senses the condition and another takes action.** The sensing processor has no action, but it signals the other processor that the condition has been sensed. The other processor has no condition, but receives a signal that the condition has occurred and performs the action. If more than one action are performed after the condition, include each action only on the diagram for the processor that performs that action.
- For each state on each State Transition Diagram apply the following procedure iteratively until all possible states have been removed:
  IF
    All outgoing transitions have no actions AND
    the conditions are signals from other processors AND
    all outward transitions go to a single destination state,
      whose outgoing transitions in turn have conditions
      that are signals from another processor

12 Real-Time

THEN
    Remove the state and its outgoing transitions AND
    Reroute the incoming transitions to the destination state AND
    Remove redirected transitions that loop to the destination AND
    Combine any logically equivalent transitions.

- Remove actions that send signals that do not result in an action by any other processor. Also remove these signals from the other processor diagrams.
- Remove states and transitions with signals that do not generate an action in the receiving processor.
- Rename states where needed for clarification.

This algorithm is illustrated by the example from Figure 12-5. Heating and temperature detection is allocated to a "heating processor" and refrigeration is allocated to a "refrigeration processor." Figures 12-13 and 12-14 illustrate the new diagrams after conditions and actions have been modified. Additional actions are shown in italic type. Signals between processors are shown as a *Signal Condition* action by the sender and a *Condition Signal* received by the receiver.

The heating processor does not change very much since refrigeration was only a single state on the original State Transition Diagram. The refrigeration processor is quite different because most of the actions have been deleted.

Figure 12-15 illustrates what happens to Figure 12-14 when the transformation rules are applied for the first time. The transformation eliminates the Gas Heating state and its outgoing transition triggered by the Cool Signal. The Cold

Figure 12-13

The State Transition Diagram for the Heating Process.

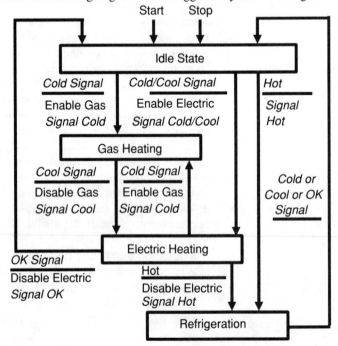

Figure 12-14

The State Transition Diagram for the Refrigeration Process.

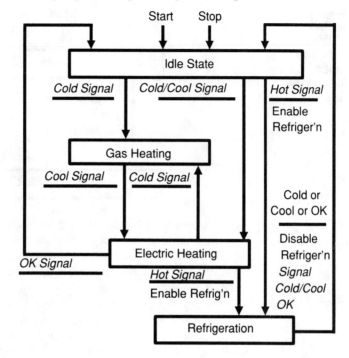

Figure 12-15

The State Transition Diagram for the Refrigeration Process after removing the Gas Heating State.

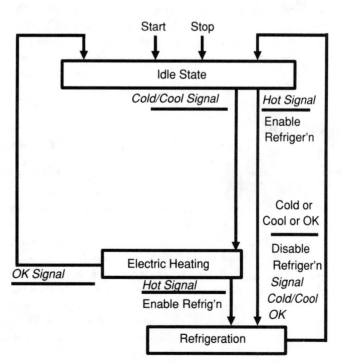

12 Real-Time

Figure 12-16

State Transition
Diagram for the
Refrigeration Process
after removing the
Electric Heating state.

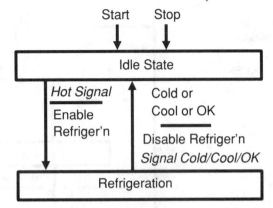

Signal coming from Electric Heating loops back to Electric Heating according to the algorithm. Thus it is not needed and can be eliminated. Similarly, the Cold Signal from the Idle State would be passed through to the Electric Heating State. However, it is logically equivalent to the Cold/Cool Signal from the Idle State so this duplication can be eliminated.

Figure 12-15 still contains signals that do not have any corresponding actions. The Cold/Cool Signal and the OK Signal have no corresponding actions so they can be removed. The Electric Heating state is not a state controlled by the Refrigeration Processor. It can be removed and the Hot Signal that it generates can be connected back to the Idle State. This then produces a duplication of the Hot Signal already coming from the Idle State so one of them can be eliminated. The final result is the simple diagram in Figure 12-16.

The same elimination process would remove the Refrigeration State and the Cold or Cool or OK Signal transition from Figure 12-13. The Hot condition transitions would return to the Idle State.

Task Allocation

Each of the State Transition Diagrams allocated to a processor is a task that can potentially run concurrently with other tasks. The problem of task allocation is a problem of scheduling potentially concurrent tasks on a single processor and providing communication between any tasks that have to be synchronized. This is a relatively simple problem if the program is implemented in a language, like ADA[1], that supports concurrent tasks. Such languages simulate concurrent operation by time-slicing, in which the processor is periodically interrupted and assigned to a different task. This happens fast enough that each task appears to have control of the processor.

If the implementation language does not support concurrent processing and communication between processes, then the designer must design a system that supports such processing. This consists of designing a combined state diagram in which there is a new state for each possible combination of states in the original diagrams. This approach can explode combinatorially for a complex system.

An alternate approach is to examine each state periodically to see if it needs to be activated. In this method, the processor maintains a clock that "ticks" at regular intervals. such as every 100 milliseconds. At each tick the conditions are examined to see if a task needs to be activated or deactivated. Any required computations are performed and the processor goes on to the next task. If the clock ticks fast enough, all active processes appear to be running concurrently.

Communication between processes is usually accomplished by setting aside an area of computer memory that is shared by processes that need to communicate with each other. The communicating processes leave messages for each other in these "mailbox"[3] areas much as people leave messages for each other on telephone answering machines. Protocols have to be established so each process knows the meaning of the message. This is an example of common coupling which is usually bad but is justified in this situation.

Module Allocation

Modules are parts of a task that do not run concurrently with other parts of the same task. These modules can be designed using Structure Charts as outlined in Chapter 9. Real-time systems add no further complications at this level.

Detailed Specification of Control Modules

The control process is documented using a State Transition Diagram. This is analogous to using a Decision Table to document an ordinary process. In the same way that there is a Structured English equivalent for a Decision Table, there is a Structured English equivalent for a State Transition Diagram. The equivalent is a case selection structure. Figure 12-17 illustrates the Structured English equivalent of the State Transition Diagram in Figure 12-5. Enable and disable operations are performed by subroutines that compute and send appropriate messages to external devices.

The events and actions are the same ones that are placed on the State Transition Diagram. The order of the cases is not important since only a single event is processed in each use of the process. Some machine efficiency may be achieved in certain languages if the events are stated in order of frequency of occurrence. Other Structured English constructs—like sequence or IF-THEN-ELSE—can be used to specify the details of an action.

One of the difficulties of real-time systems is that more than one process may be active at the same time. The computer may be required to keep track of the state of each of several subsystems simultaneously. It may even have to synchronize the activities of several processes. This implies that the processes need some way of communicating with each other.

An example of a communicating system is one in which temperature and tank level in a pressure vessel are being controlled by two separate subsystems. The temperature control system should not operate when the tank is empty. The system should not heat the tank if it is completely full because the tank might explode. The temperature control system needs to know the current state of the level control system if it is to avoid these conditions.

12 Real-Time

Figure 12-17

Structured English
equivalent of the
State Transition
Diagram in Figure 12-
5.

IF Cold and state is Idle
    Enable Gas
    Enable Electric
ELSEIF Cool and state is Idle
    Enable Electric
ELSEIF Cool and state is Gas Heating
    Disable Gas
ELSEIF Cold and state is Electric Heating
    Enable Gas
ELSEIF OK and state is Electric Heating
    Disable Electric
ELSEIF Hot and state is Electric Heating
    Disable Electric
    Enable Refrigeration
ELSEIF Hot and state is Idle
    Enable Refrigeration
ELSEIF Cold or Cool and state is Refrigeration
    Disable Refrigeration

Special Problems of Real-Time Systems

Real-time systems are different from ordinary data processing systems in a variety of ways. Some of these differences cause special problems that make it difficult to use the CASE techniques advocated in this book. The following differences are among the most significant.

- **Stringent performance requirements.** In data processing systems it is usually satisfactory to set performance criteria such as one second response time to users 90 percent of the time. Since real-time systems control active processes, it is usually not enough to be able to complete all processes only a certain percentage of the time. They must be completed on time every time or the process goes out of control. Thus the load on the system must be estimated accurately. It must not be increased by unpredictable processes such as user inquiries to a database. Simulation is usually used to verify that all processes can be performed on time. Redundancy is often used to ensure fault-tolerance.

- **Transient data.** Real-time systems often deal with very large quantities of data that arrive in a continuous stream. It is not practical or desirable to store all these data permanently. They are usually useful only for a short period around the time that they are generated. It may be much more efficient to store this current data in active memory and forget it as soon as it becomes irrelevant. This means that the data model may not actually get stored on a file. Filed data often consist of a periodic sample taken for analysis and control purposes. For example, a drug manufacturer may have to log selected manufacturing conditions to trace problems with a batch that does not pass standard tests.

- **Efficient storage.** The storage structure used in memory may differ significantly from the structure used in a Relational Database. A relational record of temperatures at three locations at regular intervals would likely consist of three columns. The columns contain location and time as the compound key and temperature as the data attribute. It is often more efficient to store these temporarily as a three column array of temperatures with the location implied by the column and the time implied by the row. Such an array may be difficult to deal with in a database environment. However, arrays are very natural in the mathematical languages, like FORTRAN, that are typically used to design real-time systems.

- **Incompatible hardware.** Real-time systems are often controlled by computers designed to work well with the sensors and actuators produced by manufacturers which specialize in this area. Database systems and 4GL languages are not always available for these machines.

- **Traceability.** The analyst must usually demonstrate that each feature in the requirements has been adequately handled by some part of the system and that no part of the system is superfluous. Some CASE tools include features for tracing requirements.

Summary

Real-time systems differ from data processing systems in several ways. Problems are formulated in scientific or engineering terms. Real-time systems contain sensors and actuators to interact with the real world. They often require concurrent processing of multiple inputs and they operate at very short time scales. They often require higher precision than do ordinary systems. Ordinary systems usually rely on some real-time environmental components, such as operating systems, database management systems, or communication systems.

Real-time systems add a third event dimension to the data and process dimensions that are used in business systems. Data Flow Diagrams are modified with new notations which distinguish control processes, control signals, control files, and continuous and discrete data flows.

The system senses physical happenings in the real world through sensors which are connected by interface technologies. The interfaces translate these real-world happenings into logical events and signals that control the system or allow the system to control the real world. The initial logical design should usually ignore the interface technology.

The control processes are documented using State Transition Diagrams. These diagrams have conventions for recording states, transitions, controls, and actions. A state is an externally observable mode of behavior. A transition is an instantaneous change from one state to another state. The change is triggered by a control, condition, or event that is sensed by the system. Actions must be performed to produce the transition to another state. An Action Table is another way of documenting the information in a State Transition Diagram.

12

Real-Time

The initial State Transition Diagram can be derived from the external events in a Context Diagram and the processes in detailed Data Flow Diagrams which correspond to states. The designer then adds an idle state, combines the events and states in a State Transition Diagram, and specifies the actions which are performed after each event.

The initial design is converted to a physical design. The conversion process involves allocating processes to processors, organizing tasks within each processor, defining the modules that support each task, designing interfaces, and adding safety features. The details of the modules are specified using the case structure from Structured English notation.

It is not always possible to use CASE methods in designing real-time systems. Stringent performance requirements, transient data, need for efficient storage, and incompatible hardware are not always supported by CASE tools.

Keywords and Phrases

Action
Action Table
Actuator
Continuous Signal
Control
Control Process
Control Signal
Discrete Signal

Manufacturing Automation Protocol
MAP
Real-Time System
Sensor
State
State Transition Diagram
Transition

Review Questions

1. Define each of the items in the list of keywords and phrases.
2. List the characteristics that distinguish real-time systems from ordinary systems.
3. Identify the extensions that must be added to a Data Flow Diagram so it can be used to document real-time systems.
4. What are the four components of a State Transition Diagram and what purpose does each component serve?
5. Identify the differences between an idealized logical real-time system and an actual system.
6. Identify the stages in the process of converting a logical model of a real-time system into an implementation model.
7. Why is it difficult to use CASE methods in implementing real-time systems?

Problems

1. The following diagram illustrates the physical arrangement of a simple tank in which the fluid level must be controlled. The tank has high and low sensors which go on when the tank has reached the highest and lowest allowable levels respectively. It has a pump that fills the tank by going on whenever the low level is sensed and stops whenever the high level is sensed. It also has an electrically operated valve that drains fluid from the tank whenever a demand sensor from another process signals that the other process needs fluid. The valve is turned off when the demand stops. The pump can fill the tank faster than the valve can drain it.

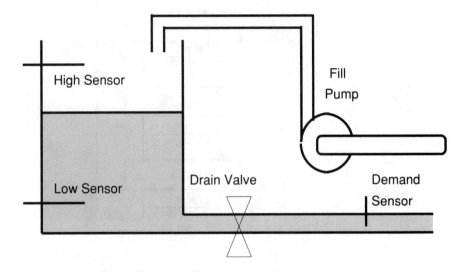

a. Draw a State Transition Diagram for the process.
b. Draw an Action Table for the process.
c. Write the Structured English equivalent of the Action Table.

2. Extend the system in Problem 1. Add a 16 character alphabetic display panel to display the current system state. This tells the operator whether the tank is filling or draining and warns the operator if the tank is not refilling properly.
a. Draw a State Transition Diagram for the revised process.
b. Draw an Action Table for the revised process.
c. Write the Structured English equivalent of the Action Table.

3. Level the process in Question 2 into a subprocess that controls the level of the tank and a subprocess that displays the states of the system. Draw the State Transition Diagram for the leveled processes.

12 Real-Time

4. The following State Transition Diagram describes the action of a common tri-lite lamp which has two filaments consuming 50 and 100 watts of electricity. By connecting none, one, or both filaments it is possible to get four different levels of light. The connections are made by a rotary switch that turns in one direction only to get off, 50, 100, or 150 watt settings.

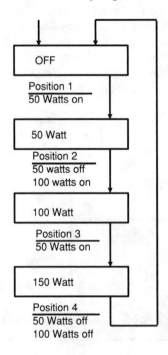

a. Convert the State Transition Diagram to an Action Table.

b. Write the Structured English equivalent of the Action Table.

5. The following describes the action of a simple microwave oven timer and control. The control panel has buttons to set a power level, an interval for cooking, a clock, and an interval timer. Each function lets the user enter numbers from a 10 key numeric input panel. The system displays numbers on a digital display as they are entered. Each function begins when the START button is pressed. The power level is reset to 10, the clock time is displayed, and the cooking time and interval timer are reset to 0 whenever the STOP button is pressed. If a power level other than 10 is desired, the power level must be set before the cooking time.

a. List all the events to which the system must respond.

b. Draw a Data Flow Diagram for the process.

c. Draw a State Transition Diagram for the control process.

d. Convert the State Transition Diagram to an Action Table.

e. Write the Structured English equivalent of the Action Table.

6. The following description documents a control system to measure the reaction time of a human machine operator. The system has three operating states: Ready, Set, and Stop.

   • The experimenter presses a READY switch to begin an experiment. The system checks all indicators to see that they have power available. If any are not functioning, the system signals the experimenter to check the condition of the indicators and restart the experiment by pressing the READY switch again. If power is available, new values are set on 5 indicators on the subject's control panel. When all indicators are set, the system is ready for an experiment.

   • The experimenter turns the SET switch on to set the experiment in motion. The system selects an indicator at random, waits a random amount of time, and resets the indicator to a dangerous level.

   • When the machine operator sees the dangerous level, the operator presses the STOP button. The system calculates the time since the indicator first showed a dangerous level and displays it for the experimenter. The system then waits for the experimenter to record the time and press the READY switch to begin a new experiment.

   a. Draw a State Transition Diagram for the process.
   b. Draw an Action Table for the process.
   c. Write the Structured English equivalent of the Action Table.

References

1. Burns, Alan, Andrew M. Lister and Andrew J. Wellings, *Lecture Notes in Computer Science: A review of ADA Tasking,* Springer-Verlag, 1986.
2. Hatley, Derek J., and Imtiaz A. Pirbhai, *Strategies for Real-Time System Specification,* Dorset House Publishing, 1988.
3. Peters, Lawrence, *Advanced Structured Analysis and Design,* Prentice-Hall, 1987.
4. SME, *MAP Applications Overview,* Society of Manufacturing Engineers, One SME Drive, P.O. Box 930, Dearborn, Michigan 48121, 1986.
5. Ward, Paul T., and Stephen J. Mellor, *Structured Development for Real-Time Systems, Volumes 1, 2, and 3,* Yourdon Press, 1985.

12
Real-Time

Chapter 13

Organizing for CASE Use

	DATABASE (WHAT)	PROGRAMS (HOW)	BENEFITS (WHY)	NETWORK (WHERE)	REAL TIME (WHEN)	SKILLS (WHO)
USER CONCEPT	Entity Relationship	Activity	Intangible Benefit	Map		Organization Design
DESIGNER CONCEPT	E-R Diagram	A-E Diagram	AHP	Network		Skills Responsibility
USER DETAIL	Forms Screens	Processes Data	Tangible Benefit	Work Volume	Discrete Events	Transition Training
DESIGNER DETAIL	EER Diagram	Data Flow Diagrams	Benefit-Cost	Partition	Transition Diagrams	Methodology Tools
BUILDER CONCEPT	Normal Form Relations	Structure Chart	Function Points	System Architecture	Specifications	Learning
BUILDER DETAIL	Files	Screens Specifications	Costs	Network Specs	Interfaces	4GL CASE

Objectives

A CASE environment can bring many capabilities and benefits to the Information Systems Department and the entire organization. However, many of these capabilities and benefits can only be realized if there are major changes in the way computer systems are implemented and used. These changes are required at the organizational, information systems, and individual employee level.

The organization needs to include information systems as part of their strategic analysis. At the organizational level, information systems must be viewed as assets rather than expenses. This involves a commitment to data sharing and a consideration of information systems development in the strategic planning process.

The Information Systems Department has to take a data-centered view of the system and learn to involve users in the development of systems. This can be done through Information Centers and End-user Computing approaches. CASE workbenches and new methodologies provide new opportunities to integrate information systems into the operations of the organization.

Individual Information Systems staff members need to learn new methods and roles. The new methods involve new techniques, new software, and a new way of thinking. The new roles include communicator, facilitator, teacher, and manager.

This chapter explains:

- Changes required at the corporate level.

- Changes required at the departmental level.

- How to convert from a 3GL to a 4GL environment.

- The functions of Information Centers and End-user Computing.

- The methods and roles that Information Systems staff need to learn.

Introduction

There are several factors which are converging to promote a change from the present 3GL environment to the 4GL and CASE environment of the future. Technology is *pulling* us in new directions by making it possible to create new, more timely, and sophisticated applications. The *pull* factors are need for integration and need for flexibility. Integration and flexibility can be offensive weapons that let an organization initiate new competitive strategies. The new technology is also *pushing* us into changing our methods. It provides more economical ways of performing current work. The *push* factors are manpower productivity, need for specialization, and machine cost. These factors push toward defending ourselves from rising costs and increased competition. Several paradoxes confront the Information Systems field. Managers have identified several issues that must be addressed to deal with these paradoxes.

Push Factors

Machine costs decrease up to 25 percent per year and people costs increase each year. This has changed the equilibrium point between using manpower and using computer power to do a particular job. In most organizations about 85 percent of the data processing manpower modifies and maintains existing systems. Management would never tolerate such a large cost of maintenance and modification in a factory environment. They would scrap any production equipment that required so much modification and replace it with new modern equipment more suited for the job. They are now beginning to realize that existing databases and software need to be treated in the same way. Many existing 3GL systems should be scrapped and replaced with 4GL systems that are flexible enough to respond to changing needs.

Major system savings can be achieved by letting the computer do a larger share of the work in the total system. The new CASE and DBMS software does cost more to buy or lease than the previous generation of software. It also may require more machine resources to operate. However, it does a lot more.

- **Documentation and training cost are reduced** by providing simpler on-line systems that are easier to use.
- **Comprehensive databases reduce effort** in designing new applications.
- **Programming is reduced** when developing new applications.
- **Maintenance cost is reduced** because the systems are conceptually simpler and more flexible and because the applications are independent of the data structure.

As systems become more complex, it becomes more difficult for any one individual to understand all parts of the system. There are two possible ways to deal with this problem. One is to make the systems simpler and the other is to divide the system into areas of specialization. Both methods are used in the 3GL environment. The environment is simplified by imposing procedural structure using the System Development Life Cycle methods. The system is also divided into independent applications so designers do not have to worry about relation-ships between applications.

The CASE environment also uses both of these strategies. Powerful 4GL languages and relational data structures simplify the system by reducing the amount of specialized knowledge needed to design and operate the system. Much of the complexity is delegated to the software environment which imposes its own structure on the system. The environment makes it possible to divide the work among specialists in database administration, programming, and user queries. Thus users can interact directly with the data they need without having to know how to organize databases or write programs.

The main difference between the two approaches is in how the required design knowledge is divided. The 3GL environment divides the system into independent applications that are then almost impossible to integrate. The CASE and 4GL environment divides the design knowledge by function while preserv-ing the ability to integrate the system. In this environment the systems staff can concentrate on the task of maintaining a consistent valid database. The users can concentrate on analyzing and using their data.

Pull Factors

As the environment becomes more turbulent, we need systems that are more flexible. There is ample evidence that product life cycles are becoming shorter and that organizations must now compete on a global scale. Technology is changing rapidly and making many existing systems obsolete in a relatively short time frame. Governments are introducing more regulations which change the way in which organizations must conduct their operations. The leisurely pace at which systems were developed in the past will not be satisfactory in the future. The window of opportunity gets narrower and organizations that cannot develop systems in time to enter the window are likely to fail.

This same turbulent environment requires that an organization be able to marshall all resources to meet new challenges. That means that integration of data resources becomes more important. An example is provided by the response of two insurance companies when the tax laws changed in the United States. Under the old tax law it was advantageous for policy holders to borrow money accumulated in their policies. Under the new law, holders would lose a tax advantage if they did not repay borrowing by a relatively short deadline. One company, using 4GL techniques, quickly generated an application that selected all customers to whom the law applied. They sent them a statement telling them exactly how much they should repay and what the advantage would be to them. Many companies using 3GL technology were unable to provide such information in time. They therefore were unable to save money for their customers or to increase their own assets by the amount of the repayment.

Oil companies find themselves in a similar situation. They are unable to predict what the next industry crisis will be. It could come from shortages caused by cartels or wars, surpluses caused by new suppliers, new competition, or from

13 Organize

government regulations designed to mitigate any of these effects. The successful companies will be those that design systems flexible enough to respond to changing circumstances quickly enough to still have an impact.

Paradoxes

Lyytinen[6] has identified several contradictory trends in the Information Systems environment.

- The significance of applications is growing while their risk increases. This is likely because most of the safe back-room applications have been done.
- The nature of applications is becoming more varied while the technical environment is becoming more uniform. The standardized environment may actually be facilitating new kinds of applications.
- Environments are changing more rapidly and getting more complex while development is getting more standardized through CASE tools. The standard tools may actually enable competitors to respond more rapidly, thus creating the more complex environment.
- Development methods are becoming more dependent on advanced tools while the success of applications becomes more independent of technological choices. The advanced tools allow the construction of complex systems in which management is the bottleneck instead of technology.

Important Issues

These apparent paradoxes lead to several important issues in the application of information systems. Moynihan[10] interviewed Chief Executive Officers, Senior Functional Managers, and Information Technology Managers to identify important issues in the implementation of information technology. Their 8 most important concerns were identified. In order of importance, they wanted:

- **More data-sharing across applications and departments.** Sharing is impeded by poor design skills, incompatible systems, and territorial jealousies.
- **Better planning and better links with business plans.** There was general agreement that more commitment from managers is needed. When information systems planning is done, it is rarely linked to business plans. Some organizations are even unwilling to reveal corporate plans to information systems groups for fear that they may be revealed to competitors.
- **Integration of core systems across plants and divisions.** Standardized data and compatible applications are required to make this happen.
- **Better cost-benefit analysis to justify projects.** This includes better evaluation of intangible benefits.
- **More user involvement in system development projects.** Users often did not know how to specify needs. They require tools like JAD to facilitate their involvement.
- **State-of-the-art systems.** Everyone wanted the apparent contradiction of state-of-the-art systems without being adventurous or using unproven technology.

- **Use of information technology to gain competitive advantage.** Many are concerned about the cost and critical importance of information technology in the delivery of their products.
- **Improved in-house technical skills.** The most serious lack of skills is in analysis and design, database design, networking, and real-time systems.

If these desires are to be satisfied, changes are required at all organization levels. The corporate level must change the way information systems are managed and evaluated. The Information Systems Department must change the way information systems are organized and developed. Individuals in the Information Systems Department must learn how to cope with new methods and roles.

Corporate Level Changes

At the corporate level, the organization needs to include information systems as part of the strategic planning process. Information systems must be viewed as a corporate resource. Organizations need to make a commitment to data-sharing. To achieve this, organizations must give their Information Systems Departments a high profile. They must make a commitment to educating both users and Information Systems staff in new ways of doing things. They must plan to redesign their organization. In summary, executives must be committed to changing the information systems.

Strategic Information Systems

Information systems were initially used to mechanize tedious clerical tasks like maintaining inventory, processing orders, and collecting payments. Such systems were usually justified by the cost savings that they produced. More recently, information systems have also been used to support the management tasks of analysis, planning, and decision-making. Such systems are usually called Decision Support Systems (DSS) or Executive Support Systems (ESS). These have typically been justified by the improved decision-making that they were supposed to produce.

Organizations have begun to treat information systems as an important part of corporate competitive strategy. Wiseman[13] describes a strategic options generator, shown in Figure 13-1. This model is designed to identify the ways in which information systems can be used to achieve a strategic advantage.

The generator identifies five strategic thrusts or directions that can be taken and five targets to which they can be applied. These targets can be competitors or they can be part of the organization and its immediate suppliers and customers.

Strategic thrusts are ways by which an organization hopes to get some sustainable advantage over its competitors. They have the following characteristics:

- **Product Differentiation.** This strategy tries to give a product some special quality that distinguishes it from the products available from competitors. This creates brand loyalty and lets the seller charge a premium price. Placing a computer order terminal in the customer's office is an example of product differentiation that makes it harder for the customer to switch suppliers.

13 Organize

Figure 13-1

The Strategic Options Generator to identify strategic thrusts and the targets they can be aimed at.

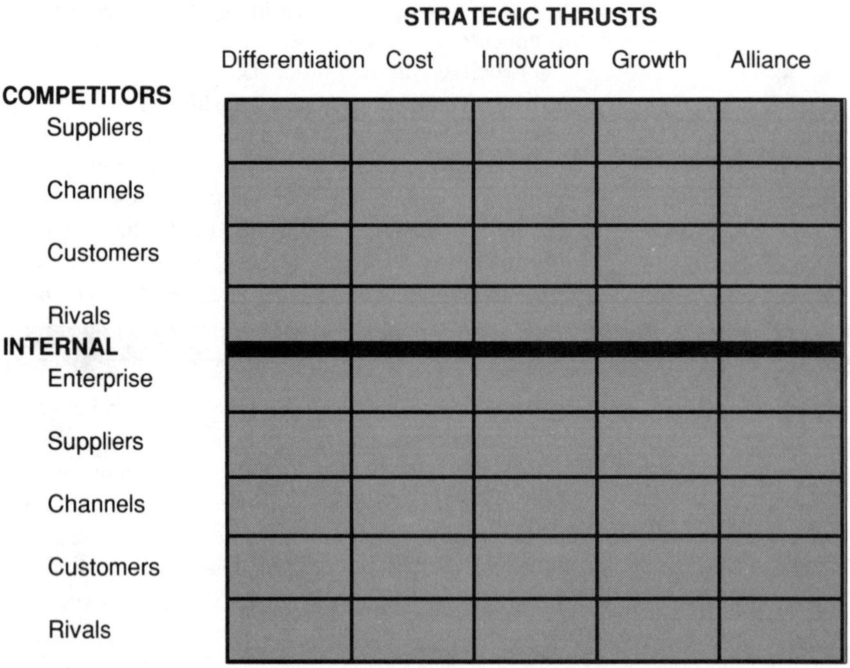

STRATEGIC THRUSTS

	Differentiation	Cost	Innovation	Growth	Alliance
COMPETITORS					
Suppliers					
Channels					
Customers					
Rivals					
INTERNAL					
Enterprise					
Suppliers					
Channels					
Customers					
Rivals					

- **Cost minimization.** In this strategy the organization tries to be the lowest cost producer. It can achieve economies of scale, economies from special knowledge of an area, or economies in information gathering. A computer system that tracks customer demand and analyzes buying patterns is an example of economies in information gathering.

- **Innovation.** This strategy produces new products, processes, services, or information that have not been available to buyers in the past. A comprehensive bank account that combines an automatic line of credit and automatic investment of surplus funds is an example of such a service.

- **Growth.** This expands the organization by expanding existing markets or penetrating new markets. This can be done by adding new products, adding new services, or entering new territories. Marketing a software package developed for internal use to customers or other organizations in the industry is an example of creating a new product and selling it in a new territory.

- **Alliance.** Alliances can be created by acquisition, joint venture, or agreement. They can exploit the information assets of one partner, the other, or some other combination. An example is an outside organization that builds a system for joint use by a consortium. An agreement that one firm will adapt a system for customers and the other will market it to their established customer base is an example of an alliance.

The strategic targets can be the internal enterprise, suppliers, channels of distribution, customers, or rival firms. They can be targets that are competing with the enterprise or they can be targets who are already linked to the enterprise. They have the following characteristics:

- **Enterprise.** Any group involved in the chain of acquisition, production, marketing, and delivery or service groups like accounting or engineering design can be targets within the enterprise. A thrust to automate production is selecting the production workforce as an enterprise target. A system to rationalize marketing effort targets the enterprise marketing function.
- **Suppliers.** Suppliers are any group that provides goods or services needed to produce the products of the enterprise. These can include such things as raw materials, finished goods, labor, capital, energy, transportation, information, or legal services. A system that tracks raw material quality or that helps suppliers to improve quality is being targeted at suppliers.
- **Distribution channels.** These groups facilitate the movement of goods from the producer to the ultimate customer. They can include distributors, retailers, transportation companies, insurers, and finance companies. A system that allows customers to connect to the seller's computer and place orders directly is targeted at the distribution channel.
- **Customers.** Customers are the ultimate purchasers of the product or service. They can be individuals, industrial buyers, resellers, governments, or foreign customers. A mileage credit system for an airline or a financial service package at a bank is targeted at a customer.
- **Rival firms.** These are organizations who compete for customers or other scarce resources. They may be selling products and services that are the same, similar, or substitutable with the enterprise's products. They may also be competing for the same raw materials, labor, or financing. An airline reservation system that links directly to travel agents is aimed at airlines who do not have such a direct link.

A strategic system can involve more than one thrust and it can be aimed at more than one target. An innovation, like a purchasing system that links the customer directly to the enterprise's computer, involves several functions. It can reduce costs, differentiate the products and services, promote growth, and lead to alliances with suppliers of non-competing goods. It can be targeted initially at customers, but impacts channels, rivals, and groups within the enterprise who are involved in marketing.

For many organizations the information system is a critical part of the competitive strategy. The information system has a pervasiveness that touches all targets of a strategy. It is also a critical part of many of the strategic thrusts. It is frequently as important as other corporate resources like money, raw materials, and human skills. It needs to be treated as a corporate resource.

Information as a Corporate Resource

In the past, organizations have rarely treated information as an important corporate resource that needs to be managed. It was usually treated as a private resource that belongs to the person or department that created it. Forms and other collected data were viewed as memory aids that remind staff about transactions.

13 Organize

They were not viewed as assets whose value increased when combined with other information in the organization to be analyzed or summarized.

The main reason for this attitude is that in the past it was physically and logically impossible to integrate all the information in an organization. Labor intensive analysis prohibits economic answers to questions that were not anticipated when a manual system—or even a computer system—was designed.

As an example, the payroll application may have salary information and the personnel system may have expected retirement dates. However, it may be virtually impossible to determine expected reductions in salaries due to retirements over the next five years. All of these data would have to be re-entered manually into a spreadsheet or personal computer database.

With modern information management technology, it is now possible to produce a design that integrates information by getting it once, getting it all, and getting it right. It is now technically and economically possible to answer questions that require information from several different sources in the organization.

There is a synergistic effect that comes from integrating information. An integrated database contains more information than the files from which it is composed. This is because it also contains implicit information about the relationships between the individual files and records.

In such an integrated environment, it becomes possible to trace flawed raw materials right to the customers who purchased the resulting flawed product. It becomes possible to trace costs to processes, products, and producers more accurately. It becomes possible to identify the most and least productive machines, methods, and manpower. It becomes possible to write monitoring programs that watch for relationships that indicate problems in a given area.

These benefits are not gained unless information is treated as a corporate asset instead of as a local expense. Yet, organizations almost universally view information as an expense rather than as an asset. They have this view because of the way corporations account for intangibles, evaluate intangible benefits, and charge for utilities.

- **Accounting treatment.** Tangible and intangible assets are usually accounted for differently. Construction of an integrated information system creates an intangible asset that has benefits over many future years. This is just like the construction of a new factory which creates tangible assets. The costs of a tangible new factory are depreciated over the life of the factory to recognize part of this cost in each year of the factory life. Yet, the cost of an intangible information system is expensed at the beginning before receiving any benefit.

  This difference in treatment occurs because information systems are not tangible assets. Accounting standards bodies are beginning to recognize the long-term nature of information systems. However, firms have rarely recognized this fact in their accounting. They still treat information systems as an expense rather than as an asset.

- **Evaluation of intangibles.** Many of the benefits of an information system are strategic and intangible. The traditional methods of evaluating projects have been based on discounted cash flow concepts. These methods evaluate the present value of all future benefits discounted at some interest rate that is adjusted for risk. This method is often unsuitable for information systems because it does not include intangible benefits with uncertain monetary value.

It is unsuitable for strategic systems because it discounts the long-term benefits so much that they get ignored. Yet one of the long term benefits may be the ultimate survival of the firm which is very difficult to put a price on.

- **Costing of utilities.** A database suffers from a further evaluation problem. It is a utility to the organization in the same way that roads and sewers are utilities to a community. Utilities are very difficult to charge for because everyone receives a benefit from them whether or not they help to pay for them. It is always to the advantage of an individual or group to claim that they should not have to pay a share of such costs. They know that they still get the benefit once the utility is provided.

The same problem arises with databases. No department wants to incur the large cost of building a centralized database, because others benefit later without paying for it. They would prefer to wait for someone else to do the job. The only way to break this log-jam is to treat the database as a corporate utility funded centrally for the benefit of all departments. It can be paid for as roads and sewers are paid for: through a central charge or tax on all users.

The organization must learn to evaluate information systems projects more carefully. It must consider the strategic, intangible, and long-term factors as well as the current economic factors during the evaluation process. To achieve the benefits of integrated information systems, information must be managed. Therefore information needs a central manager—a Chief Information Officer.

The Chief Information Officer

The Chief Information Officer has custody of all information in the organization that may be used by more than one organizational unit. This is a broad mandate with boundaries that are hard to define. In theory, any information may be useful to some other part of the organization at some time. In practice, most information is used by local users. The main responsibilities of the Chief Information Officer are strategy, architecture, access, standards, and delivery.

- **Strategy** involves development of a plan that integrates the business information needs of the organization with the opportunities presented by the available technology.
- **Architecture** consists of defining a database architecture that integrates all information so it can be accessed in any logical form.
- **Access** involves development of controls to safeguard information so only authorized users have access to it.
- **Standards** for hardware, software, databases, and communications are needed to make it easy to access data and services through the whole organization. Nonstandard facilities create barriers between systems.

13 Organize

- **Delivery** consists of developing a technology platform of hardware and software to deliver information to the users that need it. This can take several years before major benefits begin.

Finding someone who can perform such a broad function is about as difficult as finding experienced kamikaze pilots. Those who volunteer may be destroyed in the effort. The Chief Information Officer can perform these functions only if the position has enough status. This means that the position must be at the same level as the Chief Financial Officer and the Chief Operations Officer.

The position needs a mandate to develop long-term strategies. If success is defined only by short-term financial savings, it is impossible to make investments in a new architecture. Such investments typically involve several years of planning and implementation before the savings and improved operations begin to show. The organization must learn to use the same methods of justifying information systems that are used to justify a new factory. The organization expects to spend a few years building a factory with no return until completion. The same expectations must be applied to an integrated information system.

Commitment to Data-Sharing

The Chief Information Officer has the difficult job of centralizing the control of information in an environment that has typically had decentralized control. Some users may resist centralization because they perceive power loss, costs, risks, and fear of the future.

- **Power and control** may be lost if others can examine information about their operations. Having control of information is a source of power. The person who controls information can handicap those who do not have information by denying permission to see it. Similarly the controller of information can extract a price in return for giving others access to it.

  Users may not want to give up control of their information if they see themselves as losing the power that information gives them, to some "Information Elite". They may also be afraid that the Chief Information Officer can misuse the power that is conveyed by having control of information. Users may be afraid that their superiors will find out unfavorable information about their operations or misinterpret data about them. They may also feel vulnerable to innacurate inputs by others.

- **Costs** are often perceived to be large because they are initially large and easy to measure. Benefits are often deferred and hard to measure. In addition changes require a large commitment of executive time.

- **Risks** exist in any new endeavor. In information systems, there are the risks that costs may be greater than expected, that the system may not work as expected, and that there may be security problems.

- **Fear** accompanies most new endeavors. When a new information system is proposed, employees have several fears. They are afraid that they will not be able to cope with the new system or will not be able to learn how to use it. They may even fear that their job will be endangered.

Part of the solution to this problem is achieved by carefully defining the responsibilities of the Chief Information Officer. The job is not to horde and dispense information at a whim. It is to define an integrated database structure that gives everyone in the organization access to the information that they require on a need-to-know basis. The information systems staff themselves would not have access to most of the data in the system. They would only have access to the definition and structure of the data.

The information systems group normally does not set the policy on who gets access to information. They only enforce it. The policy is normally set by a high-level organizational committee in which each major user group is represented. This group must create an environment in which information-sharing is the norm. If the top management of an organization is strongly behind a policy of information-sharing, then a centralized system is easier to implement. The centralized system provides benefits to all and makes all participants into winners.

Brathwaite[1] suggests that data ownership can be dealt with by:

- **A user group** to set policy and arbitrate data access disputes. A data sharing policy supported by management is coupled with controls to ensure that data are audited to guarantee quality.
- **A hierarchy of privileges** to define ownership. Privileges are classified into property, ownership, and access privileges.
  - **Property privileges** are given to those who can determine administrative and access rights.
  - **Administrative privileges** allow the user to read, insert, update, and delete data.
  - **Access privileges** allow a user to read data without changing it.

Commitment to Education

Change to a CASE environment involves many changes in the way information is processed in the organization. The systems department must learn how to work with new technologies. The users must take more responsibility for getting information from the central system.

Much of the knowledge possessed by information systems specialists becomes obsolete in a CASE environment. Skills, such as COBOL programming, are not always transferable into the new environment.

It has been argued that a new graduate can learn 4GL languages faster than an experienced COBOL programmer. This is because a 4GL programmer has to learn to think about broader concepts. There is no need to think about how the computer executes a command. Instead, the programmer must think about the user requirements. Programmers must first unlearn many old ways of doing things. Then they can learn the new way. This takes some time.

Programmers must also learn to use CASE tools and methods. Chapter 1 showed that the old System Development Life Cycle is inappropriate in a CASE environment. Analysts and programmers have to unlearn old procedures and learn new techniques, such as graphic design tools and Joint Application Design.

13 Organize

Many traditional programmers welcome CASE tools the way master chess players welcome a program that plays chess for them. They feel that it takes all the fun out of the activity. They see the tools and techniques as a threat to the creativity they enjoy and the control they exercise in their jobs. They have developed in a culture that encourages them to see their code as a work of art resulting from their own creativity. They resist giving up the fun of coding—which they enjoy—to spend time working with users—which they do not enjoy. CASE tools may be a threat to originality instead of a liberator from drudgery.

The organization must make a commitment to re-educating their systems personnel. Otherwise, the existing staff feel frustrated when the hard-won knowledge of the past is scrapped. They may even feel that they are at a disadvantage relative to new graduates who have been introduced to these new techniques in their recent courses. If they feel frustrated, they resist the new techniques. If that happens, projects are likely to fail.

An important kind of re-education is shifting the focus from technical to business problems. This requires that Information Systems people learn to work very closely with their clients. This can be accomplished by a combination of education, reorganization, incentives, and selection.[5,8]

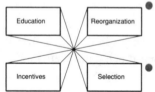

- **Education** can be external or internal. External education can take the form of management courses that serve as a "Micro MBA." Internal education can be achieved by having Information Systems people work directly beside operating personnel. For instance, application programmers may accompany sales people on calls to learn how the other half lives. This helps to build credibility with the users who then take suggestions more seriously.

- **Reorganization** involves placing IS people in the user organization and giving users more control over IS activities. A possible strategy is moving systems people directly into the user departments. Another is making the systems group into a profit center that sells services to users.

- **Incentives** involve some system of rewarding systems groups for improvements in quality, delivery time, or efficiency. Most are now rewarded for the amount of code they generate themselves. CASE tools eliminate this yardstick. Incentives work best when they are given to a team and when they reflect the contribution to the success of the end-user's mission. An example would be profit-sharing with end-users.

- **Selection** means choosing employees who are naturally inclined to work well with users. Some firms find that people with non-technical degrees can be trained in Information Systems technology more easily than technical graduates can be trained in organization and business skills. As a result, they often hire Business or Liberal Arts graduates and train them to use 4GL and CASE tools as needed.

Users also have to be educated to use the new systems. 4GL environments provide the user with more flexibility in defining information needs and getting customized reports. However, the users need to know how to use this environment if they are to gain the maximum benefit from it. This means that they need to know how to use query languages, graphics packages, spreadsheets, and other tools that are provided in this environment.

This is part of an overall trend to redeployment of human capital. Jobs are changing rapidly—partly due to the development of computer systems themselves. Most people in an organization must be prepared to learn new skills. Automation and technology make some jobs obsolete and make other new ones possible. Employees must learn more about how computers can help them. Computers will also aid in the training process.

It is no longer possible for users to delegate all development to system specialists. The organization has to provide ways for the user to learn how to capitalize on these tools. Information Centers—to be discussed later—provide a way to achieve End-User Computing.

Organizational Redesign

An organization that uses information strategically must change its structure. An information-intensive organization needs a different structure than a labor-intensive organization. Such an organization has the following characteristics:

- **Simplification.** The ideal objective is elimination of unneeded tasks. If you cannot eliminate tasks, simplify them. If you cannot simplify them, automate them. Computers help with simplification by integrating and automating tasks.
- **Reduced middle management.** Middle management is an important target for simplification. Computers allow middle managers to eliminate or automate many control tasks. They also make managers more productive by speeding data-gathering, analysis, and communication.
- **Increased communication.** As an organization gets more complex, its members need to communicate more to make sure that they are not working at crossed purposes. Most important actions have ramifications through large parts of the organization. Communication is needed to convey plans to the organization. It is also needed to hear comments and criticisms from the rest of the organization. Thus plans can be modified to consider factors that may have been neglected. Access to databases and electronic mail help to achieve better communication.
- **Increased collaboration.** Part of the communication process comes from people working together on a task. When they collaborate, they ensure that more viewpoints are considered and more creative solutions are produced. Working together makes it easier to produce the ideal product that is available any time, any place, and any way the customer needs it. Electronic communications and electronic meeting software facilitate collaboration.

Executive Commitment

Studies of the determinants of success in implementing information systems projects agree that executive commitment is one of the most important factors. Executives must commit time, money, people, and authority if they want to obtain modern integrated systems.

13 Organize

Executive time is needed during the strategic design phase. The executives of the organization are the only ones who know much of the information needed to create a strategic design. They are also the only ones with the authority to commit resources and make decisions about strategic directions. If they are not willing to commit time to understanding and supporting the development effort, integration projects are doomed to failure.

Executives must also commit their patience to the project. A major change, like CASE implementation, does not happen over night. It can take a year or two before the first CASE project is completed. It can take six months just to select methods, software, and hardware and to train analysts to use them. A strategic analysis can take another three to six months. The first project will take six months to a year.

Money is needed for analyst work stations, CASE tools, reference materials, training, and possibly new staff with special skills. In addition there may be a need for training rooms for staff and boardrooms large enough to use group methods.

Some new people with special skills may be needed. More important, existing people must be provided with time to learn new methods. The first project using CASE methods may take longer than traditional methods because of the time taken with training, organization, and experimentation. This initial investment will pay large dividends in later projects, but may make the first project look inefficient.

Many decisions must be made about development methods, hardware, software, training, and possibly hiring. The manager of the Information Systems Department must be given the authority to make these decisions. The manager must also be given the resources to acquire these facilities or authority to redeploy existing resources. This may include the authority to delay some existing work while a new system is developed.

The Information Systems Department needs an executive champion who believes in the need for changes, is willing to commit resources to the change, is willing to delegate authority to make changes, and is patient enough to wait for results.

IS Department Level Changes

The Information Systems Department also has to change the way in which it does things in the CASE environment. The first problem is to implement a CASE environment. Then the department must become more user-oriented and foster more user-involvement. This can be accomplished by using information centers, end-user computing, and group approaches to design. It must change from an application-centered approach to a data-centered approach. All of this requires new analysis, design, and development methods. The new methods, in turn, require a conversion process to accomplish the transition from the old methods to the new methods.

Implementing CASE

Hughes and Clark[4] found that CASE implementation goes through five stages: disenchantment, resignation, commitment, implementation, and maturity. Each is characterized by a different trigger point that introduces the new stage. Together the stages represent a progression from no CASE use to integrated CASE use.

- **Disenchantment** is triggered by the realization that new techniques and tools are needed to satisfy user demands. This stage consists of comparison shopping and experimentation with different CASE tools to learn more about what they can do. Typically eighty to ninety percent of the investigated tools are discarded.

- **Resignation** is triggered by the realization that some tools are useful and necessary. Specific tools are chosen to support the different stages of analysis and design. Rather than waiting for the perfect integrated product, analysts start learning how to use the tools now so they will not get left behind.

- **Commitment** is triggered by the realization that a tool must be accompanied by standard development methods. System management, project control, and possibly reverse engineering are added at this point. A Data Base Administrator is appointed. Quality assurance measures are designed to be used with the tools. Analysts who acquired tools to speed development discover that improved accuracy is the real benefit of using CASE tools.[2] One organization found that the number of errors in new systems dropped by ninety percent when CASE tools were adopted.

- **Implementation** is triggered by the realization that substantial additional resources are needed. Consultants may be hired to help implement CASE methods. Staff are trained in the methods of analysis and the use of the tools. Computers and copies of tools are acquired for the newly trained staff. Strategic planning is introduced to the development cycle. Experienced analysts and project leaders are chosen to implement the first system using CASE methods. The best initial project is a relatively simple application that can be implemented in three to six months. Consultants may be used to coach the team through the first project. While all this activity is going on, apparent productivity may temporarily drop.

- **Maturity** is triggered by the realization that one method and one set of tools cannot serve all functions. Openness and flexibility are essential features of the new methods. The lessons of the implementation phase are used to refine development methods. Software management practices are changed to reflect the greater need for analysis and the reduced need for programming and testing. Different methods and tools may be used for prototyping light applications and for developing "industrial strength" applications. Members of the first team are used to train members of teams that implement later projects. Complete conversion occurs over a period of one to two years. Programmers are gradually replaced by automatic code generators.

13 Organize

This sequence allows a department to learn in a controlled fashion without making expensive and disastrous mistakes. Mistakes that are made are relatively inexpensive. They are a cost of learning and adapting to a new environment.

User Involvement

In the past there has been a wide gulf between the technoelite who minister to the needs of computer systems and the technopeasants who go about the daily business of running the organization. The elite concentrated on mastering the technology—a task which occupied all of their available time. They had little time—and less concern—for understanding the business of the organization. As a result, many systems were constructed that were technically sophisticated, but did not do a good job of serving the users. This led to dissatisfaction among the users. When the users complained, they were usually told that programming resources were scarce and the systems could not be changed.

Meanwhile, the users have been retaliating in their own quiet way. They have been learning more about computers. This has been partly the result of formal education about computers in high school and university programs. It has been mainly the result of buying microcomputers to bypass the need for cumbersome applications developed by systems groups.

The microcomputer revolution has exposed users to a wide variety of well-designed software that combines power with user-friendliness. It is no longer possible to tell users that what they want cannot be done. They have probably seen it done in a commercial package. If the systems group does not provide what they want, users take their business elsewhere.

The increased capabilities of software—both on microcomputers and on mainframe computers—combined with the increased sophistication of the users is leading to a new style of dialog between the system group and the users. This dialog is characterized by the use of information centers, end-user computing, and group approaches to design.

Information Centers

An information center is a facility with people, equipment, and software organized to help users get access to information in the organization. It helps to solve the problem of accessing information that the organization already has, but that is not available in a form needed by the users. It usually consists of some combination of the following elements:

- **People.** Having the right kind of people in an information center is crucial. Their main task is working with the users to solve various immediate problems. They need to be friendly, helpful, and knowledgeable. They need to have knowledge about the data and systems that are available and also about the kinds of business problems that the users typically encounter. The first staff that the users meet should be generalists who can solve the variety of relatively simple problems that make up most of the load. They need to be backed up by specialists who can deal with complex problems or specialized software.

- **Advising.** The major task in the center is advising users about where to find information, how to access it, and how to manipulate it. Sometimes this role extends to advising users about acquiring their own microcomputers and software. The emphasis is usually on helping the users to do something for themselves rather than doing it for them.
- **Education.** Sometimes this advising role extends to providing formal courses in how to use particular software packages and application systems. These courses make the user self-sufficient and relieve the advisors of many of the simpler problems that users would otherwise have.
- **Hardware.** Some information centers provide a room with terminals or microcomputers that users can use to access data. Others arrange to buy and maintain microcomputers for users. This is often done through bulk-purchase arrangements that can save money for the organization. This function helps to standardize the equipment in the organization. Standardization makes it easier for advisors to trace problems that result from failed equipment.
- **Software.** Many information centers provide software in the same way that they provide hardware. They often identify standard database, spreadsheet, graphics, and analysis packages for the organization. This makes the advising task easier by reducing the number of different packages that have to be supported. It also makes it easier for users to communicate and share data if they are all using the same packages.

  The information center also usually provides query languages and statistical analysis packages on the mainframe computer. These are used for data access and for complex analyses.
- **Programming.** The information center is not designed to perform major programming tasks. However, it often writes simple programs that are beyond the user's ability to access or manipulate data. Frequently these programs are queries and summaries—like monthly reports—that are used on a regular basis.

Information centers have become the ground where users and computer specialists meet. They solve many immediate problems for users without requiring a major system analysis, design, and development effort. This reduces the workload on the systems group. Centers also alert the information systems group to problems with existing systems. This provides a good indication of the kinds of systems and databases that should be built in the future. Finally, the center performs a visible and useful function for users. This helps build credibility and respect for the systems group by creating supporters in the organization. These supporters can be very important when authorization is needed for major new initiatives.

End-User Computing

The information center facilitates the development of computing applications directly by end-users. The combination of user-friendly software with training and assistance from the information center is liberating users from the long delays that most organizations experience in getting new programs.

13 Organize

The growth of end-user computing is a mixed blessing. Users no longer need to rely on experts to implement all of their applications. They can implement some of the simpler applications themselves. This frees the experts to work on larger applications that users do not have the skill to implement. On the other hand users may tackle projects that are beyond their capability. They then repeat the mistakes that professionals made in the early days of computing: fragmented applications, inadequate testing, and non-existent documentation.

An organizational policy is needed to determine which applications should be developed by end-users and which should be developed by systems analysts. The policy has to tradeoff the convenience, speed and economy of end-user computing against the integrity and long-term support that is associated with a professionally developed application. A reasonable guideline is that analysts should develop an application when any of the following is required in the application:

- **Shared data.** When data are shared, there are several users who are relying on the integrity of the data. Such cases require assurance that the database has been designed to be compatible with other organizational data and to have adequate controls on accuracy and integrity. These are features that are frequently neglected by end-users since they often do not have the experience to recognize problems in this area. A bad design of a shared system can have a costly impact on other groups relying on the system. If the data are not being shared, then only the end-user developers stand to lose from a bad design.

- **Audited data.** If the data—usually financial data—need to be audited, there is a need for assurance that the system has adequate controls on accuracy and integrity. Otherwise the system is very vulnerable to fraud and embezzlement. Independent development and testing by the systems group helps to provide this assurance.

- **Large applications.** Large applications are likely to have many users and last a long time. As a result they need to be accurate, complete, efficient, and well-documented. They also need a sponsor who agrees to perform any maintenance that may be required in the future. This may be after the original developer has moved on to another position or another organization. Small applications typically have one or a few users in a small group. If the small system is scrapped, the cost and the number of users impacted is small.

End-user computing is most appropriate when the application is small and affects only one or a very few users in a single work group. Reports and summaries from databases developed by a central systems group are good examples of candidates for end-user computing. Reports are typically used by only a few people and they often need customizing to satisfy the specialized needs of a particular individual or group. These needs are often temporary or very individualized. There is no great loss in scrapping them when a person moves and no longer needs them. The database is still centrally developed so it provides the benefits of professional design and data-sharing.

Group Approaches

The information systems group must become familiar with group approaches to analysis and design. These approaches must involve the users at all stages of analysis and design to ensure that the system reflects their needs. Joint Application Design (JAD), as described in Chapter 5, is an example of such an approach.

Unfortunately, there is evidence that the typical analyst does not like working with other people. In a study of computer professionals, Couger[3] found that one of their most outstanding traits is their low need for social interaction. The kind of people who choose to go into the computing field apparently prefer to work alone. They do not feel a need to work with others. They are likely to design on the basis of assumptions about what users need rather than go to the users to find out whether the assumptions are correct.

The systems group must learn to recruit different kinds of people into the analysis and design area. High marks in a Computer Science Program indicate technical proficiency. They give no indication of any ability to work with users to build a system that satisfies business needs. Some organizations find that graduates from a Business or Liberal Arts program with an interest in computing often perform better as analysts and designers. This is because they are better able to understand and communicate user needs.

If this is true, then it means that the traditional career path from programmer to programmer-analyst to analyst is inappropriate. Analysts should be selected for their ability to communicate. They should learn analysis and design by working directly with good analysts as part of a team.

Data-Centered Approach

Traditional information management approaches are application-centered. Application programs are designed to deal with a particular problem, such as order-processing. Another program is designed to deal with shipping and a third is designed to deal with product costing. The result is that three systems with three different data structures are developed as shown in Figure 13-2.

If a data-centered approach is taken, the database in Figure 13-3 serves all three applications. There is no need to develop and maintain separate databases. There is no data duplication, so there are no arguments about which versions of the data are correct. Furthermore, the data are immediately available for new applications, such as inventory control or identification of customers who use specific products. In practice, a database has many more entities than are shown in the example. These are used by many more applications than are shown in the example. The savings from reduced duplication is also multiplied many times.

The application-oriented approach leads naturally to an organization that is structured by groups of applications. The Information Systems Department develops specialists who deal with groups of applications such as manufacturing, financial, or marketing programs. These separate groups may use some of the same data. They typically do not get together to define a common database because they work in separate organizations. The organizational structure is depicted by the dashed lines in Figure 13-4.

13 Organize

Figure 13-2
Three separate over-lapping systems.

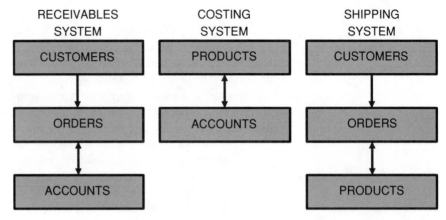

An organization structure that separates data and applications is needed. A database administrator (often called a DBA) is needed to design, implement, and control the database. Application specialists are needed to design programs that use the data defined by the DBA. This means a change in responsibilities as shown by the dashed lines in Figure 13-5. The DBA is concerned with all functions related to data including:

● **Design.** The DBA has to develop long-range plans for data architecture and detailed designs for the logical and physical database. These include standards for identification keys, data types, and data formats. Logical, physical, and application views of the data have to be maintained.

Figure 13-3
A single integrated database with multiple applications sharing the data.

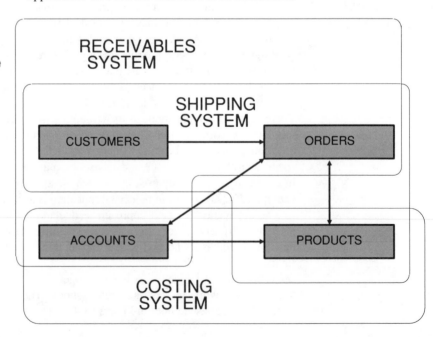

Figure 13-4
Separate organiza-
tions for each applica-
tion group consisting
of screens, programs,
and reports.

Application #1   Application #2   Application #3

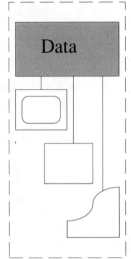
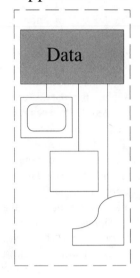
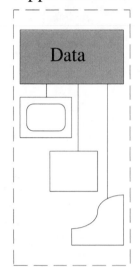

- **Integrity checks.** These include automatic checks performed by the Data
  Base Management System and others performed by the application code. The
  DBA must inspect and approve any application code that creates or updates
  data to be sure that integrity is maintained. This must happen even though the
  code is developed by the applications group.

Figure 13-5
Separate administra-
tion for database and
applications.

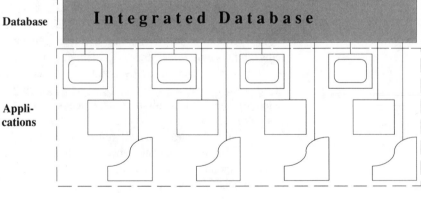

Database   Integrated Database

**Appli-
cations**

Users

13 Organize

- **Efficiency.** The DBA needs to monitor the use of the database to check on the performance and efficiency of the system. When necessary, the database must be "tuned" to improve efficiency. This can be done by using an index to improve access or changing physical placement on a disk to keep commonly needed records together.

- **Custody.** This includes security, access, and recovery. The database has to be protected with passwords or encryption to keep unauthorized people from seeing the data. Authorized users are given permission to access data as needed. Recovery procedures are used to ensure that the system recovers from disasters like power failures or accidental erasures.

The Application Administrator has a similar set of duties to perform related to the application programs. These include:

- **Standards.** Standards are required for user interfaces, reports, and program code. The standards need to address the languages to be used, the format of the screens and output, and the style of the program code.

- **Design.** The Application Administrator is responsible for designing new applications. This involves working with users to determine needs. It also involves working with the Data Base Administrator to identify changes and extensions needed in the database.

- **Efficiency.** Programs have to be tested and modified to make sure that they operate efficiently. Efficiency is usually important for only a small percentage of the code since most code is executed infrequently.

- **Maintenance.** The Application Administrator has to work closely with users to make sure that the applications continue to function satisfactorily. New extensions are added and old components may be improved or updated.

The data-centered approach also means a change in the order in which design and implementation are approached. An application-oriented approach starts with the application problem and later develops data files to support the application. A data-oriented approach starts with a database design that supports several applications. The applications are then produced to use and maintain the data.

This requires a shift in thinking and management style. The information systems group's mission changes. Under an application orientation, the systems group reacts to user needs by building isolated applications to solve specific needs. Under a data orientation, the systems group becomes proactive instead of reactive. They must anticipate user needs and include them in the database design to make future development easier. They must plan for future integration.

This does not mean that all future needs have to be anticipated. There are always unexpected changes. However, changes and extensions that can be anticipated should be incorporated into the database design. This simplifies the development of future applications.

New Methods

The systems group must learn new methods in a CASE environment. They involve changes to the selection of projects, the Systems Development Life Cycle that implements projects, and the CASE tools that support development.

Selection of Projects

A method for selecting projects was outlined in detail in Chapter 4. The main difference between this method and traditional methods is that this method includes intangible factors. Traditional methods have usually focused only on tangible financial benefits. In information systems the intangible benefits are often more important than the tangible ones. Many organizations have no procedures for evaluating intangible benefits.

Another difference is that projects are selected within a framework which considers all the information needs of the organization. Projects are not isolated. They are part of an overall plan for automating the information flows in the organization. Project selection emphasizes the order in which subsystems are to be implemented rather than deciding if systems are to be implemented at all.

This approach again implies that the Information Systems Department does more long-term planning to determine how the different systems they are building will fit together.

The first project that uses CASE tools can be crucial. If it succeeds, it will lead the way for rapid assimilation of CASE methods. If it fails, CASE tools may be abandoned. The ideal first project has strategic importance and support which provides visibility. It also has a manageable time frame so analysts will not be tempted to take disastrous shortcuts. Avoid controversial projects with unrealistic time frames or other characteristics that doom them to failure. The failure will almost certainly be blamed on the new tools.

System Development Life Cycle

The traditional System Development Life Cycle concentrates heavily on producing a detailed, voluminous, and poorly understood specification document that is officially accepted by the users. This document is then used as a basis for coding and testing, whether or not it reflects true requirements. A large part of the coding and testing phase is spent resolving errors and ambiguities in the specification document. Figure 13-6 shows the proportion of time typically spent in each phase of the System Development Life Cycle.

Coding and testing usually consumes the largest amount of development time. This is partly due to the complexity of the coding process and partly due to poor specifications. An error detected in the early Architecture and Analysis phases is much easier to correct than an error detected during the Coding and Testing phases. Figure 13-7 shows that if an error can be corrected for a dollar at the Architecture stage, the same error costs ten dollars at the Design stage, sixty dollars at the Coding stage and a hundred dollars at the Implementation stage.

The CASE environment shifts this cost structure significantly. The use of more strategic analysis increases the costs incurred in the early phases. The use of CASE tools eases the analysis task. This provides an incentive to do a more complete analysis. As a result, analysis costs may actually rise. However, overall costs fall because better analysis eliminates most of the errors that are so costly to correct in the Coding stage. Figure 13-8 shows how the effort shifts to the earlier stages of the development cycle.

13 Organize

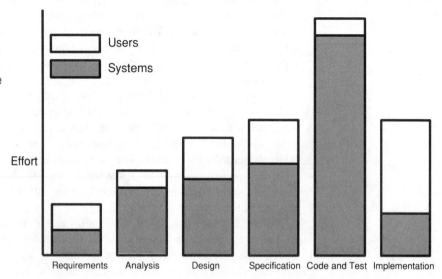

Figure 13-6

The relative effort expended in each stage of the traditional System Development Life Cycle.

CASE tools are being augmented with code generators which automate most of the coding and reduce testing significantly. This development reduces the coding cost further and shifts a higher proportion of costs to the early phases.

This shift of effort can lead to problems during the first project. Everyone expects CASE tools to decrease the time taken to implement a project. However, during the early stages of the project, the time taken actually increases. Some

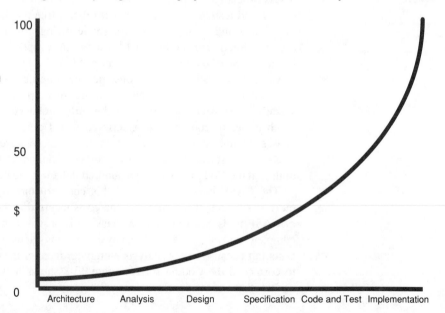

Figure 13-7

The cost of correcting errors as a function of the life cycle stages in which they are first detected.

Figure 13-8

Relative effort expended in in each stage of the CASE and 4GL System Development Life Cycle.

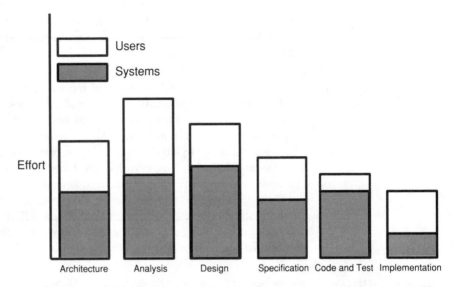

people may assume that all parts of the project will take longer. They may panic and cancel the use of CASE tools before they have a chance to get the benefits in the later stages. It takes some faith and perseverance to complete the first project and give CASE tools a fair trial.

CASE Tools

Computer Aided Software Engineering (CASE) tools have been described in Chapter 1. Their main impact is to make the analysis and design effort more systematic. Many of the benefits of CASE tools are realized only if all the tools described in this book are used. The Entity-Relationship Diagram contains information needed to design a Relational Database. The Relational Database is needed to generate a Data Flow Diagram. The Data Flow Diagram is transformed into a Structure Chart. The processes in the Structure Chart are documented with Structured English or Action Diagrams. These finally become the input to automatic code generators.

Using 3GL methods with CASE tools is like pulling a Model T with horses—it makes no use of the new technology and actually gets in the way. Such misuse of CASE tools automates the failure of projects.

Integrated CASE tools achieve their integration through the use of a Data Dictionary that describes each of the components of the design. Thus a data entity is described only once even though it is used in many parts of the design. This approach reduces the cost of using all of these documentation techniques. As a result, these analysis tools will be used pervasively.

The use of CASE tools implies a larger investment in hardware and software for use by analysts. It also implies that there must be a significant investment in training analysts. The tools are not very useful unless the analyst using them

13 Organize

knows how to identify entities, improve cohesion, eliminate coupling, and use the other techniques that have been described here. A fool with a tool is still a fool. CASE tools alone only allow the untrained analyst to make more mistakes faster.

Skills Development

Conversion to a CASE environment requires that most information systems staff must learn new skills. Both the use of CASE tools and the use of a new System Development Life Cycle have to be learned. Specific training needs depend on assessment of individual skills. Training may be triggered by requests from individuals or by needs identified by supervisors. Training may consist of vendor-provided classes, internally developed classes, or various self-paced methods such as videos and computerized tutorials.

Training should be provided before new tools and methods are introduced. Training should occur as soon as possible after a skill deficiency has been identified. Ideally, training should occur just before the skills are needed on the job so there will be no time to forget the new skills.

New Facilities

The support facilities are the software, the hardware, and the work environment used by the information systems staff. Each of them must be selected with some care.

Software Selection

The specific CASE tools needed in a given environment depend on the System Development Life Cycle that is used, the kinds of projects undertaken, and the target implementation environment. Vendors are improving their products rapidly, so the best tool today may not be the best tool tomorrow. No tool is likely to have every desired feature. The following list of factors identifies some of the more important issues that must be considered in selecting CASE tools.

- **Support for standards.** Many organizations have existing standards defining their development life cycle, their notation, and their deliverables on a project. If a tool cannot accommodate these standards, either the tool or the standards must be modified.
- **Vendor support.** Once a tool is selected, all new documentation, development, and maintenance is entered through the tool. Thus the tool should come from a vendor who is expected to provide training now and upgrades to the system later to support new methods and new hardware.
- **Network capability.** Most projects require that several people work together as a team to develop a system. Being able to connect workstations to a network facilitates communication between team members.
- **Ease of use.** The tool should be conceptually easy to use. A good tool extends the analyst's abilities to provide new capabilities. In addition it must have good documentation and good training facilities.
- **Adaptability.** Different methods are needed for small and large projects; for internally and externally sponsored projects; and for maintenance versus new

development. The tool should be able to adapt to these varying needs. It should also be possible to customize the tool to add features needed in a particular environment.

- **Interfaces to other tools.** If a tool does not have every feature needed in a particular environment, it should at least have the ability to work with other tools needed by the analyst. These include word processors, project management tools, programming languages, code generators, and testing tools.

Hardware

A CASE environment requires personal computers, monitors, printers, and networks. They must each be selected to match the needs of the people using them because it is hard to use a hammer for a task that requires a knife. The main concerns are capability and reliability.

- **Capability** means that computers, networks, and printers must be fast enough to prevent unreasonable delays. Monitors and printers must have high enough resolution to display the detail needed by the user.
- **Reliability** means that the equipment should seldom fail. When it does fail, the vendor, or a service center, should be able to detect problems easily and replace parts quickly.

Work Environment

It takes more than a desk and a personal computer to make an analyst productive. The new analysis techniques emphasize group processes. The work environment must provide space and facilities in which groups can work effectively. A large systems group will need work rooms, a conference room, a training room, and a library in addition to offices for each of the staff. Each of them must be equipped for its function.

- **Work rooms** are used for small group meetings where most communication takes place. They should seat four to six people with a work table. Each room should also have a computer, a printer, a 28 inch monitor, a white board, and a conference phone. These allow the group to work through design ideas and communicate with others.
- **A conference room** is used for JAD sessions and for decision-making. It should seat 25 or more people at conference tables with flexible seating arrangements. It also needs several white boards, a computer, and a large projection monitor.
- **A training room** is used for internal courses. it should seat ten to sixteen people and provide a computer for every two people. White boards, a printer, a large monitor, and an overhead projector are also needed.
- **A library** houses software manuals, training manuals, video tapes, system documentation, internal reports, working drafts, and other information related to the organization and its systems.

13 Organize

The Conversion Process

One of the most difficult problems the Information Systems Department faces is converting current unintegrated systems into a single integrated system. The existing separate systems typically have many overlapping functions and data elements. Most of them use files that have been defined directly in a language like COBOL rather than through a Data Base Management System.

The existing files usually suffer from three problems: homonyms, synonyms, and inconsistency.

- **Homonyms.** These are data elements with the same name, but different definitions. For instance, PRODUCT_COST may mean wholesale cost in one system and retail cost in another.

- **Synonyms.** These are elements with the same meaning, but different names. For instance, the cost of an item may be PRODUCT_COST in the manufacturing system and INVENTORY_VALUE in the inventory system.

- **Inconsistencies.** These are elements that are supposed to be the same, but are entered in different ways in different files. For instance John J. Doe may appear in different name fields as John Doe, J. Doe, J. J. Doe, and Doe, John J. The different files may also have different lengths and different rules about capitalization and punctuation. Another inconsistency results when different systems have the same data entered at different times. The files are inconsistent because totals are different and some files do not yet contain data that are in other files.

All of these problems must be eliminated during the conversion to an integrated database. Since the files are frequently used by multiple applications as shown in Figures 13-2 and 13-3, it is difficult to select a subset of files for a conversion project. Conversion of one application can require conversion of several files. Conversion of each file can then require conversion of many more applications. The conversion process spreads like a contagious disease.

The only practical way to perform most conversions is to define projects in which several related applications are converted at the same time. If the applications are chosen carefully, it is usually possible to limit the number of interactions with unconverted systems. These interactions are then handled by making duplicate copies of the converted files in a format suitable for the unconverted applications. This duplication continues until the other systems are converted.

The conversion of data and applications must be accompanied by a conversion of management structure, method, and responsibility. Yet an immediate conversion is not possible because many old applications must still be maintained by old methods for the several years that the conversion takes. Thus the conversion process must occur in parallel with the operation of the old system. The conversion process consists of several steps as illustrated in Figure 13-9.

- **Existing applications.** Unconverted applications continue to be managed as they are now. Some of the existing staff continue to maintain these applications until they are scheduled for conversion. They continue to be funded in the present manner until the conversion.

Figure 13-9
Converting separate applications into an integrated system.

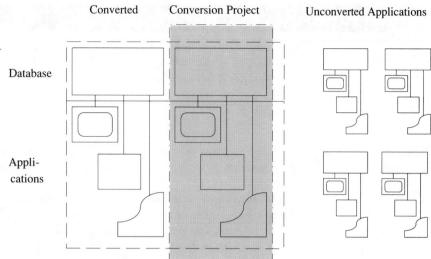

Converted   Conversion Project   Unconverted Applications

Database

Appli-
cations

- **Future applications.** All future databases and applications are managed by a Data Base Administrator and an Applications Manager. The new managers start with a small organization and grow as more converted applications are added. The Data Base Administrator function should be a centrally funded service. The cost of maintaining applications should be charged to the user group that uses each application.
- **Conversion projects.** New and conversion projects are carried out by a conversion team made up of database experts, application experts, and users. This SWAT (Specialists With Advanced Tools) team provides a focus for reorganizing data, redeveloping applications, and training staff.
- **Project completion.** Teams disband when the project is completed and join one of three groups. Some join the DBA group to help manage the enlarged central database. Some join the application group to help maintain the new application. Some start a new project team to train people currently supporting old applications so they can participate in the next conversion project. Upon project completion, the data created during the conversion project becomes a shared corporate resource.

Gradually the existing applications and the existing staff are converted to operate in the new environment. The conversion project acts as a kind of machine that takes in old applications with one organizational structure and produces a new integrated application environment. The process is gradual. The best staff start the process and deal with the initial problems of learning how to work in the new environment. The more reticent staff have longer to adjust.

13
Organize

Individual Level Changes

Changes at the corporate and at the departmental level must be accompanied by changes at the individual level. Existing staff must learn new methods of doing things. They must learn to play new roles in the organization. The changes in the way the organization does things have impacts on things that individuals have to do.

Learning New Methods

The first major impact of the CASE environment on individuals is that they have to learn new methods of doing things. This applies to analysts, programmers, and users.

Analysts must learn to use all of the methods described in this book. They normally use them in a CASE environment. As a result, there are many new things to learn. These include a new set of methods, a new set of software tools, and a new way of thinking about software problems.

The Half-Life of Knowledge

Learning a new way of thinking about problems involves forgetting an old way of thinking. This is often the hardest part of learning anything. However, one has to recognize that knowledge decays like everything else. As new knowledge is created, some of the old knowledge becomes obsolete, inapplicable, or untrue. It is replaced with new knowledge that is more appropriate for the current environment or closer to some unreachable goal called truth.

The time that it takes for half of our knowledge about an area to become obsolete is known as the half-life of that knowledge. This time depends on the field of knowledge and on the environment.

Some fields, like classical literature, may be relatively mature with only small amounts of new knowledge being generated. Their half-life is relatively long because the same knowledge is useful for a long time. Other fields, like Information Systems, change very rapidly.

The half-life in this field has been estimated to be between one and five years. Major computer shows report that about half of the exhibitors each year were not there the year before. That means that half of an organization's competitors were not there the year before. Thus half of a salesperson's knowledge of competitive conditions has to be replaced every year. A comparison of introductory information systems texts and lecture notes shows that about half of the content of books used five years ago is not being used today. This gives an upper estimate of five years for the half-life of knowledge in the field.

However half-life is measured, it is relatively short. Even using a five year half-life, people become obsolete very quickly if they do not spend a significant proportion of their time learning new material. New knowledge takes many forms. It can be about new hardware, new software, new methods of producing either of them, new uses for computing, or new ways of attacking field problems.

New Software Tools

The old analysis and design methods consisted primarily of manual drawing methods combined with some wordprocessing for producing documentation. The only significant software tools were programming languages, input editors, and debugging packages.

The new analysis and design methods use CASE tools to document the analysis in a Data Dictionary, produce graphic output for analysis by users, and generate prototypes of databases and screens. Some packages can also generate application code from the specifications.

These tools are very powerful, but they also take some time to learn. Introductory courses in their use usually take at least a week. Additional weeks of courses may be needed to learn the method well enough to understand when and how to use the tools appropriately. After that, several months of actual use are required before individuals become skilled and comfortable with them.

An organization cannot make an intelligent decision about adopting a particular CASE package unless it knows what the alternatives are. As a result, it usually is necessary to learn about the capabilities of several of these packages. It may also be necessary to use some of them in trial projects or tests to see how effective they are. These are all investments in learning about the new software.

The same process must be applied to other kinds of software, such as Data Base Management Systems, screen generators, report generators, and application generators. Some of these may require other facilities such as communications programs or new operating systems. As a result, most of the software used in the CASE environment may be new to both analysts and programmers.

This large investment in new software and in learning new methods is justified by the productivity improvements which result for analysts, programmers, and users. Analysts can generate better designs which satisfy more of the users' needs. Programmers spend less time coding and maintaining. Users waste less time learning how to use systems because the systems are more logical. Users also get better information which makes them more efficient and more effective in their jobs.

New Ways of Thinking

The new tools do not produce many improvements unless they are accompanied by new ways of thinking about problems. Analysts must undergo a paradigm shift. The most difficult change is learning to think about problems in a broader context. The new tools are usually powerful enough to solve problems that are more complex than those that have usually been tackled in the past. However, those problems are not solved unless the analysts can understand the complexities of the problem.

Understanding complexity often requires the ability to stand back and look at the forest instead of concentrating on individual trees. The analyst must comprehend the broad structure of the problem before getting immersed in details.

In a 3GL environment so much detail is required that it is impossible to step back enough to see a broad picture. A broad picture eventually requires so much

13 Organize

detailed specification and coding that it never gets implemented. Analysts deliberately confine themselves to a narrow view. The best analysts are those who eliminate lower priority items and produce a design that is deliverable.

The CASE environment handles the detail by delegating most of it to the software. There is no need to code detailed file structures, access methods, screens, or reports. Most of this detailed code is generated automatically by the software. Only high level control structures must be analyzed and programmed. This leaves more time to concentrate on the relationships between systems.

In a 3GL environment the languages and the people focus on the problem from the viewpoint of the computer. The best programmers are the ones who can see how the machine executes the code. This allows them to devise algorithms that are efficient from a machine's point of view.

With CASE, the analyst focuses on problems from the users' point of view. Instead of concentrating on how a computer does an operation, it is more important to concentrate on what operations need to be performed for the user. When these are specified, the software determines how to accomplish the operation.

As an example, the analyst and programmer must concentrate on which data items are to be retrieved in a query. They do not have to worry much about how the data are stored or how the computer accesses them. The programmer asks the Data Base Management System for data with certain characteristics and it appears. Most of the coding required to specify record formats, search for records that match conditions, store them in computer buffers, and format them for output is produced automatically.

This obsoletes a large part of the knowledge gained at great cost by programmers in the past. They may have very little competitive advantage compared to new students straight out of school. Worse still, they may actually be worse off because they still have to unlearn old ways of thinking, which students never learned. Again, this implies a need for continual learning.

Learning New Roles

In the 3GL environment the analyst plays a primarily technical role. The job consists of translating user requirements into specifications that a programmer can implement. The most difficult part of the task is perceived to be the technical part because of all the limitations imposed by available hardware and software. The challenge is to develop a technical strategy that does not severely compromise the user requirements. A system is successful if the users use the system and do not complain very loudly.

In the 3GL environment, a software company[12] can advertise—only slightly facetiously—that they want people who answer yes to the following questions:

- Do you keep a copy of the IBM S370 Principles of Operations on your bed?
- Do you know what control register 6 is used for?
- Have you ever programmed for 24 hours straight just for the fun of it?
- When you talk to IBM, do you tell THEM how the system works?
- Do you discuss channel programming at parties?

There is always a need for some of these computer wizards to develop operating systems, tune applications, and develop specialized programs. However, the emphasis is increasingly on analysts who can communicate with users. They help users by developing applications that solve business problems for their organization. Moad[9] identifies the following list of skills and attitudes that are now in demand in the job market.

- 4GLs and C language
- Personal Computer orientation
- UNIX
- Networking
- Proactive customer orientation
- Desire to work in groups

On the other hand, the following skills and attitudes are in decline.

- Mainframe orientation
- COBOL
- Reactive customer orientation
- Desire to work alone

In the CASE and 4GL environment the analyst's primary job is to support the user in operating the enterprise. This means that a large part of the job is translating technical capabilities to the user so the best system is built. The system is successful only if it satisfies all the needs of all the users, even if the user does not yet fully understand all needs.

The analyst must resist the temptation to assume that technical superiority over the user also implies intellectual superiority. The purely intellectual and emotionless Mr. Spock from Star Trek is not a good role model for an analyst. Analysts should be organizational psychoanalysts trying to identify problems and help users to discover solutions that resolve the problems.

The analyst has a proactive role that requires more investigation of needs and more selling of available services from the systems group. The analyst becomes more of a communicator, teacher, facilitator, manager, and intrapreneur.

Communicator

Analysis is primarily a communication task. The analyst must first communicate with the user to identify the real needs of the user. This is very difficult because the user frequently does not fully understand what is possible and the analyst does not fully understand what is needed. Each must learn from the other. Each must learn to see the world through the other's eyes.

The analyst must then create a design and communicate it clearly to the implementer. Again this is a difficult communication task. The user requirements have usually been stated in business terms and the implementation specifications must be communicated in technical terms. This is a translation process that is fraught with potential for communication errors because it involves two almost entirely different languages.

13 Organize

The communications role is very important. Analysis is essentially a communication process. The best analysts are people who enjoy dealing closely with and helping many other people.

Teacher

Part of the communication process is a teaching task. Users cannot specify a requirement unless they understand that they need it. They cannot understand that they need it until they are aware that it is possible. The analyst is often the person best able to identify technologies that may be of use to the client. Thus the analyst often has to teach users what they can expect of new technologies.

The analyst also must teach the user some of the techniques used to gather and analyze data. An Entity-Relationship Diagram and a Data Flow Diagram are very useful languages for sharing knowledge about a system. However, like all languages, both parties have to learn them before communication can take place.

Facilitator

The user often sees the analyst as a link to the mysterious world of information systems. The user expects the analyst to facilitate a transition to a new way of solving business problems by using technology. Again this is an intermediary role. The analyst acts as a link between two different groups—users and information systems staff—to get the groups to improve the organization's effectiveness. The facilitator role uses knowledge of needs and possibilities, ability to communicate with diverse groups, and ability to solve new and different problems.

Manager

The analyst must manage the production of new systems just as the production of any other product must be managed. The analyst must understand the needs of the users. Since many of the users are managers, the analyst must be able to think like a manager to be able to help the users.

When technical questions become relatively less important, business questions become relatively more important. The analyst and the system maintainers are likely to get moved into the user organization to develop better rapport with users. In the user organization, they are evaluated according to the user criteria. The criteria are related to the efficiency and effectiveness with which the organization delivers its product or service. Analysts must become good managers.

Intrapreneur

Gifford Pinchott III[11] defines an intrapreneur as the person "who takes hands-on responsibility for creating innovation of any kind within an organization." The intrapreneur is "the dreamer who figures out how to turn an idea into a profitable reality." This role has some significant risks and a large measure of satisfaction if successfully executed. Pinchott[11] suggests ten rules that improve an intrapreneur's chances of success.

- Come to work each day willing to be fired.
- Circumvent any orders aimed at stopping your dream.
- Do any job needed to make your project work, regardless of your job description.

- Find people to help you.
- Follow your intuition about the people you choose. Work only with the best.
- Work underground as long as you can—publicity triggers the corporate immune mechanism.
- Never bet on a race unless you are running in it.
- Remember it is easier to ask for forgiveness than for permission.
- Be true to your goals, but be realistic about the ways to achieve them.
- Honor your sponsors.

These rules are a bit extreme for people in a service department, like Information Systems. However, a number of them can be very helpful when trying to introduce innovative ideas to capitalize on new methods and technologies.

The intrapreneur encounters resistance both inside and outside the Information Systems organization. Managers outside IS may resist because they lose control of data or have to learn something new. Financial managers resist because they cannot evaluate the subjective benefits of a new system. This happens even though they have the same problems with "approved activities" like Research and Development or Accounting and Finance. Inside the IS group, most of the resistance comes about because staff may need new skills that make their present skills obsolete. Resistance can be overcome by preparation, having a mentor, and gradual infiltration.

- **Preparation** means educating interested parties to know what is involved or convince them of what is needed. A consultant can be useful. Managers are sometimes more receptive to unbiased outsiders with no interest in the outcome. Getting a consultant can also show that you are committed to a solution to the perceived problem. It also means doing the homework to make sure that the proposed project is needed and that the tools are in place. For instance, it is pointless to propose that the next project be implemented with CASE tools until someone has acquired and learned how to use CASE tools.
- **A mentor** in corporate management is essential. All projects go through difficult times. A mentor can get the top level commitment to ensure resources. A mentor can also protect the project from premature cancellation during the difficult times.
- **Gradual infiltration** means selecting projects that are most likely to succeed. The ideal project is one where opposition is low, new development is needed anyway, effectiveness will increase after implementation, and visibility is high. Success on the first project builds credibility for tackling more difficult projects.

Future Career Prospects

In the future, the analyst's job will continue to shift away from being dominantly technical. The job will take on more aspects of service to the user. As systems become integrated, there will be less need for entirely new systems and more need for analysis of existing data. The analyst's job will be to help the user in using that data. Analysts must deemphasize "coding to the bare metal" and emphasize working with high-level languages to solve user problems.

13 Organize

Those analysts who can work effectively with the users to produce useful systems to support the business of the organization have a bright future. Those who cannot adjust to the new environment are condemned to perpetual maintenance of old programs or to early—and maybe involuntary—retirement.

Summary

A need for productivity, specialization, and efficiency is pushing organizations into CASE environments. A need for flexibility and integration is also pulling organizations toward this environment.

Changes are required at all levels of the organization. The corporate level must change the way information systems are managed and evaluated. The Information Systems Department must change the way information systems are organized and developed. Individuals in the Information Systems Department must learn how to cope with new methods and roles.

At the corporate level, the organization includes information systems as part of its strategic analysis. It introduces CASE systems in stages called disenchantment, resignation, commitment, implementation, and maturity. It needs to view information systems as a corporate resource. It needs to make a commitment to data-sharing in the organization. To achieve this, the organization must give the Information Systems Department a high profile. It must make a commitment to educating both users and Information Systems staff in new ways of doing things.

The information system in many organizations becomes part of a strategy for product differentiation, cost minimization, innovation, growth, and alliance with other groups. These strategies may be applied to the internal enterprise, the suppliers, the distribution channels, the customers, or rival firms. To be part of such a strategy, information has to be considered as a corporate resource instead of a corporate expense.

The strategy is usually developed by a Chief Information Officer who is responsible for strategy, data architecture, data access, and delivery systems. The organization must have a commitment to data sharing and education if it is to make all of these changes.

The Information Systems Department must become more user-oriented and foster more user involvement. This can be accomplished by using information centers, end-user computing, and group approaches to design. It must change from an application-centered approach to a data-centered approach. There must be a conversion process to aid the transition from old methods to new methods.

Information centers are responsible for advising, education, and user-oriented hardware and software. End-user computing is most appropriate when there is no need for shared data, audited systems, or large applications.

The new organizational structure requires a Data Base Administrator who is responsible for the design, integrity checks, efficiency, and custody of the database. An applications Administrator is responsible for program standards, design, efficiency, and maintenance.

The systems group must learn new methods to implement a CASE environment. The new methods involve significant changes to the selection of projects, the Systems Development Life Cycle used to implement projects, and the CASE tools that support the development cycle.

The changes at the corporate level and at the departmental level must be accompanied by changes at the individual level. Existing staff must learn new methods of doing things. They must learn to play new roles in the organization. The changes in the way the organization does things have impacts on the things that individuals have to do.

The main changes for individual staff are that their jobs become somewhat less technical and are more closely aligned to the problems of the users. They must learn how to work more closely with the users to improve the effectiveness of the organization. The analyst must become more of a communicator, teacher, facilitator, and manager.

Keywords and Phrases

Alliance	Growth
Chief Information Officer	Information Center
Conversion	Innovation
Cost Minimization	Product
Customers	Rival Firm
Distribution Channels	Strategic Target
End-User Computing	Strategic Thrust
Enterprise	Suppliers

Review Questions

1. Define each of the items in the list of keywords and phrases.
2. Identify push and pull factors that foster a change to CASE environments.
3. What changes are required at the corporate level to implement a 4GL and CASE environment?
4. What changes are required at the Information Systems Department level to implement a 4GL and CASE environment?
5. What changes are required at the individual level to implement a 4GL and CASE environment?
6. Identify strategic thrusts an organization can make for competitive advantage.
7. Identify the possible targets towards which an organization can direct strategic thrusts.
9. In what way does viewing information systems as a corporate asset differ from viewing information systems as a corporate expense?
10. How does a commitment to data-sharing change an organization?
11. How can an organization facilitate end-user computing?
12. Under what circumstances should analysts, instead of end-users, develop information systems?

13 Organize

13. What are the main duties of a Data Base Administrator and of an Applications Administrator?
14. How do 4GL and CASE tools change the System Development Life Cycle?
15. Outline a process that can be used to convert a 3GL environment to a 4GL and CASE environment.
16. What new roles does the analyst take in a 4GL and CASE environment?

Problems

1. Hugh Mungus, The Chief Executive Officer of a large insurance company, has been to a seminar on integrated corporate databases given by a well-known information systems guru. Now he wants to develop a plan for converting the company information system into an integrated database system. The current system has about 25 major application programs which have been developed independently over a period of 15 years at an estimated cost of $75 million. Each application has its own files and programs defined in COBOL. There are also many small programs that periodically convert data from one file structure to another so application programs can share data.

   COBOL is used for all programming. None of the 100 programmers and analysts is skilled in the use of any other language. A senior programmer tried a CASE tool a couple of years ago on a project. It was abandoned because the learning and conversion of procedures took longer than the time saved on the project by the CASE tool.

   About 85% of programmer time is spent on maintaining, changing, and extending the existing systems. Non-emergency changes are saved for major revisions of application programs. Each application has a major revision scheduled every two years. Users have requested so many changes that revisions are now 10 months behind schedule. A large proportion of the revisions involve reports that combine data from more than one application.

   Each application is maintained by its own team of programmers and analysts. These people are often the ones who developed the application, so they know it intimately. Salaries and benefits are good, so there has been relatively little employee turnover.

   The IS department is under pressure to provide better service to users. However, it is unable to get budget authorization to hire the estimated 25 programmers and analysts needed to clear the backlog using existing methods. Senior management is reluctant to spend more money on a department they feel has been ineffective in the past. Meanwhile users have acquired personal computers and are demanding access to data—which they know is in the system—so they can analyze it in a wide variety of ways.

   You have been hired as a consultant by top management. Recommend a plan to accomplish the desired conversion. Specify what things have to be done, in what order, and who should do them.

2. The following manuscript is a translation from an ancient Aramaic manuscript tentatively titled ***The Book of Nemesis.*** It was recently rediscovered as a tattered manuscript in an old monastery and was immediately communicated via a computer Bulletin Board. Some of the passages are very difficult to translate into modern idiom, so the translator has apparently taken some liberties with terminology. It describes a construction project that had some problems. Using the principles of good design learned in this book, explain what went wrong with the project and how the problems could be corrected.

In the beginning there was the Requirement for a Temple and the Requirement was without form or structure and darkness was upon the face of the Client, and the face of the Client was turned away from the Company. So the Company said: "Let there be a Tender."

And lo, there was a Tender, and the Client saw that it was good, and the face of the Client was turned once more unto the works of the Company.

Then did the Company gather together all manner of creatures, and from this gathering was created the Project Team—and it was said that it was good. From the Project Team were produced Surveyors and Engineers and diverse other forms of life. And from the multitude was selected one who was raised above all others and who was called Manager. And he was to lead the Project Team along the path of productivity for the Company's sake. And it happened that the mind of the Manager was dazzled by the Tender and he thereby believed that all things were possible, even though there was, as yet, no architecture.

Thus it was that the Manager commanded all Engineers to be gathered together in one place and he spoke to their leader who was called Chief Engineer: "Let there be a Schedule, whereby I may know the Delivery Date, and I shall make you responsible for the accomplishment of this schedule." Therefore did the Chief Engineer move amongst his followers and ask of them "How shall this be done?"

Whereupon his followers withdrew, each to his own desk and estimated, as was their custom. And it came to pass that each Engineer brought forth an estimate and, after much wailing and gnashing of teeth, all estimates were consolidated and summarized into one place which was called a Project Plan.

And the Chief Engineer brought the Manager unto the Project plan saying: "Behold—it will take a full score of months to accomplish."

But the Manager was not pleased and said: "I have raised you up from the depths and given unto you many resources and even so you have not understood the Tender. Your Project Plan is too long." Whereupon the Manager hired consultants, authorized much overtime and cancelled all holidays. Then he spake unto the Chief Engineer: "Behold, see all that I have done, the Delivery Date shall be in one Year."

Then did the Chief Engineer set his followers to digging and building and there were many meetings and much time was employed in the working thereof—even though there was as yet no Architecture. And it came to pass

13 Organize

that the Manager examined the designs and he saw that they were too ambitious and he knew that they could not be accomplished by the Delivery Date.

Whereupon the Manager commanded the Chief Engineer to separate the design into two parts. One part he called the Mandatory Functions and the other part he called Options. And the Client called him names. And the Manager commanded: "Let the Vendors put forth their salesmen and let us have a Data Base Management System" and it was so.

The salesmen produced all manner of Epistles which laid claim to many and wondrous things—each according to their own file structure. And it came to pass that a Data Base Management System was selected and the Chief Engineer said that it was good and that more engineers were required if all was to be accomplished by the Delivery Date. Thus it was that the Project Team was increased almost without number.

The Manager, espying this host from afar said: "Let there be Organization" and there was Organization.

And the Project team was split into many groups that did not speak to each other, and it was said that, perhaps it was good. Some groups the Chief Engineer called Senior Engineers and others he called Junior Engineers and he gave domination to the former over the latter. And the Junior Engineers saw it differently.

Now it was said that the Chief Engineer exhorted his followers to even greater efforts because the Delivery Date was nigh and the breath of the Manager was hot upon his neck. Both Senior and Junior Engineers became sore afraid. They strove mightily to please the Chief Engineer with much overtime and copious comment and everyone excavated and constructed, each in his own manner.

The manager, seeing this, liked it not and commanded: "Let there be Standards" and there were Standards. But the Engineers liked them not and productivity fell. When he learned of this the Chief Engineer was afraid that he would be cast down from his high place and therefore commanded: "Let there be Progress Reports" and there were Progress Reports.

The Chief Engineer looked at the Progress reports and saw that the Delivery Date would not be met. Therefore, on the tenth month, the Chief Engineer rose up, pressed his garments, washed his beard, and went unto the Manager, grovelling and pointing his fingers and causing much blame to issue forth unto all manner of creatures who sold both materials and tools.

And the Chief Engineer asked for an extension whereat the Manager was exceedingly angry and caused doubt to be cast on the legitimacy of the Chief Engineer's ancestors—even to the third and fourth generation. And there was much beating of breasts and tearing of hair—mostly the Chief Engineer's. And the Manager commanded the Chief Engineer to release all the Consultants. But the Chief Engineer refused saying that all were needed, that there was no documentation and that there was, as yet, no architecture.

And it came to pass that an extension was granted and the Chief Engineer returned to his followers bearing these tidings and there was rejoicing and revelry among the workers. On the twentieth month the Chief Engineer said: "Let the components be integrated, one with another, so that the testing can begin." And it was so and great difficulties were experienced and many hours of overtime were employed in finding out why the components would not integrate—for there was no documentation and, as yet, no architecture.

Then on the twenty fourth month, the Chief Engineer did go to the Manager and say unto him: "Behold I give you good tidings of great joy for you and for your Client, for on this day the work is complete." And suddenly there was all about them a host, a multitude of Salesmen praising the Chief Engineer and singing: "Glory to the Company, the Manager, and the Chief Engineer and, please, can you make this small change?" And the Chief Engineer rose up and spake thus unto them: "We dare not for there is no documentation and, as yet, no architecture."

References

1. Brathwaite, Kenmore S., "Resolution of Conflicts in Data Ownership and Sharing in a Corporate Environment," *Data Base,* Fall 1983, pp. 37-42.
2. Burkhard, Donald L. and Per V. Jenster, "Applications of Computer-Aided Software Engineering Tools: Survey of Current and Prospective Users," *Data Base,* Fall, 1989, pp. 28-37.
3. Couger, J. Daniel, Robert A. Zawacki, and Edward B. Oppermann, "Motivation Levels of MIS Managers versus those of Their Employees", *MIS Quarterly,* Sept. 1979, pp. 47-56.
4. Hughes, Cary T. and Jon D. Clark, "The Stages of CASE Usage," *Datamation,* Feb. 1, 1990, pp. 41-44.
5. Lodahl, Thomas M., and Kay Lewis Redditt, "Aiming IS at Business Targets", *Datamation,* Feb. 15, 1989, pp. 93-100.
6. Lyytinen, Kalle, "New Challenges of Systems Development: A Vision of the 90's," *Data Base,* Fall 1989, pp. 1-12.
7. Martin, James, *Application Development Without Programmers,* Prentice-Hall Inc., 1982.
8. Moad, Jeff, "Out of the Glass House," *Datamation,* Aug. 1, 1989, pp. 71-72.
9. Moad, Jeff, "It's Time to Retrain," *Datamation,* Aug. 1, 1990, pp. 20-24.
10. Moynihan, Tony, "What Chief Executives and Senior Managers Want From Their IT Departments," *MIS Quarterly*, March 1990, pp. 14-25.
11. Pinchott III, Gifford, *Intrapreneuring,* Harper and Row, 1985.
12. VM Software, Inc. Career Quiz, Advertisement in *Datamation,* Nov. 1. 1985, p. 76.
13. Wiseman, Charles, *Strategic Information Systems,* Irwin, 1988.

13

Organize

GLOSSARY

Abstraction. This is the process of collecting subtypes of entities that share some attributes into higher level entities that contain the shared attributes. The subtypes may be overlapping or they may be mutually exclusive.

Action. Thing that has to be done during the transition from one state to another. More than one action can be associated with a control condition, but all are assumed to occur instantly during the transition to the next state.

Action Bar. A horizontal menu of actions on a screen. The action can be selected by pointing, cursoring, or entering a key letter.

Action Diagram. A diagramming technique used to document the logic of a computer program or module. Vertical brackets are used to group lines of instructions that are executed together in sequence.

Action Table. A table that identifies all the possible states, signals, and outcomes that can occur for a process.

Activities. The tasks that have to be performed to achieve the mission of an organization. Activities are arranged in hierarchical levels: resources, life cycle stages, and functions.

Activity-Entity Matrix. A table with activities listed down the side and entities listed across the top. The intersections of the rows and columns record whether an activity uses information from an entity. If each cell contains ones for use or zeros for disuse, it is called a binary Activity-Entity Incidence Matrix. If each cell contains the frequency with which each entity is used by the corresponding activity, it is called an Activity-Entity Frequency Matrix. If each cell contains C, R, U, or D to indicate Creation, Reading, Updating, and Deletion of data, it is called an Activity-Entity Usage Matrix.

Actuator. A device that can make direct changes to the environment without going through a human intermediary. An example is a computer controlled valve that can change a flow rate in a pipe.

Aggregation Abstraction. See Overlapping Subtype.

AHP. See Analytic Hierarchy Process.

Alias. See Synonym.

Alliance. A strategic thrust involving a joint undertaking by two or more independent parties. Alliances can be created by acquisition, joint venture, or agreement. They can exploit the information assets of one partner, the other, or some other combination such as an outside organization that will build a system for joint use by a consortium.

Alternate Key. An alternate key is a unique identifier that could be used as a primary key, if the chosen primary key were not being used.

Analysis. The process of breaking down the whole of a complex system into its component parts by a series of progressive refinements. It proceeds from the general to the particular as compared to synthesis.

Analytic Hierarchy Process. A method of evaluating projects which are judged by multiple criteria. It is similar to the Criterion Function, but has procedures for generating criterion weights by pairwise comparison. This makes it possible to evaluate the consistency of the weight estimates. See Criterion Function.

ASCII. American Standard Code for Information Interchange. A standard mapping of binary patterns into alphanumeric and other characters.

Atomic Key. A unique identifier consisting of a single attribute.

Attribute. An attribute is an elementary item of recordable data that cannot be further subdivided into meaningful data items. An attribute does not have further recordable attributes. It is a characteristic that describes a property of, or provides detailed information about, the thing described by an entity type. It is also called a field in a file record or a column in a table.

Back-end CASE. See Computer Aided Software Engineering.

Backup. A snapshot copy of a data file that can be used to reconstruct a file if the file is lost or damaged. Backup copies are usually stored at a site away from the computer so that it will not be destroyed by a disaster that destroys the main copy.

Balanced Diagram. A Data Flow Diagram which has the same interface data flows as the parent process which was exploded to produce the diagram.

Bar Code Scanner. A device that uses a laser beam to scan bars printed on a product or object to determine the numeric code that identifies the product or object.

Batch Process. A process that manipulates multiple transactions or records on a file in a single computer run with no human intervention in the process. The alternative is an interactive process that processes single transactions at a screen as an operator enters each transaction.

Black Box. Anything that can be used without needing to know the internal contents or structure. It is characterized only by its inputs and outputs.

Boss. A software module that controls another module called a worker. A boss may be a worker for another higher-level boss.

Bottom-Up Analysis. This is an approach that gathers a lot of detail and then tries to organize it into a general structure.

Bottom-Up Testing. A form of integration testing in which the lowest level worker modules are implemented first. Then a temporary driver module is coded to call the workers to make sure that the worker modules function correctly when called.

Boyce-Codd Normal Form. A relational table is in Boyce-Codd Normal Form if and only if all attributes depend only on a candidate key.

Brainstorming. A group process for generating a list of ideas that are related to a problem. The process is designed to encourage idea-generation by deliberately avoiding criticism of any of the ideas that are suggested.

Business Information Control Study (BICS). A model of an enterprise that identifies generic entities, relationships, and activities using seven questions about transactions in the organization.

Call. An arrow on a Structure Chart that passes control from a boss module to a worker module that it points to.

Cardinality. A characteristic of relationships between entity types. It indicates the relative number of entity occurrences in each entity type that are related to occurrences in the other related entity type.

CASE. See Computer Aided Software Engineering. Sometimes also stands for Cute Antonym for Software Engineering.

Case Structure. A programming selection structure in which one of several cases is selected depending on the value of a selection parameter. See IF-THEN-ELSE Structure.

Certification Information. This is information on forms—such as date of issue, signatures, sequential form numbers, and stamps—which certify the existence, correctness, or authenticity of a form.

Characteristic Entity. An entity type that is below a kernel entity in a hierarchy of entity types. It depends on the kernel entity for its existence. It inherits the attributes of the kernel entity. The key attribute of the kernel is part of the key of the characteristic entity type.

Check Box. A method of selecting options or actions from a list on a form or computer screen. The user places a mark in a box corresponding to the selected choice.

Check Digit. A digit or character that is computed by some transformation of the characters of an identification code. This check digit is made part of the identification code. The check digit is recomputed during data entry, using the same transformation, to check whether all of the original characters have been entered correctly.

Chief Information Officer. A person who has custody of all information in the organization that may be used by more than one organizational unit. This person is usually responsible for a strategic Information Systems plan, a database architecture, access rules, and a technology platform of hardware and software to deliver information to the users that need it.

CIO. Chief Information Officer.

Clear Box. A representation of a black box module which reveals its state information and the logical machine inside the box.

Clustering. A process of grouping items into subsets that are as similar as possible while keeping the groups as different as possible. There are many methods of clustering. The differences between them depend on the definitions of similarity and difference used by the analyst.

Code Generator. A high level specification language that produces a program in a 3GL such as COBOL.

Code Re-Engineer. A software tool that can take badly written 3GL programs and reorganize them automatically to have a more maintainable structure.

Code Translator. A program that can translate a program written in one computer language into another language.

Cohesion. A measure of how closely the instructions, processes, or statements within a module are related. It is the degree to which a module serves a single purpose rather than a multiplicity of purposes. In a module with high cohesion, all instructions contribute toward the complete performance of a single well-defined function. The kinds of cohesion, ordered from best to worst, are: functional, sequential, communicational, procedural, temporal, logical, and coincidental.

Glossary

Coincidental Cohesion. A level of cohesion in which there is no clear reason for placing the functions in a module together.

Common Coupling. A level of coupling in which modules share data by leaving it in an agreed global area of memory that is accessible to all participating modules. Sharing files does not cause common coupling. The type is named after the COMMON statement in the FORTRAN language which creates such an area.

Communication. The exchange of messages with some permissible content within some context to produce a conversation.

Communicational Cohesion. A level of cohesion in which subtasks in a module use the same data, but are not sequentially related. The various functions of the module happen to use the same input data or produce outputs for use by the same next module. The functions are otherwise unrelated and the output of one is not input to the next.

Compound Key. This is a primary key that consists of more than one attribute.

Computer Aided Software Engineering. A variety of computer programs and software tools that support some or all of the tasks in the System Development Life Cycle. A collection of tools creates a work-bench for the system analyst. The tools can help with any of analysis, design, data modelling, prototyping, coding, testing, and implementation. The tools are sometimes divided into Upper CASE (or Front-end CASE) tools which support analysis and design and Lower CASE (or Back-end CASE) tools which support coding, testing, and implementation.

Concatenated Key. A key made up by concatenating two or more attributes to create a unique identifier.

Concurrent Structure. A code structure that allows two processes to be performed simultaneously. This can happen physically if there is more than one computer in the system. It can also happen logically if the physical order of the processes is unimportant.

Connection Trap. A false relationship that is implied when two entities share the same key.

Constant. A kind of pressure experienced by system analysts.

Content Coupling. A level of coupling in which one module reaches into the internals of another module to deposit data or control its function.

Context Diagram. A simple Data Flow Diagram that shows only the terminators and the data flows that go into and out of a system. It shows the context that the system operates in, but not the processes or files.

Context Sensitivity. The ability of a program or screen to modify its actions or options depending on the current state of the program or screen. Used particularly to describe menus and help information.

Continuous Signal. A signal that has a value at all times. The value may change smoothly over time. See Discrete Signal.

Control. A condition or event that causes a system to make a transition between states.

Control Break. A point in a long sorted report where new values of the sorted variable begin. New headings and summary data are inserted at this break point.

Control Coupling. A level of coupling in which the calling module sends a control flag to the called module directing it to perform one of several possible actions.

Control Flag. A flag used by a boss module to tell a worker module which of several options to select.

Control Process. A special process that controls the activity of all other processes in a real-time system.

Control Signal. Data flow created by a control process to enable or disable a process. It acts as a switch or level settings to determine the behavior of a process.

Conversion. The process of converting from an old processing method to a new one. This often involves training, installing new equipment, and translating data into a new format.

Cost Minimization. A strategic thrust in which an organization tries to be the lowest cost producer. It can achieve economies of scale, economies from special knowledge of an area, or economies in information gathering.

Coupling. A measure of the strength of the connections between modules. The degree of coupling is the probability that the contents of another module will have to be taken into account while designing, implementing, or modifying a module. The greater the interdependence between modules, the higher the coupling between them. The kinds of coupling, ordered from greatest to least, are: data, stamp, tramp, control, and common.

Criteria. Measurable outcomes which can be used to determine whether an objective has been reached. See Objective.

Criterion Function. A method of evaluating projects which are judged by multiple criteria. Each criterion is given a weight. All of the weights sum to 1. Each project is given a value for each criterion. The product of the weights and corresponding values are summed for each project. These sums are ranked to determine the order of priority of the projects. See Analytic Hierarchy Process.

Critical Success Factors (CSF). These are those few things that must be done well if a particular organization is to survive and prosper.

CRUD. A mnemonic for the four operations that can be performed on a database: Create, Read, Update, and Delete.

CSF. See Critical Success Factors.

Cursor. An indicator on a computer screen that shows which action will be taken or where the next entry will occur.

Customers. Strategic targets that are the ultimate purchasers of the product or service. They can be individuals, industrial buyers, resellers, governments, or foreign customers.

Data Base Machine. A computer designed for the sole purpose of executing database operations requested by programs on one or more other computers. SQL is often the language used for generating the request.

Data Base Management System (DBMS). A generalized software system that is used to create manage, and protect the data used by an organization. It allows the designer to define data files; issue commands to insert, update, and delete data; and maintain data by performing validation, backup, and recovery operations. The characteristics of the database are permanently described in a Data Dictionary that is part of the DBMS. It is independent of other application programs, so many programs can share the use of the data without having to design new files for each program.

Data Coupling. A level of coupling in which only required data are passed between modules and they are passed through explicit, elemental, calling parameters. An elemental parameter cannot consist of other parameters arranged in a structure. There are no possible interactions created by data from other sources not in the parameter list.

Data Dictionary. A set of tables or files that describe the properties of the objects in a database or CASE tool. In a Relational Data Base Management System, the Data Dictionary is commonly stored in the same kind of table used to store application data. Then it is special part of the database used to describe the design of the application database.

Data Flow. Any information coming into a process or going out of it in a Data Flow Diagram. Data flow is symbolized by an arrow and the flow is in the direction that the arrow points. Data flows can connect terminators or files to processes. They cannot connect terminators to files. The data can be in any form, including forms, magnetic tapes, electronic signals, or verbal messages. The content of the data flow can be in any degree of detail or aggregation.

Data Flow Diagram. A diagram used to record the behavior of a system. The diagram consists of symbols for terminators, data flows, processes, and files.

Data Navigation Diagram. An Entity-Relationship Diagram that has been annotated to show what actions will be taken as an application program navigates from one data table to another.

Data Structure. The logical arrangement of entities, attributes, keys, and integrity rules that define a database.

Database. Any collection of files or tables that are used together by one or more applications.

Decision Support System (DSS). A system that supports managerial decision making by providing tools to model and interpret information.

Decision Table. A decision table is a formal technique for presenting all of the possible choices in a situation. The decision table contains three categories of information: conditions, actions, and rules.

Decision Tree. A decision tree consists of a set of branches that lead from the root or start of the decision process to leaves which each contain a decision. A condition is evaluated at each branch of the tree.

Decomposition Diagram. This is a hierarchical chart that shows how an activity, or other object, is decomposed into subactivities.

Deletion Anomaly. This is an error that occurs when desired information is deleted along with undesired information in an unnormalized table.

Dendrogram. A graph which shows when each cluster merges in a hierarchical clustering process. It looks somewhat like a tree in which branches successively join to form a single trunk.

Descriptive Information. This information provides directions and constraints on the use of a form.

Design. What you will later regret not doing properly.

DFD. See Data Flow Diagram.

Directive Flag. A flag used by a worker module to tell the boss module which of several options to select.

Disassembly. An approach to analysing the functions of a new system. An output is factored into its components by removing successive parts until all the elements that make up the final result have been identified. See Forward Assembly.

Discrete Signal. A signal that has a value only at discrete points in time. It has no value between discrete points in time. The value may change abruptly between points. See Continuous Signal.

Distributed System. Two or more processors that are designed to work together to support the information needs of an organization.

Distribution Channels. Strategic targets that facilitate the movement of goods from the producer to the ultimate customer. They can include distributors, retailers, transportation companies, insurers, and finance companies.

Documentation. Instructions translated from German into English by someone who is Chinese.

Domain Integrity. A database constraint that ensures that the value stored in an occurrence of an attribute is of the proper data type and contains a value from the domain of possible values.

Dot Matrix Printer. Printers that print individual characters by the impact of a vertical row of wires through an inked ribbon. The character is constructed from an array of dots.

Driver. A temporary module used during testing to simulate the behavior of a boss module so the calling behavior of the worker module can be tested.

DSS. See Decision Support System.

Encapsulation. The process of hiding the internal state, messages, and actions of an object in an Object Oriented Programming System.

End-User Computing. Computer applications developed by end-users instead of information systems professionals. This is practical if the users have access to Fourth Generation Languages and the application is small, does not need to be audited, and uses data needed only by the end-user.

Enterprise. Strategic targets within an enterprise are any group involved in the chain of acquisition, production, marketing, and delivery or service groups like accounting or engineering design.

Entity Integrity. This is a rule that ensures that each occurrence of an entity will be uniquely identifiable. This is accomplished by ensuring that the key is always non-null and unique.

Entity Occurrence. An entity occurrence is a single instance of the thing described by an entity type. It is also called a record in a file, a row in a table, or a tuple in a relation.

Entity-Relationship Diagram. A diagram that maps entity types, the relationships between them, and the cardinality of each relationship.

Entity Type. Entity types are the PRIMARY THINGS of a business about which data are recorded. Since they are things, they must have names that are NOUNS and should have the properties of a noun. An entity must have an identifying key and it must have some attributes or characteristics that need to be recorded about it. It is sometimes also called an object, file, table, relation, or data store.

Essential Model. See Logical Model.

Event. The trigger that initiates a data flow into a system. The event may be initiated by a person or organization, or it may be triggered by a timed deadline.

Event Diagram. A Data Flow Diagram that has one process to handle each event on the Event List. It is used to partition the system into independent processes.

Executive Support System (ESS). A system that supports executive activities such as planning and communication.

Existence Dependency. Existence dependency is another way of describing the relationship between characteristic entities and kernel entities. It occurs when a relationship is mandatory, the existence of one entity depends on the existence of a parent entity, and the entity inherits the identification keys of the parent entity.

Extended Entity-Relationship Model (EER). A version of the Entity-Relationship model that adds symbols for optionality, overlapping subtypes, mutually exclusive subtypes, and kernel and characteristic entities.

Extensional Information. This is the part of a form that is to be filled in. It usually consists of blanks to be written in or boxes to be checked.

Explosion. The process of expanding processes, data flows, or files in a Data Flow Diagram to see their detailed contents.

Fifth Normal Form. A table is in Fifth Normal Form if and only if every join dependency in it is a consequence of its candidate keys. A join dependency exists if and only if the relation is the join of its projections on X, Y, ..., Z where X, Y, ..., Z are subsets of the attributes of the relation.

File. A physical collection of records that have the same attributes and structure. Files (sometimes called stores) store data for use at a later time, by another process, or in a different place. A relational table is an example of a file.

File Diagram. The most detailed level of Data Flow Diagram. It shows how the detailed processes interact with the files in the database.

Firmware. Programs and logical instructions that are made a permanent part of the physical components of a computer. Firmware is between hardware and software in that it is a series of instructions like software, but is part of the physical computer, like hardware. See Hardware and Software.

First Generation Language. A computer language that consists of binary codes for each operation that the computer can perform. This is the language which the central processing unit of the computer understands. See Second Generation Language.

First Normal Form. A table is in First Normal Form if it is a flat structure with rows and columns. A hierarchy of data is not in First Normal Form.

Flag. A variable that is used to communicate internal processing information between modules in a program.

Font. A complete set of print characters with the same face, size, and style. Face refers to the shape of the characters. Size refers to the height of the characters. Style refers to the thickness of the characters (thin, normal, and bold) and whether the characters are slanted (italic).

Foreign Key. A foreign key is used to create a link with another entity. The primary key of one entity is also used as a foreign key in another entity to provide a logical link between the two entities.

Forms. Standardized documents on paper or screen with descriptions of attributes and blank areas in which to record the values of attributes. A form contains certification information, extensional information, intentional information, and descriptive information.

Forms Analysis. A procedure for analyzing forms to produce a logical Entity-Relationship model. The procedure consists of identifying structural parts, locating data areas, extracting elements from each area, and assigning each element to an attribute in an entity of the Entity-Relationship Diagram.

Forward Assembly. An approach to analysing the functions of a new system. Successive processes are applied to inputs until the desired result is achieved as in an assembly line.

Fourth Generation Language (4GL). A computer language that simplifies the production of information systems compared to production with Third Generation Languages. The language operates from the point of view of the user. It has syntax for the specification of requirements. It gets the details required to construct a program from a Data Dictionary that contains details about the database used by the system. The 4GL instructions are translated into first, second, or third generation languages before they can be executed by the computer. See First Generation Language.

Fourth Normal Form. A table is in Fourth Normal Form if, when there is a multivalue dependency $A \rightarrow \rightarrow B$ all other attributes are single value dependent on A, the key.

Front-end CASE. See Computer Aided Software Engineering.

Function. The task that has to be performed to accomplish the activities in each life cycle stage for each resource. Functions are self-contained. They process information, and lead to single step automation. They have identifiable results, identifiable workers, and clear boundaries. Function Testing. Testing to make sure that an integrated system performs all of the functions defined in the specifications.

Functional Cohesion. A level of cohesion in which everything in the module contributes to accomplishing the same specific, discernable, easily specified task. The task may be simple or complex, but there is a single task.

Gateway. A device that can translate and transfer signals sent on one network so they can be received on another network.

Generalization Abstraction. See Mutually Exclusive Subtypes.

Goal. The ultimate object or end that one strives to attain. See Objective.

Graphics Screen. A screen that can display arbitrary graphic elements of any size, made up of an array of dots on the screen. The alternative is a character-

Glossary

oriented screen that can display only alphabetic characters.

Graphic User Interface. A graphics screen interface using pop-up windows, pull-down menus, scroll bars, icons, and a pointing device, such as a mouse. Different vendors provide additional features.

Growth. A strategic thrust that expands the organization by expanding existing markets or penetrating new markets. This can be done by adding new products, adding new services, or entering new territories.

GUI. See Graphic User Interface.

Hardware. The physical components of a computer system that can be touched. See Software and Firmware.

HICCUP. Horribly Inconvenient Computer Crash Under Pressure.

Hierarchy. A structure in which the components are organized by importance into a set of successively more detailed levels. The highest level provides a very general summary of the situation. Each successive lower level reveals more detail about the previous level.

Homonym. A name that has different meanings to different people in the organization. e.g. cost may mean different things to different people.

Horizontal Table Partitioning. Maintaining the same table structure with different instances in the rows at two or more locations in a distributed system. See Vertical Table Partitioning and Replicated Table.

Hypertext. An online documentation technique which automatically cross-references topics in a document. Topics and keywords are highlighted in the text. Clicking on the highlighted words jumps to a definition or explanation of the topic or to related topics. The trail of jumps is recorded so the user can return to the original topic. Hypertext allows the user to easily explore the details of a subject or to skip over uninteresting parts.

Icon. A picture on a screen that represents an action or application that the computer can implement. The icon is activated by clicking a mouse cursor on it.

IF-THEN-ELSE Structure. A programming selection structure in which one of two cases is selected depending on whether a selection parameter is true or false. See Selection Structure.

Information Center. A facility with people, equipment, and software organized to help users get access to information in the organization. It helps to solve the problem of accessing information that the organization already has, but that is not available in a form that the users need. It usually provides some combination of advising, education, hardware, software, and programming.

Information Hiding. The design of program modules so that a user only needs to know the inputs and outputs of the module. The user does not have to know the detailed internal structure of the module to be able to use it.

Information Processing. The name you give to the data processing department when people are so disgusted with it that they will not let it be discussed in their presence.

Information Systems Architect. A designer who focuses on the analysis and design of an integrated system rather than on the parts. The architect acts as an intermediary between the user-client and the programmers who build the system. The architect identifies the framework and context of the system and the needs of the user. These are then translated into specifications to be implemented by programmers.

Inheritance. The ability of an object to have the same characteristics as another object from which it was derived in an Object Oriented Programming System.

Ink Jet Printer. A printer in which the image is created by droplets of ink that are directed at the paper by electrostatic charges. Ink jet printers can produce graphic images but they cannot print multipart forms.

Innovation. A strategic thrust that produces new products, processes, services, or information that have not been available to buyers in the past.

Insertion Anomaly. This is an error that occurs when desired information cannot be inserted in an unnormalized table without also inserting undesired information. See Update Anomaly.

Intangible Benefits. Benefits whose value is very difficult to estimate in dollar terms. They have qualitative characteristics that improve an activity or process. The usual method of estimating their value is to compare their value to something with a known economic value. See Tangible Benefits.

Integration Testing. A test of program modules to make sure that they work together when integrated into a group.

Integrity Controls. Controls that prevent the insertion of incorrect or inconsistent data, the deletion of data that should be preserved, or the preservation of data that should be deleted.

Intentional Information. This is the labels or descriptions for each field on a form. Instructions for filling the form may be explicit or implicit.

Interface. Any boundary between which two systems communicate. The systems could be two programs, two computers, or a person and a computer.

Intersection Entity. An entity inserted between two other entities to split an M:N relationship into two 1:N relationships.

Isolated Process. A process or group of processes, in a Data Flow Diagram, that interact only with terminators and files, but not with other processes.

JAD. See Joint Application Design.

Join. A join is a procedure which links the attributes of two relational tables by matching rows that share one or more common attributes. The result is a new table with all the attributes of the constituent tables. There is a row for each of the possible combinations of the common attributes.

Joint Application Design (JAD). This is a process in which all interested parties to a design get together in a group for a few days to specify the design requirements. With the help of a session leader, they identify data, processing needs, organizational rules, and political constraints that determine the parameters of the design.

Kernel Entity. The highest entity type in a hierarchy of entities. It has a unique identity that does not depend on the existence of any other entity type. The lower entities are called characteristic entities.

Key Attribute. An attribute, or set of attributes, that uniquely identifies an entity occurrence. It is also called an identifier or a determinant.

Keyword. A word which is part of the vocabulary of a specific computer language.

LAN. See Local Area Network.

Laser Printer. A printer that creates images using a technology similar to that of an electrostatic photocopier. The image is generated by a laser beam, or by light emmiting diodes, on a photosensitive drum. Grains of toner are attracted to the drum and are then transferred to the paper.

Life Cycle Stages. The stages in the life of a resource during which it is planned, acquired, maintained, and disposed of.

Line Printer. A printer that prints a whole line at a time by the impact of hammers through an inked ribbon on a band, drum, or chain of letters that rotates past the paper.

Local Area Network. A network that connects a number of computers that are in close proximity. The computers are usually microcomputers. The distances are usually less than a few thousand feet.

Logical Cohesion. A level of cohesion in which a module performs several functions that are logically similar but procedurally different.

Logical Model. A model of the processes in a system which leaves out all processes that would not be required if implemented using an ideal technology that costs nothing, takes no time to do its job, has no size, and never makes mistakes. The model concentrates only on *what* must be done and not on *how* it is done. The model ignores physical processes that store and transport data, the people and machines that perform the processes, the media on which data are stored, and any error-checking processes. It is sometimes called an Essential Model.

Lower CASE. See Computer Aided Software Engineering.

Machine. A logical module within a black box that responds to both the external inputs and the internal state of the box.

Machine-Independent Program. A program that will not run on any machine.

Magnetic Ink Character Recognition (MICR). A system that reads specially shaped alphabetic characters that have been printed with magnetic ink. The characters are read in a manner similar to reading an audio or video tape.

Management. Running after programmers to make them fill out time sheets. This usually fails because the managers do not get to the office until after the programmers have gone home.

Management Information System (MIS). A system that provides reports for managing the operations of an organization.

Manufacturing Automation Protocol (MAP). A standard specification developed by General Motors Corporation for communication between equipment components in automated factories.

MAP. See Manufacturing Automation Protocol.

Menu. A list on a screen or window that contains one or more choices that a user can select. The list may be arranged either vertically or horizontally.

MICR. See Magnetic Ink Character Recognition.

Microfilm. An output medium in which a laser-generated image is projected onto a piece of photographic film which is then processed like any other film. A magnifying viewer is needed to view the result.

Module. A set of programming instructions that can be invoked by name. Its symbol on a Structure Chart is a rectangular box.

Multivalue Dependency. B is multivalue dependent on A if there are more than one value of B which correspond to one value of A.

Murphy's Law. Whatever can go wrong, will go wrong. And at the most inopportune time.

Mushware. Software of poor quality that behaves as if some of the instructions have been scrambled.

Mutually Exclusive Subtypes. Mutually exclusive subtypes occur when the general entity must be one, and only one, of the more specific entities. The relationship between the entities is that the subtype entity IS_A supertype entity. Mutually exclusive subtypes have thick arrows that join before pointing to the supertype entity. Mutually exclusive subtypes have a mandatory relationship because the subtype entity occurrence must belong to one, and only one, of the supertype occurrences. See Overlapping Subtypes.

N-ary Relationship. A simultaneous relationship between N entity types instead of two entity types.

Nominal Group Process. A process for generating goals and criteria for the evaluation of a set of projects. It has two basic phases: generation and prioritization. The generation phase is used to generate a list of important factors or goals. The prioritization phase consolidates the factors and specifies the importance of each factor.

Object Oriented Programming System (OOPS). A class of programming languages in which independent objects perform specific tasks. The objects work together by passing messages to each other to invoke specific actions. The key features of Object-Oriented Programming are message passing, encapsulation, and inheritance.

Objective. A specific accomplishment that contributes to the achievement of a goal. See Goal and Criteria.

On-Line. The concept that a computer should have access to a human whenever it needs one.

OOPS. See Object Oriented Programming System.

Operating System. A program which controls interactions between a computer and the external environment. It may contain features that determine which program may currently use the computer, where data will be stored, displayed, or transmitted, and how data are communicated to other computers.

Operational Level. The operational level of the organization has specific tasks that need to be performed to achieve the goals of the enterprise. These tasks are relatively narrow, short-term, structured, and internally oriented. The information needs at this level are stable and predictable if the strategic goals of the enterprise do not change. See Strategic Level and Tactical Level.

Optical Scanner. An input device that can read printed or typed characters from a page as if they had been entered at a keyboard. Some can also read hand printed characters.

Optional Attribute. This is an attribute that is allowed to have a null value in a physical occurrence.

Optionality. This property determines whether every occurrence of an entity must be linked to an instance of a related entity. An optional relationship does not have to have a link. A mandatory relationship must have a link.

Organization Chart. A diagram that shows the management levels and hierarchical relationship between the different members of an organization.

Overlapping Subtypes. Overlapping subtypes of entities occur when the more abstract supertype entity can describe more than one of the subtype entities at the same time. An overlapping subtype is sometimes called an aggregation abstraction. The relationship between the entities is that the subtype entity IS_PART_OF the supertype. Subtype relationships are symbolized with thick arrows. Overlapping subtypes have separate arrows with the arrowhead pointing to their supertype entity. All have an optional relationship. See Mutually Exclusive Subtypes.

Panel. An area on a computer screen devoted to data about a single subject or from a single table.

Partitioned Database. A database in which different tables are stored in two or more locations in a distributed system. See Horizontal Table Partitioning, Vertical Table Partitioning, and Replicated Table.

Pascal. A programming language named after a man who would turn over in his grave if he knew about it.

Peak Load. The amount of work that a computer must perform during the period of highest use.

Peer Review. An examination of the overall program design and specifications by programmers who are not on the design team. They provide a critique of the design to identify possible problems. They usually do not make suggestions for improvement because this would cast them in the role of designers. This is often used for a high-level review of the initial design.

Pen Plotter. A printing device that has one or more pens that move over a sheet of paper to draw continuous lines. Flatbed plotters have a flat sheet and pens that move vertically and horizontally across the sheet. Drum plotters wrap the paper around a cylinder. An arm moves the pen across the cylinder and the cylinder rotates to move the pen in the perpendicular direction.

Pop-Up Window. A panel or portion of a screen that pops up to extend the dialog to a new level. A pop-up window is used when a specific task must be accomplished before returning to regular processing.

Primary Key. This is the identifier that is used to uniquely identify each occurrence of an entity. This is often an identification number or code. More than one attribute may be needed to uniquely identify an entity occurrence. Multiple attributes used as a primary key are called a ***compound key***.

Procedural Cohesion. A level of cohesion in which the functions in a module are grouped on the basis of the order of their occurrence. They are together because they are part of the same sequence or repetitive loop in a program. They are *not* linked by data fed from one to the other as in sequential cohesion. They do *not* work on the same data as in communicational cohesion.

Process. A thing that transforms incoming data flows into one or more outgoing data flows. Each process name should be a strong active verb with a single explicit object.

Product Differentiation. A strategic thrust that attempts to give a product some special quality that distinguishes it from the products available from competitors. This can create brand loyalty and permit the seller to charge a premium price.

Project. This is a procedure which eliminates some columns in a relational table. If part of a compound key is eliminated, then only the rows with unique combinations of the remaining subkeys are retained.

Prototyping. Sometimes defined as simulated execution of non-existent software. It is an iterative design process in which the analyst and the user work together to determine the features required in the design. It is usually used to design visible components, such as screens and reports. A model of the system, called a prototype, is produced to show the user what the system will look like. Prototyping is done in stages of identification, formatting, and en-

hancing. The identification stage identifies all data elements that must be present on the screen. The formatting stage determines the position, label, and emphasis of each element. The enhancement stage adds validity checks, operator aids, and help facilities.

Pseudocode. A specification language, similar to Strucured English, that resembles the code of a computer language, but allows terms not permitted in the computer language.

Pull-Down Menu. A menu in a window that drops down from a command selected in a menu bar. The menu normally disappears when a command is selected.

Quality Control. Assuring that the quality of a program does not get out of hand and add to the cost of analysis, design, and implementation.

Real-Time System. A computer system that interacts with some external system that is usually dominated by laws of physics, chemistry, and biology. It typically requires high precision, rapid response, and concurrent processing of multiple inputs.

Recursive Relationship. A relationship between occurrences of an entity type and other occurrences of the same entity type. Thus *"parts IS_A_COMPONENT_OF parts"* is a recursive relationship.

Referential Integrity. On of several database integrity constraints that ensure that rows in related tables are still correctly related after insertion, update, or deletion. As an example, rows of a characteristic entity must be deleted when the corresponding row of the kernel entity is deleted. These rules apply to intersection entities that implement M:N associations, kernel to characteristic existence dependencies, and subtype relationships.

Relation. A relation is a table with a fixed set of columns called attributes and a set of time-varying rows called tuples. The attributes and the tuples have no specific order. There are no duplicate tuples.

Relationship. A business action between two associated entity types. The relationship represents some interaction between the corresponding entity types in the real world. The relationship is named by an active verb that relates the two entities.

Repeat Structure. A program structure which repeats a process until some condition is met, such as processing all items on a list. The Repeat While structure tests before the logic is executed, so the process may not get executed at all. The Repeat Until structure tests after the logic is executed, so the program logic gets executed at least once.

Replicated Table. Maintaining a separate copy of a database table in two or more different locations in a distributed system. The tables have the same structure and contain the same entity instances. See Horizontal Table Partitioning and Vertical Table Partitioning.

Reporting Flag. A flag that passes status information from a worker module to its boss module.

Resolution. A measure of the amount of detail that can be printed by an output device. It is usually measured in dots per inch (dpi). Visual clarity increases as the number of dots per inch increases.

Resources. These are the different things that an enterprise requires to operate successfully. They include money, materials, equipment, personnel, suppliers, customers, intangibles, and information.

Response. The output that results when a rule is applied in a system.

Reusable Code. A program module that has been designed to perform a generic function. It can be reused in any place where the generic function is required.

Rival Firms. Strategic targets who compete for customers or other scarce resources. They may be selling products and services that are the same, similar, or substitutable with the enterprise's products. They may also be competing for the same raw materials, labor, or financing.

Rollback. The process of undoing a transaction on a file. It requires the use of historic images of the involved records before and after the transaction. These images are stored in a historic log file of all transactions in sequence.

Rollforward. The process of rebuilding a series of transactions that occurred after a snapshot copy of the files was taken for backup purposes. It requires a backup snapshot copy and a log of all transactions since the backup was taken.

Rule. A natural or organizational law that determines how a stimulus to a system is converted into a response.

Scroll Bar. A bar at the side of a scroll list. A highlighted part of the bar rides up and down, like an elevator, to show which part of the list is visible. The highlight can be moved with a mouse to scroll to another part of the list. Both horizontal and vertical scroll bars are used to control the portion of a large area, such as a map, that is visible.

Scroll List. A list of items that is too long to fit into a window. A portion of the list is displayed in the window. The rest of the list can be scrolled through the visible window by using a scroll bar.

SDLC. See System Development Life Cycle.

Second Generation Language. A computer language which uses mnemonic symbols for each of the operations that a computer can perform and for each of the locations at which information is stored. The symbols are easier for programmers to understand than binary codes. They also relieve the programmer of the task of assigning memory locations for data storage. An assembler is used to translate this language into the First Generation Language that a computer understands. See Third Generation Language.

Second Normal Form. A relational table is in Second Normal Form if all of its attributes depend on the whole key. The whole key includes all subkeys in a compound key.

Selection Structure. A program structure used when only one of several processes is to be chosen depending on some logical condition. The IF-THEN-ELSE Structure selects between two logical options that are either true or false. The Case Structure selects among more than two options.

Sensor. A device to sense important physical parameters such as temperature, pressure, or speed directly without getting the information from human operators.

Sequence Structure. A program structure used when two or more processes must be performed in a required sequence.

Sequential Cohesion. A level of cohesion in which the functions of a module are in the same module because they must be executed in sequence. The result of one function becomes the input to the next function.

Similarity. A measure of how much two things resemble each other. The measure ranges from 0 for things that have no elements in common to 1 for things that are identical.

Single Value Dependency. B is single value dependent on A if there is only one value of B which correspond to one value of A.

SLOC. See Source Lines of Code.

Software. The programs of instructions that control a computer to make it perform all of the tasks that are required to provide computer support for a business activity. See Hardware.

Software Engineering. A discipline whose goal is to produce reliable software products in a cost-effective method. Many of the techniques of the discipline are adapted from the engineering of hardware products. Some see Software Engineering as an oxymoron, like military intelligence or telephone service.

Source Lines of Code. A count of the number of logical lines of code written in the original source language. Comment lines are usually not included. This count is often used for estimating the cost of programming or evaluating programmer productivity.

Span of Control. The number of worker modules that a boss module calls in performing its function. In organizations it is the number of immediate subordinates that a single manager supervises.

SQL. See Structured Query Language.

Stamp Coupling. A level of coupling in which structured parameters are used to pass data. The data have to be arranged in the required structure. Some parts of the structure may not be used.

State. A stable condition in which a system exists. A stimulus triggers the system to perform some action which brings about a new stable condition. A state is an externally observable mode of behavior.

State Information. A record of the past history of a black box that allows historic events to alter the behavior of the box.

State Machine Diagram. A representation of a black box module which reveals its state information and the logical machine inside the box.

State Transition Diagram. A model of the different states that a system can be in and the control signals and actions that cause the transition to another state. The four components of a State Transition Diagram are states, transitions, controls, and actions.

Statement of Purpose. A single paragraph that defines what is included and what is not included in a system being designed. It provides a reference which can be used to delineate a boundary in the gray area between the system and the rest of the universe.

Stimulus. An input that triggers a system to change its state.

Strategic Level. The level of an organization which does planning for the future of the enterprise and organizes the resources of the enterprise to achieve that planned future. The main concerns of this layer are broad, long-term, unstructured, and externally oriented. Their in-formation needs are volatile and unpredictable. See Tactical Level and Operational Level.

Strategic Target. Organizations at which a strategic thrust can be directed. The strategic targets can be the internal enterprise, suppliers, channels of distribution, customers, or rival firms. They can be targets that are competing with the enterprise or they can be targets who are already linked to the enterprise.

Strategic Thrust. Ways by which an organization may hope to get some sustainable advantage over its competitors. See Alliance, Cost Minimization, Growth, Innovation, and Product Differentiation.

Strategy. A long range plan whose merits cannot be evaluated until long after its creators have left the organization.

Structure. One of the five basic categories of logical machines that can be used to construct all logical programs. The five basic structures are: sequence, selection, repeat-while, repeat-until, and concurrent structures.

Structure Chart. A diagram that identifies the modules in a program and shows the relationships between them. The relationships are modelled by the data and flags that flow between the modules and by the call relationship which passes control between modules.

Structured Analysis. A method for identifying the processes need to automate an existing system. the conceptual stages are documenting the existing physical system, extracting the essential logical model, designing a new logical model, and designing a new physical system. In practice the existing physical and logical models may not always be documented.

Structured English. A restricted form of English that removes features that cause ambiguity and confusion. These features are adjectives, adverbs, compound sentence structures, non-imperative moods, punctuation, and footnotes. See Pseudocode.

Structured Query Language. A standard database language that is used to define a database, modify it, control access to it, and retrieve data through query statements. It has been implemented on many computers by many vendors.

Structured Walkthrough. A process designed to check the validity of an analysis or design. A group of users and analysts examine the Data Flow Diagrams to check for missing or incorrect descriptions of processes, data, files, or terminators.

Stub. A temporary module used during testing to simulate the behavior of a worker so that the calling behavior of the boss module can be tested.

Subtype Entity. An entity that is one of a group of entities that share some common attributes. The common attributes are stored in a common supertype entity from which the subtypes inherit their properties. See Mutually Exclusive Subtypes and Overlapping Subtypes.

Summary Data. An aggregation of data to summarize many instances with one value. Common summary statistics are count, total, average, standard deviation, minimum, and maximum.

Supertype Entity. An entity used to store common attributes of subtype entities that each have their own different attributes. See Mutually Exclusive Subtypes and Overlapping Subtypes.

Suppliers. Strategic targets in any group that provides goods or services needed to produce the products of the enterprise. These can include such things as raw materials, finished goods, labor, capital, energy, transportation, information, or legal services.

Synonym. A name that refers to the same entity type or process as another existing name. It is also called an alias.

Synthesis. The process of building a complex system from its component parts. The process proceeds from the particular to the general as compared to analysis.

System. A set of things or processes that are linked together by rules to form a unified process. A system has boundaries and interacts with the universe beyond the boundary by passing data across the boundary.

System Analysis. The process of identifying the components of a system that are required to perform some desired task or function.

System Design. The process of selecting among alternate methods of implementing the components of a system identified during a system analysis.

System Development Life Cycle (SDLC). A series of stages through which the development of a computer system progresses. The stages vary in different organizations, but the cycle usually contains the following stages: requirements definition, analysis, design, specification, coding, testing, and implementation. When CASE tools are used, the SDLC is often modified to include architecture, analysis, prototyping, and implementation with coding and testing performed in each of the stages.

System Testing. System testing determines whether the system can perform all of it functions in a realistic operating environment. It must be able to handle peak loads, store all required data, respond rapidly, and recover from mechanical failures.

Table. See Relation.

Tactical Level. The level of an organization which concerns itself with managing the specific departments of the enterprise. These middle managers try to organize the tasks of the enterprise as efficiently as possible. They try to convert the broad goals that are defined at the strategic level into tactics that can be implemented to achieve these goals. The viewpoint and information needs of this layer are intermediate between those of the strategic level above and the operational level below.

Tangible Benefits. Benefits whose value can be easily estimated in dollars. See Intangible Benefits.

Temporal Cohesion. A level of cohesion in which functions are placed in the same module only because they have to be performed at the same time. It is commonly used for initialization and termination modules.

Terminator. An external person, organization, or machine that provides data or receives data in a Data Flow Diagram. Terminators are named with a noun. All terminators must have at least one data flow entering or leaving the terminator. The terminator is symbolized by a shadowed rectangle.

Third Generation Language. A computer language that provides instructions for generic operations such as reading, writing, and calculating formulas. These instructions are translated by a compiler into many more detailed instructions in a first or second generation language. The instructions must be written from the point of view of the computer. All operations and decisions are specified in the sequence in which they are to be performed. These languages are much simpler to use than Second Generation Languages. See Fourth Generation Language.

Third Normal Form. A relational table is in Third Normal Form if all of its attributes depend on the whole key and nothing but the key. The whole key includes all subkeys in a compound key.

Three Tier Architecture. A network architecture consisting of microcomputers on desks, minicomputers to serve departments, and mainframe computers to serve the entire organization.

Time Savings Times Salary. A method of estimating the savings that will result from the implementation of a computer system. The hours saved by all people who use the system is multiplied by their hourly salary, with benefits, to get the total savings.

Top-Down Analysis. This is an approach that works down from the general to the particular. As each level of the problem is understood, it is expanded into more detail.

Top-Down Testing. An integration testing method in which the top boss module is coded first. Calls are tested by calling a stub module that simulates the action of the called module. Then the stubs are replaced with fully coded modules and the process is repeated.

Tramp Coupling. A level of coupling in which data flows through several modules to get from where it is produced to where it is used. The intermediate modules must carry the data even though it serves no function within them. This is another version of stamp coupling.

Transform Analysis. The process of identifying the major inputs, major outputs, and the central transform in a Data Flow Diagram, which are then used to construct a Structure Chart.

Transition. A change from a previous state to another state. A state can have one or more transitions coming into it and one or more transitions leaving it. Each transition has a control and one or more actions associated with it.

TSTS. See Time Savings Times Salary.

Tuple. A row in a relational table. See Relation.

Upper CASE. See Computer Aided Software Engineering.

Unit Testing. Unit tests are performed on individual modules to detect errors in interfaces, input, output, data structure, arithmetic, comparisons, and control logic.

Update Anomaly. This is an error that occurs when two different values can be inserted for the same logical occurrence of an attribute in an unnormalized table. It occurs because the same item is stored in more than one place. See Insertion Anomaly.

Utility Module. A program module used to perform standard tasks that are needed in many parts of a program.

Validation. The process of evaluating sofware at the end of the development process to ensure compliance with the requirements. Sometimes it is the process of verifying that a program does what your lawyer thinks it should.

Validity Check. Checks for mandatory relationships, unique keys, allowable values, and other constraints that are made whenever data are inserted, updated, or deleted.

Vaporware. A software product which is like vapor: the vendor says that it is there, but nobody has ever seen it. This is a term used for software that has not yet been delivered, and might never be delivered.

Verification. The process of ensuring that software performs all of its functions correctly.

Vertical Table Partitioning. Maintaining tables with different columns, but with the same instances of entities in the rows at two or more locations in a distributed system. The identification keys are the same in all tables so the tables can be joined. See Horizontal Table Partitioning and Replicated Table.

Worker. A program module that performs a service for a boss module. It may also be a boss to other worker modules.

WORM. Write Once, Read Many. Used to describe non-erasable optical storage disks.

WORN. Written Once, Ran Never. Used to describe poor quality storage disks. See Vaporware.

Glossary of Graphic Notation

The Extended Entity-Relationship Model

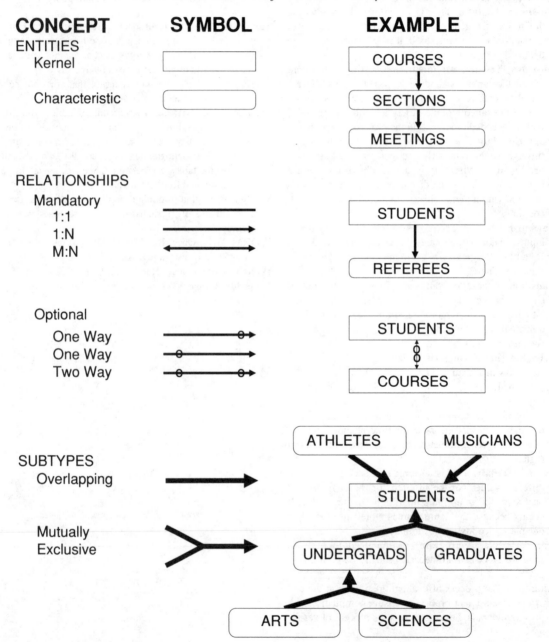

CONCEPT	SYMBOL	EXAMPLE

ENTITIES
  Kernel

  Characteristic

RELATIONSHIPS
  Mandatory
    1:1
    1:N
    M:N

  Optional
    One Way
    One Way
    Two Way

SUBTYPES
  Overlapping

  Mutually
  Exclusive

COURSES
SECTIONS
MEETINGS

STUDENTS
REFEREES

STUDENTS
COURSES

ATHLETES   MUSICIANS
STUDENTS
UNDERGRADS   GRADUATES
ARTS   SCIENCES

English Equivalents of the Extended Entity-Relationship Model

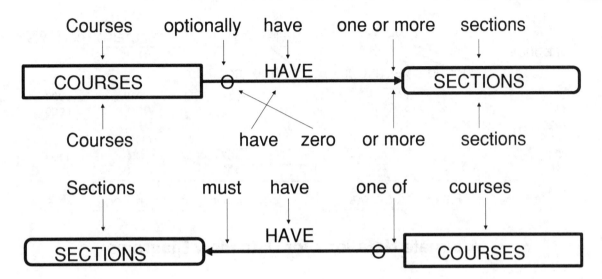

Alternate Notations for Entity-Relationship Models

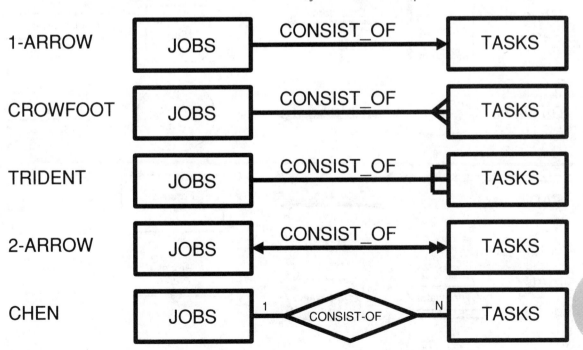

Notation for Relational Data Tables

| ENTITY | | KEYS | | FOREIGN KEYS | | ATTRIBUTES OR COLUMNS | |

MEETINGS

COURSE_ID	SECTION_ID	MEETING_ID	BUILDING_ID	ROOM_ID	DAY	TIME
1021	01	1	19	212	MON	0900
1021	01	2	19	212	WED	0900
1021	02	1	19	214	TUE	1400
1021	02	2	19	214	THU	1400
2202	01	1	21	107	MON	1100
2202	01	2	21	109	WED	1100

| RELATION OR TABLE | ROW, TUPLE, OR ENTITY OCCURENCE |

Alternate Notations for Data Flow Diagrams

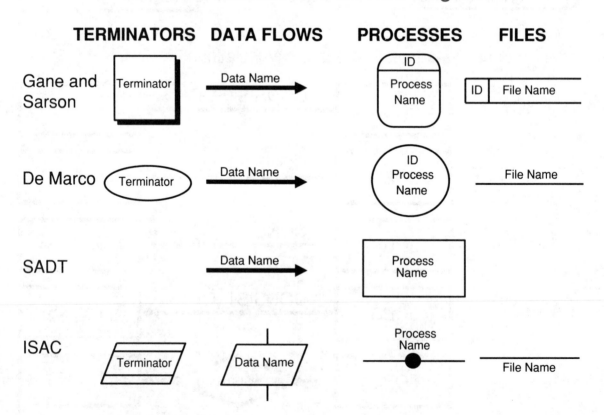

	TERMINATORS	**DATA FLOWS**	**PROCESSES**	**FILES**
Gane and Sarson	Terminator	Data Name →	ID / Process Name	ID | File Name
De Marco	Terminator	Data Name →	ID Process Name	File Name
SADT		Data Name →	Process Name	
ISAC	Terminator	Data Name	Process Name ●	File Name

Real-Time Extensions for Data Flow Diagrams

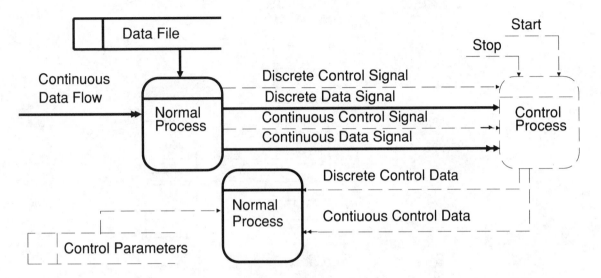

Elements of a State Transition Diagram for Real-Time Systems

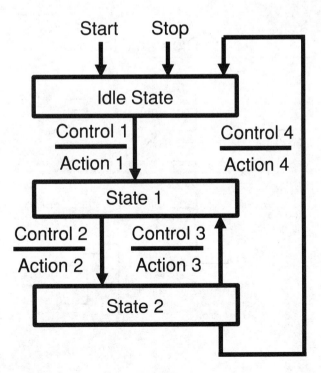

Equivalence Between Data Flow Diagrams and Structure Charts

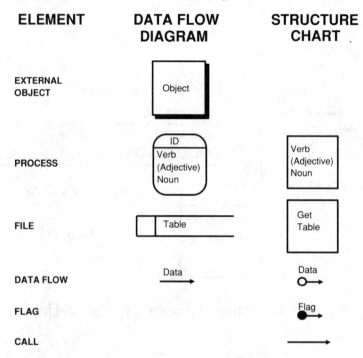

Action Diagram Notation

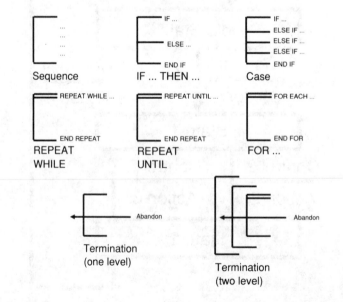

Index